March 14–15, 2015
Istanbul, Turkey

Association for Computing Machinery

Advancing Computing as a Science & Profession

VEE'15

Proceedings of the 11th ACM SIGPLAN/SIGOPS International Conference on

Virtual Execution Environments

Sponsored by:
ACM SIGPLAN and ACM SIGOPS

In-cooperation with:
USENIX

Supported by:
Intel, Microsoft Research, and VMware

Association for Computing Machinery

Advancing Computing as a Science & Profession

The Association for Computing Machinery
2 Penn Plaza, Suite 701
New York, New York 10121-0701

Notice to Past Authors of ACM-Published Articles
ACM intends to create a complete electronic archive of all articles and/or other material previously published by ACM. If you have written a work that has been previously published by ACM in any journal or conference proceedings prior to 1978, or any SIG Newsletter at any time, and you do NOT want this work to appear in the ACM Digital Library, please inform permissions@acm.org, stating the title of the work, the author(s), and where and when published.

ISBN: 978-1-4503-3450-1 (Digital)

ISBN: 978-1-4503-3765-6 (Print)

Additional copies may be ordered prepaid from:

ACM Order Department
PO Box 30777
New York, NY 10087-0777, USA

Phone: 1-800-342-6626 (USA and Canada)
+1-212-626-0500 (Global)
Fax: +1-212-944-1318
E-mail: acmhelp@acm.org
Hours of Operation: 8:30 am – 4:30 pm ET

Printed in the USA

VEE 2015 Foreword

It is our great pleasure to welcome you to the 2015 ACM SIGPLAN/SIGOPS Conference on Virtual Execution Environments (VEE'15).

This year's conference continues its tradition of providing a forum for researchers and practitioners to interact, share ideas, and discuss the latest work on virtualization. The conference brings together people from different domains of computer science, from the top of the software stack down to the micro-architectural level.

This year's call for papers attracted 60 submissions. Out of these, the program committee accepted 17 papers. Reviewing was double-blind and was done entirely by the program committee members. All submissions received 3-4 reviews, and authors were given the opportunity for rebuttal before the PC meeting.

Submissions	Reviewed	Accepted	
Full Technical Papers	50	16	32%
Short Papers	10	1	10%
Total	60	17	28%

In addition to the papers, this year's technical program includes two invited keynote presentations.

Putting together VEE'15 was a team effort. We first thank the authors for providing the content of the program. We are very grateful for the hard work of the program committee in reviewing papers and providing feedback for authors. We also want to recognize the organizers of ASPLOS 2015 as being instrumental in coordinating local arrangements, registration, and logistics for the conference. Lastly, we are thankful for the conference sponsors, ACM SIPLAN and ACM SIGOPS, for the cooperation with Usenix, and for our generous corporate supporters, Intel, Microsoft Research, and VMware, for their continued support.

We hope that you will find the symposium interesting and thought-provoking and that it provides you with opportunity to meet and engage with other researchers and practitioners from institutions from around the world.

Ada Gavrilovska   **Angela Demke Brown**   **Bjarne Steensgaard**
Georgia Tech, USA   *University of Toronto, Canada*   *Microsoft, USA*
VEE'15 General Chair   VEE'15 Program Chair   VEE'15 Program Chair

Table of Contents

Session: Improving and Exploiting I/O Virtualization

Session: Address Space Management

Session: Managing Virtual Clusters

Session: VM Testing and Introspection

Session: User-facing Applications

Session: Security and Reliability

VEE 2015 Organization

General Chair: Ada Gavrilovska *(Georgia Tech)*

Program Co-Chairs: Angela Demke Brown *(University of Toronto)*
Bjarne Steensgaard *(Microsoft)*

Program Committee: Jonathan Appavoo *(Boston University)*
Haibo Chen *(Shanghai Jiao Tong University)*
Dilma Da Silva *(Texas A&M University)*
Amer Diwan *(Google)*
Daniel Frampton *(Microsoft)*
David Gregg *(Trinity College Dublin)*
David Grove *(IBM Research)*
Vishakha Gupta *(Intel)*
Tomas Kalibera *(Purdue University)*
Kenichi Kourai *(Kyushu Institute of Technology)*
Priya Nagpurkar *(IBM Research)*
Donald Porter *(Stony Brook University)*
Jennifer Sartor *(Ghent University and Vrije Universiteit Brussel)*
Ravi Soundararajan *(VMware)*
Gaël Thomas *(LIP6)*
Timothy Wood *(George Washington University)*

Steering Committee Chair: Dilma Da Silva *(Texas A&M University)*

Steering Committee: Steve Blackburn *(Australian National University)*
Marc Fiuczynski *(Akamai)*
Steven Hand *(Microsoft Research)*
Gernot Heiser *(NICTA and UNSW)*
Steve Muir *(Comcast)*
Brian Noble *(University of Michigan)*
Erez Petrank *(Technion)*
Andrew Warfield *(University of British Columbia)*
Dan Tsafrir *(Technion)*

VEE 2015 Sponsors & Supporters

Sponsors

SIGPLAN

SIGOPS
ACM SIG on Operating Systems

In cooperation with

usenix
THE ADVANCED
COMPUTING SYSTEMS
ASSOCIATION

Supporters

intel

Microsoft Research

vmware

A Comprehensive Implementation and Evaluation of Direct Interrupt Delivery

Cheng-Chun Tu

Oracle Labs

cheng-chun.tu@oracle.com

Michael Ferdman

Stony Brook Univieristy

mferdman@cs.stonybrook.edu

Chao-tung Lee

Industrial Technology
Research Institute, Taiwan

marklee@itri.org.tw

Tzi-cker Chiueh

Industrial Technology
Research Institute, Taiwan

tcc@itri.org.tw

Abstract

As the performance overhead associated with CPU and memory virtualization becomes largely negligible, research efforts are directed toward reducing the I/O virtualization overhead, which mainly comes from two sources: DMA set-up and payload copy, and interrupt delivery. The advent of SRIOV and MRIOV effectively reduces the DMA-related virtualization overhead to a minimum. Therefore, the last battleground for minimizing virtualization overhead is how to directly deliver every interrupt to its target VM without involving the hypervisor.

This paper describes the design, implementation, and evaluation of a KVM-based direct interrupt delivery system called DID. DID delivers interrupts from SRIOV devices, virtual devices, and timers to their target VMs directly, completely avoiding VM exits. Moreover, DID does not require any modifications to the VM's operating system and preserves the correct priority among interrupts in all cases. We demonstrate that DID reduces the number of VM exits by a factor of 100 for I/O-intensive workloads, decreases the interrupt invocation latency by 80%, and improves the throughput of a VM running Memcached by a factor of 3.

Categories and Subject Descriptors C.0 [*General*]: Hardware/software interfaces

Keywords SR-IOV, I/O Virtualization, Interrupts, I/O Performance

1. Introduction

With increasingly sophisticated hardware support for virtualization, the performance overhead associated with CPU and memory virtualization is largely negligible. The only remaining non-trivial virtualization overhead is due to I/O virtualization. The I/O virtualization overhead itself mainly comes from two sources: setting up DMA operations and copying DMA payloads, and delivering interrupts when I/O operations are completed. The advent of SRIOV [12] and MRIOV [32] allows a VM to interact with I/O devices directly and thus effectively reduces the DMA-related virtualization overhead to a minimum [25, 27]. Therefore, the last I/O virtualization performance barrier is due to interrupt delivery. Because the main overhead of interrupt delivery are VM exits, a key approach to reduce the overhead of virtualized server I/O is to deliver interrupts destined to a VM directly to that VM, bypassing the VM exit and avoiding involving the hypervisor. Direct delivery of interrupts to their target VMs not only minimizes the performance overhead associated with I/O virtualization, but also decreases the *interrupt invocation latency*, a key consideration in real-time virtualized computing systems. This paper describes the design, implementation, and evaluation of a KVM-based direct interrupt delivery system called DID, which offers a comprehensive solution to eliminate interrupt delivery performance overhead on virtualized servers.

DID solves two key technical challenges for direct interrupt delivery. The first challenge is how to directly deliver interrupts to their target VMs without invoking the hypervisor on the delivery path. The second challenge is how to signal successful completion of an interrupt to the interrupt controller hardware without trapping to the hypervisor. We set the following goals at the onset of this project:

- If a VM is running, all interrupts for this VM, including those from emulated devices, SRIOV devices, timers, and other processors, are delivered directly.

- When a target VM is not running, its associated interrupts must be delivered indirectly through the hypervisor, but the priority among all interrupts, both directly and indirectly delivered, is correctly preserved.

- The number of VM exits required to deliver and complete an interrupt is zero.

• No paravirtualization or modification to the VM's OS is needed.

To satisfy these goals, DID leverages several architectural features available on modern Intel x86 servers. First, DID takes advantage of the *interrupt remapping table* on the IOMMU to route interrupts to their target VM directly when the target VM is running and to the hypervisor when the target VM is not running, without requiring any changes to the guest OS. Moreover, the hypervisor can run on any of the available CPU cores. If an interrupt is delivered via the hypervisor, it becomes a *virtual interrupt* when it is delivered to the target VM. Second, DID leverages the inter-processor interrupt (IPI) mechanism to inject virtual interrupts from the hypervisor directly into a VM running on another core. This virtual interrupt delivery mechanism effectively converts a virtual interrupt back into a physical interrupt, eliminating a well-known problem of existing virtual interrupt delivery mechanisms, where lower-priority virtual interrupts may override higher-priority directly delivered interrupts because virtual interrupts do not pass through the local interrupt controller (local APIC). Additionally, DID employs special handling of timer interrupts, which do not pass through the IOMMU, and also avoids VM exits when delivering timer interrupts, regardless of whether they are being delivered to a VM or to the hypervisor. This is achieved through careful installation of timer interrupts that the hypervisor sets up on a dedicated core and migration of timer interrupts that a VM sets up when the VM is suspended and migrated.

Existing approaches to this interrupt delivery problem include software patches in guest OSes and host's kernel to enable hypervisor bypassing [18, 19, 31] when interrupts arrive, or vendor-specific hardware upgrades such as Intel's interrupt APIC virtualization support (APICv) [1]. DID takes a software-only approach and is proven to be more effective in reducing the number of VM exits as compared to the existing hardware solutions. After carefully examining existing software-based solutions [18, 19, 31], we have identified several major limitations in these solutions and removed all of them in DID. Specifically, existing solutions distinguish between *assigned interrupts* and *non-assigned interrupts*, and are able to directly deliver only assigned interrupts, which are usually from SRIOV devices. Moreover, these solutions suffer from a cascade effect in which the hypervisor has to turn off the direct interrupt mechanism of a VM while injecting a virtual interrupt to the VM and in the process creates more virtual interrupts. Finally, legacy or closed-sourced OSes cannot enjoy the benefits of these solutions because they require guest OS modification.

The current DID prototype is built into the KVM hypervisor [24] that supports direct pass-through for SRIOV devices. We demonstrate the following performance advantages of DID for virtualized x86 servers equipped with SRIOV NICs:

• The interrupt invocation latency of a cyclictest benchmark is reduced by 80%, from $14\mu s$ down to $2.9\mu s$.

• The intra-machine TCP-based iperf throughput is improved by up to 21%.

• The Memcached throughput, in terms of bounded-latency requests per second, is improved by 330% as a result of reducing the VM exit rate from 97K per second to less than 1K per second.

2. Background

On Intel x86 servers, system software performs the following sequence of steps to carry out a transaction with an I/O device, such as a NIC. First, the system software issues I/O instructions to set up a DMA operation for copying data from memory to the I/O device. Then, the DMA engine on the I/O device performs the actual copy and signals completion by sending an interrupt to the CPU. Finally, the corresponding interrupt handler in the system software is invoked to process the completion interrupt and to send an acknowledgement to the interrupt controller hardware.

In a naive I/O virtualization implementation, at least three VM exits are required to execute an I/O transaction: one when the I/O instructions are issued, another when the completion interrupt is delivered, and the third when the interrupt handler finishes. If an I/O device supports single-root I/O virtualization (SRIOV), a VM is able to issue I/O instructions directly to the device in a way that is isolated from other VMs, and therefore VM exits are avoided when I/O instructions are issued. However, despite SRIOV, the other two VM exits remain. The goal of DID is to eliminate the remaining two VM exits associated with each I/O transaction by delivering completion interrupts to their VMs directly and allowing the VMs to directly acknowledge interrupts, in both cases without involving the hypervisor.

2.1 Intel x86's Interrupt Architecture

On x86 servers, interrupts are asynchronous events generated by external components such as I/O devices. The currently executing code is interrupted and control jumps to a pre-defined handler that is specified in an in-memory table called IDT (Interrupt Descriptor Table). The x86 architecture defines up to 256 interrupt vectors, each of which corresponds to the address of an interrupt handler function that is going to be invoked when the corresponding interrupt is triggered.

It used to be the case that an I/O device interrupts the CPU by sending a signal on a wire connecting itself to the CPU's programmable interrupt controller (PIC). However, modern x86 servers adopt a more flexible interrupt management architecture called *message signaled interrupt* (MSI) and its extension MSI-X. An I/O device issues a message signaled interrupt to a CPU by performing a memory write operation to a special address, which causes a physical interrupt to be sent to the CPU. When a server starts up, the system software is responsible for allocating the MSI address and MSI data for each I/O device detected in the server. MSI addresses are allocated from the address ranges assigned to the local APICs (LAPICs) and MSI data are the payloads used in the memory write operations that trigger a message signaled interrupts. An interrupt's MSI address specifies the ID of the interrupt's destination CPU core and its MSI data contains the interrupt's vector number and delivery mode.

MSI is compatible with PCIe, which is the dominant I/O interconnect architecture used on Intel x86 servers. Each memory write operation used to trigger an MSI interrupt is a PCIe memory write request which is issued by a PCIe device and which traverses the PCIe hierarchy to the root complex [7]. An x86 server employs a LAPIC for each CPU core, an IOAPIC for each I/O subsystem, and an IOMMU to isolate the PCIe address space from the server's physical memory space. IOAPIC supports an *I/O redirection table* and IOMMU supports an *interrupt remapping table*. Both tables allow the system software to specify the destination ID, trigger mode, and delivery mode for each PCIe device interrupt. The trigger mode of an interrupt specifies whether the interrupt's signal to the CPU is edge-triggered or level-triggered. Possible delivery modes of an interrupt are (1) the *fixed* mode, in which an interrupt is delivered to all CPUs indicated in the destination ID field, (2) the *lowest priority* mode, in which an interrupt is delivered only to the destination CPU that executes at the lowest priority, (3) the *NMI* (Non-Maskable Interrupt) mode, in which an interrupt is delivered to the destination CPU core at the highest priority and cannot be masked.

IOMMU is an important building block of the I/O virtualization technology built into modern x86 servers [6, 20] that ensures that only authorized interrupts from authorized PCIe devices are allowed to enter a system. Each interrupt remapping table (IRT) entry specifies the interrupt information associated with an MSI address, including a source ID field called SID. When the IOMMU's interrupt remapping mechanism is turned on, a field in an MSI address is used to reference an entry in the IRT. An unauthorized MSI interrupt either points to an invalid IRT entry or an valid IRT entry with a mismatched SID, and is thus blocked by the IOMMU [34].

When an MSI interrupt arrives at its destination CPU, the corresponding interrupt handler in the IDT is invoked. Specifically, an x86 CPU maintains two 256-bit bitmaps: the Interrupt Request Register (IRR) and In-Service Register (ISR). The arrival of an interrupt X with the vector v sets the v-th bit of the IRR (i.e., IRR[v]=1). As soon as X's interrupt handler is invoked, IRR[v] is cleared and ISR[v] is set to indicate that X is currently being serviced. When the interrupt handler associated with X completes, it writes to the end-of-interrupt (EOI) register of the corresponding LAPIC to acknowledge interrupt X to the hardware. Typically, the write to EOI does not contain vector information because

it implicitly assumes the completion of the currently highest interrupt. The interrupt controller in turn clears the corresponding bit in the ISR, and delivers the highest-priority interrupt among those that are currently pending, if any.

Finally, an x86 CPU core can send an interrupt to another CPU core via a special type of interrupt called an interprocessor interrupt (IPI). Applications of IPI include booting up, waking up or shutting down another CPU core for more power-efficient resource management, and flushing another CPU core's TLB to maintain TLB consistency. When a CPU core sends an IPI, it writes to the Interrupt Command Register (ICR) of its LAPIC a payload consisting of the IPI's parameters (e.g., the delivery mode, trigger mode, interrupt vector, destination ID, priority, etc). A CPU core is able to send an IPI to its own destination ID, thereby triggering a *self IPI*, an interrupt on the sending core.

2.2 Virtual Interrupt

An x86 CPU core is in *host* mode when the hypervisor runs on it and in *guest* mode when a VM runs on it. A CPU core stays in guest mode until any event configured to force a transition into host mode. When transitioning to host mode, the hypervisor takes over, handles the triggering event, and then re-enters guest mode to resume the VM's execution. The transition from guest mode to host mode is called a *VM exit* and the transition from host mode to guest mode is a *VM entry*. The performance overhead of a VM exit/entry lies in the cycles spent in saving and restoring execution contexts and the associated pollution of CPU caches when executing hypervisor code.

VT support [33] in the x86 architecture enables a hypervisor to set a control bit in the VMCS (Virtual Machine Control Structure) called the *external interrupt exiting* (EIE) bit, which specifies whether or not a VM exit is triggered in the event of a hardware interrupt. More concretely, if the EIE bit is cleared, an interrupt arriving at a CPU core with a running VM causes a direct invocation of the interrupt handler address in the VM, without incurring a VM exit. When EIE is set, the interrupt forces a VM exit and is handled by the hypervisor. The VT support of the x86 architecture also supports another control bit in the VMCS called *NMI exiting* bit, which specifies whether an NMI interrupt triggers a VM exit when it is delivered to a CPU core on which a VM is running, or if the NMI is also delivered directly into the VM.

When an interrupt is directly delivered to a VM, the CPU core uses a different Interrupt Descriptor Table (IDT) than the IDT used in host mode. On the other hand, when an interrupt destined for a VM triggers a VM exit and is delivered by the hypervisor, it is the hypervisor's responsibility to convert this interrupt into a virtual interrupt and inject it into the target VM when the VM resumes execution. Note that a VM exit does not always result in a virtual interrupt injection. For example, if a VM exit is caused by an interrupt whose target is not the running VM (e.g., a timer interrupt set up by the hypervisor), then this interrupt is not converted to a virtual interrupt and no virtual interrupt injection is performed.

KVM injects virtual interrupts into a VM by emulating the LAPIC registers with an in-memory data structure, mimicking a hardware LAPIC by setting up the emulated registers, such as IRR and ISR, prior to resuming the VM. When a VM is resumed, it checks the IRR, and services the highest-priority pending interrupt by looking up the VM's IDT and invoking the corresponding interrupt handler. After the interrupt handler completes, it acknowledges the virtual interrupt by writing to the (emulated) EOI register, which triggers another VM exit to the hypervisor to update the software-emulated IRR and ISR registers. This design has two drawbacks. First, a virtual interrupt could potentially override the service of a direct interrupt with a higher priority. Second, each EOI write incurs a VM exit in addition to the one that originally triggered interrupt delivery.

2.3 Virtual Device

A VM interacts with an I/O device directly if it is an SRIOV device and indirectly through the hypervisor if it is a virtual device. For an SRIOV device deployed on a server, every VM on the server is assigned a *virtual function* of the SRIOV device. When a virtual function on the SRIOV device issues an interrupt, the hypervisor handles the interrupt and then injects the corresponding virtual interrupt into the target VM. Modern hypervisors split virtual device drivers into front-end drivers, which reside in a guest, and back-end drivers, which reside in the hypervisor. When a VM performs an I/O transaction with a virtual device, the hypervisor terminates the transaction at the virtual device's back-end driver and injects a completion interrupt into the requesting VM via an IPI, because a VM and its backend driver typically run on different CPU cores. Asynchronously, the hypervisor performs the requested transaction with the corresponding physical device and handles the completion interrupt from the physical device in the normal way.

The completion interrupts from both SRIOV devices and virtual devices are handled by the hypervisor and are transformed and delivered to their target VMs as virtual interrupts. Moreover, the current mechanism for handling the EOI write of a virtual interrupt requires the involvement of the hypervisor. As a result, each completion interrupt from an I/O device entails at least two VM exits.

2.4 APIC Virtualization

Since one of the major reasons for VM exits is due to the hypervisor maintaining the states of a VM's emulated LAPIC, the recently released Intel CPU feature, APICv, is aimed to address the issue by virtualizing the LAPIC in the processor. In general, APICv virtualizes the interrupt-related states and APIC registers in VMCS. APICv emulates APIC-access so that APIC-read requests no longer cause exits and APIC-write requests are transformed from fault-like VM exits into trap-like VM exits, meaning that the instruction completes

before the VM exit and that processor state is updated by the instruction. APICv optimizes the virtual interrupt delivery process by its *posted interrupt* mechanism, which allows the hypervisor to inject virtual interrupts by programming the posted interrupt related data structures of VMCS in *guest mode*. Traditionally, delivering virtual interrupts requires VM exits into host mode because data structures maintained by VMCS are not allowed to be modified in guest mode. However with APICv, there is no such restriction and hypervisor is able to update the VM's interrupt state registers, such as IRR and ISR, while the VM is running.

Specifically, APICv enables delivering virtual interrupts without VM exits by adding two registers as guest interrupt status, the RVI (Requesting Virtual Interrupt) and the SVI (Servicing Virtual Interrupt), and allows them to be updated in *guest mode*. APICv's virtual interrupt, or posted interrupt, is delivered by setting up the 256-bit PIR (Posted Interrupt Request) registers and the ON (Outstanding Notification) bit. The PIR indicates the vector number of the posted interrupt to be delivered and the ON bit shows that there is an posted interrupt pending. The posted interrupt is delivered to the currently running guest-mode VM and the corresponding states of RVI and SVI are updated by the processor without hypervisor involvement. At the end of the posted interrupt handling, APICv's EOI virtualization keeps a 256-bit EOI-Exit bitmap, allowing the hypervisor to enable trap-less EOI write of the corresponding posted interrupt's vector number. Finally, posted interrupts can be configured in the interrupt remapping table so not only virtual interrupts but also external interrupts can directly injected into a guest.

3. Related Work

Interrupts and LAPIC have been identified as the major sources of I/O virtualization overhead, especially pronounced in I/O intensive workloads [13, 15, 18, 19, 25, 27]. To reduce the number of VM exits, hardware vendors are pursuing hardware virtualization support for the APIC, such as Intel's APICv [1], AMD's AVIC [3], and ARM's VGIC [16]. While these techniques may offer an alternative in future hardware generations, DID can achieve the same or better goals of minimizing the VM exits overheads today, without requiring advanced vendor-specific hardware support.

Ole Agesen et al. [14] propose a binary rewriting technique to reduce the number of VM exits. The mechanism dynamically optimizes the VM's code by identifying instruction pairs that cause consecutive VM exits and dynamically translating the guest code to a variant that incurs fewer VM exits. Jailhouse [4] is a partitioning hypervisor that pre-allocates the hardware resources and dedicates them to guest OSes in order to achieve bare-metal performance. However, due to lack of hardware virtualization for all types of physical resources, this approach generally requires heavy guest modifications and loses the benefits of virtualization. On the

	Virtual Interrupt	External Device Interrupt	Timer Interrupt	End-Of-Interrupt	Guest Modification
ELI/ELVIS	Mixed HW/emulated LAPIC	Partially Direct	Indirect	Partially Direct	No/Yes
Jailhouse	Not Support	Direct	Direct	Direct	Yes
APICv	Posted Interrupt	Indirect	Indirect	Direct	No
DID	HW LAPIC	Direct	Direct	Direct	No

Table 1. *Comparison of the interrupt delivering mechanisms between ELI/ELVIS, Jailhouse, APICv, and DID.*

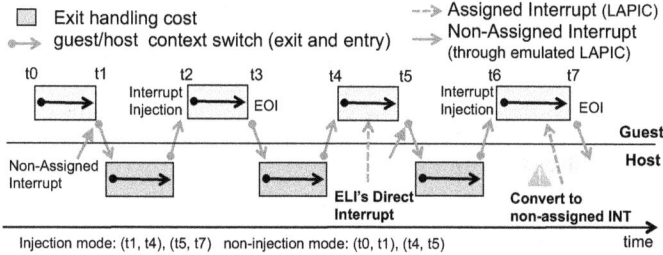

Figure 1. *ELI's mechanism takes effects only at its non-injection mode period, which are between (t0, t1) and (t4, t5), while DID direct delivers all interrupts as long as the CPU is in guest mode.*

other hand, NoHype [22, 29] addresses the VM exit from the perspective of security, because VM exits are the point where control transfers from guest to the host/hypervisor. Unlike NoHype, DID is built for performance rather than security.

ELI and ELVIS are the most well-known software solution for achieving direct interrupt delivery. While ELI directly delivers only SRIOV device interrupts to the VM, DID improves upon ELI by also directly delivering *all* interrupts including timer, virtualized, and paravirtualized device interrupts. ELI solved the mis-delivery problem by using a shadow IDT, modifying the VM's IDT such that all interrupt vectors allocated to the hypervisor and other VMs are made invalid, causing the corresponding interrupts to always force the a VM exit. In the case of paravirtual I/O device interrupts, DID is more general than ELVIS, because it does not require modifications to the guest OS, a major deployment advantage for VMs using closed-sourced OSes and binary OS distributions. Finally, DID leverages the IPI mechanism to inject virtual interrupts into target VMs, thus forcing virtual interrupts to be managed by the HW LAPIC in the same way as directly delivered interrupts. This unifies the delivery mechanisms of virtual and direct interrupts, avoiding priority inversion.

Additionally, the direct interrupt delivery mechanism proposed by ELI/ELVIS takes effects only at its non-injection mode, as illustrated in Figure 1. Specifically, ELI separates interrupt sources to be either assigned interrupts, which is delivered directly, and non-assigned interrupts, which falls back to KVM's virtual interrupt. Non-assigned interrupts must be handled by the emulated LAPIC at the injection mode, which disables the direct delivery. As non-assigned interrupts arrive at $t1$ and until its completion $t4$, the ELI's direct interrupt mechanism is fully off. Even if an assigned

interrupt arrives at the injection mode, ($t6$, $t7$), ELI/ELVIS has to convert it to non-assigned interrupt, making the direct interrupt mechanism *partially direct* and the system staying longer handling traditional interrupt injection. We summarize the existing approaches in Table 1 and present the design of DID in the next section.

4. Proposed Direct Interrupt Delivery Scheme

In this section, we describe the mechanisms comprising our Direct Interrupt Delivery approach and prorotype implementation.

4.1 Overview

The main challenge we address to support direct interrupt delivery on x86 servers is in avoiding the *mis-delivery* problem, the problem of delivering an interrupt to an unintended VM. The mis-delivery problem mainly results from the following architectural limitations. First, the x86 server architecture dictates that either every external interrupt causes a VM exit or none of the external interrupts cause a VM exit. This limitation makes it difficult to deliver an interrupt differently depending on whether its target VM is currently running or not. One possible solution is shadow IDT [18, 19]. However, it carried several security issues. Second, the hypervisor is able to inject a virtual interrupt into a VM only when the hypervisor and the VM both run on the same CPU core. For virtual devices, this causes a VM exit for every interrupt from a back-end driver to one of its associated front-end drivers, because these drivers tend to run on different CPU cores. Third, LAPIC timer interrupts do not go through the IOMMU and therefore cannot benefit from the interrupt remapping table. As a result, existing mechanisms for timer interrupt delivery trigger VM exits to the hypervisor. This incurs significant performance overheads as high-resolution timers are used in ever more applications. Moreover, triggering VM exits on timer interrupts increases the variance of the interrupt invocation latency because an additional software layer (i.e., the hypervisor) is involved in the interrupt delivery.

DID leverages the flexibility provided by x2APIC [11] to remove unnecessary VM exits when programming timers and signaling completion of interrupts. With x2APIC, the hypervisor can specify which registers in the LAPIC area can be directly read or written by the VM without triggering a VM exit. Specifically, DID exposes two model-specific register to the VMs, the x2APIC EOI register and

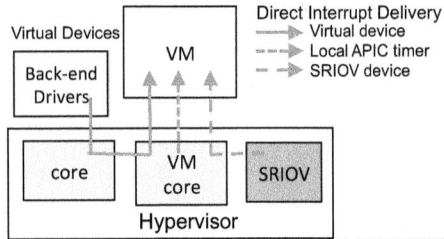

Figure 2. *DID delivers interrupts from SRIOV devices, virtual devices, and timers directly to the target VM.*

the TMICT (Initial Timer Count) register. As a result, a VM can program the LAPIC timer and write to the associated EOI register directly, without incurring a VM exit and associated performance overheads.

In the following subsections, we will go into the details of how DID delivers interrupts from SRIOV devices, virtual devices, and timers directly to their targets, and how to support direct EOI write while preserving the priority among interrupts regardless of how they are delivered.

4.2 SRIOV Device Interrupt

When a VM M is started on a server with an SRIOV device (e.g., a NIC), it is given a virtual function F on the SRIOV device. Once the binding between M and F is established, M can issue memory-mapped I/O instructions directly to F and F can only interrupt M. In DID, when F generates an interrupt, if M is running, this interrupt goes through the PCIe hierarchy, an IOMMU, and eventually reaches the LAPIC of the CPU core on which M is running in guest mode; otherwise, DID arranges to deliver the interrupt to the hypervisor, which then injects a virtual interrupt into M.

To achieve the above behavior, for every VMCS, we clear the EIE bit, so that delivery of an interrupt to a running VM does not cause a VM exit. We also set the NMI exiting bit, so that an NMI interrupt forces a VM exit, even when the EIE bit is cleared. When our DID hypervisor schedules a VM M to run on a CPU core C, it modifies the IOMMU's interrupt remapping table entries assigned to M's virtual functions so that the destination of the interrupts generated by these virtual functions is C. This ensures that every SRIOV device interrupt of M is routed directly to the CPU core assigned to M when M is running. Additionally, when the DID hypervisor deschedules a VM M, it modifies the IOMMU's interrupt remapping table entries assigned to M's virtual functions so that the delivery mode of the interrupts generated by these virtual functions is changed to the NMI mode. This ensures that every SRIOV device interrupt for M causes a VM exit and is delivered to the hypervisor as an NMI interrupt when M is not running. The additional modifications to the interrupt remapping table at the time when the hypervisor schedules and deschedules a VM enable direct delivery of an SRIOV device interrupt only when the interrupt's target VM is running.

When an SRIOV device interrupt is delivered indirectly through the DID hypervisor, the hypervisor runs on the CPU core on which the interrupt's target VM originally ran, rather than on a dedicated CPU core. This allows the processing overhead of our indirectly-delivered interrupts to be uniformly spread across all CPU cores.

In our design, even when a VM M is running on a CPU core C, it is possible that, when a directly-delivered SRIOV device interrupt reaches C, C is in fact in host mode (i.e., the hypervisor is running, rather than M). In this case, the DID hypervisor converts the received interrupt into a virtual interrupt and injects it into M when resuming M's execution.

4.3 Virtual Device Interrupt

To exploit parallelism between physical I/O device operation and VM execution, modern hypervisors, such as KVM, dedicate a thread to each virtual device associated with a VM. Normally, a VM's virtual device thread runs on a different CPU core than the CPU core on which the VM runs. On a DID system, when a virtual device thread delivers a virtual device interrupt I to its associated VM M, the virtual device thread first checks if M is currently running, and, if so, issues an IPI to the CPU core on which M runs with the IPI's interrupt vector set to I's interrupt vector. Because we clear the EIE bit, this IPI is delivered to M without causing a VM exit. The end result is that a virtual device interrupt is directly delivered into its associated VM without a VM exit.

Even though the DID hypervisor tries to deliver a virtual device interrupt to its associated VM only when the VM is running, there is a possible race condition. An IPI-based virtual device interrupt can only be delivered to a CPU core on which its associated VM should be running, but it is possible for the CPU core to be in host mode rather than in guest mode when the interrupt is delivered. In this situation, the hypervisor accepts the IPI on behalf of the associated VM, converts the IPI-based virtual device interrupt into a virtual interrupt and injects it into the associated VM before resuming guest execution.

4.4 Timer Interrupt

For direct delivery of SRIOV device interrupts, we solve mis-delivery problem in DID by taking advantage of the flexibility offered by hardware support for interrupt remapping. In direct delivery of virtual device interrupts, DID solves the mis-delivery problem by making sure that the target VM is running on the target CPU core before sending an IPI to that core. However, on x86 servers, timer interrupts are associated with the LAPIC and do not pass through an interrupt remapping table before reaching their target CPU core. As a result, the hypervisor does not have the flexibility of modifying how a timer interrupt is delivered after it is set up. Consequently, if a timer interrupt is delivered directly, without involving the hypervisor, a timer set up by a VM can be erroneously delivered to the hypervisor, if the target CPU core is in host mode or it can be delivered to the wrong

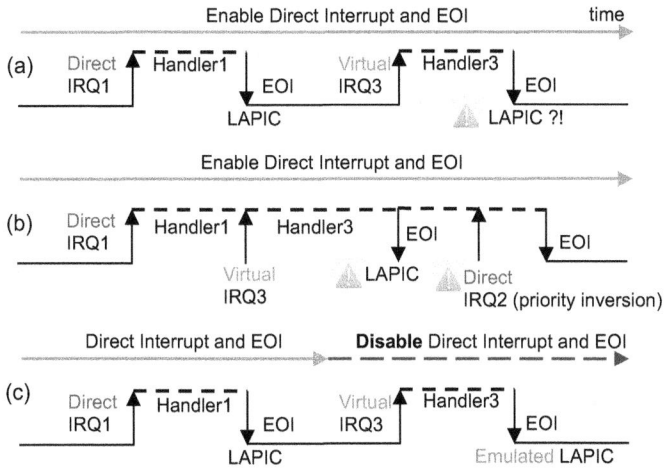

Figure 3. *(a) The LAPIC may receive an EOI write when it thinks there are no pending interrupts. (b) The LAPIC may dispatch an interrupt (IRQ2) when the current interrupt (IRQ1) is not yet done because it receives an EOI write. (c) ELI [18, 19] avoids the confusions caused by direct EOI write by turning off direct interrupt delivery and EOI write whenever at least one virtual interrupt is being handled.*

VM if another VM is running on the target CPU core at the time of timer expiration.

To support direct delivery of timer interrupts while avoiding the mis-delivery problem in DID, we restrict timers set up by the hypervisor to a designated core. Moreover, when the hypervisor schedules a VM M on a CPU core C, the timers that M configured are installed on C's hardware timer; when the hypervisor deschedules a VM M from CPU core C, the timers that M configured are removed from C's hardware timer and installed on the hardware timer of the designated CPU core.

Our design enforces the invariant that, except for the designated CPU core, the only timers installed on a CPU core's hardware timer are set up by the VM currently running on that CPU core. Therefore, this invariant guarantees that no mis-delivery problem is possible when timer interrupts are delivered directly. On the designated CPU core, the DID hypervisor is prepared to service timer interrupts configured by the hypervisor and by those VMs that are not currently running. The timer interrupts destined to non-running VMs are delivered to them as virtual interrupts when those VMs are resumed.

4.5 Direct End-of-Interrupt Write

When an interrupt handler completes servicing an interrupt in DID, it writes to an x2APIC EOI register on the associated LAPIC to acknowledge to the interrupt controller that the service of the current interrupt is finished and the interrupt controller is allowed to deliver the next pending interrupt. The x86 architecture allows our system software to choose whether to trigger a VM exit or not when a VM writes to the

associated EOI register. Although it is desirable to avoid a VM exit when a VM writes to the associated EOI register, there may be undesirable side effects if writing to the EOI register does not involve the hypervisor, depending on the mechanism used by the hypervisor to inject virtual interrupts into VMs.

A common way to inject virtual interrupts into a VM, as implemented by KVM, is to properly set up the emulated LAPIC of the VM's VMCS before resuming the VM. However, this emulated LAPIC approach requires EOI writes to trigger VM exits to ensure the consistency in the states of the emulated and physical APICs. If the handler of a virtual interrupt directly writes the EOI, the LAPIC may receive an EOI notification when it thinks there is no pending interrupt, as shown in Figure 3 (a), or may think the currently pending interrupt is already completed when in fact it is still on-going, as shown in Figure 3 (b). Moreover, the LAPIC may incorrectly dispatch a lower-priority interrupt (e.g., IRQ2 in Figure 3) (b) to preempt a higher-priority interrupt (e.g., IRQ1), because the handler for the virtual interrupt IRQ3 writes to the EOI register directly.

The root cause of this priority inversion problem is that virtual interrupts are not visible to the LAPIC when they are injected via software emulation of IRR/ISR. To solve this problem, existing direct interrupt delivery solutions [18, 19, 31] disable direct interrupt delivery and direct EOI writes for a VM whenever the VM is handling any virtual interrupt, as shown in Figure 3 (c) and as called *injection mode* in ELI/ELVIS. Our approach to this problem in DID is different, in that we use a self-IPI to inject a virtual interrupt into a VM. Specifically, before the DID hypervisor resumes a VM, it issues an IPI to its own CPU core. This IPI is then delivered to the injected VM directly after the VM resumes. If multiple virtual interrupts need to be injected into a VM, our DID hypervisor sets up multiple IPIs, each corresponding to one virtual interrupt.

DID's IPI-based virtual interrupt injection mechanism completely eliminates the priority inversion problem due to direct EOI write. When a virtual interrupt is delivered in the form of an IPI, it becomes visible to the target CPU core's LAPIC, enabling it to compete with other direct and virtual interrupts. Because a LAPIC observes every interrupt delivered to its associated CPU core and every EOI write, it allows our system to not mistake an in-service interrupt for being completed when in fact it is not and to not deliver a new interrupt prematurely.

Because DID uses IPIs for direct delivery of virtual interrupts, regular IPIs no longer trigger VM exits in our system. For the original applications of IPIs, such as shutting down CPU cores or flushing remote TLBs, we use special IPIs in DID whose delivery mode is set to NMI. The NMI setting forces a VM exit on the target CPU core, enabling the DID hypervisor to regain control and take proper actions corresponding to the special IPIs.

Regardless of whether or not the DID hypervisor runs on the same CPU core as the VM into which a virtual interrupt is being injected, our DID design uses the same IPI-based mechanism (with proper interrupt vector setting) to deliver the virtual interrupt. There are two key advantages of our IPI-based virtual interrupt delivery mechanism. First, when the source and destination involved in a virtual interrupt delivery run on different CPU cores, no VM exit is needed. Second, because each virtual interrupt takes the form of a hardware interrupt (i.e., IPI) and goes through the target CPU core's LAPIC, the priority among interrupts delivered to a CPU core is correctly preserved no matter how these interrupts are delivered, directly or otherwise.

5. Performance Evaluation

5.1 Evaluation Methodology

To quantify the effectiveness of DID, we measured the reason for and the service time spent in each VM exit using a variety of workloads. We then calculated the time-in-guest (TIG) percentage by summing up the time between each VM entry and VM exit as the total time in guest, and dividing the total time in guest by the total elapsed time.

The hardware testbed used in the evaluation of our DID prototype consists of two Intel x86 servers that are connected back to back with two Intel 10GE 82599 NICs. DID is installed on one of the servers, which is a Supermicro E3 tower server and has an 8-core Intel Xeon 3.4GHz CPU with hardware virtualization (VT-x) support and 8GB memory. The other server acts as a request-generating host, which is equipped with an 8-core Intel i7 3.4GHz CPU and 8GB memory. The server on which DID is installed runs KVM with Intel's VT-d support enabled so that multiple virtual machines could directly access an SRIOV device without interference.

We run Fedora 15 with Linux kernel version 3.6.0-rc4 and qemu-kvm version 1.0 on both servers. We provision each VM with a single vCPU, pinned to a specific core, 1GB memory, one virtual function from the Intel SRIOV NIC, and one paravirtualized network device using virtio and the vhost [10, 26] kernel module.

We boot each VM with the same CPU type setting as the host and enable x2APIC support. The virtual machine started into the graphical user interface mode since the console mode (with -nographic) carried extra performance overhead due to VM exits triggered by MMIOs [23]. We also set idle=poll to prevent a HLT instruction from causing a VM exit. For timer experiments, we enable the kernel parameter "NO_HZ".

We configure all CPU cores to run at their maximum frequency, because the *cyclictest* program tends to report longer latency when the CPU core runs in a power efficient or on-demand mode. For all network experiments, we set the Maximum Transmission Unit (MTU) to its default size of 1500 bytes.

For each configuration, we turn DID on and off to evaluate the benefits of DID. The following benchmark programs are used in this study.

- *WhileLoop*: a loop running for 2^{34} iterations, where each iteration performs one integer addition.

- *Cyclictest*: program for measuring the *interrupt invocation latency* (the average time interval between the moment a hardware interrupt is generated and the moment the corresponding handler in the user-level cyclictest program receives control). We run cyclictest with the highest priority on a dedicated core, measuring 100,000 interrupts at a rate of one per millisecond.

- *PacketGen*: a UDP-based program that sends 128-byte UDP packets to a UDP-based receiver at the rate of 100K, 250K, 400K, and 600K packets per second, where both the sender and receiver programs run at the lowest priority level.

- *NetPIPE* [28]: a ping-pong test to measure the half round-trip time between two machines. In our experiments, we vary the message size from 32 bytes to 1024 bytes.

- *Iperf* [30]: program for measuring the TCP throughput between two machines. We report the average of five 100-second runs.

- *Fio* [2]: single-threaded program performing 4KB random disk reads and writes to a virtual disk backed via virtio by a 1GB ramdisk with cache disabled.

- *DPDK l2fwd* [21]: user-level network device drivers and libraries that support line-rate network packet forwarding.

- *Memcached* [5, 17]: key-value store server. We emulate a twitter-like workload and measure the peak requests served per second (RPS) while maintaining 10ms latency for at least 95% of requests.

- *SIP B2BUA [9]*: a SIP (Session Initiation Protocol) Back-to-Back User Agent server software which maintains complete call states and requests. We use SIPp [8] to establish 100 calls per second with each call lasting 10 seconds.

5.2 Reduction in VM Exit Rate

In the 64-bit Intel x86 architecture with VT-x, there are 56 possible reasons for a VM exit. Each VM exit leads to its corresponding exit handler in the hypervisor and reduces the number of CPU cycles spent in the VM. We identify the most-frequently occurring reasons for triggering a VM exit under I/O-intensive workloads as (1) EXTINT: Arrival of an external interrupt, which includes IPIs sent from the hypervisor's I/O thread and hardware interrupts from SRIOV and para-virtualized devices, (2) PENDVINT: Notification of a pending virtual interrupt to a VM that was previously uninterruptible, (3) MSRWR: Attempt by a VM to write to a

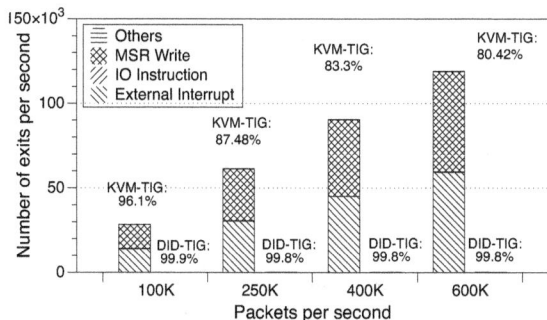

Figure 4. *The breakdown of VM exit reasons for a test VM running on KVM when it is receiving UDP packets through an SRIOV NIC at different rates and when DID is turned on or off*

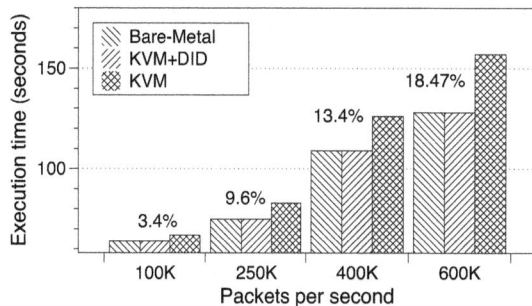

Figure 5. *The execution time of a while-loop program on a bare metal machine, a VM running on KVM, and on KVM with DID, when there is a background load of receiving UDP packets through an SRIOV at different rates.*

model-specific register (MSR) (e.g., programming LAPIC registers and EOI registers), and (4) IOINSR: Attempt by a VM to execute an I/O instruction (e.g., configuring a hardware device).

To assess the effectiveness of DID under a network-intensive workload, we measure the VM exit rate of a running VM when it is receiving UDP packets at different rates. Specifically, we measured vanilla KVM Linux against a system with DID on a test server equipped with an SRIOV NIC. We used a test VM provisioned with a VF on the SRIOV NIC and ran a UDP receiver program in the test VM, collecting the VM exit statistics using the Linux kernel's ftrace facility while a separate program sends UDP packets to the receiver inside the test VM. As shown in Figure 4, when the UDP packet rate at the test VM reaches 100K packets per second, the VM exit rate reaches 28K exits per second, with 96.1% of the time spent in guest mode (TIG). The two dominant reasons for VM exits are external interrupts (EXTINT) and writes to model-specific registers (MSRWR). Because the NIC used in this test supports SRIOV, most external interrupts come from the MSI-X interrupts generated by the VF assigned to the test VM when it receives UDP packets. When using para-virtualized network device, the external interrupt exit is caused by an IPI (inter-processor interrupt) sending from the backend driver, usually the QEMU I/O thread. Additionally, by analyzing the target of each MSR write operation, we conclude that writing to the EOI (End-Of-Interrupt) register accounts for more than 99% of MSR writes. The fact that only 28K VM exits per second are observed when the test VM is receiving 100K packets per second demonstrates that the NIC supports interrupt coalescing. As the packet rate is increased to 250K, 400K, and 600K, the VM exit rate increases to 62K, 90K and 118K, respectively, and the time in guest (TIG) decreases to 87.48%, 83.3%, and 80.42%, respectively. Because the NIC coalesces interrupts more aggressively at higher packet rates, the VM exit rate grows less than linearly with the packet rate.

Figure 4 shows that DID eliminates almost all VM exits due to external interrupts and EOI writes, and reduces

the VM exit rate to under 1K per second regardless of the UDP packet rate. With DID, the main reason for VM exits is the I/O instructions (IOINSR) that the guest VM's drivers (i.e., SRIOV VF driver and virtio-net/virtio-blk) use to program the assigned VF's configuration registers, such as the descriptors in the transmission/reception ring buffers. When the test VM is receiving packets at 600K per second, DID saves $(99.8 - 80.42) = 19.38\%$ of the CPU time by avoiding unnecessary VM exits.

5.3 Application-Level CPU Saving

To quantify DID's performance benefits at the application level, we ran the WhileLoop program on a physical machine running Linux (bare metal), on a Linux VM under KVM without DID (vanilla KVM), and on a Linux VM under KVM with DID (KVM+DID). The WhileLoop program does not execute any privileged instruction and thus incurs no VM exit overhead during its execution. At the same time, we ran the UDP receiving program in the background, receiving UDP packets at different rates. Figure 5 shows that for all tested packet rates, the total elapsed time of WhileLoop in the KVM+DID configuration is nearly identical to that of the bare metal configuration. This is because DID eliminates almost all VM exit overheads, allowing the vast majority of the CPU time to be spent in guest mode while executing the WhileLoop program. In contrast, the elapsed time of WhileLoop in the vanilla KVM configuration increases with the UDP packet rate because higher packet rates lead to more VM exit overhead and thus lower TIGs. Accordingly, the WhileLoop performance gains of KVM+DID over vanilla KVM for the tested packet rates are 3.4%, 9.6%, 13.4%, and 18.47%. As shown in Figure 5, the performance gains are closely correlated with the reductions in TIGs that DID enables, 3.8%, 11.42%, 16.6%, and 19.38%, respectively.

5.4 Interrupt Invocation Latency

In addition to reduced VM exit overheads, another major performance benefit of DID is reduction in the interrupt in-

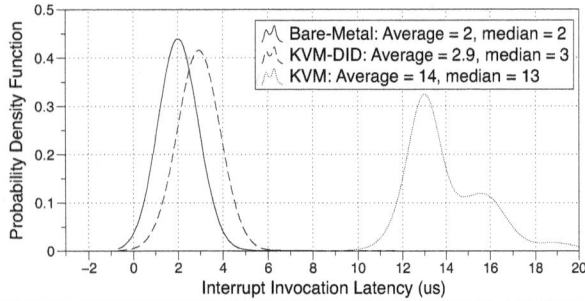

Figure 6. *The probability density function of the interrupt invocation latency of the bare metal, vanilla KVM and KVM+DID configuration during a 100-second cyclictest run*

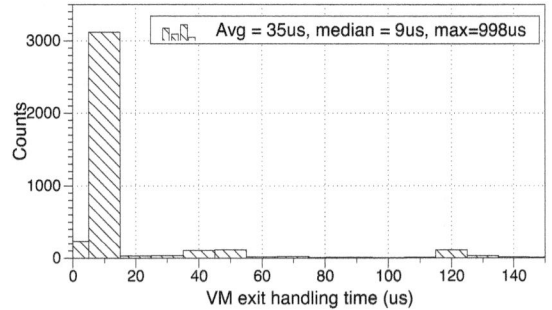

Figure 7. *Service time distribution of the VM exits during which a timer interrupt of a cyclictest program run is delivered*

vocation latency, the time between when a hardware interrupt is generated and when the corresponding interrupt handler starts processing it. Cutting down the interrupt invocation latency is crucial to real-time computing systems because it reduces their worst-case delay bound. DID reduces the interrupt invocation latency by removing the hypervisor from the interrupt delivery path. We used the cyclictest program to evaluate DID's interrupt invocation latency, which in this case is specifically defined as the time difference between when a timer generates an interrupt and when the user-level cyclictest program is invoked to handle it. In the vanilla KVM configuration, where interrupts are delivered indirectly through the hypervisor, factors that affect the interrupt invocation latency are:

1. The hypervisor may temporarily disable interrupt delivery and thus delay the delivery of interrupts from hardware devices to the hypervisor.

2. The hypervisor may introduce additional delays before converting a received interrupt into a virtual interrupt and injecting it into its target VM.

3. A VM's guest OS may disable interrupts and thus delay the delivery of virtual interrupts from the hypervisor to the guest OS.

4. There may be delays in scheduling the cyclictest program after the guest OS handles an incoming virtual interrupt.

In this test, we raised the scheduling priority of the cyclictest program to the highest possible, thus decreasing the variation in the fourth factor above. However, the first three factors are determined by the interrupt mechanisms in the hypervisor and guest OS.

Figure 6 plots the probability density function of the interrupt invocation latency of the bare metal, vanilla KVM, and KVM+DID configuration after running 100,000 timer operations of the cyclictest program. The average interrupt invocation latency of vanilla KVM is $14\mu s$. As expected, this configuration exhibits the highest interrupt latency, because each timer operation in the cyclictest program takes at least three VM exits to set-up the LAPIC timer (specifically TMICT register), receive a timer interrupt, and acknowledge

the completion of a timer interrupt. The VM exits are chiefly responsible for the increase in the delay and variability associated with the second factor above.

The average interrupt invocation latency of KVM+DID is $2.9\mu s$, because DID eliminates all VM exits due to TMICT register programming, timer interrupt delivery, and EOI write. Although close to bare metal, the average interrupt invocation latency of KVM+DID is $0.9\mu s$ higher. Although most timer interrupts are delivered directly to the CPU core under DID, it is possible that the target CPU core is in host mode rather than in guest mode at the time of interrupt delivery. When this happens, the hypervisor sets up the self-IPI bitmap to generate a timer interrupt to the target VM when guest execution is resumed. Therefore, the interrupt invocation latency is increased by the amount of time that the hypervisor takes to complete the operation in progress when it receives the interrupt. In our tests, even in an idle VM, there remain approximately 500 VM exits per second, most of which are due to I/O instructions and extended page table (EPT) violations in the VM. The service times for these VM exits account for the small interrupt invocation latency gap between bare metal and KVM+DID.

In a 100-second cyclictest run, there were 100,000 timer interrupts, of which 991 VM exits were due to EPT violations with an average VM exit service time of $9.9\mu s$, and 6550 VM exits were due to I/O instructions, with an average VM exit service time of $8.65\mu s$. During this time, only 3,830 timer interrupts were delivered to the target CPU core when it is in host mode or during a VM exit; the service time distribution of these VM exits is shown in Figure 7. 1782 of the 3830 timer interrupts land in VM exits due to EPT violations, with an average VM exit service time of $11.07\mu s$, while the remaining timer interrupts land in VM exits due to I/O instructions, with an average VM exit service time of $24.11\mu s$. As a result, the total contribution of these VM exit service times to the timer interrupt's invocation latency is $84,300\mu s$ over the 100-second run. Because the average interrupt invocation latency of the bare metal configuration is $2\mu s$, the average interrupt invocation latency in KVM+DID can be approximated by $((100,000-3,830) * 2 + 84,289) /$

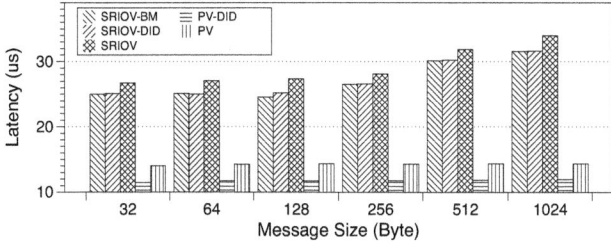

Figure 8. *One-way packet latency between an external server and another server running in the bare metal configuration (SRIOV-BM), the KVM+SRIOV+DID configuration (SRIOV-DID) and the KVM+SRIOV configuration (SRIOV), and between a process running directly on top of a Linux-KVM machine and another process running inside a VM that in turn runs on the same Linux-KVM machine with DID turned on (PV-DID) or off (PV)*

$100,000 = 2.76\mu s$, which is close to the measured result, $2.9\mu s$.

5.5 Network Performance Benefits

To measure DID's impact on packet latency, we used the NetPIPE benchmarking tool [28], which employs ping-pong tests to measure the half round-trip time between two servers. Figure 8 shows the latency measurements reported by NetPIPE as we vary the message size from 32 bytes to 1024 bytes. The left-most three bars for each message size correspond to NetPIPE results measured between an external server and another server running in a bare-metal configuration (SRIOV-BM), the KVM+SRIOV+DID configuration (SRIOV-DID), and the KVM+SRIOV configuration (SRIOV). When the SRIOV NIC is used, programming the VFs does not trigger a VM exit. As a result, there is no noticeable difference between the packet latency of the SRIOV-BM configuration and the SRIOV-DID configuration, because the latter does not incur a VM exit on interrupt delivery. In the SRIOV configuration, the only VM exits observed are due to interrupts generated by the VFs and EOI writes, resulting in the average service times for these VM exits being $0.85\mu s$ and $1.97\mu s$, respectively. Under the case of SRIOV, we observe two types of VM exits per packet received when executing the NetPIPE benchmark. The first exit is due to the arrival of the external interrupt, indicating the packet arrival, and the second VM exit is due to acknowledgement of interrupt (EOI). The average exit handling time of EOI takes 0.85us, while the eixt handling time of the external interrupt is 1.97us. Consequently, the average packet latency of the SRIOV configuration is higher than that of the SRIOV-BM configuration by approximately $2.44\mu s$, which is comparable to $1.97 + 0.85 = 2.82\mu s$. When the packet size is increasing, the latency also increases as the per-byte overhead starts to dominate the packet latency and accordingly the packet latency increases with the packet size.

The two right-most bars for each message size in Figure 8 correspond to the NetPIPE results measured between

a process running on a Linux-KVM host and another process running inside a VM that, in turn, runs on the same Linux-KVM machine with DID turned on (PV-DID) or off (PV). These processes communicate with each other through a para-virtualized front-end driver, a virtio-net back-end driver, and a Linux virtual bridge. In theory, each packet exchange requires three VM exits, one for interrupt delivery, another for EOI write, and a third for updating the back-end device's internal state. In practice, the virtio-net implementation batches the device state updates required by the processing of multiple packets and significantly cuts down the number of VM exits due to I/O instructions, as compared to the number of VM exits caused by EOI writes and interrupt delivery. Consequently, the average packet latency of the PV configuration is higher than that of the PV-DID configuration by at most $2.41\mu s$, which is comparable to the sum of the average service times of the VM exits caused by EOI writes and interrupt delivery. Whereas the packet latencies of SRIOV and SRIOV-DID increase with the message size, the packet latencies of PV and PV-DID are independent of the message size, because the latter does not copy the message's payload when packets are exchanged within the same physical server [10, 26].

To quantify the network throughput benefits of DID, we used the iperf tool [30]. Our results show that, over a 10Gbps link, the iperf throughput of the SRIOV-DID configuration is 9.4Gbps, which is 1.1% better than that of the SRIOV configuration (9.3Gbps), even though the TIG improvement of SRIOV-DID over SRIOV is 16.8%. The CPU-time savings cannot be fully translated into network throughput gain, because the physical network link's raw capacity is nearly saturated. Over an intra-machine connection, the iperf throughput of the PV-DID configuration is 24Gbps, which is 21% better than that of the PV configuration (19.8Gbps), even though the TIG improvement of PV-DID over PV is only 11.8%. The CPU-time savings are more than the network throughput gain, because no payload is actually copied for intra-machine communication and therefore reduction of CPU time does not directly translate to throughput gain.

On the other hand, we also found that DID does not show observable improvement over the DPDK l2fwd benchmark. For DPDK, we set-up the SRIOV NIC and executed DPDK's layer 2 forwarding program, l2fwd, using a VM's VF device. We generate the forwarding traffic from the request generating server to the VM using DPDK's version of Pktgen, and measure the maximum number of received and forwarded packets processed by l2fwd program. Due to the polling nature of DPDK, all network packets are delivered to the l2fwd program via VF device without triggering any interrupt. As a result, either with or without DID, l2fwd shows capable of forwarding 7.9 millions of 128-byte packets per second.

5.6 Block I/O Performance Benefits

To analyze the performance benefits of DID under a high-performance directly-attached disk I/O system, such as an

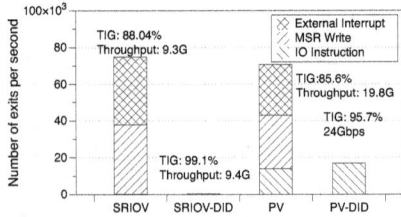

Figure 9. *The iperf throughput improvement of DID when a SRIOV NIC is used for inter-server communication and a paravirtualized NIC is used for intra-server communication*

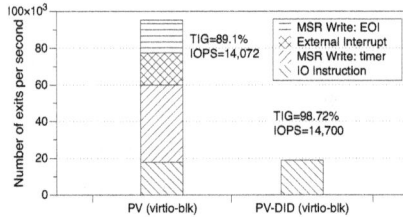

Figure 10. *The VM exit rate and the breakdown of VM exit reasons of the Fio benchmark*

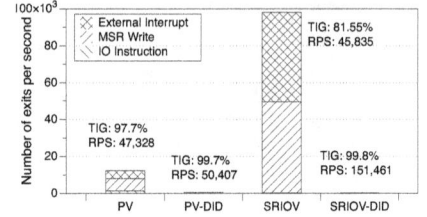

Figure 11. *The VM exit rate and the breakdown of VM exit reasons of a Memcached server under the PV, PV-DID, SRIOV, and SRIOV-DID configurations*

array of solid state disks, we configured a 1GB ramdisk on the host, exposing it to the test VM running on the host using virtio-blk, and ran the Fio benchmark inside the test VM. We measured the IOPS and the I/O completion time, which is the time difference between when Fio issues an I/O request and when that request is completed and returned to Fio. Figure 10 shows that, when DID is turned off, the IOPS is 14K with an average I/O completion time of $34\mu s$. When DID is turned on, the IOPS increases to 14.7K with an average I/O completion time of $32\mu s$. These performance differences again result from the fact that DID eliminates VM exits due to interrupt delivery (EXTINT) and MSRWR writes. As expected, the performance gain of DID is limited by the block I/O rate and thus the associated interrupt rate is generally much lower.

Unlike iperf, where the number of VM exits due to interrupt delivery is approximately the same as the number of MSRWR writes, Fio observes three times the number of VM exits due to MSRWR writes compared to the number of VM exits due to interrupt delivery. Analysis of the Fio benchmark reveals that the program sets up a timer before submitting an I/O request to protect itself from unresponsive disks and clears the timer after each request is completed. Therefore, for every I/O request, three MSRWR writes are needed, one for EOI write, and two for TWICT writes. DID successfully eliminates all VM exits due to these MSR writes.

5.7 Memcached Workload

To evaluate the performance improvement of DID on a popular server workload, we set up a dual-threaded Memcached 600MB server inside a VM (the test VM is configured with one vCPU and 1GB of RAM). We generated a 600MB twitter dataset and warmed up the server by preloading the dataset. We then run a Memcached client simulator that creates eight threads and 200 TCP/IP connections with a get/set ratio of 4:1. To guarantee quality of service in each experiment, we empirically find the peak request rate that allows the server to complete 95% of all requests within 10 msec. We turn off Nagle's algorithm (TCP nodelay option) on both client and server ends.

Figure 11 shows the VM exit rate of the PV, PV-DID, SRIOV, and SRIOV-DID configurations, whose RPS are 47.3K, 50.4K, 45.8K, and 151.5K, respectively. SRIOV-DID outperforms all other configurations by a large margin, because it enjoys the benefits of both SRIOV and DID and removes the majority of VM exits, with a TIG of 99.8%. We compared the performance of the Memcached server on a bare-metal setup of the same hardware, observing a 152.3K RPS, which is only 0.6% higher than SRIOV-DID. The second best setup is PV-DID, with a TIG of 99.7%, followed by the PV configuration, with a TIG of 97.7%. Notably, SRIOV comes in last, with a TIG of 81.55%. Even though SRIOV does not incur any VM exit overhead due to I/O instructions, SRIOV still performs worse than PV, because it incurs a larger number of VM exits due to interrupt delivery and EOI writes than PV. In the PV configuration, the vhost thread periodically polls the physical NIC, batches incoming packets, and then interrupts the front-end driver in the target VM. As a result, the number of packets delivered to a target VM per interrupt is noticeably higher in the PV configuration than in the SRIOV configuration.

One way to achieve the same interrupt aggregation benefit as a polling vhost thread in the PV configuration is to leverage Linux's NAPI facility, which is designed to mitigate the interrupt overhead through polling when the incoming interrupt rate exceeds a certain threshold. To confirm that interrupt rate reduction via polling is the reason behind the inferior performance of SRIOV, we reduced the NAPI threshold of the Linux VM from its default value of 64 down to 32, 16, 8, and 4, essentially increasing the likelihood that the guest's SRIOV VF driver runs in polling mode. When the NAPI threshold is set to 4 or 8, the resulting RPS of the SRIOV configuration rises to 48.3K, improving over the PV configuration. However, the price for lowering the NAPI threshold to 4 or 8 is an increase in CPU utilization by 3% and 6%, respectively. These results confirm that careful tuning can mitigate VM exit overheads of SRIOV in some cases, making them comparable to PV.

In addition to higher CPU utilization, the PV and PV-DID configurations also increase the request latency due to request batching. Because of the increased request latency, the quality-of-service target cannot be achieved at the same request rate. This explains why, even though the TIG difference between PV-DID and SRIOV-DID is only 0.1%, the RPS of SRIOV-DID is about three times higher than that of PV-DID.

5.8 VoIP Workload

To evaluate the performance benefits of DID in a B2BUA system, we configured the SIPp [8] UAC (User Agent Client) as the call originating endpoint at the request-generating host, the B2BUA server inside a VM at the DID server, and the SIPp UAS (User Agent Server) as the call answering endpoint at the DID server's hypervisor domain. All the SIP messages between UAS and UAC are processed and forwarded by B2BUA's call control logic. Specifically, a call between UAC and UAS is initiated from the UAC by sending an INVITE message to the B2BUA's call control Logic, which performs authentication and authorization. Then, B2BUA forwards the INVITE message to the UAS, the answering endpoint. The UAS receiving the INVITE message will start ringing and sending back an 180 SIP provisional response. As soon as the answering endpoint picks up the phone, an 200 OK SIP message is sent to the originating endpoint and the session is established. Since we set-up 100 calls per second with each call lasting 10 second, the maximum simultaneous call sessions maintained in B2BUA is 1000.

Table 2 shows the call session set-up latency under five configurations. For each experiment, we configured the UAC to make 10,000 calls and measured the call session set-up latency, which is from the UAC sending an INVITE message to the UAC receiving 200 OK message. We observed that although the UAC generates 100 calls per second, the best average call rate we can achieve is 90.9 from the Bare-Metal configuration, and 90.8 from the SRIOV-DID configuration. An important factor affecting the call rate result is the number of retransmitted INVITE messages. PV shows the lowest call rate of 85.5, because it incurs a higher number of INVITE message retransmissions. For session set-up latencies, except the Bare-Metal configuration, SRIOV-DID achieves the best performance with 9061 call set-ups that are completed under 10ms, while PV performs the worst, with 8159 call set-ups that are completed under 10ms and 1335 call set-ups that are completed over 200 ms. The measured VM exit rates for SRIOV, SRIOV-DID, PV, and PV-DID are 4608, 1153, 6815, and 1871. Overall, DID's improvement over SRIOV and PV comes from keeping more CPU time in guest mode by avoiding VM exits and as a result, allowing B2BUA server to process more SIP messages and lower the overall session set-up latency.

5.9 VM Exits Analysis of APIC Virtualization

To analyze the performance benefits of APICv, we set up a server equipped with Intel Xeon E5-2609v2 CPU, 16GB

	<10	10-100	100-200	>200	Call Rate	INVITE Retrans.
Bare-Metal	9485	112	147	256	90.9	79
SRIOV	8342	186	248	1224	86.8	5326
SRIOV-DID	9061	159	242	538	90.8	2440
PV	8159	243	263	1335	75.6	5961
PV-DID	8473	280	61	1186	85.5	4920

Table 2. *Call session set-up latency (ms) distribution of 10,000 calls processed by SIP B2BUA server .*

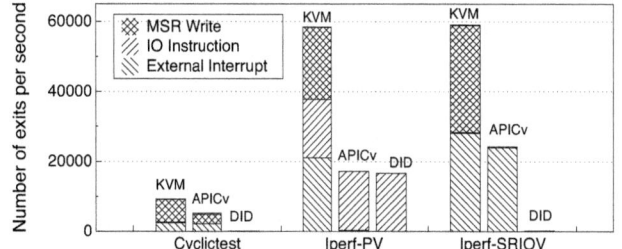

Figure 12. *The VM exit rate and the breakdown of exit reasons under KVM, KVM with APICv support, and DID.*

memory and installed Linux kernel 3.14 with the latest support for APICv in KVM. We present the VM exit rates under three types of workloads: the cyclictest workload representing the LAPIC timer interrupts, the Iperf-PV TCP workload for virtual interrupts, and the Iperf-SRIOV TCP workload for external interrupts. Figure 12 shows the result, with each bar from left to right representing vanilla KVM set-up, KVM with APICv enabled, and KVM with DID enabled and APICv disabled.

The cyclictest result shows that the number of MSR Write VM exits associated with APICv is half of that of vanilla KVM. This is because APICv avoids the EOI exit with EOI virtualization, while the rest of the MSR Write exits are caused by programming the timer register (TMICT). In contrast, DID completely eliminate these types of VM exits. For Iperf-PV experiment, APICv gives the same improvement in reducing the number of VM exits as DID. This is because APICv's posted interrupt mechanism enables delivering virtual interrupts from the back-end driver to the VM running core without triggering VM exits, whereas DID achieves the same effect without modifying the guest OS or requiring hardware support. Finally, in the Iperf-SRIOV experiment, APICv shows that although EOI virtualization helps to eliminate the MSR Write exits, external interrupts arriving at the VM running core still trigger VM exits. As a comparison, DID disables the EIE bit in VMCS so that external interrupts do not trigger any VM exit.

6. Discussion

Interrupts are triggered and handled in one of two scenarios. Interrupts are either triggered by direct-passthrough devices configured for VMs or they are triggered by devices configured for the host. When the system is not fully loaded (has spare physical cores available), DID directs interrupts for the host to the spare physical cores, avoiding interference on the cores where VMs are executing. As a result, interrupts from the host's devices are never delivered to cores which run VMs. However, when the system is oversubscribed, it is possible that interrupts destined for the host arrive at a core which is executing a VM, because the host and VMs are time-sharing a physical core. Under such circumstances, DID configures the host devices to deliver interrupts in NMI-mode. When a device triggers interrupts destined for the host, but this interrupt arrives at a core which is running a VM, the NMI forces a VM exit and passes control to the host. The host's interrupt handler (do_IRQ in Linux) examines the vector number of the interrupt and dispatches the interrupt to the host's interrupt handler based on the host's IDT. Note that configuring an interrupt for NMI mode does not lose the interrupt's original vector number. As a result, when the control is passed to the host, the host is aware of the source of the interrupt.

DID configures NMI not only for hardware interrupts, but also for IPIs triggered by the hypervisor. Because DID uses IPIs to send virtual interrupts directly to the target VM, the host's original use of IPIs, intended for operations such as rescheduling interrupts and TLB shutdown, must use NMI-mode interrupts to force a VM exit. The NMI-mode IPI triggers a VM exit and invokes the host's interrupt handler by using the interrupt's original vector number. Note that it is possible for the NMI to arrive at a core already running in the host mode instead of guest mode. Because DID is capable of identifying the source device or core of the interrupt, it can correctly distinguish whether the interrupt is intended for the guest and requires generating a self-IPI, or if the interrupt is intended for the host and requires directly invoking the corresponding interrupt handler.

7. Conclusion

The performance overhead of I/O virtualization stems from VM exits due to I/O instructions and interrupt delivery, which in turn comprise interrupt dispatch and end-of-interrupt (EOI) acknowledgement. Whereas SRIOV is meant to remove VM exits due to I/O instructions, this paper presents DID, a comprehensive solution to the interrupt delivery problem on virtualized servers. DID completely eliminates most of the VM exits due to interrupt dispatches and EOI notification for SRIOV devices, para-virtualized devices, and timers. As a result, to the best of our knowledge, DID represents one of the most efficient, if not the most efficient, interrupt delivery systems published in the literature. DID achieves this feat by leveraging the IOAPIC's interrupt remapping hardware, avoiding mis-delivery of direct interrupts, and employs a self-IPI mechanism to inject virtual interrupts, which enables direct EOI writes without causing priority inversion among interrupts. In addition to improved latency and throughput, DID significantly reduces the interrupt invocation latency, and thus forms a crucial technology building block for *network function virtualization*, which aims to run telecommunication functions and services on virtualized IT infrastructure.

References

[1] Enabling Optimized Interrupt/APIC Virtualization in KVM. KVM Forum 2012.

[2] Fio - Flexible I/O Tester. http://freecode.com/projects/fio.

[3] Introduction of AMD Advanced Virtual Interrupt Controller. XenSummit 2012.

[4] Jailhouse Partitioning Hypervisor. https://github.com/siemens/jailhouse.

[5] Memcached: memory object caching system. http://memcached.org/.

[6] Secure virtual machine architecture reference manual. AMD.

[7] Single-Root I/O Virtualization and Sharing Specification, Revision 1.0, PCI-SIG.

[8] SIPp: traffic generator for the SIP protocol. http://sipp.sourceforge.net/.

[9] Sippy B2BUA. http://www.b2bua.org/.

[10] virtio- and vhost-net need for speed performance challenges. KVM Forum 2010.

[11] Intel 64 Architecture x2APIC Specification, Intel Corporation, 2008.

[12] Single-Root I/O Virtualization and Sharing Specification, Revision 1.0, PCI-SIG, 2008.

[13] Keith Adams and Ole Agesen. A comparison of software and hardware techniques for x86 virtualization. In *ACM ASPLOS'06*.

[14] Ole Agesen, Jim Mattson, Radu Rugina, and Jeffrey Sheldon. Software techniques for avoiding hardware virtualization exits. In *USENIX Annual Technical Conference*, pages 373–385, 2012.

[15] Muli Ben-Yehuda, Michael D Day, Zvi Dubitzky, Michael Factor, Nadav Har'El, Abel Gordon, Anthony Liguori, Orit Wasserman, and Ben-Ami Yassour. The turtles project: Design and implementation of nested virtualization. In *OSDI*, volume 10, pages 423–436, 2010.

[16] Christoffer Dall and Jason Nieh. Kvm/arm: Experiences building the linux arm hypervisor. 2013.

[17] Michael Ferdman, Almutaz Adileh, Onur Kocberber, Stavros Volos, Mohammad Alisafaee, Djordje Jevdjic, Cansu Kaynak, Adrian Daniel Popescu, Anastasia Ailamaki, and Babak Falsafi. Clearing the Clouds: A Study of Emerging Scale-out Workloads on Modern Hardware. volume 40, pages 37–48. ACM, 2012.

[18] Abel Gordon, Nadav Amit, Nadav Har'El, Muli Ben-Yehuda, Alex Landau, Assaf Schuster, and Dan Tsafrir. Eli: bare-metal performance for i/o virtualization. *ACM SIGARCH Computer Architecture News*, 40(1):411–422, 2012.

[19] Nadav Har'El, Abel Gordon, Alex Landau, Muli Ben-Yehuda, Avishay Traeger, and Razya Ladelsky. Efficient and scalable paravirtual i/o system. In *USENIX Annual Technical Conference*, pages 231–242, 2013.

[20] R. Hiremane. Intel Virtualization Technology for Directed I/O (Intel VT-d). *Technology@ Intel Magazine, 2007.*

[21] DPDK Intel. Intel data plane development kit.

[22] Eric Keller, Jakub Szefer, Jennifer Rexford, and Ruby B Lee. Nohype: virtualized cloud infrastructure without the virtualization. In *ACM SIGARCH Computer Architecture News*, volume 38, pages 350–361. ACM, 2010.

[23] Jan Kiszka. Towards linux as a real-time hypervisor. *RTLWS11, 2009.*

[24] Avi Kivity, Yaniv Kamay, Dor Laor, Uri Lublin, and Anthony Liguori. kvm: the linux virtual machine monitor. In *Proceedings of the Linux Symposium*, volume 1, pages 225–230, 2007.

[25] Kaushik Kumar Ram, Jose Renato Santos, Yoshio Turner, Alan L Cox, and Scott Rixner. Achieving 10 gb/s using safe and transparent network interface virtualization. In *Proceedings of the 2009 ACM SIGPLAN/SIGOPS international conference on Virtual execution environments*, pages 61–70. ACM, 2009.

[26] Rusty Russell. virtio: towards a de-facto standard for virtual i/o devices. *SIGOPS Oper. Syst. Rev. 2008.*

[27] Jose Renato Santos, Yoshio Turner, G John Janakiraman, and Ian Pratt. Bridging the gap between software and hardware techniques for i/o virtualization. In *USENIX Annual Technical Conference*, pages 29–42, 2008.

[28] Quinn O Snell, Armin R Mikler, and John L Gustafson. Netpipe: A network protocol independent performance evaluator. In *IASTED International Conference on Intelligent Information Management and Systems*, volume 6. Washington, DC, USA), 1996.

[29] Jakub Szefer, Eric Keller, Ruby B Lee, and Jennifer Rexford. Eliminating the hypervisor attack surface for a more secure cloud. In *Proceedings of the 18th ACM conference on Computer and communications security*, pages 401–412. ACM, 2011.

[30] Ajay Tirumala, Feng Qin, Jon Dugan, Jim Ferguson, and Kevin Gibbs. Iperf: The tcp/udp bandwidth measurement tool. *http://dast.nlanr.net/Projects*, 2005.

[31] Hitachi Tomoki Sekiyama, Yokohama Research Lab. Improvement of real-time performance of kvm.

[32] Cheng-Chun Tu, Chao-tang Lee, and Tzi-cker Chiueh. Secure i/o device sharing among virtual machines on multiple hosts. In *Proceedings of the 40th Annual International Symposium on Computer Architecture*, pages 108–119. ACM, 2013.

[33] Rich Uhlig, Gil Neiger, Dion Rodgers, Amy L Santoni, Fernando CM Martins, Andrew V Anderson, Steven M Bennett, Alain Kagi, Felix H Leung, and Larry Smith. Intel virtualization technology. *Computer*, 38(5):48–56, 2005.

[34] Rafal Wojtczuk and Joanna Rutkowska. Following the white rabbit: Software attacks against intel vt-d technology.

A Hybrid I/O Virtualization Framework
for RDMA-capable Network Interfaces

Jonas Pfefferle*, Patrick Stuedi*, Animesh Trivedi*,
Bernard Metzler*, Ioannis Koltsidas* and Thomas R. Gross‡

IBM Research*, ETH Zuerich‡
{jpf,stu,atr,bmt,iko}@zurich.ibm.com, trg@inf.ethz.ch

Abstract

RDMA-capable interconnects, providing ultra-low latency and high-bandwidth, are increasingly being used in the context of distributed storage and data processing systems. However, the deployment of such systems in virtualized data centers is currently inhibited by the lack of a flexible and high-performance virtualization solution for RDMA network interfaces.

In this work, we present a hybrid virtualization architecture which builds upon the concept of separation of paths for control and data operations available in RDMA. With hybrid virtualization, RDMA control operations are virtualized using hypervisor involvement, while data operations are set up to bypass the hypervisor completely. We describe HyV (Hybrid Virtualization), a virtualization framework for RDMA devices implementing such a hybrid architecture. In the paper, we provide a detailed evaluation of HyV for different RDMA technologies and operations. We further demonstrate the advantages of HyV in the context of a real distributed system by running RAMCloud on a set of HyV-enabled virtual machines deployed across a 6-node RDMA cluster. All of the performance results we obtained illustrate that hybrid virtualization enables bare-metal RDMA performance inside virtual machines while retaining the flexibility typically associated with paravirtualization.

1. Introduction

RDMA-capable interconnects like Infiniband or iWARP are increasingly being considered in deployments of large distributed data processing systems. Examples of this sort are RAMCloud [22], FaRM [5] and Pilaf [18]. RDMA networks provide ultra-low latency and high-bandwidth – two properties that are of highest interest when processing large data sets under time constraints.

As of today, all of the existing systems we are aware of that use RDMA networks in larger deployments do so in a strictly bare-metal environment. This is unfortunate since many of the systems would benefit from the advantages of virtualization (higher utilization of physical resources due to hardware multiplexing, flexibility due to virtual machine migration, snapshotting, etc.) [3, 12].

Currently, virtualization support for RDMA network interfaces is available in the form of single-root I/O virtualization (SR-IOV) [25]. SR-IOV delivers close to bare-metal performance in virtualized environments but lacks some of the flexibility aspects one typically associates with virtualization. For instance, SR-IOV requires device and platform support, which, compared to software solutions, has higher development costs and is harder to maintain. Additionally, setting up SR-IOV is inherently static which complicates virtual machine migration later on (see Section 2.2).

In this paper, we argue that the very nature of RDMA's separation of control and data path allows for virtualizing RDMA capable NICs entirely in software while still achieving bare-metal performance. We introduce the notion of hybrid virtualization, a I/O virtualization scheme for RDMA interconnects. With hybrid virtualization, virtual RDMA devices running in the guest interact with the hypervisor using a paravirtual interface solely for control operations such as when creating network resources like queue pairs or completion queues. These network resources are then mapped into the guest virtual machine for direct access. Consequently, any subsequent access to these resources during data transmission and reception bypasses the hypervisor completely.

We present HyV, a virtualization framework for RDMA-capable network interfaces implementing such a hybrid architecture for the Linux kernel virtual machine (KVM). We show that HyV is able to achieve highest performance while still retaining maximum flexibility. As an example, HyV permits applications in one virtual machine to read or write

VEE '15, March 14–15, 2015, Istanbul, Turkey.
Copyright © 2015 ACM 978-1-4503-3450-1/15/03... $15.00.
http://dx.doi.org/10.1145/2731186.2731200

memory from remote virtual machines on different physical hosts within 1-2 microseconds.

By using the HyV framework, virtual RDMA devices can be implemented very similar to implementing paravirtual devices. Thereby, the key challenge in HyV was (1) to separate the hardware-dependent part from the hardware-independent part and (2) to facilitate and ease the effort for vendors to implement their own virtual RDMA NICs with very little effort. The paper presents the design and implementation of HyV and discusses three specific RDMA devices which we virtualized using HyV.

To demonstrate the advantages of HyV for real applications, we have deployed RAMCloud – a DRAM-based distributed key-value store – on a set of HyV-enabled virtual machines. Our measurements show that by leveraging HyV we can achieve native throughput and latency on the cluster with no change to the application.

In summary, this paper's contributions include (1) a hybrid I/O architecture to virtualize RDMA network devices, (2) the design and implementation of HyV as a generic framework for virtual RDMA devices, and (3) the demonstration of how to use HyV to achieve bare-metal latency and throughput between virtual machines interconnected with a RDMA capable network.

2. Background

In this section we provide the relevant background on RDMA networking and network virtualization.

2.1 Remote Direct Memory Access (RDMA)

RDMA capable network interface controllers or RNICs offer high-bandwidth, ultra low-latency network operations for accessing data in remote memories. The performance advantages of RDMA are mainly achieved by separating the *control path* from the *data path* while completely eliminating the OS/CPU involvement from the latter. This separation of paths frees network I/O from overheads otherwise associated with resource management, multiplexing, scheduling etc. [6]. Instead, network and application resources are pre-allocated and registered with the RNIC on the control path. A control path to the RNIC consists of calls to setup resources and context in the device that – during data path operations – enable moving data in a zero-copy fashion between the network and an application buffer. This separation philosophy is also reflected in the way applications interact with the RNIC. Applications typically identify and create necessary resources upfront and outside of performance critical sections, but benefit from fast RDMA data operations when performance really matters. In comparison, the traditional BSD socket interface has intertwined control and data paths where resources are allocated, associated, used and then released all as part network I/O operations.

Thus, the critical aspect of RNIC's is that the control paths are used to directly map device provided, connection-specific, structures into an applications address space. For example, RDMA gives each application its own private and virtual network interface consisting of transmission (TX) and reception (RX) work queues called *queue pairs* (QP). This approach eliminates software and protection overheads, however, it also entangles application code with device details that are usually encapsulated by an OS device driver. To mitigate this burden and ensure portability a device's specific memory layout and protocol for interaction is encapsulated by a vendor provided user-level library. The library exposes a standardized RDMA interface (verbs) to the application while managing and interacting with mapped structures unique to a particular device [9, 11]. To issue a data transfer, applications use the verbs interface to asynchronously post I/O requests on the QP. These I/O requests contain pointers to application buffers that are accessed by the RNIC through DMA. I/O completion events are put on a separate notification queue which applications can poll or block on.

2.2 Network I/O Virtualization

Virtualization enables efficient hardware utilization by multiplexing server hardware among virtual machines (VMs). As virtual machines can be created, snapshotted, replicated, and resumed very quickly, they give great flexibility in resource planning, provisioning and administration to handle workload spikes. Despite many advantages, one of the key challenges in virtualization is efficient network I/O virtualization. The two most prominently used techniques for network I/O virtualization are (a) direct device assignment and (b) paravirtualization. Direct device assignment can be achieved by passthrough or hardware assisted virtualization (e.g. PCIe SR-IOV). In both cases a dedicated NIC instance is exclusively assigned to a virtual machine. While this mode avoids any involvement of the hypervisor, it lacks flexibility. For example, setting up direct device assignment is typically a static task where the number of NIC instances need to be configured upfront and cannot be changed thereafter. This requires careful consideration to not waste resources on the hardware for unused virtual interfaces. Further, direct device assignment needs special platform support for memory translation and complicates VM live migration [24].

In contrast to hardware-assisted virtualization, a paravirtualized network stack offers great flexibility at lower performance. It uses a split driver model with a frontend driver in the virtualization aware guest OS and a backend driver on the host. Frontend and backend driver interact over a dedicated communication channel[7]. With paravirtualization, the software network state is maintained in the hypervisor which simplifies migrating and checkpointing of the network state. These flexibility aspects of paravirtualization are the main reason why paravirtualization is widely used in todays virtualization environment. The downside of paravirtualization is that crossing the guest/hypervisor boundaries imposes some overhead during data path operations.

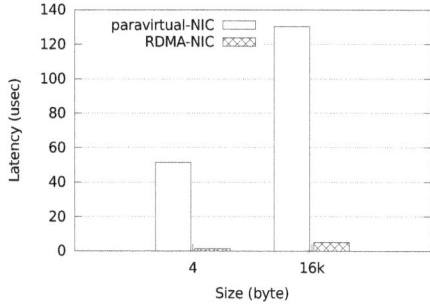

Figure 1: Performance gap between paravirtualized socket/tcp, and bare-metal verbs/rdma

In the following, we discuss our hybrid virtualization scheme tailored to RDMA-capable interfaces. Hybrid virtualization inherits some of the flexibility advantages of paravirtualization, but at the same time, achieves a performance comparable to hardware-assisted virtualization.

3. Hybrid RDMA Virtualization Architecture

Paravirtualized network devices use a single channel to communicate between the guest and the host operating system. Both data and control transfer funnel through the channel and many layers of abstractions, requiring data copies, hypervisor accesses, scheduling, network buffer allocation and management etc. This design originates from the fact that traditional network controllers do not implement a sufficient form of isolation and context to allow network resources to be multiplexed across hypervisor/guest boundaries. A trusted entity (i.e. hypervisor) has to process data and control operations in software before transfer to or from untrusted guests (Figure 2a). This is in a sharp contrast to RDMA operations where the data and control paths are completely separated even at the device interface level (Figure 2b). The separation helps to deliver high-performance with isolation to the applications. Consequently, there exists a large performance gap between RDMA performance and the performance of a paravirtualized network stack (Figure 1). To enable RDMA performance inside virtual machines, it will therefore be absolutely key to continue separating the control from the data path. The traditional paravirtualized architecture is not sufficient since it does not include the notion of path separation, and as such cannot deliver the full performance advantages of RDMA.

Design: A natural way to extend RDMA's philosophy of separation of paths into virtualization is to virtualize RDMA network devices at the function interface of RDMA verbs, instead of at the level of the PCI device. We define a hybrid virtualization architecture for RDMA interfaces in which verbs-level control operations are virtualized in a paravirtual fashion, while data operations are executed on guest-private data channels (Figure 2c).

3.1 Paravirtualized Control Path

On the control path, network resources are mapped to and from the RDMA controller into the application memory inside a VM. With hybrid virtualization, these network resources are created using a frontend/backend driver pair. Control operations issued from an RDMA-enabled application – such as create_qp() to create a queue pair, or create_cq() to create a completion notification queue – are executed by performing a system call into the frontend driver running in the guest. This mechanism is similar to the one used for control operations in the native RDMA stack. After having intercepted the call, the frontend driver forwards the control operation to the backend driver using a paravirtual communication channel. The backend driver, if needed, enforces the isolation, security and resource limits for VMs by modifying/filtering operations before forwarding them to the *unmodified* host device driver. After approval from the host OS, the host device driver creates the requested network resources on the RNIC. Finally, the backend driver maps the newly created resource (e.g., queue pair) into the address space of the guest RDMA application. Application resources such as memory buffers are also registered (*reg_mr()*) with the RNIC using the split drivers.

In order for hybrid virtualization to work together with unmodified host RDMA drivers, some control operations – in particular the ones that interact with the memory management subsystem – require modifications in the host. Specifically, extra memory translations are needed in two directions:

1. **Top Down:** Translating guest virtual memory areas into the host address space such that they can be used with the host device driver and RNIC.

2. **Bottom Up:** Mapping host physical memory areas to guest virtual memory such that it can be used by a guest application to directly access the RNIC.

These two kinds of mappings cover scenarios for both data path setup and user memory registration. However, the implementation depends on how the hypervisor handles virtual machine memory as well as on the interface to the host device driver, details of which are discussed in the Section 4.2.

3.2 Direct Data I/O Path

The data path consists of posting I/O requests and reaping completion notifications from the RNIC. With hybrid virtualization, this is achieved by directly reading and writing memory-mapped hardware queues from within the guest. The RDMA application in the guest OS prepares an I/O request and writes it in the queue pair using the post_send() or post_recv() verbs call. Since the queue pair is mapped into guest memory, the unmodified user-space device-driver can be used for posting I/O requests.

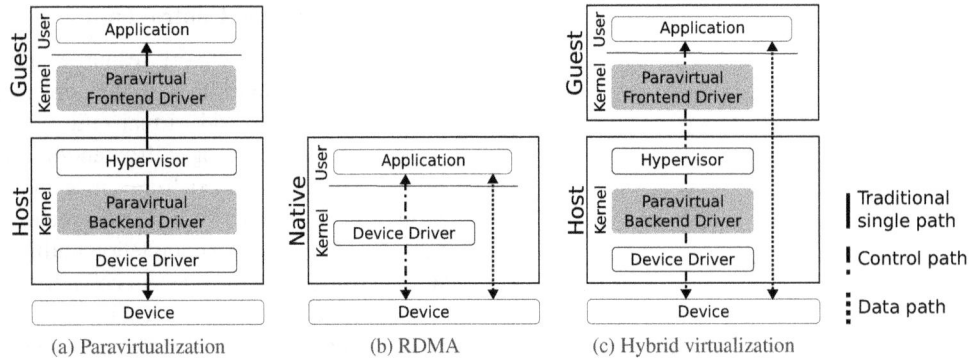

Figure 2: Virtualization architectures

A transmission work request triggers the RNIC to prepare and transmit data from the pre-registered application buffer inside the guest OS in a zero-copy manner. For incoming packets, the destination memory is resolved by the RDMA controller after RDMA protocol processing and data is directly DMA'ed into the final application buffer. Since network and packet processing, multiplexing etc. happens in the RDMA controller, the hypervisor (as well as the guest/host OS) is completely eliminated from the fast data path. Upon the I/O completion, the RNIC generates a work completion (WC) element and puts that into the completion queue. The application can poll (`poll_cq()`) or block (`get_cq_event()`) on this queue to receive completion notification. The blocking mode requires further support from the underlying virtualization framework to raise events for notifications. Event notification is discussed in more detail in Section 4.

3.3 Advantages

Hybrid virtualization has advantages over both direct assignment based virtualization and paravirtualization. Clearly, when compared to paravirtualization, the advantage of hybrid virtualization is the improved performance due to less hypervisor involvement. By eliminating the guest OS and the hypervisor from the fast data path, the hybrid virtualization architecture can deliver a performance that is very close to the network hardware limits.

On the other hand, when compared to direct devices assignment, the advantage of hybrid virtualization is that it puts the hypervisor back in charge of network resource creation, management and accounting on the RNIC. Now these operations can be implemented by taking any necessary operating system and virtual machine state into consideration. Consequently, the hypervisor can enforce various firewall, quota, and isolation rules while creating network resources on the RNIC. The hybrid architecture is also more resource efficient. Instead of statically partitioning network resources between virtualized instances, in the hybrid architecture these resource can be assigned on-demand to VMs. For example, SR-IOV with IOMMU requires allocation and

pinning of all memory of the guest VM for DMA. With hybrid virtualization, only application buffers which are involved in RDMA are pinned.

4. Implementation

We developed HyV, a proof-of-concept implementation of the hybrid virtualization architecture. HyV offers an easy to use, flexible, and generic RDMA virtualization framework implemented for the Linux kernel virtual machine (KVM) as the hypervisor [14]. The system runs on the x86-64 architecture, however, our source code does not have any architecture dependencies and, although not tested, should run on other platforms as well. The ultimate goal of HyV is to provide a virtualization solution for RDMA that fulfills the following requirements:

1. *Direct hardware access:* For full performance, applications inside a VM should be able to directly access the RDMA network interface.

2. *Standardization and extensibility:* The framework should make it easy for vendors of RDMA hardware to get their devices virtualized.

3. *Unmodified kernel and userspace components:* Existing native RDMA applications should run unmodified in a HyV-enabled virtual machine.

Requirement (1) is achieved by implementing the hybrid virtualization architecture as discussed in the previous section. Requirements (2) and (3) are achieved through a modular implementation of HyV. In the following, we first provide a brief overview of the software architecture of HyV, and then discuss several aspects in more detail.

4.1 Overview

HyV is implemented as a plugin component for the Linux OFED RDMA software stack. OpenFabrics is an effort by different vendors to integrate RDMA interconnect technologies and provide a standard RDMA verbs programming interface [19]. Their OpenFabrics Enterprise Distribution (OFED) is a widely used RDMA software stack which spans both user- and kernel-space. User-space applications link against the *libibverbs* library which forwards control verbs operations to the *OFED core* in the kernel; from there they are further forwarded to a device-specific kernel-driver. Data verb calls are forwarded to a device-specific user-space driver where network resources are directly accessed, bypassing the operating system. By programming against the OFED provider API, vendors can enable their devices with a user- and kernel-space driver.

Figure 3 shows the architecture of HyV as it is embedded in the OFED stack. HyV allows the unmodified OFED stack to be used by both guest and host OS. Applications inside a virtual machine will use the regular components comprising of libibverbs, OFED core and user-space device drivers. Instead of running the real kernel-level provider, however, HyV requires a virtual provider to be loaded inside the guest. The virtual provider interacts with the HyV frontend to relay verbs control operations to the hypervisor. At the hypervisor, a HyV backend receives the control operations and feeds them into the OFED core at the host.

The virtual provider loaded in the guest is device-specific and is the only component in HyV that needs to be implemented to virtualize a given RDMA network interface. A virtual provider inside the guest is necessary because setting up the memory-mapped data path during control operations is device-specific. Vendors of RDMA hardware develop a virtual provider by implementing the standard OFED function calls that are otherwise implemented by their real kernel-device driver. For instance, by implementing the `create_qp()` interface, a vendor is given the opportunity to implement a device specific mapping of the QP resource. The HyV framework provides a set of API functions which makes the development of a virtual provider for a given hardware easier. As an example, HyV provides generic functions to map and unmap host memory into the guest address space. Later, we discuss the implementation of virtual providers for one Infiniband and two iWARP RDMA devices.

As discussed earlier and also illustrated in Figure 3, only control operations are relayed through the hypervisor (via virtual provider), data operations are executed directly on the RDMA hardware using the previously established mapped resources in the guest.

Control Path: We use the virtio paravirtualization framework as a basic mechanism to pass control operations from the guest to the hypervisor [29]. virtio uses a queue abstraction for the transport layer, called virtqueue, which allows buffers to be exchanged between guest and host. Hypercalls are used to notify the host of newly available buffers that are ready to be transmitted, and injected interrupts are used to notify the guest of newly received data buffers. On x86, notifications require VM exits and therefore add some extra

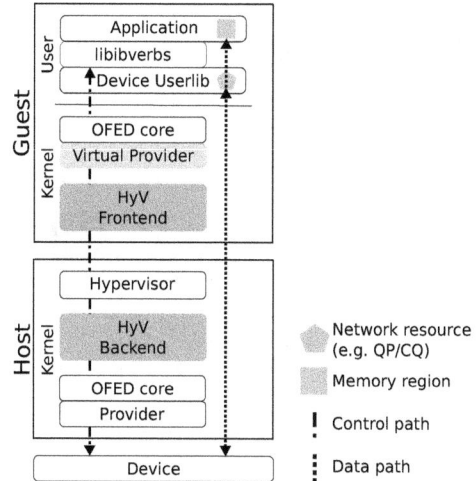

Figure 3: HyV architecture

latency. We will evaluate the effect of interrupt injection and hypercall VM exits in Section 5.

Data Path Work Completions: Remember that RDMA offers two ways of notifying the application about a completed RDMA operation, polling and blocking. With HyV, no hypervisor interactions are necessary when polling is used. In the case of blocking, the situation is different. Here, the application is put to sleep and woken up as soon as work completions are put on the CQ. One possible way to implement such a notification mechanism is to forward callback operations using the virtio framework. However, we found the virtio framework to be inefficient at handling small buffer events (e.g., completion events of 4 bytes). Namely, virtio uses extra work queues to notify a guest of a consumed buffer which adds latency to the performance critical event path. Consequently, we decided to use a shared ring-buffer instead of virtqueue buffers to forward events to the guest. The ring-buffer is an implementation of a single consumer/producer queue [15] which is protected by guest and host private locks to allow for multiple consumers/producers. These additional locks are necessary because Linux defers interrupt processing to software interrupt handlers which can run in parallel on different CPU cores [17].

4.2 Resource Mapping

The fundamental task of RDMA control operations like `create_qp()` or `reg_mr()` is to map resources (e.g., queue pair, or user memory) either from the host into the application inside the virtual machine, or, from the guest application to the host.

Our observation with RDMA devices is that there are two basic schemes used to setup such a resource mapping: *bottom up* - the application reserves virtual memory in the form of a memory map call to a special file and the kernel device driver backs them by physical pages (e.g. DMA-

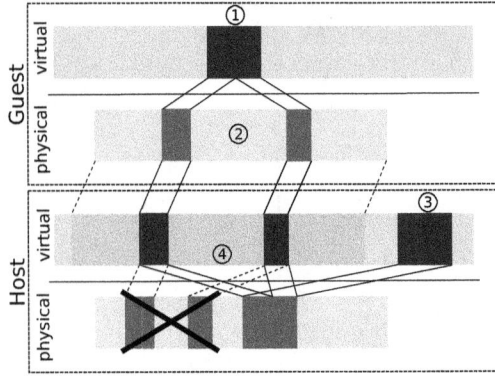

Figure 4: Bottom up memory mapping

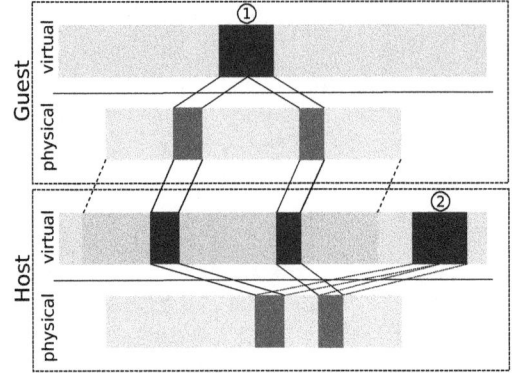

Figure 5: Top down memory mapping

enabled pages or PCI I/O memory); *top down* - memory is allocated in the application and pinned by the kernel device driver to enable DMA transfers.

It turned out that implementing such a mapping functionality in case of virtualization is challenging due to several assumptions made by the OFED host drivers. In the following we describe the challenges and explain how we addressed them in HyV. Note that we cannot use an IOMMU to perform these mappings because we share a single device across virtual machines with different physical address spaces. Devices can initiate DMAs to any address spaces at any time.

Bottom up: The provider on the host expects a contiguous (host) virtual memory region, ready to back it with physical pages. Unfortunately, a contiguous virtual memory region in the guest might not be contiguous in the host virtual memory (HVM). This is because in KVM virtual machines are essentially regular Linux processes, each of which with its own virtual address space.

To overcome this problem in HyV, we remap guest physical memory (GPM) to the actual physical pages of the network resource. The various steps of this process are illustrated in Figure 4. First, the application performs the mapping as is (step 1), which ends up in the virtual provider. From there the call is forwarded to the HyV frontend where the reserved virtual memory region is backed by physical pages (step 2). Subsequently, the HyV frontend passes the list of physical pages and the initial mapping parameters to the HyV backend where the pages are translated to the corresponding virtual memory regions on the host (offset calculation). Using the initial mapping parameters, the HyV backend creates a mapping into host virtual memory (HVM) to extract the physical pages of the network resources by walking the page table (step 3). Finally, the backend remaps the virtual memory regions that correspond to the mapping in the guest, to the extracted pages of the actual network resource (step 4). The HVM mapping is not needed anymore and can be destroyed.

Top down: Here, the provider also expects a contiguous (host) virtual memory region, but unlike in *bottom up* it

does not back the region itself but relies on the operating systems to do so. Thus, the provider only pins the memory to ensure that the pages can be used for DMA transfers and extracts them for installation on the device. Unfortunately, in the virtualized environment we have the same problem as in *bottom up* that the virtual memory region from the guest is not contiguous on the host.

Again, in HyV we implement a memory remapping between the guest and host. The various steps are illustrated in Figure 5. This time we have to use the underlying physical pages that back the virtual memory region in the guest (step 1). Thereafter, we pin the physical pages in both the guest and the host in order to create a new contiguous mapping into HVM (step 2). This mapping can then be used by the provider to extract and pin the physical pages as described previously. After registration the HVM mapping can be destroyed. HyV does not need to perform a remapping into contiguous HVM if the memory region is already contiguous, i.e. contiguous in GPM. Currently, we do not fully leverage this fact, but avoid remapping if the memory region fits inside a single page.

4.3 RDMA Devices Supported by HyV

A virtual provider for a specific RDMA network interface needs to implement various handlers for verb control operations like `create_qp()` or `create_cq()`. These handlers are invoked by the OFED runtime everytime an application issues a corresponding verb control operation. A virtual provider can implement a given handler in two ways. Either – for instance when implementing the `reg_mr()` handler – it can relay the operation directly to the real kernel-level provider by using the matching relay API function available in HyV. Or – for instance when implementing the `create_qp()` handler – a provider may use the mapping API functions available in HyV to map network resources into the guest in a device specific way. Table 1 shows the most important API functions available in HyV for implementing virtual providers.

To emphasize the framework aspect of HyV and to show that it is not limited to a particular interconnect technology

API functions	Description
hyv_reg_mr()	forward reg_mr() operation
hyv_create_qp()	forward create_qp() operation
hyv_mmap_gvirt()	top down memory mapping
hyv_mmap_hphys()	bottom up memory mapping

Table 1: Most prominent HyV API for implementing virtual providers

we implemented virtual providers for both Infiniband and iWARP devices. With these providers we are able to support the following devices:

Mellanox ConnectX-1/2/3 VPI/Pro: The ConnectX device supports Infiniband [9] and RDMA over converged Ethernet (RoCE) [10]. Its driver allocates resources in the userspace driver and requires a *top-down* mapping in the virtual provider. Additionally, its driver requires a user accessible region (UAR), e.g. used for doorbells. The UAR is allocated in a *bottom up* manner and can be easily mapped by the provided mapping API.

Chelsio Terminator 4/5: This is a 10GbE NIC with a fully offloaded RDMA iWARP [27] engine. iWARP implements RDMA functionality on top of a TCP/IP transport. The T4/5 device allocates network resource in a *bottom up* manner. Therefore, the resource mappings for T4/5 could easily be implemented using the aforementioned mapping API available in HyV.

SoftiWARP: This device is a software implementation of iWARP on top of kernel TCP sockets [30]. Applications using SoftiWARP benefit from zero-copy data transmission. However, data operations do involve the kernel and require a system call to kick of processing. This system call is implemented by a special post_send() operation to the kernel. The virtual provider for SoftiWARP therefore has to virtualize the post_send() operation which is done by forwarding the operations the same way as control operations. Unfortunately, this also adds extra latency during data operations. We are going to evaluate the latency overhead of virtualized SoftiWARP in Section 5.

5. Evaluation

In this section we evaluate HyV at the level of raw RDMA operations. We demonstrate HyV in two different experimental setups.

Experimental setup (A): A 6-node Infiniband cluster where each machine contains a dual Intel Xeon E5-2650 v2 (2.6Ghz, 20MB Cache) CPU and 160GB DDR3 RAM. The machines are connected using a dual port Mellanox ConnectX-3 VPI 56Gb/s FDR Infiniband RNICs. We use two back-to-back connected interfaces on different physical machines for microbenchmarks. Experiments in Section 6 use all machines with both ports connected through a Mellanox SX6036

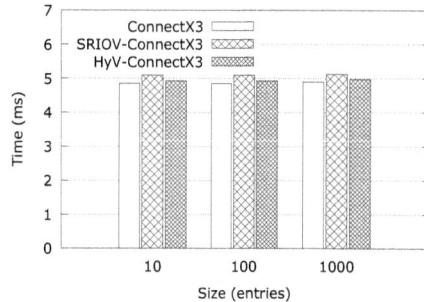

Figure 6: Create QP

Switch. On these systems we use the KVM hypervisor of a 3.13.11 vanilla Linux kernel with a QEMU frontend [4]. All virtual machines are configured with six virtual CPUs and 16GB memory and they run a 3.13.11 vanilla Linux kernel with *KVM_GUEST* kernel configuration enabled. We compare three configurations: native, SR-IOV and with HyV.

Experimental setup (B): Two machines with dual Intel Xeon E5-2690 (2.9Ghz, 20MB Cache) CPU and 96GB DDR3 RAM. The machines are connected using Chelsio T420-CR 10GbE RNICs with jumbo frames (9K MTU). The NICs are connected through an IBM G8264 Switch. Kernel versions and configuration are the same as above.

5.1 Control Path

In the following, we quantify the performance overhead of control operations in HyV which is required to enable complete bypass on the data path. All experiments are performed using experimental setup (A).

The create_qp() verbs call creates a queue pair and installs it on the RNIC for direct access. In this test we create QPs that can hold 10, 100 and 1000 work request entries and compare the virtual device's control path to the control path of the native device. We measure the performance by counting the number of transactions (creating and destructing QPs) over a period of 10 seconds. As can be observed from Figure 6, HyV shows slightly lower performance than native, as it has to double pin and remap the QP memory (*top-down* mapping, cf. Section 4). This shows that creation time is actually dominated by installing the resource on the device. SR-IOV has similar but slightly worse performance than HyV. We suspect more complex communication and resource management on the device when dealing with virtual functions (VF) to account for lower performance on the control path.

The reg_mr() verbs call registers a memory region for later use, causing the NIC driver to pin the memory region and install its physical pages onto the NIC. Figure 7 shows the registration cost for memory regions with sizes from 1KB to 256MB. Memory allocation and population cost is not included in the measurement. For sizes smaller or equal to 64KB, the memory registration time is more or

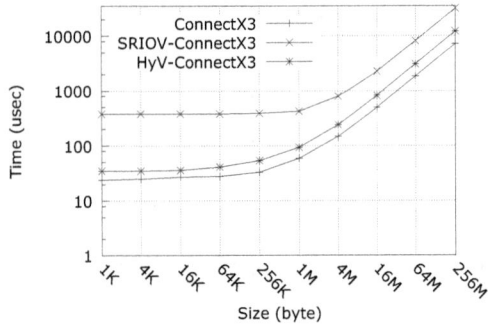

Figure 7: Memory Registration

less constant and is determined by the cost of processing the system call and manipulating the process address space. Except for SR-IOV where, as above, registering seems to be limited by communication overhead with the device. For larger sizes, the registration cost is dominated by the number of pages being registered. Registering a MR with HyV-ConnectX3 takes approximately 2 times as long as with native ConnectX3. For small sizes this overhead mainly comes from forwarding the command over the paravirtual control path. For larger transfer sizes the overhead can be accounted to the double-pinning of pages (guest and host) as well as to the cost of remapping memory. SR-IOV takes approximately 4 times as long as compared to native ConnectX3. To get a better understanding if this is a general PCI passthrough/SR-IOV issue we conducted the same experiments on a passthrough-T4 device (not shown) and observed that this setup only shows minor performance overhead on the control path. We plan to further investigate the exact cause that limits the ConnectX-3 SR-IOV control path performance.

A memory region (MR) can be unregistered with the dereg_mr() verbs, which unpins the memory and removes the physical page list from the NIC. We have also measured the cost of unregistering memory regions, but we omit discussing these results in detail as they were very similar to the results we got for memory registration.

5.2 I/O Performance

One key metric of interest is the raw I/O performance of HyV in terms of RDMA data operations. In the following, we look at throughput and latency of RDMA operations in HyV, and compare the results with the performance obtained natively and with passthrough. The benchmarks are performed either VM-to-VM or host-to-host.

Latency: To measure latency we use RDMA read operations with 4B and 16KB message size respectively. The reported numbers are round-trip times, i.e. work completions of read operations are generated after the remotely read memory has been stored locally. To determine the completion of a RDMA operation we use CQ polling. Experiments

lasts 10 seconds and numbers reported are the average over 5 runs.

As can be observed from Figure 8a, the three different configurations, native, SR-IOV and HyV using experimental setup (A) show very similar performance for both 4B and 16KB message size. This is because in all three cases, the network resources (queue pairs, completion queues) are being accessed directly from the application in the guest, with no operating system or hypervisor involvement.

Figure 8c compares read latency of 4B and 16KB message size for the native and HyV-enabled T4 device when polling for completions using experimental setup (B). As seen in the previous Section, due to complete bypass of the hypervisor HyV-T4 is able to achieve equal to native latencies.

Throughput: To measure throughput we use RDMA write operations with message sizes from 1B to 64KB. The test starts with 10 outstanding work requests and posts a new work request each time a request has completed. The intention behind the small number of outstanding work requests is to capture a potential overhead introduced by the virtual environment. Benchmarks in Figure 9a are performed on experimental setup (A). We observe that HyV does not impose any overhead in terms of throughput. Due to hypervisor bypassing, passthrough and HyV show equal performance compared to their native counterpart. In each of the cases linespeed is reached at 4KB message size.

Throughput tests using experimental setup (B) with HyV-T4 (not shown) confirmed the above results. T4 is able to reach linespeed at 2KB transfer size as native (10 outstanding).

5.3 Virtualization Overheads

VM exits are one of the main sources of overhead in I/O virtualization in general. With HyV, VM exits occur as part of forwarding control operations or when using completion events. Fortunately, RDMA semantics allow completion event interrupts per operation, in contrast to traditional networking where in the worst case, interrupts are generated per packet.

Completion Events: Figure 8b shows the RDMA read latency with 4B and 16KB message sizes for the case where blocking is used instead of CQ polling on experimental setup (A). As can be seen, both SR-IOV and HyV show equal latency for 4B message size, but their latencies are higher compared to the latency in the native setup. For 16KB message size, HyV shows slightly higher latency than SR-IOV. The performance overhead for completion events can be explained by the need for an emulated advanced programmable interrupt controller (APIC) to allow interrupt injection with the current x86 architecture [8]. This introduces VM exits to inject interrupts into the VM on each completion event (see Section 4). However, as expected, the interrupt injection latency of $3\mu s$ for 4B remains constant with increasing

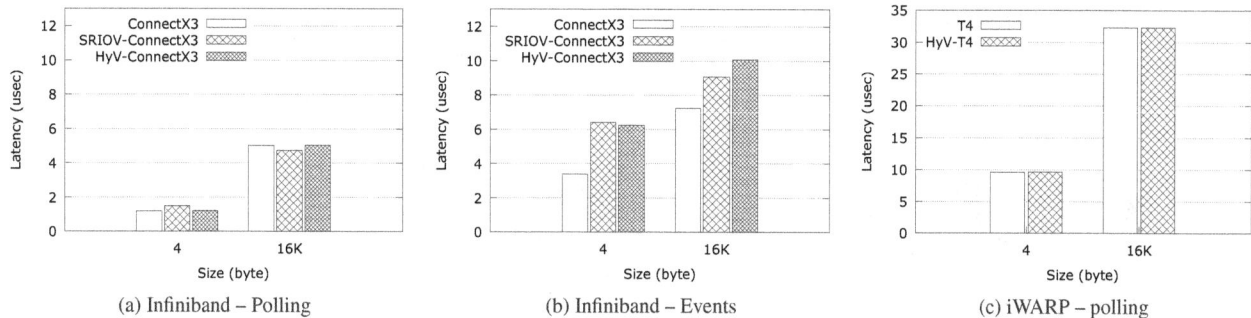

(a) Infiniband – Polling (b) Infiniband – Events (c) iWARP – polling

Figure 8: RDMA Read Latency

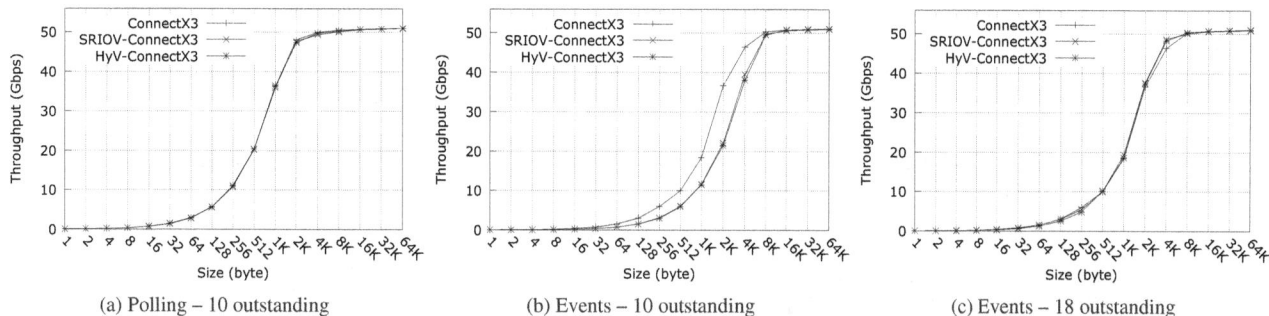

(a) Polling – 10 outstanding (b) Events – 10 outstanding (c) Events – 18 outstanding

Figure 9: RDMA Write Throughput on Infiniband

message size and thus, becomes negligible for large message sizes.

We further investigate the effect of CQ blocking on RDMA write throughput. Figure 9b-c shows write throughput for the two different batch sizes. In a configuration with just 10 outstanding work request, ConnectX3 reaches linespeed at 8KB. The performance gap for up to 8KB between the native and virtualized environment is due to interrupt injection overhead, cf. above. As we increase the number of outstanding work requests to 18, the overhead is amortized.

Memory footprint: The size of the memory footprint is an important metric in a virtualized environment and directly affects the level of consolidation that can be achieved. We ran an experiment where we register a memory region of 1MB and count the the number of pinned pages in the system. What we observed is that with the passthrough configuration the entire virtual machine memory was locked and held in the host RAM. In particular, we noticed that the virtual machine resident set size was 16GB, which is the maximum RAM the VM was permitted to use in the given configuration. The reason for this behavior is that passthrough requires locking of the complete guest physical memory to support direct DMA anywhere into the VM memory.

For the same experiment, but using a HyV-enabled VM, we observed only 1MB of memory being pinned and a res-

ident set size of 205MB (guest application + kernel). HyV allows for a more efficient memory usage because all the RDMA memory (which is DMA'able) is explicitly registered through the hypervisor. Consequently, HyV has a much lower memory footprint than passthrough, and thereby allows packing more VMs on to a single physical machine.

CPU load: CPU load is also an important metric to be considered in the context of I/O virtualization. Table 2 shows the host CPU load during RDMA operations (initiating side) for different configurations (100% is equivalent to 1 loaded core).

All configurations fully load a single CPU if RDMA operation are used in combination with polling. When using events, the CPU load is generally much lower since the application is temporarily put to sleep (as opposed to executing a busy wait polling loop). However, events lead to interrupt injections in a virtualized environment and therefore increase the CPU load for both passthrough and HyV.

5.4 Software Devices

In the following we show that VMs can directly benefit from HyV-enabled software RDMA devices where hardware is not available.

In Figure 10a we compare native and virtualized TCP request/response performance against Software RDMA send/

25

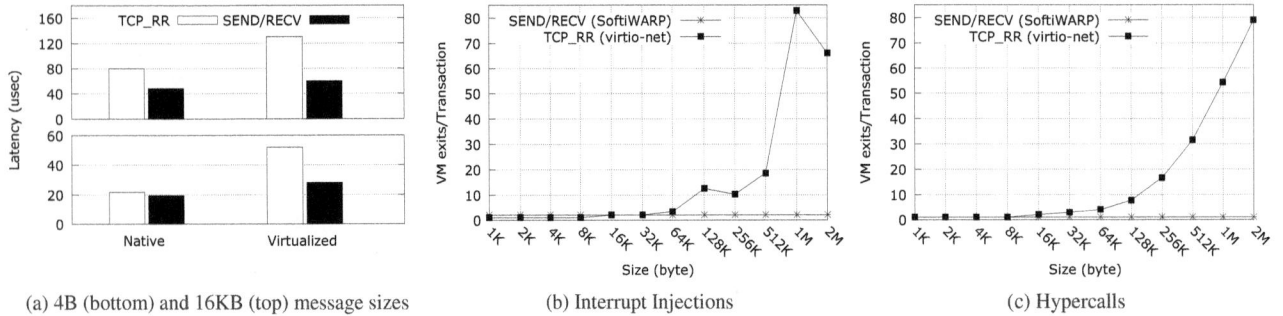

(a) 4B (bottom) and 16KB (top) message sizes   (b) Interrupt Injections   (c) Hypercalls

Figure 10: Send/receive on Software RDMA compared to TCP request/response

	read latency		write throughput	
	polling	events	polling	events
ConnectX3	100%	4%	100%	46%
sriov-ConnectX3	100%	35%	100%	96%
HyV-ConnectX3	100%	22%	100%	98%

Table 2: CPU load

Device	Provider	Virtual provider
ConnectX1/2/3	9165	357
SoftiWARP	7923	279
Chelsio T4/5	11483	536

Table 3: Virtual provider lines of code

receive on experimental setup (B). RDMA send/receive has similar semantics to socket `write()`/`read()`. All configurations run on a Chelsio T4 (RDMA offloading disabled) NIC. For virtualized TCP we use the virtio-net device with a vhost kernel backend. As software RDMA device we use SoftiWARP a iWARP implementation on top of kernel TCP sockets. HyV is used to virtualize the SoftiWARP device.

Our results show that SoftiWARP is capable of delivering lower latencies than TCP sockets. In the virtualized setup this performance benefit over TCP becomes more significant as HyV-SoftiWARP only introduces an overhead of approximately $10\mu s$. In contrast virtio-net is up to 2.5 times slower than native TCP and, thus, can be outperformed by HyV by a factor of 2. This can be explained by additional copies in virtio-net and network stack traversals on both guest and host. In contrast, HyV offloads the TCP/IP processing onto the host.

We show interrupt injection exits in Figure 10b, hypercall exits in Figure 10c. HyV only requires two VM exits for interrupt injection per transaction, i.e. one for each operation (send/receive), independent of the transfer size. Moreover, HyV-SoftiWARP requires only one hypercall exit per operation. In contrast, the packet-based nature of virtio-net results in much larger numbers of VM exits. Note that Virtio-net does implement a certain level of batching to mitigate this problem, nevertheless the interrupt rate and VM exits is much higher compared to HyV.

These results show the direct benefit of having Software RDMA devices in a virtualized environment. While interrupt injection and hypercalls add up to a large amount of VM exits respectively computation overhead on a traditional paravirtual NIC, HyV can totally avoid interrupt exits on data

operations if polling is used, and even when using events only one VM exit per operation is required.

5.5 Virtualization Effort

As discussed, to virtualize a device with HyV, a vendor has to write a virtual provider. Table 3 shows lines of code for the original provider (running in the host) and their virtual counterpart for Mellanox ConnectX1/2/3, SoftiWARP and Chelsio T4/5. In all cases, the code size of the virtual providers is less than 5 percent of the original provider. Due to the framework API available in HyV, the virtual providers are easy to implement and do not require a deep understanding of the original provider. For example, it took us only 3 days to implement a virtual provider for the Chelsio T4/5 RDMA NIC.

6. Application: RAMCloud

RAMCloud [23] is a distributed DRAM-based key-value store. Durability and availability are provided by fast failure recovery from disks, instead of main-memory replication, due to cost and energy [21]. RAMCloud is built for large scale and low latency. The latter is achieved by performing RPCs over RDMA. This allows, for example, to execute a 100B read in under $5\mu s$. RAMCloud's cluster architecture consists of three components: master and backup, coordinator and client. A storage server runs a master which holds all the data in DRAM and, typically, a backup of the data on disk. The coordinator is a centralized service managing metadata and cluster membership. Clients perform RPCs to the coordinator and to masters. In our experiments we run masters without backup, as our focus is on network I/O. We evaluate RAMCloud on experimental setup (A), cf. Section

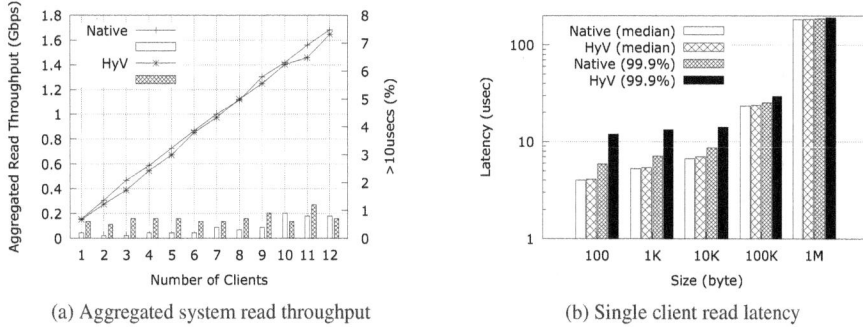

(a) Aggregated system read throughput   (b) Single client read latency

Figure 11: RAMCloud deployed in virtual machines using HyV

5, both in a native deployment and virtualized with HyV. Two aspects of the system are measured: aggregated read bandwidth and single client latency.

Aggregated Read Bandwidth: In this experiment we run 12 masters and 1 coordinator co-located on 6-machines leveraging all 12 IB ports available. Each master is initialized with one table holding one entry with a 30B key and 100B payload. Clients perform random reads across all servers. We run clients co-located to the masters on all 6-machines with increasing number to show the scalability of the system network I/O. For HyV we use two VMs per physical machine and give each machine access to one IB port. Figure 11a shows aggregated read throughput (lines/left) and the percentage of operations which take longer than $10\mu s$ (bars/right). RAMCloud's performance increases linearly with the number of clients, and HyV shows near native performance. The higher percentage of operations which finished after 10 microseconds with HyV can be explained by general virtualization overhead (e.g. scheduling [13, 20], APIC [8], etc.).

Single Client Latency: Figure 11b shows single client read latency of varying object sizes (30B key) in a single server setup. HyV is able to achieve equal to native latencies. The 99.9 percentile in the virtualized environment is slightly higher due to general virtualization overhead, cf. above.

Summary and Experience: In the above experiments we show that HyV imposes a minimum performance overhead on a distributed RAMCloud deployment by retaining key performance properties of RDMA. Such deployments could directly benefit from virtualization, e.g. by putting standby nodes for recovery in VMs. These nodes can be booted in seconds and moved around at system administrator's discretion. Moreover, by leveraging the VM image provisioning feature, which is only made possible by putting RAMCloud inside a VM, we significantly reduced the system setup and deployment time.

7. Related Work

vRDMA is a paravirtual RDMA device for the OFED RDMA stack [1]. Like HyV, vRDMA allows direct access to application buffers in VMs by RDMA NICs. However, in contrast to HyV, vRDMA uses a paravirtual communication channel to perform data operations. That is, vRDMA cannot completely bypass the hypervisor on data operations. The benefit of such a design is that no device specifics have to be exposed to the VM which may simplify VM checkpointing or VM migration. Additionally, there is no need for memory remapping in vRDMA because it directly uses the OFED kernel Verbs API on the host to forward work requests from the guest to the NIC's work queue. However, it trades these properties for performance (especially latency). From our experience with SoftiWARP we estimate a performance overhead of $3\mu s$ on the send path. On the receive path polling for completions cannot be implemented trivially. Either events have to be used on the host or both host and guest have to perform polling which significantly increases the CPU load. In any way, we estimate a total performance overhead of $4\mu s$, in the best case, which e.g. results in up to 4 times higher read latency with IB.

The closest to our solution is "High-performance VMM-bypass I/O in Virtual Machines" [16]. It uses a paravirtual approach to support complete bypass of the hypervisor on data operations. Our work on HyV contributes the following: (1) memory mapping API to allow using unmodified drivers on both guest and host, (2) generic, interconnect independent, RDMA verbs forwarding API to ease development of lightweight virtual providers, (3) demonstration of a real distributed application on a HyV-enabled cluster

Paradice is a I/O paravirtualization framework to virtualize devices that use a (unix-style) device file interface to applications [2]. Like HyV, Paradice virtualizes at a high-level interface ("paravirtualization boundary") to target a larger number of devices in a generic way. Isolation between VMs is achieved by assigning the device to a dedicated driver VM (requires IOMMU) and runtime checks on memory operations. Unfortunately, device drivers have to be modified to perform these checks (tool assisted).

	Direct I/O Path	Hypervisor Awareness	Resource Efficiency	Virtualization Features
Paravirtualization	✗	✓	1st	1st
HyV	✓	✓	2nd	2nd
SR-IOV	✓	✗	3rd	3rd

Table 4: Comparison of virtualization architectures.

8. Discussion and On-Going Work

In the evaluation, we have quantified certain advantages of HyV compared to paravirtualization and direct assignment (e.g., better memory consolidation). In this section, we are discussing both, limitations and potential further advantages of HyV, in the context of traditional virtualization aspects such as resource management, security, isolation or VM migration. Table 4 summarizes some of the findings discussed in this section.

Efficient Resource Management: In comparison to SR-IOV, one key advantage of HyV is its efficient resource management. While it is the explicit resource management of RDMA that allows for efficient resource management in the first place, it is the fact that HyV re-instantiates the hypervisor's role as the global resource manager which extends this feature to virtual machines. RDMA requires explicit resource management where all networking resources such as memory regions, queue pairs, and completion queues etc., are created, managed, and destroyed by the applications running inside a VM. By relaying these resource management calls on the paravirtualized control path, HyV explicitly informs hypervisor of a VM's networking requirements. This is beneficial, considering that hypervisors often struggle to predict a VM's resource usage. For example, as demonstrated, HyV's VM memory footprint can be accounted accurately and efficiently in comparison to SR-IOV/IOMMU's static memory assignment. Similarly, the numbers of QPs – representing connections associated offloaded state on the NIC – can be created and assigned dynamically on-demand to a VM based upon its requirement. Hence, a connection-heavy VM will end up consuming more networking resources on NIC than a connection-light VM. This explicit resource awareness in the hypervisor can also be used for a better VM scheduling and provisioning.

Security and Isolation of VMs: By virtualizing an RDMA NIC, HyV brings the NIC into the security domain of the virtualized infrastructure. HyV depends upon RDMA security mechanisms, which are similar in spirit to what can be found in modern operating systems. All RDMA resources belong to an application allocated protection domain. RDMA hardware enforces isolation by identifying associated protection domains for every resource and restricting access to it, if necessary. Memory access rights (read or write, local or remote etc.) are controlled by the application and enforced by RDMA hardware. The hypervisor can check the validity of these rights at memory registration time. Certain implementation related bugs such as a buggy DMA engine etc., can be contained by using platform virtualization technologies such as IOMMU.

To achieve performance isolation, RDMA provides a number of settings at different granularity depending on the interconnect technology [28]. These facilities can be used to provide QoS, rate limiting etc. among VMs [26] and we are currently exploring similar ideas in the context of HyV.

VM Migration and Checkpointing: VM migration and checkpointing remain challenging issues even for HyV. The complexity arises from the blackbox nature of the offloaded I/O processing in the network card. Clean checkpointing can be achieved by moving a VM into a stable state, where no more offloaded I/O operations are in progress. This state can be achieved by unmapping RDMA resources (or making them read only) inside the VM, and then waiting until all I/O operations and associated completion/error notification events are generated by the RNIC.

VM migration requires explicit support from the RNIC and involves moving network state (QPs, CQs) as well as memory resources (registered memory areas and STAGs). A device-specific hypervisor driver can assist with the state export, migration, and import logic. An alternative approach is to recreate RDMA state and resources on the newly migrated machine [31]. However, implementation complexity of such approaches prohibits their deployment in a distributed, general-purpose virtualized infrastructure.

To our knowledge, neither checkpointing nor VM migration is supported by any RDMA vendor yet. However, we believe that a HyV-like hybrid virtualization architecture retaining control in the hypervisor will be beneficial for implementing these features in the future.

9. Conclusion

RDMA networks – due to their ultra-low latency and high bandwidth – are attractive not only in the HPC domain but also for distributed systems processing cloud workloads in data centers. In this work, we presented HyV, a virtualization framework that unleashes the full performance advantages of RDMA interconnects to virtual machines. HyV implements a hybrid virtualization architecture where network resources are mapped into the guest VM for direct access. We have shown that HyV achieves close-to bare-metal performance inside virtual machines. We further demonstrated the usefulness of HyV in the context of a real distributed system such as RAMCloud, which we deployed on a HyV-enabled cluster equipped with RDMA interconnects.

References

[1] Adit Ranadive and Bhavesh Davda. Toward a Paravirtual vRDMA Device for VMware ESXi Guests. VMware, 2012.

[2] Ardalan Amiri Sani, Kevin Boos, Shaopu Qin, and Lin Zhong. I/O Paravirtualization at the Device File Boundary. In *Proceedings of the 19th International Conference on Architectural Support for Programming Languages and Operating Systems*, ASPLOS '14, pages 319–332, New York, NY, USA, 2014. ACM.

[3] Nadav Amit, Dan Tsafrir, and Assaf Schuster. VSwapper: A Memory Swapper for Virtualized Environments. In *Proceedings of the 19th International Conference on Architectural Support for Programming Languages and Operating Systems*, ASPLOS '14, pages 349–366, New York, NY, USA, 2014. ACM.

[4] Fabrice Bellard. QEMU, a Fast and Portable Dynamic Translator. In *Proceedings of USENIX Annual Technical Conference*, pages 41–46, 2005.

[5] Aleksandar Dragojević, Dushyanth Narayanan, Miguel Castro, and Orion Hodson. FaRM: Fast Remote Memory. In *11th USENIX Symposium on Networked Systems Design and Implementation (NSDI 14)*, pages 401–414, Seattle, WA, April 2014. USENIX Association.

[6] Thorsten Von Eicken, Anindya Basu, Vineet Buch, and Werner Vogels. U-net: A user-level network interface for parallel and distributed computing. In *In Fifteenth ACM Symposium on Operating System Principles*, 1995.

[7] Keir Fraser, Steven H, Rolf Neugebauer, Ian Pratt, Andrew Warfield, and Mark Williamson. Safe hardware access with the Xen virtual machine monitor. In *In 1st Workshop on Operating System and Architectural Support for the on demand IT InfraStructure (OASIS)*, 2004.

[8] Abel Gordon, Nadav Amit, Nadav Har'El, Muli Ben-Yehuda, Alex Landau, Assaf Schuster, and Dan Tsafrir. ELI: Bare-metal Performance for I/O Virtualization. In *Proceedings of the Seventeenth International Conference on Architectural Support for Programming Languages and Operating Systems*, ASPLOS XVII, pages 411–422, New York, NY, USA, 2012. ACM.

[9] InfiniBand Trade Association. InfiniBand Architecture Specification, Volume 1, Release 1.2.1. 2007.

[10] InfiniBand Trade Association. Annex A16: RDMA over Converged Ethernet (RoCE). 2010.

[11] J. Pinkerton J. Hilland, P. Culley and R. Recio. RDMA Protocol Verbs Specification. http://www.rdmaconsortium.org/home/draft-hilland-iwarp-verbs-v1.0-RDMAC.pdf, 2003.

[12] Hwanju Kim, Sangwook Kim, Jinkyu Jeong, Joonwon Lee, and Seungryoul Maeng. Demand-based Coordinated Scheduling for SMP VMs. In *Proceedings of the Eighteenth International Conference on Architectural Support for Programming Languages and Operating Systems*, ASPLOS '13, pages 369–380, New York, NY, USA, 2013. ACM.

[13] Hwanju Kim, Hyeontaek Lim, Jinkyu Jeong, Heeseung Jo, and Joonwon Lee. Task-aware Virtual Machine Scheduling for I/O Performance. In *Proceedings of the 2009 ACM SIG-PLAN/SIGOPS International Conference on Virtual Execution Environments*, VEE '09, pages 101–110, New York, NY, USA, 2009. ACM.

[14] Avi Kivity, Yaniv Kamay, Dor Laor, Uri Lublin, and Anthony Liguori. kvm: the Linux Virtual Machine Monitor. In *Proceedings of the Linux Symposium*, volume 1, pages 225–230, Ottawa, Ontario, Canada, June 2007.

[15] L. Lamport. Proving the correctness of multiprocess programs. *IEEE Trans. Softw. Eng.*, 3(2):125–143, March 1977.

[16] Jiuxing Liu, Wei Huang, Bulent Abali, and Dhabaleswar K. Panda. High Performance VMM-bypass I/O in Virtual Machines. In *Proceedings of the Annual Conference on USENIX '06 Annual Technical Conference*, ATEC '06, pages 3–3, Berkeley, CA, USA, 2006. USENIX Association.

[17] Matthew Wilcox. I'll Do It Later: Softirqs, Tasklets, Bottom Halves, Task Queues, Work Queues and Timers. In *Linux.Conf.Au*, 2003.

[18] Christopher Mitchell, Yifeng Geng, and Jinyang Li. Using One-sided RDMA Reads to Build a Fast, CPU-efficient Key-value Store. In *Proceedings of the 2013 USENIX Conference on Annual Technical Conference*, USENIX ATC'13, pages 103–114, Berkeley, CA, USA, 2013. USENIX Association.

[19] OFED. The Open Fabric Alliance, at https://www.openfabrics.org/.

[20] Diego Ongaro, Alan L. Cox, and Scott Rixner. Scheduling I/O in Virtual Machine Monitors. In *Proceedings of the Fourth ACM SIGPLAN/SIGOPS International Conference on Virtual Execution Environments*, VEE '08, pages 1–10, New York, NY, USA, 2008. ACM.

[21] Diego Ongaro, Stephen M. Rumble, Ryan Stutsman, John Ousterhout, and Mendel Rosenblum. Fast Crash Recovery in RAMCloud. In *Proceedings of the Twenty-Third ACM Symposium on Operating Systems Principles*, SOSP '11, pages 29–41, New York, NY, USA, 2011. ACM.

[22] John Ousterhout, Parag Agrawal, David Erickson, Christos Kozyrakis, Jacob Leverich, David Mazières, Subhasish Mitra, Aravind Narayanan, Diego Ongaro, Guru Parulkar, Mendel Rosenblum, Stephen M. Rumble, Eric Stratmann, and Ryan Stutsman. The Case for RAMCloud. *Commun. ACM*, 54(7):121–130, July 2011.

[23] John Ousterhout, Parag Agrawal, David Erickson, Christos Kozyrakis, Jacob Leverich, David Mazières, Subhasish Mitra, Aravind Narayanan, Guru Parulkar, Mendel Rosenblum, Stephen M. Rumble, Eric Stratmann, and Ryan Stutsman. The Case for RAMClouds: Scalable High-performance Storage Entirely in DRAM. *SIGOPS Oper. Syst. Rev.*, 43(4):92–105, January 2010.

[24] Zhenhao Pan, Yaozu Dong, Yu Chen, Lei Zhang, and Zhijiao Zhang. CompSC: Live Migration with Pass-through Devices. In *Proceedings of the 8th ACM SIGPLAN/SIGOPS Conference on Virtual Execution Environments*, VEE '12, pages 109–120, New York, NY, USA, 2012. ACM.

[25] PCI SIG. Single Root I/O Virtualization, at https://www.pcisig.com/specifications/iov/single_root/.

[26] A Ranadive, A Gavrilovska, and K. Schwan. FaReS: Fair Resource Scheduling for VMM-Bypass InfiniBand Devices.

In *Cluster, Cloud and Grid Computing (CCGrid), 2010 10th IEEE/ACM International Conference on*, pages 418–427, May 2010.

[27] R. Recio, B. Metzler, P. Culley, J. Hilland, and D. Garcia. A Remote Direct Memory Access Protocol Specification. RFC 5040, October 2007.

[28] S. A. Reinemo, T. Skeie, T. Sodring, O. Lysne, and O. Trudbakken. An Overview of QoS Capabilities in Infiniband, Advanced Switching Interconnect, and Ethernet. *Comm. Mag.*, 44(7):32–38, September 2006.

[29] Rusty Russell. virtio: Towards a De-facto Standard for Virtual I/O Devices. *SIGOPS Oper. Syst. Rev.*, 42(5):95–103, July 2008.

[30] Animesh Trivedi, Bernard Metzler, and Patrick Stuedi. A case for RDMA in clouds: turning supercomputer networking into commodity. In *Proceedings of the Second Asia-Pacific Workshop on Systems*, APSys '11, pages 17:1–17:5, New York, NY, USA, 2011. ACM.

[31] Vangelis Tasoulas. Prototyping Live Migrationn With SR-IOV Supported InfiniBand HCAs. `http://www.bsc.es/sites/default/files/public/mare_nostrum/2013hpcac-04.pdf`, 2012.

Notes: IBM is a trademark of International Business Machines Corporation, registered in many jurisdictions worldwide. Intel and Intel Xeon are trademarks or registered trademarks of Intel Corporation or its subsidiaries in the United States and other countries. Linux is a registered trademark of Linus Torvalds in the United States, other countries, or both. Other products and service names might be trademarks of IBM or other companies.

Supporting High Performance Molecular Dynamics in Virtualized Clusters using IOMMU, SR-IOV, and GPUDirect

Andrew J. Younge[1], John Paul Walters[2], Stephen P. Crago[2], Geoffrey C. Fox[1]

[1] School of Informatics and Computing
Indiana Univerisity
Bloomington, IN 47408
{ajyounge,gcf}@indiana.edu

[2] Information Sciences Institute
University of Southern California
Arlington, VA 22203
{jwalters,crago}@isi.edu

Abstract

Cloud Infrastructure-as-a-Service paradigms have recently shown their utility for a vast array of computational problems, ranging from advanced web service architectures to high throughput computing. However, many scientific computing applications have been slow to adapt to virtualized cloud frameworks. This is due to performance impacts of virtualization technologies, coupled with the lack of advanced hardware support necessary for running many high performance scientific applications at scale.

By using KVM virtual machines that leverage both Nvidia GPUs and InfiniBand, we show that molecular dynamics simulations with LAMMPS and HOOMD run at near-native speeds. This experiment also illustrates how virtualized environments can support the latest parallel computing paradigms, including both MPI+CUDA and new GPUDirect RDMA functionality. Specific findings show initial promise in scaling of such applications to larger production deployments targeting large scale computational workloads.

Keywords Cloud computing; IaaS; Virtualization; KVM; IOMMU; SR-IOV; GPUDirect; Molecular Dynamics; OpenStack

1. Introduction

The cloud computing paradigm has become pervasive for commodity computing, but has not yet become widely accepted in the High Performance Computing (HPC) community. Various platform tools such as Hadoop and MapReduce, among others, have already percolated into data intensive computing within HPC [20]. In addition, there are efforts to support traditional HPC-centric scientific computing applications in virtualized cloud infrastructure. There are a multitude of reasons for supporting parallel computation in the cloud[12], including features such as dynamic scalability, specialized operating environments, simple management interfaces, fault tolerance, and enhanced quality of service, to name a few. There is a growing effort to support advanced scientific computing using virtualized infrastructure which can be seen by a variety of new efforts, including the Comet resource within XSEDE at San Diego Supercomputer Center [25].

Nevertheless, there exists a past notion that virtualization used in cloud infrastructure is inherently inefficient. Historically, cloud infrastructure has done little to provide the necessary advanced hardware capabilities that have become almost mandatory in supercomputers today, most notably advanced GPUs and high-speed, low-latency interconnects. Instead, cloud infrastructure providers have favored commodity homogeneous systems. The result of these notions has hindered the use of virtualized environments for parallel computation, where performance is paramount.

This is starting to change, however, as today's cloud providers seek improved performance at lower power. This has resulted in a heterogeneous cloud. Amazon EC2 supports GPU accelerators in EC2 [5], and OpenStack supports heterogeneity using flavors [8]. These advancements in cloud level support for heterogeneity combined with better support for high-performance virtualization makes the use of cloud for HPC much more feasible for a wider range of applications and platforms.

Still, performance remains a concern within virtualized environments. To that end, a growing effort is currently underway that looks to systematically identify and reduce any overhead in virtualization technologies. While some of the first efforts to investigate HPC applications on cloud infrastructure like the DOE Magellan project [37] documented many shortcomings in performance, recent efforts

VEE '15,   March 14–15, 2015, Istanbul, Turkey..
Copyright © 2015 ACM 978-1-4503-3450-1/15/03... $15.00.
http://dx.doi.org/10.1145/2731186.2731194

have proven to be largely successful [24, 38], though further research is needed to address issues of scalability and I/O.

Thus, we see constantly diminishing overhead with virtualization, not only with traditional cloud workloads [18] but also with HPC workloads. While virtualization will almost always include some additional overhead in relation to its dynamic features, the eventual goal for supporting HPC in virtualized environments is to minimize what overhead exists whenever possible. To advance the placement of HPC applications on virtual machines, new efforts are emerging which focus specifically on key hardware now commonplace in supercomputers. By leveraging new virtualization tools such as I/O memory management unit (IOMMU) device passthrough and Single Root I/O Virtualization (SR-IOV), we can now support such advanced hardware as the latest Nvidia Tesla GPUs [36] as well as InfiniBand fabrics for high performance networking and I/O [21, 26]. While previous efforts have focused on single-node advancements, our contribution in this paper is to show that real-world applications can operate efficiently in multi-node clusters and cloud infrastructure.

The remainder of this paper is organized as follows. In Section 2 we describe the background and related work necessary for high performance virtualization. In Section 3, we describe a heterogeneous cloud platform, based on Open-Stack. This effort has been under development at USC/ISI since 2011 [14]. We describe our work towards integrating GPU and InfiniBand support into OpenStack, and we describe the heterogeneous scheduling additions that are necessary to support not only attached accelerators, but any cloud composed of heterogeneous elements.

In Sections 4 and 5 we describe the LAMMPS and HOOMD benchmarks and our experimental setup. In Section 6 we characterize the performance of LAMMPS and HOOMD in a virtual infrastructure complete with both Kepler GPUs and QDR InfiniBand. Both HOOMD and LAMMPS are used extensively in some of the world's fastest supercomputers and represent example simulations that HPC supports today. We show that these applications are able to run at near-native speeds within a completely virtualized environment. Furthermore, we demonstrate the ability of such a virtualized environment to support cutting edge technologies such as RDMA GPUDirect, illustrating that the latest HPC technologies are also possible in a virtualized environment. In Section 7, we provide a brief discussion before concluding in Section 8.

2. Background and Related Work

Virtualization technologies and hypervisors have seen widespread deployment in support of a vast array of applications. This ranges from public commercial cloud deployments such as Amazon EC2 [1], Microsoft Azure [19], and Google's Cloud Platform [6] to private deployments within colocation facilities, corporate data centers, and even na-

tional scale cyberinfrastructure initiatives. All these look to support various use cases and applications such as web servers, ACID and BASE databases, online object storage, and even distributed systems, to name a few.

The use of virtualization and hypervisors to support various HPC solutions has been studied with mixed results. In [38], it is found that there is a great deal of variance between hypervisors when running various distributed memory and MPI applications, and that overall, KVM performed well across an array of HPC benchmarks. Furthermore, some applications may not may fit well into default virtualized environments, such as High Performance Linpack [24]. Other studies have looked at interconnect performance in virtualization and found the performance of conventional techniques to be lacking even in the best-case scenario, with up to a 60% performance penalty [28].

Recently, various CPU architectures have added support for I/O virtualization mechanisms in the CPU ISA through the use of an I/O memory management unit (IOMMU). Often, this is referred to as PCI Passthrough, as it enabled devices on the PCI-Express bus to be passed directly to a specific virtual machine (VM). Specific hardware implementations include Intel's VT-d [29], AMD's IOMMU [9] for x86_64 architectures, and recently ARM System MMU [11]. All of these implementations effectively look to aid in the usage of DMA-capable hardware to be used within a specific virtual machine. By using these features, a wide array of hardware can be utilized directly within VMs and enable fast and efficient computation and I/O capabilities.

2.1 GPU Passthrough

Nvidia GPUs comprise the single most common accelerator in the Nov 2014 Top 500 List [15] and represent an increasing shift towards accelerators for HPC applications. Historically, GPU usage in a virtualized environment has been difficult, especially for scientific computation. Various front-end remote API implementations have been developed to provide CUDA and OpenCL libraries in VMs, which translate library calls to a back-end or remote GPU. One common implementation of this is rCUDA [16], which provides a front-end CUDA API within a VM or any compute node, and then sends the calls via Ethernet or InfiniBand to a separate node with 1 or more GPUs. While this method provides the desired functionality, it has the drawback of relying on the interconnect itself and the bandwidth available, which can be especially problematic on an Ethernet based network. Furthermore, as this method consumes bandwidth, it can leave little remaining for MPI or RDMA routines, thereby constructing a bottleneck for some MPI+CUDA applications that depend on inter-process communication. Another mechanism of using GPUs in VMs is hypervisor based virtualization [33].

Recently efforts have been seen to support such GPU accelerators within VMs using IOMMU technologies, with implementations now available with KVM, Xen, and VMWare

[34–36, 39]. These efforts have shown that GPUs can achieve up to 99% of their bare metal performance when passed to a virtual machine using PCI Passthrough. While it has been demonstrated that using PCI Passthrough results in high performance across a range of hypervisors and GPUs, the efforts have been limited to investigating single node performance until now.

2.2 SR-IOV and InfiniBand

With almost all parallel HPC applications, the interconnect fabric which enables fast and efficient communication between processors becomes a central requirement to achieving good performance. Specifically, a high bandwidth link is needed for distributed processors to share large amounts of data across the system. Furthermore, low latency becomes equally important for ensuring quick delivery of small message communications and resolving large collective barriers within many parallelized codes. One such interconnect, InfiniBand, has become the most common implementation used within the Top500 list.

Supporting I/O interconnects in VMs has been aided by Single Root I/O Virtualization (SR-IOV), whereby multiple virtual PCI functions are created in hardware to represent a single PCI device. These virtual functions (VFs) can then be passed to a VM and used by the guest as if it had direct access to that PCI device. SR-IOV allows for the virtualization and multiplexing to be done within the hardware, effectively providing higher performance and greater control than software solutions.

SR-IOV has been used in conjunction with Ethernet devices to provide high performance 10Gb TCP/IP connectivity within VMs [23], offering near-native bandwidth and advanced QoS features not easily obtained through emulated Ethernet offerings. Currently Amazon EC2 offers a high performance VM solution utilizing SR-IOV enabled 10Gb Ethernet adapters. While SR-IOV enabled 10Gb Ethernet solutions offers a big forward in performance, Ethernet still does not offer the high bandwidth or low latency typically found with InfiniBand solutions.

Recently SR-IOV support for InfiniBand has been added by Mellanox in the ConnectX series adapters. Initial evaluation of SR-IOV InfiniBand within KVM VMs has demonstration point-to-point bandwidth to be near-native, but with up to 30% latency overhead for very small messages [21, 30]. However, even with the noted overhead, this still signifies up to an order of magnitude difference in latency between InfiniBand and Ethernet with VMs. Furthermore, advanced configuration of SR-IOV enabled InfiniBand fabric is taking shape, with recent research showing up to a 30% reduction in the latency overhead [26]. However, real application performance has not yet been well understood until now.

2.3 GPUDirect

NVIDIA's GPUDirect technology was introduced to reduce the overhead of data movement across GPUs [2, 32]. Currently, there exists three distinct versions of GPUDirect. GPUDirect v1 adds accelerated communication with network and storage devices through the use of a single CPU buffer, and GPUDirect v2 provides peer-to-peer communication between discrete GPUs on a single node. GPUDirect v3, the most recent version and what is used in this manuscript, provides support for direct RDMA between GPUs across an InfiniBand interconnect for Kepler-class GPUs. This alleviates the need for staging data to/from host memory in order to transmit data via InfiniBand between GPUs on separate nodes, although it does require application code to target GPUDirect.

GPUDirect relies on three key technologies: CUDA 5 (and up), a CUDA-enabled MPI implementation, and a Kepler-class GPU (RDMA only). Both MVAPICH and OpenMPI support GPUDirect. Support for RDMA over GPUDirect is enabled by the MPI library, given supported hardware, without requiring changes to the MPI calls. In this paper, we demonstrate scaling a MD simulation to 4 nodes connected via QDR InfiniBand and show that GPUDirect RDMA improves both scalability and overall performance by approximately 9% at no cost to the end user.

3. A Cloud for High Performance Computing

With support for GPU Passthrough, SR-IOV, and GPUDirect, we have the building blocks for a high performance, heterogeneous cloud. In addition, other common accelerators (e.g. Xeon Phi [4]) have similarly been demonstrated in virtualized environments. We envision a heterogeneous cloud that supports both high speed networking and accelerators for tightly coupled applications.

To this end we developed a heterogeneous cloud based on OpenStack [7]. In our previous work, we demonstrated the ability to rapidly provision GPU, bare metal, and other heterogeneous resources within a single cloud [14]. Building on this effort we have added support for GPU passthrough to OpenStack as well as prototyped SR-IOV support for ConnectX-2 and ConnectX-3 Infiniband devices. Mellanox has since added an OpenStack InfiniBand networking plugin for OpenStack's Neutron service [3]. While OpenStack supports services for networking (Neutron), compute (Nova), identity (Keystone), storage (Cinder, Swift), and others, our work focuses entirely on the compute service.

Scheduling is implemented at two levels: the cloud level and the node level. In our earlier work, we have developed a cloud level heterogeneous scheduler for OpenStack that allows scheduling based on architectures and resources [14]. In this model, the cloud level scheduler dispatches jobs to nodes based on resource requirements (e.g. Kepler GPU) and node level resource availability.

At the node, a second level of scheduling occurs to ensure that resources are tracked and not over-committed. Unlike traditional cloud paradigms, devices passed into VMs cannot be over-committed. We treat devices, whether GPUs or InfiniBand virtual functions, as schedulable resources. Thus, it is the responsibility of the individual node to track resources committed and report availability to the cloud level scheduler. For reporting, we augment OpenStack's existing reporting mechanism to provide a low overhead solution.

4. Benchmarks

We selected two molecular dynamics (MD) applications for evaluation in this study: LAMMPS and HOOMD [10, 27]. These MD simulations are chosen to represent a subset of advanced parallel computation for a number of fundamental reasons:

- MD simulations provide a practical representation of N-Body simulations, which are one of the major computational *Dwarfs* [13] in parallel and distributed computing.

- MD simulations are one of the most widely deployed applications on large scale supercomputers today.

- Many MD simulations have a hybrid MPI+CUDA programming model, which has become commonplace in HPC as the use of accelerators increase.

As such, we look to LAMMPS and HOOMD to provide a real-world example for running cutting-edge parallel programs on virtualized infrastructure. While these applications by no means represent all parallel scientific computing efforts (see 13 Dwarfs [13]), we hope these MD simulators offer a more pragmatic viewpoint than traditional synthetic HPC benchmarks such as High Performance Linpack.

LAMMPS The Large-scale Atomic/Molecular Parallel Simulator is a well-understood highly parallel molecular dynamics simulator. It supports both CPU and GPU-based workloads. Unlike many simulators, both MD and otherwise, LAMMPS is heterogeneous. It will use both GPUs and multicore CPUs concurrently. For this study, this heterogeneous functionality introduces additional load on the host, allowing LAMMPS to utilize all available cores on a given system. Networking in LAMMPS is accomplished using a typical MPI model. That is, data is copied from the GPU back to the host and sent over the InfiniBand fabric. LAMMPS does not include GPUDirect support, and no RDMA is used for these experiments.

HOOMD-blue The Highly Optimized Object-oriented Many-particle Dynamics – Blue Edition is a particle dynamics simulator capable of scaling into the thousands of GPUs. HOOMD supports executing on both CPUs and GPUs. Unlike LAMMPS, HOOMD is homogeneous and does not support mixing of GPUs and CPUs. HOOMD supports GPUDirect using a CUDA-enabled MPI. In this paper we focus on

HOOMD's support for GPUDirect and show its benefits for increasing cluster sizes.

5. Experimental Setup

Using two molecular dynamics tools, LAMMPS[27] and HOOMD [10], we demonstrate a high performance *system*. That is, we combine PCI passthrough for Nvidia Kepler-class GPUs with QDR Infiniband SR-IOV and show that high performance molecular dynamics simulations are achievable within a virtualized environment. For the first time, we also demonstrate Nvidia GPUDirect technology within such a virtual environment. Thus, we look to not only illustrate that virtual machines provide a flexible high performance infrastructure for scaling scientific workloads, including MD simulations, but also that the latest HPC features and programming environments are available and efficient in this same model.

5.1 Node configuration

To support the use of Nvidia GPUs and InfiniBand within a VM, specific host configuration is needed. This node configuration is illustrated in Figure 1. While our implementation is specific to the KVM hypervisor, this setup represents a design that can be hypervisor agnostic.

Each node in the testbed uses CentOS 6.4 with a 3.13 upstream Linux kernel for the host OS, along with the latest KVM hypervisor, QEMU 2.1, and the *vfio* driver. Each guest VM runs CentOS 6.4 with a stock 2.6.32-358.23.2 kernel. A Kepler GPU is passed through using PCI Passthrough and directly initiated within the VM via the Nvidia 331.20 driver and CUDA release 5.5. While this specific implementation used only a single GPU, it is also possible to include as many GPUs as one can fit within the PCI Express bus if desired. As the GPU is used by the VM, an on-board VGA device was used by the host and a standard Cirrus VGA was emulated in the guest OS. OFED version 2.1-1.0.0 drivers are used with Mellanox ConnectX-3 VPI adapter with firmware 2.31.5050. The host driver initiates 4 VFs, one of which is passed through to the VM where the default OFED mlnx_ib drivers are loaded.

5.2 Cluster Configuration

Our test environment is composed of 4 servers each with a single Nvidia Kepler-class GPU. Two servers are equipped with K20 GPUs, while the other two servers are equipped with K40 GPUs, demonstrating the potential for a more heterogeneous deployment. Each server is composed of 2 Intel Xeon E5-2670 CPUs, 48GB of DDR3 memory, and Mellanox ConnectX-3 QDR InfiniBand. CPU sockets and memory are split evenly between the two NUMA nodes on each system. All InfiniBand adapters use a single Voltaire 4036 QDR switch with a software subnet manager for IPoIB functionality.

For these experiments, both the GPUs and InfiniBand adapters are attached to NUMA node 1 and both the guest

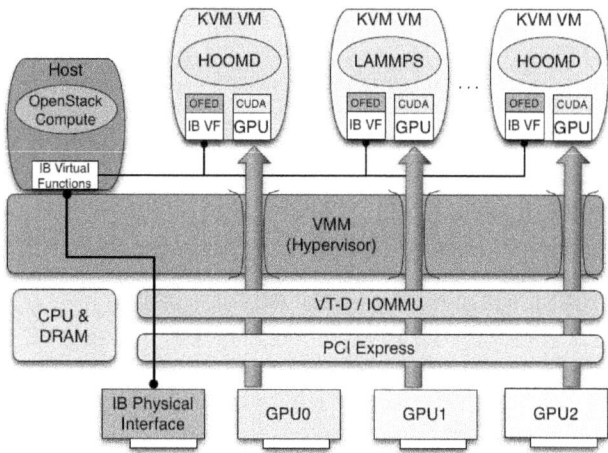

Figure 1. Node PCI Passthrough of GPUs and InfiniBand

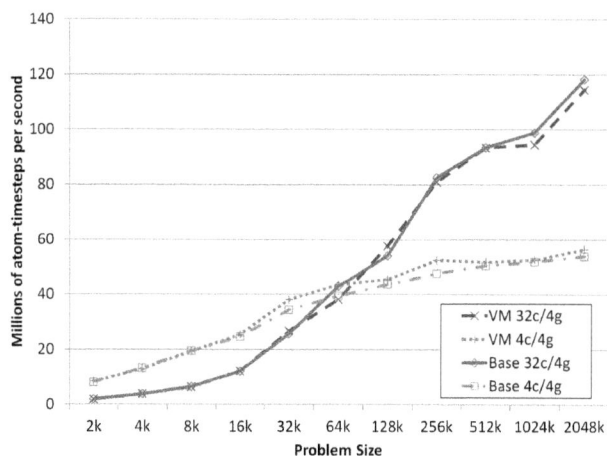

Figure 3. LAMMPS RHODO Performance

VMs and the base system utilized identical software stacks. Each guest was allocated 20 GB of RAM and a full socket of 8 cores, and pinned to NUMA node 1 to ensure optimal hardware usage. For a fair and effective comparison, we also use a native environment without any virtualization. This native environment employs the same hardware configuration, and like the Guest OS runs CentOS 6.4 with the stock 2.6.32-358.23.2 kernel.

6. Results

In this section, we discuss the performance of both the LAMMPS and HOOMD molecular dynamics simulation tools when running within a virtualized environment. Each application set was run 10 times, with the results averaged accordingly.

6.1 LAMMPS

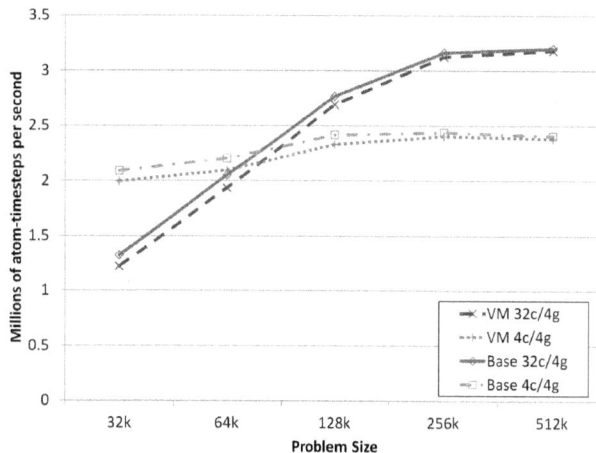

Figure 2. LAMMPS LJ Performance

Figure 2 shows one of the most common LAMMPS algorithms used - the Lennard-Jones potential (LJ). This algorithm is deployed in two main configurations - a 1:1 core

to GPU mapping and a 8:1 core to GPU mapping, labeled in Figures 2 and 3 as 4c/4g and 32c/4g, respectively. With the LAMMPS GPU implementation, a delicate balance between GPUs and CPUs is required to find the optimal ratio for fastest computation, however here we just look at the two most obvious choices. With small problem sizes, the 1:1 mapping outperforms the more complex core deployment, as the problem does not require the additional complexity provided with a multi-core solution. As expected the multi-core configuration quickly offers better performance for larger problem sizes, achieving roughly twice the performance with all 32 available cores. This is largely due to the availability of all 8 cores to keep the GPU fully utilized.

The important factor for this manuscript is the relative performance of the virtualized environment. From the results, it is clear the VM solution performs very well compared to the best-case native deployment. For the multi-core configuration across all problem sizes, the virtualized deployment averaged 98.5% efficiency compared to native. The single core per GPU deployment reported better-than-native performance at 100% native. This is likely due to caching effects, but further investigation is needed to fully identify this occurrence.

Another common LAMMPS algorithm, the Rhodopsin protein in solvated lipid bilayer benchmark (Rhodo), was also run with results given in Figure 3. As with the LJ runs, we see the multi-core to GPU configuration resulting in higher computational performance for the larger problem sizes compared to the single core per GPU configuration, as expected.

Again, the overhead of the virtualized configuration remains low across all configurations and problem sizes, with an average 96.4% efficiency compared to native. We also see the gap in performance decrease as the problem size increases, with the 512k problem size yielding 99.3% of native performance. This finding leads us to extrapolate that a virtualized MPI+CUDA implementation could scale to a larger computational resource with similar success.

6.2 HOOMD

In Figure 4 we show the performance of a Lennard-Jones liquid simulation with 256K particles running under HOOMD. HOOMD includes support for CUDA-aware MPI implementations via GPUDirect. The MVAPICH 2.0 GDR implementation enables a further optimization by supporting RDMA for GPUDirect. From Figure 4 we can see that HOOMD simulations, both with and without GPUDirect, perform very near-native. The GPUDirect results at 4 nodes achieve 98.5% of the base system's performance. The non-GPUDirect results achieve 98.4% efficiency at 4 nodes. These results indicate the virtualized HPC environment is able to support such complex workloads. While the effective testbed size is relatively small, it indicates that such workloads may scale equally well to hundreds or thousands of nodes. The advantage of using GPUDirect RDMA is also evident in Figure 4, with a 9% performance boost realized for both virtualized and non-virtualized experiments.

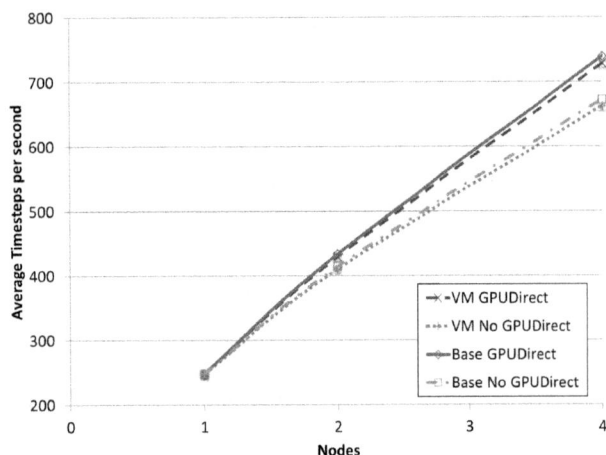

Figure 4. HOOMD LJ Performance with 256k Simulation

7. Discussion

From the results, we see the potential for running HPC applications in a virtualized environment using GPUs and InfiniBand interconnect fabric. Across all LAMMPS runs, we found only a 1.9% overhead between the KVM virtualized environment and native. For HOOMD, we found a similar 1.5% overhead, both with and without GPU Direct. These results go against conventional wisdom that HPC workloads perform poorly in VMs. In fact, we show two N-Body type simulations programmed in an MPI+CUDA implementation perform at roughly near-native performance in tuned KVM virtual machines.

With HOOMD, we see how GPUDirect RDMA shows a clear advantage over the non-GPUDirect implementation, achieving a 9% performance boost in both the native and vir-

tualized experiments. While GPUDirect's performance impact has been well evaluated previously [2], it is the authors' belief that this manuscript represents the first time GPUDirect has has been utilized in a virtualized environment.

Another interesting finding of running LAMMPS in a virtualized environment is that as workload increases from a single node to 32 cores, the overhead does not increase. These results lend credence to the notion that this solution would also work for a much larger deployment, assuming system jitter can be minimized [31]. Specifically, it would be possible to expand such computational problems to a larger deployment in FutureGrid [17], Chameleon Cloud [22], or even the planned NSF Comet machine at SDSC, scheduled to provide up to 2 Petaflops of computational power. Effectively, these results provide evidence that HPC computations can be supported in virtualized environment with minimal overhead.

8. Conclusion

The ability to run large-scale parallel scientific applications in the cloud has become possible, but historically has been limited by both performance concerns and infrastructure availability. In this work we show that advanced HPC-oriented hardware such as the latest Nvidia GPUs and InfiniBand fabric are now available within a virtualized infrastructure. Our results find MPI + CUDA applications, such as molecular dynamics simulations, run at near-native performance compared to traditional non-virtualized HPC infrastructure, with just an averaged 1.9% and 1.5% overhead for LAMMPS and HOOMD, respectively. We also show the utility of GPUDirect RDMA for the first time in a cloud environment with HOOMD. The support of these workloads coalesce to provide an open source Infrastructure-as-a-Service framework using OpenStack. Our future efforts will be twofold. We first hope to increase the scale to significantly larger cloud infrastructure on a new experimental system and confirm near-native performance is acheivable in a virtualized environment. We also look to expand the workload diversity and support many other HPC and big data applications running efficiently in virtual clusters.

Acknowledgments

This work was developed with support from the National Science Foundation (NSF) under grant #0910812 to Indiana University and with support from the Office of Naval Research under grant #N00014-14-1-0035 to USC/ISI. Andrew J. Younge also acknowledges support from The Persistent Systems Fellowship of the School of Informatics and Computing at Indiana University.

References

[1] Amazon elastic compute cloud (Amazon EC2). Website, August 2010. URL http://aws.amazon.com/ec2/.

[2] NVIDIA GPUDirect. Website, November 2014. URL `https://developer.nvidia.com/gpudirect`.

[3] Mellanox Neutron Plugin. Website, November 2014. URL `https://wiki.openstack.org/wiki/Mellanox-Neutron`.

[4] Getting Xen working for Intel(R) Xeon Phi(tm) Coprocessor. Website, November 2014. URL `https://software.intel.com/en-us/articles/getting-xen-working-for-intelr-xeon-phitm-coprocessor`.

[5] AWS high performance computing. Website, November 2014. URL `http://aws.amazon.com/hpc/`.

[6] Google Cloud Platform. Website, November 2014. URL `https://cloud.google.com/`.

[7] OpenStack cloud software. Website, November 2014. URL `http://openstack.org`.

[8] OpenStack flavors. Website, November 2014. URL `http://docs.openstack.org/openstack-ops/content/flavors.html`.

[9] AMD Corporation. AMD I/O virtualization technology (IOMMU) specification. Technical report, AMD Corporation, 2009.

[10] J. Anderson, A. Keys, C. Phillips, T. Dac Nguyen, and S. Glotzer. HOOMD-blue, general-purpose many-body dynamics on the GPU. In *APS Meeting Abstracts*, volume 1, page 18008, 2010.

[11] ARM Limited. ARM system memory management unit architecture specification. Technical report, ARM Limited, 2013.

[12] M. Armbrust, A. Fox, R. Griffith, A. D. Joseph, R. Katz, A. Konwinski, G. Lee, D. Patterson, A. Rabkin, I. Stoica, and M. Zaharia. A view of cloud computing. *Commun. ACM*, 53 (4):50–58, Apr. 2010. ISSN 0001-0782.

[13] K. Asanovic, R. Bodik, B. C. Catanzaro, J. J. Gebis, P. Husbands, K. Keutzer, D. A. Patterson, W. L. Plishker, J. Shalf, S. W. Williams, et al. The landscape of parallel computing research: A view from Berkeley. Technical report, Technical Report UCB/EECS-2006-183, EECS Department, University of California, Berkeley, 2006.

[14] S. Crago, K. Dunn, P. Eads, L. Hochstein, D.-I. Kang, M. Kang, D. Modium, K. Singh, J. Suh, and J. P. Walters. Heterogeneous cloud computing. In *Cluster Computing (CLUSTER), 2011 IEEE International Conference on*, pages 378–385. IEEE, 2011.

[15] J. Dongarra, H. Meuer, and E. Strohmaier. Top 500 supercomputers. Website, November 2014. URL `http://top500.org/`.

[16] J. Duato, A. J. Pena, F. Silla, J. C. Fernández, R. Mayo, and E. S. Quintana-Orti. Enabling CUDA acceleration within virtual machines using rCUDA. In *High Performance Computing (HiPC), 2011 18th International Conference on*, pages 1–10. IEEE, 2011.

[17] G. Fox, G. von Laszewski, J. Diaz, K. Keahey, J. Fortes, R. Figueiredo, S. Smallen, W. Smith, and A. Grimshaw. FutureGrid—a reconfigurable testbed for Cloud, HPC and Grid computing. *Contemporary High Performance Computing: From Petascale toward Exascale, Computational Science*. Chapman and Hall/CRC, 2013.

[18] N. Huber, M. von Quast, M. Hauck, and S. Kounev. Evaluating and modeling virtualization performance overhead for cloud environments. In *CLOSER*, pages 563–573, 2011.

[19] R. Jennings. *Cloud Computing with the Windows Azure Platform*. John Wiley & Sons, 2010.

[20] S. Jha, J. Qiu, A. Luckow, P. K. Mantha, and G. C. Fox. A tale of two data-intensive paradigms: Applications, abstractions, and architectures. In *Proceedings of the 3rd International Congress on Big Data*, 2014.

[21] J. Jose, M. Li, X. Lu, K. C. Kandalla, M. D. Arnold, and D. K. Panda. SR-IOV support for virtualization on InfiniBand clusters: Early experience. In *Cluster, Cloud and Grid Computing (CCGrid), 2013 13th IEEE/ACM International Symposium on*, pages 385–392. IEEE, 2013.

[22] K. Keahey, J. Mambretti, D. K. Panda, P. Rad, W. Smith, and D. Stanzione. NSF Chameleon cloud. Website, November 2014. URL `http://www.chameleoncloud.org/`.

[23] J. Liu. Evaluating standard-based self-virtualizing devices: A performance study on 10 GbE NICs with SR-IOV support. In *Parallel Distributed Processing (IPDPS), 2010 IEEE International Symposium on*, pages 1–12, April 2010.

[24] P. Luszczek, E. Meek, S. Moore, D. Terpstra, V. M. Weaver, and J. Dongarra. Evaluation of the HPC challenge benchmarks in virtualized environments. In *Proceedings of the 2011 International Conference on Parallel Processing - Volume 2*, Euro-Par'11, pages 436–445, Berlin, Heidelberg, 2012. Springer-Verlag.

[25] R. L. Moore, C. Baru, D. Baxter, G. C. Fox, A. Majumdar, P. Papadopoulos, W. Pfeiffer, R. S. Sinkovits, S. Strande, M. Tatineni, et al. Gateways to discovery: Cyberinfrastructure for the long tail of science. In *Proceedings of the 2014 Annual Conference on Extreme Science and Engineering Discovery Environment*, page 39. ACM, 2014.

[26] M. Musleh, V. Pai, J. P. Walters, A. J. Younge, and S. P. Crago. Bridging the virtualization performance gap for HPC using SR-IOV for InfiniBand. In *Proceedings of the 7th IEEE International Conference on Cloud Computing (CLOUD 2014)*, Anchorage, AK, 2014. IEEE.

[27] S. Plimpton, P. Crozier, and A. Thompson. LAMMPS-large-scale atomic/molecular massively parallel simulator. *Sandia National Laboratories*, 2007.

[28] L. Ramakrishnan, R. S. Canon, K. Muriki, I. Sakrejda, and N. J. Wright. Evaluating interconnect and virtualization performance for high performance computing. *SIGMETRICS Perform. Eval. Rev.*, 40(2):55–60, Oct. 2012. ISSN 0163-5999.

[29] M. Righini. Enabling Intel® virtualization technology features and benefits. Technical report, Intel Corporation, 2010.

[30] T. P. P. D. L. Ruivo, G. B. Altayo, G. Garzoglio, S. Timm, H. Kim, S.-Y. Noh, and I. Raicu. Exploring InfiniBand hardware virtualization in OpenNebula towards efficient high-performance computing. In *CCGRID*, pages 943–948, 2014.

[31] S. Seelam, L. Fong, A. Tantawi, J. Lewars, J. Divirgilio, and K. Gildea. Extreme scale computing: Modeling the impact of

system noise in multicore clustered systems. In *Parallel Distributed Processing (IPDPS), 2010 IEEE International Symposium on*, pages 1–12, April 2010. .

[32] G. Shainer, A. Ayoub, P. Lui, T. Liu, M. Kagan, C. R. Trott, G. Scantlen, and P. S. Crozier. The development of Mellanox/NVIDIA GPUDirect over InfiniBand—a new model for GPU to GPU communications. *Computer Science-Research and Development*, 26(3-4):267–273, 2011.

[33] Y. Suzuki, S. Kato, H. Yamada, and K. Kono. GPUvm: why not virtualizing GPUs at the hypervisor? In *Proceedings of the 2014 USENIX conference on USENIX Annual Technical Conference*, pages 109–120. USENIX Association, 2014.

[34] K. Tian, Y. Dong, and D. Cowperthwaite. A full GPU virtualization solution with mediated pass-through. In *Proc. USENIX ATC*, 2014.

[35] L. Vu, H. Sivaraman, and R. Bidarkar. GPU virtualization for high performance general purpose computing on the ESX hypervisor. In *Proceedings of the High Performance Computing Symposium*, HPC '14, pages 2:1–2:8, San Diego, CA, USA, 2014. Society for Computer Simulation International.

[36] J. P. Walters, A. J. Younge, D.-I. Kang, K.-T. Yao, M. Kang, S. P. Crago, and G. C. Fox. GPU-Passthrough performance: A comparison of KVM, Xen, VMWare ESXi, and LXC for CUDA and OpenCL applications. In *Proceedings of the 7th IEEE International Conference on Cloud Computing (CLOUD 2014)*, Anchorage, AK, 2014. IEEE.

[37] K. Yelick, S. Coghlan, B. Draney, R. S. Canon, et al. The Magellan report on cloud computing for science. Technical report, US Department of Energy, 2011.

[38] A. J. Younge, R. Henschel, J. T. Brown, G. von Laszewski, J. Qiu, and G. C. Fox. Analysis of Virtualization Technologies for High Performance Computing Environments. In *Proceedings of the 4th International Conference on Cloud Computing (CLOUD 2011)*, Washington, DC, 2011. IEEE.

[39] A. J. Younge, J. P. Walters, S. Crago, and G. C. Fox. Evaluating GPU passthrough in Xen for high performance cloud computing. In *High-Performance Grid and Cloud Computing Workshop at the 28th IEEE International Parallel and Distributed Processing Symposium*, Pheonix, AZ, 05 2014. IEEE.

Proactively Breaking Large Pages to Improve Memory Overcommitment Performance in VMware ESXi

Fei Guo, Seongbeom Kim, Yury Baskakov, Ishan Banerjee

VMware, Inc

{fguo, skim, ybaskako, ishan}@vmware.com

Abstract

VMware ESXi [28] leverages hardware support for MMU virtualization available in modern Intel/AMD CPUs. To optimize address translation performance when running on such CPUs, ESXi preferably uses host large pages (2MB in x86-64 systems) to back VM's guest memory. While using host large pages provides best performance when host has sufficient free memory, it increases host memory pressure and effectively defeats page sharing. Hence, the host is more likely to hit the point where ESXi has to reclaim VM memory through much more expensive techniques such as ballooning or host swapping. As a result, using host large pages may significantly hurt consolidation ratio.

To deal with this problem, we propose a new host large page management policy that allows to: a) identify 'cold' large pages and break them even when host has plenty of free memory; b) break all large pages proactively when host free memory becomes scarce, but before the host starts ballooning or swapping; c) reclaim the small pages within the broken large pages through page sharing. With the new policy, the shareable small pages can be shared much earlier and the amount of memory that needs to be ballooned or swapped can be largely reduced when host memory pressure is high. We also propose an algorithm to dynamically adjust the page sharing rate when proactively breaking large pages using a VM large page shareability estimator for higher efficiency.

Experimental results show that the proposed large page management policy can improve the performance of various workloads up to 2.1x by significantly reducing the amount of ballooned or swapped memory when host memory pressure

is high. Applications still fully benefit from host large pages when memory pressure is low.

Categories and Subject Descriptors D.4.2 [*Operating Systems*]: Storage Management—Main memory

General Terms Measurement, Performance, Design

Keywords Virtualization; memory overcommitment; resource management; page sharing; large page

1. Introduction

Many contemporary hypervisors enable high server consolidation by allowing memory overcommitment. In a memory overcommitted host, the total used guest memory of all virtual machines (VMs) exceeds the host memory size. With an effective memory overcommitment support, hypervisor can provide high hardware availability, low operational cost and optimal resource utilization. Despite the benefits, memory overcommitment should be used wisely as it may degrade the applications performance.

VMware ESXi hypervisor utilizes page sharing, ballooning, host swapping, and some other techniques [11, 28] to efficiently reclaim VM memory when host free memory is scarce. Compared to ballooning and host swapping, which typically incur high performance penalty [19], page sharing is proven to be a light weight technique that can significantly reduce the memory footprint of a VM. Due to the low overhead of page sharing, ESXi can afford constantly performing sharing pages to acquire as much free memory as possible. However, the use of page sharing is largely limited in systems using host large pages because the likelihood of finding two identical large pages is fairly low.

ESXi preferentially maps guest physical pages to host large pages when running in servers with the hardware-assisted MMU virtualization techniques, such as Intel EPT and AMD NPT [13]. In such systems, using host large pages significantly reduces the cost of hardware TLB misses hence improves VM performance. For example, experiments have shown that the performance can be improved by up to 30% for certain workloads when using host large pages (Section 2).

Note that extensively using host large pages puts more pressure on memory system and may hurt server consolidation ratio. First, it amplifies memory allocation requests: even if the guest requests a 4KB page, ESXi eagerly allocates a large page (2MB in x86-64 systems) to *back* the guest page. As a result, the host free memory is consumed at a much higher rate. Secondly, using host large pages effectively defeats page sharing and defers it until host free memory is severely low, to the point where ESXi has to quickly reclaim memory using ballooning or swapping. When this happens, host large pages start to be *broken* to accommodate the reclamation requests, and the small pages within the broken large pages can be shared thereafter. As discussed in Section 2, deferring page sharing can lead to suboptimal performance because the amount of ballooned and swapped pages could be largely reduced had the shareable memory been reclaimed through page sharing in advance. Therefore, how to use host large pages efficiently in a memory over-committed host is a challenge to hypervisor memory management.

In this paper, we propose a new host large page management policy, referred to as *LPageBreak*, in ESXi hypervisor. Compared to the existing policy, the major contributions of the LPageBreak policy include:

1. Identify large pages that are infrequently used, i.e., 'cold' large pages, and allow them to be broken even when host free memory is plenty. Basically, we implement a simple 'cold' large page detector by periodically scanning the *Accessed* bits of large pages that are available in many modern CPUs. Hypervisor then breaks the 'cold' large pages that contain shareable small pages to share them right away.

2. Add a new memory state called `clear` in current ESXi memory management policy before the state where ESXi reclaims memory using ballooning or swapping (i.e., the `low` state as described in Section 3.1). When host free memory drops to the `clear` state, all large pages including the 'hot' ones are allowed to be broken. As a result, the host memory pressure can be relieved with the help of page sharing so that the amount of memory to be ballooned or swapped later is reduced, if not avoided at all.

3. Implement an adaptive policy to adjust page sharing rate in the `clear` state. This is critical for good performance because if the sharing rate is not high enough, hypervisor may not be able to reclaim the majority of shareable pages before it reaches the `low` state. In the prototype, the sharing rate is adjusted based on the host memory consumption rate and the VM large page shareability. The latter is obtained through a proposed estimator which predicts how much guest memory in VM large pages are shareable had they been backed by host small pages.

4. Lastly, we observe that for best performance, the `clear` state threshold, which determines whether to break 'hot'

large pages or not, should be adjusted when the host constantly stays in the `clear` state without entering the `low` state. We implement a dynamic threshold adjustment mechanism which effectively preserves host large pages if host memory consumption stops growing while in the `clear` state.

We evaluated the proposed LPageBreak policy using a 32GB, 16 core AMD Opteron 8378 server against SPECjbb, Swingbench, VDI, DVDstore2 and Olio workloads. The major findings are summarized as follows. First, we found that proactively breaking 'cold' large pages incurs negligible performance impact on workload while saving memory. Secondly, the proposed page shareability estimator can provide accurate predictions for various workloads with less than 13% errors, which are small enough for the page sharing speed adjustment algorithm. Thirdly, by dynamically adjusting the `clear` state threshold, Swingbench performance can be improved by 9.8% when host stays in the `clear` state without triggering ballooning or swapping. Finally, by using the LPageBreak policy in memory overcommitment tests, the overall performance can be improved by up to 2.1x for various workloads compared to the performance with default policy where large pages are preserved until ballooning or swapping happens.

The rest of the paper is organized as follows. We present the motivation for improving ESXi large page management policy in Section 2. In Section 3, we discuss the design of various techniques used in the proposed LPageBreak policy. Section 4 provides the implementation details of the prototype. Section 5 and Section 6 present the experiment environment and the evaluation results which show how LPage-Break improves performance in memory overcommitment cases. Section 7 discusses the related work and Section 8 concludes the work.

2. Motivations

In this section, we assess the benefits of using host large pages in virtualization environment and demonstrate why using host large pages can lead to suboptimal performance when host is memory overcommitted.

2.1 Impact of Host Large Page Backing

In virtualization environment, if the hypervisor uses large pages to back guest pages, the cost of address translation between guest virtual memory and host physical memory can be significantly reduced. For example, in a system with four level nested page tables, the number of memory accesses due to a TLB miss can drop from 24 to 15 when large pages are used [1]. TLB intensive workloads will greatly benefit from the use of large pages due to fewer TLB misses and faster page table lookup. Table 1 compares the performance of various workloads when using guest large pages and/or host large pages. The experiments are conducted using a single VM running on an Intel Xeon X5570 system. The results

Benchmark	SPEC-jbb	Swing-bench	DVD-store2
Guest large+Host large	1.30	1.12	1.02
Guest small+Host large	1.12	1.07	1
Guest large+Host small	1.06	1	1
Guest small+Host small*	1	1	1

Table 1. Performance of different workloads when the guest uses large pages vs. small pages and the host uses large pages vs. small pages. For each workload, * is used as the baseline case and all results are normalized to the baseline.

are normalized to the baseline case where both the guest and the host use small pages.

There are several interesting observations from this table. First, it is clear that the effect of using large pages is application dependent. For SPECjbb workload, using both guest large pages and host large pages can boost throughput by 30% compared to the baseline case, while for DVDstore2 [2] workload, using large pages improves performance by only 2%. Secondly, while the best performance is achieved when both the guest and the host use large pages, significant performance gain is still attained even if large page backing is used only by the host. For example, compared to the baseline performance, SPECjbb and Swingbench obtain 12% and 7% performance improvement respectively when only host large pages are used. Due to the above advantages, ESXi eagerly allocates host large pages to back guest memory by default.

2.2 Host Large Pages in Memory Overcommitment

When host memory pressure is low, using host large pages achieves the best performance for many workloads. However, when host memory pressure is high, using host small pages allows reclaiming memory through page sharing so that the amount of memory to be reclaimed through ballooning or swapping can be significantly reduced or avoided at all. This would achieve better performance because the performance penalty of ballooning or host swapping is high enough to negate the benefits of using host large pages. Although small pages within a large page can still be shared after the large page is broken, the sharing happens too late as previously ballooned or swapped pages have already negatively impacted the performance.

To illustrate this problem, Figure 1 compares the average operation latency of six VMs running VDI workloads in two setups. The first one (referred to as Lpage) uses host large pages to back VMs memory. The second one (referred to as SPage) uses host small pages. In the beginning with zero *memhog* VMs (described in Section 5), the host has plenty of free memory. We then incrementally add extra *memhog* VMs to increase the level of memory overcommitment, effectively putting more pressure on host memory. Other details of the experimental setup can be found in Section 5.

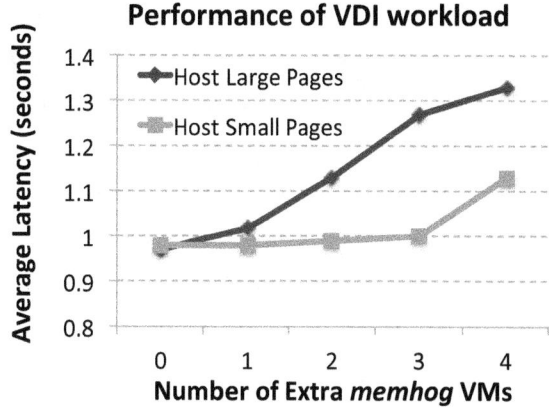

Figure 1. Average 95 percentile operation latency of VDI VMs when increasing the host memory pressure. The smaller the latency, the better the performance.

From this figure we can see that when host memory pressure is low, LPage performs similarly to SPage. As VDI workload generates few TLB misses with host small pages, the benefit of using large pages is not significant. However, as the level of host memory overcommitment increases, SPage consistently outperforms LPage. In the case where three extra *memhog* VMs are added, the average operation latency is smaller by as much as 27% when using host small pages. This is because the amount of memory reclaimed using ballooning or host swapping is largely reduced by sharing small pages in advance.

One solution to mitigate the above performance problem is to let hypervisor disable large page backing for VMs that are not TLB intensive. However, the hypervisor needs very costly instrumentations to check whether guest applications are TLB intensive or not. Manually turning off host large page backing for VMs that are known to be not TLB intensive is also an option. However, in large scale enterprise and cloud environments, manual tuning is not feasible at all. A more robust solution is to make hypervisor deal with large pages more adaptively and transparently when host memory is overcommitted. To achieve this, we propose the new LPageBreak policy in ESXi hypervisor. The design of LPageBreak is presented in next section.

3. Design

In this section, we briefly summarize ESXi memory management basics in Section 3.1. In Section 3.2, we present our proactive approach to breaking large pages even if the host has enough free memory. Section 3.3 introduces a new `clear` state into ESXi memory management. In this state, large pages are broken more aggressively to enable memory reclamation via page sharing. We also present a scheme to dynamically adjust the threshold for transitioning into the `clear` state. Finally, in Section 3.4, we present an algorithm

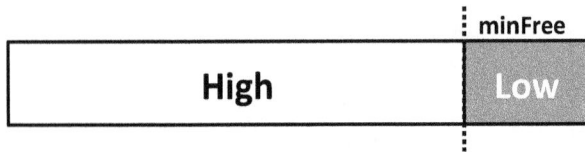

Figure 2. The illustration of free memory states in ESXi.

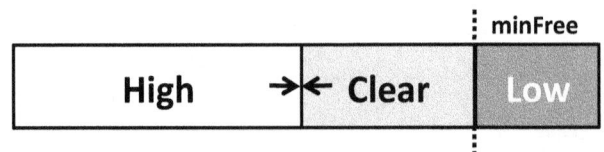

Figure 4. The illustration of ESXi free memory states with the new `clear` state.

for adjusting page sharing scan rate based on the estimated VM large page shareability.

3.1 VMware ESXi Memory Management Basics

ESXi has an associated free memory *state* which is determined by the amount of free memory on the host. The use of different reclamation techniques depends on the state. Although the actual states are more fine-grained, for the sake of simplicity they can be roughly condensed to two states: high and low, as illustrated in Figure 2. The state transition threshold is called *minFree* and preset based on the host memory size.

When host is in the high state, only page sharing is used to reclaim memory. By running the page sharing scanning thread, hypervisor tries to identify and collapse multiple memory pages with identical content into a single memory page. If a shared page is written in the future, the virtual machine monitor (VMM) will break the sharing. To limit the CPU overhead of the page sharing scanning thread, its scan rate is set to a fairly low value by default.

ESXi starts to reclaim memory using ballooning and host swapping when host memory is in the low state. In this case, if a ballooned or swapped guest page is backed by a host large page, the host large page is broken. The performance impact of ballooning is typically small, but it may lead to guest level swapping which can significantly hurt application performance [19]. Host swapping is the last resort for reclaiming VM memory. It incurs the highest performance penalty because the future swap-in activities involve slow and synchronous disk operations. To mitigate the performance impact of host swapping, ESXi attempts to share or compress the swap candidate pages to avoid costly swapping.

3.2 Breaking 'Cold' Large Pages

As discussed in Section 2, ESXi preferentially uses host large pages to back guest memory. This is critical for certain applications to obtain high performance. However, not all large pages are *actively* used by VMs. To illustrate the problem, we present the large page activeness profiles for VDI and SPECjbb VMs respectively in Figure 3. For profiling, we periodically scan the status of the *Accessed* bits in the page directory entries and clear those bits thereafter. Each page directory entry corresponds to a 2MB contiguous guest physical memory region, which is referred to as

a large page region [1], hence a single access to a small page would appear as an access to the large page region. In Figure 3, each horizontal slice represents a minute of execution as the time goes from the top to the bottom. A dot in each horizontal line stands for a large page region. Empty (no color) means the large page region is not accessed and gray color means the large page region is accessed in the last one minute interval. From the figure, we can see that SPECjbb workload constantly accesses some large page regions (mostly JVM heap) throughout the entire workload run time while all other large page regions are rarely accessed. For VDI workload, there also exist quite a lot of large page regions that have very few or no accesses at all for a considerable amount of time. By breaking the host large pages with few or no accesses, i.e., 'cold' large pages, the shareable small pages within the broken large page can be shared to relieve the host memory pressure. If any of the small pages in a broken 'cold' large page is accessed again, the host large backing will be reestablished because ESXi hypervisor provides a large page promotion mechanism which attempts to automatically remap all the small pages in a large page region to a host large page upon access. Therefore, breaking 'cold' large pages typically brings negligible impact on a VM's performance.

3.3 `clear` Memory State

Breaking 'cold' large pages reduces host memory consumption with negligible performance impact when host memory pressure is low. However, it may not be sufficient when host memory pressure increases, making host eventually reach the low state. In this case, it is beneficial to break all large pages (including the 'hot' ones) in advance so that hypervisor can preemptively reclaim memory through page sharing. Then the amount of memory reclaimed through ballooning or swapping can be minimized. To achieve this, we propose a new state called `clear` between the high state and the low state in ESXi memory scheduler.

As illustrated in Figure 4, the threshold for switching from the `clear` state to the low state is fixed to be the *minFree* value, hence the existing memory scheduler behavior is not changed. The threshold for switching from the high state to the `clear` state, referred to as `high-to-clear`

---

[1] In x86-64 architecture, a large page is typically referred to a page size of 2MB. Note that a host large page backs a large page region but a large page region is not necessarily backed by a host large page.

(a) VDI

(b) SPECjbb

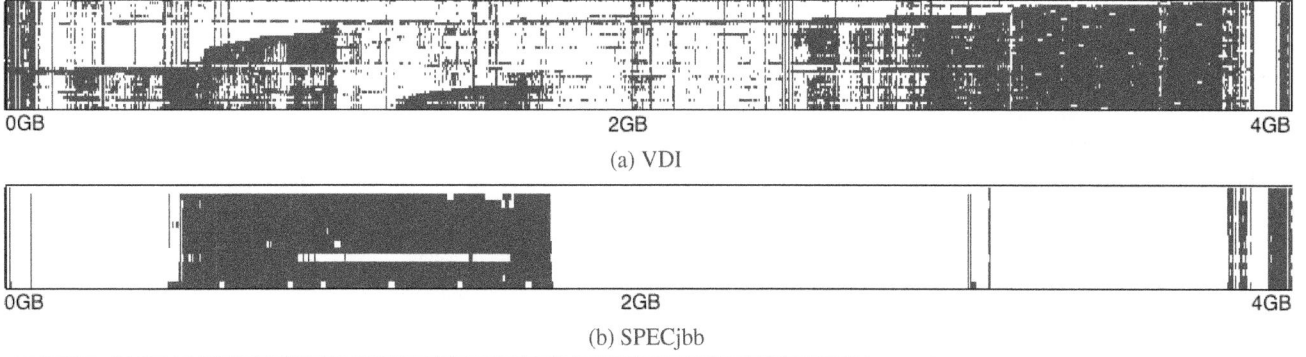

Figure 3. Large page activeness profiles for VDI (a) and SPECjbb (b). Both VMs are configured with 4GB memory. The y axis represents the runtime. The x axis represents the contiguous large page regions in VM's memory. Grey dot means that the large page region has been accessed in the past minute.

threshold, becomes a variable which can be dynamically changed based on the host free memory consumption rate. Detailed algorithm is presented in the next section. In the `clear` state, any large page can be broken if it contains shareable small pages and the large pages that do not contain shareable small pages are still preserved. Large page allocation and promotion in ESXi are both disabled as well. Note that once host goes back to the `high` state, large page allocation and promotion are re-enabled. The hypervisor will promote all the small pages back to large pages again if VM accesses them. As a result, VMs can still benefit from host large pages when memory pressure decreases.

3.3.1 `high-to-clear` Threshold Adjustment

The `clear` state can be considered as a free memory buffer to prevent the host from reaching the `low` state. The size of the buffer is determined by the `high-to-clear` threshold. Using a fixed threshold simplifies the design, but it is suboptimal if host enters the `clear` state but never reaches the `low` state. In this case, unnecessarily breaking large pages can hurt VM performance if some of them are accessed frequently by the guest.

We propose a `high-to-clear` threshold adjustment mechanism based on the free memory consumption rate. Essentially, if the host free memory increases in the `clear` state (e.g., the memory reclaimed through page sharing compensates for the VM memory consumption increase), we reduce the `high-to-clear` threshold to allow the host to re-enter the `high` state in the future. Once we detect that host free memory drops rapidly, the `high-to-clear` threshold is reverted to the default value. More specifically, ESXi hypervisor periodically (with $\Delta Time$ interval) executes the CLEARTHRESHOLDADJUST function, shown in Algorithm 1, when host is in the `clear` state. The function takes the difference in host free memory (the unit is number of pages), denoted as $\Delta Free = curFree - prevFree$, as the input parameter. A positive $\Delta Free$ value means host free memory increases and vice versa. If the host free memory increases

---

Algorithm 1 `high-to-clear` Threshold Adjustment

1: **procedure** CLEARTHRESHOLDADJUST($\Delta Free$)
2:     $newThresh \leftarrow curThresh$
3:     **if** $\Delta Free > prevFree \times \frac{MinPct}{100}$ **then**
4:         $newThresh \leftarrow \frac{curThresh+minFreeThresh}{2}$
5:     **else if** $\Delta Free < 0$ **then**
6:         $distance \leftarrow curFree - minFree$
7:         $timeToLow \leftarrow \frac{distance}{(-1) \times \Delta Free} \times \Delta Time$
8:         **if** $timeToLow <$ MinAllowTime **then**
9:             $newThresh \leftarrow Default$
10:         **end if**
11:     **end if**
12:     **if** $newThresh \neq curThresh$ **then**
13:         CommitClearThreshold($newThresh$)
14:     **end if**
15: **end procedure**

---

by more than $MinPct$ percentage compared to the free memory in last epoch, the `high-to-clear` threshold is reduced to the middle between the current `high-to-clear` threshold and the minFree threshold. Note that $MinPct$ is used to avoid frequent threshold changes due to small free memory variations. Otherwise, if the host free memory drops, we estimate the time to reach the `low` state given the current free memory consumption rate (line 6 and line 7). If the time is smaller than a certain threshold $MinAllowTime$, the `high-to-clear` threshold is reset to the default value. The threshold remains unchanged if the time to `low` state is long enough assuming the memory pressure can be stabilized or even reduced in the near future.

3.4 Page Scanning Rate Adjustment

In ESXi, the rate of memory reclamation through page sharing highly depends on the page sharing scan rate. In the `high` state, memory reclamation is not critical, hence the default scan rate is low to avoid any noticeable CPU overhead. However, after the host enters the `clear` state, the scan rate might need to be higher to reclaim memory faster and to prevent the host from entering the `low` state. Although a higher scan

43

rate leads to a higher CPU overhead, the benefit of reducing the amount of ballooned or swapped memory can easily compensate the higher CPU overhead.

In general, the scan rate should be set based on the host memory consumption rate and the VM memory shareability. For example, if fewer small pages in the backing large pages are shareable, the scan rate needs to be higher in order to pick up enough shareable small pages from the broken large pages and vice versa. Since the memory shareability in VM large pages is unknown in ESXi, we propose an estimator which uses a sampling technique to predict how much guest memory is shareable had the backing large pages been broken. The estimator periodically performs the following operations:

1. Randomly check $nTotalLargeRegion$ number of large page regions. If the large page region is backed by a host large page, the host large page is sampled and a counter ($nSampledLPage$) is incremented.

2. Scan the content of all small pages within the sampled large pages and compute their page signatures (called *hints*). For each small page, if its content matches a shared page or another hint, a counter ($nDuplicate$) is incremented.

3. The percentage of VM large pages in the host, denoted as $P(L)$, is estimated as $P(L) = \frac{nSampledLPage}{nTotalLargeRegion}$ and the percentage of small pages backed by host large pages that have duplicate copies, denoted as $P(D)$, is computed as $P(D) = \frac{nDuplicate}{nTotalSmall}$, where $nTotalSmall$ is the total number of small pages in the sampled large pages.

Note that $P(D)$ largely overestimates the percentage of shareable small pages because its calculation does not consider the fact that a memory write to a shared page will immediately break the sharing. If a workload generates a lot of memory writes, the amount of shareable pages would be small even if many small pages in the VM can find other pages with identical content. By leveraging the existing VM working set estimator in ESXi [28], we can easily obtain the estimated percentage of written pages per minute, denoted as $P(W)$, from the hypervisor. Assuming that the written pages follow identical and independent distribution, the predicted percentage of shareable small pages, denoted as $P(S)$, is computed as $P(S) = P(D) \times (1 - P(W))$.

Given the above $P(L)$ and $P(S)$ estimations, we propose a simple algorithm, as shown in Algorithm 2, to adjust the $ShareScanRate$ parameter in ESXi which specifies the total number of scanned pages per second in the host. Basically, the scheduler periodically (with $\Delta Time$ interval) monitors the host free memory reduction (the unit is number of pages), denoted as $Reduced = max(prevFree - curFree, 0)$. Its exponential moving average value is passed to function SCAN-RATEADJUST along with $P(S)$ and $P(L)$ when host enters the clear state. If the estimated shareable small pages in VM large pages are scarce (e.g., almost all large pages have

---

Algorithm 2 Page Sharing Scanning Rate Adjustment

1: **procedure** SCANRATEADJUST($P(S), P(L), Reduced$)
2:     **if** $HostMem \times P(L) \times P(S) < Reduced$ **then**
3:         $newScanRate \leftarrow Default$
4:     **else**
5:         $newScanRate \leftarrow \frac{Reduced}{\Delta Time \times P(L) \times P(S)}$
6:         $newScanRate \leftarrow \min(8k, newScanRate)$
7:     **end if**
8:     **if** $newScanRate \neq curScanRate$ **then**
9:         CommitShareScanRate($newScanRate$)
10:     **end if**
11: **end procedure**

---

already been broken), the scan rate is set to the default to avoid the unnecessary CPU overhead. Otherwise, the scan rate is set to allow the page sharing rate to keep up with the host memory consumption rate. Note that the scan rate is bounded to 8K pages per second and when host moves back to the high state, the scan rate is reset to the default value as well.

4. Implementation

We use the *Accessed* bits scanning mechanism to identify the 'cold' large pages. The results are saved in a bitmap where each bit corresponds to a guest large page region. Basically, we periodically scan the page directory entries for entire VM memory in a timer call back function in VMM. If the *Accessed* bit of an inspected entry is set, the bit, corresponding to this large page in the bitmap, is also set. A host large page is treated as a 'cold' large page if its corresponding bit in the bitmap is clear, i.e., the host large page is not accessed in previous check interval.

The implementation of proactively breaking large pages largely facilitates the existing page sharing algorithm in ESXi which is summarized as follows:

1. The page sharing scan thread periodically selects several guest small pages. For each page, it computes the page hint, based on the page content and then checks if the page should be shared, or its hint should be added to a global hash table.

2. If a guest page has a content that matches the content of any of the existing shared pages or hints, **and** the page is not backed by a host large page, the scan thread will post an invalidation request to VMM. Upon receiving the invalidation request, VMM will remove all the mapping of the shareable page on all vCPUs. The new mapping to the shared common host page will be established when the shareable page is accessed again. More rigorous checks are performed to make sure the sharing is valid. However, if the guest page is backed by a host large page, no invalidation request is posted to VMM.

3. If a guest page's hint does not match existing hints, the hint hash table is updated with the new hint regardless

whether the guest page is backed by a host large page or not. This is to expedite future page sharing once the backing large page is broken for any reason.

When host memory is in the `low` state, the algorithm works slightly differently. In step 2, the invalidation request will be posted to VMM even if the guest page is backed by a host large page. When VMM receives the invalidation request, it breaks the large page backing so that the small pages within the large page can be shared.

In the prototype, page sharing algorithm in step 2 is slightly modified to support breaking 'cold' large pages and the new `clear` state. More specifically, when host is in the `high` state, the hypervisor checks against the *Accessed* bits scan results bitmap for each scanned shareable small page and the invalidation request is sent to VMM even if the small page is backed by a 'cold' large page. As a result, the backing 'cold' large page is broken and the shareable small pages can be shared right away. When host enters the `clear` state, the invalidation request is posted to VMM unconditionally for each shareable small page. Then all the backing large pages including the 'hot' ones are broken as a result. Note that if a host large page does not contain any shareable small pages, it is preserved in the `clear` state.

The VM large page shareability estimator runs in a dedicated global kernel thread throughout the entire server life time running the algorithm described in Section 3.4. It randomly samples eight large page regions per GB of host memory every minute (i.e., $nTotalLargeRegion = 8$). The sampling rate is set to limit the scanning overhead. Dynamic `high-to-clear` threshold adjustment and page sharing scan rate adjustment algorithms are implemented in main memory scheduler thread which is invoked at every second. Overall, implementing the proposed techniques needs fairly simple code changes to the existing ESXi scheduler (less than 500 lines of code).

5. Environment

The experiments are conducted using an AMD Opteron 8378 server running a modified vSphere ESXi hypervisor. The host has 32GB RAM and 4 quad-core AMD Opteron CPUs. The server connects to a SAN backed by an EMC CX4-120 storage system. The `high-to-clear` threshold is set to be four times of *minFree* value (~3.8GB) initially. The workloads used to evaluate the proposed techniques are VDI, SPECjbb2005, DVDstore2, Olio and Swingbench. These workloads are commonly used in examining the CPU, memory and I/O performance in virtualized environment. We briefly describe the workloads as follows:

1. The VDI [9] VM (1 vCPU, 4GB memory) runs a set of commonly used applications like *Word*, *Excel*, *Internet Explorer*, etc in a Windows 7 OS. The individual time of performing various operations against these applications

Workload	VDI	Swing-bench	SPEC-jbb	DVD-store2	Olio
# of instances	6	8	12	6	4
memhog size	4GB	8GB	9GB	7GB	2GB

Table 2. Test configurations.

are recorded. The measured performance metric is the 95th percentile latency value of all operations.

2. The Swingbench [4] is a load generator designed to stress an Oracle database. The database VM (1vCPU, 4GB memory) runs an Oracle 11R database in RedHat 5.4 OS. The performance metric is the total operations per minute for all database VMs.

3. The SPECjbb2005 [3] VM (1vCPU, 4GB memory) evaluates the server side Java performance by emulating a client/server system. The guest OS is Redhat 5.4 and the JVM is Sun7. The performance metric is the total throughput of all VMs.

4. The DVDstore2 [2] VM (4 vCPUs, 4GB memory) runs an online e-commerce test application against a SQL server 2008 database. The guest OS is Windows Server 2008 and we measure the total throughput of all VMs.

5. The Olio workload is one application from VMMark 2.x suite [5]. It emulates a web 2.0 social-events application. Each Olio tile is composed of a database VM (2 vCPUs, 2GB memory) and an application server VM (4 vCPUs, 6GB memory). We run multiple Olio tiles in the host and measure the average response latency of all tiles.

In the experiments, besides the workload VMs, we run additional *memhog* VMs to control the degree of host memory overcommitment. Each *memhog* VM, running Windows 2008 server, is configured with one vCPU and full memory reservation. It stays idle after guest OS is booted. We intentionally disable page sharing and ballooning for the *memhog* VMs. Since Windows 2008 guest writes zero content to all the memory during booting, the configured memory of the *memhog* VMs are all allocated and preserved during the entire workload run time, pushing significant memory pressure to the host. To evaluate the overall performance impact of the proposed policy (Section 6.4), the experiments are conducted to mimic the case of adding new VMs to a memory overcommitted host. Basically, we power on all the workload VMs plus one *memhog* VM with a specific memory size which makes the host enter the `clear` state. Table 2 lists the number of VMs and the *memhog* VM memory sizes for different workloads. After fifteen minutes, we start to gradually power on extra 3GB *memhog* VMs [2] with five minutes interval to increase the degree of host memory overcommit-

---

[2] The memory size of the extra *memhog* VMs is set to make sure there are enough data points for various levels of memory overcommitment.

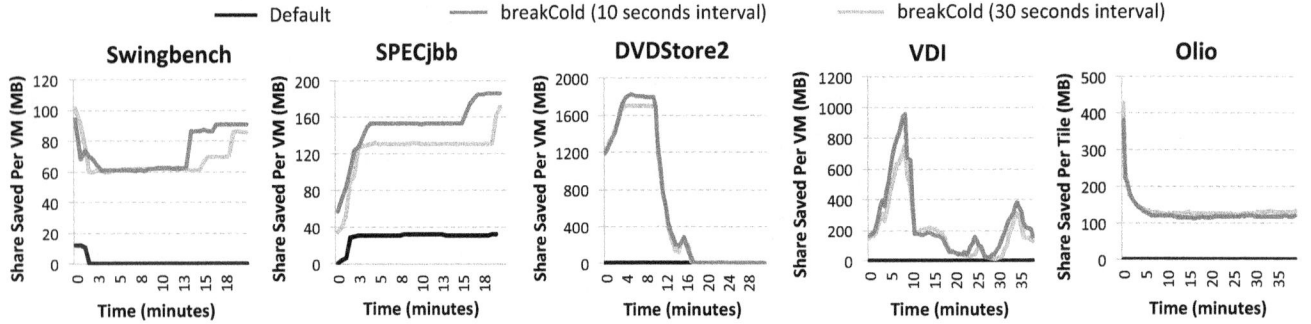

Figure 5. The amount of saved memory from page sharing for each VM when breaking 'cold' large pages in the `high` state compared to the default case where all host large pages are preserved. The *Accessed* bits check intervals are 10 and 30 seconds.

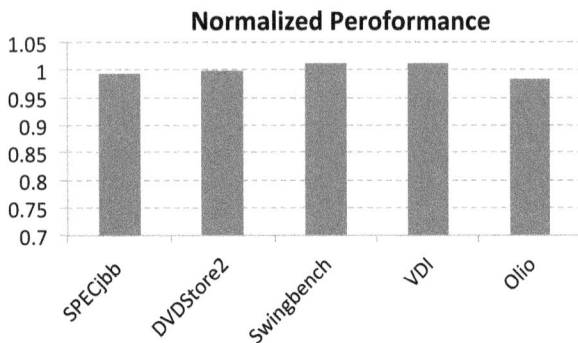

Figure 6. The performance of different workloads when breaking 'cold' large pages in the `high` state. The results are normalized to the default cases where all large pages are preserved.

ment. For Swingbench and SPECjbb workloads, the guest OS is configured with 3GB of large pages for database/JVM to use.

6. Evaluation

In this section, we evaluate the impact of breaking 'cold' large pages on the amount of memory saved from page sharing and application performance in Section 6.1. Section 6.2 presents the benefit of changing the `high-to-clear` threshold dynamically based on the host memory consumption rate. We evaluate the accuracy of the VM large page shareability estimator in Section 6.3. In Section 6.4, we present the overall workload performance improvement of using the new LPageBreak policy (combining all the proposed techniques) compared to the performance of using the default policy. Finally, we discuss the overhead of the proposed techniques in Section 6.5.

6.1 Impact of Breaking 'Cold' Large Pages

To evaluate the memory saving from breaking 'cold' large pages, we run four workload VMs in the host (host stays in the `high` state all the time) with different *Accessed* bits check intervals. The results are presented in Figure 5. As expected, the memory saving from breaking 'cold' large pages is highly workload dependent. For Swingbench, SPECjbb and Olio workloads, the average amount of the memory saved through page sharing ranges between 50MB and 150MB per VM and the memory saving is relatively stable throughout the workload run time. For DVDstore2 and VDI workloads, the memory saving from sharing can be as high as 1.8GB and 1GB per VM respectively in the beginning, while dropping to a few hundred MB or even less later. Note that unlike the traditional page sharing mechanism where only memory writes break sharing, memory reads also defeat page sharing in the experiments because ESXi automatically promotes the small pages to a large page when they are accessed in the `high` state. Hence, the saved memory reduction can be due to the fact that VMs start to touch most of the allocated memory. In the default cases, ESXi uses large pages to back VM memory hence the amount of shared pages are almost zero for most of the workloads while SPECjbb shows a small amount (∼30MB) of shared memory per VM.

To evaluate the impact of the *Accessed* bits check interval on the amount of shared memory, we tried 10 seconds and 30 seconds intervals in the experiments. As shown in Figure 5, changing the *Accessed* bits check interval does not drastically impact the amount of memory saved through page sharing for most of the workloads. Hence, we use 30 seconds interval in the rest of the experiments to minimize the CPU overhead. Figure 6 presents the normalized workload performance when breaking 'cold' large pages in the `high` state. From the figure, we can see that the performance varies within ±1.5% noise range for all workloads compared to the default cases where all large pages are preserved. Overall, breaking 'cold' large pages saves VM memory with negligible performance impact.

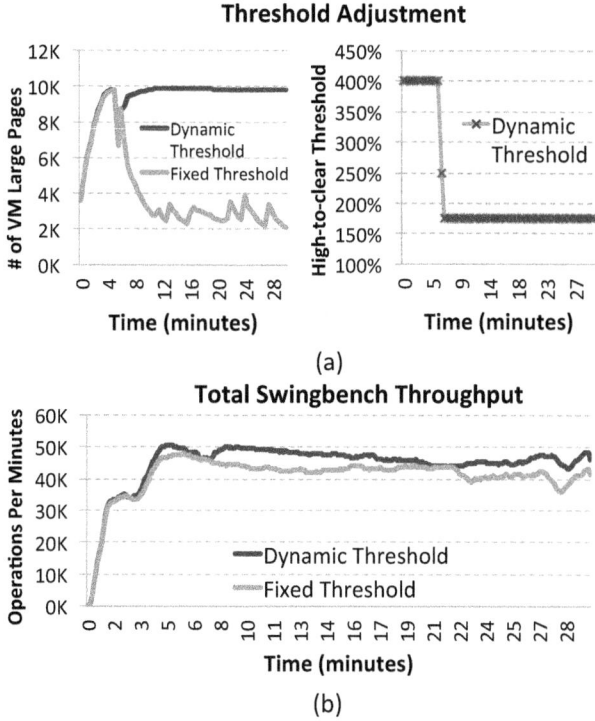

Threshold Adjustment

(a)

Total Swingbench Throughput

(b)

Figure 7. The amount of VM large pages (a) and Swingbench workload performance (b) using a fixed vs. dynamic `high-to-clear` threshold when host is in the `clear` state. The `high-to-clear` threshold is normalized to the *minFree* value.

6.2 Impact of `high-to-clear` Threshold

We choose to use Swingbench workload to demonstrate the advantage of using dynamic `high-to-clear` threshold adjustment since it largely benefits from host large pages and its active memory is highly shareable. In the experiment, we run six Swingbench VMs for five minutes and then power on an 8GB *memhog* VM. When the `high-to-clear` threshold is fixed to the initial value, host enters the `clear` state while not reaching the `low` state. In this case, as shown in the Figure 7(a), only 20% of VM large pages remain after the *memhog* VM is powered on because hypervisor reclaims shareable memory by breaking large pages in the `clear` state. Instead, when the `high-to-clear` threshold is dynamically adjusted, hypervisor detects the increase of host free memory and then quickly reduces the `high-to-clear` threshold twice (from 400% to 250% and then from 250% to 175%, as shown in Figure 7(a)). As a result, host immediately switches back to the `high` state and the broken large pages are recovered once the small pages are accessed. By recovering the broken large pages, the total Swingbench VMs throughput is improved by 9.8% compared to that of using a fixed `high-to-clear` threshold (Figure 7(b)), matching the performance of using the default policy with-

out the `clear` state (not shown in the figure). Overall, the dynamic `high-to-clear` threshold adjustment mechanism overcomes the drawback of using a static threshold such that the performance can be degraded when host stays in the `clear` state.

6.3 VM Large Page Shareability Estimation

The VM large page shareability estimator runs in a dedicated kernel thread. It randomly samples 256 host large pages every minute in the 32GB host. To evaluate the estimation accuracy, we run the estimator against various workloads and compare the estimated percentages of shareable memory to the 'actual' percentages of shareable memory during the workload run time. In the experiments, four 4GB VMs run in the host, i.e., host stays in the `high` state with the 'cold' large pages broken. The estimated percentage of shareable memory, denoted as $ShareEstPct$, is computed as:

$$ShareEstPct = \frac{HostMem \times P(L) \times P(S) + curShared}{HostMem}$$

where $P(L)$ and $P(S)$ are defined in Section 3.4 and $curShared$ counts the current shared pages including the ones from the broken 'cold' large pages. The 'actual' percentages of shareable memory, denoted as $ActualPct$, are obtained by running workloads using host small pages with the highest page sharing scan rate. The results are presented in Figure 8.

For Swingbench and DVDstore2, the amount of shared pages is high in the beginning and decreases over time because the workload generates a lot of memory writes when updating database tables which break sharing. Since we have accounted for the percentage of written pages in the page shareability estimation ($P(S)$ in Section 3.4), the estimator closely tracks the actual behavior. VDI workload shows large amount of shareable memory because the host large pages contain many small pages with identical content. The workload mostly runs small applications with few memory write operations hence its shareable memory is mostly greater than 50% during the workload run time. SPECjbb workload shows relatively low percentage of shareable memory because the JVM heap contains random content which provides very few shareable pages. Most of the sharing in this workload comes from the common guest OS pages. Olio workload shows the largest prediction error where the estimator overestimates the percentage of shareable memory. We found that this workload generates quite a lot memory writes and apparently those memory writes do not follow our assumption that they are independent and identically distributed across VM memory. This could be the main reason why the estimator mispredicts the shareability. On average, the absolute prediction errors ($|ShareEstPct - ActualPct|$) are 2%, 1%, 4%, 7% and 13% for Swingbench, SPECjbb, DVDstore2, VDI and Olio respectively. Overall, the estimator can provide accurate prediction on VM large page shareability to guide the page sharing scan rate adjustment.

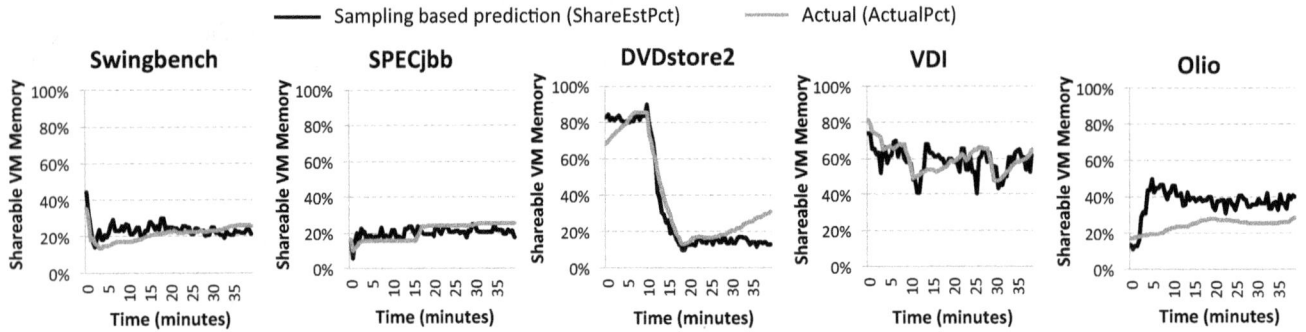

Figure 8. The accuracy of the VM large page shareability estimator for different workloads over workload run time.

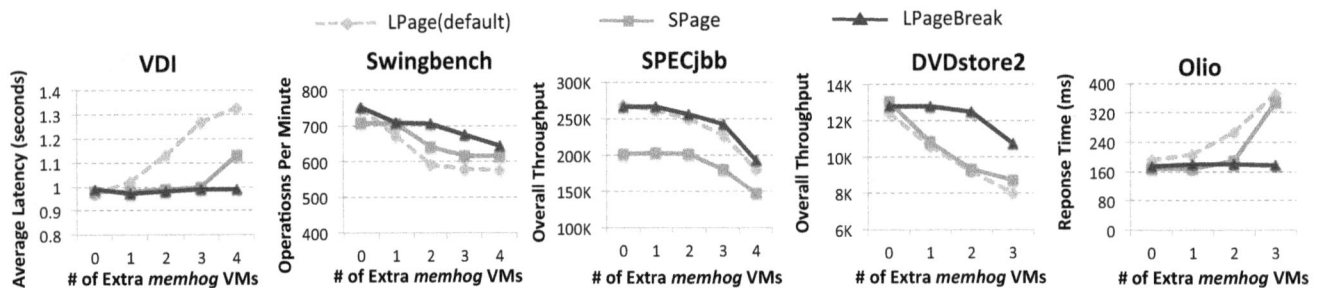

Figure 9. Performance of different workloads under different levels of memory overcommitment. Note that the performance metrics is the operation latency for VDI and Olio, hence the smaller, the better.

6.4 Overall Performance Impact

For simplicity, in this section, the new host large page management policy is referred to as 'LPageBreak'. The default of using and preserving host large pages in the `high` state is referred to as 'LPage'. Using host small pages is referred to as 'SPage'.

Figure 9 compares the performance of LPageBreak, LPage and SPage for various workloads under different levels of memory overcommitment. For VDI workload, as the memory pressure increases, the average operation latency keeps increasing up to 34% in the LPage case. In contrast, LPageBreak works extremely well for VDI workload such that it achieves almost no latency increase with high memory pressure. The reason why LPageBreak significantly improves performance for VDI workload can be explained by Figure 10. This figure shows the total amount of ballooned plus swapped memory and the total amount of shared memory of VDI VMs over the workload run time in the highest memory overcommitment case (four extra *memhog* VMs). In the default LPage case, when the first extra *memhog* VM is powered on, host immediately enters the `low` state where ballooning and swapping occur. Every time an additional *memhog* VM is powered on, we can observe a burst increase in total ballooned and swapped memory (Figure 10(a)). With LPageBreak, memory is reclaimed through page sharing

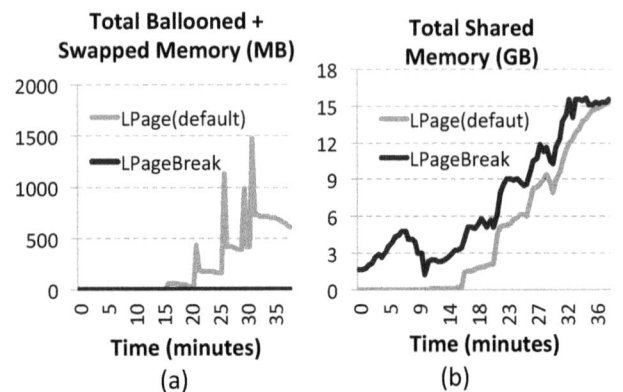

Figure 10. The total amount of ballooned and swapped memory (a) and the total amount of shared memory (b) for VDI VMs when four extra *memhog* VMs are continuously powered on in the host.

much earlier compared to the LPage case (Figure 10(b)) so that powering on a new *memhog* VM does not cause any ballooned or swapped memory at all. Therefore, the VDI workload performance is not impacted by the increase of memory pressure.

It is interesting to see that LPageBreak even outperforms SPage by 13% in the highest memory overcommitment case. We found that since the default page sharing scan rate used in SPage case is not high enough, the speed of reclaiming memory through page sharing is slower than the memory consumption rate. As a result, a small amount of swapping and ballooning occur since the fourth extra *memhog* VM is powered on, which hurts the workload performance. In the LPageBreak case, page sharing scan rate is adjusted to be more than 10x faster than the default using Algorithm 2 so that small pages can be quickly shared to avoid ballooning or host swapping.

For other workloads, LPageBreak also performs the best as the host memory pressure increases. Compared to the LPage cases, LPageBreak improves performance by up to 20%, 34%, 8% and 2.1x for Swingbench, DVDstore2, SPECjbb and Olio workloads respectively. It significantly outperforms SPage for Swingbench, DVDStore and Olio workloads due to the share scan rate increase. For SPECjbb workload, the results are quite interesting such that SPage performs the worst in all configurations. This is mainly because: 1) SPECjbb workload does not produce many shareable pages so using small pages does not reclaim much memory through page sharing; 2) SPECjbb workload is TLB intensive hence the advantage of using host large pages dominates the performance in those configurations.

Overall, LPageBreak policy combines the benefits of both LPage and SPage. When host is in the `high` state, the actively used VM large pages are preserved for best performance. When host approaches the `low` state, large pages are proactively broken so that VMs avoid the performance penalty from memory ballooning or host swapping.

6.5 Overhead

In the prototype, the CPU and storage overhead of the proposed techniques are negligible. For example, the memory overhead of the bitmap that stores the *Accessed* bits scan results is $\frac{1}{2^{24}}$ of the configured VM memory size. A 4KB page can store the bitmap for 64GB VM memory. The *Accessed* bits scan runtime overhead is proportional to the VM memory size. In our testbed, scanning the *Accessed* bits for each one GB VM memory takes around 10 microseconds. As long as the check interval is long enough, VM performance is unlikely to be affected by the *Accessed* bits scanning. However, if the VM memory is huge (e.g., TB memory), the scanning overhead can be non-negligible. In the future, we plan to use a background kernel thread to asynchronously scan the *Accessed* bits without blocking VM execution to mitigate the performance impact. In the prototype, since the memory sizes of our workload VMs are typically small, *Accessed* bits scan is implemented in VMM context for simplicity. For the VM large page shareability estimator, the process of scanning all the small pages in the sampled large pages is CPU intensive. However, with the current sample rate, the estima-

tor consumes around 1% of one core which is a fixed and trivial overhead in a 16-core system.

7. Related Work

To efficiently use large pages and handle problems like allocation amplification and defragmentation, researchers have proposed to manage multiple page sizes in general purpose operating systems [15, 16, 25, 27]. For example, Navarro [25] et al. proposed a large page management system in which the page size can be promoted when the small pages in a large page region are all accessed, and demoted speculatively to find proper small pages for swapping out or in response to large page defragmentation activity. Fabien [17] et al. studied the impact of large pages on page level false sharing in NUMA system and proposed a mechanism to control the large page enablement for better memory locality. In this work, we proposed to proactively demote (i.e., break) a large page in a virtualized server based on its activeness and host free memory availability. The purpose is to allow hypervisor to reclaim memory through page sharing in order to improve server consolidation without affecting VM performance.

In virtual memory management, LRU approximated page replacement policies such as CLOCK are widely used in general purpose operations systems. Jiang [21] et al. proposed CLOCL-PRO algorithm which uses reuse distance instead of recency to classify pages into 'hot' or 'cold' pages. The algorithm works on small pages and is driven by page faults. In this work, we attempt to identify 'cold' large by periodically scanning the large pages' *Accessed* bits in page directory entries. The large pages are considered to be 'cold' if they are not accessed in the last check interval. Using this approach, code changes to page fault handlers are avoided and by carefully setting the scan rate, the classification overhead can be negligible.

There were many studies in analyzing and exploiting page sharing opportunities in virtualization environments [10, 12, 14, 18, 20, 23, 24, 26]. All these work assume small pages are used in the system and the interaction between page sharing and large page backing is not considered.

Contemporary hypervisors such as Hyper-V, KVM and Xen support large pages and memory overcommitment. Hyper-V [7] uses host level swapping in some rare and restricted cases. Since Hyper-V does not support page sharing, optimizations like sharing pages before swapping them out are not available. KVM treats VMs as regular processes hence conventional memory reclamation technique such as host swapping applies. It requires certain kernels and guests to support KSM [10] which works similarly to ESXi page sharing. KVM does not consider the interaction between page sharing and large pages in its memory management. Xen uses Dynamic Memory Control(DMC) [8] to manage memory, but it does not allow to overcommit the physical host memory. However, Xen recently introduces transcendent memory management [6] which supports a ballooning technique to reclaim idle guest memory and use it as a pool for all VMs. There were proposals to implement sharing of guest memory in Xen (e.g., [22, 24]), but they have not been incorporated into product yet. To the best of our knowledge, this paper is the first attempt to study the interaction between host large pages and page sharing in virtualization environment.

8. Conclusion

In this paper, we measure the impact of host large pages on workload performance when host is heavily memory overcommitted. Since using host large pages noticeably increases VM memory consumption and defeats page sharing, the workload performance may be significantly degraded compared to when host small pages are used. However, disabling host large pages typically degrades the performance of many workloads when host has plenty of free memory.

To deal with such a dilemma, we propose a new host large page management policy. Basically, we identify 'cold' large pages and allow breaking them when host free memory is sufficient. A new clear state is added to ESXi memory management in which all large pages can be proactively broken. We implement a policy to adjust the clear state threshold based on the host memory consumption rate. In the clear state, page sharing scan rate is adjusted using the proposed VM large page shareability estimator to efficiently reclaim memory through page sharing. Overall, by sharing small pages earlier, the amount of memory that needs to be reclaimed through expensive ballooning or swapping later can be reduced.

Experimental results show that the proposed host large page management policy is quite effective while being totally transparent to the user. It achieves up to 2.1x performance improvement for some workloads under high memory pressure while not causing any noticeable performance degradation when memory pressure is low. In a word, the proposed policy significantly improves server consolidation by combining the benefits of using only host large pages and only host small pages.

References

[1] AMD-V™ Nested Paging. http://developer.amd.com/wordpress/media/2012/10/NPT-WP-1%201-final-TM.pdf.

[2] Dell DVD Store. http://en.community.dell.com/techcenter/extras/w/wiki/dvd-store.aspx.

[3] SPECjbb2005. http://www.spec.org/jbb2005/.

[4] Swingbench. http://www.dominicgiles.com/swingbench.html.

[5] Vmmark 2.x. http://www.vmware.com/products/vmmark/.

[6] Xen transcendent memory. https://oss.oracle.com/projects/tmem/, 2010.

[7] Hyper-v dynamic memory overview. http://technet.microsoft.com/en-us/library/hh831766.aspx.

[8] Xcp faq dynamic memory control. http://wiki.xenproject.org/wiki/XCP_FAQ_Dynamic_Memory_Control, 2013.

[9] B. Agrawal, R. Bidarkar, S. Satnur, L. Spracklen, T. M. Ismail, U. Kurkure, and V. Makhija. Vmware view planner: Measuring true virtual desktops experience at scale. *VMware Tech Journal*, December 2012.

[10] A. Arcangeli, I. Eidus, and C. Wright. Increasing memory density by using KSM. In *Proceedings of the Linux Symposium*, pages 313–328, 2009.

[11] I. Banerjee, F. Guo, K. Tati, and R. Venkatasubramanian. Memory overcommitment in the esx server. https://labs.vmware.com/vmtj/memory-overcommitment-in-the-esx-server, 2013.

[12] S. Barker, T. Wood, P. Shenoy, and R. Sitaraman. An Empirical Study of Memory Sharing in Virtual Machines. In *Proceedings of the USENIX Annual Technical Conference*, 2012.

[13] N. Bhatia. Performance evaluation of intel ept hardware assit. https://www.vmware.com/pdf/Perf_ESX_Intel-EPT-eval.pdf, 2009.

[14] C. Chang, J. Wu, and P. Liu. An empirical study on memory sharing of virtual machines for server consolidation. In *IEEE 9th International Symposium on Parallel and Distributed Processing with Applications (ISPA)*, pages 244–249, 2011.

[15] Z. Fang, L. Zhang, J. B. Carter, W. C. Hsieh, and S. A. Mckee. Reevaluating online superpage promotion with hardware support. In *Proceedings of the International Symposium on High Performance Computer Architecture*, pages 63–72, 2001.

[16] N. Ganapathy and C. Schimmel. General purpose operating system support for multiple page sizes. In *Proceedings of the USENIX Annual Technical Conference*, 1998.

[17] F. Gaud, B. Lepers, J. Decouchant, J. Funston, A. Fedorova, and V. Quema. Large pages may be harmful on numa systems. In *Proceedings of the USENIX Annual Technical Conference*, pages 231–242, 2014.

[18] K. Govil, D. Teodosiu, Y. Huang, and M. Rosenblum. Cellular disco: resource management using virtual clusters on shared-memory multiprocessors. In *Proceedings of the seventeenth ACM symposium on Operating systems principles*, SOSP '99, pages 154–169, 1999.

[19] F. Guo. Understand memory resource management in vmware vsphere 5.0. http://www.vmware.com/files/pdf/mem_mgmt_perf_vsphere5.pdf, 2010.

[20] D. Gupta, S. Lee, M. Vrable, S. Savage, A. C. Snoeren, G. Varghese, G. M. Voelker, and A. Vahdat. Difference engine: harnessing memory redundancy in virtual machines. *Commun. ACM*, 53(10):85–93, Oct. 2010.

[21] S. Jiang, F. Chen, and X. Zhang. Clock-pro: An effective improvement of the clock replacement. In *Proceedings of the USENIX Annual Technical Conference*, 2005.

[22] J. F. Kloster, J. Kritensen, and A. Mejlholm. Efficient memory sharing in the xen virtual machine monitor. http://mejlholm.org/uni/pdfs/dat5.pdf.

[23] K. Miller, F. Franz, M. Rittinghaus, M. Hillenbrand, and F. Bellosa. XLH: More Effective Memory Deduplication Scanners Through Cross-layer Hints. In *Proceedings of the USENIX Annual Technical Conference*, pages 279–290, 2013.

[24] G. Miłós, D. Murray, S. Hand, and M. Fetterman. Satori: Enlightened page sharing. In *Proceedings of the USENIX Annual Technical Conference*, 2009.

[25] J. Navarro, S. Iyer, P. Druschel, and A. Cox. Practical, transparent operating system support for superpages. *SIGOPS Operating System Review*, 36(SI):89–104, Dec. 2002.

[26] P. Sharma and P. Kulkarni. Singleton: system-wide page deduplication in virtual environments. In *Proceedings of the 21st international symposium on High-Performance Parallel and Distributed Computing*, HPDC '12, 2012.

[27] I. Subramanian, C. Mather, K. Peterson, and B. Raghunath. Implementation of multiple pagesize support in hp-ux. In *Proceedings of the USENIX Annual Technical Conference*, 1998.

[28] C. A. Waldspurger. Memory resource management in VMware ESX server. *SIGOPS Operating System Review*, 36(SI):181–194, Dec. 2002.

HSPT: Practical Implementation and Efficient Management of Embedded Shadow Page Tables for Cross-ISA System Virtual Machines

Zhe Wang[1,2], Jianjun Li[1], Chenggang Wu[1] *, Dongyan Yang[3] †, Zhenjiang Wang[1], Wei-Chung Hsu[4], Bin Li[5] ‡, Yong Guan[6]

[1]State Key Laboratory of Computer Architecture, Institute of Computing Technology, Chinese Academy of Sciences,
[2]University of Chinese Academy of Sciences, [3]China Systems and Technology Lab, IBM, Beijing, China,
[4]Dept. Computer Science & Information Engineering, National Taiwan University, [5]Netease, Hangzhou, China,
[6]College of information Engineering, Capital Normal University, Beijing, China
[1]{wangzhe12, lijianjun, wucg, wangzhenjiang}@ict.ac.cn, [3]dyyang@cn.ibm.com, [4]hsuwc@csie.ntu.edu.tw,
[5]richardustc@gmail.com, [6]guanyong@mail.cnu.edu.cn

Abstract

Cross-ISA (Instruction Set Architecture) system-level virtual machine has a significant research and practical value. For example, several recently announced virtual smart phones for iOS which run smart phone applications on x86 based PCs are deployed on cross-ISA system level virtual machines. Also, for mobile device application development, by emulating the Android/ARM environment on the more powerful x86-64 platform, application development and debugging become more convenient and productive. However, the virtualization layer often incurs high performance overhead. The key overhead comes from memory virtualization where a guest virtual address (GVA) must go through multi-level address translation to become a host physical address (HPA). The Embedded Shadow Page Table (ESPT) approach has been proposed to effectively decrease this address translation cost. ESPT directly maps GVA to HPA, thus avoid the lengthy guest virtual to guest physical, guest physical to host virtual, and host virtual to host physical address translation.

However, the original ESPT work has a few drawbacks. For example, its implementation relies on a loadable kernel module (LKM) to manage the shadow page table. Using LKMs is less desirable for system virtual machines due to portability, security and maintainability concerns. Our work proposes a different, yet more practical, implementation to address the shortcomings. Instead of relying on using LKMs, our approach adopts a shared memory mapping scheme to maintain the shadow page table (SPT) using only "**mmap**" system call. Furthermore, this work studies the support of SPT for multi-processing in greater details. It devices three different SPT organizations and evaluates their strength and weakness with standard and real Android applications on the system virtual machine which emulates the Android/ARM platform on x86-64 systems.

Categories and Subject Descriptors C.0 [*General*]: System Architectures; D.4.2 [*Operating Systems*]: Storage Management—main memory, virtual memory

General Terms Management, Measurement, Performance, Design, Experimentation, Security

Keywords memory virtualization; cross-ISA virtualization; Embedded Shadow Page Table; HSPT; Hosted Shadow Page Table; practical implementation; loadable kernel module; Security; Portability

---

* To whom correspondence should be addressed.

† This work was done when Dongyan Yang attended Institute of Computing Technology, CAS.

‡ This work was done when Bin Li attended Institute of Computing Technology, CAS.

VEE '15, March 14–15, 2015, Istanbul, Turkey.
Copyright © 2015 ACM 978-1-4503-3450-1/15/03...$15.00.
http://dx.doi.org/10.1145/2731186.2731188

1. Introduction

System virtualization has regained its popularity in recent years and has been widely used for cloud computing [15, 17]. It allows multiple guest operating systems to run simultaneously on one physical machine. The guest operating systems (OS) on such virtual machines are agnostic about the host OS and hardware platforms. System virtualization can be divided into same-ISA and cross-ISA categories depending on whether the guest and the host are of different instruction-set architecture (ISA). Same-ISA system virtualization is commonly used for server consolidation, for example, VMware Workstation [13], VMware ESX Server [23], XEN [8], KVM [25] and VirtualBox [6] support same-ISA system virtual machines. Cross-ISA system virtualization is also important and commonplace. For example, applications and OSes compiled for one ISA can run on platforms with another ISA. Recently announced virtual smart phones for iOS which run Apple iPhone applications on x86 based PCs are based on cross-ISA system level virtual machines. The Android Emulator [2] emulates the Android/ARM environment on the x86-64 platforms is yet another example, it offers great convenience in development and debugging to Android application developers. This paper focuses on the performance of cross-ISA system virtual machines.

QEMU [5] is a very commonly used cross-ISA virtual machine. Since the ISA of the guest (e.g. ARM) is different from that of the host (i.e. x86 based PC). Dynamic Binary Translation (DBT) is often used to speed up emulation [18]. One challenge in system virtualization is the large memory virtualization overhead where the virtual address of the guest must be mapped to the guest physical address, then the guest physical address be mapped to the host physical address during program execution (as shown in Figure 1(a)). For example, on average QEMU spends 23%~43% of the total execution time in memory translation for SPEC CINT2006 benchmarks when running in system mode emulation [14]. So optimizations to minimize such memory virtualization overhead are the key to enhance the performance of the system-level emulator.

Hardware-assisted memory virtualizations, such as Intel Extended Page Tables [19] and AMD Nested Paging [9], are effective ways to reduce this overhead for same-ISA virtual machines. But they do not support cross-ISA system virtualization. Software-based memory virtualization (e.g. Software MMU) has been used in existing system virtual machines, such as QEMU. However, software MMU is one major contributor to sluggish simulation. Some recent approaches, such as the Embedded Shadow Page Table (ESPT) [14] exploits a combination of software MMU and hardware MMU to significantly cut down the memory virtualization cost. ESPT utilizes the larger address space on modern 64-bit processors and creates a loadable kernel module (LKM) to embed the shadow page entries into the host page table. Those shadow page table (SPT) entries are used to store the mapping between guest virtual address and host physical address. This table can be used by the hardware walker to resolve TLB misses. In [14], ESPT has achieved significant speed up (>50%).

However, the original ESPT work has a few drawbacks. For example, its implementation relies on a LKM to manage SPTs. Using LKMs is less desirable for system virtual machines due to portability, security and maintainability

concerns. For instance, 1) most of LKMs use the internal kernel interface and different kernel versions may have different interfaces. For example, there have been 47 Linux kernel versions after version 2.0 and 12 of them had updated MMU-related modules. If the LKM approach is adopted to manage ESPT, we would have to update the kernel modules of ESPT management for 10 out of the 12 kernel versions. So it would be difficult to have one LKM supporting all kernel versions. 2) To enforce security, modern OS only allows the user who has root privilege to load LKMs. So the original ESPT can only be used by the privilege users. We believe it is important to allow all users to have access to system virtual machines. This is the case for many Android application developers. 3) Using LKMs, the kernel would be less secure. For example, for the Linux kernel, many kernel exploits have been reported, and often these exploits attack LKMs instead of the core kernel [16]. CVE is a list of information security vulnerabilities and exposures provided for public [3]. In the 306 Linux kernel vulnerabilities listed on CVE from January 2013 to November 2014, 112 vulnerabilities are located in the core kernel, while 194 vulnerabilities are in LKMs or drivers.

The main reason for using LKMs in ESPT is to operate on the SPT which is created and maintained at privileged level. We divided the operations on SPT into three types: creating SPT, synchronizing with guest page table (GPT) and switching SPT for different processes. The application scenario of the first type is that when the guest creates a new process, we should create a new SPT accordingly. The second is that because SPT is the shadow of the GPT, we must synchronize the SPT with the GPT to ensure consistency. The third is that when the guest switches process, the emulator should also switch to its corresponding SPT. Based on these three types of operations, we have come up with a different implementation to manage SPTs without using LKMs. To distinguish our new implementation from the original ESPT, we call our approach "Hosted Shadow Page Table" (HSPT). HSPT uses three methods to accomplish these operations with no LKMs. First, it uses a portion of the host page table as SPT to accomplish the operation of creating SPT. Second, it uses the shared memory mapping scheme where multiple virtual pages can be mapped to the same physical page to synchronize the SPT with GPT. Third, it uses Shared SPT to handle multi-processing in guest OSes. As for Shared SPT, it has also investigated on three variations for performance improvements.

The main contributions of this paper are as follows:

1. Proposed a practical implementation of ESPT to speed up cross-ISA system virtual machines without using loadable kernel modules thus avoid the accompanying portability, usability and security problems.

2. Proposed an efficient synchronization mechanism between SPT and GPT based on shared memory mapping methods.

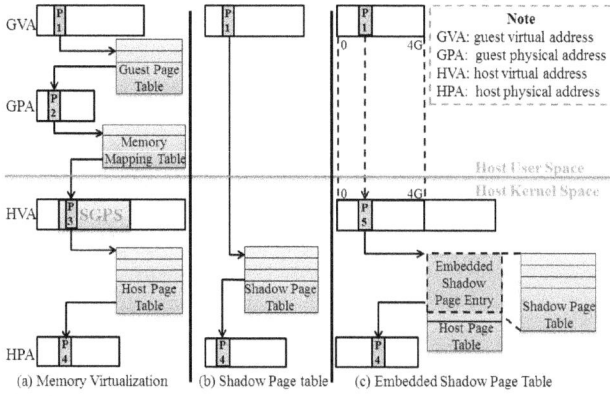

Figure 1. Address translation of (a) Traditional memory virtualization, (b) Shadow Page Table and (c) Embedded Shadow Page Table

Guest memory instruction: ldr R0, [fp] // register fp stores the GVA

| GVA is in %edi;
lookup software TLB to find HVA;
If(miss)
  walk GPT and MMT to find HVA;
HVA is set into %edi;
mov %eax, (%edi) //load data
Next Instruction   (a) | GVA is in %edi;
mov %eax, (%edi) //load data
jmp to Label
Software MMU instructions;
Label:
Next Instruction
       (b) |
| GVA is in %edi;
add %esi, %edi, *GDVAS_base*
mov %eax, (%esi) //load data
Next Instruction   (c) | GVA is in %edi;
//%gs stores the *GDVAS_base*
mov %eax, %gs:%edi //load data
Next Instruction
       (d) |

Guest platform is ARM-32, Host platform is x86-64

Figure 2. Target translation codes of guest memory access instruction with (a) Software MMU, (b) ESPT and HSPT. Target translation codes in (c) HSPT are generated by general translation method. Target translation codes in (d) HSPT are generated by optimized translation method.

3. Proposed and evaluated three SPT organizations, including Shared, Private and Group Shared SPT to handle multi-processing in guest OSes. A guideline on how to select each variation is provided.

4. All schemes proposed and studied have been carefully implemented and evaluated on a system emulator which emulates the Android/ARM environment on the x86-64 platform. Experiments with SPEC CINT2006 benchmarks and multiple practical Android applications show that our technology can achieve comparable performance as the original ESPT while making the system emulator more portable, secure and maintainable. With our new SPT organization varations, our approach can efficiently handle applications with multi-processing.

The rest of the paper is organized as follows: Section 2 gives our motivation; Section 3 focuses on the framework and details of HSPT; Section 4 presents the settings of our experiment and results. Section 5 briefly discusses related work and Section 6 concludes this paper.

2. Motivation

Memory virtualization is an important part of system virtualization. In a hosted system virtual machine, such as KVM [25] based virtual machines, multiple guest OSes and the host OS share the same machine physical memory and are isolated from each other. Consider the x86 platform, as an example, if running as a standalone machine, the OS needs provide the page table which maps the Virtual Address (VA) to the Physical Address (PA). The hardware MMU uses TLB to speed up page table lookup. When a TLB miss occurs, a hardware table walker searches the page table to find the page table entry, and insert it into the TLB. If running on a virtual machine, the PA of a guest machine is not the true machine PA. It is actually mapped to the virtual address of the host machine, so another level of translation is required. Figure 1(a) shows the address translation of traditional mem-

ory virtualization. A virtual machine usually allocates a large chunk of virtual space to simulate the guest physical memory, we call this space "Simulated Guest Physical Space" (SGPS) (as indicated in the figure). When the guest accesses the machine memory, it goes through three-level of address translation. It works as follow: When the guest code accesses a guest virtual page P1, it goes through the guest page table (GPT) to obtain the guest physical page P2 and then look up the internal memory mapping table (MMT) which is created for recording the location of guest physical memory at the host virtual address to find the corresponding host virtual page P3. Next, it searches the host page table (HPT) to obtain the host physical page P4. After these three steps, the guest can finally access the machine memory.

For same-ISA system virtual machines, a Shadow Page Table (SPT) [10] is often created, which maps the guest VA to the machine physical address. When a guest process is running, the hypervisor switches the HPT to this SPT so that only one level of address translation is performed. Figure 1(b) shows the traditional SPT. When running the guest code, the page table base pointer, such as the CR3 register in x86, will be changed to the SPT and then it can directly use hardware MMU to accomplish the address translation.

For cross-ISA system virtual machines, such memory translation process is simulated in software, so it is often called "software MMU". QEMU [5] uses software MMU to translate a guest virtual address (GVA) to the host virtual address (HVA), and let the host machine to handle the HVA translation afterwards. In QEMU, a software-TLB contains the recently used map from GVA to HVA. Each memory access instruction of the guest is translated into several host instructions by the internal dynamic binary translator [5] of QEMU. Suppose ARM-32 is the guest and x86-64 is the host, an ARM memory load instruction "ldr R0,[fp]" is translated into several host instructions with software MMU, as shown in Figure 2(a). These generated host instructions are used to search the software-TLB and can get the target

HVA if hit. If miss, the GVA will go through the aforementioned three-level of address translation (i.e. P1 to P2, P2 to P3 and P3 to P4). In other words, to emulate a single memory access instruction of the guest, 10 to 20 native instructions will be executed when the search hits in the software-TLB or hundreds of instructions to execute when it misses. However, the advantage of using software MMU is platform and OS independent, thus more portable.

Embedded Shadow Page Table (ESPT) proposes to adopt the SPT approach from same-ISA virtual machine. Adopting SPT directly in cross-ISA machines is much more difficult than it initially looks. This is because the guest architecture is emulated. For example a guest register is emulated as a host memory location, so when running the guest code, it needs to access both the guest addresses and the host addresses in the same translated code block, each requires a different page table. So frequently switching back and forth between SPT and HPT is needed. This excessive overhead of page table switching is intolerable, therefore, ESPT proposes to embed the SPT into the HPT to avoid such table switching [14]. In ESPT, LKMs are used to create and manage embedded shadow page entries in HPT (as shown in Figure 1(c)). The consistency between GPT and SPT is also maintained by using LKMs. ESPT first sets all the 4G memory space dedicated for the shadow page entries as protected, when certain pages are accessed, SIGSEGV will be triggered to invoke a registered signal handler. In the signal handler, ESPT will use the fault GVA to go through the aforementioned three-level of address translation to find HPA and then create the mapping from GVA to HPA into the SPT. Finally, it resumes from the fault instruction. ESPT maintains a SPT for each guest process, when the guest process switches, ESPT will use LKMs to set the host directory page table base pointer for the lower 4G space to the targeted SPT. For example, Figure 1(c) shows that "Embedded Shadow Page Entry" points to a SPT, when the guest process switches, ESPT will set "Embedded Shadow Page Entry" to point to the guest's new SPT.

Taking ARM-32 as guest and x86-64 as host, as shown in Figure 2(b), we can see that ESPT will translate one guest access memory instruction to a 'mov', a 'jmp' and several Software MMU instructions. There are two types of page faults in this approach: one is shadow page fault and another is guest page fault. Shadow page fault occurs when the requested GVA is not in the SPT. It is handled by LKMs. A guest page fault is handled by Software MMU. Those instructions work as follow: the 'mov' instruction will first try to access the GVA by using SPT. If hit in SPT, the obtained HVA will go through the hardware MMU to execute and then jump to execute the next guest instruction. If miss in SPT, LKMs will be invoked to fill the SPT and resume execution, and if guest page fault occurs, ESPT will replace the 'jmp' with 'nop' and execute Software MMU instructions to fill the GPT.

ESPT can significantly reduce the address translation overhead. SPEC CINT2006 benchmark results indicate that ESPT achieves an average speed up of 1.51X in system mode when emulating ARM-32 on x86-64 and a 1.59X for emulating IA32 on x86-64 against the original software MMU [14].

ESPT and Software MMU both have their own strength and weakness. To avoid the shortcomings of relying on LKMs, we have come up with a different way to incorporate the idea of SPT. It is non-trivial to avoid using LKMs for two reasons: 1) Our new approach must be able to create and maintain SPT in kernel space without using LKMs; 2) Multi-processing emulation with the same address space must be supported by our method. The technical details of HSPT will be described in the following section.

3. The Framework of HSPT for Cross-ISA System Emulation

Similar to ESPT, our HSPT focuses on the widespread scenario where the virtual space of the host is larger than the guest, such as ARM 32bit to x86 64bit. This scenario is very common to system virtualization since the 64bit architecture is more powerful in both functionality and performance, making it an ideal host machine. Taking advantage of the larger host's address space, we can use a portion of the host page table as our SPT to avoid frequent switching between the shadow and the host page table. We also believe our approach could be applied to the scenario where the guest is an ARM 64bit architecture. The user address space of x86-64 is 256TB (48-bit). Although ARM 64bit also supports 64-bit virtual address, the current AArch64 OS only uses 39-bit of virtual address (512GB), so there are room left for embedding SPTs.

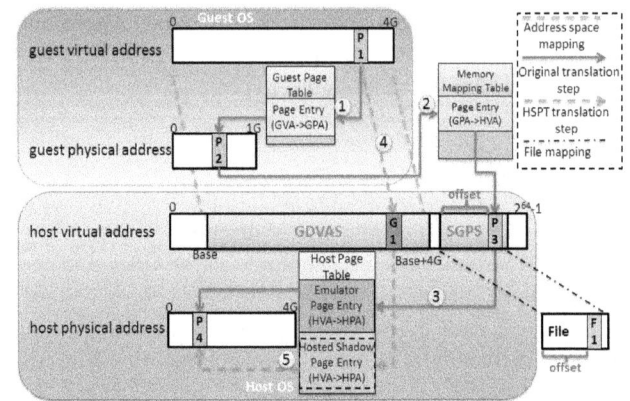

Figure 3. Address translation and the method of creating shadow page mapping of HSPT

Figure 3 shows the address translation process under HSPT. We set aside a fixed virtual space called "Guest-Dedicated Virtual Address Space" (GDVAS) from the host virtual space (as indicated in the figure). When we set aside GDVAS, each page in the guest virtual space is mapped to a page in the GDVAS. For example, the memory accesses of guest virtual page P1 would be translated to the accesses of host virtual page G1 in GDVAS (labelled as step 4). A traditional virtual machine would transform the accesses of P1 to the accesses of host physical page P4 after going through GPT, MMT and HPT (step 1, 2, 3) translation steps. In our approach, P1 is mapped to G1 with an offset which is also the base address of the allocated GDVAS (step 4). By mapping G1 to P4 which was mapped from P3 (step 5), the guest can also access data from G1. Thus we can convert the basic translation process from $P1 \xrightarrow{GPT} P2 \xrightarrow{MMT} P3 \xrightarrow{HPT} P4$ to $P1 \xrightarrow{+offset} G1 \xrightarrow{SPT} P4$. The translation from P1 to G1 does not need table lookup, they only differ by a fixed offset. Compared with the basic memory translation, our approach can reduce three rounds of table lookup down to only once.

Figure 2(c, d) show the general and optimized translation where the optimized translation is only applicable to the platform with segment registers. Since there is only a constant offset from P1 to G1, when translating a guest memory access instruction, we just add the GVA (e.g. P1) to the base of GDVAS. As shown in Figure 2(c), an ARM memory instruction 'ldr R0,[fp]' is translated into 'add %esi, %edi, *GDVAS_base*' and 'mov %eax, (%esi)', where *GDVAS_base* represents the base of GDVAS. Moreover, when the host has the support of segment registers, we can utilize one segment register to hold the base address of GDVAS and optimize the translation. As shown in Figure 2(d), the segment register 'gs' is used to finish the first-layer address translation from P1 to G1. After that, hardware MMU will finish the translation from G1 to P4 automatically. HSPT based translation can reduce the address translation process from 10 to 20 native instructions down to only one or two, thus eliminating most of the address translation overhead.

So far, we have introduced the framework of HSPT, but there are still several issues to address:

1. We had described the memory accesses to guest virtual page P1 can be transformed to accessing the host virtual page G1. Section 3.1 will discuss how to create the mapping from G1 to P4.

2. SPT keeps the direct maps from guest virtual address to host physical address, so it must keep pace with the guest page table. Section 3.2 will discuss a mechanism to maintain the consistency between SPT and GPT.

3. When a guest process switch happens, both the traditional SPT and ESPT must also change the SPT. Section 3.3 will discuss three new SPT variations in our HSPT to support the guest multi-process.

3.1 Creating Shadow Page Mapping

As shown in Figure 3, creating shadow page mapping means creating the mapping from G1 to P4 into the SPT. After basic translation process, we know that P3 is mapped to P4. What we need to do is to make G1 to share P4 mapped from P3.

HSPT uses a mechanism which maps two or more virtual pages to the same physical page to accomplish this shared operation. In the virtual machine initialization phase, the virtual machine allocates a host virtual space which is the so-called "SGPS" space (as indicated in the figure) and used as the guest physical space. When doing this, we use the "**mmap**" system call with 'MAP_SHARED' flag to map this space to a file. Then when the virtual machine starts to run and needs to create the SPT entry for G1, what we need to do is to map G1 with proper protection to the same host physical page P4. This is done by using the "**mmap**" system call and map G1 to the same offset F1 of the target file with P3. After this, the host OS will automatically map G1 and P3 to the same host physical page P4 with isolated page protection.

3.2 Consistency between HSPT and GPT

To make sure each GPT has a correct SPT and the entries in SPT are not outdated, we need to capture the creation and modification of GPT and then set the respective SPT mappings. The main reason for GPT changes include: 1) creation of a new GPT by guest OS due to initiating a new process; 2) modification of GPT by guest OS. These two scenarios are discussed respectively in the following sections.

3.2.1 Guest Page Table Created by Guest OS

When the guest OS creates a process, we need to correspondingly prepare a SPT for it. Since there are so many entries in each guest page table and only a small portion of these entries are actually used, it would be inefficient to synchronize every entry at this time. Therefore, we adopt a lazy synchronization approach which uses the SIGSEGV signal to inform which entry needs update and is similar to ESPT.

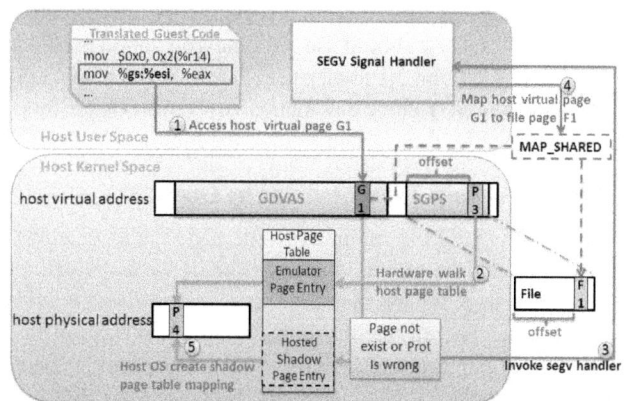

Figure 4. Signal notification mechanism for creating HSPT and synchronizing shadow page entries

Signal based Lazy Synchronization When a new SPT is created, we do not create mappings for all the entries. Instead, we only set the page protection value of all the entries as 'NONE'. Thus when a shadow page entry is accessed at the first time, the SIGSEGV exception will be raised and we

Algorithm 1 SEGV signal handler

Input:
   Faulted host virtual address, $SegvAddress$;
   The base of current GDVAS, $BaseAddress$;
   The current guest page table, GPT;
   The Memory Mapping Table, MMT;

Output:
   None;

1: Host virtual page $G1 = SegvAddress\&PAGE\_MASK$;
2: Guest virtual page $P1 = G1 - BaseAddress$;
3: **if** Is guest page fault **then**
4:    Jump to execute guest exception handler code;
5: **else**
6:    Walk the GPT and look up the MMT to find host virtual page $P3$;
7:    Find $P3$'s corresponding file page $F1$;
8:    Map $G1$ to the same file page $F1$;
9:    Return to restart the faulted insruction;
10: **end if**

have the chance to synchronize for this entry. The execution flow of the SIGSEGV signal handle is shown in Figure 4 and the algorithm of signal handler is shown in Algorithm 1. When the guest first accesses the host virtual page G1 (labelled as step 1), a SIGSEGV signal will be raised since the page is protected in SPT (step 2). The host kernel will throw a signal to the virtual machine process and the control goes into our previously registered SIGSEGV signal handler (step 3). The handler will first compute the guest virtual page P1 (indicated in signal handler) and then walk the GPT to decide whether it is caused by the guest page fault or the inconsistency of SPT. If it is caused by the guest page fault, the handler will jump to execute the guest exception related handler. Otherwise, this exception is caused by the inconsistency of SPT and we should use the synchronization method mentioned in Section 3.1 to map G1 (Step 4) and the host OS will update the SPT entry automatically (Step 5). After this, the signal handler returns and resume the fault instruction.

3.2.2 Guest Page Table Modified by Guest OS

When the guest OS is running, all the page tables of guest processes could be modified at any time. If we monitor the whole guest page tables' memory space, the overhead would be excessive. Therefore, we intercept TLB-invalidation instructions to capture which entry requires synchronization. This approach is similar to the mechanism used in ESPT.

Intercepting the Guest TLB-invalidation instructions When the guest OS updates a page table entry, it should inform TLB to invalid the corresponding entry to ensure the consistency between the GPT and the TLB. Therefore, we can intercept TLB-invalidation instructions to capture the GPT updates indirectly. When we intercept these instructions, we do not modify the shadow page entry to the newest mapping, instead, we just clear the outdated mapping in SPT by using

"**mmap**" system call with 'PROT_NONE' flag. When such pages are accessed, a SIGSEGV signal will be raised and we could synchronize at that time.

3.3 Support for Multi-Process

Multi-processing is very common in real Android apps. Without proper support for multi-processing, the cross-ISA system virtual machine using HSPT will have inadequate performance. We investigate three variations of SPT organizations: Shared SPT which makes all the guest process sharing one single SPT, Private SPT which provides a separate SPT for each guest process and Group Shared SPT which makes a group of the guest processes sharing a SPT. These three methods will be detailed in the following subsections.

3.3.1 Shared SPT

Shared SPT represents that all the guest processes uses the same SPT. It works as follows: When the emulator detects a guest process is switching out (this can be detected by monitoring the page table pointer), we should clear the SPT by using "**mmap**" system call with 'PROT_NONE' flag to get them ready for the next switched-in process. Figure 5 gives the illustration of this process. When guest process A first accesses a page, a SIGSEGV signal will be raised due to the inconsistency and we will update the corresponding entry in SPT(labelled as step 1). Then when the guest OS switches process A out and B in(step 2), we clear the SPT entries belong to process A to get ready for the new process B(step 3). After some time, process B would also be switched out(step 4) and process A back to active(step 5). Similarly, we clear the SPT entries of process B(step 6). When process A first accesses its SPT, SIGSEGV signals will be raised and SPT will be properly synchronized.

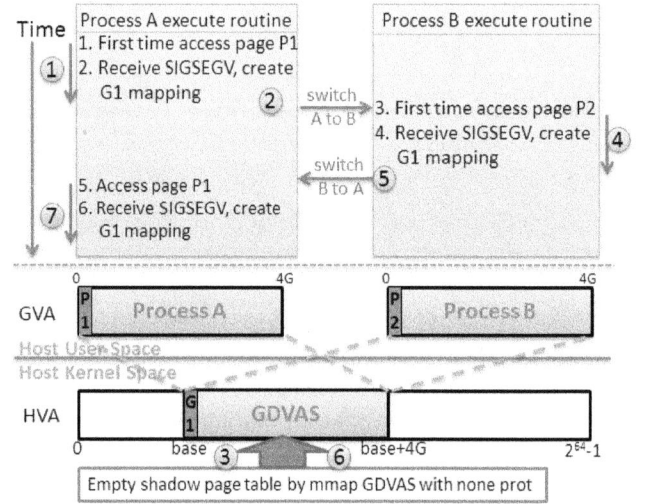

Figure 5. Shared SPT for handling guest multi-process

From this illustration, we can see that in the Shared SPT strategy, when a process is switched back again, the information of the filled SPT entries in the last timeslot is lost and the SPT of the switched-in process has to be warmed up again. Such repeated filling would result in a significant increase in the number of SIGSEGV and the runtime overhead. To reduce such repeated signal, we explored an optimization strategy called "Prefill Optimization".

Prefill Optimization Consider temporal locality that the entries accessed in the past may likely be accessed again in the future, we choose to prefill SPT entries when a process is switched in. Because the page table entries could be changed during the time of switched out, we only record which entries were accessed but not with full detailed information. Moreover, the number of filled entries will accumulate as the process keeps executing and only a small part of the entries filled may be accessed in this timeslot, so if we prefill all the past entries at the resumption of each process, the overhead incurred may exceed the benefit. Based on this observation, we set a window for each guest process. Each time a new SPT entry is synchronized, we'll record the index of this entry in the window. When the window is full, it is flushed to restart recording. After done this, when a certain process is switched in, we'll first synchronize all the entries recorded in this processs window. The impact of the window size to performance will be evaluated in the experiment section.

3.3.2 Private SPT

Prefill optimization can reduce the overhead of warming up in Shared SPT during frequent guest process switches. However, the prefill operation itself could be expensive. If the host machine has enough virtual memory space, the virtual machine could be benefit from Private SPT to avoid page table refill. As mentioned before, each SPT is bound to a separate GDVAS. Private SPT would consume a greate amount of virtual address space.

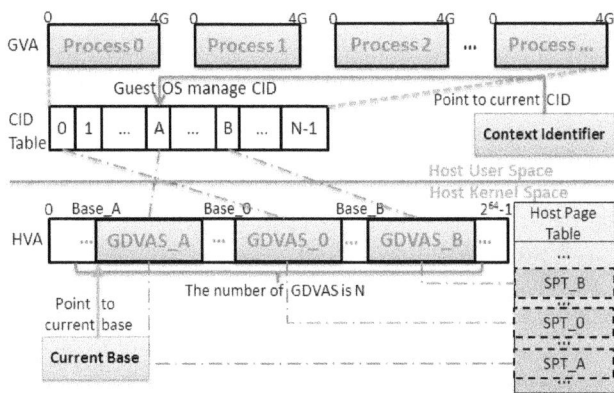

Figure 6. Private SPT for handling guest multi-process

Setting write-protection to the switched-out GPTs is a common but expensive method to monitor the modification of GPT [24]. To reduce this overhead, we again intercept the TLB-invalidation instructions to identify modified page entries. Consider x86 and ARM, as an example, they use PCID (Process Context Identifier) [4] and ASID (Address Space Identifier) [1, 20] respectively to identify TLB entries

for each process. We call this kind of identifier as "Context Identifier" (CID). Same virtual address of different processes can be distinguished in the TLB due to CID. Based on this, when the process switching happens, there is no need to flush the whole TLB.

Principles of TLB structure with CID Under this structure, OS must obey the following principles: 1) At the time of process switching, CID register which contains the CID of the current active process should be modified. 2) When the OS modifies the page table, TLB must be informed with the CID and the address. 3) There are a limited number of available CIDs. We assume this number is N. So when the number of processes exceeds N, the sharing of CID between new processes and certain old processes would happen.

Management of Private SPTs Based on the principles above, we can tell which entry of a process, and the process CID is modified from the TLB-invalidation instructions. Therefore, when setting up each private SPT, we choose to bind each SPT with a CID (as shown in Figure 6) rather than the process ID so that we can use the TLB-invalidation instructions to maintain consistency between SPT and the corresponding guest page table.

Switching SPT As mentioned above, the CID register would be updated when the guest process switch happens. Since SPT is correlated with CID, we should also switch SPT at this time. Before describing activities involved in SPT switching, there is an issue needs to be addressed about the instruction translation which is shown in Figure 2(c). Since the translated instructions may be shared by different guest processes, when each process has a different SPT, in order to make each process access their own data through the same translated native instructions, we need to load the GDVAS base address of the current executing process before adding it to GVA. This base address can be stored in a global memory area and switched when the guest process is switched. Similarly, when the host has the segment register support, there is no need for this load operation and we can simply use the segment register to contain this base and modified this register when the guest process switches in. Based on the above, when the guest process switches what need to be done is only modifying the active GDVAS base address which can be kept in a global memory area or in the segment register on certain host platforms.

3.3.3 Group Shared SPT

Although Private SPT can avoid frequent SPT-clear problem of Shared SPT, it consumes too much host virtual space. Taking ARM as the guest, a virtual space size of 256*4G=1TB (upto 256 different processes allowed) would be needed. There may not be enough host virtual space. To address this problem, we proposed Group Shared SPT that the number of SPTs do not based on the available CID. Instead, we set up a fix number of SPTs depending on the size of host virtual space. Each time a process switches in, if this process already has a corresponded SPT, then we'll just use this SPT. Other-

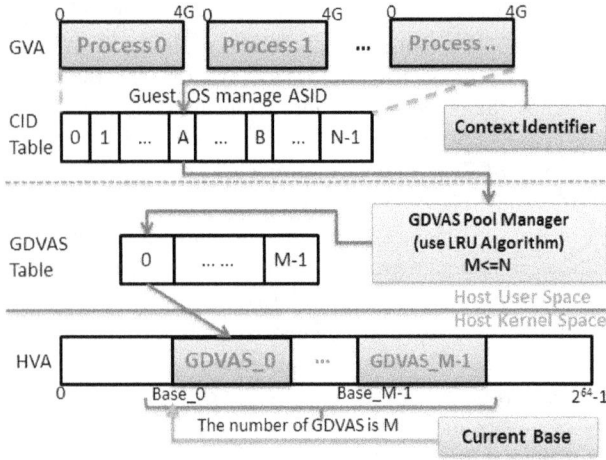

Figure 7. Group Shared SPT for handling guest multi-process

wise, if there's still an available SPT, it will be allocated. If not, we'll pick up one from the SPT pool based on certain strategies. This specific strategy is the LRU (Least Recently Used) algorithm which chooses the process which is least recently scheduled and clear its SPT for this new process. In Group Shared SPT, a group of processes share the same SP-T. It is a compromise between Shared SPT and Private SPT. As long as the virtual space is sufficient, it works as Private SPT, when the virtual address space is short, it works like Shared SPT for a small number of processes.

Figure 7 shows the framework of Group Shared SPT. We can see that SPT is allocated from a GDVAS Table rather than correlated with CID as used in Private SPT. When the new switched-in process has no corresponding SPT and need to allocate a new one from the GDVAS table, we also adopt the prefill optimization used in Shared SPT. The performance under different number of SPTs will be evaluated in the experiment section.

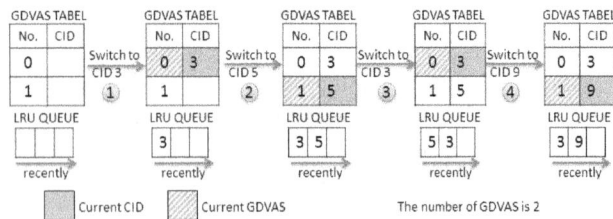

Figure 8. Example of managing shadow page tables with Group Shared SPT

Figure 8 shows an example of how Group Shared SPTs are managed during process switching. In this example, we assume the virtual machine only allocates two GDVASs from the host. When the guest runs the first process with CID 3, GDVAS_0 will be allocated to this process. The current base is set to Base_0 and the LRU queue is updated accordingly (labeled as step 1). Next, when guest switches to the process with CID 5, GDVAS_1 will be allocated to

this process. The current base is set to Base_1 and the LRU queue is updated accordingly (step 2). Next, when guest switches back to the process with CID 3, the current base is set back to Base_0 and the LRU queue updated (step 3). Next, when the guest switches to another process with CID 9, no free GDVAS are available, so the virtual machine must select one GDVAS as victim. In this case, GDVAS_1 will be selected since it is least recently scheduled according to the LRU queue. Hence, GDVAS_1 will be allocated to this newly switched-in process (step 4).

4. Experimental Evaluation

4.1 Experimental setup

We implement HSPT based memory virtualization framework on an Android Emulator which uses a modified QE-MU to emulate the Android/ARM environment on the x86-64 platform. The host experimental platform is Intel E7-4807 machine with 1064MHZ, 15G RAM, and Ubuntu 12.04.3 LTS(x86-64). We use Android 4.4(Kernel: 3.4.0-gd853d22nnk) as our guest and run test cases in guest VM.

Two suites of programs we selected to run as the guest applications are SPEC CINT2006 benchmarks and Android applications.

SPEC CINT2006 benchmarks SPEC CINT2006 is a CPU-intensive benchmark suite, stressing system's processor and memory subsystem. The source code of these benchmarks uses the GNU standard lib, but Android uses its own native lib. So in our experiments, we use static linked benchmarks. We only test the train input dataset instead of ref due to the limitation of available memory. Android Emulator uses QE-MU which can only provide a maximum of 1GB of memory for guest when emulating the ARM platform, some benchmarks of CINT2006 with ref input require more than 1GB of memory during execution.

Android applications In order to test whether HSPT can enhance the actual user experience, we also test the Android system boot and applications start-up time. We select some generally used apps, including Clock, Calendar, Messages, Calculator, Phone and Contacts. The reason why we test the app start-up time is that running apps needs user interaction, it is difficult to test precisely. The startup latency is an important aspect to consider in many applications, especially for embedded systems. At the startup of an Android application, intensive interaction with the OS will occur to request for system resources. Many operations in the startup-phase might also get used afterwards. To avoid averaging with testing outliers, we ran each application test multiple times and take the average of three middle scores as the final result.

4.2 Evaluation of Shared SPT

4.2.1 Shared SPT without prefill optimization

Figure 9(a) shows the performance of the CINT2006 benchmarks. The x-axis is the benchmarks and y-axis is the execution time in seconds. Figure 9(b) shows the speedup. We can

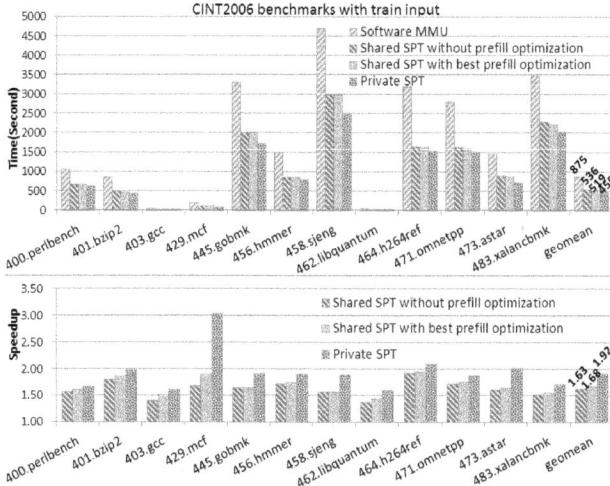

Figure 9. (a) Execution time and (b) Speedup by Private SPT and Shared SPT against Software MMU for SPEC CINT2006 benchmarks

see that our Shared SPT without prefill optimization can enhance the performance of Android Emulator for each benchmark and can achieve a 1.63X speedup on average.

4.2.2 Shared SPT with Prefill Optimization

In order to test the impact of the prefill optimization with different window sizes on the performance, we set ten values (shadow page entries) including 0, 100, 200, 300, 400, 500, 600, 700, 800 and 900 for window size. Figure 10 shows the speedup achieved by prefill optimization with different window sizes against Shared SPT without this optimization. The x-axis represents different window sizes and the y-axis is the speedup against shared SPT without prefill optimization. We can see that with increasing window size, the speedup of Shared SPT firstly keeps going up and then starts to decrease when the window size exceeds 300 entries. At window size 300, we have achieved a maximum speedup of 1.68X (1.033*1.63X).

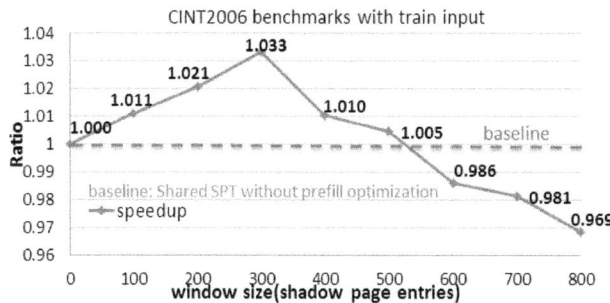

Figure 10. Speedup by prefill optimization with different window size against Shared SPT without prefill optimization

To explain the reason of the drop of performance when the window size exceeds 300, we did a profile of the number of SEGV exceptions for uninitialized page table entries and

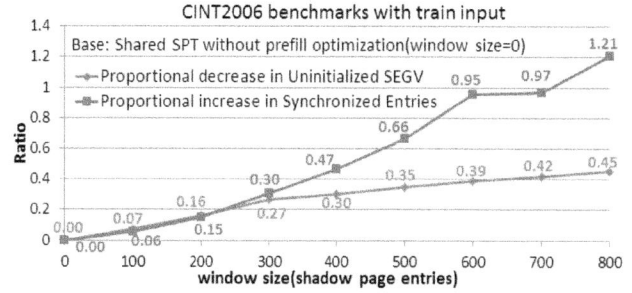

Figure 11. The number of Uninitialized SEGV and synchronized shadow page entries with different window sizes

synchronized SPT entries. Figure 11 shows the result, the x-axis is different window sizes and y-axis is the ratio against window size 0 (that also represents the Shared SPT without prefill optimization). There are two types of SEGVs in HSPT that one is the SEGV due to uninitialized SPT entries and the other is raised by guest page faults. 'Uninitialized SEGV' represents the first type of SEGV and 'Synchronized Entries' represents the number of SPT entries synchronized including activities from both the prefill operation and the SIGSEGV signal handling. The 'Proportional decrease in Uninitialized SEGV' legend is computed by the following formula:

$$\frac{Base\,SEGV\,num \;-\; Current\,SEGV\,num}{Base\,SEGV\,num}$$

, where 'Base SEGV num' and 'Current SEGV num' represent the number of 'Uninitialized SEGV' under window size 0 and the current window size respectively. The legend of 'Proportional increase in Synchronized Entries' is computed similarly. We can see that the two ratios have minuscule differences when window size is less than 300. But when window size exceeds 300, the gap between these two ratios start to diverge which means that many prefilled SPT entries are not used before this process is switched out. Since the prefill comes with overhead, such unused prefilled entries will be a waste. When this overhead exceeds the profit, the performance goes down.

4.2.3 Shared SPT for Android Practical Applications

Figure 12(a) shows the experimental result of Android system boot and applications start-up time. The x-axis is the Android system and applications, the y-axis is the boot time of system and the start-up time of applications in seconds. Figure 12(b) shows the speedup. The 'Shared SPT with best prefill optimization' is the prefill optimized Shared SPT when window size is 300. From this figure we can see that no matter whether we adopt prefill optimization or not, Shared SPT does not outperform the Software MMU for the system boot time and start-up time of each application. For practical Android apps, what is needed is Private SPT. Nevertheless, prefill optimization for Shared SPT clearly outperforms basic Shared SPT on both CINT2006 and practical apps.

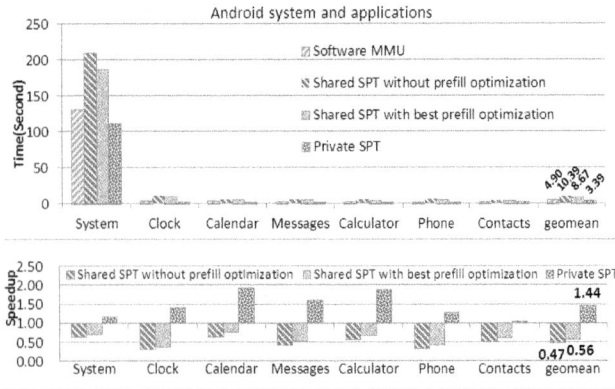

Figure 12. (a) Execution time and (b) Speedup by Private SPT and Shared SPT against Software MMU for Android system boot and applications start-up

The different outcomes between Figure 9 and Figure 12 come from the fact that each CINT2006 benchmark needs only one process but each Android app may need multiple service processes. So the performance of process switching dominates practical apps more than CINT2006 benchmarks. In Shared SPT, frequent process switching can causes frequent SPT-clear operations. So Shared SPT is not ideal for emulating applications with multi-processing.

4.3 Evaluation of Private SPT

4.3.1 Private SPT for SPEC CINT2006 benchmarks

From Figure 9(b), we can see that Private SPT achieves an average speedup of 1.92X against Software MMU. We can also see that compared with other benchmarks, 429.mcf has the largest speedup. In order to explain this, we also did an experiment that profiled the TLB miss rates of Software MMU. Figure 13 shows the result, the y-axis is the TLB-miss rate. We can see that the TLB miss rate of 429.mcf is higher than others. There are two main reasons of TLB miss in Software MMU that one is that software-TLB needs to be cleared each time a guest process switches out (it does not use the ASID feature of ARM TLB) and the other is that software-TLB is not big enough (it has only 256 entries). Because Private SPT does not need to clear the SPT when a guest process switches and each page in guest virtual space is covered in SPT, so it can effectively solve the problem of

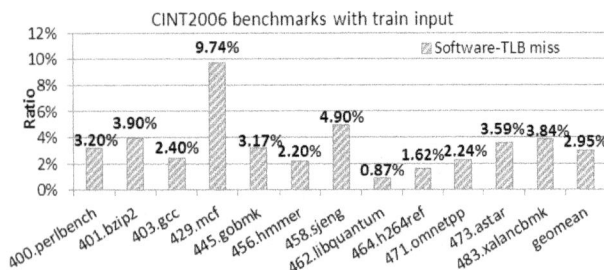

Figure 13. TLB miss ratio of Software MMU

high TLB miss rate and this explains why this benchmark can achieve a greater speedup.

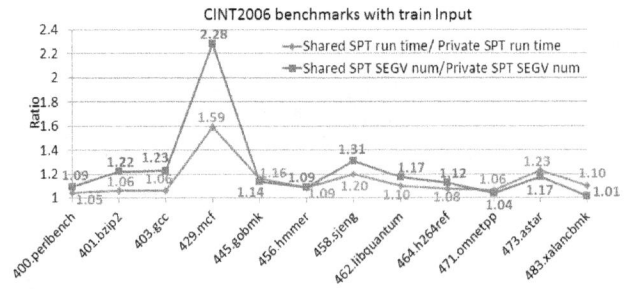

Figure 14. Impact on the performance of the total number of SEGV with uninitialized reason

From Figure 9(b), we can also see that 429.mcf achieves the highest speedup when comparing Private SPT against Shared SPT. To explain the reason, we give both Private SPT and Shared SPT a profile of the number of SEGV due to uninitialized reason. The results are shown in Figure 14. The y-axis is the ratio which represents statistics of Private SPT against Shared SPT with best prefill optimization. As we can see from the figure, the performance improvement tracks the same trend with the proportional decrease in Uninitialized SEGV numbers. The benchmark 429.mcf reduces most of the SEGV caused by uninitialized SPT entries so as to improve the performance the greatest.

4.3.2 Private SPT for Android Practical Applications

From Figure 12(b), we can see that compared with Software MMU, Private SPT has a significant performance boost of Android emulator and can achieve an average of 1.44X speedup for Android system and practical applications.

4.4 Evaluation of Group Shared SPT

We also evaluate the performance of Group Shared SPT with different number of SPTs against Software MMU. Group Shared SPT is implemented with the prefill optimization with 300 as the window size and we test the performance when the number of SPTs is 1, 4, 8, 16 and 32. Note that the more SPT used, the performance would be closer to Private SPT, but the more virtual space will be consumed. The fewer SPT used, the performance will be closer to Shared SPT.

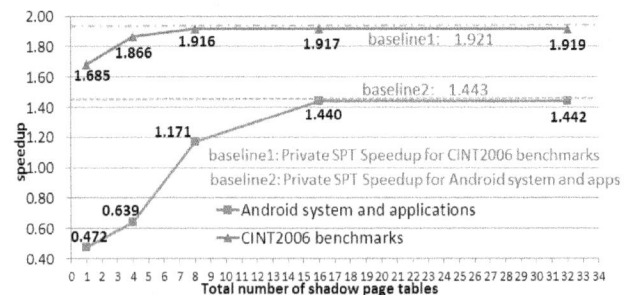

Figure 15. Performance of Group Shared SPT with different number of SPTs

The experimental result is shown in Figure 15. The x-axis represents different number of SPTs and the y-axis is the average speed-up against Software MMU. The performance is compared with the average speedup of Private SPT with 256 SPTs which is shown in the upper baseline. We can see obviously from the figure that the performance of CINT2006 benchmarks keeps improving with the increasing number of SPTs and when the number of SPTs exceeds 8, the performance of Group Shared SPT is very close to Private SPT. For Android system and applications, when the number exceeds 8, Group Shared SPT can perform better than Software MMU and when the number exceeds 16, Group Shared SPT becomes competitive with Private SPT.

We can see that for CINT2006 benchmarks and Android practical applications, 8 and 16 of SPTs would be sufficient to obtain the performance benefit of Private SPT without suffering insufficient virtual address space. Since the Android apps need more service processes while running, they need a larger number of SPTs than CINT2006 benchmarks.

4.5 Discussion

The observed performance of HSPT on CINT2006 is similar to ESPT [14]. We did not compare the performance of HSPT side-by-side with ESPT since we need to implement the LKMs in order to reproduce the performance numbers of ESPT in an identical experimental setup. This work does not claim HSPT will yield greater performance than ESPT, it is motivated for better platform portability, higher system security, and improved usability for application developers since non-root users can also benefit from HSPT technology. Another major difference is that we noticed the importance of synchronizing SPT for multi-processing in Android environment. While Private SPT works well for multi-processing, it may take too much virtual address space. We come up with a Group Shared SPT approach which preserved most of the performance gain from Private SPT without its downsides.

In this paper, we only introduce the implementation of HSPT on Linux OS. Actually, our HSPT can be implemented on any host OS with shared memory mapping capability. For example, since Windows has an API "**CreateFileMapping**" [7] to implement the shared memory mapping, HSPT can also be implemented on Windows OS.

5. Related Work

The primary memory virtualization methods for same-ISA system-level virtual machine include the software-based method such as Shadow Page Table (SPT) and the hardware-assisted method such as Intel Extended Page Tables [19] and AMD Nested paging [9]. SPT [10] has been widely used, it maps GVA directly to HPA to avoid levels of virtual address translations. The method to improve the performance of emulator used by hardware-assisted memory virtualization is mainly on two dimensional (2D) page walks [10] which us-

es hardware to walk both guest and nested page table to accomplish the address translation.

Xiaolin Wang and Jiarui Zang show that neither hardware-assisted method nor SPT can be a definite winner. SPT will result in expensive VM exits whenever there is a page fault that requires synchronization between the guest and shadow page tables. Hardware assists can solve this problem well, but compared with SPT, it has a disadvantage that the page walk yields more memory accesses and thus longer latency to resolve TLB misses [21, 22]. So they propose a dynamic switching mechanism between these two methods [24].

To reduce the overhead of many memory references to resolve TLB misses by 2D page walkers, some architectures use a page walk cache (PWC), which is an extra hardware table to hold intermediate translations [9, 12]. Jeongseob Ahn and Seongwook Jin discover that nested page table sizes do not impose significant overheads on the overall memory usage. So they propose a flat nested page table to reduce unnecessary memory references for nested walks. Further, they also adopt a speculative mechanism to use the SPT to accelerate the address translation [11]. Compared with SPT, they eliminate the shadow page table synchronization overheads.

There are two memory virtualization technologies for cross-ISA system virtualization. One is ESPT [14] and another is Software MMU such as the one used in QEMU [5]. ESPT embeds shadow page entries into the host page table (HPT) to avoid frequent page table switching between SPT and HPT. Software MMU designs a software-TLB which contains the recently used map from guest virtual address to host virtual address. Each memory instruction of the guest is translated into several host instructions to search the software-TLB. If hit, the mapped host virtual address can be used, if miss, the emulator must go through the three-level address translation. The advantage of Software MMU is platform portability. ESPT can reduce the software-TLB search time since the SPT can directly work with the hardware MMU. However, ESPT uses LKMs to manage the embedded SPT, and the use of LKMs decreases platform portability, system usability and introduces possible security concerns [16]. To combine these two methods' advantage, we propose HSPT which exploits all the advantages of ESPT with no LKMs.

6. Conclusion

In this paper, we proposed an practical implementation of Shadow Page Table (SPT) for cross-ISA virtual machines without using Loadable Kernel Modules (LKMs). Our approach uses part of the host page table as SPT and rely on the shared memory mapping schemes to update SPT, thus avoid the use of LKMs. Our implementation and management of the SPT avoids some shortcomings of using LKMs, making the virtual machines more portable, usable and secure. When test the Android emulator, we noticed the importance of reducing SPT update cost. Initially, a Shared SPT was used. We introduced a prefill optimization to cut down the cost of SPT updates during process resumptions. However, the best way to support multi-processing is to use Private SPT. Since Private SPT consumes too much virtual address space (VAS), it could fail in cases where there are many processes. So we come up with an elegant compromise, called Group Shared SPT where a group of processes could share the same SPT. With a given number of SPTs, limited by the available VAS supported by the platform, if the number of processes is relatively small, each process can obtain its own SPT, thus enjoy the full benefit of Private SPT. When the number of processes increases beyond the number of SPTs, some processes must share a SPT. So Group Shared SPT works adaptively to balance between high performance and limited VAS. With sufficient host virtual space, our approach has achieved up to 92% speedup for CINT2006 benchmarks and 44% improvement for the Android system boot and practical applications start-up on the Android emulator.

Acknowledgments

We would like to thank the anonymous reviewiers for their useful feedback. This research is supported by the National High Technology Research and Development Program of China under grant 2012AA010901, the National Natural Science Foundation of China (NSFC) under grants 61303051, 61303052, 61332009 and 60925009, the Innovation Research Group of NSFC under grant 61221062.

References

[1] ARM®Architecture Reference Manual.

[2] Android emulator. URL http://developer.android.com/tools/help/emulator.html.

[3] Cve. URL http://www.cvedetails.com.

[4] Intel®64andIA-32 ArchitecturesSoftwareDeveloperManual.

[5] Qemu emulator. URL http://wiki.qemu.org/Manual.

[6] Virtualbox. URL http://www.virtualbox.org/.

[7] Windowsapi. URL http://msdn.microsoft.com/en-us/library.

[8] Xen. URL http://www.xen.org.

[9] Amd-v nested paging, 2008.

[10] K. Adams and O. Agesen. A comparison of software and hardware techniques for x86 virtualization. SIGARCH Comput. Archit. News, 34(5):2–13, Oct. 2006. ISSN 0163-5964.

[11] J. Ahn, S. Jin, and J. Huh. Revisiting hardware-assisted page walks for virtualized systems. In Proceedings of the 39th Annual International Symposium on Computer Architecture, ISCA '12, pages 476–487, 2012. ISBN 978-1-4503-1642-2.

[12] R. Bhargava, B. Serebrin, F. Spadini, and S. Manne. Accelerating two-dimensional page walks for virtualized systems. SIGPLAN Not., 43(3):26–35, Mar. 2008. ISSN 0362-1340.

[13] E. Bugnion, S. Devine, M. Rosenblum, J. Sugerman, and E. Y. Wang. Bringing virtualization to the x86 architecture with the original vmware workstation. ACM Trans. Comput. Syst., 30 (4):12:1–12:51, Nov. 2012. ISSN 0734-2071.

[14] C.-J. Chang, J.-J. Wu, W.-C. Hsu, P. Liu, and P.-C. Yew. Efficient memory virtualization for cross-isa system mode emulation. In Proceedings of the 10th ACM SIGPLAN/SIGOPS International Conference on Virtual Execution Environments, VEE '14, pages 117–128, 2014. ISBN 978-1-4503-2764-0.

[15] H. Chen and B. Zang. A case for secure and scalable hypervisor using safe language. In Proceedings of the 2012 International Workshop on Programming Models and Applications for Multicores and Manycores, PMAM '12, 2012.

[16] H. Chen, Y. Mao, X. Wang, D. Zhou, N. Zeldovich, and M. F. Kaashoek. Linux kernel vulnerabilities: State-of-the-art defenses and open problems. In Proceedings of the Second Asia-Pacific Workshop on Systems, APSys '11, 2011.

[17] J. Park, D. Lee, B. Kim, J. Huh, and S. Maeng. Locality-aware dynamic vm reconfiguration on mapreduce clouds. In Proceedings of the 21st International Symposium on High-Performance Parallel and Distributed Computing, HPDC '12, pages 27–36, 2012. ISBN 978-1-4503-0805-2.

[18] J. Smith and R. Nair. Virtual Machines: Versatile Platforms for Systems and Processes (The Morgan Kaufmann Series in Computer Architecture and Design). 2005.

[19] R. S. M. A. B. K. L. Uhlig, Neiger and Smith. Intel virtualization technology. Computer, 2005.

[20] P. Varanasi and G. Heiser. Hardware-supported virtualization on arm. In Proceedings of the Second Asia-Pacific Workshop on Systems, APSys '11, 2011.

[21] VMware. Performance evaluation of amd rvi hardware assist. Technical report, Technical report, 2009.

[22] VMware. Performance evaluation of intel ept hardware assist. Technical report, Technical report, 2009.

[23] C. A. Waldspurger. Memory resource management in vmware esx server. In Proceedings of the 5th Symposium on Operating Systems Design and implementation, OSDI '02, pages 181–194, 2002. ISBN 978-1-4503-0111-4.

[24] X. Wang, J. Zang, Z. Wang, Y. Luo, and X. Li. Selective hardware/software memory virtualization. SIGPLAN Not., 46 (7):217–226, Mar. 2011. ISSN 0362-1340.

[25] S. Yang. Extending kvm with new intel®virtualization technology. In Intel Open Source Technology Center., 2008.

GPUswap: Enabling Oversubscription of GPU Memory through Transparent Swapping

Jens Kehne   Jonathan Metter   Frank Bellosa

Operating Systems Group, Karlsruhe Institute of Technology (KIT)

os@itec.kit.edu

Abstract

Over the last few years, GPUs have been finding their way into cloud computing platforms, allowing users to benefit from the performance of GPUs at low cost. However, a large portion of the cloud's cost advantage traditionally stems from oversubscription: Cloud providers rent out more resources to their customers than are actually available, expecting that the customers will not actually use all of the promised resources. For GPU memory, this oversubscription is difficult due to the lack of support for demand paging in current GPUs. Therefore, recent approaches to enabling oversubscription of GPU memory resort to software scheduling of GPU kernels – which has been shown to induce significant runtime overhead in applications even if sufficient GPU memory is available – to ensure that data is present on the GPU when referenced.

In this paper, we present GPUswap, a novel approach to enabling oversubscription of GPU memory that does not rely on software scheduling of GPU kernels. GPUswap uses the GPU's ability to access system RAM directly to extend the GPU's own memory. To that end, GPUswap transparently relocates data from the GPU to system RAM in response to memory pressure. GPUswap ensures that all data is permanently accessible to the GPU and thus allows applications to submit commands to the GPU directly at any time, without the need for software scheduling. Experiments with our prototype implementation show that GPU applications can still execute even with only 20 MB of GPU memory available. In addition, while software scheduling suffers from permanent overhead even with sufficient GPU memory available, our approach executes GPU applications with native performance.

Categories and Subject Descriptors   D.4.2 [*Operating Systems*]: Storage Management—Virtual Memory, Swapping

Keywords   Virtualization; Memory Overcommitment; Oversubscription; Swapping; GPU

1. Introduction

Over the last few years, the use of GPUs as compute accelerators has been constantly growing. Especially in the field of high performance computing (HPC), GPUs are delivering unprecedented levels of performance for certain classes of applications. Most recently, GPUs have also been finding their way into cloud computing platforms, allowing users to benefit from the performance of GPUs at low cost by relieving them of the burden of purchasing and maintaining a dedicated supercomputer.

Cloud providers often oversubscribe the resources of their cloud platforms in order to reduce costs: In case of GPUs, the provider can rent out more GPU memory to customers than is actually available, expecting that the customers will not actually use all of the promised memory. In doing so, cloud providers carefully assign virtual machines to physical hosts such that the actual demand for GPU memory will be close to – but not more than – the physical capacity of the GPU in order to maximize utilization and application performance at the same time. However, customers do not always behave as expected and may choose to fully utilize the promised memory at any time, possibly exceeding the GPU's physical capacity. Though this kind of over-utilization may rarely occur in practice, the cloud platform must ensure that all applications still function correctly and with acceptable performance even if memory is over-utilized.

Currently, handling over-utilization of GPU memory is difficult since current GPUs do not support precise exceptions and therefore cannot seamlessly continue execution after page faults. As a result, these GPUs typically treat page faults as fatal errors. Previous attempts to handle over-utilization of GPU memory, such as Gdev [11] and GDM [18] therefore rely on software scheduling of GPU kernels in order to multiplex the available GPU memory. When dispatching a kernel to the GPU, these solutions copy the working set of the application that launched the kernel into GPU memory, evicting memory from other kernels if necessary. On the downside, these systems typically software-schedule the GPU even while GPU memory is not fully utilized. Since GPU software scheduling has been shown to induce considerable overhead [11], such software scheduling should be avoided.

In this paper, we present GPUswap, a novel approach to extending GPU memory, which uses the GPU's ability to directly access system RAM to transparently extend applications' GPU address spaces. GPUswap relocates data from applications over-using their memory quota to system RAM, and then redirects the page table entries for the relocated data to the copy in system RAM. Our approach keeps all data permanently accessible to the GPU and does therefore not require software scheduling of GPU kernels. In contrast to previous approaches, our approach does not induce overhead unless the GPU's memory is actually over-utilized. Experiments with our prototype implementation show that when sufficient GPU memory is available, software scheduling suffers from 3.5 – 30 % overhead, while GPUswap executes GPU applications with native performance.

The rest of this paper is organized as follows: We first provide a short overview of current GPUs in Section 2 and introduce our design goals in Section 3. Then, we present our proposed design in Section 4. Section 5 describes the prototypical implementation of our approach, while Section 6 presents our initial performance evaluation of our prototype. Finally, Section 7 presents related work and Section 8 concludes the paper.

2. GPU Background

Modern GPUs are asynchronous in nature: Applications submit small tasks called *GPU kernels* to the GPU and are then free to perform other work while the GPU processes these kernels. Applications can submit work to the GPU by writing commands into *command submission channels*. Recent GPU generations from both AMD and Nvidia feature multiple such command submission channels that can be used by different applications concurrently. To guarantee protection between those applications, these GPUs confine every application to its own *address space*, thus ensuring that an application cannot access memory of other applications.

In this section, we give an overview of the relevant mechanisms for CPU-GPU interaction and protection. We start with a description of GPU memory management, including address spaces, in Section 2.1, followed by a description of the GPU command submission process in Section 2.2.

2.1 Memory management

Modern GPUs assign an address space to each application in order to guarantee protection between GPU kernels from different applications. Each address space is defined by a page table containing GPU-virtual to GPU-physical mappings.

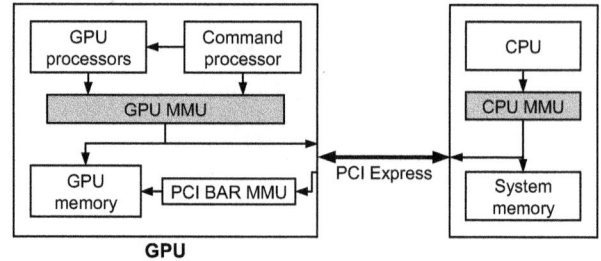

Figure 1: Access paths to GPU memory. GPU kernels access both system RAM and GPU memory through the GPU's MMU. (© 2013 IEEE. Taken from [5] with permission)

For the GPUs we examined, these page tables can contain two types of memory pages: Regular pages of 4 kb and large pages of 128 kb. GPU kernels only operate on GPU-virtual addresses, which a dedicated MMU, depicted in Figure 1, transparently translates to GPU-physical addresses.

Current GPU software stacks manage memory using *Buffer Objects* (BO). BOs are contiguous regions of GPU-virtual memory spanning one or more page table entries. While a BO is always contiguous in virtual memory, the same does not necessarily apply to physical memory, as the page table can map each page of the BO to an arbitrary page in physical memory.

The memory management of current GPUs lacks some features found commonly in CPUs: Current GPUs typically treat page faults as fatal errors, and their page tables do not contain reference- or dirty-bits. Therefore, well-known memory management techniques like demand paging or traditional page replacement algorithms cannot be applied to GPUs.

The GPU's page tables are typically not limited to GPU-physical memory. Instead, they can also contain physical addresses in system RAM. In that case, the GPU's MMU translates any access to a GPU-virtual address mapped to system RAM into a PCI-e bus transaction. Mapping system RAM into GPU address spaces this way is transparent to GPU kernels as these GPU kernels operate on virtual addresses only. The only distinction between GPU memory-backed and system RAM-backed virtual memory is speed: Operations targeting system RAM are limited by the bandwidth of the PCI-express bus, which is about 25x slower than the GPU's native memory bus. In essence, a GPU using both system RAM and it's own memory can thus be considered a NUMA system.

While extending the GPU's memory with system RAM is supported by current GPU software stacks, the application must typically decide at allocation time where to store a given buffer object. This implies that a single BO may not span both GPU memory and system RAM. However, this limitation stems purely from the current GPU software stacks since BOs are a software construct. The GPU hardware can map GPU-virtual addresses to GPU- or system RAM with page granularity, independent of BO boundaries.

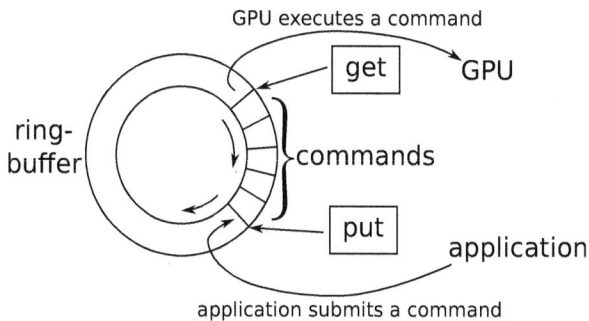

Figure 2: The GPU command submission process (© 2013 IEEE. Taken from [5] with permission)

2.2 Command submission

For most modern GPUs, applications submit GPU commands using command submission channels as depicted in Figure 2. Each channel consists of a ring buffer holding the actual GPU commands, and two pointers – *get* and *put* – which reside in memory-mapped device registers and point to the head and tail of the command queue inside the ring buffer. The GPU driver can memory-map these command submission channels – including both ring buffer and pointers – into the application's CPU address space. Applications can thus submit commands directly to the GPU, without invoking the GPU driver. An application wishing to send commands to the GPU first writes these commands into the next free slot in the command submission channel's ring buffer, and then advances the *put*-pointer, which signals the GPU that a command was just submitted. The GPU processes the commands queued in the ring buffer sequentially and advances the *get*-pointer whenever a command has been consumed.

On the downside, granting applications direct access to the command submission channels also implies that all scheduling decisions for commands from different channels are left to the GPU alone. Therefore, if multiple applications access the GPU concurrently, neither the applications nor the GPU driver have any information about the ordering of commands from different applications. In addition, once a command has been written into the command submission channel, it must execute to completion – it is not possible to un-submit a command even if that command has not yet begun to execute. Since applications cannot be sure when exactly a submitted command will execute, each application must thus ensure uninterrupted access to all data needed by each of its commands until those commands have finished execution.

3. Design goals

The main goal of GPUswap is to enable oversubscription of GPU memory. However, in doing so, GPUswap should not sacrifice application performance or compatibility with existing applications. Besides enabling oversubscription, we thus define the following objectives for our design:

Fairness From the GPU's perspective, system RAM is significantly slower than the GPU's own memory. Relocating application data to system RAM can thus result in significant runtime overhead for the application owning the data. Ideally, this overhead should be distributed fairly among applications. Unfortunately, we can not yet estimate the performance impact of storing a given data structure in system RAM. Therefore, our current goal is to guarantee a fair share of GPU memory to each application. In the future, we will investigate other relocation policies to instead divide the overhead more evenly.

Performance Our goal is thus to optimize for the common case: GPUswap should not induce overhead unless there is a shortage in GPU memory. Our reasoning behind this goal is that we expect relocation of data to system RAM to be relatively rare. The goal of sharing GPU memory is to increase the utilization of that memory. However, such sharing is ineffective when a single application fully utilizes the available memory by itself. Therefore, we expect GPU memory to be shared mainly among applications using relatively small amounts of GPU memory. In that scenario, system RAM is only used to cope with the exceptional case that an application requests more GPU memory than expected. However, if GPUswap must relocate data to system RAM, overhead is unavoidable due to the difference in speed between GPU memory and PCI-e bus. GPUswap is therefore intended as a short-term solution only. If a shortage in GPU memory persists for an extended period of time, the cloud provider should take additional action, such as migrating a VM to a different host.

Transparency Most GPU applications are written under the assumption that the application has exclusive access to the GPU. In addition, modern GPU drivers map the GPU's command submission channels directly into the application to maximize application performance. Our solution should maintain this illusion of exclusive and direct GPU access by keeping any relocation of GPU memory fully transparent to the application in order to remain compatible with existing applications. Specifically, the application should be able to submit commands to the GPU at any time, without being affected by memory relocation. Therefore, from the application's point of view, GPU memory should never become inaccessible, and the contents of GPU memory should never change unexpectedly.

4. Architecture

GPUswap uses system RAM as an extension to GPU memory. Modern GPUs can map system RAM into applications' GPU address spaces, allowing GPU kernels transparent access to system RAM. If applications allocate more GPU memory than available, GPUswap transparently copies data

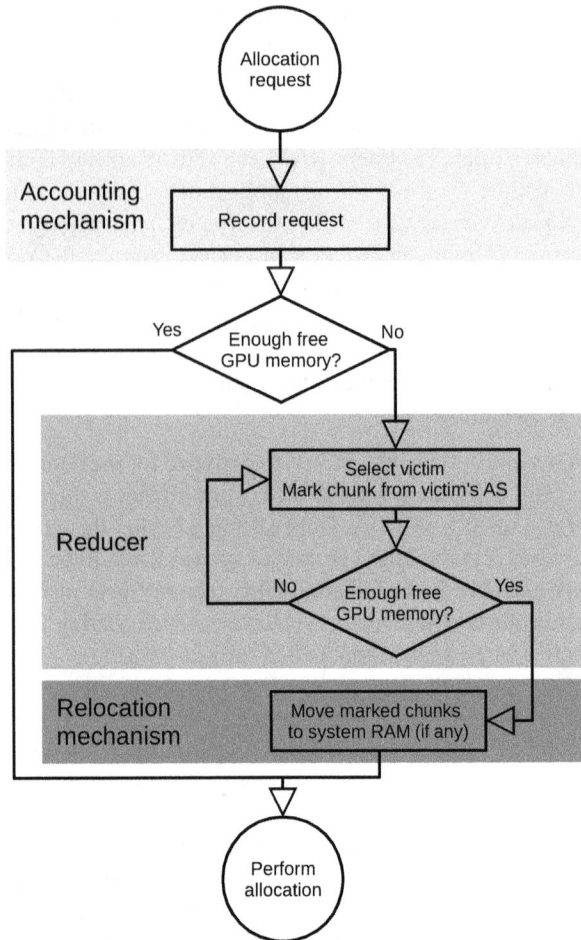

Figure 3: The main components of GPUswap and their operation

from GPU memory to system RAM, and subsequently maps that data in system RAM to the same virtual address it originated from. Applications can thus allocate more GPU memory than is physically available, while GPUswap ensures that all data remains permanently accessible, even if it does not reside in GPU memory. Therefore, in contrast to previous approaches, GPUswap does not depend on software scheduling of GPU kernels to enable oversubscription of GPU memory.

4.1 Overview

GPUswap consists of three main components as depicted in Figure 3: An accounting mechanism which tracks information about each application's allocated memory, a reducer that, based on information from the accounting mechanism, decides which memory to move to system RAM, and a swapping mechanism which executes the reducer's decisions. Whenever an application requests GPU memory, the accounting mechanism takes note of that request in order to track the BOs and the total amount of GPU memory allocated by each application. If there is insufficient free GPU

memory to serve the request, the reducer then decides which memory should be relocated to system RAM to free up GPU memory for the request. Finally, the relocation mechanism performs the actual relocations. Conversely, whenever an application frees GPU memory, GPUswap selects relocated memory fitting into the available space on the GPU and moves that memory back onto the GPU in order to maintain good memory utilization. GPUswap's operation is completely transparent to applications, apart from a small delay in the application's GPU command execution during the operation of the relocation mechanism.

GPUswap is designed to operate in the context of the operating system kernel, either as an add-on to an existing GPU driver, or as a separate module wrapping calls from userspace into the GPU driver. Operating inside the kernel gives GPUswap both information about and control over all applications in the system, without requiring cooperation from those applications. Therefore, running in the kernel allows GPUswap to enforce allocation policies even against uncooperative applications.

4.2 Memory accounting

Our accounting mechanism intercepts every request for GPU memory. These requests are sent to the GPU driver by the user-space CUDA runtime whenever that runtime needs additional memory, for example to satisfy a call to cudaMalloc(). Once activated, our accounting mechanism logically divides the allocated BO into fixed-size chunks. The chunk size is 2 MB by default, but can be configured to different values if desired. The accounting mechanism maintains a list of all allocated chunks as well as the total amount of memory allocated for each application. Whenever GPU memory is relocated, the reducer informs the accounting mechanism to keep each application's total GPU memory usage accurate.

GPUswap manages GPU memory in chunks rather than pages or entire BOs. Relocating memory with BO granularity could result in poor memory utilization since BOs can be hundreds of megabytes in size: If GPUswap relocates a large BO in order to make room for a small allocation, most of the relocated memory would remain unused. Managing memory with page granularity limits the amount of wasted memory to the page size, but can result in high computational overhead if each page of a large BO must be processed individually. We chose to manage GPU memory in chunks as a compromise between the conflicting goals of minimizing wasted GPU memory and minimizing computational overhead: The amount of wasted memory is limited to the chunk size – which is much smaller than the typical BO size – while at the same time, the computational overhead is limited since there are far fewer chunks than pages to process. Note that the chunk size can be configured to the page size or the size of the GPU's memory – the latter resulting in each BO consisting of one chunk – should the need arise.

68

4.3 Victim selection

If there is not enough free GPU memory for a request, the reducer decides which memory to relocate to system RAM in two steps: i) Select which application should give up GPU memory (*victim selection*), ii) selecting a chunk of GPU memory owned by that application for relocation (*chunk selection*). The reducer repeats these two steps until the size of the selected memory plus the size of the pre-existing free memory is larger than or equal to the size of the new request.

The reducer uses data from the accounting mechanism to select a victim. Since it is our goal to spread the available GPU memory evenly among applications, the reducer currently chooses the application consuming most GPU memory as the victim. To determine which application uses most GPU memory, the reducer considers all data currently residing in GPU memory as well as the newly allocated BO. Considering that new BO as well as existing memory ensures that the reducer can relocate memory owned by the requesting application in case the new request causes that application to exceed its fair share of GPU memory.

Once the reducer has selected a victim, the second step is to select a chunk of GPU memory owned by that victim for relocation. Ideally, since any access to the selected memory will incur a significant performance penalty after relocation, the reducer should select a chunk that the application will not use in the near future. Unfortunately, typical algorithms used to achieve a good selection – such as LRU or LFU – are unusable on GPUs since the GPU's MMU does not implement a reference bit and is therefore unable to track page accesses. Consequently, we currently revert to selecting a random chunk owned by the victim. Once a chunk has been selected, the reducer marks that chunk for relocation and reduces the victim's accounted GPU memory consumption by the size of the selected chunk.

4.4 Relocation mechanism

Once the reducer has selected appropriate chunks, the relocation mechanism actually moves these chunks to system RAM. During relocation, the mechanism must ensure the consistency of the chunks' contents. To that end, the relocation mechanism performs the following steps:

1. Temporarily suspend GPU access for the application owning the chunk

2. Copy the chunk's contents to system RAM

3. Modify the application's GPU page tables so that the chunk's location in the application's GPU-virtual address space maps to the new location of the BO in system RAM

4. Return to 2 if the application owns another marked chunk

5. Restore GPU access for the application

Suspending GPU access for the application is necessary to ensure the consistency of the chunks' contents during relocation: If the application is allowed to execute GPU kernels during copying, one of these kernels could write to a chunk while that chunk is being copied. If such a write occurs in a region of the chunk that has already been copied, this modification is lost upon switching the page table to the now outdated version of the chunk in system RAM. Unfortunately, we cannot apply the classical techniques for solving this problem to GPUs due to the limited capabilities of the GPU's MMU. For example, using write faults to detect changes to the copied memory, as is typically done for virtual machine migration [2], does not work on current GPUs since these GPUs treat write faults as fatal errors. Therefore, there is currently no alternative to suspending the application's GPU access altogether.

Our swapping mechanism uses the same technique as LoGV [5] to suspend GPU access for an application: The mechanism transparently unmaps all command submission channels from the application's address space, replaces those channels with shadow copies in system RAM, and waits for all commands in the unmapped command submission channels to finish execution. For the application, the shadow copies are indistinguishable from regular command submission channels, which maintains the illusion of uninterrupted GPU access and thus keeps memory relocation transparent to the application. In particular, the application can still submit commands without blocking, since these commands are transparently written to a shadow copy. After the relocation finishes, the mechanism restores the application's GPU access by synchronizing the contents of the shadow copies with the physical channels – causing all GPU commands submitted to a shadow copy to begin execution – before remapping the physical channels back into the application's address space. Our relocation mechanism only suspends GPU access for one application at a time to prevent the GPU from idling, and copies all marked buffers in the disabled application's address space at once while the application is suspended.

Our relocation mechanism assumes that there is sufficient system RAM to hold all selected chunks. We consider this assumption reasonable since current server machines typically contain much more system RAM than GPU memory. However, the mechanism cannot use ordinary application memory for relocating chunks: The memory holding these chunks must be non-pageable and DMA-accessible to make the relocated chunks accessible to the GPU. Since appropriate memory is easy to allocate for a device driver, we chose to allocate the memory for relocated chunks in the driver's memory space for simplicity. In principle, however, GPUswap can use any memory with the desired properties for relocation. Allocating memory for relocation in the driver is thus not a strict requirement if appropriate memory can be obtained by other means.

4.5 Returning memory to the GPU

Before any data is relocated, the GPU memory must be fully utilized to minimize the overhead associated with the use of system RAM. Therefore, GPUswap attempts to move suitable chunks from system RAM back to GPU memory whenever an application frees GPU memory. GPUswap considers a chunk suitable if i) that BO resides in system RAM, and ii) the chunk's size is less than or equal to the amount of free GPU memory. GPUswap chooses which chunks to move back to the GPU in two steps: First, GPUswap selects one application owning at least one suitable chunk as the winner. That winner is currently the application owning the least amount of GPU memory to distribute GPU memory fairly among applications. Then, GPUswap randomly chooses one of that winner's suitable chunks and marks that chunk for relocation back onto the GPU. GPUswap repeats these two steps until no suitable chunks remain.

Once GPUswap has selected a set of chunks, we employ the relocation mechanism described in Section 4.4 to move the marked chunks back to the GPU. In essence, the relocation mechanism repeats the same steps as for relocating chunks to system RAM, only this time using GPU memory as the destination. First, the mechanism chooses an application owning at least one marked chunk and suspends that application's access to the GPU. Then, the mechanism copies all marked chunks owned by that application back into GPU memory, and modifies the application's GPU page tables to keep the chunks accessible in the same (virtual) locations. Finally, the swapping mechanism restores the application's GPU access, and advances to the next application owning marked chunks.

5. Prototype implementation

We integrated our prototype implementation of GPUswap into the PathScale GPU driver (pscnv) [13]. Pscnv is currently the only open-source GPU driver capable of mapping the GPU's command submission channels into user space. Unfortunately, pscnv limits our current implementation to Nvidia Fermi GPUs. In principle, however, our approach applies to all GPUs that feature virtual address spaces and multiple command submission channels, which includes newer GPU generations from both Nvidia and AMD. We are currently working on an implementation based on the Nouveau driver which will support Nvidia Kepler- and Maxwell-generation GPUs.

Most of GPUswap's functionality is implemented as an add-on separate from the main components of the original pscnv driver. GPUswap is activated through a hook in pscnv's memory allocator which invokes GPUswap once for each memory allocation request. GPUswap then operates as described in Section 4.1: The reducer selects appropriate chunks of GPU memory to relocate, before the relocation mechanism copies the selected chunks into system RAM. This process frees up enough memory to subsequently allow pscnv's original memory allocator to serve the original request. Since this entire process is implemented inside pscnv

without requiring changes to the driver's API, GPUswap's operation is completely transparent to applications.

5.1 Memory accounting and management

The original pscnv driver manages memory as BOs, which are contiguous in virtual GPU memory and can be hundreds of megabytes in size. However, we prefer a smaller entity of memory management as explained in Section 4.2. Therefore, we split each allocated BO into fixed-size chunks. If the size of the BO cannot be evenly divided by the chunk size, the remainder is put into a separate chunk that is smaller than the configured size. We ensure that these chunks appear as contiguous BOs towards user space to keep this modification transparent to applications. Internally, we compose the chunks of large pages whenever possible to minimize the amount of page table manipulation.

Since each chunk may be placed in GPU or system memory individually, our accounting mechanism maintains per-application lists of GPU memory chunks which GPUswap can potentially move to system RAM, as well as chunks that have already been moved. Since pscnv lacked any per-application resource accounting, we introduced a new data structure that contains these two lists as well as general memory consumption statistics for each application. Whenever an application allocates a BO, the allocator adds all chunks of that BO to the application's list of chunks that can be moved to system RAM. Similarly, whenever our relocation mechanism moves chunks to system RAM, it also moves the appropriate entries to the list of already relocated chunks.

5.2 Reducer

On each request for GPU memory, our reducer executes in the kernel context of the thread that submitted the request. Since relocating memory requires suspending GPU access for the application owning that memory – which is a costly operation – to guarantee the consistency of the relocated memory's contents, the reducer does not perform the relocation immediately. Instead, it adds each selected chunk to a list attached to the state data structure of the application owning the selected chunk. After enough memory has been selected, the reducer triggers the relocation mechanism which then performs the actual relocations. The reducer then waits for all enqueued relocation operations to complete, in order to ensure that pscnv's memory allocator will subsequently find sufficient free GPU memory.

5.3 Suspending applications

GPUswap uses a similar mechanism as LoGV [5] to suspend GPU access for applications: GPUswap unmaps all GPU command submission channels from the application's address space and replaces those channels with identical shadow copies in system RAM. To restore GPU access after relocation, GPUswap copies all newly submitted GPU commands from the shadow copies to the physical channels and subsequently maps the physical channels back into the application's address space.

To avoid creating inconsistencies while a shadow copy is being created or synchronized with a physical channel, we must prevent the application from modifying both the physical channel and the shadow copy while the operation is in progress. Therefore, we perform these operations while neither the command submission channel nor the shadow copy are mapped into the application's address space. If the application accesses the unmapped channel, the resulting page fault is directed to GPUswap, which stalls its response until the operation is complete. Except for a possible delay in the page fault handler, both suspending and resuming GPU access are thus completely transparent to applications.

5.4 Relocation mechanism

After our reducer finishes operation, the relocation mechanism iterates over all applications owning at least one selected chunk, suspends each application's GPU access using the mechanism described in Section 5.3, and copies all chunks from the application's selected chunk list to system RAM. Note that only chunks that already exist in GPU memory are copied in this way: If chunks from the newly allocated BO are selected for relocation, these chunks are allocated in system RAM directly.

Since GPUswap is a part of pscnv, our relocation mechanism can use utility functions that are part of pscnv, for example to manipulate the GPU's page tables. However, pscnv assumes that the GPU's command submission channels are mapped into the application, and thus does not include important pieces of application logic. For example, pscnv itself cannot submit commands to the GPU, which is necessary to initiate DMA transfers. We therefore backported the missing pieces necessary for DMA transfers from gdev and pscnv's userspace library into the pscnv kernel module. Our current implementation supports asynchronous DMA, which allows our relocation mechanism to relocate all queued chunks in parallel while the application is suspended.

5.5 Returning memory to the GPU

GPUswap performs return operations in a separate thread executing in kernel space. Since the GPU applications we examined tend to free multiple BOs in short succession, that thread checks for unused GPU memory in regular intervals. These intervals should be as long as necessary to capture each set of free operations in a single interval with high probability, but otherwise as short as possible to ensure that GPU memory does not remain unused for extended periods of time. We currently set the interval to 50 ms, which fulfills both conditions to our satisfaction. If our thread detects unused GPU memory at the end of an interval, the thread chooses a set of chunks to relocate back into GPU memory and executes the appropriate relocation operation, which involves the same steps as relocation into system RAM.

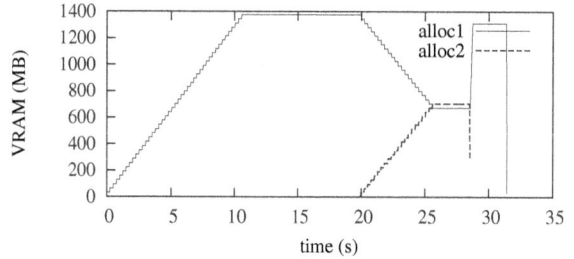

(a) Total amount of allocated GPU memory

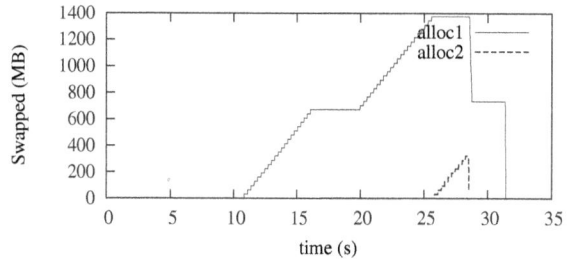

(b) Total amount of allocated system RAM

Figure 4: Total amount of memory allocated by two memory-intensive processes over time

6. Experimental Evaluation

GPUswap's main goal is to enable oversubscription of GPU memory while maintaining fairness, performance and transparency. As described in Section 5, our approach achieves transparency by operating completely inside the driver, not requiring any changes to applications. To show the fairness and performance of our approach, we conducted a number of experiments using our prototype implementation.

6.1 Experimental setup

We used a Nvidia GeForce GTX 480 GPU as a testbed for our experiments. The GPU is based on the Fermi microarchitecture and features 480 cores and 1.5 GB of GDDR5 memory. Our host system consists of a Intel Core i7-4470 CPU and 16 GB of system RAM. For our experiments, we locked both CPU and GPU at the highest available clock frequency. For our benchmarks, we used Gdev's CUDA implementation (ucuda) [9], which supports both Gdev and pscnv. Our host system ran Ubuntu 12.04.5, which is based on Linux 3.5.7.33.

6.2 Fairness

Since GPU memory offers much higher performance than system RAM, the available GPU memory should be distributed fairly among applications. To that end, GPUswap attempts to guarantee a fair amount of GPU memory to each application. We created a synthetic benchmark application called *alloc* to evaluate whether our approach fulfills that guarantee. Alloc performs no computation, but instead con-

Application	Area
backprop	Machine learning
bfs	Graph computation
heartwall	Image processing
hotspot	Physics simulation
lud	Linear algebra
srad2	Image processing

Table 1: The benchmarks used in our evaluation

tinuously allocates BOs of 32 MB until it possesses a total of 2 GB of virtual GPU memory. Alloc then waits a pre-defined amount of time before freeing all allocated memory at once. Our reasoning behind this benchmark was to simulate the behavior of a program containing a memory leak. In our experiment, we started two instances of alloc – named alloc1 and alloc2 – with alloc2 starting 20 seconds after alloc1. We then recorded the total amount of both GPU memory and system RAM allocated by both instances combined. We set the chunk size to 32 MB to make the relocation operations more visible.

The results are shown in Figure 4. Alloc1 starts at time 0 and gradually fills up all available GPU memory. When no more GPU memory is available, our reducer starts moving data to system RAM in response to new allocations. As a result, the amount of allocated system RAM starts to increase until alloc1 owns a total of 2 GB of memory. 20 seconds after the launch of alloc1, alloc2 starts and attempts to allocate memory. As the entire GPU memory has been allocated by alloc1, our reducer chooses chunks owned by alloc1 – which obviously exceeds its fair share of memory – for relocation. As a result, alloc1's amount of GPU memory decreases at the same rate as the amount of GPU memory allocated to alloc2 increases until both instances own approximately the same amount of GPU memory. Note that the amounts of memory owned by both instances are not exactly equal: Since the 1400 MB of GPU memory available to applications do not divide equally by 32 MB, alloc2 ends up with one more chunk than alloc1. Since this kind of imbalance is limited to one chunk, we consider the amount of unfairness acceptable.

6.3 Performance

We used six benchmark applications from the rodinia benchmark suite [1] – which have been previously adapted to ucuda [8] – to evaluate the performance of our prototype. The resulting set of benchmarks is listed in Table 1.

We ran each of our benchmark applications multiple times while gradually increasing the amount of available GPU memory in 50 MB increments to evaluate the effect of using system RAM instead of GPU memory. To limit the available GPU memory, we modified the pscnv kernel module, forcing pscnv's memory allocator to ignore all GPU memory above a configurable address. At each memory size we tested, we started two instances of each benchmark ap-

plication simultaneously. Since our reducer selects 2 MB chunks for relocation at random, we ran each benchmark application 10 times to allow our reducer to select different combinations for chunks. In addition, we modified our benchmark applications to repeat their main computation step 100 times in order to make the effect of using system RAM in place of GPU memory more visible. To that end, we added a loop comprising all GPU kernel launches and as much of the application's I/O as possible to each of our benchmark applications. The only exception to this modification was hotspot: Hotspot already executes its GPU kernels for a number of iterations, which allowed us to repeat the main computation step by simply setting the desired number of iterations appropriately.

For comparison, we ran this experiment on both GPUswap and gdev. We chose gdev since it is currently the only freely available tool for enabling oversubscription of GPU memory that we are aware of. Gdev enables oversubscription by transparently sharing BOs between applications: Whenever memory pressure occurs, Gdev selects two BOs of similar size owned by different applications. Gdev then copies the contents of one of those BOs into system RAM, and maps the other BO into the GPU address space of both applications. Whenever a GPU kernel of one of the two applications is then scheduled for execution, Gdev copies that application's data into the shared BO before starting the kernel. To implement limiting of GPU memory, we added the same modification we made to pscnv to the gdev kernel module.

Figure 5 shows the runtime for each of our benchmark applications for various GPU memory sizes on both GPUswap and gdev. For each application, we recorded the runtime of the slower of the two instances. As expected, our solution induces less runtime overhead than gdev for most of our benchmark applications if all application data resides on the GPU, which is the case for all applications at 500 MB GPU memory. Most notably, gdev's overhead for backprop was more than 30% compared to GPUswap, followed by srad2, lud and heartwall with 14%, 10% and 3.5% overhead, respectively. The only notable exception was hotspot, for which GPUswap showed an average overhead of 1.5% compared to gdev. Bfs did not show any significant difference in runtime between GPUswap and gdev. Overall, we conclude that GPU software scheduling, as implemented by gdev, causes significant runtime overhead for most applications, while GPUswap – which only interrupts GPU computation in case of memory pressure – does not induce overhead for most applications as long as sufficient GPU memory is available.

On the downside, our benchmarks also show the cost of relocating application data to system RAM: At a total GPU memory size of 20 MB – at which almost all application data resides in system RAM – the runtime of all applications increases significantly – from 50% for backprop to 786% for bfs. For most applications, however, the overhead ap-

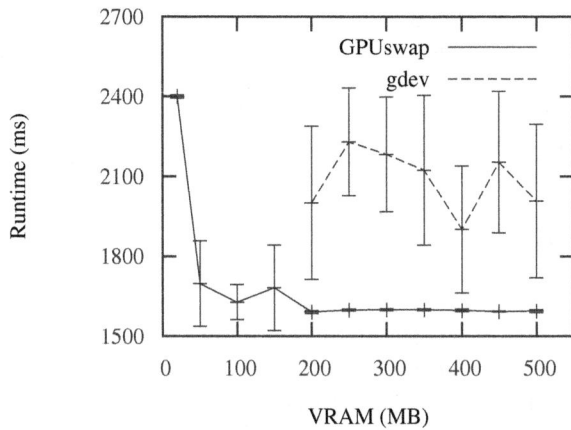

(a) backprop

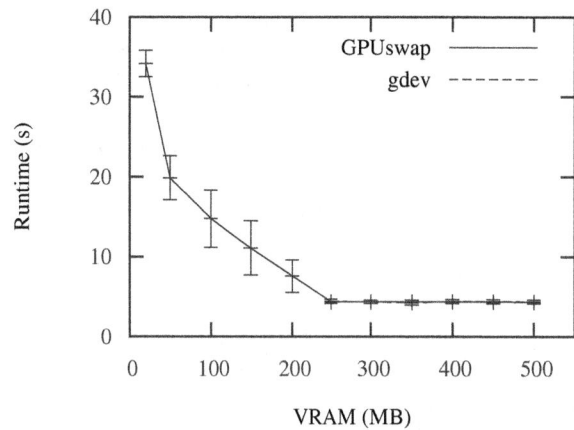

(b) bfs

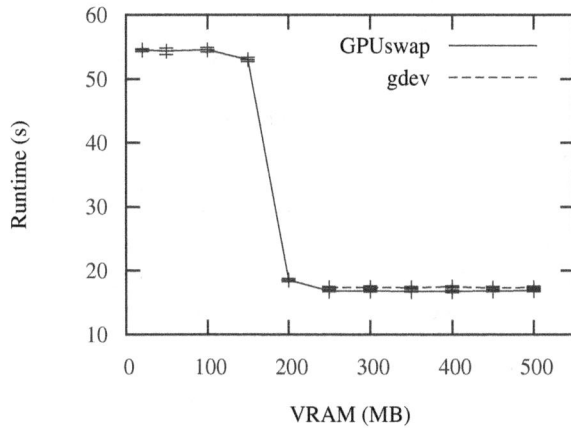

(c) heartwall

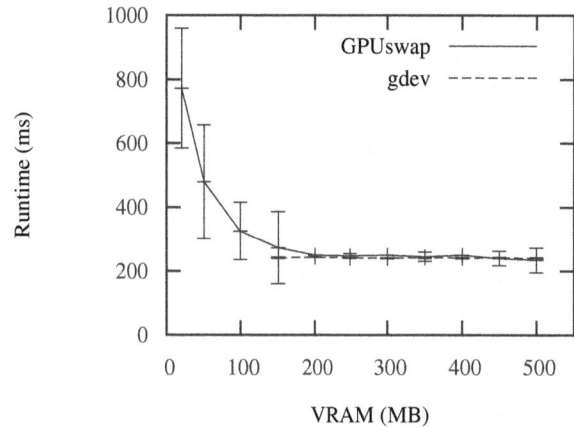

(d) hotspot

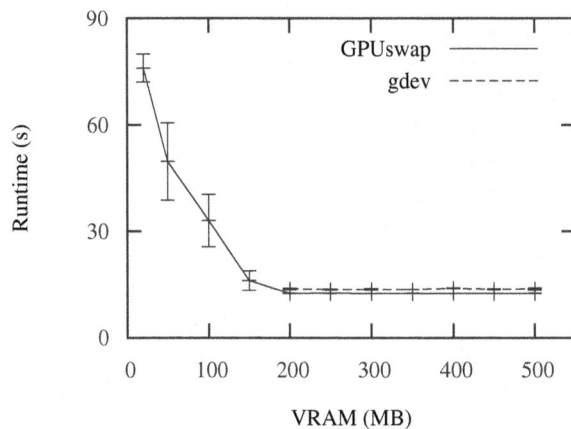

(e) lud

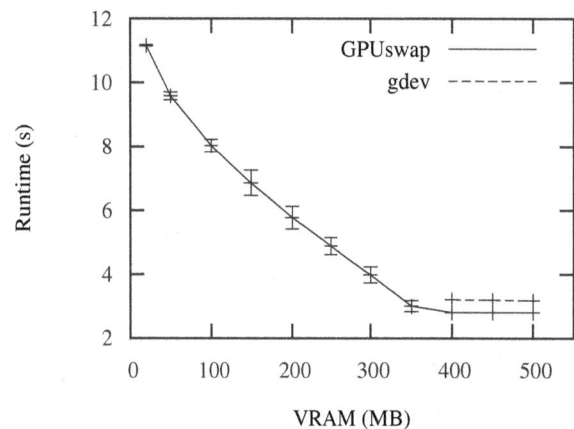

(f) srad2

Figure 5: The runtime of two instances of each benchmark application for various amounts of GPU memory. The x-axis shows the amount of GPU memory available to applications, while the y-axis shows the average runtime of the slower of the two instances. Unfortunately, Gdev caused all benchmark applications to crash under memory pressure. Therefore, results for Gdev are only shown for cases where sufficient GPU memory is available.

pears to decrease exponentially as we add more GPU memory. Consequently, if only a small amount of application data is relocated, the overhead becomes relatively small as well. Unfortunately, we could not compare these results to Gdev since all benchmark applications invariably crashed as soon as Gdev detected memory pressure. However, since we expect all application data residing in system RAM to be an exceptionally rare case and GPUswap is intended mainly as a short-term solution, we consider GPUswap's overhead acceptable overall.

Since GPUswap selects memory chunks for relocation randomly, and different chunks may have a different impact on performance when relocated, the runtimes of most of our benchmark applications fluctuate heavily as soon as any application data is relocated to system RAM. This fluctuation is shown by the error bars in Figure 5, which show the standard deviation of the benchmark runtimes across all runs at each memory size. It is important to note that for some benchmarks, the low end of this standard deviation comes close to the application's runtime with sufficient GPU memory available, which indicates that GPUswap's random selection sometimes selects chunks for relocation which have only a negligible impact on performance. Unfortunately, it is currently not possible to detect these chunks beforehand since current GPUs lack appropriate hardware support, such as reference bits in the GPU's page tables. However, we believe that hardware support for detecting rarely accessed chunks has the potential to greatly improve GPUswap's performance.

We repeated some of our experiments with up to five concurrent instances of our benchmark applications to assess the scalability of GPUswap. Our results indicate that the increase in computational overhead due to the larger number of applications can be neglected – in practice, the runtime overhead appears to depend only on the amount of relocated application data. Our experiments also show that the overhead is spread evenly among all running applications. These results are consistent with our expectations: Since Fermi GPUs run GPU kernels from different applications sequentially, there is no additional contention on the PCI-e bus if more applications are started in parallel. However, bus contention could be a problem on GPUs capable of running kernels from different applications concurrently.

6.4 Relocation delay

In addition to the direct cost of using system RAM in place of GPU memory, GPUswap can also cause delays in applications while memory is being relocated. Specifically, each allocation request can cause two types of delay: i) The allocating application itself may have to wait for a relocation to complete before the actual allocation can take place, and ii) the GPU access for another application may be suspended if memory owned by that application is relocated in response to an allocation request.

We ran the same benchmark applications as in the previous experiment with the total amount of GPU memory limited to 100 MB to measure the impact of these delays. We ran each benchmark application five times, again starting two instances of each application simultaneously. While the applications were running, we recorded the amount of memory relocated and the delay caused by each individual relocation operation. The results are depicted in Figure 6. Figure 6a shows the delay experienced by applications requesting GPU memory, depending on the amount of GPU memory that must be relocated to make room for the request. Note that each of our benchmark applications allocates the same buffers in each run, which is why the memory sizes appear quantized in this figure. Figure 6b shows the delay experienced by applications that must give up memory in response to an allocation request. Finally, Figure 6c shows the time taken for the raw DMA transfers taking place during relocation, depending on the size of the transfer. The chunk size in this experiment was set to the default of 2 MB, which causes the apparent quantization in Figures 6b and 6c.

The allocation requests we observed were generally delayed by less than 100 ms. We consider this delay acceptable since most GPU applications tend to re-use previously allocated memory instead of allocating and freeing buffers frequently. However, the delay did not always mirror the time needed for a DMA transfer of the same size. The reasons for this result are twofold: First, GPUswap performs work of its own in addition to the DMA transfer – for example to select which chunks should be relocated – which can cause allocation requests to be delayed longer than the time needed for the DMA transfer. Second, the delay may be shorter than the time for a DMA transfer if chunks from the newly requested memory are selected for relocation, which results in those chunks being allocated in system RAM directly, without the need for a DMA transfer.

The delays we observed in applications not allocating memory themselves were even shorter on average than the delay for allocation requests. This shorter delay is owed to the fact that GPUswap performs almost all of its computation – such as chunk selection – in the context of the application requesting memory. Therefore, the delay experienced by other applications is dominated by the time needed for the DMA transfer, which can be seen from the mostly linear relationship between the amount of relocated memory and the delay in Figure 6b and Figure 6c. However, we observed that some relocations delayed the application longer than average. We assume that these relocations ran concurrently with computation on previously relocated memory and thus suffered from contention on the PCI-e bus. However, even these longer relocations generally completed in under 50 ms.

We again repeated these experiments with more than two applications. Our results indicate that multiple concurrent applications can introduce considerable jitter to the dura-

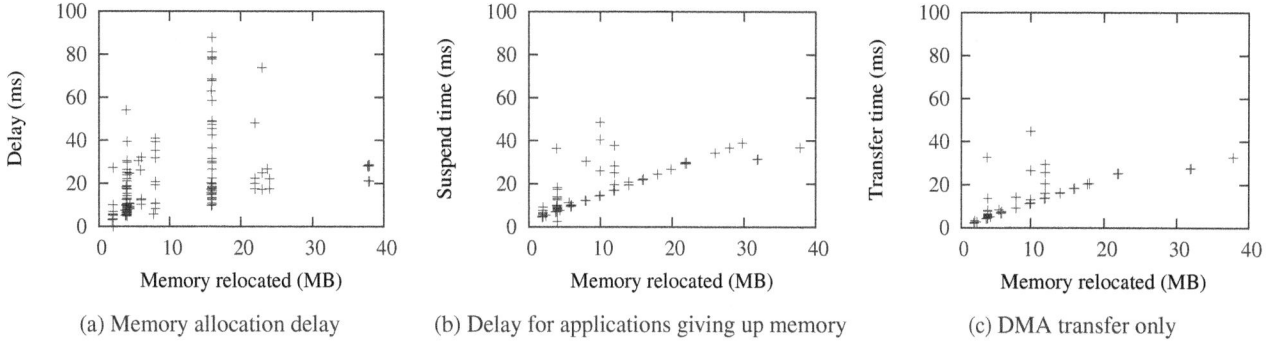

| (a) Memory allocation delay | (b) Delay for applications giving up memory | (c) DMA transfer only |

Figure 6: The results of our measurements of relocation delay. The plots show the relocation delay experienced by an application allocating memory (left) and an application that must give up memory due to an allocation request from another application (center). The plot on the right shows only the time for the DMA transfer that takes place during relocation.

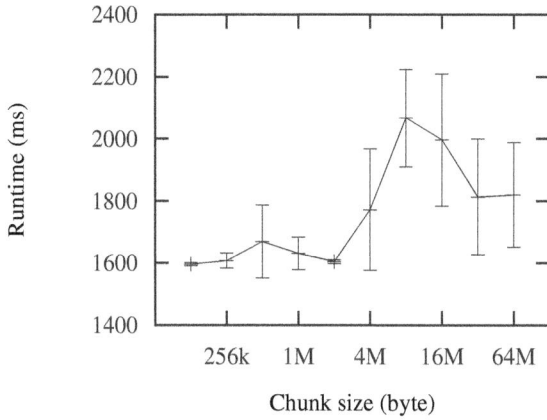

Figure 7: Total runtime of backprop for various chunk sizes

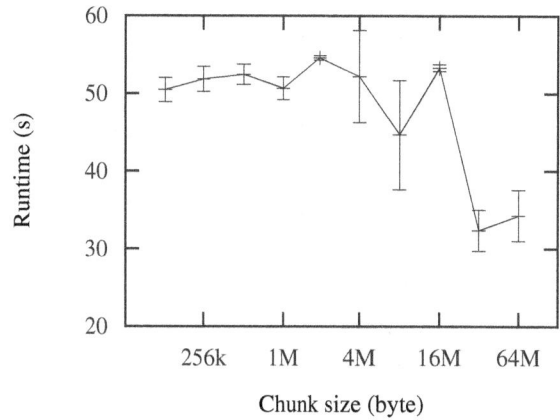

Figure 8: Total runtime of heartwall for various chunk sizes

tion of the DMA transfers, and hence to both applications requesting memory and applications losing memory due to allocation requests from other applications. This increased jitter was to be expected since more concurrent applications increase the potential for contention on the PCI-e bus.

6.5 Chunk size

GPUswap manages GPU memory in chunks as a compromise between granularity and computational overhead. In order to study the runtime effects of the chunk size, we ran two instances of each of our benchmark applications with the available GPU memory limited to 100 MB, while gradually increasing the chunk size from 128 kb – which equals one large page – to 64 MB. For each chunk size, we started each application ten times. We first measured the total runtime of each application's main computation step as described in our second experiment (Section 6.3). Our results indicate that the effect of different chunk sizes on the application runtime depends heavily on the application. Some applications, such as backprop (Figure 7), benefit from small chunk sizes, while others, such as heartwall (Figure 8), prefer larger chunks. As

the effect of the chunk size on the other applications was generally weaker than on backprop and heartwall, we chose not to show these results for brevity. However, the results do not indicate a clear trend towards a specific chunk size. We therefore conclude that there is no single chunk size that is optimal for all applications in terms of total runtime. In the future, we plan to investigate why specific chunk sizes are optimal for certain applications, which will allow us to select an appropriate chunk size dynamically for each application.

We also measured the average delay experienced by memory allocation requests across all applications as described in Section 6.4 for chunk sizes from 128 kb to 64 MB. Our results, which are depicted in Figure 9, indicate that a chunk size of 2 MB minimizes the allocation delay. At smaller chunk sizes, GPUswap must consider a large number of chunks, which leads to a high computational overhead if a large amount of memory must be relocated, while at larger chunk sizes, the delay is dominated by long DMA transfer times. For the moment, we therefore chose 2 MB as GPUswap's default chunk size.

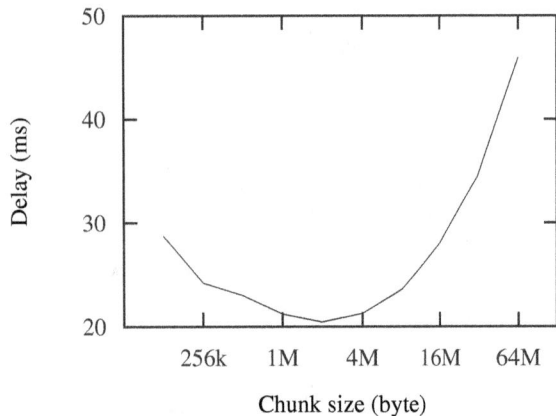

Figure 9: The average allocation delay across all benchmark applications for various chunk sizes

7. Related Work

Several previous projects have considered the use of GPUs in a shared environment. GViM [6], gVirtuS [4], rCUDA [3] and vCUDA [15] all work by intercepting high-level (e.g., CUDA or OpenCL) GPU commands in the guest VM and forwarding those commands to the hypervisor. Time-Graph [10] and PTask [14] instead intercept GPU commands at the operating system level, either by trapping accesses to the GPU's command submission channels, or by offering a custom API. GPUvm [16], gVirt [17] and LoGV [5] take a hybrid approach, intercepting only commands related to GPU resource allocation, while granting the application direct access to the GPU's command submission channels. Though all of these projects enable sharing of a GPU between multiple guest VMs, to our knowledge, none of them specifically address GPU memory. Note that while GPUswap re-uses some techniques from LoGV – most notably unmapping of command submission channels – the two are completely separate projects: LoGV does not address memory fairness, while GPUswap is not aware of guest applications. However, the two could likely be integrated for use in production cloud environments.

Gdev [11] implements software scheduling of low-level GPU commands, and uses its control over GPU command execution to enable a limited form of GPU buffer sharing between applications. Gdev extends the available GPU memory by alternating the contents of shared buffers between applications during scheduling, always copying the content of the next application to run onto the GPU. GDM [18] later removed virtually all of Gdev's restrictions by instead copying the entire application memory to the GPU during scheduling. Both Gdev and GDM can thus allocate more GPU memory than physically available; however, both also rely on software scheduling, thus inducing considerable runtime overhead even if enough free GPU memory is available.

Nvidia's Unified Memory, which was integrated into the CUDA SDK [12] in version 6, creates a single address space shared between CPU and GPU by transparently synchronizing the contents of system RAM and GPU memory. However, to the best of our understanding, Unified Memory does not enable oversubscription of GPU memory since all GPU memory shared in this fashion must be allocated on the GPU. In addition, Unified Memory is implemented in the user-space CUDA runtime and can thus not evict other applications' memory from the GPU, which makes it impossible to enforce fairness.

RSVM [7] also manages GPU memory on the application level. RSVM consists of a shared library which hides the complexity of GPU memory management from the application and is able to extend GPU memory using system RAM. However, applications must use the RSVM library explicitly. RSVM thus depends on cooperation from the application and is therefore not suitable for a cloud environment containing multiple, mutually untrusted applications.

8. Conclusion

In this paper, we presented GPUswap, a novel approach to enabling oversubscription of GPU memory that does not depend on software scheduling of GPU kernels. GPUswap transparently relocates application data from the GPU into system RAM, while keeping this data permanently accessible to the application. Therefore, GPUswap allows applications to submit commands to the GPU directly at any time, without involving the GPU driver or GPUswap. Experiments with our prototype implementation indicate that the avoidance of software scheduling in GPUswap increases performance while sufficient GPU memory is available. However, relocating large portions of application data to system RAM has a significant impact on application performance.

GPUswap is under active development, and there are two main issues that we plan to address in the future. First, since GPUswap is still limited to Nvidia Fermi GPUs, we are working on porting our prototype to the Nouveau driver, which will allow us to evaluate GPUswap on Nvidia's latest GPU hardware. Second, it is currently difficult to select appropriate memory for relocation due to the lack of appropriate hardware support – such as reference bits – in current GPUs. We are currently exploring ways to limit the performance impact of GPUswap by detecting particularly poor selections – for example, the GPU's built-in performance counters could allow us to detect an increased number of bus transactions in response to a chunk relocation.

References

[1] S. Che, M. Boyer, J. Meng, D. Tarjan, J. Sheaffer, S.-H. Lee, and K. Skadron. Rodinia: A benchmark suite for heterogeneous computing. In *Proceedings of the 5th International Symposium on Workload Characterization*, IISWC '09, pages 44–54, Austin, TX, Oct. 2009. IEEE.

[2] C. Clark, K. Fraser, S. Hand, J. G. Hansen, E. Jul, C. Limpach, I. Pratt, and A. Warfield. Live migration of virtual machines. In *Proceedings of the 2nd Symposium on Networked Systems Design & Implementation*, NSDI '05, pages 273–286, Boston, MA, USA, May 2005. USENIX Association.

[3] J. Duato, A. Pena, F. Silla, J. Fernandez, R. Mayo, and E. Quintana-Orti. Enabling CUDA acceleration within virtual machines using rCUDA. In *Proceedings of the 18th International Conference on High Performance Computing*, HiPC '11, pages 1–10, Bengaluru, India, Dec. 2011.

[4] G. Giunta, R. Montella, G. Agrillo, and G. Coviello. A GPGPU transparent virtualization component for high-performance computing clouds. In *Proceedings of the 16th International Euro-Par Conference on Parallel processing*, Euro-Par '10, pages 379–391, Naples, Italy, Sept. 2010. Springer.

[5] M. Gottschlag, M. Hillenbrand, J. Kehne, J. Stoess, and F. Bellosa. LoGV: Low-overhead GPGPU virtualization. In *Proceedings of the 4th International Workshop on Frontiers of Heterogeneous Computing*, FHC '13, pages 1721–1726, Zhangjiajie, China, Nov. 2013. IEEE.

[6] V. Gupta, A. Gavrilovska, K. Schwan, H. Kharche, N. Tolia, V. Talwar, and P. Ranganathan. GViM: GPU-accelerated virtual machines. In *Proceedings of the 3rd ACM Workshop on System-level Virtualization for High Performance Computing*, HPCVirt '09, pages 17–24, Nuremberg, Germany, Apr. 2009. ACM.

[7] F. Ji, H. Lin, and X. Ma. RSVM: A region-based software virtual memory for GPU. In *Proceedings of the 22nd International Conference on Parallel Architectures and Compilation Techniques*, PACT '13, pages 269–278, Edinburgh, Scotland, Sept. 2013. IEEE.

[8] S. Kato. Rodinia for gdev. `https://github.com/shinpei0208/gdev-bench`, Nov. 2014.

[9] S. Kato. Gdev. `https://github.com/shinpei0208/gdev`, Nov. 2014.

[10] S. Kato, K. Lakshmanan, R. R. Rajkumar, and Y. Ishikawa. TimeGraph: GPU scheduling for real-time multi-tasking environments. In *Proceedings of the 2011 USENIX Annual Technical Conference*, USENIX ATC '11, pages 17–30, Portland, OR, USA, June 2011. USENIX Association.

[11] S. Kato, M. McThrow, C. Maltzahn, and S. Brandt. Gdev: First-class GPU resource management in the operating system. In *Proceedings of the 2012 USENIX Annual Technical Conference*, USENIX ATC '12, pages 401–412, Boston, MA, USA, June 2012. USENIX Association.

[12] Nvidia Corporation. CUDA toolkit. `https://developer.nvidia.com/cuda-toolkit`, 2014.

[13] PathScale. Pscnv. `https://github.com/pathscale/pscnv`, Nov. 2014.

[14] C. J. Rossbach, J. Currey, M. Silberstein, B. Ray, and E. Witchel. PTask: Operating system abstractions to manage GPUs as compute devices. In *Proceedings of the 23th Symposium on Operating System Principles*, SOSP '11, pages 233–248, Cascais, Portugal, Sept. 2011. ACM.

[15] L. Shi, H. Chen, J. Sun, and K. Li. vCUDA: GPU-accelerated high-performance computing in virtual machines. *IEEE Transactions on Computers*, 61(6):804–816, June 2012.

[16] Y. Suzuki, S. Kato, H. Yamada, and K. Kono. GPUvm: Why not virtualizing GPUs at the hypervisor? In *Proceedings of the 2014 USENIX Annual Technical Conference*, USENIX ATC '14, pages 109–120, Philadelphia, PA, June 2014. USENIX Association.

[17] K. Tian, Y. Dong, and D. Cowperthwaite. A full GPU virtualization solution with mediated pass-through. In *Proceedings of the 2014 USENIX Annual Technical Conference*, USENIX ATC '14, pages 121–132, Philadelphia, PA, June 2014. USENIX Association.

[18] K. Wang, X. Ding, R. Lee, S. Kato, and X. Zhang. GDM: Device memory management for GPGPU computing. In *Proceedings of the 2014 ACM International Conference on Measurement and Modeling of Computer Systems*, SIGMETRICS '14, pages 533–545, Austin, TX, USA, June 2014. ACM.

HeteroVisor: Exploiting Resource Heterogeneity to Enhance the Elasticity of Cloud Platforms

Vishal Gupta

VMware

vishalg@vmware.com

Min Lee

Intel

min.lee@intel.com

Karsten Schwan

Georgia Institute of Technology

schwan@cc.gatech.edu

Abstract

This paper presents HeteroVisor, a heterogeneity-aware hypervisor, that exploits resource heterogeneity to enhance the elasticity of cloud systems. Introducing the notion of 'elasticity' (E) states, HeteroVisor permits applications to manage their changes in resource requirements as state transitions that implicitly move their execution among heterogeneous platform components. Masking the details of platform heterogeneity from virtual machines, the E-state abstraction allows applications to adapt their resource usage in a fine-grained manner via VM-specific 'elasticity drivers' encoding VM-desired policies. The approach is explored for the heterogeneous processor and memory subsystems evolving for modern server platforms, leading to mechanisms that can manage these heterogeneous resources dynamically and as required by the different VMs being run. HeteroVisor is implemented for the Xen hypervisor, with mechanisms that go beyond core scaling to also deal with memory resources, via the online detection of hot memory pages and transparent page migration. Evaluation on an emulated heterogeneous platform uses workload traces from real-world data, demonstrating the ability to provide high on-demand performance while also reducing resource usage for these workloads.

Categories and Subject Descriptors D.4.0 [*Operating Systems*]: General

General Terms Design, Performance

Keywords Heterogeneous platforms, Cloud elasticity

1. Introduction

Elasticity in cloud infrastructures enables 'on-demand' scaling of the resources used by an application. Resource scaling

VEE '15, March 14–15, 2015, Istanbul, Turkey.
Copyright © 2015 ACM 978-1-4503-3450-1/15/03... $15.00.
http://dx.doi.org/10.1145/2731186.2731191

techniques used by modern cloud platforms like Amazon's Elastic Compute Cloud (EC2), involving the use of different types of virtual machines (VMs), however, are coarse-grained, both in space and in time. This has substantial monetary implications for customers, due to the costs incurred for limited sets of fixed types of VM instances and the frequencies at which heavy-weight scaling operations can be performed. Customers could implement their VM-internal solutions to this problem, but a *truly elastic* execution environment should provide 'fine-grained' scaling capabilities able to *frequently* adjust the resource allocations of applications in an *incremental* manner. Given the competition among cloud providers for better services, fine-grained resource management may prove to be a compelling feature of future cloud platforms [1, 13].

An emerging trend shaping future systems is the presence of heterogeneity in server platforms, including their processors, memories, and storage. Processors may differ in the levels of performance offered [12, 24], like the big/little cores commonly found in today's client systems. Memory heterogeneity can arise from the combined use of high speed 3D die-stacked memory, slower off-chip DRAM, and non-volatile memory [11, 30, 40, 44]. Such heterogeneity challenges system management, but we view it as an opportunity to improve future systems' scaling capabilities, by making it possible for execution contexts to move among heterogeneous components via dynamic 'spill' operations, in a fine-grained manner and driven by application needs.

The *HeteroVisor* virtual machine monitor presented in this paper hides the underlying complexity associated with platform heterogeneity from applications, yet provides them with a highly elastic execution environment. Guest VMs see what appears to be a homogeneous, yet scalable, virtual resource, which the hypervisor maintainsby appropriately mapping the virtual resource to underlying heterogeneous platform components. Specifically,HeteroVisor presents to guests the abstraction of *elasticity (E) states*, which provides them with a channel for dynamically expressing their resource requirements, without having to understand in detail the heterogeneity present in underlying hardware. Inspired by the already existing P-state interface [38] usedto scale the frequency and voltage of processors, E-states generalizes that concept to address with one unified abstraction the multiple types of resource heterogeneity seen in future servers, including their processors and memory. As with P-state changes, E-state transitions triggered by applications provide hints to the hypervisor on managing the resources assigned to each VM, but for E-state changes, guests can further refine those hints via system- or application-level modules called *elasticity drivers* (like the Linux CPU governor in the case of P-states) to indicate preferences concerning such management. HeteroVisor uses them to better carry out the fine-grain adjustments needed by dynamic guests.

With heterogeneous CPUs, E-states are used to provide the abstraction of a scalable virtual CPU (vCPU) to applications desiring to operate at some requested elastic speed that may differ from that of any one of the actual heterogeneous physical cores. Such fine-grained speed adjustments are achieved by dynamically mapping the vCPUs in question to appropriate cores and in addition, imposing *usage caps* on vCPUs. For heterogeneous memories, E-states provide the abstraction of performance-scalable memory, with multiple performance levels obtained by adjusting guests' allocations of fast vs. slower memory resources.

E-states are challenging to implement. Concerning CPUs, fine-grained E-state adjustments seen by the hypervisor shouldbe honored in ways that efficiently use underlying cores, e.g., without unduly high levels of core switching.The issue is addressed by novel vCPU scaling methods in HeteroVisor. Concerning memory, previous work has shown that application performance is governed not by the total amount of fast vs. slow memory allocated to an application, but instead, by the fast vs. slow memory speeds experienced by an application's current memory footprint [27]. HeteroVisor addresses this by maintaining a page access-bit history for each VM, obtained by periodically scanning the access-bits available in page tables. This history is used to detect a guest's 'hot' memory pages, i.e., the current memory footprints of the running applications. Further, by mirroring guest page tables in the hypervisor, it can manipulate guest page mappings in a guest-transparent manner, thus making possible hot page migrations (between slower vs. faster memories), by simply changing mappings in these mirror page tables, without guest involvement. A final challenge is to decide which resources should be scaled to what extent, given the potential processor- vs. memory-intensive nature of an application. HeteroVisor'ssolution is to permit guest VMs to express their scaling preferences in per-VM 'elasticity drivers'.

HeteroVisor's implementation in the Xen hypervisor [4] is evaluated with realistic applications and workloads onactual hardware, not relying on architectural simulators. CPU and memory controller throttling are used to emulate processor and memory subsystem heterogeneity. For workloads derived from traces of Google cluster usage data [18], exper-

imental results show that by exploiting heterogeneity in the unobtrusive ways advocated by our work, it becomes possible to achieve on-demand performance boosts as well as cost savings for guest applications with diverse resource requirements. The CPU and memory scaling mechanisms provide up to 2.3x improved quality-of-service (QoS), while also reducing CPU and memory resource usage by an average 21% and 30%, respectively. Elasticity drivers are shown useful via comparison of two different guest usage policies, resulting in different trade-offs between QoS and cost.

2. Elasticity via Heterogeneity

2.1 Elasticity in Clouds

Elasticity, i.e., the ability to scale resources on-demand to minimize cost, is an attractive feature of cloud computing systems. Resources can be scaled in a 'scale out' or 'scale up' manner. Table 1 shows a comparison summary of these two approaches. Scale-out varies the number of VM instances used by an application. It is used in commercial cloud services like Amazon EC2 AutoScaleto increase capacity in the form of additional VMs of fixed instance types, where instances can be rented in the order of several minutes to a full hour, and users are charged for the whole instance even if it is only partially used. Thus, scale out is a rather heavy-weight and coarse-grained operation with high end-user cost implications.

Table 1: Elastic resource scaling in clouds

	Scale out	Scale up
Scaling Method	VM Instances	Resource Shares
Resource Granularity	Coarse	Fine
Time Granularity	Slow	Fast
Software Changes	High	Minimal

'Scale up' operations entail adjusting the shares of platform resources to which a VM is entitled. Such fine-grained elasticity enables a user to start a VM with some basic configuration and dynamically alterthe platform configuration it needs. Such scaling may be sufficient for and in fact, preferable to VM-level scaling, e.g., when a VM experiences sudden short bursts requiring temporarily higher levels of resources. For current cloud users, the presence of such functionality would mean shorter rent durations (on the order of seconds)and reduced costs. Another advantage is that such scaling can be transparent to the VM, not requiring sophisticated software changes or VM-level management methods to deal with varying resource needs.

2.2 Resource Heterogeneity

HeteroVisor enhances the scaling capabilities of future cloud computing systems by exploiting the increasing levels of resource heterogeneity seen in server platforms. Evidence of such heterogeneity abounds. Heterogeneous processors, i.e., CPU cores that differ in their performance/power capabilities (as shown in Figure 1), are known to be energy-efficient alternatives to homogeneous configurations [12, 24, 48], underlined by commercial implementations from CPU vendors [16, 35]and encouraged by research demonstrating the utility of low-powered cores for datacenter applications [3, 20] and by methods that efficiently utilize brawny cores [5, 26]. Schedulers for heterogeneous cores have seen extensive exploration [23, 24, 39, 41, 45].

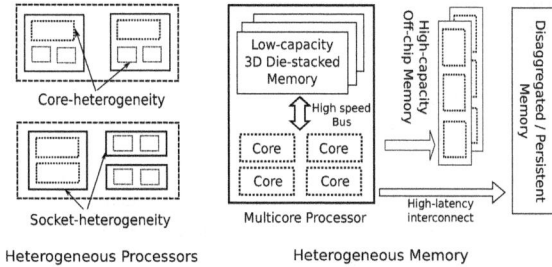

Figure 1: Platforms with heterogeneous resources

Heterogeneity in memory technologies has gone beyond the NUMA properties seen in high-end server platforms.New memory technologies like die-stacked 3D memories and non-volatile memories, in addition to traditional DRAM, can result in a hierarchy of heterogeneous memory organization, as shown in Figure 1. 3D stacked memories can provide lower latency and higher bandwidth, in comparison to traditional off-chip memories [29]. But since the capacity of such memories is limited [30], future servers expect to have a combination of both fast on-chip memory and additional slower off-chip memory. Moreover, inclusion of disaggregated memory or persistent memory technologies will further extend memory heterogeneity [11, 28, 40, 44].

Heterogeneity is already present in storage subsystems when using local vs. remote storage, SSDs vs. hard drives, andfuture persistent memory. HeteroVisor is concerned with heterogeneity in platforms' CPU and memory subsystems, but its general approach is applicable to other resources, as well.

2.3 Exploiting Heterogeneity

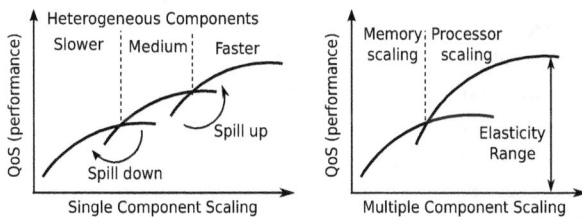

Figure 2: Using heterogeneity to enable resource scaling

HeteroVisor enhances a server's elastic resource scaling capabilities with an approach in which 'spill' operations change the heterogeneity of VMs' resource allocations. Consider a resource like memory with heterogeneous components with three different performance characteristics, i.e.,

die-stacked DRAM as the fast resource, off-chip DRAM as the medium-performance resource, and non-volatile memory as the slow resource. With each of these components supporting a different performance range, the performance of the memory subsystem seen by each guest VM can be adjusted across a wide range, by varying the allocation mix given to the application. As a higher share of a VM's resources are allocated in faster memory (e.g., by moving application data to on-chip memory from off-chip DRAM), its performance increases. This is denoted as a 'spill up' operation, as shown in Figure 2. Similarly, by 'spilling down' the application resource (e.g., ballooning out VM pages to persistent memory), performance can be lowered, perhaps in response to an application-level decrease in the memory intensity of its activities. In this manner, the hypervisor provides to guest VMs the abstraction of scalable memory, internally using spill operations over the underlying heterogeneous components. Further, by appropriately allocating various amounts of slower vs. faster memory to applications, memory scaling can extend beyond the three different physical speeds present in physical hardware (i.e., 3D die stacked RAM, off-chip DRAM, NVRAM) to offer what appear to be finer grain scaled memory speeds andbandwidths.

The scaling mechanisms outlined for memory above can be applied to other platform resources, including processor andstorage components, to provide an overall extended elasticity range to an application, as shown in Figure 2. Furthermore, this elasticity extends across multiple resource types,so that HeteroVisor can offer guest VMs slow processors with rapidly accessible memory for data-intensiveapplications, while a CPU-intensive guest with good cache behavior may be well-served with slower memory components. When doing so, the different components' use is governed by spill operations: (i) processor scaling is achieved by appropriate scheduling of vCPUs to heterogeneous cores and capping their usage of these cores to achieve a target speed, and (ii) memory spill operations manage memory usage. Note that considerable complexity for the latter arises from the facts that page migrations may incur large overheads and more importantly, because the hypervisor does not have direct visibility into a VM's memory access pattern (to the different memory allocated to it) determining its performance. HeteroVisor addresses this issue by developing efficient mechanismsto detect a guest VM's 'hot' pages, i.e., frequently accessed pages, and then moving those between different memories without guest involvement. The next section describes the various mechanisms incorporated into HeteroVisor to implement resource scaling.

3. Design

Using heterogeneous platform resources, HeteroVisor provides fine-grained elasticity for cloud platforms. To incorporate heterogeneity into the scaling methods, there are several principles that we follow in our design.

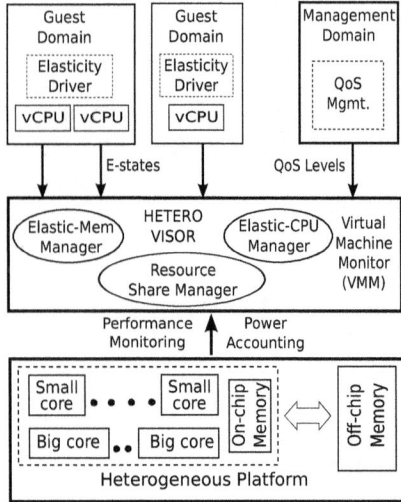

Figure 3: System architecture for HeteroVisor

- Adhering to the philosophy that cloud platforms should sell resources and not performance, VMs should explicitly request resources from the cloud provider. This design requiring application VMs to specify their resource requirements is common to IaaS platforms where users select different types of VM instances.

- Typically special software support is required for managing heterogeneity. Diversity across vendors and rapidly changing hardware make it difficult for operating systems to incorporate explicit mechanisms for managing these components. Thus, the complexity of managing heterogeneous components should be hidden from the users.

- The resource scaling interface should be generic and extensible to allow its use on various platforms with different heterogeneous configurations. It should allow scaling of resources in incremental ways and should be lightweight in nature for frequent reconfiguration. It should also work with multiple resources.

Figure 3 depicts HeteroVisor, its various components, and their interactions. The underlying server platform consists of heterogeneous CPUs and memory, and it provides capabilities for online performance and power monitoring. The platform is shared by multiple guest virtual machines, where each VM communicates with the hypervisor about its resource requirements through the *elasticity (E) state* interface (detailed in Section 3.1). E-states are controlled by an *E-state driver* module, allowing the guest VM to communicate its changing resource needs and usage as state transitions. The hypervisor contains heterogeneity-aware elastic resource managers including a CPU scheduler and, memory manager. It also contains a resource share manager which is the higher-level resource allocator that takes into account various E-state inputs from the VMs and QoS related policy constraints from the management domain, to partition resources across all VMs, whereas the CPU and memory man-

agers enforce these partitions and manage them efficiently for each VM. These components are described in more detail next.

3.1 Elasticity States

Inspired by the P-state (performance-state) interface [38] defined by the ACPI standard and used to control CPU voltage and frequency (DVFS), the E-state (elasticity-state) abstraction permits VMs to provide hints to the hypervisor, governed by VM-specific E-state drivers.

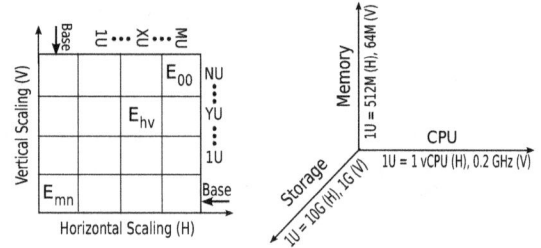

Figure 4: Elasticity state abstraction for resource scaling

The E-state interface defines multiple states, where each state corresponds to a different resource configuration. E-states are arranged along two dimensions, corresponding to horizontal and vertical scaling as shown in Figure 4. Horizontal scaling makes it possible to add virtual resources to the application, using hot-plug based mechanisms; vertical scaling implies boosting the performance of existing platform resources. Both horizontal and vertical scaling are scale up methods, separate from the scale out methods varying the number VM instances. As in the case of P-states, a higher numbered E-state (E_{mn}) represents a lower resource configuration, while a lower numbered E-state (E_{00}) implies a higher performance mode. Further, these states are specific to each scalable component, resulting in separate state specifications for processor, memory, and storage subsystems. For all resource types, however, a change in E-state implies a request to change the allocation of resources to that VM by a certain number of resource units (U). For the CPU component, a horizontal E-state operation changes the number of vCPUs, while vertical scaling adjusts vCPU speed in units of CPU frequency. Similarly, for the memory subsystem, horizontal scaling is achieved by changing its overall memory allocation, while vertical scaling adjusts its current allocation in terms of usage of fast/slow memory (at page granularity). HeteroVisor's current policies are concerned with vertical scaling in the presence of heterogeneous resources, explainedin more detail next.

3.2 Elastic CPU Manager

Heterogeneous resources consisting of components with different performance levels can be used to provide a virtual, highly elastic server system. We next describe how this can be achieved for heterogeneous cores,with a formulation specialized for the case of two different types of cores (this can be generalized to multiple performance levels). Section 3.3 extends the approach to heterogeneous memory systems.

3.2.1 Virtual Core Scaling:

Given a platform configuration with heterogeneous cores, the objective of the elastic CPU manager is to provide to a guest VMhomogeneous virtual cores running at some desired speed that may be different from the speeds of the physical cores being used. This can be achieved by appropriate scheduling of the vCPUs on these heterogeneous cores and assigning a *usage cap* to each vCPU, limiting its usage of physical resources. For such scaling, our current approach schedules all vCPUs on slow cores initially, with fast cores kept idle, the assumption being that slow cores have lower ownership costs for the cloud usersrequesting resources for their VMs. As vCPUs are scaled up, the slow core cap of vCPUs is increased to meet the desired scaling speed.When slow core cycles are saturated, further scaling results in vCPUs being scheduled to fast cores, providing higher scaled speeds than what is possible with slow cores only.

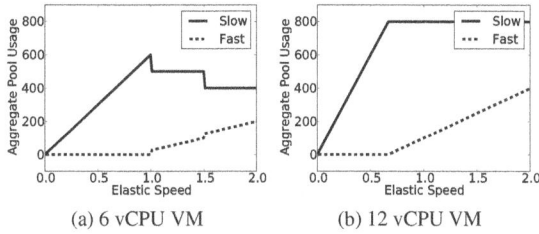

(a) 6 vCPU VM   (b) 12 vCPU VM

Figure 5: Models for vCPU scaling using heterogeneity

The expressions for the corresponding usage caps of various cores for achieving a given effective processing speed can be obtained by formulating a linear optimization problem, solvable using standard solvers. Since allocations must be computed in kernel-space, instead of relying on external solvers, we obtain a closed-form solution for the special case of two types of cores, slow (s) and fast (f), where slow cores have lower ownership cost than fast cores, thereby prioritizing allocations to use slow cores before using fast cores. We omit the formulation and derivation of these expressions due to space constraints. Instead, Figure 5 plots the resultant equations for a configuration with 8 slow cores with 1x speed and 4 fast cores with 4x speed. The figure shows the aggregate slow and fast pool usage for a VM (total percentage utilization caps are assigned collectively to all vCPUs) as we vary the elastic core speed. Two different VM configurations are plotted, by varying the number of vCPUs in the VM to 6 and 12.

In both the cases, slow pool usage first increases linearly as we increase the elastic core speed (solid lines). Once slow cores are saturated at usage values 600 for 6 vCPUs and 800 for 12 vCPUs (constrained by 8 physical slow cores), fast pool usage gradually increases (see the dotted lines) to obtain the requested elastic scaling. For example, a VM with

12 vCPUs at speed 1U exhibits 800% slow pool utilization (8 slow cores fully utilized) and 100% fast pool usage (1 fast core with speed 4x). We also see jumps in the CPU usage with v_n equal to 6 at speed 1 and 1.5, which happens due to the shift of a slow pool vCPU to the fast pool.

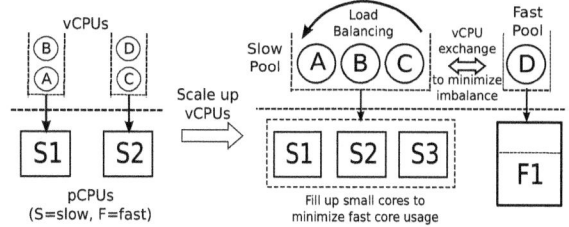

Figure 6: Virtual core scaling using heterogeneous cores

For elastic scaling, vCPUs are partitioned into two pools, one corresponding to the each type of core, i.e., slow and fast pool. Each vCPU executes within a particular pool and is load-balanced among other vCPUs belonging to that pool, as shown in Figure 6. Because of this partitioning of vCPUs into pools, there may arise performance imbalances among vCPUs. To deal with this, a rotation is performed periodically among pools to exchange some vCPU, thus giving every vCPU a chance to run on the fast cores, resulting in better balanced performance. Such migrations have very little cost if done infrequently and particularly if the cores involved share a last-level cache.

3.2.2 Implementation:

Virtual core scaling is implemented by augmenting Xen's CPU credit scheduler by adding two different types of credits: slow and fast. Credits represent the resource right of a VM to execute on the respective types of cores and are distributed periodically (30ms) to each running VM. A vCPU owns one type of credits during one accounting period. As the VM executes, its credits are decremented periodically (every 30ms) based upon the type of cores it uses. A vCPU can execute as far as it has positive credits available. Once it has consumed all credits, it goes offline by being placed into a separate 'parking queue' until the next allocation period. At this point, the credits are redistributed to each VM, and its vCPUs are again made available for scheduling. Further, a circular queue of vCPUs is maintained to periodically rotate vCPUs between slow and fast cores.We find it sufficient to use a granularity of 10 scheduler ticks, i.e., at a frequency of 300ms, for this purpose,for the long-running server workloads used in our experimental evaluation.

3.3 Elastic Memory Manager

HeteroVisor realizes performance-scalable memory by changing a VM's memory allocation across underlying heterogeneous components, i.e., use of fast memory for high-performance E-states and slow memory for slower E-states. This section describes elasticity management for heterogeneous memories involving fast die-stacked memory and slow off-chip DRAMs. Since die-stacked memory is small in capacity in comparison to off-chip DRAM, a subset of pages from the application's memory must be chosen to be placed into stacked-DRAM. For this purpose, it is important to detect and manage the application's 'hot' pages that are critical to its performance. This requires the hypervisor to efficiently track each guest's memory accesses.

3.3.1 Memory Access Tracking:

Modern processors provide only limited hardware support for detecting application' memory access patterns. On the x86 architecture, each page table entry has an access bit, which is set by the hardware when the corresponding page is accessed. Software is responsible for clearing/using this bit. We use this single-bit information to build an access bit history to determine a VM's memory access pattern. Specifically, we periodically scan and collect the access bits, forming a bitmap, called an 'A-bit history' (access-bit history), shown in Figure 7. A 32-bit word and a 100ms time interval is used for scanning, implying 3.2 seconds of virtual time corresponding to one word. If the A-bit history has many ones, i.e., it is a dense A-bit history, this indicates that the page is hot and frequently accessed. A threshold of 22, obtained experimentally, is used in our work for marking a page as hot.

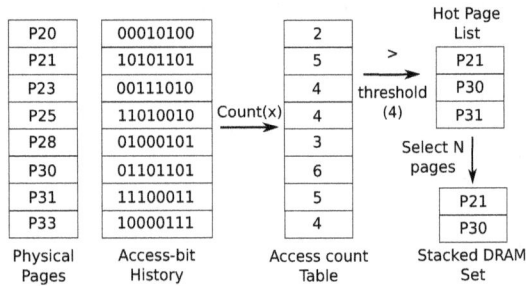

Figure 7: Tracking hot pages using access-bits

Since application processes within a guest VM run in virtual time, page tables are scanned over virtual time – every 100ms –rather than wall-clock time, for an accurate A-bit history.For accurate accounting, events like timer tick (TIMER), address space switches (NEW_CR3), and vCPU switches (SCHEDULE) are also taken into account.Our implementation collects and maintains an A-bit history for all machine frames for all guest VMs, including the management domain.

3.3.2 Hot Page Management:

Detected with the A-bit history, hot pages are actively managed by moving them in and out of fast/slow memories. There are four categories of pages and associated actions, depending on their residencies and status, as shown in Table 2. Active hot pages should be migrated to or maintained in fast memory, and inactive cold pages should be discarded.

While Cases 2 & 3 are relatively easy tasks, Actions 1 and 4 are the primary determinants of the overhead of page migrations, handled as described below.

Table 2: Hot page management actions

	Residency	Status	Action
1	Off-Chip	Active	Migrate to on-chip DRAM
2	Off-Chip	Inactive	Drop from the list
3	On-Chip	Active	Keep in on-chip DRAM
4	On-Chip	Inactive	Migrate to off-chip DRAM

Hot pages are managed to form a linked list (see Figure 8). Since this list can be quite long, its inspectioncan cause substantial overheads for scanning and migrating such pages. To efficiently manage this list, only parts of the list are considered at one time, where MAX_SCAN (currently 512) determines the number of pages that are scanned in a time window (every 100ms). Further, the removal of inactive pages may incur page migrations to off-chip memory, causing potentialperturbation seen by co-running applications. In addition, since pages freed by the guest are likely to be used again by the next job(since memory allocators in guest VMs often reuses previously freed pages), it is beneficial to employ 'lazy' page migrations, that is, to delay the eviction of selected pages from stacked DRAM. We do so by migrating only MAX_MFNS pages from the hot page list every time the list is scanned. Finally, TIME_WINDOW macro (3000ms) defines when a page in the list becomes inactive. Thus, if a page in the list is not accessed for 3000ms, it is considered inactive and eventually discarded.

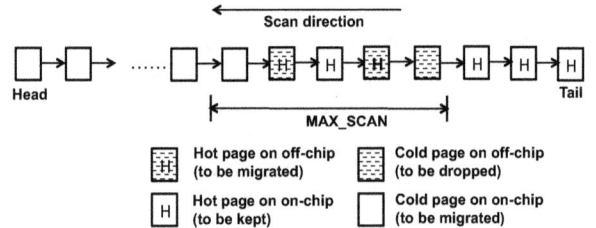

Figure 8: Hot page management and associated actions

A final note concerning hot page list management is that scanning happens in the reverse direction, as new pages are added to the front of the list, and the tail typically contains the oldest pages. This further reduces overhead, since it avoids unnecessary page migrations.

3.3.3 Transparent Page Migration:

Memory spill operations are performed by migrating pages between different memories. Such migrations require remapping guest page tables, which are hidden from the hypervisor. In order to do this in a guest-transparent way, HeteroVisor*mirrors* guest page tables.For para-virtualized guests, page tables are write-protected and require the hypervisor's involvement in updating page table entries through a hypercall. We simply intercept these calls and re-create a mirror version of the page tables as shown in Figure 9 and install them in the CR3 hardware register, forcing the guest to use these mirrors. This allows us to freely change virtual-to-physical mappings, without any changes to the guest OS. For fully virtualized guests, these mechanisms may be simplified by hardware supports such as NPT (nested page table) or EPT (Extended page table). These architectural extensions implement an extra level of address translation so this extra layer can be used to implement transparent page migrations.

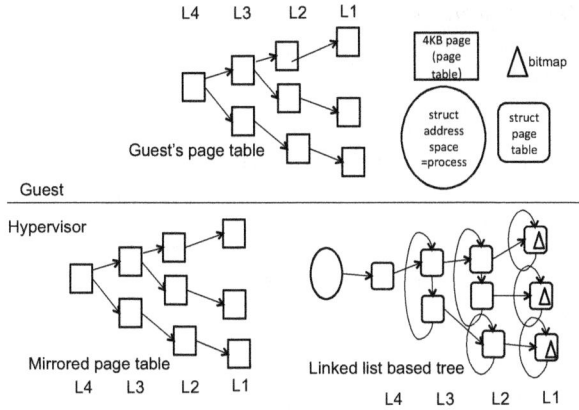

Figure 9: Mirror page tables for page migrations

Additional optimizations serve to minimize negative impacts on cache behavior. Rather than scanning page tables completely, separate metadata structures using linked lists and pointers (see Figure 9) are used for easy iteration over page table entries, optimizing page table scanning for access bits. Without this optimization, the whole 4KB of each page table would be scanned, thus trashing cache real estate (i.e., 4KB-worth cache lines). This is particularly important for interior (L2, L3, L4) page tables. Further, only existing mappings are managed in this list, thereby effectively eliminating unnecessary scans. Finally, L1 page tables (leaf node) use a bitmap to quickly detect present pages. This again eliminates unnecessary scans on the L1 page table and prevents valuable cache lines from being evicted.

3.3.4 Handling Shared Pages:

Since any machine frame can be shared between multiple processes/guests, all of the corresponding page table entries must be updated when migrating such a page. To do this efficiently, we employ *reverse maps* (Rmaps) that store this reverse mapping information, i.e., from a page in physical memory to entries in various page tables. We can iterate over this Rmap list to find all of the mappings to a given page, thus enabling efficient remapping for any given page. Each machine page (mfn) is associated with one Rmap_list that contains pointers to page table and page table index.

3.4 Elasticity Driver

Elasticity drivers are the guest-specific components of the HeteroVisor stack, allowing guest VMs to guide resource al-

location by triggering E-state transitions, in a manner similar to the CPU governor making P-state (performance-state) changes in the context of DVFS (dynamic voltage and frequency scaling) [38]. Interesting resource management policies can be implemented by using different implementations of the driver, thus permitting each application (i.e., guest VM orsome set of guest VMs – a VM ensemble) to choose a specific driver catering to its requirements. Various solutions (e.g., RightScale) are already available to implement resource scaling controllers for applications, and by making it easy to employ such solutions, the E-state driver is a step forward in giving applications fine-grained controlover how their resources are managed. HeteroVisor does not require guests to specify E-state drivers, of course, thus also able to support traditional VMs with static configurations, but such VMs will likely experience cost/performance penalties due to over/under-provisioning oftheir resources.

We note that it should be clear from these descriptions that guest VMs can use custom and potentially, quite sophisticated controllers in their E-state drivers, including prediction-based mechanisms [42] that model application behavior to determine the resultant E-state changes. The E-state driver used in our current work implements a simple reactive heuristic for illustration. The driver performs the scaling in two steps:

Step 1: First pick a resource for scaling (CPU, memory) for the current epoch

Step 2: Request scaling operation (up, down, or no change) for the selected resource

To select a resource for scaling, it needs to consider two factors in making this decision: the application's sensitivity to the resource and the cost of the resource to obtain best performance for minimum cost. The current driver uses IPC (instructions-per-cycle) as the metric to determine an application's sensitivity to CPU or memory. If IPC is high, scaling is performed along the CPU axis for that epoch; otherwise, it picks the memory resource for scaling. It currently assigns equal cost to both types of resources (CPU and memory), but any cost values can be incorporated in the heuristic to obtain the desired cost/performance trade-off.

The scaling heuristic used employs a combination of utility factor (*util*) and application performance (*qos*) to form the E-state transition logic shown in Algorithm 1. The utility factor is analogous to CPU/memory utilization, i.e., the percentage of resources (CPU usage cap or memory pages) consumed by a VM against its assigned usage. Similarly, the QoS metrics, such as response time or response rate, can be obtained from the application. Specifically, for these metrics, the E-state driver defines four thresholds: qos_{hi}, qos_{lo}, $util_{hi}$, and $util_{lo}$. If *qos* is lower than the minimum required performance qos_{lo} or if the utility factor is higher than $util_{hi}$ mark, an E-state scaleup operation is requested. Scale down logic requires *qos* to be higher than qos_{hi} and *util* to be lower than the $util_{lo}$ threshold.

Intuitively, if the application performance is lower than its SLA or if the utility factor is too high, which may cause SLA violations, a scale up operation is issued to request more resources. On the other hand, if application performance is higher than its desired SLA, a scale down operation can be issued, given that the utility factor is low to avoid violations after scaling. In order to avoid oscillations due to transitory application behavior, history counters are used to dampen switching frequency. Specifically, a switch is requested only after a fixed number of consecutive identical E-state change requests are received. The history counter is a simple integer counter, which is incremented whenever consecutive intervals generate the same requests and reset otherwise.

Algorithm 1: Elasticity-Driver Scaling Heuristic

---

if $util > util_{hi}$ OR $qos < qos_{lo}$ **then**
    $E_{next} \leftarrow E_{cur-1}$;   `// Scale up`
else if $util < util_{lo}$ AND $qos > qos_{hi}$ **then**
    $E_{next} \leftarrow E_{cur+1}$;   `// Scale down`
else
    $E_{next} \leftarrow E_{cur}$;   `// No change`

The E-state driver is implemented as a Linux kernel module that periodically changes E-states by issuing a hypercall to Xen. The driver uses a QoS interface in the form of a proc file to which the application periodically writes its QoS metric. In addition, it reads the VM utility factor from the hypervisor through a hypercall interface. The E-state driver runs once every second, with a value of three for the history counter and 1.25 as the IPC cut-off for resource selection.

3.5 Resource Share Manager

HeteroVisor uses a tiered-service model where different clients can receive different levels of quality of service. Clients requesting higher QoS and thus paying higher cost, obtain better guaranties in terms of resource allocation, by prioritizing allocations to their VMs. In comparison, clients with lower QoS requirements obtain resources as they become available. Such clients with different QoS levels can be co-run, to minimize resource waste while maintaining QoS. An example of such a service is Amazon EC2 Spot instances which run along with standard EC2 instances and receive resources when unused by standard instances. In such scenarios, each VM is assigned a QoS-level (similar to Q-states [34]) by the administrator that states its willingness to pay. The allocation is then performed for each resource to determine the share of each VM, taking into account any E-state and Q-state changes, as shown in Algorithm 2. The allocation happens periodically and proceeds in multiple phases, as described below.
Phase 1: to ensure fairness in allocation, a minimum share value is assigned to each application (if given), so that no high QoS application can starve lower QoS applications. **Phase 2:** the allocation is done in sorted order of VM Q-states. For each VM, it increases or decreases its resource

allocation by a fixed fraction (δ) depending on the desired E-state change by that VM as 'up' or 'down', respectively. Otherwise, the allocation is kept constant. **Phase 3:** After allocating shares to all the applications, any remaining resource shares are assigned to low QoS instances which are willing to accept as many resource as available.

Algorithm 2: Resource Share Allocation Algorithm

Input: $estate(vm_i), qstate(vm_i)$
Output: $share(vm_i)$
$share_{avail} = share_{total}$
foreach $VM\ vm_i$ (in order $qstate(vm_i)$ high $\rightarrow$ low) **do**
    if $share_{avail} > 0$ **then**
        if $estate(vm_i) == estate_{up}$ **then**
            `// Assign more shares`
            $share(vm_i) = share(vm_i) + \delta$
        end
        else if $estate(vm_i) == estate_{down}$ **then**
            `// Reduce resource shares`
            $share(vm_i) = share(vm_i) - \delta$
        end
        $share_{avail} = share_{avail} - share(vm_i)$
    end
end

The paper's current experimental evaluation considers only single-VM scenarios. The allocation problem across competing VMs can be solved using various statistical techniques including bidding mechanisms and priority management [2].We do not experiment with such methods because this paper's focus is on ways to manage heterogeneity in cloud environmentsrather than on allocation and scheduling techniques.

4. Experimental Evaluation

4.1 Setup

Our experimental platform consists of a dual-socket 12 core Intel Westmere server with 12GB DDR3 memory, with heterogeneity emulated as follows. Processor heterogeneity is emulated using CPU throttling, by writing to CPU MSRs, which allows changing the duty cycle of each core independently. Memory throttling is used to emulate heterogeneous memory. It is performed by writing to the PCI registers of the memory controller, thus slowing it down. This allows us to experiment with memory configurations of various speeds, such as M1 and M2, which are approximately 2x and 5x slower than the original M0 configuration with no throttling.

In all experiments, response time is chosen as the QoS metric (lower is better), implying that an inverse value of latency is used in the QoS thresholds for the driver. A latency value of 10ms is chosen as the SLA, corresponding to which two policies are evaluated by using different thresholds for the scaling algorithm as shown in Table 3. These thresholds are obtained after experimenting with several different values. The first QoS-driven policy (ES-Q) is performance-sensitive, while the second resource-driven policy (ES-R) favorslower speeds, and thus, higher resource savings.

Table 3: Thresholds for scaling policies

	qos_{hi}	$util_{lo}$	qos_{lo}	$util_{hi}$
ES-Q	1/5	40	1/10	90
ES-R	1/5	50	1/15	95

For CPU experiments, a platform configuration consisting of eight slow cores and four fast cores is considered, where slow and fast cores are distributed uniformly on each socket to minimize migration overheads. The performance ratio between fast and slow cores is kept at 4x. Experiments are conducted using a VM with 12 vCPUs, providing an elasticity range up to 2U. Having an E-state step of 0.2U gives us 10 CPU E-states from E0 (2U) to E9 (0.2U), which are exported by the E-state interface. Similarly, memory evaluation is done using a platform configuration with 512MB of fast memory and an E-state step of 64MB, resulting in 8 memory E-states. Elastic scaling mechanisms are compared against a base case configuration with a static allocation of 1U CPU resources (E5 CPU state) and 256MB stacked memory (E4 memory state).

4.2 Workloads

Experimental runs use a web server and an in-house memcached-like (memstore) application, which service a stream of incoming requests from a client machine. The web server launches a CPU-intensive computation kernel, while memstore performs a memory lookup operation in response to each request. The memstore application allows us to load the memory subsystem to its peak capacity, avoiding CPU and network bottlenecks associated with standard memcached implementation. In addition, several other benchmarks, including SPEC CPU2006 and modern datacenter applications, are also included in the analysis.

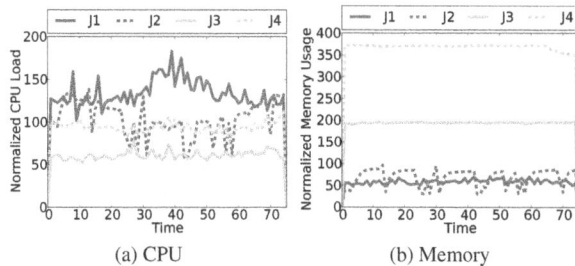

(a) CPU   (b) Memory

Figure 10: Traces based on Google cluster data [18]

In order to simulate dynamically varying resource usage behavior, workload profiles based on data from Google cluster traces are used [18]. Specifically, this data provides the normalized CPU utilization of a set of jobs over several hours from one of Google's production clusters. The dataset consists of four types of jobs from which we obtain

the average CPU load and memory usage of each type of job, with resultant data shown in Figure 10. As seen from the figure, workload J1 has constant high CPU usage, while J2 has varying behavior, with phases of high and low usage. In comparison, workloads J3 and J4 have uniform CPU usage, with J3 having significant idle components. Similarly, the memory usage behavior of these jobs shows J1 and J2 having low memory footprints, while J3 and J4 have higher usage profiles. These traces are replayed by varying the input request rate in proportion to the CPU load and changing the data-store size of the memstore workload in proportion to the memory usage of each trace, with each data point maintained for 20 seconds. It is to be noted that the data presented in the graphs is averaged across the entire cluster rather than being retrieved from a single server instance, because the dataset does not provide the machine mapping. We believe, however, that these jobs offer a good mix to test different dynamic workload scenarios present in server systems.

4.3 Experimental Results

Evaluations analyze the gains in performance and resource cost attainable from using fine-grained elastic scaling, compared to static allocation schemes.

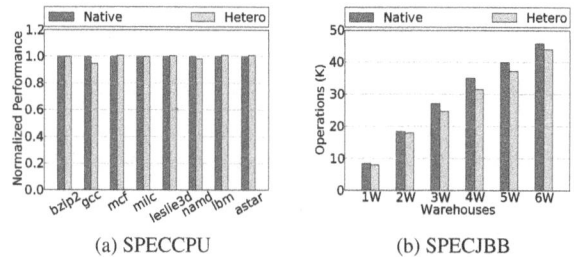

(a) SPECCPU   (b) SPECJBB

Figure 11: Performance comparison of heterogeneous configurations with the native platform

Figure 11 evaluates the overheads associated with scaling operations. Specifically, Figure 11a compares the performance of several SPEC CPU2006 benchmarks with composed virtual platforms using heterogeneous cores (8S+4F) against standard homogeneous configurations (12S). Both configurations operate at an elastic core speed of 1U and memory is allocated completely from off-chip DRAM. The data shows comparable performance for both the configurations, implying that the overhead associated with its scaling operations are small. In order to evaluate multi-threaded execution scenarios, Figure 11b shows the performance score for SPECjbb2005, a Java multi-tier warehouse benchmark, at different configurations, by increasing the number of warehouses. As seen from the figure, performance results for the both cases closely follow each other with increasing threads, showing its applicability to multi-threaded applications as well.

E-state scaling is first evaluated by running the web server application with increasing load and withdynamic scaling of

E-states (see Figure 12). Figures 12a and 12b show the response rate and response time for this workload. As apparent in the figures, throughput rises gradually as load is increased. The corresponding latency curve is relatively flat, as the E-state driver scales E-states to maintain latency within the SLA (10ms). We also notice a few spikes in the latency graph; these occur in response to an increase in the input load, whereupon the E-state is scaled up to reduce latency. The corresponding E-state graph is shown in Figure 12c, where E-states are scaled from from E9 to E4 in multiple steps.

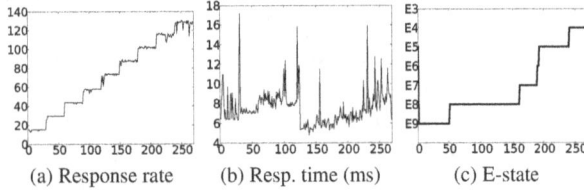

(a) Response rate   (b) Resp. time (ms)   (c) E-state

Figure 12: Elastic scaling experiment using the webserver workload (x-axis = time (s))

Evaluating the impact of memory heterogeneity, Figure 13 compares the performance of several SPEC CPU2006 applications (see Figure 13a) and various modern cloud application benchmarks, including graph database, graph search, key-value store, Lucene search engine, Tomcat server, kmeans, page-rank, and streamcluster algorithms (see Figure 13b) on different memory configurations. Specifically, it shows normalized performance at the base M0 configuration (without throttling) and for the M1 and M2 memory configurations (by applying different amounts of memory controller throttling). As evident from the figure, several applications experience severe performance degradation due to low memory performance, including 14x (5x) and 7x (4x) performance loss for the mcf and kvstore (key-value store) applications for the two memory configurations: M2 and M1. Other applications, like bzip and page-rank, exhibit less sensitivity. Overall, these results suggest that memory performance is critical to realistic applications which can therefore, benefit from the elastic management of heterogeneous memory resources.

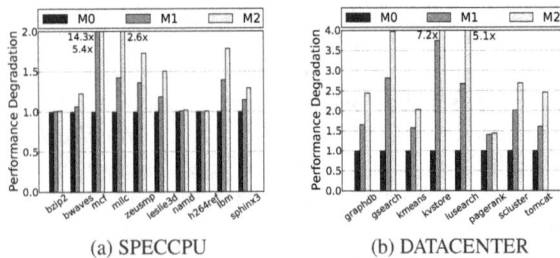

(a) SPECCPU   (b) DATACENTER

Figure 13: Impact of memory performance

Showing the use of the A-bit history based mechanisms to obtain the working set sizes (WSS) of applications, Fig-

ure 14 plots WSS graphs as a function of time for several SPEC CPU2006 workloads. As seen in the figure, working set size varies across applications from ~10MB for omnetpp to a much larger value of ~200MB for memory-intensive mcf. Further, WSS dynamically changes over time for these applications, thereby showing the need for runtime memory elasticity.

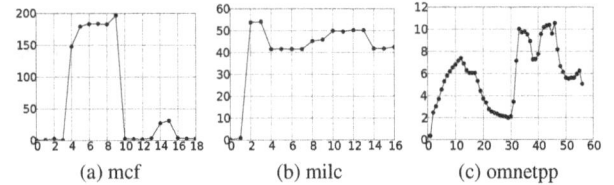

(a) mcf   (b) milc   (c) omnetpp

Figure 14: Working set size detection using access-bit history (x-axis = time (s), y-axis = WSS (MB))

Figure 15 shows the performance impact of memory E-state scaling on the memstore application, by gradually scaling E-states from E7 to E0, i.e., increasing the size of the fast memory allocation, where each state is maintained for five seconds before scaling to the next state. The non-scaling scenario (NS) shows a flat latency graph at 34ms and 42ms for the M1 and M2 configurations, respectively. In comparison, when E-states are scaled up from E7 (left) to E0 (right) in Figure 15a, the average latency for each memory operation decreases gradually to 8ms. The reduced access times with elastic scaling causes a 4.3x increase in application throughput (from 0.28M to 1.2M) (see Figure 15b). Also, the performance of the NS and ES configurations are comparable when no fast memory is used, signifying negligible overheads due to management operations like page table scans, mirroring, and maintaining other data structures. These results demonstrate that resource scaling on heterogeneous memory systems can be applied to obtain desired QoS for memory-sensitive applications.

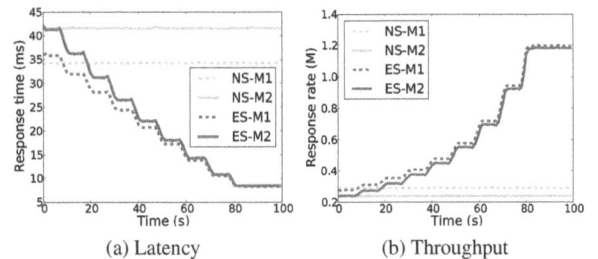

(a) Latency   (b) Throughput

Figure 15: Impact of elastic memory scaling on the performance of memstore application

We next evaluate the four workloads based on Google cluster traces shown in Figure 10. The results in Figure 16 compare the QoS and resource usage for the base configuration without any elastic scaling (NS-B) with elastic CPU scaling for the two policies ES-Q and ES-R given in Table 3. The base platform configuration consists of 12 slow cores, each with an elastic speed of 1U. The QoS score graph shows the fraction of queries for which service latency falls within the SLA (10ms). Similarly, the resource usage graphs compare the relative usage of various configurations, assuming a linear relationship between E-states and resource usage.

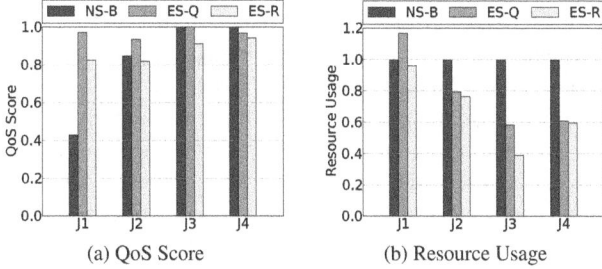

(a) QoS Score   (b) Resource Usage

Figure 16: Experimental results for CPU E-state scaling

As the results show, both policies provide much higher QoS than the base system for workload J1. Specifically, the QoS-sensitive policy ES-Q results in a 97% QoS score, with a 17% resource usage penalty, while the resource-driven policy ES-R provides lower QoS (83%), with lower usage (0.96x). In comparison, the base platform can only sustain a 43% QoS level. It is clear, therefore, that HeteroVisor can scale up resources to provide better performance when system load is high. For workload J2, ES-Q exhibits 9% higher and ES-R results in 3% lower QoS, while also reducing resource usage by 21% and 24%, respectively. Thus, resources are scaled up and down to meet the desired performance requirement. For J3 with low input load, HeteroVisor yields resource savings while also maintaining QoS, i.e., it generates 100% and 91% QoS scores with 42% and 61% lower resource usage for the two policies. In this manner, scaling down resources during low load periods produces savings for these jobs. Finally, the uniformly behaving workload J4 also shows comparable performance with significant resource savings across these configurations (~40%). In summary, E-states enable dynamic scaling of resources providing high-performance when required (as for J1) and resource savings for low activity workloads like J3 and J4.

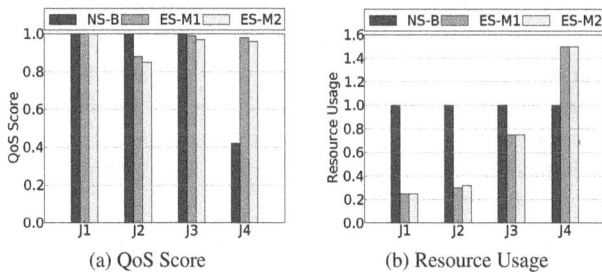

(a) QoS Score   (b) Resource Usage

Figure 17: Results for memory E-state scaling

Concerning memory elasticity, Figure 17 shows the memstore application, using the load traces depicted in Figure 10b to vary the datastore size. The figure compares the QoS score and resource usage for the base configuration

(NS-B) with the QoS-driven policy (ES-Q) under the M1 and M2 memory configurations. Additional experimentswith the resource-driven ES-R policy shows only minor variation for the memory scaling experiments. With a base case configuration consisting of 256MB of stacked DRAM (state E4), as the data in Figure 17a suggests,ES provides a 2.3x better QoS score for job J4, while performance is comparable for J1 and J3. J2 shows a 15% performance loss with scaling due to its varying memory usage, causing frequent scaling operations. Comparable behavior is seen across the two memory configurations (M1 and M2). The resource usage results in Figure 17b illustrate that ES policies significantly reduce the use of fast memory of jobs J1, J2, and J3 (75%, 70%, and 25%, respectively). In comparison, J4 observes a 50% increase in its resource usage due to its large memory footprints. Overall, elastic resource scaling using HeteroVisor provides a 30% lower stacked memory usage while maintaining performance.

Figure 18 shows the residency distribution (%) in each E-state for each of the four jobs, for the CPU scaling experiments. The states are color coded by their gray-scale intensity, meaning that a high-performance E-state is depicted by a darker color in comparison to a low-performing E-state. The graphs in Figures 18a and 18b correspond to the ES-Q and ES-R policies. As seen in the figures, different E-states dominate different workloads. J1 has large shares of E-states E2, E4, and E5 due to its high activity profile. For the low-CPU workload J3, the slower states E7 and E8 are dominant under the ES-Q and ES-R policies respectively. Similarly, J4 spends the majority of its execution time in states E7 and E5,while J2 makes mixed use of the E8, E7, E6, and E5 states. The results show the rich use of E-states, differing across andwithin workloads.

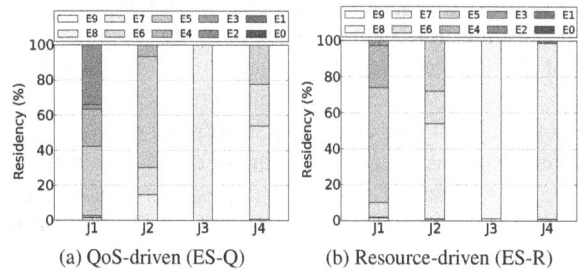

(a) QoS-driven (ES-Q)   (b) Resource-driven (ES-R)

Figure 18: E-state residencies for two scaling policies

The corresponding E-state switch profiles for the ES-Q policy are shown in Figure 19. Both J1 and J4 stay in lower E-states initially and scale up when demand increases. J3 stays in a single E-state, while J2 has several E-state transitions due to its variable load. In summary, results make clear that HeteroVisor successfullyand dynamically scales resources to match the varying input load requirements seen by guest VMs.

Interesting about these results is that HeteroVisor exploits platform heterogeneity for dynamically scaling the resources neededby guests to meet desired application perfor-

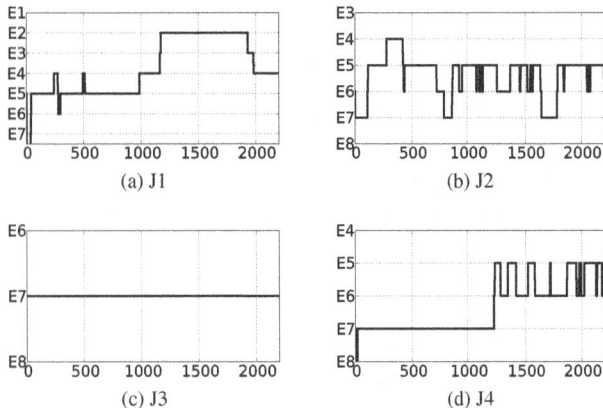

Figure 19: E-state switch profiles showing usage of various states (x-axis = time (s), y-axis = E-states)

mance/cost trade-offs. As shown by the experimental data, the approach not only better services load peaks in comparison to homogeneous platforms (up to 2.3x), but it also provides savings (an average 21% for CPU and 30% for memory) to applications by scaling down their resources during idle periods. For all of these activities, E-state drivers can be customized to meet different user requirements, which we demonstrate experimentally with policies that either meet high QoS requirement using an aggressive policy or that reduce resource usage while maintaining performance by using a conservative policy.

5. Related Work

Resource Management in Clouds: There has been substantial prior work on elastic resource scaling for server systems. In comparison to cluster-level scaling solutions [14, 19], HeteroVisor focuses on platform-level, fine-grained resource scaling. RaaS [1] and Kaleidoscope [6] argue in favor of fine-grained resource management for future cloud platforms, as also explored in our work. Q-Clouds, VirtualPower, AutoPilot, and CloudScale propose hypervisor-level mechanisms for elastic scaling of cloud resources [32, 34, 37, 42]. However, none of these address the effective use of platform-level heterogeneity in multiple platform resources. Several techniques have been developed for fair sharing of resources in cloud environments [15, 49]. Similarly, market-based allocation methods for datacenter applications have also been analyzed [17, 43, 47]. Such methods can be incorporated into HeteroVisor to ensure efficient operation and provide fairness.

Heterogeneous Processor Scheduling: Earlier work has demonstrated the need for compute heterogeneity advocating wimpy and brawny cores to efficiently support a wide variety of applications [3, 5, 20, 26, 48], as well as shown its presence in datacenters [36]. Several implementations of heterogeneous processor architectures have been released by various CPU vendors [16, 35]. In order to manage these platforms, appropriate OS-level [7, 23, 24, 39, 41, 45] and

VMM-level [22, 25] techniques have been developed to efficiently run applications on heterogeneous cores. HeteroVisor adopts an alternative approach that hides heterogeneity from the OS scheduler, exposing a homogeneous scalable interface. Finally, several heterogeneity-aware cloud schedulers have also been proposed [8, 33] which are complementary to HeteroVisor that works at the platform level.

Heterogeneous Memory Management: The detection of memory usage behavior of virtual machines has been exploredin previous work [21, 31, 46]. In comparison, we usepage-table access bits to detect not only the working set sizes but also provide 'hotness' informationabout each page to guide page placement. Similarly, various methods for balancing memory allocation among competing VMs also exist which can be incorporated into our design for improving efficiency [2, 50]. Concerning heterogeneous memory, several architectural solutions have been proposed for page placement strategies in such systems involving NVRAM, DRAM caches, and disaggregated memory [11, 28, 40, 44]. In comparison, our work focuses on software-controlled memory management to more efficiently utilize stacked DRAM. There is also increasingly more emphasis on memory voltage scaling efforts [9, 10]. HeteroVisor approach goes beyond voltage scaling to support heterogeneous resources for efficient operation.

6. Conclusions & Future Work

This paper presents the HeteroVisor system for managing heterogeneous resources in elastic cloud platforms, providing applicationswith fine-grained scaling capabilities. To manage heterogeneity, it provides the abstraction of elasticity (E) states to the guestvirtual machine, which an E-state driver can use to elastically request resources on-demand. The proposed abstractions generalizeto managing multiple resource types and levels of resource heterogeneity. Demonstrating its application to CPU and memory, we present techniques to manage these heterogeneous resources in an elastic manner. The HeteroVisor solution is implemented in the Xen hypervisor along with a simple E-state driver realizing two scaling policies, QoS-driven and resource-driven. Experimental evaluations are carried out using real-world traces on an emulated heterogeneous platform. They show that HeteroVisor can provide VMs with the capabilities to quickly obtain resources for handling load spikes and/or to minimize cost during low load periods.

There are multiple possible directions for future work. Investigating challenges with the design of fine-grain resource management policies for requesting and allocating resources in the presence of multiple competing users is one future direction. Market based allocation mechanisms based on game theory become relevant in this context. In addition, using elasticity-states with multiple platform resources and multiple levels of heterogeneity is also interesting.

References

[1] O. Agmon Ben-Yehuda, M. Ben-Yehuda, A. Schuster, and D. Tsafrir. The resource-as-a-service (RaaS) cloud. In *Proceedings of the 4th USENIX conference on Hot Topics in Cloud Ccomputing*, HotCloud'12, pages 12–12, Berkeley, CA, USA, 2012. USENIX Association.

[2] O. Agmon Ben-Yehuda, E. Posener, M. Ben-Yehuda, A. Schuster, and A. Mu'alem. Ginseng: Market-driven memory allocation. In *Proceedings of the 10th ACM SIGPLAN/SIGOPS International Conference on Virtual Execution Environments*, VEE '14, pages 41–52, New York, NY, USA, 2014. ACM. .

[3] D. G. Andersen, J. Franklin, M. Kaminsky, A. Phanishayee, L. Tan, and V. Vasudevan. FAWN: a fast array of wimpy nodes. In *Proceedings of the ACM SIGOPS 22nd symposium on Operating systems principles*, SOSP '09, pages 1–14. ACM, 2009. .

[4] P. Barham, B. Dragovic, K. Fraser, S. Hand, T. Harris, A. Ho, R. Neugebauer, I. Pratt, and A. Warfield. Xen and the art of virtualization. In *Proceedings of the nineteenth ACM symposium on Operating systems principles*, SOSP '03, pages 164–177, New York, NY, USA, 2003. ACM. .

[5] L. A. Barroso. Brawny cores still beat wimpy cores, most of the time. *Micro, IEEE*, 30(4):20 –24, july-aug. 2010. ISSN 0272-1732. .

[6] R. Bryant, A. Tumanov, O. Irzak, A. Scannell, K. Joshi, M. Hiltunen, A. Lagar-Cavilla, and E. de Lara. Kaleidoscope: cloud micro-elasticity via VM state coloring. In *Proceedings of the sixth conference on Computer systems*, EuroSys '11, pages 273–286, New York, NY, USA, 2011. ACM. .

[7] T. Cao, S. M. Blackburn, T. Gao, and K. S. McKinley. The yin and yang of power and performance for asymmetric hardware and managed software. In *Proceedings of the 39th Annual International Symposium on Computer Architecture*, ISCA '12, pages 225–236, Washington, DC, USA, 2012. IEEE Computer Society.

[8] C. Delimitrou and C. Kozyrakis. Paragon: QoS-aware scheduling for heterogeneous datacenters. In *Proceedings of the 18th international conference on Architectural support for programming languages and operating systems*, ASPLOS '13, pages 77–88, New York, NY, USA, 2013. ACM. .

[9] Q. Deng, D. Meisner, L. Ramos, T. F. Wenisch, and R. Bianchini. MemScale: active low-power modes for main memory. In *Proceedings of the sixteenth international conference on Architectural support for programming languages and operating systems*, ASPLOS XVI, pages 225–238. ACM, 2011. .

[10] Q. Deng, D. Meisner, A. Bhattacharjee, T. F. Wenisch, and R. Bianchini. CoScale: Coordinating CPU and memory system DVFS in server systems. In *Proceedings of the 2012 45th Annual IEEE/ACM International Symposium on Microarchitecture*, MICRO '12, pages 143–154. IEEE, 2012. .

[11] X. Dong, Y. Xie, N. Muralimanohar, and N. P. Jouppi. Simple but effective heterogeneous main memory with on-chip memory controller support. In *Proceedings of the 2010 ACM/IEEE International Conference for High Performance Computing, Networking, Storage and Analysis*, SC '10. IEEE, 2010. .

[12] A. Fedorova, J. C. Saez, D. Shelepov, and M. Prieto. Maximizing power efficiency with asymmetric multicore systems. *Commun. ACM*, 52(12):48–57, Dec. 2009. .

[13] G. Galante and L. C. E. d. Bona. A survey on cloud computing elasticity. In *Proceedings of the 2012 IEEE/ACM Fifth International Conference on Utility and Cloud Computing*, UCC '12, pages 263–270. IEEE Computer Society, 2012. .

[14] A. Gandhi, T. Zhu, M. Harchol-Balter, and M. A. Kozuch. SOFTScale: stealing opportunistically for transient scaling. In *Proceedings of the 13th International Middleware Conference*, Middleware '12, pages 142–163, New York, NY, USA, 2012. Springer-Verlag New York, Inc.

[15] A. Ghodsi, M. Zaharia, B. Hindman, A. Konwinski, S. Shenker, and I. Stoica. Dominant resource fairness: fair allocation of multiple resource types. In *Proceedings of the 8th USENIX conference on Networked systems design and implementation*, NSDI'11. USENIX Association, 2011.

[16] P. Greenhalgh. Big.LITTLE Processing with ARM CortexTM-A15 & Cortex-A7. White paper, ARM, Sept 2011.

[17] M. Guevara, B. Lubin, and B. C. Lee. Navigating heterogeneous processors with market mechanisms. In *High Performance Computer Architecture (HPCA2013), 2013 IEEE 19th International Symposium on*, pages 95–106, 2013. .

[18] J. L. Hellerstein. Google cluster data. Google research blog, Jan. 2010. Posted at /urlhttp://googleresearch.blogspot.com/2010/01/google-cluster-data.html.

[19] Y.-J. Hong, J. Xue, and M. Thottethodi. Dynamic server provisioning to minimize cost in an IaaS cloud. In *Proceedings of the international conference on Measurement and modeling of computer systems*, SIGMETRICS '11, pages 147–148, New York, NY, USA, 2011. ACM. .

[20] V. Janapa Reddi, B. C. Lee, T. Chilimbi, and K. Vaid. Web search using mobile cores: quantifying and mitigating the price of efficiency. In *Proceedings of the 37th annual international symposium on Computer architecture*, ISCA '10, pages 314–325, New York, NY, USA, 2010. ACM. .

[21] S. T. Jones, A. C. Arpaci-Dusseau, and R. H. Arpaci-Dusseau. Geiger: monitoring the buffer cache in a virtual machine environment. In *Proceedings of the 12th international conference on Architectural support for programming languages and operating systems*, ASPLOS XII, pages 14–24. ACM, 2006. .

[22] V. Kazempour, A. Kamali, and A. Fedorova. AASH: an asymmetry-aware scheduler for hypervisors. In *Proceedings of the 6th ACM SIGPLAN/SIGOPS international conference on Virtual execution environments*, VEE '10, pages 85–96, New York, NY, USA, 2010. ACM. .

[23] D. Koufaty, D. Reddy, and S. Hahn. Bias scheduling in heterogeneous multi-core architectures. In *Proceedings of the 5th European conference on Computer systems*, EuroSys '10, pages 125–138, New York, NY, USA, 2010. ACM.

[24] R. Kumar, K. I. Farkas, N. P. Jouppi, P. Ranganathan, and D. M. Tullsen. Single-ISA heterogeneous multi-core architectures: The potential for processor power reduction. In *Proceedings of the 36th annual IEEE/ACM International Symposium on Microarchitecture*, MICRO 36. IEEE, 2003.

[25] Y. Kwon, C. Kim, S. Maeng, and J. Huh. Virtualizing performance asymmetric multi-core systems. In *Proceedings of the 38th annual international symposium on Computer architecture*, ISCA '11, pages 45–56, New York, NY, USA, 2011. ACM. .

[26] W. Lang, J. M. Patel, and S. Shankar. Wimpy node clusters: what about non-wimpy workloads? In *Proceedings of the Sixth International Workshop on Data Management on New Hardware*, DaMoN '10, pages 47–55. ACM, 2010. .

[27] M. Lee and K. Schwan. Region scheduling: efficiently using the cache architectures via page-level affinity. In *Proceedings of the seventeenth international conference on Architectural Support for Programming Languages and Operating Systems*, ASPLOS '12, pages 451–462. ACM, 2012. .

[28] K. Lim, Y. Turner, J. R. Santos, A. AuYoung, J. Chang, P. Ranganathan, and T. F. Wenisch. System-level implications of disaggregated memory. In *Proceedings of the 2012 IEEE 18th International Symposium on High-Performance Computer Architecture*, HPCA '12, pages 1–12. IEEE, 2012. .

[29] G. H. Loh. 3D-stacked memory architectures for multi-core processors. In *Proceedings of the 35th Annual International Symposium on Computer Architecture*, ISCA '08, pages 453–464. IEEE Computer Society, 2008. .

[30] G. H. Loh, N. Jayasena, K. McGrath, M. O'Connor, S. Reinhardt, and J. Chung. Challenges in heterogeneous die-stacked and off-chip memory systems. In *In Proc. of 3rd Workshop on SoCs, Heterogeneity, and Workloads (SHAW)*, Feb 2012.

[31] P. Lu and K. Shen. Virtual machine memory access tracing with hypervisor exclusive cache. In *2007 USENIX Annual Technical Conference on Proceedings of the USENIX Annual Technical Conference*, ATC'07, pages 3:1–3:15, Berkeley, CA, USA, 2007. USENIX Association.

[32] R. Nathuji and K. Schwan. VirtualPower: coordinated power management in virtualized enterprise systems. In *Proceedings of twenty-first ACM SIGOPS symposium on Operating systems principles*, SOSP '07, pages 265–278. ACM, 2007. .

[33] R. Nathuji, C. Isci, and E. Gorbatov. Exploiting platform heterogeneity for power efficient data centers. In *Proceedings of the Fourth International Conference on Autonomic Computing*, ICAC '07, pages 5–. IEEE Computer Society, 2007. .

[34] R. Nathuji, A. Kansal, and A. Ghaffarkhah. Q-clouds: managing performance interference effects for QoS-aware clouds. In *Proceedings of the 5th European conference on Computer systems*, EuroSys '10, pages 237–250. ACM, 2010. .

[35] Nvidia. Variable SMP: A multi-core CPU architecture for low power and high performance. White paper, 2011.

[36] Z. Ou, H. Zhuang, J. K. Nurminen, A. Ylä-Jääski, and P. Hui. Exploiting hardware heterogeneity within the same instance type of Amazon EC2. In *Proceedings of the 4th USENIX conference on Hot Topics in Cloud Ccomputing*, HotCloud'12, pages 4–4, Berkeley, CA, USA, 2012. USENIX Association.

[37] P. Padala, K.-Y. Hou, K. G. Shin, X. Zhu, M. Uysal, Z. Wang, S. Singhal, and A. Merchant. Automated control of multiple virtualized resources. In *Proceedings of the 4th ACM European conference on Computer systems*, EuroSys '09, pages 13–26, New York, NY, USA, 2009. ACM. .

[38] V. Pallipadi and A. Starikovskiy. The ondemand governor: Past, present and future. *Linux Symposium*, 2:223–238, 2006.

[39] S. Panneerselvam and M. M. Swift. Chameleon: operating system support for dynamic processors. In *Proceedings of the 17th international conference on Architectural Support for Programming Languages and Operating Systems*, ASPLOS XVII, pages 99–110, New York, NY, USA, 2012. ACM. .

[40] L. E. Ramos, E. Gorbatov, and R. Bianchini. Page placement in hybrid memory systems. In *Proceedings of the international conference on Supercomputing*, ICS '11, pages 85–95, New York, NY, USA, 2011. ACM. .

[41] J. C. Saez, M. Prieto, A. Fedorova, and S. Blagodurov. A comprehensive scheduler for asymmetric multicore systems. In *5th EuroSys*, pages 139–152, New York, NY, USA, 2010. .

[42] Z. Shen, S. Subbiah, X. Gu, and J. Wilkes. CloudScale: elastic resource scaling for multi-tenant cloud systems. In *Proceedings of the 2nd ACM Symposium on Cloud Computing*, SOCC '11, pages 5:1–5:14, New York, NY, USA, 2011. ACM. .

[43] T. Somu Muthukaruppan, A. Pathania, and T. Mitra. Price theory based power management for heterogeneous multi-cores. In *19th Conference on Architectural Support for Programming Languages and Operating Systems*, ASPLOS, pages 161–176. ACM, 2014. .

[44] K. Sudan, K. Rajamani, W. Huang, and J. Carter. Tiered memory: An iso-power memory architecture to address the memory power wall. *Computers, IEEE Transactions on*, 61 (12):1697–1710, Dec 2012. ISSN 0018-9340. .

[45] K. Van Craeynest, A. Jaleel, L. Eeckhout, P. Narvaez, and J. Emer. Scheduling heterogeneous multi-cores through performance impact estimation (PIE). In *Proceedings of the 39th Annual International Symposium on Computer Architecture*, ISCA '12, pages 213–224, Washington, DC, USA, 2012. IEEE Computer Society.

[46] C. A. Waldspurger. Memory resource management in VMware ESX server. In *Proceedings of the 5th USENIX conference on Operating systems design and implementation*, OSDI'02, Berkeley, CA, USA, 2002. USENIX Association. .

[47] W. Wang, B. Liang, and B. Li. Revenue maximization with dynamic auctions in IaaS cloud markets. In *Quality of Service (IWQoS), 2013 IEEE/ACM 21st International Symposium on*, pages 1–6, 2013. .

[48] D. Wong and M. Annavaram. KnightShift: Scaling the energy proportionality wall through server-level heterogeneity. In *Proceedings of the 2012 45th Annual IEEE/ACM International Symposium on Microarchitecture*, MICRO '12, pages 119–130. IEEE Computer Society, 2012. .

[49] S. M. Zahedi and B. C. Lee. REF: Resource elasticity fairness with sharing incentives for multiprocessors. In *International Conference on Architectural Support for Programming Languages and Operating Systems*, ASPLOS '14, pages 145–160. ACM, 2014. .

[50] W. Zhao and Z. Wang. Dynamic memory balancing for virtual machines. In *Proceedings of the 2009 ACM SIGPLAN/SIGOPS international conference on Virtual execution environments*, VEE '09, pages 21–30. ACM, 2009. .

A-DRM: Architecture-aware Distributed Resource Management of Virtualized Clusters

Hui Wang[†*], Canturk Isci[‡], Lavanya Subramanian[*], Jongmoo Choi[♭*], Depei Qian[†], Onur Mutlu[*]

[†]Beihang University, [‡]IBM Thomas J. Watson Research Center, [*]Carnegie Mellon University, [♭]Dankook University

{hui.wang, depeiq}@buaa.edu.cn, canturk@us.ibm.com, {lsubrama, onur}@cmu.edu, choijm@dankook.ac.kr

Abstract

Virtualization technologies has been widely adopted by large-scale cloud computing platforms. These virtualized systems employ distributed resource management (DRM) to achieve high resource utilization and energy savings by dynamically migrating and consolidating virtual machines. DRM schemes usually use operating-system-level metrics, such as CPU utilization, memory capacity demand and I/O utilization, to detect and balance resource contention. However, they are oblivious to microarchitecture-level resource interference (e.g., memory bandwidth contention between different VMs running on a host), which is currently not exposed to the operating system.

We observe that the lack of visibility into microarchitecture-level resource interference significantly impacts the performance of virtualized systems. Motivated by this observation, we propose a novel architecture-aware DRM scheme (*A-DRM*), that takes into account microarchitecture-level resource interference when making migration decisions in a virtualized cluster. *A-DRM* makes use of three core techniques: 1) a profiler to monitor the microarchitecture-level resource usage behavior online for each physical host, 2) a memory bandwidth interference model to assess the interference degree among virtual machines on a host, and 3) a cost-benefit analysis to determine a candidate virtual machine and a host for migration.

Real system experiments on thirty randomly selected combinations of applications from the CPU2006, PARSEC, STREAM, NAS Parallel Benchmark suites in a four-host virtualized cluster show that *A-DRM* can improve performance by up to 26.55%, with an average of 9.67%, compared to traditional DRM schemes that lack visibility into microarchitecture-level resource utilization and contention.

VEE '15, March 14–15, 2015, Istanbul, Turkey.
Copyright is held by the owner/author(s). Publication rights licensed to ACM.
ACM 978-1-4503-3450-1/15/03...$15.00.
http://dx.doi.org/10.1145/2731186.2731202

Categories and Subject Descriptors   C.4 [*Performance of Systems*]: Modeling techniques, measurement techniques; D.4.8 [*Operating Systems*]: Performance – Modeling and prediction, measurements, operational analysis

Keywords   virtualization; microarchitecture; live migration; performance counters; resource management

1. Introduction

Server virtualization and workload consolidation enable multiple workloads to share a single physical server, resulting in significant energy savings and utilization improvements. In addition to improved efficiency, virtualization drastically reduces operational costs through automated management of the distributed physical resources. Due to these attractive benefits, many enterprises, hosting providers, and cloud vendors have shifted to a virtualization-based model for running applications and providing various services (e.g., Amazon EC2 [2], Windows Azure [1]).

A key feature of virtualization platforms is the ability to move a *virtual machine (VM)* between physical hosts. This feature enables the migration of VMs to the appropriate physical hosts such that overall cluster efficiency is improved and resource utilization hot-spots are eliminated [15, 35, 43, 53]. In order to derive efficiency benefits from virtualization, the distributed resources should be managed effectively using an automated *Distributed Resource Management (DRM)* scheme. Such a scheme employs the VM migration feature judiciously to migrate VMs to the appropriate physical hosts such that VMs do not interfere with each other or significantly degrade each other's performance.

Many current DRM schemes [23, 27–31, 34, 56, 70, 72], including commercial products [31], manage VMs based solely on operating-system-level metrics, such as CPU utilization, memory capacity demand and I/O utilization. Such schemes do not consider interference at the microarchitecture-level resources such as the shared last level cache capacity and memory bandwidth. In this work, we observe that operating-system-level metrics like CPU utilization and memory capacity demand that are often used to determine which VMs should be migrated to which physical hosts cannot accurately characterize a workload's microarchitecture-level shared resource interference behavior. We observe that VMs may exhibit similar CPU utilization and memory capacity demand but very different memory bandwidth usage. Hence, DRM schemes that operate solely based on operating-system-level metrics could make migration decisions that leave the underlying microarchitecture-level interference unsolved or make it worse, leading to more interference at the microarchitecture-level and thus degrade the overall performance.

Some VM scheduling approaches (e.g., [75]) attempt to account for microarchitecture-level interference offline by employing a profiling phase to build a workload interference matrix that captures the interference characteristics when different pairs of applications are co-run. They then build constraints into the DRM scheme to forbid the co-location of workloads that heavily interfere with each other. We observe that such an *offline profiling* approach to incorporate microarchitecture-level interference into VM management at a cluster level has two major drawbacks. First, obtaining an interference matrix through profiling might not be feasible in all scenarios. For instance, it is not feasible for hosting providers and cloud vendors such as Amazon EC2 [2] and Microsoft Azure [1] to profile jobs from all users in advance, since it would incur prohibitive overhead to do so. Second, even if workloads can be profiled offline, due to workload phase changes and changing inputs, interference characteristics could change over execution. Hence, the interference matrix compiled from offline profiling might not accurately capture interference behavior during runtime.

Our goal, in this work, is to design a DRM scheme that takes into account interference between VMs at the microarchitecture-level shared resources, thereby improving overall system performance. To this end, we propose an architecture-aware DRM scheme, *A-DRM*. *A-DRM* takes into account two main sources of interference at the microarchitecture-level, 1) shared last level cache capacity and 2) memory bandwidth by monitoring three microarchitectural metrics: last level cache miss rate, memory bandwidth consumption and average memory latency. Specifically, *A-DRM* monitors the memory bandwidth utilization at each host. When the memory bandwidth utilization at a host exceeds a threshold, the host is identified as contended. Once such contention has been identified, the next key step is to identify which VMs should be migrated and to which hosts. In order to identify this, *A-DRM* performs a cost-benefit analysis to determine by how much each potential destination host's performance would be impacted if each VM on the contended host were migrated to it. Specifically, the cost-benefit analysis first estimates the increase in the last level cache miss rate at each potential destination host if each VM on the contended host were moved to it and then uses this miss rate increase to quantify the performance impact on the destination host.

We implement *A-DRM* on KVM 3.13.5-202 and QEMU 1.6.2, and perform comprehensive evaluations using a four-host cluster with various real workloads. Our experimental results show that *A-DRM* can improve the performance of a cluster by up to 26.55% with an average of 9.67%,

and improve the memory bandwidth utilization by 17% on average (up to 36%), compared to a state-of-the-art DRM scheme [34] that does not take into account microarchitecture-level interference.

This paper makes the following contributions:

- We show that many real workloads exhibit different memory bandwidth and/or LLC usage behavior even though they have similar CPU utilization and memory capacity demand. Therefore, for effective distributed resource management, we need to consider not only operating-system-level metrics but also microarchitecture-level resource interference.

- We propose a model to assess the impact of interference on a host and perform a cost-benefit analysis to measure the impact of migrating every VM from a contended source host to a destination host.

- We propose *A-DRM*, which to our best knowledge, is the first DRM scheme that takes into account the characteristics of microarchitecture-level interference in making VM migration decisions, thereby mitigating interference and improving overall system (cluster) performance.

- We implement and evaluate our proposal on real hardware using diverse workloads, demonstrating significant performance improvements.

- We discuss several practical challenges that we encounter when implementing our *A-DRM* scheme, such as the effect of socket migration and the interconnection traffic.

2. Background and Motivation

In this section, we provide background on the main sources of microarchitecture-level interference. We then discuss the limitations of current DRM schemes that perform VM management using only operating-system-level metrics such as CPU utilization and memory capacity demand.

2.1 Microarchitecture-level Interference

The shared last level cache (LLC) capacity and main memory bandwidth are two major resources that are heavily contended between VMs sharing a machine [41, 42, 50, 51, 63]. Applications/VMs evict each other's data from the last level cache, causing an increase in memory access latency, thereby resulting in performance degradation [57, 58, 61]. Applications'/VMs' requests also contend at the different components of main memory, such as channels, ranks and banks, resulting in performance degradation [39, 41, 42, 47, 50, 51, 63, 64]. Different applications have different sensitivity to cache capacity and memory bandwidth [57, 63]. An application/VM's performance degradation depends on the application/VM's sensitivity to shared resources and the co-running applications/VMs [20, 63].

Today's servers typically employ a Non-Uniform Memory Access (NUMA) architecture, which has multiple sockets that are connected via interconnect links (e.g. QPI [33]). Several previous works propose to mitigate interference by migrating VMs *across* sockets such that applications/VMs

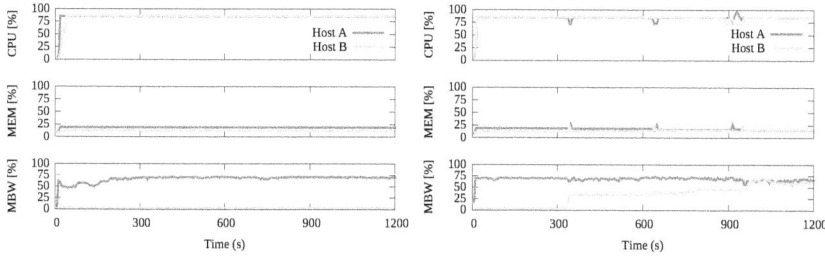

Figure 1: Resource utilization of Traditional DRM

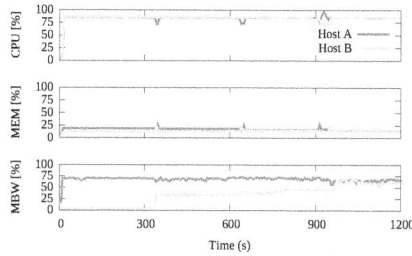

Figure 2: Resource utilization of Traditional DRM + MBW-awareness

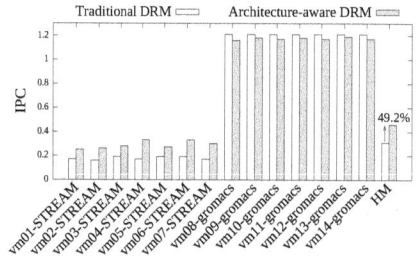

Figure 3: IPC Performance (HM is harmonic mean.)

that do not contend for the same shared resource are mapped to the same socket [12, 45, 60]. Our focus, in this work, is not on a single server, but on a *cluster of servers*. We explore VM migration across nodes, which is complementary to migrating applications/VMs across sockets.

2.2 Limitations of Traditional DRM Schemes

To address the VM-to-Host mapping challenge, prior works [23, 27–31, 34, 56, 72] have proposed to manage the physical resources by monitoring operating-system-level metrics (such as CPU utilization, memory capacity demand) and appropriately mapping VMs to hosts such that the utilization of CPU/memory resources is balanced across different hosts. While these schemes have been shown to be effective at CPU/memory resource scheduling and load balancing, they have a fundamental limitation – they are not aware of the microarchitecture-level shared resource interference.

2.2.1 Lack of Microarchitecture-level Shared Resource Interference Awareness

Prior works, including commercial products, base migration decisions on operating-system-level-metrics. However, such metrics cannot capture the microarchitecture-level shared resource interference characteristics. Our real workload profiling results (detailed in Section 6.1) show that there are many workloads, e.g., STREAM and gromacs, that exhibit similar CPU utilization and demand for memory capacity, but have very different memory bandwidth consumption. Thus, when VMs exhibit similar CPU and memory capacity utilization and the host is not overcommitted (i.e., CPU or memory is under-utilized), traditional DRM schemes that are unaware of microarchitecture-level shared resource interference characteristics would not recognize a problem and would let the current VM-to-host mapping continue. However, the physical host might, in reality, be experiencing heavy contention at the microarchitecture-level shared resources such as shared cache and main memory.

2.2.2 Offline Profiling to Characterize Interference

Some previous works [31, 37, 75] seek to mitigate interference between applications/VMs at the microarchitecture-level shared resources by defining constraints based on *offline profiling* of applications/VMs, such that applications that contend with each other are not co-located. For instance, in VMware DRS [31], rules can be defined for VM-to-VM or VM-to-Host mappings. While such an approach based on offline profiling could work in some scenarios, there are two

major drawbacks to such an approach. First, it might not always be feasible to profile applications. For instance, in a cloud service such as Amazon EC2 [2] where VMs are leased to any user, it is not feasible to profile applications offline. Second, even when workloads can be profiled offline, due to workload phase changes and changing inputs, the interference characteristics might be different compared to when the offline profiling was performed. Hence, such an offline profiling approach has limited applicability.

2.3 The Impact of Interference Unawareness

In this section, we demonstrate the shortcomings of DRM schemes that are unaware of microarchitecture-level shared resource interference with case studies. We pick two applications: gromacs from the SPEC CPU2006 benchmark suite [6] and STREAM [7]. STREAM and gromacs have very similar memory capacity demand, while having very different memory bandwidth usage: STREAM has high bandwidth demand, gromacs has low (more workload pairs that have such characteristics can be found in Section 6.1).

We run seven copies (VMs) of STREAM on Host A and seven copies (VMs) of gromacs on Host B (initially). Both of the hosts are SuperMicro servers equipped with two Intel Xeon L5630 processors running at 2.13GHz (detailed in Section 5). Each VM is configured to have 1 vCPU and 2 GB memory.

Figure 1 shows the CPU utilization (CPU), total memory capacity demand of VMs over host memory capacity (memory capacity utilization - MEM), and memory bandwidth utilization (MBW) of the hosts when a traditional DRM scheme, which relies on CPU utilization and memory capacity demand, is employed. We see that although the memory bandwidth on Host A is heavily contended (close to achieving the practically possible peak bandwidth [21]), the traditional DRM scheme does nothing (i.e., does not migrate VMs) since the CPU and memory capacity on Host A and Host B are under-utilized and Host A and Host B have similar CPU and memory capacity demands for all VMs.

Figure 2 shows the same information for the same two hosts, Host A and Host B. However, we use a memory-bandwidth-contention-aware DRM scheme to migrate three VMs that consume the most memory bandwidth from Host A to Host B at 300 seconds, 600 seconds and 900 seconds. To keep the CPU resources from being oversubscribed, we also migrate three VMs that have low memory bandwidth requirements from Host B to Host A. We see that after the three migrations, the memory bandwidth usage on Host A and Host B are balanced, compared to when employing the traditional DRM scheme (Figure 1).

Figure 3 shows the performance comparison between the traditional DRM and memory-bandwidth-contention-aware schemes, measured in IPC (Instructions Per Cycle). We see that the IPC of the VMs running STREAM increases dramatically (close to 2x in some cases). The harmonic mean of the IPC across all VMs improves by 49.2%, compared to the traditional DRM scheme. These results show that traditional DRM schemes that base their migration decisions solely on CPU utilization and memory capacity demand could leave significant performance potential unharnessed.

Our goal, in this work, is to design a DRM scheme that considers microarchitecture-level shared resource interference when making VM migration decisions such that interference is mitigated and resource utilization and performance are improved in a virtualized cluster.

3. *A-DRM*: Design

In this section, we describe the design of *A-DRM*, our proposed distributed resource management scheme that incorporates awareness of microarchitecture-level shared resource interference.

3.1 Overview

Figure 4 presents an overview of *A-DRM*, which consists of two components: a *profiler* deployed in each physical host and a *controller* that is run on a dedicated server.

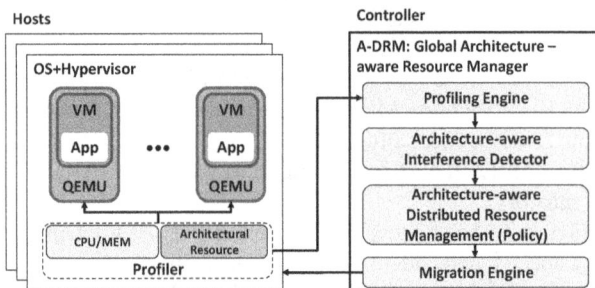

Figure 4: Prototype implementation

The primary objective of the *profiler* is to monitor resource usage/demands and report them to the *controller* periodically (at the end of every *profiling interval*). The *profiler* consists of two main components: 1) a CPU and memory profiler, which interacts with the hypervisor to get the CPU utilization and memory capacity demand of each VM and 2) an *architectural resource* profiler that leverages the hardware performance monitoring units (PMUs) to monitor the last level cache (LLC) capacity and memory bandwidth (MBW) usage of each VM. The *architectural resource* profiler also monitors the total memory bandwidth utilization and the average DRAM read latency, at each socket, to be used in detecting and managing interference.

The *controller* is the centerpiece of our distributed resource management framework. It is designed to detect microarchitecture-level shared resource interference and leverage this information to perform VM migration. The

controller consists of four components: 1) A *profiling engine* that stores the data collected by the *profiler*. In order to improve accuracy and robustness in profiling data, a sliding window mechanism is used to calculate the moving average and smooth the profiled statistics. 2) An *architecture-aware interference detector* is invoked at each *scheduling interval* to detect microarchitecture-level shared resource interference. It detects hosts whose memory bandwidth utilization is greater than a threshold and classifies such hosts as contended. 3) Once such interference is detected, the *architecture-aware DRM policy* is used to determine new VM-to-Host mappings to mitigate the detected interference. The *architecture-aware DRM policy* computes the increase in LLC miss rates at each potential destination host, if each VM on a contended host were to be moved to it. It uses these miss rate increases to quantify the cost and benefit, in terms of performance impact at the source and destination hosts for every <contended host, VM, potential destination> tuple. This cost-benefit analysis is used to determine the best VM-to-host mappings. 4) The *migration engine* is then invoked to achieve the new VM-to-Host mappings via VM migration. These migrations could be configured to happen automatically or with the approval of the administrator.

3.2 Profiling Engine

The *profiling engine* stores the data collected by the *profiler* to quantify LLC and memory bandwidth interference, such as memory bandwidth consumption and LLC miss rate. The list of the monitored performance events and how exactly these are employed to quantify LLC and memory bandwidth interference are described in Table 1 and Section 4.

3.3 Architecture-aware Interference Detector

The *architecture-aware interference detector* detects the microarchitecture-level shared resource interference at each host. As we discussed in Section 2.1, the LLC capacity and main memory bandwidth are two major sources of microarchitecture-level shared resource interference. When VMs contend for the limited LLC capacity available on a host, they evict each other's data from the LLC. This increases data accesses to main memory, thereby increasing memory bandwidth consumption and interference. Furthermore, VMs' requests also contend for the limited main memory bandwidth at different main memory components such as channels, ranks and banks. Since the impact of both cache capacity and memory bandwidth interference is an increase in memory bandwidth utilization, the *architecture-aware interference detector* uses the memory bandwidth consumed at each host to determine the degree of microarchitecture-level shared resource interference. It computes the memory bandwidth utilization at each host as

$$MBW_{util} = \frac{ConsumedMemoryBandwidth}{PeakMemoryBandwidth}. \quad (1)$$

When the MBW_{util} at a host is greater than a threshold, $MBW_{Threshold}$, we identify the host as experiencing interference at the microarchitecture-level shared resources. We provide more details on how we measure memory bandwidth in Section 4.1.

3.4 Architecture-aware DRM policy

The *architecture-aware DRM policy* is at the core of our *controller* and is invoked at the beginning of each *scheduling interval*. In this section, we present the high level design of our *architecture-aware DRM policy*. We provide more implementation details in Algorithm 1 and Section 4.2. Our DRM policy employs a two phase algorithm to determine an alternate VM-to-host mapping that mitigates interference.

Algorithm 1 *A-DRM*'s memory bandwidth based VM migration algorithm

---

1: Input: *Metrics* (Snapshot of the measured metrics of entire cluster)
2: $RecommendedMigrations \leftarrow null$
3:
4: /* First phase: find a set of migrations to mitigate memory bandwidth interference */
5: **for each** MBWContendedHost src in the cluster **do**
6:     **while** MBW_{util} of $src > MBW_{Threshold}$ **do**
7:         $MaxBenefit \leftarrow 0$
8:         $BestMigration \leftarrow null$
9:         **for each** VM v in src **do**
10:             **for each** host dst with $MBW_{util} < MBW_{Threshold}$ **do**
11:                 $Benefit \leftarrow Benefit_{vm} + Benefit_{src}$
12:                 $Cost \leftarrow Cost_{migration} + Cost_{dst}$
13:                 **if** $Benefit - Cost > MaxBenefit$ **then**
14:                     $MaxBenefit \leftarrow Benefit$
15:                     $BestMigration \leftarrow$ migrate v from src to dst
16:                 **end if**
17:             **end for**
18:         **end for**
19:         **if** $BestMigration \neq null$ **then**
20:             $RecommendedMigrations.add(BestMigration)$
21:             Update $Metrics$ to reflect $BestMigration$
22:         **end if**
23:     **end while**
24: **end for**
25:
26: /* Second phase: balance CPU and memory utilization */
27: **for each** CPU/MemoryCapacityContendedHost src in the cluster **do**
28:     **while** src still CPU or Memory Capacity contended **do**
29:         $MinMBWRatio \leftarrow 1$ /* $0 \leq Ratio \leq 1$ */
30:         $BestMigration \leftarrow null$
31:         **for each** VM v in src **do**
32:             **for each** host dst with $CPU_{util} < CPU_{Threshold}$ or $MEM_{util} < MEM_{Threshold}$ **do**
33:                 $MBWRatio \leftarrow$ *the MBW ratio on dst after migration*
34:                 **if** $MBWRatio < MinMBWRatio$ **then**
35:                     $MinMBWRatio \leftarrow MBWRatio$
36:                     $BestMigration \leftarrow$ migrate v from src to dst
37:                 **end if**
38:             **end for**
39:         **end for**
40:         **if** $BestMigration \neq null$ **then**
41:             $RecommendedMigrations.add(BestMigration)$
42:             Update $Metrics$ to reflect $BestMigration$
43:         **end if**
44:     **end while**
45: **end for**
46: **return** $RecommendedMigrations$

In the first phase, we use a greedy hill-climbing technique to determine the best VM-to-host mapping with the goal of mitigating microarchitecture-level shared resource interference. For each host that is detected as contended

by the *architecture-aware interference detector* (MBWContendedHost in Algorithm 1 line 5), we aim to determine a set of migrations that provides the most benefit, while incurring the least cost. The *Benefit (line 11)* is an estimation of the improvement in performance if a VM were migrated, for both the VM under consideration to be migrated ($Benefit_{vm}$) and the other non-migrated VMs at the source host ($Benefit_{src}$). The *Cost (line 12)* is an estimation of the migration cost ($Cost_{migration}$) and degradation in performance at each potential destination host due to the migration ($Cost_{dst}$). We present detailed descriptions of these costs and benefits in Section 4.2. We employ a non-aggressive migration scheme that i) only migrates the least number of VMs to bring the host's MBW_{util} under the $MBW_{Threshold}$ (line 6), and ii) does not migrate at all if a good migration that has greater benefit than cost cannot be identified (line 13). For each contended host, after we determine a migration that provides the maximum benefit, we will accordingly update the memory bandwidth demand of the corresponding dst/src hosts by adding/subtracting the VM's bandwidth demand (line 21). The result of this phase is a set of recommended migrations that seek to mitigate microarchitecture-level interference. While the recommended migrations from this phase tackle the problem of microarchitecture-level shared resource interference, they do not take into account CPU utilization and memory capacity demand. This is done in the second phase.

The second phase, which is similar to traditional CPU and memory demand based DRM, balances the CPU and memory capacity utilization across all hosts, preventing CPU/memory capacity from being overcommitted, while keeping the cluster-wide memory bandwidth utilization balanced. Only after both phases are completed will the recommended migrations be committed to the *migration engine*.

3.5 Migration Engine

The *migration engine* performs the migrations generated by the *architecture-aware DRM policy*. We design the *migration engine* to avoid unnecessary migrations. Specifically, our *migration engine* has the ability to identify dependencies among recommendations and eliminate avoidable migrations. For instance, if *A-DRM* issues two migrations $VM_A: Host_X \rightarrow Host_Y$ (migrate VM A from host X to Y) and $VM_A: Host_Y \rightarrow Host_X$ (migrate VM A from host Y to X)[1], the *migration engine* would not issue them, since the second migration nullifies the effect of the first migration. Furthermore, if *A-DRM* issues two migrations $VM_A : Host_X \rightarrow Host_Y$ and $VM_A : Host_Y \rightarrow Host_Z$, the *migration engine* will combine them into one: $VM_A: Host_X \rightarrow Host_Z$, thereby improving the efficiency of migrations. After such dependencies have been resolved/combined, the remaining recommended migrations are executed.

---

[1] This is possible because $Metrics$ are continuously updated based on recommended migrations. As a result, future recommended migrations may contradict past recommended migrations.

4. *A-DRM*: Implementation

We prototype the proposed *A-DRM* on KVM 3.13.5-202 [43] and QEMU 1.6.2 [5]. The host used in our infrastructure is a NUMA system with two sockets (Section 5). We use the Linux performance monitoring tool *perf* to access the hardware performance counters, and the hardware performance events we use are listed in Table 1. To estimate the CPU demand of a VM, we use the mechanism proposed by [34]. The memory capacity metrics of a VM are obtained via libvirt [3]. We describe the details of our memory bandwidth measurement scheme and cost-benefit analysis in Sections 4.1 and 4.2 respectively.

4.1 Memory Bandwidth Measurement in NUMA Systems

In a NUMA system, the host contains several sockets and each socket is attached to one or more DIMMs (DRAM modules). For each socket, we measure the memory bandwidth using hardware performance events UNC_QMC_NORMAL_READS and UNC_QMC_WRITES, which includes any reads and writes to the attached DRAM memory. Thus the bandwidth consumption of the socket can calculated as

$$ConsumedMemoryBandwidth$$
$$= \frac{64\text{B} \times (\text{UNC\_QMC\_NORMAL\_READS} + \text{UNC\_QMC\_WRITES})}{ProfilingInterval}$$

since each of these reads and writes access 64 bytes of data. This bandwidth consumption is used along with the peak bandwidth to calculate memory bandwidth utilization (MBW_{util}), as shown in Equation 1. A host is identified as experiencing contention for microarchitecture-level shared resources only when all sockets on a host have MBW_{util} greater than the $MBW_{Threshold}$. While it is possible that only some of the sockets in a host could be contended, in a NUMA system, such interference can usually be mitigated by migrating VMs across sockets [12, 19, 45, 59, 60], which is orthogonal to our proposal.

We also estimate the bandwidth for each VM using OFFCORE_RESPONSE (in Table 1), which tracks the number of all requests from the corresponding VM to the DRAM. The per-VM bandwidth metrics are correspondingly added/subtracted from the socket-level bandwidth utilization metrics to estimate the new memory bandwidth utilizations during the execution of Algorithm 1.

4.2 Cost-Benefit Analysis

The main objective of the cost-benefit analysis is to filter out migrations that do *not* provide performance improvement or that degrade performance. For a given migration tuple <*src*, *vm*, *dst*>, indicating migration of *vm* from host *src* to host *dst* the costs include: 1) the VM migration cost and 2) performance degradation at the destination host due to increased interference. The benefits include: 1) performance improvement of the migrated VM and 2) performance improvement

Table 1: Hardware Performance Events

Hardware Events	Description
OFFCORE_RESPONSE	Requests serviced by DRAM
UNC_QMC_NORMAL_READS	Memory reads
UNC_QMC_WRITES	Memory writes
UNC_QMC_OCCUPANCY	Read request occupancy
LLC_MISSES	Last level cache misses
LLC_REFERENCES	Last level cache accesses
INSTRUCTION_RETIRED	Retired instructions
UNHALTED_CORE_CYCLES	Unhalted cycles

of the other VMs on the source host due to reduced interference. To quantitatively estimate the costs and benefits, all four types of costs/benefits are modeled as time overheads.

4.2.1 Cost: VM Migration

VM migration incurs high cost since all of the VM's pages need to be iteratively scanned, tracked and transferred from the host to the destination. *A-DRM* models the cost of VM migration by estimating how long a VM would take to migrate. This cost depends mainly on the amount of memory used by the VM, network speed and how actively the VM modifies its pages during migration.

The VM migration approach used in *A-DRM* is a *precopy*-based live migration [15, 43, 53] with timeout support. Initially, live migration (that does not suspend the operation of the VM) is employed. If the migration does not finish within a certain time (*live migration timeout*), *A-DRM* switches to an offline migration approach, which suspends the entire VM and completes the migration.

A-DRM calculates the time required for VM migration ($Cost_{migration}$ in Algorithm 1) based on the VM's current active memory size, the dirty page generation rate and the data transfer rate across the network.

$$Cost_{migration} = \frac{ActiveMemorySize}{DataTransferRate - DirtyRate}$$

4.2.2 Cost: Performance Degradation at *dst*

By migrating a VM to a host, the VM would compete for resources with other VMs on the destination host. The main sources of contention at the destination host are the shared LLC capacity and memory bandwidth. The VMs at the destination host would experience interference from the migrated VM at these shared resources, thereby stalling for longer times. The *Stall cycles* (*Stall* for short) indicates the latency experienced by a VM from waiting for requests to the LLC and DRAM, during the previous *scheduling interval*. It is calculated as:

$$Stall = NumLLCHits * LLCLatency +$$
$$NumDRAMAccesses * AvgDRAMLatency$$

We measure the $NumLLCHits$ as the difference between the performance events LLC_REFERENCES and LLC_MISSES (in Table 1). We use a fixed $LLCLatency$ in our system [32]. We use the performance event OFFCORE_RESPONSE to estimate $NumDRAMAccesses$. We estimate the $AvgDRAMLatency$ using performance events UNC_QMC_OCCUPANCY and

UNC_QMC_NORMAL_READS (in Table 1) as:

$$AvgDRAMLatency = \frac{UNC\_QMC\_OCCUPANCY}{UNC\_QMC\_NORMAL\_READS}$$

For every migration tuple $<src, vm, dst>$, A-DRM uses a simple linear model to estimate the new *Stall* of each VM on the destination host after the migration, as a function of last level cache misses per kilo cycles (MPKC), as follows:

$$NewStall_i = Stall_i \times \frac{MPKC_{dst} + MPKC_{vm}}{MPKC_{dst}}, \forall i \in dst$$

$MPKC_{vm}$ is the MPKC of the migrated *vm*, while $MPKC_{dst}$ is the sum of MPKCs of all VMs on the destination host. This simple linear model assumes that the *Stall* for each VM on the destination host, *dst*, increases linearly as the increase in MPKC (LLC miss rate) at the destination host, if *vm* were moved from *src* to *dst*.

The increase in stall time for each individual VM, i, on the destination host (from the linear model above) is

$$DeltaStall_i = \frac{Stall_i \times MPKC_{vm}}{MPKC_{dst}}$$

The overall cost (performance degradation) on the destination host, in terms of time overhead, of migrating *vm* to *dst* is calculated as the sum of the stall time increase of each VM:

$$Cost_{dst} = \sum_{i \in dst} DeltaStall_i$$

4.2.3 Benefit: Performance Improvement of *vm*

A similar linear model as the previous subsection can be used to model the performance benefit experienced by the migrated *vm*:

$$Benefit_{vm} = \frac{Stall_{vm} \times MPKC_{src}}{MPKC_{dst}}$$

$MPKC_{src}$ is the sum of the MPKCs of all VMs on the source host. The migrated *vm*'s stall time reduces/increases proportionally to the ratio of the source and destination's memory bandwidth demand (MPKC), using a linear model.

4.2.4 Benefit: Performance Improvement at *src*

The performance improvement experienced by the VMs remaining on the *src* host can be estimated as:

$$Benefit_{src} = \sum_{j \in src} \frac{Stall_j \times MPKC_{vm}}{MPKC_{src}}$$

The *Stall* of the remaining VMs on the source host reduces proportionally to the memory bandwidth demand (MPKC) of the migrated VM (*vm*), using our linear model.

5. Methodology

We conduct our experiments on a cluster of four homogeneous NUMA servers and a Network-Attached Storage (NAS). All servers and the shared NAS are connected via a 1 Gbps network. Each server is dual-socket with a 4-core Intel Xeon L5630 (Westmere-EP). Each core has a 32KB private L1 instruction cache, a 32KB private L1 data cache, a 256KB private L2 cache, and each socket has a shared 12MB L3 cache. Each socket is equipped with one 8GB DDR3-1066 DIMM. We disable turbo boost and hyper-threading to maximize repeatability. The hypervisor is KVM. The OS is Fedora release 20 with Linux kernel version 3.13.5-202. The QEMU and libvirt versions are 1.6.2 and 1.1.3.5, respectively. Each virtual machine is configured to have 1 vCPU and 2 GB memory.

Workloads. Our workloads are shown in Table 2. We use applications from the SPEC CPU2006 [6], PARSEC [11], NAS Parallel Benchmark [4] suites and the STREAM Benchmark [7, 47]. We also include two microbenchmarks: *MemoryHog* and *CPUUtilization*, which saturate the memory capacity and CPU resources, respectively. We first profile the microarchitecture-level shared resource usage of each application by running it alone inside a VM and pinning the CPU and memory to the same socket. We classify an application as memory-intensive if its memory bandwidth consumption is beyond 1 GB/s, and memory-non-intensive otherwise (details in Section 6.1). Except for the profiling experiments, applications are iteratively run inside VMs.

Metrics. We use the harmonic mean of Instructions Per Cycle (IPC) and weighted speedup [22, 62] to measure performance. We use the maximum slowdown metric [16, 41, 42, 69] to measure unfairness.

Comparison Points and Parameters. We compare A-DRM to a traditional CPU and memory demand based DRM policy [34] (*Traditional DRM* in short). We employ the same methodology to estimate the CPU utilization and memory capacity demand for *A-DRM* and *Traditional DRM*. When the total demand of all the VMs is beyond the host's capacity, it migrates the VMs to other under-utilized hosts. The parameters used in our experiments are summarized below:

Parameter Name	Value
CPU overcommit threshold ($CPU_{Threshold}$)	90%
Memory overcommit threshold ($MEM_{Threshold}$)	95%
Memory bandwidth threshold ($MBW_{Threshold}$)	60%
DRM scheduling interval (*scheduling interval*)	300 seconds
DRM sliding window size	80 samples
Profiling interval (*profiling interval*)	5 seconds
Live migration timeout (*live migration timeout*)	30 seconds

6. Evaluation

In this section, we present our major evaluation results. First, we present the characteristics of workloads, namely, memory bandwidth, LLC hit ratio and memory capacity demand. Afterwards, we revisit our motivational example (Section 2.3), demonstrating the resource utilization behavior and benefits with *A-DRM*. We then evaluate the effectiveness of *A-DRM* with a variety of workload combinations. Finally, we present sensitivity to different algorithm parameters and summarize the lessons learned from our evaluations.

6.1 Workload Characterization

Figure 5 and Figure 6 show the memory capacity demand, memory bandwidth and LLC hit ratio for each workload considered in this study (Note the CPU utilization for each

Table 2: Workloads

Suites	Benchmarks (55 total)	Memory Intensity
SPEC CPU2006	bwaves, mcf, milc, leslie3d, soplex, GemsFDTD, libquantum, lbm (8 total)	memory-intensive
	perlbench, bzip2, gcc, gamess, zeusmp, gromacs, cactusADM, namd, gobmk, dealII, provary, calculix, hmmer, sjeng, h264ref, tonto, omnetpp, astar, sphinx3, xalancbmk (20 total)	memory-non-intensive
PARSEC 2.1	streamcluster (1 total)	memory-intensive
	blackscholes, bodytrack, canneal, dedup, facesim, ferret, fluidanimate, swaptions, x264 (9 total)	memory-non-intensive
NAS Parallel Benchmark	cg.B, cg.C, lu.C, sp.B, sp.C, ua.B, ua.C (7 total)	memory-intensive
	bt.B, bt.C, ep.C ft.B, is.C, lu.B, mg.C (7 total)	memory-non-intensive
STREAM	STREAM (1 total)	memory-intensive
Microbenchmark	MemoryHog, CPUUtilization (2 total)	memory-non-intensive

VM is always above 95%, which is not shown in the figures). The reported values are measured when we run each workload alone and pin the vCPU and memory to the same socket. We make the following observations.

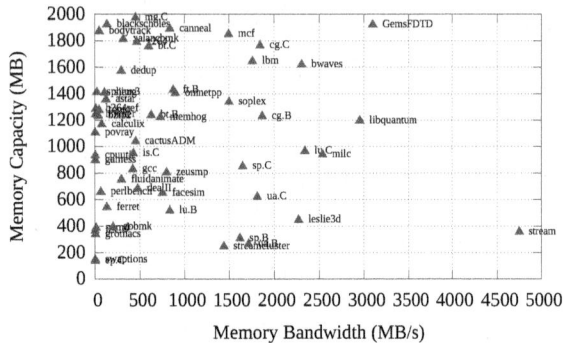

Figure 5: Memory capacity vs. memory bandwidth consumption

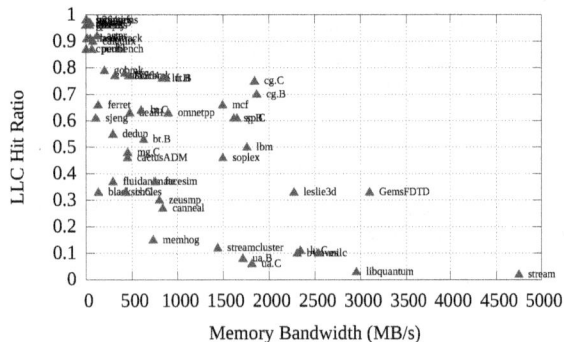

Figure 6: LLC hit ratio vs. memory bandwidth consumption

First, there is no strong correlation between memory capacity demand and memory bandwidth (Figure 5). For instance, the workloads STREAM and gromacs have similar memory capacity demand (around 400MB) while their memory bandwidth requirements are quite different (memory bandwidth requirement of STREAM is 4.5 GB/s while that of gromacs is 0.1 GB/s). There are more such pairs (e.g., blackscholes vs. GemsFDTD, perlbench vs. facesim), indicating that several workloads exhibit different memory bandwidth requirements, while having similar memory capacity demand.[2] Second, generally, workloads that consume

low memory bandwidth exhibit a high LLC hit ratio (Figure 6). However, there exist cases where workloads consume very different amounts of memory bandwidth even when they exhibit similar LLC hit ratios (e.g., leslie3d and blackscholes). This is because the hit ratio only captures what fraction of accesses hit in the cache, whereas the absolute number of requests to the shared memory hierarchy could be very different for different applications. Third, when workloads that have high bandwidth requirements (often due to a low LLC hit ratio) are co-located on the same host, they tend to interfere (as they both access memory frequently), degrading performance significantly. To prevent this contention, we need to consider memory bandwidth and LLC usage behavior in making co-location decisions, as we describe in Equation (1) and Section 4.2.

6.2 A-DRM Case Study

We revisit the example discussed in Section 2.3 and demonstrate the effectiveness of A-DRM on the workloads in the example. Figure 7 shows the impact (over time), of applying A-DRM on our workloads. At the bottom, the evolution of VM-to-host mappings is shown (labeled from Ⓐ to Ⓓ). There are two hosts and seven VMs on each host. Each VM runs either the STREAM benchmark which is represented as a rectangle with vertical lines (denoted as "H", meaning that it has high memory bandwidth demand) or the gromacs benchmark which is represented as a rectangle with horizontal lines (denoted as "L", meaning it has low memory bandwidth demand). The figure also shows the variation of the total CPU utilization (CPU), memory capacity demand utilization (MEM) and memory bandwidth utilization (MBW) (normalized to the total capacity of the host) on each of the hosts, as time goes by. The timeline is labeled from ① to ⑥.

In the initial state (labeled as Ⓐ), we configure all VMs (VM01-VM07) in Host A to run the STREAM benchmark, while all VMs (VM08-VM14) in Host B run the gromacs benchmark. Since STREAM has high memory bandwidth demand, Host A becomes bandwidth-starved, while Host B which executes gromacs (an application with low memory bandwidth demand) has ample unused bandwidth. At the end of the first scheduling interval (300 seconds, ①), A-DRM detects that the memory bandwidth utilization of Host A is above the $MBW_{Threshold}$ (60%).

---

[2] Similarly, we observed no correlation between the memory bandwidth demand and CPU utilization of a workload.

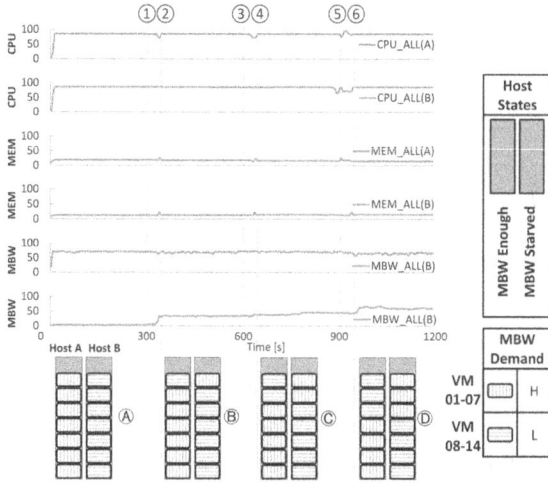

Figure 7: *A-DRM* execution timeline

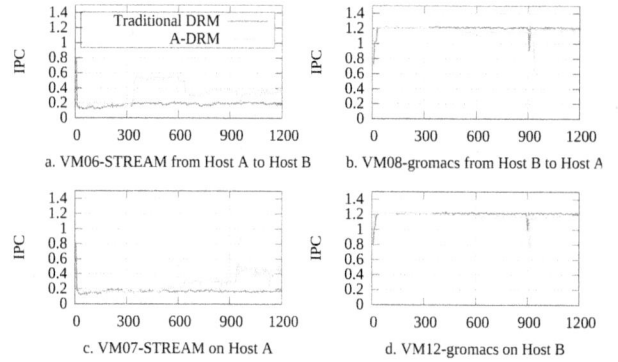

a. VM06-STREAM from Host A to Host B   b. VM08-gromacs from Host B to Host A

c. VM07-STREAM on Host A   d. VM12-gromacs on Host B

Figure 8: IPC of VMs with *A-DRM* vs. Traditional DRM

The *architecture-aware DRM policy* is then invoked. Upon execution of the first phase of Algorithm 1, *A-DRM* selects one VM on Host A, which provides the maximum benefit based on our cost-benefit analysis and migrates it to Host B. Then, upon execution of the second phase of the algorithm, *A-DRM* selects a VM from Host B to re-balance the CPU utilization between the two hosts. As a result of the execution of both phases, the VM-to-host mapping changes, as shown in Ⓑ. Note that after time ②, when this migration is completed, the memory bandwidth usage of Host B increases due to the migrated VM.

Furthermore, it is important to note that while the bandwidth usage of Host B increases, the bandwidth usage of Host A does not decrease even though *gromacs* has lower memory-bandwidth usage than *STREAM*. This is because the freed up memory bandwidth is used by the remaining VMs. Hence, at the next scheduling point (600 seconds, ③), *A-DRM* detects bandwidth contention and invokes the two phases of the *architecture-aware DRM policy* and performs another migration. The result is the VM-to-host mapping in Ⓒ. This process then repeats again at the 900 second scheduling point (⑤), resulting in the VM-to-host mapping in Ⓓ. At this point, the memory bandwidth utilization of the two hosts are similar. Hence, the cost-benefit analysis prevents *A-DRM* from migrating any further VMs, since there is no benefit obtainable from such migrations.

Figure 8 shows the performance of four representative VMs from this experiment. VM06 and VM08 are initially located on Host A and Host B respectively. At the 300-second scheduling point in Figure 7, VM06 is migrated from Host A to Host B, while VM08 is migrated from Host B to Host A. VM07 and VM12 remain on Host A and Host B respectively and are not migrated.

Figure 8a presents the IPC for VM06, which runs *STREAM* and has high memory bandwidth demand. After migration (at 300 seconds), the IPC of VM06 increases significantly. At the 600-second scheduling point, VM06's performance degrades since another VM is migrated from Host A to Host B. As VMs are migrated away from Host A,

VM07's (which remains on Host A) performance (Figure 8c) improves significantly (at 600 and 900 seconds).

A potential concern is that the VMs running *gromacs* may experience performance degradation when co-located on the same host as *STREAM*. However, Figure 8b and Figure 8d show that VM08 , the VM migrated from Host B to Host A and VM12, the VM remaining on Host B experience only a slight drop in performance, since *gromacs* does not require significant memory bandwidth.[3] Therefore, we conclude that by migrating VMs appropriately using online measurement of microarchitecture-level resource usage, *A-DRM* alleviates resource contention, achieving better performance for contended VMs. Furthermore, the cost-benefit analysis prevents migrations that would not provide benefit.

6.3 Performance Studies for Heterogeneous Workloads

Our evaluations until now have focused on a homogeneous workload, to help better understand the insights behind *A-DRM*. In a real virtualized cluster, however, there exist a variety of heterogeneous workloads, showing diverse resource demands. In this section, we evaluate the effectiveness of *A-DRM* for such heterogeneous workloads.

Figure 9 presents the improvement in harmonic mean of IPCs (across all VMs in a workload) for 30 workloads, from our experiments on a 4-node cluster. We run 7 VMs on each node, making up a total of 28 VMs. Each VM runs a benchmark, which is selected randomly from Table 2. Each workload *i*X*n*Y-Z, consists of X VMs that run memory-intensive applications and Y VMs that run *n*on-intensive applications. We evaluate two different workloads for each intensity composition, the number of which is denoted by Z. For instance, *i*12*n*16-1 means that 12 VMs are memory-intensive and 16 VMs are memory-non-intensive (randomly selected from Table 2), and this is the first workload with this particular intensity composition.

We draw three main conclusions from Figure 9. First, *A-DRM* improves performance by up to 26.55%, with an average improvement of 9.67% across all our 30 workloads, compared to traditional DRM [34]. Second, *A-DRM* outperforms traditional DRM for *all* 30 workloads, indicating that microarchitecture-level interference-awareness is an impor-

---

[3] The IPC of VM08 and VM12 drops for a brief period around 900 second since we run gromacs repeatedly throughout the experiment and its first run finishes at 900 seconds.

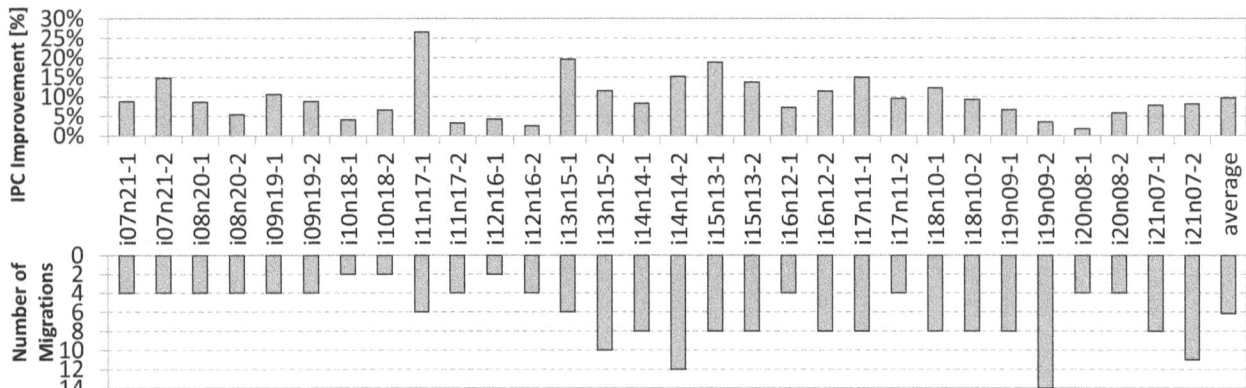

Figure 9: IPC improvement compared to Traditional DRM for different workloads (top), and number of migrations (bottom)

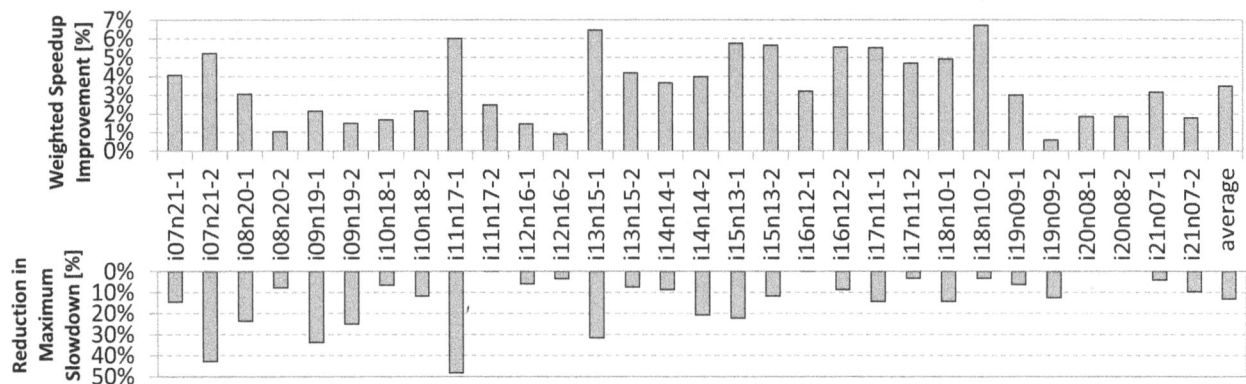

Figure 10: Weighted Speedup (top) and Maximum Slowdown (bottom) normalized to Traditional DRM for different workloads

tant factor to consider for effective virtualized cluster management. Third, *A-DRM* provides the highest improvements when the number of memory-intensive and memory-non-intensive benchmarks is similar, since it is possible to derive significant benefits from balancing demand for cache capacity and memory bandwidth effectively in such workloads.

Figure 9 also shows the number of migrations with *A-DRM*. The number of migrations with traditional DRM is zero, since the CPU/memory capacity utilization among the four hosts are similar, as a result of which no migrations are initiated. On the contrary, for *A-DRM*, this number ranges from 2 to 14 (6 on average).

Figure 10 shows each workload's weighted speedup and maximum slowdown (experienced by any VM in a workload) with *A-DRM* normalized to traditional DRM. *A-DRM*'s average weighted speedup improvement is 3.4% (maximum 6.7%). *A-DRM* reduces the maximum slowdown by 13% (up to 48%). These results indicate that *A-DRM* provides high performance benefits, while also ensuring that VMs are not slowed down unfairly.

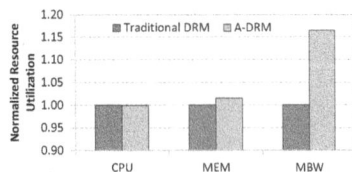

Figure 11: Cluster-wide resource utilization

Figure 11 shows the cluster-wide utilization of CPU, memory capacity and memory bandwidth. We observe that

A-DRM enhances the memory bandwidth utilization by 17% on average, compared to traditional DRM, while maintaining comparable CPU and memory capacity utilization.

6.4 Parameter Sensitivity

The performance of *A-DRM* can be affected by control knobs such as the $MBW_{Threshold}$, *live migration timeout*, and the sliding window size (see Section 4). To evaluate the impact of these different parameters, we conduct several sensitivity studies with the workload we use in our case study (Figure 7), composed of *STREAM* and *gromacs* (on a two-node cluster).

Memory bandwidth threshold. Figures 12 and 13 show the performance and the number of migrations when we vary the $MBW_{Threshold}$ from 50% to 80%. When $MBW_{Threshold}$ is too small (50%), *A-DRM* identifies a host as bandwidth-starved too often, thereby triggering too many migrations, which can incur high overhead. On the contrary, if $MBW_{Threshold}$ is too large ($> 60\%$), contention might go undetected. In fact, we see that there are no migrations when the $MBW_{Threshold}$ is 70% or 80%. We see that an $MBW_{Threshold}$ of 60% achieves a good tradeoff.

Live migration timeout. Figure 14 shows how the live migration timeout parameter affects *A-DRM*. We vary the parameter from 5 to 60 seconds. When it is too small, the migration essentially defaults to a *stop and copy* technique [35], causing very long downtime. On the other hand, when it is too large, the tracking and transferring of modified pages could consume significant resources, which aggravates the interference problem. We use a live migration timeout of 30 seconds that balances these two factors.

Sliding window size. Figure 15 shows the performance when we set the size of the sliding window to 20, 40, 60 and 80 samples respectively. The sliding window mechanism is applied to get smooth moving average values of the profiled metrics. If the size of the sliding window is too small, the moving average of the profiled data will be sharp, causing spurious changes to trigger *A-DRM* to migrate VMs. On the contrary, if the size of the sliding window is too large, the moving average will change slowly, resulting in *A-DRM* being less adaptive. We see that a value of 80 provides good performance.

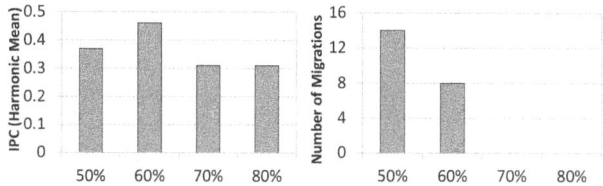

Figure 12: Perf. sensitivity to $MBW_{Threshold}$

Figure 13: Migrations sensitivity to $MBW_{Threshold}$

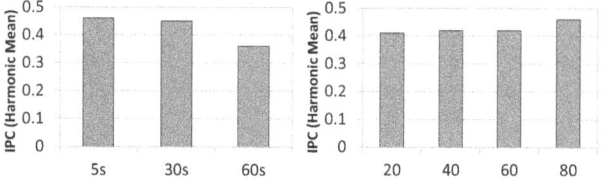

Figure 14: Sensitivity to *live migration timeout*

Figure 15: Sensitivity to sliding window size

6.5 Sensitivity to Workload Intensity

Figure 16 shows the IPC improvement when we vary the memory intensity of the workload. Specifically, we use the same benchmarks and the same two-node cluster used in Figure 7, but change the number of VMs that run the memory-*intensive* workload. Note that in Figure 7, we only conduct experiments for the *i07n07* case.

This figure shows that when the number of memory-intensive VMs in a workload is less than 5, *A-DRM* hardly performs any migrations, achieving similar performance as traditional DRM. When the number of memory-intensive VMs ranges from 5 to 10, *A-DRM* performs a number of migrations and improves performance significantly. When the number of memory-intensive VMs increases beyond 10, there are very few migrations. Upon further investigation, we discovered the reason for this behavior. Our experimental host has two sockets and each socket has 4-cores, its own on-chip memory controller and local memory (8GB DRAM). Hence, when the number of VMs running memory-intensive applications is smaller than or equal to 4, the socket-level migration (enabled by the NUMA_AUTO_BALANCING feature in the Linux kernel) places each memory-intensive VM on a different socket. Therefore, *A-DRM* does not need to do any migrations. On the contrary, when the number of memory-intensive VMs is larger than 10, all sockets/hosts are similarly congested, which does not offer opportunity for *A-DRM* to kick in and migrate VMs. We conclude that *A-*

DRM provides the highest benefits for workloads that have a mix of both memory-intensive and memory-non-intensive applications.

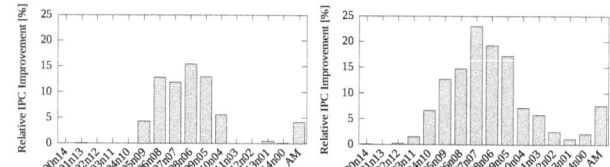

Figure 16: *A-DRM* Performance improvement for different workload intensities

Figure 17: *A-DRM* Performance improvement using socket and host-level migration

6.6 Detecting Per-Socket Contention

While analyzing these results, we were curious to observe what would happen if we turned off the NUMA_AUTO_BALANCING feature and instead, detected contention at a per-socket level and initiate migrations even when a *single socket* on a host is contended (rather than *all* sockets contended). Figure 17 presents results from this experiment.

Comparing Figure 17 with Figure 16 shows that when we detect and respond to socket level interference (while turning off NUMA_AUTO_BALANCING), we achieve better IPC improvement than using just host-level migration. As the number of VMs that run intensive workload increases, the on-chip resources such as LLC and memory controller become greater bottlenecks and socket-level microarchitectural resource contention detection and appropriate VM migration is able to effectively mitigate this interference. We still need to address some issues such as migration cost for socket-level migration and interactions between the hypervisor's NUMA-aware mechanisms and VM migration. We will investigate these issues further as part of our future work.

Another key lesson we learn from this study is that the contention at the inter-socket interconnection network (such as QPI [33] in our system) is not very high. During the initial stages of designing *A-DRM*, we considered the interconnect as one of the contended resources. However, when we measured the QPI traffic, it was always low and hardly ever contended. On analyzing this further, we see that the NUMA_AUTO_BALANCING feature provided by the Linux kernel tries to reduce the remote memory accesses by employing appropriate vCPU scheduling and page migration mechanisms, leading to low interconnect traffic.

7. Related Work

Our work tackles the problem of virtual machine management in a cluster. We have already compared qualitatively and quantitatively to traditional distributed resource management (DRM) schemes (e.g., [31, 34, 72]) that take into account only OS-level metrics such as CPU and memory capacity utilization in making VM-to-host mapping decisions, showing that our proposed *A-DRM* scheme provides significant performance benefits over them.

DRM schemes. To our knowledge, there are few previous works on distributed resource management in a cluster that are aware of microarchitecture-level interference. One work by Ahn et al. [8] explores this direction by simply sorting all the VMs in a cluster by last level cache misses, and remapping the VMs to minimize the number of LLC misses cluster-wide. Our proposed *A-DRM* scheme is more comprehensive with a detailed cost-benefit analysis, taking into account both memory bandwidth utilization and cache misses.

Various DRM polices have been proposed to manage a virtualized cluster [31, 34, 72]. Wood et al. [72] propose to use CPU, memory and network utilization to detect hot spots and migrate VMs. Isci et al. [34] propose an accurate method to estimate the runtime CPU demand of a workload. Based on this, they design a dynamic resource management policy that consolidates the VMs on under-utilized hosts to other hosts to save energy. VMware DRS [31] is a commercial product that enables automated management of virtualized hosts. DRS constructs a CPU and memory resource pool tree, and estimates the CPU and active memory demand of each VM, each host and each pool. After this estimation phase, a top-down phase is invoked where each child's resource requirement and allocation is checked and maintained. DRS uses an aggressive load balancing policy that minimizes the standard deviation of all hosts' CPU and memory utilization. However, unlike *A-DRM*, none of these schemes are aware of the underlying microarchitecture-level shared resource contention.

Mitigating microarchitecture-level interference through task and data mapping. Several research efforts have developed task and data migration mechanisms within a host, that take into account microarchitecture-level interference [9, 10, 18, 19, 24, 46, 49, 52, 67, 68, 70, 71, 74, 76]. Tang et al. [66] develop an adaptive approach to achieve good thread-to-core mapping in a data center such that threads that interfere less with each other are co-located. Blagodurov et al. [12] observe that contention-aware algorithms designed for UMA systems may hurt performance on NUMA systems. To address this problem, they present new contention management algorithms for NUMA systems. Rao et al. [59, 60] observe that the penalty to access the uncore memory subsystem is an effective metric to predict program performance in NUMA multicore systems. Liu et al. [45] observe the impact of architecture-level resource interference on cloud workload consolidation and incorporate NUMA access overhead into the hypervisor's virtual machine memory allocation and page fault handling routines.

While all these works seek to tune performance within a single node, we focus on a *cluster* of servers in a virtualized environment. In such a virtualized cluster setting, VM migration *across* hosts and DRM schemes that are aware of microarchitecture-level interference enable the ability to mitigate interference that *cannot* be mitigated by migrating VMs within a single host.

Other approaches to mitigate microarchitecture-level interference. Other approaches have been proposed to mitigate microarchitecture-level interference. Some examples of such approaches are interference-aware memory scheduling [39, 41, 42, 48, 50, 51, 63, 64], cache partitioning [36, 40, 57, 65, 73], page coloring [14, 44] and source throttling [13, 20, 38, 54, 55]. These works likely enable more efficient VM consolidation as they enable more efficient and controllable utilization of the memory system, and therefore are complementary to our proposal.

8. Conclusion

We present the design and implementation of *A-DRM*, which, to our knowledge, is the first distributed resource management (DRM) scheme that is aware of and that mitigates microarchitecture-level interference via VM migration. Unlike traditional DRM schemes that operate solely based on operating-system-level metrics, *A-DRM* monitors the microarchitecture-level resource usage (in particular, memory bandwidth and shared last level cache capacity usage) of each virtualized host via an on-chip resource profiler, in addition to operating-system-level metrics like CPU and memory capacity utilization. *A-DRM* then performs a cost-benefit analysis to determine which VMs should be mapped to which hosts and achieves the new mapping through VM migration.

We implement *A-DRM* on a KVM and QEMU platform. Our extensive evaluations show that *A-DRM* can enhance the performance of virtual machines by up to 26.55% (average of 9.67%), under various microarchitecture interference levels, compared to a traditional DRM scheme that is not aware of microarchitecture-level interference [31, 34, 72]. *A-DRM* also improves the average cluster-wide memory bandwidth utilization by 17% (up to 36%).

Our work demonstrates a promising path to achieve substantial improvements through microarchitectural-interference-aware distributed resource management for virtualized clusters. Our results show that being aware of microarchitecture-level shared resource usage can enable our *A-DRM* scheme to make more effective migration decisions, thus improving performance and microarchitecture-level resource utilization significantly. We propose to explore more sources of microarchitectural interference (e.g., interconnect bandwidth [16–18, 25, 26]) to further improve performance and resource utilization in virtualized clusters, as part of future work.

Acknowledgments

We thank the anonymous reviewers for their constructive feedback. We acknowledge the support of our industrial partners, including Facebook, Google, IBM, Intel, Microsoft, Qualcomm, Samsung, and VMware. This work is partially supported by NSF (awards 0953246, 1212962, 1065112), the Intel Science and Technology Center on Cloud Computing, the National High-tech R&D Program of China (863) under grant No. 2012AA01A302, National Natural Science Foundation of China (NSFC) under Grant Nos. 61133004, 61202425, 61361126011. Hui Wang is partially supported by the China Scholarship Council (CSC). Lavanya Subramanian is partially supported by a Bertucci fellowship.

References

[1] Windows Azure. http://www.windowsazure.com/en-un/.

[2] Amazon EC2. http://aws.amazon.com/ec2/.

[3] libvirt: The virtualization API. http://libvirt.org.

[4] NAS Parallel Benchmarks. http://www.nas.nasa.gov/publications/npb.html.

[5] QEMU. http://qemu.org.

[6] SPEC CPU2006. http://www.spec.org/spec2006.

[7] STREAM Benchmark. http://www.streambench.org/.

[8] J. Ahn, C. Kim, J. Han, Y.-R. Choi, and J. Huh. Dynamic virtual machine scheduling in clouds for architectural shared resources. In *HotCloud*, 2012.

[9] M. Awasthi, D. W. Nellans, K. Sudan, R. Balasubramonian, and A. Davis. Handling the problems and opportunities posed by multiple on-chip memory controllers. In *PACT*, 2010.

[10] N. Beckmann, P.-A. Tsai, and D. Sanchez. Scaling distributed cache hierarchies through computation and data co-scheduling. In *HPCA*, 2015.

[11] C. Bienia. *Benchmarking Modern Multiprocessors*. PhD thesis, Princeton University, January 2011.

[12] S. Blagodurov, S. Zhuravlev, M. Dashti, and A. Fedorova. A case for NUMA-aware contention management on multicore systems. In *USENIX ATC*, 2011.

[13] K. K. Chang, R. Ausavarungnirun, C. Fallin, and O. Mutlu. HAT: heterogeneous adaptive throttling for on-chip networks. In *SBAC-PAD*, 2012.

[14] S. Cho and L. Jin. Managing distributed, shared L2 caches through OS-level page allocation. In *MICRO*, 2006.

[15] C. Clark, K. Fraser, S. Hand, J. G. Hansen, E. Jul, C. Limpach, I. Pratt, and A. Warfield. Live migration of virtual machines. In *NSDI*, 2005.

[16] R. Das, O. Mutlu, T. Moscibroda, and C. Das. Application-aware prioritization mechanisms for on-chip networks. In *MICRO*, 2009.

[17] R. Das, O. Mutlu, T. Moscibroda, and C. R. Das. Aérgia: exploiting packet latency slack in on-chip networks. In *ISCA*, 2010.

[18] R. Das, R. Ausavarungnirun, O. Mutlu, A. Kumar, and M. Azimi. Application-to-core mapping policies to reduce memory system interference in multi-core systems. In *HPCA*, 2013.

[19] M. Dashti, A. Fedorova, J. Funston, F. Gaud, R. Lachaize, B. Lepers, V. Quema, and M. Roth. Traffic management: A holistic approach to memory placement on NUMA systems. In *ASPLOS*, 2013.

[20] E. Ebrahimi, C. J. Lee, O. Mutlu, and Y. N. Patt. Fairness via Source Throttling: A configurable and high-performance fairness substrate for multi-core memory systems. In *ASPLOS*, 2010.

[21] D. Eklov, N. Nikoleris, D. Black-Schaffer, and E. Hagersten. Bandwidth Bandit: Quantitative characterization of memory contention. In *PACT*, 2012.

[22] S. Eyerman and L. Eeckhout. System-level performance metrics for multiprogram workloads. *IEEE Micro*, (3), 2008.

[23] D. Gmach, J. Rolia, L. Cherkasova, G. Belrose, T. Turicchi, and A. Kemper. An integrated approach to resource pool management: Policies, efficiency and quality metrics. In *DSN*, 2008.

[24] S. Govindan, J. Liu, A. Kansal, and A. Sivasubramaniam. Cuanta: Quantifying effects of shared on-chip resource interference for consolidated virtual machines. In *SoCC*, 2011.

[25] B. Grot, S. W. Keckler, and O. Mutlu. Preemptive virtual clock: a flexible, efficient, and cost-effective QOS scheme for networks-on-chip. In *MICRO*, 2009.

[26] B. Grot, J. Hestness, S. W. Keckler, and O. Mutlu. Kilo-NOC: a heterogeneous network-on-chip architecture for scalability and service guarantees. In *ISCA*, 2011.

[27] A. Gulati, I. Ahmad, and C. A. Waldspurger. PARDA: Proportional allocation of resources for distributed storage access. In *FAST*, 2009.

[28] A. Gulati, C. Kumar, I. Ahmad, and K. Kumar. BASIL: Automated IO load balancing across storage devices. In *FAST*, 2010.

[29] A. Gulati, A. Merchant, and P. J. Varman. mClock: Handling throughput variability for hypervisor IO scheduling. In *OSDI*, 2010.

[30] A. Gulati, G. Shanmuganathan, I. Ahmad, C. Waldspurger, and M. Uysal. Pesto: Online storage performance management in virtualized datacenters. In *SoCC*, 2011.

[31] A. Gulati, A. Holler, M. Ji, G. Shanmuganathan, C. Waldspurger, and X. Zhu. VMware distributed resource management: Design, implementation, and lessons learned. *VMware Technical Journal*, 1(1):45–64, 2012.

[32] Intel. Performance Analysis Guide for Intel Core i7 Processor and Intel Xeon 5500 processors.

[33] Intel. An Introduction to the Intel QuickPath Interconnect, 2009.

[34] C. Isci, J. Hanson, I. Whalley, M. Steinder, and J. Kephart. Runtime demand estimation for effective dynamic resource management. In *NOMS*, 2010.

[35] C. Isci, J. Liu, B. Abali, J. Kephart, and J. Kouloheris. Improving server utilization using fast virtual machine migration. *IBM Journal of Research and Development*, 55 (6), Nov 2011.

[36] R. Iyer. CQoS: a framework for enabling QoS in shared caches of CMP platforms. In *ICS*, 2004.

[37] M. Kambadur, T. Moseley, R. Hank, and M. A. Kim. Measuring interference between live datacenter applications. In *SC*, 2012.

[38] O. Kayiran, N. C. Nachiappan, A. Jog, R. Ausavarungnirun, M. T. Kandemir, G. H. Loh, O. Mutlu, and C. R. Das. Managing GPU concurrency in heterogeneous architectures. In *MICRO*, 2014.

[39] H. Kim, D. de Niz, B. Andersson, M. H. Klein, O. Mutlu, and R. Rajkumar. Bounding memory interference delay in cots-based multi-core systems. In *RTAS*, 2014.

[40] S. Kim, D. Chandra, and Y. Solihin. Fair cache sharing and partitioning in a chip multiprocessor architecture. In *PACT*, 2004.

[41] Y. Kim, D. Han, O. Mutlu, and M. Harchol-Balter. ATLAS: A scalable and high-performance scheduling algorithm for multiple memory controllers. In *HPCA*, 2010.

[42] Y. Kim, M. Papamichael, O. Mutlu, and M. Harchol-Balter. Thread cluster memory scheduling: Exploiting differences in memory access behavior. In *MICRO*, 2010.

[43] A. Kivity, Y. Kamay, D. Laor, U. Lublin, and A. Liguori. kvm: the Linux Virtual Machine Monitor. In *Proceedings of the Linux Symposium*, volume 1, 2007.

[44] J. Lin, Q. Lu, X. Ding, Z. Zhang, X. Zhang, and P. Sadayappan. Gaining insights into multicore cache partitioning: Bridging the gap between simulation and real systems. In *HPCA*, 2008.

[45] M. Liu and T. Li. Optimizing virtual machine consolidation performance on NUMA server architecture for cloud workloads. In *ISCA*, 2014.

[46] J. Mars, L. Tang, R. Hundt, K. Skadron, and M. L. Soffa. Bubble-Up: Increasing utilization in modern warehouse scale computers via sensible co-locations. In *MICRO*, 2011.

[47] T. Moscibroda and O. Mutlu. Memory performance attacks: Denial of memory service in multi-core systems. In *USENIX Security*, 2007.

[48] T. Moscibroda and O. Mutlu. Distributed order scheduling and its application to multi-core DRAM controllers. In *PODC*, 2008.

[49] S. P. Muralidhara, L. Subramanian, O. Mutlu, M. Kandemir, and T. Moscibroda. Reducing memory interference in multicore systems via application-aware memory channel partitioning. In *MICRO*, 2011.

[50] O. Mutlu and T. Moscibroda. Stall-time fair memory access scheduling for chip multiprocessors. In *MICRO*, 2007.

[51] O. Mutlu and T. Moscibroda. Parallelism-aware batch scheduling: Enhancing both performance and fairness of shared DRAM systems. In *ISCA*, 2008.

[52] R. Nathuji, A. Kansal, and A. Ghaffarkhah. Q-clouds: Managing performance interference effects for QoS-aware clouds. In *EuroSys*, 2010.

[53] M. Nelson, B.-H. Lim, and G. Hutchins. Fast transparent migration for virtual machines. In *USENIX ATC*, 2005.

[54] G. Nychis, C. Fallin, T. Moscibroda, and O. Mutlu. Next generation on-chip networks: What kind of congestion control do we need? In *HotNets*, 2010.

[55] G. Nychis, C. Fallin, T. Moscibroda, and O. Mutlu. On-chip networks from a networking perspective: Congestion and scalability in many-core interconnects. In *SIGCOMM*, 2012.

[56] P. Padala, K.-Y. Hou, K. G. Shin, X. Zhu, M. Uysal, Z. Wang, S. Singhal, and A. Merchant. Automated control of multiple virtualized resources. In *EuroSys*, 2009.

[57] M. K. Qureshi and Y. N. Patt. Utility-based cache partitioning: A low-overhead, high-performance, runtime mechanism to partition shared caches. In *MICRO*, 2006.

[58] M. K. Qureshi, A. Jaleel, Y. N. Patt, S. C. Steely, and J. Emer. Adaptive insertion policies for high performance caching. In *ISCA*, 2007.

[59] J. Rao and X. Zhou. Towards fair and efficient SMP virtual machine scheduling. In *PPoPP*, 2014.

[60] J. Rao, K. Wang, X. Zhou, and C.-Z. Xu. Optimizing virtual machine scheduling in NUMA multicore systems. In *HPCA*, 2013.

[61] V. Seshadri, O. Mutlu, M. A. Kozuch, and T. C. Mowry. The evicted-address filter: A unified mechanism to address both cache pollution and thrashing. In *PACT*, 2012.

[62] A. Snavely and D. M. Tullsen. Symbiotic jobscheduling for a simultaneous multithreaded processor. In *ASPLOS*, 2000.

[63] L. Subramanian, V. Seshadri, Y. Kim, B. Jaiyen, and O. Mutlu. MISE: Providing performance predictability and improving fairness in shared main memory systems. In *HPCA*, 2013.

[64] L. Subramanian, D. Lee, V. Seshadri, H. Rastogi, and O. Mutlu. The blacklisting memory scheduler: Achieving high performance and fairness at low cost. In *ICCD*, 2014.

[65] G. E. Suh, L. Rudolph, and S. Devadas. Dynamic partitioning of shared cache memory. *Journal of Supercomputing*, 28(1), 2004.

[66] L. Tang, J. Mars, N. Vachharajani, R. Hundt, and M. L. Soffa. The impact of memory subsystem resource sharing on datacenter applications. In *ISCA*, 2011.

[67] L. Tang, J. Mars, and M. L. Soffa. Compiling for niceness: Mitigating contention for QoS in warehouse scale computers. In *CGO*, 2012.

[68] A. Tumanov, J. Wise, O. Mutlu, and G. R. Ganger. Asymmetry-aware execution placement on manycore chips. In *SFMA*, 2013.

[69] H. Vandierendonck and A. Seznec. Fairness metrics for multi-threaded processors. *IEEE CAL*, February 2011.

[70] C. A. Waldspurger. Memory resource management in VMware ESX server. In *OSDI*, 2002.

[71] C. Weng, Q. Liu, L. Yu, and M. Li. Dynamic adaptive scheduling for virtual machines. In *HPDC*, 2011.

[72] T. Wood, P. Shenoy, A. Venkataramani, and M. Yousif. Black-box and gray-box strategies for virtual machine migration. In *NSDI*, 2007.

[73] Y. Xie and G. H. Loh. PIPP: Promotion/insertion pseudo-partitioning of multi-core shared caches. In *ISCA*, 2009.

[74] H. Yang, A. Breslow, J. Mars, and L. Tang. Bubble-flux: Precise online QoS management for increased utilization in warehouse scale computers. In *ISCA*, 2013.

[75] K. Ye, Z. Wu, C. Wang, B. Zhou, W. Si, X. Jiang, and A. Zomaya. Profiling-based workload consolidation and migration in virtualized data centres. *TPDS*, 2014.

[76] S. Zhuravlev, S. Blagodurov, and A. Fedorova. Addressing shared resource contention in multicore processors via scheduling. In *ASPLOS*, 2010.

Towards VM Consolidation Using a Hierarchy of Idle States

Rayman Preet Singh, Tim Brecht, and S. Keshav

Cheriton School of Computer Science, University of Waterloo

{rmmathar, brecht, keshav}@uwaterloo.ca

Abstract

Typical VM consolidation approaches re-pack VMs into fewer physical machines, resulting in energy and cost savings [13, 19, 23, 40]. Recent work has explored a just-in-time approach to VM consolidation by transitioning VMs to an inactive state when idle and activating them on the arrival of client requests [17, 21]. This leads to increased VM density at the cost of an increase in client request latency (called *miss penalty*). The VM density so obtained, although greater, is still limited by the number of VMs that can be hosted in the one inactive state. If idle VMs were hosted in *multiple* inactive states, VM density can be increased further while ensuring small miss penalties. However, VMs in different inactive states have different capacities, activation times, and resource requirements.

Therefore, a key question is: How should VMs be transitioned between different states to minimize the expected miss penalty? This paper explores the hosting of idle VMs in a hierarchy of multiple such inactive states, and studies the effect of different idle VM management policies on VM density and miss penalties. We formulate a mathematical model for the problem, and provide a theoretical lower bound on the miss penalty. Using an off-the-shelf virtualization solution (LXC [2]), we demonstrate how the required model parameters can be obtained. We evaluate a variety of policies and quantify their miss penalties for different VM densities. We observe that some policies consolidate up to 550 VMs per machine with average miss penalties smaller than 1 ms.

Categories and Subject Descriptors D.4.7 [*Operating Systems*]: Organization and Design, Distributed Systems

Keywords Virtualization, virtual machines, cloud computing, VM density, VM consolidation, VM hierarchy

VEE '15, March 14–15, 2015, Istanbul, Turkey..
Copyright © 2015 ACM 978-1-4503-3450-1/15/03... $15.00.
http://dx.doi.org/10.1145/2731186.2731195

1. Introduction

Virtual machine (VM) consolidation [13, 19, 23, 40] allows cloud-providers to pack multiple VM instances running on underutilized physical machines into fewer machines, enabling some machines to be turned off, resulting in energy and cost savings. This allows cloud-providers to minimize costs, and maximize profits, while continuing to meet SLAs.

Typical VM consolidation approaches simply re-pack VMs into fewer physical machines using VM migration. The VM density (average number of VMs/machine) such methods yield is bounded by the maximum number of VMs that can be co-hosted on a single machine. However many VM workloads exhibit frequent, often long, and uncorrelated idle periods. Examples of such workloads include certain web-hosting workloads [21], cyber-foraging workloads [28], and personal servers [14, 25, 31]. When multiple VMs with such workloads are co-hosted on a machine, decreasing the resource footprint of idle VMs allows for a much denser VM packing, thus reducing hosting costs for both tenants and cloud-providers. For such workloads, it is possible to reclaim resources from idle VMs by transitioning them to inactive state(s), and activating them on the arrival of client requests. Table 1 shows inactive states proposed or supported in a few virtualization solutions. Such a consolidation effort is compatible with existing migration-based consolidation methods since it incurs little network overhead. Moreover, this type of consolidation is able to leverage transient idle periods to reclaim resources whereas conventional VM migration-based consolidation methods rely solely on long idle periods.

Virtualization Solution	Inactive states
LXC [2]	Frozen(stock) [24], Shutdown (stock)
Xen	Suspended, Shutdown (stock), Substrates [35]
VMWare ESXi	Suspended, Shutdown (stock), Fast-resume [38, 39]
KVM	Suspended, Shutdown (stock)

Table 1: Proposed and natively supported (denoted "stock") inactive states for a few virtualization solutions.

Recent work [17, 21] has explored the use of one inactive state (e.g., substrate [35], fast-resume [38, 39]) for managing idle VMs. In doing so, VM density is limited by the maximum number of VMs (per machine) in that inactive state that can be hosted on a machine. If idle VMs were hosted in more than one such inactive state (Table 1), VM density can be increased. Unfortunately, due to differences in their design and resource requirements, different inactive states have varying VM activation and deactivation times, and VM capacities. Consequently, miss penalties for idle VMs in different inactive states vary significantly. This leads to the following questions: 1) How should idle VMs be transitioned across different inactive states? In other words, when a VM becomes idle which inactive state should it be transitioned to? 2) Subsequently, when should an idle VM be transitioned to other state(s) in anticipation of client requests? Therefore, what is needed is a policy that governs the transitions of idle VMs across inactive states so as to minimize the miss penalties and maximize VM density. We refer to these policies as *idle VM management policies*. Existing mechanisms (Section 2) can then be used to implement such policies and dynamically transition idle VMs across the inactive states.

In this work we study the effect of different idle VM management policies on VM density and miss penalties. First, we formally model the problem of multiplexing idle VMs across multiple inactive states. We divide the policy space into two parts, (i) *demand-based* (or reactive) policies, and (ii) *proactive* policies. Using our model formulation, we provide a lower-bound on the miss penalty incurred by demand-based policies. Then, by finding similarities between this problem and the problems of page replacement and multi-level cache management, we propose *SlidingWindow*, a proactive policy which leverages inter-arrival time prediction to further reduce miss penalties. We obtain the model parameters (i.e., inactive state capacities, and transition times) for LXC [2], a widely used OS-level virtualization solution. We then use the measured parameters to evaluate different reactive and proactive policies, while using *personal servers* as a sample low duty-cycle workload. Our evaluation shows that at low-to-medium VM densities, a simple proactive policy can deliver up to an order of magnitude lower average miss penalty than widely known reactive policies, whereas reactive policies perform better under higher VM density.

This work makes the following key contributions:

- We present a formal model for idle VM management policies, and provide a lower bound on the miss penalty of reactive policies.
- With LXC [2] as our example virtualization solution, we demonstrate the measurement of model parameters using microbenchmarks.
- We study a few representative VM management policies, quantify their miss penalties using a simulation-based evaluation, and provide insight into their behaviour.

2. Background and Related work

Target Applications: Numerous rapidly-emerging applications are designed to execute (either completely or in part) on a per-user VM to provide a variety of services such as cloud-backed mobile applications (cyber-foraging) [17, 28],

private data collection [16] and mining [25, 31], private online social networks [11], and other private VM-based applications [20]. Remote management of home sensors [10], and privacy-preserving community-wide sensing [14] are other examples. These VM-hosted applications service workloads where each VM is idle for large periods of time, and at any instant, only a small fraction (across a given number of VMs) are actively serving clients. Hence these idle periods can be leveraged to increase VM density and lower hosting costs. Similarly, recent work [21] has focused on *lower-end* consumers hosting user-facing services with frequent idle-periods, that can tolerate relinquishing of resources, when idle, in exchange for lower hosting costs.

Inactive states for VMs: Traditionally, VMs hosted on a machine are thought of as always being in a booted active state, and thus utilizing the host's CPU, memory, and disks [13, 19, 23, 40]. Inactive states are additional states providing a middle ground between the booted and shutdown states, where VMs consume only a fraction of resources of the booted state. This presents an opportunity for further increasing VM density. As different states utilize different amounts of each resource, it is possible to have a hierarchy of states where, at any instant, VMs actively serving workloads are in the booted state, while each idle VM is in one of the inactive states. Note also that a VM in the shutdown state only consumes the host's disk.

Recent work has proposed inactive states for VMs to reduce their resource footprint, albeit for different reasons e.g., for reducing VM activation time. Wang et al. [35] propose stateful in-memory *VM substrates* which are less resource-intensive than a running VM, and have small VM activation times. Knauth et al. [22] propose a fast-resume state which leverages lazy disk reads to lower VM activation time. Likewise, Twinkle [41] demonstrates the use of different optimizations–working set estimation, demand prediction, and free page avoidance, to lower VM resume (from suspended) times. This body of existing work focuses on reducing resource footprint of inactive VM states and/or reducing activation times, and does not study the multiplexing of VMs across inactive states, and its impact on miss penalties and VM density. To our knowledge, no prior work has studied the design of policies to transition VMs between different states, even for a two-state hierarchy.

Just-in-time provisioning of VMs: Existing work has explored using one inactive state for hosting idle VMs. Dream-Server [21] demonstrates the use of a lazy, eager, and hybrid VM resume [22, 38, 39] for just-in-time provisioning of VMs for web-hosting workloads exhibiting idle periods. Similarly, Ha et al. [17] explore just-in-time VM provisioning for offloading computation from a mobile device. This body of existing work leverages only a single inactive state, which limits VM density to the maximum number of inactive VMs that can co-exist in that particular state. Since inactive states differ in their resource requirements, VM density can be improved by multiplexing idle VMs across multiple inactive states, which is the focus of our work.

Existing work has also demonstrated activation of VMs on request arrival, using different mechanisms, such as a reverse-proxy server running on the host [21]. Other possible mechanisms include using a DNS server running on the host [32], or a host-kernel module which uses the target IP address in a request to identify and activate the target VM.

Determining VM idleness: The amount of time a VM is idle depends entirely on the workload it serves. For instance, if a VM hosts application servers, once an active VM stops serving clients, it can be classified as being idle. Existing work has shown how such rules to determine VM idle time can be created. For instance, in case of server-client workloads such rules can use the number of connected TCP clients [32], or can use CPU and memory utilization [37] (for a variety of workloads, e.g., involving server-client jobs, or VM-initiated jobs). Example mechanisms to implement such rules include *VM introspection* [18, 32, 37], and *client-request monitoring* using a DNS server [32].

3. Model Formulation

Once a VM becomes idle it can either be left in the booted state, or can be transitioned (either immediately or at a suitable later time) to one of the inactive states, depending on the VM management policy in place. Since different inactive states, due to differences in their design and resource intensiveness, have different transition-to-booted times, the policy's actions can significantly affect miss penalties for subsequent requests for this VM. Similarly, because the maximum number of VMs possible in each state is limited (typically by a certain system resource), the policy's actions may also affect miss penalties for other VMs depending on which state it chooses to place them in. Due to such implications on miss penalties, it is important to choose a VM management policy which minimizes miss penalties across all VMs while maximizing VM density.

Many cloud environment workloads today exhibit a great deal of VM heterogeneity. VMs may have varying resource demands, workloads, and SLAs. In this work, as a starting point, we study scenarios where VMs are relatively homogeneous in resource requirements, workloads, and SLAs (e.g., VMs for personal servers in Section 2). We defer the study of heterogeneous scenarios to future work.

To better understand and reason about different possible policies, we formulate a simple mathematical model of the problem. Such a formulation gives a sound theoretical foundation to the problem, and as we show, can be used to provide a lower bound on the miss penalty incurred by any demand-based policy.

Let $S_1, S_2 \ldots S_n$ (as shown in Figure 1) be the n inactive states, in addition let S_0 be the booted state, and S_{n+1} be the shutdown state. Similarly, let $V_1, V_2 \ldots V_v$ be v VMs pro-

visioned on a machine. Let the maximum number of VMs feasible in state S_i be B_i. Let matrix $T_{(n+2) \times (n+2)}$ be the time to transition VMs across different states, i.e. $t_{i,j}$ is time to transition from S_i to state S_j where $i, j \in \{0, 1, \ldots n, n+1\}$. We realize that in practice, the transition times are stochastic variables (associated with some distribution). Our model can be viewed as a mean value analysis. We view B_i as a soft bound, i.e., if the number of VMs in S_i exceeds B_i, transition times ($\forall j, t_{i,j}$ and $t_{j,i}$) may degrade. To simplify the notation in a later proof, let t_i be the time to transition from S_i to S_0 (booted), i.e. $t_i = t_{i,0}, i \in \{0, 1, \ldots n, n+1\}$.

Let VM requests received over a time period t be denoted as $\omega = r_1, r_2 \ldots r_t$, a string of tuples r_i, where $r_i = (V_j, d_i)$ where V_j, and d_i denotes the duration for which V_j is active (serving request r_i). We refer to ω as the *request string*. For a given ω, let $P_\pi(\omega)$ denote the total miss penalty incurred by VM management policy π. Thus for an optimal VM management policy θ, $\forall \omega \forall \pi, P_\theta(\omega) \leq P_\pi(\omega)$.

Policies can be divided into two classes: i) reactive (or demand-based) policies, and ii) proactive policies. We now address each class separately and describe how VM management policies are related to other types of resource management policies.

3.1 Reactive policies

Reactive policies configure, transition, or provision a system resource, such as a memory page, only when a demand for that resource is received, and are also referred to as *demand-based* policies. Examples include the widely used demand-based page replacement policies such as LRU, FIFO, Clock, and others [12]. Another prominent example is multi-level cache management policies such as DEMOTE [36]. Belady's OPT algorithm [9], which simply evicts the page referenced furthest in the future, is provably the optimal demand-based policy for single-level caches [7, 15] (e.g., page replacement). However the optimal demand-based policy for multi-level caches remains unknown [15]. Nevertheless, we build upon existing results on page replacement and caching policies and formulate a lower bound on the miss penalty $P_\pi(\omega)$ incurred by any demand-based VM manage-

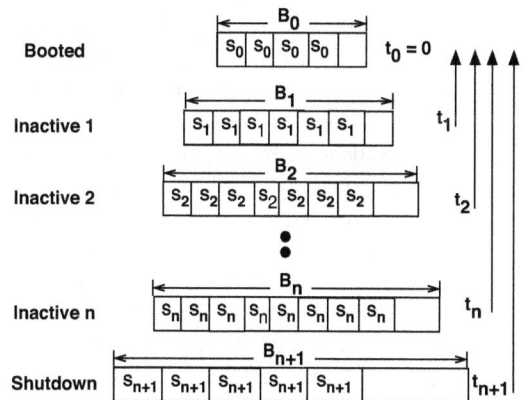

Figure 1: Hierarchy of VM states.

ment policy π. Policies can be either *online*, which only use information about the past, or *offline*, which also use information about the future. Our lower bound assumes knowledge of future arrivals and cannot be implemented in an online fashion. It serves as a theoretical lower bound for comparison with other demand-based policies.

For any given ω, a VM management policy π is a demand-based policy if, π transitions a VM V_i to the booted state at time t (if not already booted), only if $\exists r_t \in \omega$, such that, $r_t = (V_i, d)$ for some duration d. For any given ω, we define $h_i, i \in \{0, 1, \dots n, n+1\}$ to be the number of requests $r_t \in \omega$, such that the target VM was in state S_i on arrival of the request. On arrival of the request r_t the target VM is transitioned to the booted state from its current state. Since the maximum number of VMs in each state is limited (B_i), this transition *may* require additional transitions for (a) transitioning other VMs from the booted state into inactive states, and (b) transitioning other VMs from one inactive state to another. Even if all transitions are conducted in parallel, these additional transitions, depending upon their duration, may contribute towards increasing the miss penalty. For instance, an additional transition may take more time than the time to transition the target VM to the booted state. Thus for any demand-based VM management policy π,

$$P_\pi(\omega) \geq Min_\pi(\omega),$$

where $Min_\pi(\omega) = \sum_{i=0}^{n+1} h_i.t_i$.

3.1.1 Lower bound on demand-based policies

Gill et al. [15] propose a demand-based multi-level cache management policy which provides the lowest average response time and lowest inter-cache bandwidth. Along the same lines, we define a VM management policy ϕ such that

$$\forall \pi, \forall \omega, Min_\phi(\omega) \leq Min_\pi(\omega),$$

and hence, $\forall \pi, Min_\phi(\omega) \leq P_\pi(\omega)$. That is $Min_\phi(\omega)$ forms a lower bound on the total miss penalty for any demand-based VM management policy π, for any request string ω for length $|\omega|$.

We now compute the lower bound $Min_\phi(\omega)$. First, consider a state hierarchy which consists only of the booted and shutdown states (i.e., $n = 0$). Consider the application of Belady's OPT algorithm on this hierarchy for managing VMs, i.e., when a VM needs to be transitioned to the booted state and the number of booted VMs equals B_0, the booted idle VM which will receive a request farthest in the future is shut down. Using this algorithm on a two-state hierarchy, for any given ω, let the optimal number of hits $hOPT(\omega, B_0)$ be the number of requests in ω such that the target VM is in the booted state (S_0) on arrival of the request, where B_0 is the maximum number of VMs possible in the booted state.

Let ϕ be a demand-based VM management policy which, for a reference string ω, for each state S_i ($i \in 0, 1, \dots n$),

exhibits h_i (number of hits to state S_i), such that

$$h_i = hOPT(\omega, \sum_{j=0}^{i} B_j) - hOPT(\omega, \sum_{j=0}^{i-1} B_j). \quad (1)$$

We show that amongst all demand-based policies, ϕ minimizes $Min_\pi(\omega)$, and hence $Min_\phi(\omega)$ forms the lower bound on the total miss penalty of any demand-based policy.

Lemma I Among all demand-based policies, policy ϕ maximizes $\sum_{i=0}^{k} h_i, \forall k \in \{0, 1 \dots n\}$.

Proof: Summing (1) over the range $i = 0, 1 \dots k$ we get,

$$\sum_{i=0}^{k} h_i = hOPT(\omega, \sum_{j=0}^{k} B_j).$$

This is the same as operating Belady's OPT algorithm on a hierarchy with just two states– booted and shutdown, with the maximum possible number of VMs in booted equal to $\sum_{j=0}^{k} B_j$. Since Belady's algorithm is known to be optimal demand-based policy on a two-state hierarchy, $\sum_{i=0}^{k} h_i$ is maximized.

Lemma II For any ω, no other demand-based policy π has $Min_\pi(\omega) < Min_\phi(\omega)$.

Proof: We prove by contradiction. Let $\widehat{\pi}$ be a demand-based policy (with respective $\widehat{h_i}$), such that $Min_{\widehat{\pi}}(\omega) < Min_\phi(\omega)$. Therefore,

$$\sum_{i=0}^{n+1} \widehat{h_i}.t_i < \sum_{i=0}^{n+1} h_i.t_i$$

Or, $\sum_{i=0}^{n} \widehat{h_i}.(t_i - t_{n+1}) + (\sum_{i=0}^{n+1} \widehat{h_i}).t_{n+1} <$

$$\sum_{i=0}^{n} h_i.(t_i - t_{n+1}) + (\sum_{i=0}^{n+1} h_i).t_{n+1}.$$

Since $\sum_{i=0}^{n+1} \widehat{h_i} = \sum_{i=0}^{n+1} h_i = |\omega|$,

$$\sum_{i=0}^{n} \widehat{h_i}.(t_{n+1} - t_i) > \sum_{i=0}^{n} h_i.(t_{n+1} - t_i). \quad (2)$$

Or, $\sum_{i=0}^{n} \widehat{h_i}.(t_n - t_i + t_{n+1} - t_n) > \sum_{i=0}^{n} h_i.(t_n - t_i + t_{n+1} - t_n).$

Or, $\sum_{i=0}^{n} \widehat{h_i}.(t_n - t_i) > \sum_{i=0}^{n} h_i.(t_n - t_i) + (\sum_{i=0}^{n} h_i - \sum_{i=0}^{n} \widehat{h_i}).(t_{n+1} - t_n).$

The second term on right hand side is non-negative because $t_{n+1} \geq t_n$, and by Lemma I, $\sum_{i=0}^{n} h_i \geq \sum_{i=0}^{n} \widehat{h_i}$. This means,

$$\sum_{i=0}^{n} \widehat{h_i}.(t_n - t_i) > \sum_{i=0}^{n} h_i.(t_n - t_i).$$

Since the nth term in the summation on either side is zero, we get,

$$\sum_{i=0}^{n-1} \widehat{h_i}.(t_n - t_i) > \sum_{i=0}^{n-1} h_i.(t_n - t_i). \quad (3)$$

In reducing (2) to (3), the summation reduces from n to $(n-1)$. Since $\forall j \in \{1, \ldots n\}, t_{j-1} \leq t_j$, these steps can be repeated until the summation reduces to $n=1$. That is, $\widehat{h_0}.(t_1 - t_0) > h_0.(t_1 - t_0)$, which implies $\widehat{h_0} > h_0$, which contradicts Lemma I (which states that ϕ maximizes $\sum_{i=0}^{k} h_i, \forall k \in \{0, 1, \ldots n\}$).

Note that the lower bound $Min_{\phi}(\omega)$ assumes future knowledge and cannot be implemented in an online fashion. Nevertheless, it serves as theoretical lower bound for comparing with other demand-based policies. In Section 5, we compare a few widely used demand-based policies with the lower bound and compare them with proactive policies.

3.2 Proactive Policies

Proactive policies configure, transition, or provision a system resource prior to a demand for it being received. They have previously been explored in the context of page replacement, with the goal of producing lower page faults than demand-based page replacement. Existing work [34] has shown that Belady's OPT algorithm is the optimal demand-based policy that minimizes the number of page fetches but does not minimize the number of page faults, because it does not prefetch pages. Trivedi et al. [34] explored the use of proactive policies to lower the number of page faults, and proposed and proved DPMIN [34] as the optimal pre-paging algorithm. DPMIN proceeds as follows: at the time of a page fault, DPMIN scans the future page reference string and fetches the first m pages that will be referenced in the future (including the page that caused the page fault), where m is the number of memory page frames. For the purposes of this paper, we define *proactive policy* as any policy that is not a demand-based policy (as defined above).

SlidingWindow: We extend the DPMIN algorithm and define the SlidingWindow policy for managing VMs across different states. Our rationale is that, since VMs can be transitioned in parallel, provisioning VMs in anticipation of requests would reduce average miss penalties. SlidingWindow proceeds as follows: whenever a request $r_t \in \omega$ is received such that the target VM is not in the booted state, it computes a new state configuration for all VMs. To compute this new configuration, SlidingWindow scans the future reference string (illustrated in Figure 2). All VMs that are currently active are placed in the booted state in the new configuration. If A is the number of currently active VMs, the first $(B_0 - A)$ VMs that will be requested in the future are placed into the booted state (S_0) (illustrated as a time window W_0) in the new configuration. Similarly, the next B_1 VMs that will be requested next are placed into S_1 (illustrated as time window W_1). This process continues up to state S_n (time window W_n), and the remaining $(v - \sum_{i=0}^{n} B_i)$ VMs are placed in the shutdown state. After the new configuration is computed, VMs are moved from their existing to this new configuration.

When VM V_i becomes idle, SlidingWindow re-scans the future reference string to compute t_{next}, i.e., the time at which

V_i will be requested next. If t_{next} falls in the time window W_j it transitions V_i into S_j, and one VM from S_k to S_{k-1} (the one that is referenced the soonest) $\forall k \in \{j, j-1, \ldots 1\}$. In effect, it slides the windows $W_0, W_1 \ldots W_{j-1}$ to the right. If t_{next} falls in the window W_0, V_i remains in the booted state.

Similar to DPMIN, our SlidingWindow policy assumes knowledge of the future reference string, and cannot be implemented in an online fashion. Therefore, in addition to the offline implementation of the policy, we provide an online implementation (called *SlidingWindow+ARMA*) which uses a predictor to estimate t_{next}, and uses the predicted value to perform its proactive VM provisioning. We describe SlidingWindow+ARMA in further detail in Section 5.2, and compare with demand-based policies in Section 5.5.

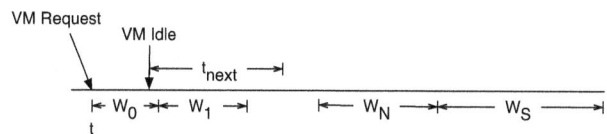

Figure 2: Proactive management, SlidingWindow policy.

4. Obtaining Model Parameters

Our formal model (described in Section 3) relies on a few input parameters, namely the transition times ($T_{(n+2)\times(n+2)}$) and the maximum number of VMs possible in each state (B_i). We use LXC [2], a widely used OS-level virtualization solution, as an example virtualization solution, and conduct an experimental analysis to obtain the model parameters. Note that we continue to refer to execution environments created using LXC as VMs, since our formal model (Section 3) is applicable to any virtualization solution. We now describe our methodology in detail and justify our choices.

4.1 LXC as a Case Study

OS-level virtualization approaches have been shown to incur 40-50% lower virtualization overhead than other approaches such as Xen paravirtualization [27, 33], thus promising potentially higher density. Example OS-level virtualization solutions include LXC [2], OpenVZ [3], and VServer [5]. We choose LXC as our example virtualization solution for several reasons: i) it is open source, allowing easy analysis of its implementation, ii) it is in production use and is part of the mainstream Linux kernel, iii) it offers a low latency inactive VM state called "frozen", iv) it is being used in other projects which can benefit from increased VM density, such as Docker [1] (to provide "frozen in state apps"), and Confidential Commuting [14] (to provide per-user private VEEs).

As noted, in addition to the booted (S_0) and shutdown state (S_2), LXC implements a *frozen* state (S_1) which forms a middle ground between booted and shutdown states. When an idle VM in the booted state is transitioned to the frozen state, it retains its memory and disk footprint, while relinquishing CPU cycles. In addition, frozen-to-booted transition times are significantly smaller than shutdown-to-booted transitions. Thus, LXC provides us with a three-state hierarchy with the booted, frozen, and shutdown states. Menage [24] provides a detailed description of the implementation of the frozen state.

4.2 Experimental Setup

We use LXC [2] (v.0.8.0) to create VMs. VMs are hosted on a machine which has four Intel Xeon processors with six 3.46 GHz cores each, and 128 GB RAM. It uses a 7200 RPM 1 TB SATA hard disk to store VMs OS images. All experiments are repeated 50 times and experiment results are reported using averages with 95% confidence intervals.

VMs in an OS-level virtualization solution, such as LXC, share the host kernel's process pool, data structures, and devices. Therefore, when increasing VM density, some host kernel parameters need to be increased. For instance, since all processes of all LXC VMs share the host kernel's pool of open file descriptors (FD) the total number of open FDs allowed by the host kernel limits the number of VMs. Similarly, the kernel's maximum allowed process identifier (PID) (set to a default of 32,767), and the number of Unix98 pseudoterminals (set to a default of 4,096), also limit the number of VMs. For conducting our experiments we increased these values to 14,000,000, 65,535, and 8,000 respectively.

4.3 Quantifying Density

We first determine the maximum number of booted, frozen, and shutdown VMs that can be supported in our testbed.

Shutdown VMs: The only system resource consumed by shutdown VMs is disk space. It is required for storing their OS image, applications, and libraries. In our testbed, each VM consumes 476 MB of disk space. Thus, 2,000 VMs can be created on a 1 TB disk, using the EXT4 filesystem.

Booted VMs: To determine the maximum number of booted VMs (B_0) we conduct a simple experiment where the number of booted but idle VMs on the machine is gradually increased, while all other VMs are shutdown. VMs are transitioned from shutdown to booted sequentially, with a delay of 30 seconds between successive VMs to ensure that the system reaches a steady state; essential for recording system measurements. Measurements are recorded using *vmstat*.

We observe that the system memory consumption increases steadily with increasing number of VMs. This is because each additional VM consumes approximately 42 MB of memory for initializing its processes (such as its SSH server, and other daemons). Figure 3 shows the CPU system time (time spent running kernel code), and CPU idle time (time spent idle) averaged over all 24 cores on the server machine, with increasing number of booted idle VMs. We observe that up to 250 VMs, the CPU is largely idle. This is because idle VMs do not perform any significant computation, and only a few VM processes (such as udevd, and other daemons) are running, causing a small increase in CPU idle time, while other processes remain blocked. Note that,

all VM processes are in user space. However, beyond 250 VMs, we observe an increase in CPU system time, eventually reaching 100% at 450 VMs. At this stage, no additional VMs can be booted as all 24 cores are completely busy. We believe that this is because of the inability of LXC's cgroup handler [24] to scale with increasing number of processes. LXC uses the cgroup handler for bookkeeping of resources used by processes of different VMs and to maintain isolation. As a result, this limits the number of booted idle VMs to approximately 250.

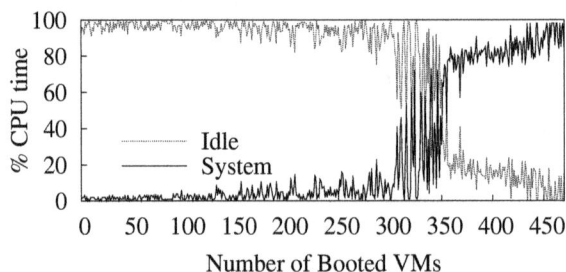

Figure 3: CPU utilization versus booted VMs.

Frozen VMs: We now determine the maximum number of frozen VMs (B_1), by conducting a simple experiment where the number of frozen VMs on the machine is gradually increased. Each VM is booted, allowed to initialize, and then transitioned to frozen. To determine when a VM has finished booting, we use *netcat* to detect if the VM's SSH server has started. We measure the time taken to boot-up the VM and start its SSH server. All other VMs remain in the shutdown state.

We observe a steady increase in the system memory consumption (at approximately 42 MB per VM; figure omitted due to space constraints). This is because processes in a frozen VM retain their memory footprint (due to the absence of memory pressure). Moreover, we observe that the time to transition a VM from shutdown to booted (before transitioning to frozen) increases considerably as the number of frozen VMs on the machine increases. This is because many system calls used by LXC for booting a VM, such as fork, wait, and open, take more time to complete, as the number of frozen VMs increases. As described in Section 4.4, this increase in transition time eventually limits the number of frozen VMs (to approximately 300 frozen VMs).

4.4 Impact of Density on Transition Time

We study the effect of VM density in each state on the transition times. We vary the number of booted VMs and measure the different state transition times (while keeping the number of frozen VMs at zero). Similarly we vary the number of frozen VMs and measure the transition times.

Varying Number of Booted VMs: The number of booted VMs is increased in steps of 50. At each step the different transition times are measured (for a given VM). All other VMs are in the shutdown state.

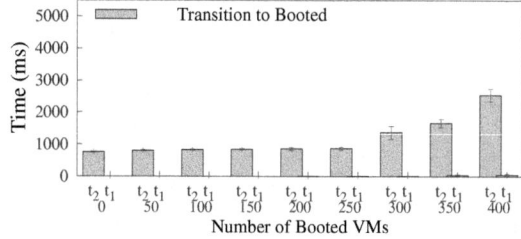

(a) Transition times for Shutdown-to-Booted (t_2) and Frozen-to-Booted (t_1).

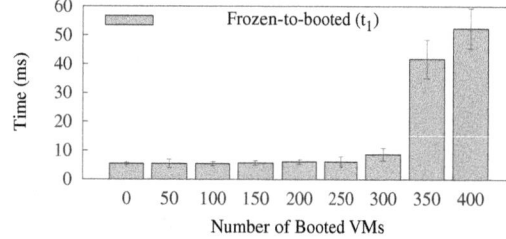

(b) Transition times for Frozen-to-Booted (t_1).

Figure 4: Transition times with increasing number of booted VMs.

Figure 4a shows the shutdown-to-booted (denoted t_2) and frozen-to-booted (denoted t_1) transition times. We observe that up to 250 VMs, the shutdown-to-booted transition time remains largely constant. However, beyond 250 booted VMs we see a considerable increase in boot-up time. This is due to a surge in CPU system time at 300 VMs and beyond (as explained in Section 4.3, Figure 3), which reduces available CPU time to zero. Figure 4b shows the frozen-to-booted transition time (denoted t_1 in Figure 4a), with a magnified time axis. We observe that frozen-to-booted transition times increase only slightly with increasing number of booted VMs, and is considerably smaller than shutdown-to-booted transition time (because frozen-to-booted is a comparatively faster and less resource-intensive transition). The abrupt rise beyond 300 booted VMs, is attributed to the surge in CPU system time, as explained in Section 4.3. Along the same lines we also measure the booted-to-shutdown ($t_{0,2}$) and booted-to-frozen ($t_{0,1}$) transition times with increasing number of booted VMs. However, we do not observe any significant variation in these transition times, remaining constant at approximately 640 ms and 0.15 ms respectively (not shown).

Varying Number of Frozen VMs: In a fashion similar to the previous experiment, the number of frozen VMs is gradually increased, and the different transition times are measured.

Figure 5a shows the shutdown-to-booted (denoted t_2) and frozen-to-booted (denoted t_1) transition times. We observe that the shutdown-to-booted transition time increases only slightly up to 300 frozen VMs, and are considerably larger beyond that point. This is because, as discussed in Section 4.3, certain system calls used by LXC for booting, require more time to complete when the number of frozen VMs increases, leading to increased transition times. Figure 5b shows the frozen-to-booted transition times (denoted as t_1 in Figure 5a) with a magnified time axis. We observe that below 300 VMs, the transition time is largely constant. However, beyond 300 frozen VMs, the transition time increases considerably. This is because LXC's cgroup freezer [24] mechanism begins consuming more time for unfreezing a VM, and hence does not scale. Therefore, the number of frozen VMs is limited by this increased transi-

tion time, to approximately 300. As in the previous experiment, we find that the booted-to-shutdown ($t_{0,2}$) and booted-to-frozen ($t_{0,1}$) transition times do not change significantly with increasing number of frozen VMs (measured at approximately 642 ms, 0.17 ms respectively, which is nearly identical to their values in case of varying number of booted VMs).

4.5 Deriving Model Parameters

Using the experimental analysis (described above), we derive the model parameters as follows.

Due to observed density and transition time with increasing number of booted VMs (as explained above, Figures 3, 4), we define the maximum number of VMs possible in the booted state (B_0) to be approximately 250. Similarly, given the variation in transition times with increasing number of frozen VMs (Figure 5), the maximum number of VMs possible in the frozen state (B_1) is approximately 300. Note that both B_0 and B_1 values derive from limitations in LXC's design and implementation (described above). While it may be interesting to explore these limitations in greater detail (and alleviate them), it lies outside the scope of this work.

We compare the shutdown-to-booted (t_2) and frozen-to-booted (t_1) transition times in the two sensitivity analysis experiments (i.e., Figure 4a and Figure 5a). Interestingly, we find that within the operating range of up to 250 booted VMs, and up to 300 frozen VMs, the respective transition times in either experiments differ insignificantly. For instance, shutdown-to-booted transition time when varying only the number of booted VMs (up to 250 booted VMs, Figure 4a), is comparable to shutdown-to-booted transition time when varying only the number of frozen VMs (up to 300 frozen VMs, Figure 5a). Other transitions times (frozen-to-booted $t_{1,0}$, booted-to-frozen $t_{0,1}$, and booted-to-shutdown $t_{0,2}$) exhibit similar behaviour. Thus, we believe that within this operating range (up to 250 booted, 300 frozen VMs) all transition times remain largely constant, *regardless of the number of booted and frozen VMs*. Therefore, we represent the average transition times (within the operating range) as the transition matrix $T_{3\times3}$ (shown in Table 2, where $t_{i,j}$=time to transition from state S_i to S_j). To transition a frozen LXC VM to shutdown (and vice versa), it must first be transitioned to booted.

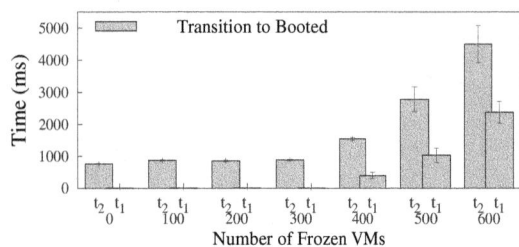

(a) Transition times for Shutdown-to-Booted (t_2) and Frozen-to-Booted (t_1).

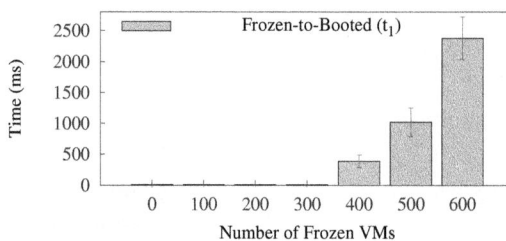

(b) Transition times for Frozen-to-Booted (t_1).

Figure 5: Transition times with increasing number of frozen VMs.

To From	Booted (S_0)	Frozen (S_1)	Shutdown (S_1)	B_i
Booted (S_0)	0.00 ms	0.17 ms	641.64 ms	250
Frozen (S_1)	4.43 ms	0.00 ms	-	300
Shutdown (S_2)	802.16 ms	-	0.00 ms	2000 (Disk limited)

Table 2: Transition matrix ($T_{3\times3}$) and B_i values for LXC.

5. Policy Comparison

Using the parameters obtained above we study the effect of different policies using a simulation-based analysis, which makes exploring a large design space feasible.

In the next section, we discuss the design and implementation of our simulator, followed by the description of the policy implementations (Section 5.2), personal server workloads (Section 5.3), our evaluation metric (Section 5.4), and simulation results (Section 5.5).

5.1 Simulator Design and Implementation

Our simulator consists of a *policy module*, a *cost-model module*, and a *workload module*. The cost-model module encapsulates the VM hierarchy parameters (B_i and $T_{3\times3}$). The policy module encapsulates all logic pertaining to a particular policy and maintains any in-memory state required for implementing that policy, e.g., any per-VM bookkeeping. The workload module encapsulates all logic required for simulating the VMs' workloads such as distributions for request inter-arrival time and request durations. Such modularity allows us to easily extend the simulator to study different workloads, different VM management policies, as well as different VM hierarchies, simply by implementing the respective module. The simulator maintains the current state assignment for each VM. In addition, it contains a single time-sorted event queue, and a single thread which processes events in this queue. Events are either of type VMrequest or VMidle.

At initialization time, the workload module generates the simulated VMrequest events for the required number of VMs, and populates the event queue. When processing a VMrequest event, the simulator passes the current state assignment, the request event, and event queue to the policy module, and receives the updated state assignment. It then compares the updated state assignment with the current one, and computes a list of required VM transitions. It then computes the time required to perform the transitions, updates the state assignment, and enqueues a VMidle event with a later timestamp (derived using the request duration in the VMrequest event) into the event queue. Note that, all invocations of the policy module are serialized. For instance, if a VMrequest event occurs while the policy module is computing the updated VM state assignment, it is processed after the policy module finishes its computation. Lastly, when computing the time taken to perform a set of transitions, the simulator assumes that different VMs' transitions take place in parallel. This assumption is justified because in doing so we are able to measure the best case behavior of any policy. Any additional overhead in the system in performing parallel transitions would only serve to increase the transition times, and the miss penalty so obtained would still be bounded by the best case scenario. VMidle events are processed in the same fashion as VMrequest events. However, certain policies (e.g, demand-based policies) may choose to not take any action when a VM becomes idle.

Implementation: We have implemented the simulator using C# over the .NET v4.5 framework. We have implemented policy modules for different reactive and proactive policies, the workloads described in the next section, and a cost-model module for LXC. We validate the simulator using sample deterministic workloads and state hierarchies. The implementation is publicly available online [4].

5.2 Policy Implementations

LRU: Least Recently Used (or LRU) [12] is a policy that is widely studied for page replacement. We apply it to idle VM management in a cascaded fashion. For each VM, it maintains the timestamp of the last request (t_r). All VMs are initially in the shutdown state. As requests for different VMs start arriving, they are transitioned to the booted state. Eventually, as the number of VMs in the booted state (i.e., including active and idle VMs) reaches the limit B_0, for each VM transitioning into booted thereafter, LRU chooses to transition the booted VM with the minimum t_r into the frozen state. In effect, for each VM it uses the "time since last request" to estimate the likelihood that it will be requested again. Similarly, as the number of VMs in the frozen state reaches B_1, for each VM transitioning into frozen thereafter, the frozen VM with the minimum t_r is shut down. Note that, unlike traditional implementations of LRU (e.g., in page replacement) where all timing information of the resource is deleted after its eviction, we maintain t_r for each VM after eviction in order to apply it across multiple states.

Cascaded Belady's OPT: This policy is simply an extension of Belady's OPT algorithm to multiple states. We apply it to idle VM management. That is, when number of VMs in any state S_i exceeds B_i, the VM that is referenced the furthest in the future is transitioned to S_{i+1}. This version of Belady's OPT algorithm is known to suboptimal [15]. However, we implement it in order to compare it with demand-based policies that have no future knowledge (e.g., LRU) and the lower bound $Min_\phi(\omega)$. To the best of our knowledge, such a comparison has not been conducted in previous work.

Lower Bound on demand-based policies: As explained in Section 3.1.1, $Min_\phi(\omega)$ forms the lower bound on demand-based policies. We first obtain the h_0, h_1, h_2 values for LXC as per Eq. 1 for the different workloads we study (i.e., different ω values). For each ω, we obtain $h_0 = hOPT(\omega, B_0)$, $h_1 = hOPT(\omega, B_0 + B_1) - hOPT(\omega, B_0)$, and $h_2 = |\omega| - h_0 - h_1$. We then determine the lower bound $Min_\phi(\omega) = (h_0.t_0 + h_1.t_1 + h_2.t_2)$.

SlidingWindow: As explained in Section 3.2, our Sliding-Window policy requires knowledge of the future. Therefore we provide an online implementation of this policy (called *SlidingWindow+ARMA*) which implements a predictor to predict the inter-arrival time for each VM, and updates the prediction model at each request for that VM. We employ the widely-used *auto regressive moving average* (ARMA) time-series model for predicting the inter-arrival times. To find the order of the ARMA model we employ the Bayesian information criterion and at each model update we perform a maximum likelihood fit on the inter-arrival times. The policy then uses the predicted inter-arrival time for each VM to perform its proactive actions. Therefore, its miss penalty greatly depends on the prediction error of the ARMA model.

To evaluate SlidingWindow+ARMA, we also implement the offline version of SlidingWindow which uses knowledge of the future (called *SlidingWindow+GroundTruth*).

5.3 Workload Analysis: Personal Servers

In order to perform a comparison of the miss penalties incurred by different policies, we chose the personal server workload. As outlined in Section 2, in these workloads each user owns and controls a separate private VM, which hosts application instances that serve client requests from that user. We chose this workload because a) they are low duty-cycle in nature [32], i.e. private VMs have uncorrelated idle times, thus allowing greater multiplexing across inactive states, b) they are a topic of active research with numerous applications such as privacy-preserving online social networks [11, 29, 30], private sensor data collection and processing [14, 16, 31], and privacy-preserving offloading from mobile devices [17].

We use three categories based on the requests' inter-arrival and duration times. We believe that such categorization (as opposed to a mixed workload) allows us to better understand the behavior of different policies.

Fixed inter-arrival time, Fixed duration: A common use of personal VMs is for periodic and fixed amount of data uploads from in-home sensors [31], or a user's smartphone [14, 25]. This leads to a request sequence where requests have fixed inter-arrival times and durations. For such requests both the arrival and departure of requests are highly predictable, and form an interesting point of comparison between proactive and reactive policies.

Stochastic inter-arrival time, Fixed duration: Recent work has proposed using personal VMs as *virtual individual servers* [11, 29, 30] where users host their private instances of common application servers. Due to the user-facing nature of these application servers, the requests they receive have stochastic inter-arrival times, and commonly involve downloading or uploading fixed amounts of data, thus leading to requests with a relatively fixed duration.

Stochastic inter-arrival time, Stochastic duration: A new and evolving use of personal VMs is as personal data and compute environments, which host and process user data. Examples include private data analytics [31], VM-backed mobile applications [28], and other similar applications [20]. In these applications the requests are user-generated, and thus have stochastic inter-arrival times. In addition these requests have a varying nature, e.g., size of data processed, and type of computation performed, which results in them having stochastic durations.

5.4 Metric

In order to compare different policies for a request string ω, we use the *average miss penalty* incurred by any policy π.

$$\text{Average miss penalty} = \frac{P_\pi(\omega)}{|\omega|}.$$

This metric i) captures the miss penalty across all VMs in the system, ii) allows us to observe the behavior of any policy with increasing number of total VMs, and iii) allows us to easily observe the differences between reactive and proactive policies. Note that the lower bound on average miss penalty of reactive policies is simply $\frac{Min_\phi(\omega)}{|\omega|}$.

5.5 Simulation Results

We now study the effect of increasing VM density on the average miss penalty for different policies. The request string ω in all simulations contains 100 arrivals per VM, i.e., $|\omega|$=Total #VMs $\times$ 100.

In order to simulate stochastic inter-arrival times, we use the request inter-arrival times from publicly available web trace data [8], since it has been used in evaluating on-demand VM provisioning in existing work [21]. Similarly in order to simulate stochastic request durations, we use the web connection duration characterization provided by Newton et al. [26], since we believe it to be a representative request duration characterization for personal servers. Lastly, we use the respective mean values from the two datasets for generating the fixed inter-arrival time (of 50 s) and fixed duration (of 10 s) workload. Table 3 shows the variability of inter-arrival times for the three cases we study. We do not include details for duration because the policies we consider do not utilize duration (policies that do so will be considered in future work). In each workload experiment (below), we start the x-axis at 250 VMs since it is the maximum number of VMs possible in the booted state (and there are no miss penalties below 250 VMs). We increase VM density to the point that the total number of simultaneously active VMs increases above 250 (equal to B_0) and cannot be hosted using this hierarchy. Note that this limit is a result of the current workload (longer idle times would increase this limit).

Case		Mean	Standard deviation	Min	Max
Duration	Inter-arrival				
Fixed	Fixed	50.0 s	0.0 s	50.0 s	50.0 s
Fixed	Stochastic	50.0 s	160.5 s	10.0 s	941.2 s
Stochastic	Stochastic	50.0 s	163.0 s	0.9 s	941.2 s

Table 3: Variation of inter-arrival times.

5.5.1 Fixed inter-arrival time, fixed duration

Figure 6 shows the average miss penalty for a request string ω with a fixed inter-arrival time of 50 seconds, and a fixed request duration of 10 seconds, for different policies with increasing VM density. Figure 6 also shows the shutdown-to-booted and frozen-to-booted transition times for comparison. For each VM, the time at which its first request is received is chosen uniformly at random from [0,50 s]. Later in this section, we analyze the behavior of policies under other inter-arrival time and duration values.

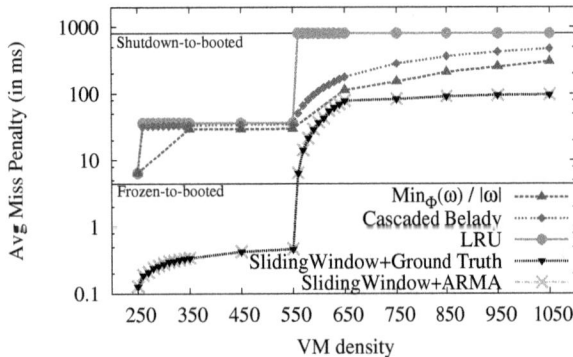

Figure 6: Fixed inter-arrival time and duration.

We first explain the behaviour of the reactive policies. We observe that at a VM density of 250, both reactive policies, LRU and Cascaded Belady's OPT, incur the same average miss penalty which matches the lower bound. This is because in this case, all reactive policies transition each VM into booted once its first request is received, and no idle VMs need to be transitioned out of the booted state thereafter, since VM density equals B_0. As VM density increases further, not all VMs can remain booted. Depending

on the policy, some VMs are transitioned to frozen (when idle), and are transitioned to the booted state when their request arrives, which increases the average miss penalty. Similarly, as VM density increases beyond 550, not all VMs can be in either booted or frozen states. That is, all other VMs are transitioned to the shutdown state (when idle), and are brought into the booted state when their request arrives, which contributes to increase the average miss penalty. Since shutdown-to-booted transition times are significantly higher than frozen-to-booted (approximately 800 ms vs. 4 ms), we see a much larger increase in the average miss penalty at VM density $\geq$ 550 (than at 250 VMs). Note that, LRU has significantly higher average miss penalty than the cascaded Belady's algorithm because LRU has no knowledge of the future reference string. In case of LRU, when VM density is greater than 550, at each request the target VM is always in the shutdown state thus incurring the maximum miss penalty. This is because in this workload, between two consecutive requests to any VM V_i, there are (v-1) requests for other VMs (i.e., one per VM). Since LRU evicts the least recently used VM from booted to frozen, and frozen to shutdown, when $v > 550$, V_i will get transitioned to shutdown after the intermediate (v-1) requests are serviced.

We now explain the behavior of proactive policies. Due to easily predictable fixed request inter-arrival times and durations, the average miss penalty of the SlidingWindow policy using our ARMA predictor (denoted 'SlidingWindow+ARMA') equals that of SlidingWindow with future knowledge (denoted 'SlidingWindow+Ground Truth'). We observe that either policy incurs a significantly lower average miss penalty than the reactive policies. This is because whenever a request whose target VM is not in the booted state is received, in addition to transitioning that VM to booted, SlidingWindow also transitions other VMs (as many as possible) to booted and frozen states (as explained in Section 3.2). Note that the proactive transitions in SlidingWindow are triggered by a request whose target VM is not in the booted state. Therefore, as VM density increases up to 550, VMs span the booted and frozen states, and beyond 550, VMs span all three states. This increases the average miss penalty (since the shutdown-to-booted transition time is significantly larger than the frozen-to-booted time). Moreover, the number of idle VMs that SlidingWindow can proactively transition to booted, depends on the number of active VMs at that instant (since the number of active booted + the number of idle booted = 250). As VM density increases, the number of simultaneously active VMs increases, and hence the number of VMs that can be proactively transitioned to booted decreases. This reduction in the number of possible proactive transitions also contributes to increase the average miss penalty.

For this workload, comparing the two online (implementable) policies (LRU and SlidingWindow+ARMA), we conclude that SlidingWindow+ARMA incurs the lower average miss penalty. It increases VM density from 250 to 550 (a gain of more than 2.2×), while keeping average miss penalty under 1 ms, for a fixed inter-arrival time of 50 seconds and fixed duration of 10 sec. Note that each VM is active for 10 sec, then becomes idle for 40 seconds before being active again, i.e., a *mean duty-cycle* of 20%. If the maximum number of frozen VMs was not limited to 300 by LXC's implementation, for up to 250 simultaneously active VMs, a maximum of $\frac{250}{0.2}$ or 1250 VMs can be hosted using this state hierarchy while keeping the average miss penalty under 1 ms. Similarly, for an idle time of 10 seconds and active time of 40 seconds (duty cycle=0.8), the maximum VM density with average miss penalty under 1 ms, would be $\frac{250}{0.8}$ or 312 VMs. To generalize, maximum VM density, for average miss penalty ≤ 1 ms with maximum number of simultaneously active VMs ≤ 250, equals $\text{MIN}\left(B_0 + B_1, \frac{B_0}{\text{mean duty-cycle}}\right)$.

5.5.2 Stochastic inter-arrival time, fixed duration

Figure 7 shows the average miss penalty for a request string ω with stochastic inter-arrival time (as described above), and a fixed request duration of 10 seconds, for different policies with increasing VM density. Figure 7 also shows the shutdown-to-booted and frozen-to-booted transition times for comparison.

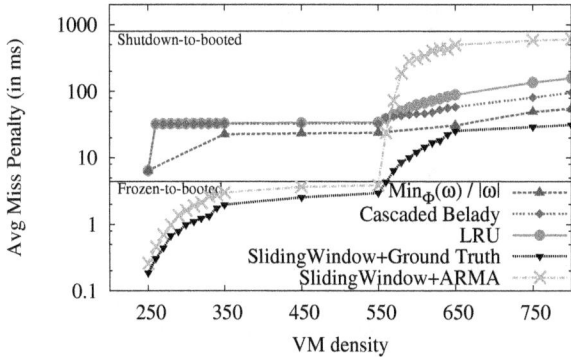

Figure 7: Stochastic inter-arrival time, fixed duration.

We observe that the behaviour of reactive policies in this case is similar to that in the case of fixed inter-arrival fixed duration workloads (as described above in Section 5.5.1). That is, their average miss penalty is equal and lowest at VM density of 250 VMs, thereafter it increases with VM density (and remains higher than the lower bound). Miss penalty is significantly higher at VM density level of 550 VMs (and more) than that at 250-550 VMs. This is because at VM density more than 550, VMs span booted, frozen, and shutdown states (and shutdown-to-booted transition time is significantly larger than frozen-to-booted time).

We now explain the behaviour of the proactive policies. Due to reasons explained above in Section 5.5.1, the average miss penalty of the SlidingWindow with future knowledge (denoted 'SlidingWindow+Ground Truth') increases as VM density increases. The increase is large at

VM density of more than 550 VMs due to the shutdown-to-booted transition time being significantly larger than frozen-to-booted. Our online implementation of SlidingWindow which uses the ARMA predictor, SlidingWindow+ARMA, incurs a higher average miss penalty than SlidingWindow+GroundTruth. This is because SlidingWindow+ARMA uses the predicted inter-arrival time for each VM to make proactive transition decisions, and thus error in prediction causes some VMs to be transitioned to sub-optimal states, which increases the average miss penalty. We observe significantly larger average miss penalties beyond VM density of 550 VMs, even though the normalized root mean square error of the prediction remains largely constant (at 0.04) with increasing VM density. This is because beyond a VM density of 550, VMs span all three booted, frozen, shutdown states (as compared to only booted and frozen below 550), and the shutdown-to-booted, booted-to-shutdown transition times are significantly higher than the frozen-to-booted, frozen-to-shutdown transition times respectively. Hence, with increasing number of VMs, for a relatively constant degree of mis-predictions, the number of VMs that get transitioned sub-optimally to the shutdown state due to a mis-predicted inter-arrival time increases. It is the large transition times for the shutdown state that causes the significant increase in average miss penalty. Due to this increase the average miss penalty of SlidingWindow+ARMA exceeds that of reactive approaches (beyond 560 VMs).

For this workload, when comparing the two online policies, LRU and SlidingWindow+ARMA, we conclude that for a desired VM density of up to 550 VMs (2.2 × the density of current solutions), SlidingWindow+ARMA incurs a much lower average miss penalty (less than 4 ms). However, for all VM density levels larger than 560, LRU outperforms SlidingWindow+ARMA. At these density levels, some idle VMs need to be in the shutdown state (which has large transition times), and any error in inter-arrival time prediction, causes a significant increase in the average miss penalty.

5.5.3 Stochastic inter-arrival time, stochastic duration

Figure 8 shows the average miss penalty for a request string ω with stochastic inter-arrival time and stochastic duration, for different policies with increasing VM density. Figure 8 also shows the shutdown-to-booted and frozen-to-booted transition times for comparison.

We observe that the stochastic request duration has little effect on the average miss penalty, which is very similar to that in case of stochastic inter-arrival time and fixed duration (described above in Section 5.5.2). We believe that this is because both the reactive and proactive policies we study (LRU, Cascaded Belady's algorithm, and SlidingWindow), only use request inter-arrival time in making their reactive or proactive transition decisions. It may be possible to formulate policies which also take expected request durations into account, which we defer to future work. The behaviour of our current policies can be explained using reasoning similar to that in Section 5.5.2.

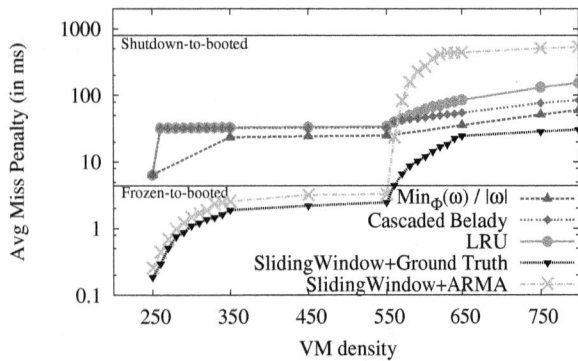

Figure 8: Stochastic inter-arrival time and duration.

5.5.4 Summary of Simulation Results

The key findings of the policy comparison (described above) can be summarized as follows:

- Online proactive policies such as SlidingWindow+ARMA are highly sensitive to prediction error. Thus for any given hierarchy, to ensure low miss penalties such policies should be used only when the desired VM density is such that all VMs can be accommodated within inactive states with low transition times. That is, when the penalties for mis-predictions are relatively small. Under all other conditions (e.g., larger VM density levels), reactive and stateless policies such as LRU should be used.
- Miss penalties of proactive and reactive (online or offline) policies which only make use of request inter-arrival times, are largely unaffected by request durations being fixed or stochastic.
- For certain workloads, using an online per-VM predictor based proactive policy results in up to a 2.2× gain in VM density with average miss penalty less than 1 ms.

6. Discussion, Limitations, and Future Work

We demonstrate multiplexing of idle VMs across inactive states using LXC as our example virtualization solution. However, our model formulation and lower bound on demand-based policies (Section 3) is applicable to any virtualization solution. Similarly, our experimental analysis to determine the model parameters (Section 4) can also be adapted to any virtualization solution. Our simulator can then easily be used (after encoding a cost-model module), to observe the effect of policies on any VM hierarchy, and policies already implemented can be re-used. We defer such extension of this work to other virtualization solutions (e.g. Xen, KVM) to future work. Nevertheless, we believe our evaluation of VM density and miss penalty can benefit existing projects [1, 14] which use LXC.

Our work is not without limitations. We have implemented only a few sample, well-known, reactive and proactive policies (i.e., LRU, Cascaded Belady's, SlidingWindow, SlidingWindow+ARMA), and have studied only one example workload (i.e., personal servers). Our goal in this work was to understand and compare the behaviour of reactive and proactive policies for idle VM management, and to compare reactive policies with our theoretical lower bound, on a given workload. We chose the personal server workload since they are a topic of active research in many areas [11, 14, 29, 31] (Section 5.3). Using this workload, we provide valuable insights into the behaviour of a few policies. However, we plan to extend our work to a broader range of policies and workloads in future work. Our modular simulator design, which isolates policy, workload, cost-model modules (Section 5.1), ensures that such a broader analysis can be conducted easily.

We have provided only one online implementation of the SlidingWindow policy (using the ARMA model). We chose the ARMA predictor since it delivered relatively small prediction error for the current workload. To use the SlidingWindow policy on other workloads other prediction methods may need to be considered, while demand-based policies such as LRU can be applied directly.

We model the problem by using a mean value analysis of transition times. Hence we derive the model parameters by defining an operating range of state capacities within which transition times are largely constant. We also assume that different VMs transitions can take place in parallel, and transition times remain unchanged. Stochastic analysis can be leveraged to model any variations in transition times. However, additional experimental analysis of density and transition times will be required to obtain parameters for a stochastic value model, which we defer to future work. Additionally, our current experimental analysis of LXC (Section 4) identifies a number of barriers to state capacities in LXC, which we plan to address in future work.

7. Conclusion

We examine the problem of multiplexing idle VMs across a hierarchy of inactive states. Our simulation-based evaluation and comparison of different policies, shows that VM density can be increased by multiplexing VMs across multiple inactive states, at the cost of a negligible increase in client request latency. Therefore, we encourage virtualization solution providers to natively support such inactive states, to allow cloud providers to increase VM density, leading to reduced hosting costs for providers (by increasing consolidation levels) and tenants (through fine-grained billing based on VM active time [6]).

Acknowledgments

Tim Brecht's research is partially supported by NSERC Discovery and Discovery Accelerator Supplement Grants. S. Keshav is supported by NSERC Discovery and CRD grants. Rayman Preet Singh is partially supported by an NSERC PGS-D scholarship, and University of Waterloo Cheriton and President's scholarships. This work is also partially funded by Microsoft Research.

References

[1] Docker: An Open Platform for Distributed Applications for Developers and Sysadmins. http://www.docker.com.

[2] Linux Containers. http://lxc.sourceforge.net/.

[3] OpenVZ. http://openvz.org.

[4] VMSim. http://github.com/rayman7718/VMSim.

[5] Linux vServer. http://linux-vserver.org.

[6] O. Agmon Ben-Yehuda, M. Ben-Yehuda, A. Schuster, and D. Tsafrir. The Resource-as-a-Service (RaaS) cloud. In *USENIX HotCloud*, 2012.

[7] A. V. Aho, P. J. Denning, and J. D. Ullman. Principles of Optimal Page Replacement. *Journal of the ACM (JACM)*, 1971.

[8] M. F. Arlitt and C. L. Williamson. Web Server Workload Characterization: The Search for Invariants. In *ACM SIGMETRICS Performance Evaluation Review*, 1996.

[9] L. A. Belady. A Study of Replacement Algorithms for a Virtual-storage Computer. *IBM Systems Journal*, 1966.

[10] A. B. Brush, E. Filippov, D. Huang, J. Jung, R. Mahajan, F. Martinez, K. Mazhar, A. Phanishayee, A. Samuel, J. Scott, and R. P. Singh. Lab of Things: A Platform for Conducting Studies with Connected Devices in Multiple Homes. In *ACM UbiComp 2013, Adjunct Proceedings*, 2013.

[11] R. Cáceres, L. Cox, H. Lim, A. Shakimov, and A. Varshavsky. Virtual Individual Servers as Privacy-Preserving Proxies for Mobile Devices. In *Proc. of ACM MobiHeld, 2009*.

[12] E. G. Coffman, Jr. and P. J. Denning. *Operating Systems Theory*. Prentice Hall Professional Technical Reference, 1973.

[13] A. Corradi, M. Fanelli, and L. Foschini. VM Consolidation: A Real Case Based on OpenStack Cloud. *Future Generation Computer Systems*, 2014.

[14] C. Elsmore, A. Madhavapeddy, I. Leslie, and A. Chaudhry. Confidential Carbon Commuting. In *Proc. of the First Workshop on Measurement, Privacy, and Mobility*, 2012.

[15] B. S. Gill. On Multi-level Exclusive Caching: Offline Optimality and Why Promotions are Better Than Demotions. In *Proc. of USENIX FAST*, 2008.

[16] T. Gupta, R. P. Singh, A. Phanishayee, J. Jung, and R. Mahajan. Bolt: A Storage System for Connected Homes. In *Proc. of NSDI*, 2014.

[17] K. Ha, P. Pillai, W. Richter, Y. Abe, and M. Satyanarayanan. Just-in-time Provisioning for Cyber Foraging. In *Proc. of ACM MobiSys*, 2013.

[18] J. Hizver and T.-c. Chiueh. Real-time Deep Virtual Machine Introspection and its Applications. In *Proc. of ACM VEE*, 2014.

[19] B. Jennings and R. Stadler. Resource Management in Clouds: Survey and Research Challenges. *Journal of Network and Systems Management*, 2014.

[20] J. Kannan, P. Maniatis, and B.-G. Chun. A Data Capsule Framework For Web Services: Providing Flexible Data Access Control To Users. *CoRR*, 2010.

[21] T. Knauth and C. Fetzer. DreamServer: Truly On-Demand Cloud Services. In *Proc. of SYSTOR*, 2014.

[22] T. Knauth and C. Fetzer. Fast Virtual Machine Resume for Agile Cloud Services. In *Proc. of IEEE ICCGC*, 2013.

[23] S. Lee, R. Panigrahy, V. Prabhakaran, V. Ramasubramanian, K. Talwar, L. Uyeda, and U. Wieder. Validating Heuristics for Virtual Machines Consolidation. *Microsoft Research, MSR-TR-2011-9*, 2011.

[24] P. B. Menage. Adding Generic Process Containers to the Linux Kernel. In *Ottawa Linux Symposium*, 2007.

[25] R. Mortier, C. Greenhalgh, D. McAuley, A. Spence, A. Madhavapeddy, J. Crowcroft, and S. Hand. The Personal Container, or Your Life in Bits. *Digital Futures*, 2010.

[26] B. Newton, K. Jeffay, and J. Aikat. The Continued Evolution of Web Traffic. In *IEEE MASCOTS*, 2013.

[27] P. Padala, X. Zhu, Z. Wang, S. Singhal, and K. G. Shin. Performance Evaluation of Virtualization Technologies for Server Consolidation. *HP Labs Technical Report*, 2007.

[28] M. Satyanarayanan, P. Bahl, R. Caceres, and N. Davies. The Case for VM-Based Cloudlets in Mobile Computing. *IEEE Pervasive Computing*, 2009.

[29] A. Shakimov, H. Lim, R. Caceres, L. Cox, K. Li, D. Liu, and A. Varshavsky. Vis-a-Vis: Privacy-preserving Online Social Networking via Virtual Individual Servers. In *Proc. of COMSNETS, 2011, .*

[30] A. Shakimov, A. Varshavsky, L. P. Cox, and R. Cáceres. Privacy, Cost, and Availability Tradeoffs in Decentralized OSNs. In *Proc. of ACM WOSN, 2009, .*

[31] R. P. Singh, S. Keshav, and T. Brecht. A Cloud-Based Consumer-centric Architecture for Energy Data Analytics. In *Proc. of ACM e-Energy, 2013*.

[32] R. P. Singh, T. Brecht, and S. Keshav. IP Address Multiplexing for VEEs. *ACM SIGCOMM CCR*, April 2014.

[33] S. Soltesz, H. Pötzl, M. E. Fiuczynski, A. Bavier, and L. Peterson. Container-based Operating System Virtualization: A Scalable, High-performance Alternative to Hypervisors. In *Proc. of ACM EuroSys 2007*.

[34] K. S. Trivedi. Prepaging and Applications to Array Algorithms. *IEEE Transactions on Computers*, 1976.

[35] K. Wang, J. Rao, and C.-Z. Xu. Rethink the Virtual Machine Template. In *Proc. of ACM VEE 2011*.

[36] T. M. Wong and J. Wilkes. My Cache Or Yours?: Making Storage More Exclusive. In *USENIX ATC*, 2002.

[37] T. Wood, P. Shenoy, A. Venkataramani, and M. Yousif. Blackbox and Gray-box Strategies for Virtual Machine Migration. In *Proc. of NSDI 2007*.

[38] I. Zhang, A. Garthwaite, Y. Baskakov, and K. C. Barr. Fast Restore of Checkpointed Memory Using Working Set Estimation. In *Proc. of ACM VEE*, 2011.

[39] I. Zhang, T. Denniston, Y. Baskakov, and A. Garthwaite. Optimizing VM Checkpointing for Restore Performance in VMware ESXi. In *Proc. of USENIX ATC*, 2013.

[40] Q. Zhang, L. Cheng, and R. Boutaba. Cloud Computing: State-of-the-Art and Research Challenges. *Journal of Internet Services and Applications*, 2010.

[41] J. Zhu, Z. Jiang, and Z. Xiao. Twinkle: A Fast Resource Provisioning Mechanism for Internet Services. In *Proc. of IEEE INFOCOM*, 2011.

Application of Domain-aware Binary Fuzzing to Aid Android Virtual Machine Testing

Stephen Kyle   Hugh Leather
Björn Franke

University of Edinburgh
s.kyle@ed.ac.uk, hleather@inf.ed.ac.uk,
bfranke@inf.ed.ac.uk

Dave Butcher
Stuart Monteith

ARM Ltd.
dave.butcher@arm.com,
stuart.monteith@arm.com

Abstract

The development of a new application virtual machine (VM), like the creation of any complex piece of software, is a bug-prone process. In version 5.0, the widely-used Android operating system has changed from the Dalvik VM to the newly-developed ART VM to execute Android applications. As new iterations of this VM are released, how can the developers aim to reduce the number of potentially security-threatening bugs that make it into the final product? In this paper we combine domain-aware binary fuzzing and differential testing to produce DEXFUZZ, a tool that exploits the presence of multiple modes of execution within a VM to test for defects. These modes of execution include the interpreter and a runtime that executes ahead-of-time compiled code. We find and present a number of bugs in the in-development version of ART in the Android Open Source Project. We also assess DEXFUZZ's ability to highlight defects in the experimental version of ART released in the previous version of Android, 4.4, finding 189 crashing programs and 15 divergent programs that indicate defects after only 5,000 attempts.

Categories and Subject Descriptors D.2.5 [*Software Engineering*]: Testing and Debugging—testing tools; D.3.4 [*Programming Languages*]: Processors—run-time environments, compilers

General Terms   virtual machines; testing; reliability; security

Keywords   testing; compiler testing; virtual machine testing; fuzzing; Android; DEX; ART; random testing

VEE '15,   March 14–15, 2015, Istanbul, Turkey..
Copyright is held by the owner/author(s). Publication rights licensed to ACM.
ACM 978-1-4503-3450-1/15/03…$15.00.
http://dx.doi.org/10.1145/2731186.2731198

1. Introduction

The creation of a new application virtual machine (VM) is a complicated task and, like the development of any piece of complex software, is bound to create bugs during the process. Once the initial development is complete, there is the potential for new features and performance improvements to introduce bugs as well. VMs may typically have multiple methods of executing a supplied program, such as an interpreter or using a just-in-time (JIT) compiler. The developers may wish to optimize such methods of execution further, or even add new ones. When this happens, how can the developers easily test that new bugs are not being introduced? While scrupulous developers will always aim to cover every corner case, it must be assumed that bugs will inevitably make their way into software.

In this paper, we will focus on the development of the new ART runtime that is used to execute Android applications. The Android mobile operating system continues to enjoy increasing popularity, recently reaching over a billion active users measured over a 30-day period. It is therefore important to use rigorous testing to find and remove as many defects that were introduced during development as possible, before the new software is released to the public.

Test suites are a good way to catch bugs during development, but are typically limited in size, and cannot easily capture all possible interactions between code optimizations in a compiler. The unit test suite of the ART runtime we discuss in this paper currently stands at around 200 tests, taken and extended from the test suite of the original VM that Android previously used. Meanwhile, GCC's unit test suite numbers over 100,000 tests, although GCC has been in development for over 25 years. How can we get from 200 to 100,000 test cases without waiting for 25 years of bug reports? Indeed, regardless of size, these test cases are usually created when bugs are found, and are only intended to prevent regressions. How do we test for bugs that we are not aware of?

When multiple modes of execution are available within a VM, differential testing can be used, where all modes of execution are given the same program, and are expected to

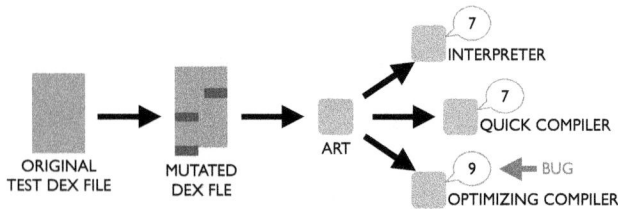

Figure 1. An overview of differential fuzz testing for VMs. A DEX program is run using multiple methods of execution, and in this example, one of the methods—the *optimizing* compiler—reveals a defect in the way it has compiled and executed the program.

```
1  // The array-length bytecode reads the length
2  // field of an array object, 8 bytes offset
3  // from the start of the object.
4  //
5  // Original DEX code:
6  // v0 = undef, v1 = undef, v2 = array
7  const/4 v0, 8
8  array-length v1, v2
9  // v0 = 8, v1 = array.length (LD [array, 8])
10 //   v2 = array
11
12 // Mutate array-length from v2 to v0:
13 const/4 v0, 8
14 array-length v1, v0
15 // v0 = 8, v1 = ??? (LD [8, 8]), v2 = array
```

Listing 1. An example of a DEX mutation leading to a compilation bug, due to incorrect bytecode verification. The compiler will always produce code that reads from the provided array pointer plus 8 bytes. By mutating the array-length instruction to take v0 as an input, we now illegally read from address $8 + 8 = 16$.

form a consensus about how the program should have been executed. With a VM that is supposed to provide a single platform and set of semantics regardless of the underlying execution platform, this is a sound expectation. Figure 1 visualises how we can use this to test for bugs in the VM. As there is no single canonical reference specification for the ART VM, we assume that the conceptually simplest (and so typically slowest) mode can be considered to be the reference mode, as it will not contain many performance-increasing optimizations that have the potential to introduce incorrect behaviour.

Another common approach to testing is fuzzing, creating random test cases through either *generative* means, where a new test is produced from no initial seed, or *mutative*, where a test is mutated from a seed program. The combination of fuzzing and differential testing, while applied to domains such as C compilers in the past[12, 16], seems a good candidate for testing a VM with the desired rigor that Android's VM would need.

We present DEXFUZZ, a tool that takes an existing test suite and performs mutative fuzzing in order to produce new tests, in an attempt to explore the boundaries of the VM. These tests are executed by the various methods of execution of ART, such as the completed *quick* compiler, the interpreter, and the in-development *optimizing* compiler. In the rest of this paper, we will refer to these modes of execution as "backends" of the VM. We use differences in how these backends execute the mutated tests to identify bugs within in the VM. Some of these bugs are present in the common verification phase of the runtime, while others have been found in the compilation phase. In this paper, we present examples of how these bugs were found, how they came to be, and how they were fixed.

We ran DEXFUZZ on the experimental version of ART released in Android KitKat (v4.4). Even after only 5,000 iterations from one seed program, we had produced 189 programs that crashed the VM and 15 programs that led to divergent behaviour. We checked and confirmed that one of the divergent programs arose from the same bug that we later patched in ART, as described in Section 3.1.1. If DEXFUZZ had been available during the initial development of ART, it might have been possible to find and fix these issues earlier.

1.1 Motivating Example

The ART VM is a new implementation of the "Dalvik VM" that executes register-based DEX bytecode on Android. In Figure 1, we see an example of DEX bytecode that loads the constant 8 into virtual register v0 at line 7. On line 8, the *array-length* instruction then reads into v1 the length of the array whose reference is stored in v2. If we mutate the *array-length* bytecode to instead read from whatever "reference" is stored in v0, then ART's bytecode verifier should reject this bytecode, because v0 does not contain an array reference at this point. However, the verifier previously failed to do this. The compiler backend for ART would then assume that it was safe to produce code that reads from *(v0+8), and so the resulting code allowed arbitrary reading of the VM process' address space, if the constant loaded into v0 was also modified. With the error checking done by the verifier reducing the complexity of the compiler, this requires that verification be sound, which was not always the case, and was a common source of issues.

The Java language aims to provide a "security sandbox" for any program that executes within it. It is still possible to construct pointers and read memory arbitrarily if a mechanism such as the Java Native Interface (JNI) is used, so more trust can be placed in an application being "well-behaved" if it contains no JNI code. Therefore such an application may come under less scrutiny by security analysts, while a piece of crafted DEX code as presented in Figure 1 could be used in combination with other exploits to read private data. With the open model of Android, and ease with which applications can be accepted into the various application stores that use Android, there is a significant possibility of encountering accidentally or even maliciously malformed DEX files.

Using DEXFUZZ, we have found a number of bugs during the development of ART, and have submitted patches to the Android Open Source Project (AOSP) code base where ART is developed. We focussed our efforts on finding and reporting bugs in the *quick* compiler, as this is the default mode of execution for ART. It is our expectation that DEX-FUZZ will become more useful as the *optimizing* compiler becomes more sophisticated. As the compiler surpasses the complexity of the *quick* compiler, optimizations are likely to introduce subtle bugs as they are initially developed. We hope that use of this tool may help prevent these bugs ever being put into released versions of the ART VM.

1.2 Contributions

The contributions presented in this paper are the following:

1. the description of domain-aware binary fuzzing for DEX bytecode, improving over *i.* naive approaches that have a greatly reduced chance of ever producing valid programs; *ii.* approaches that may only produce valid programs; *iii.* approaches that are limited to only source code generation, and therefore potentially fail to test as many bytecode sequences in a VM.

2. an application of differential testing to the ART virtual machine in Android, that exploits the multiple execution methods available in the VM to find bugs using mutated test programs.

3. a presentation of bugs found in the Android Open Source Project using these approaches, and how they were fixed.

1.3 Overview

In Section 2, we present an overview of our fuzzing and testing strategy for finding bugs in the ART VM. In Section 3 we present an analysis of the mutation process, as well as giving examples of some bugs that were found using our system and how they were found. In Section 4 we provide some discussion of the impact of our system, and look at related work in the field in Section 5. Finally, we consider potential future work for DEXFUZZ in Section 6 and conclude in Section 7.

2. DEXFUZZ

Fuzz testing as a concept initially referred to the random creation of input to test the capabilities of a program or Application Programming Interface (API), particularly to test its ability to gracefully handle erroneous input. Fuzz testing is typically divided into two categories: *generative*, and *mutative*, where generative does not require a seed to generate a new piece of input, while mutative does.

2.1 Naive fuzz testing

The most basic form of mutative fuzzing is to take some seed input and randomly flip bits in order to produce some new, mutated input. We could apply this technique immediately to producing test programs for the VM, but this isn't likely to yield very useful results. The ART VM is supposed to provide a secure sandbox for program execution, and so it must verify any bytecode that it is expected to execute. This verification forms a hierarchy of checks that range from checking that the two input registers to an `add-float` bytecode actually contain float values, to calculating an Adler-32 checksum on the file, and checking this against a provided checksum in the header. Because of these checks, it is extremely likely that any bytecode that is produced through random bitflips will fail some part of verification, if not at least the checksum that protects the entire DEX file.

We tested this claim by producing a simple fuzzer that fuzzed a test program a million different ways for three different fuzzing strategies. In all cases, the DEX file header is untouched, and then the Adler-32 checksum is recalculated after fuzzing, to ensure that we are checking that such simple fuzzing will be rejected by some other aspect of verification aside from the checksum. We ran each program through the DEX code viewing tool (*dexdump*) as this reports when a DEX file has basic structural errors.

The first strategy iterated through every byte after the header, with a 50% chance of having its value varied by +/- 30. This produced no programs that passed structural verification, out of a million programs. The second strategy changed the chance to 1%, and still no programs passed structural verification. The final strategy used a chance of 0.1%. This strategy did produce programs that passed structural verification - 14%. With further testing, 4% passed full verification when executed with ART, and of those that passed, 97% ran successfully and 0.14% showed divergent behaviour between different ART backends - 0.006% of the million programs that were generated. Focussed mutation could achieve a much higher rate of divergence than this - we stated in Section 1 that we were able to find 15 divergent programs in only 5,000 attempts, compared to the rate of 60 in 1,000,000 seen here. Additionally, this approach doesn't have the potential to insert or delete instructions, or insert even more complex constructs such as new methods or classes.

Typical generative approaches to fuzz testing for compilers have focussed on producing valid programs in the relevant source language. In the case of Csmith[16], this desire for valid program generation stemmed from the presence of undefined behaviour with certain sequences of C code. With a bytecode format like DEX, the concept of undefined behaviour does not exist. Either a sequence of bytecode has a well-defined set of semantics, or the sequence must not verify. Therefore, we are not concerned with the threat of undefined behaviour, and would actually prefer to generate some invalid programs, in a bid to ensure the verifier of ART is robust. Additionally, prior generative approaches have found it difficult to produce a system that fully utilises all features of the language that they are generating code for[16]. Using a set of programs from a test suite that should at the very least contain all features of the language as a seed basis for testing seems a better approach.

Neither of the above strategies are ideal for fuzzing bytecode, so in DEXFUZZ we adopt an approach that applies some degree of intelligence to the use of mutations.

2.2 Mutating DEX Bytecode

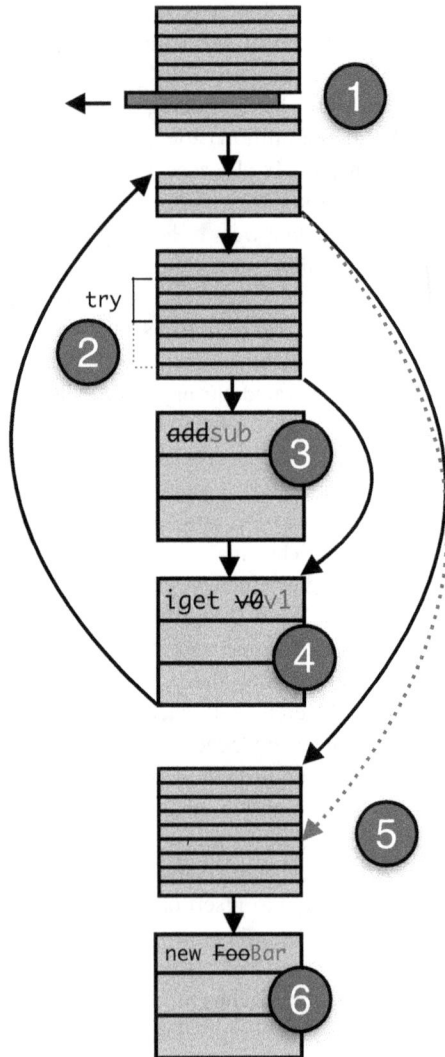

Figure 2. Some examples of DEX bytecode mutations applied to a method formed of six basic blocks. In ①, an instruction is deleted. In ②, the boundaries of a try block are expanded. In ③, an add operation is replaced with a subtract operation, operating on the same types and virtual registers. In ④, the virtual register specified by an *iget* instruction is changed. In ⑤, the branch from the 2nd basic block to the 6th is shifted forward by a few instructions. Finally, in ⑥, a new instance of an object of class Bar is created instead of Foo.

Our fuzzing process can be characterised as domain-aware mutation of bytecode. Figure 2 provides an example

of some mutations performed within a single method. Our hope is that the application of a small number of relatively simple, but domain-aware, mutations can lead to both programs that verify, but also highlight bugs in the ART VM through unexpected handling of mutated bytecode.

```
parse DEX file into mutatable methods;
Methods = set of mutatable methods;
Mutators = set of mutators;
methodCount = random(2,10);
for i in methodCount do
    method = selectRandom(Methods);
    mutationCount = random(1,3);
    while mutationCount > 0 do
        mutator = selectRandom(Mutators);
        if mutator.canMutate(method) then
            method = mutator.applyMutation(method);
            mutationCount = mutationCount - 1;
        else
            if reached mutation attempt threshold then
                give up mutating method;
            end
        end
    end
end
write methods and mutated methods into new DEX file;
```

Algorithm 1: Mutative fuzzing process for DEX files.

Algorithm 1 shows pseudo code for the mutation process. DEXFUZZ will parse a program's DEX file and produce a set of mutatable code items, each of which represent a method within the program. In order to increase the likelihood that the program will successfully verify, DEXFUZZ limits the number of methods that will be mutated to a random value between 2 and 10. A random subset of the available mutatable methods are then selected using this value, and each in turn is mutated. Each method has between 1 and 3 mutations applied to it by default, although this value can be configured. DEXFUZZ randomly selects from the list of available mutators that are listed in Table 1. Because each mutator checks and reports if it is able to mutate the given method (for example, BranchShifter will only mutate methods containing branches), this process repeats until the desired number of mutations has been applied, or a maximum number of attempts is reached. After all mutations have been applied to the correct number of methods, a new, mutated DEX file is produced by DEXFUZZ.

Why does this mutation strategy improve over simple bit-flipping fuzzing? At the very least, this allows us to add and remove instructions within the method. Additionally, we can ensure that branches always remain within the code area, type or field pool indices fall within the range of types of fields available in the DEX file, and a specified virtual register in an instruction is actually allocated in the given method. These are what we consider to be simple structural constraints that the verifier can easily check for.

Why does it improve over generative or mutative fuzzing that only produces legal programs? While we have highlighted some verifier constraints as simple, others are more complicated, such as checking the types of values in virtual registers are valid wherever they are used. It is important to test these constraints, and so we do not provide any guarantee that a mutation will leave the bytecode in a completely legal state. Indeed a few of the bugs we have found in ART were found in the verifier, and this was made possible by allowing the production of invalid programs.

2.3 Differential Testing of Multiple VM Backends

Test suite programs are typically used to test for VM correctness by executing the program, and comparing its output against what it is expected to produce. However, with the generation of new test programs, the expected output is unknown. Therefore, we rely on the fact that the multiple methods of execution available to a VM are intended to produce the same result—one of the design goals of many VMs, but particularly ones related to executing Java code—to test our mutated programs.

Figure 1 visualises our differential testing strategy. We can run mutated programs using the *quick* and *optimizing* compilers, as well as the interpreter. Additionally, in our search for bugs, we ran mutated programs on both 32 and 64-bit variants of the VM. When they fail to reach a consensus about the output of the program, it is highly likely that one of the modes of execution has discovered a bug.

3. Results

We have used DexFuzz to find defects in the in-development version of ART when running on an ARMv8 platform, in both AArch32 and AArch64 execution modes. The version of DexFuzz we have used to find bugs is designed to send programs to the target platform via the Android Debug Bridge (ADB) for execution. Because of the overhead involved in sending programs to the platform, we verify all mutated programs on the host machine first using the DEX compiler, `dex2oat`, that has been compiled for the host machine, and only upload programs that pass this initial test. The host and target versions of `dex2oat` verify all DEX files the same way.

3.1 Finding Bugs

In this section we present some examples of bugs that we have found in the ART VM in AOSP, and explain both how they were discovered by DexFuzz, and what caused their presence. Some bugs we report were found in the verifier. Although we do not have two verifiers to perform differential testing with, the use of such testing can still lead to bugs being found in the verifier. This typically occurred when a

hole in the verifier would lead to the *quick* compiler and interpreter producing different results for the falsely verified code. This was usually because the *quick* compiler would make assumptions about the code it could produce based on properties of the DEX bytecode that the verifier had allegedly proven.

3.1.1 Reading the instance field of a non-reference bearing virtual register

In DEX bytecode, there exist instructions such as *iget*, that allow the reading and writing of instance fields of objects. The verifier of ART checks that the data currently in input virtual registers for a given bytecode have the correct types, with respect to the types the bytecode operates on.

```
const/4 v2, 1
iget v0, v1, MyClass.counter
add-int/2addr v0, v2
iput v0, v1, MyClass.counter
```

This piece of DEX bytecode represents the increment of the *counter* field of a MyClass object whose reference resides in *v1*. When mutated by the VirtualRegisterChanger mutation, which changed the *v1* on line 2 to *v2*, the verifier accepted this bytecode, despite *iget* now attempting to read the instance field of the constant 1 in *v2* rather than any reference to an object. The *quick* compiler would then assume that it was safe to emit native code that loads from the address stored in the input to *iget*, plus the offset of counter. If the constant loaded into *v2* initially was modified, then memory could be arbitrarily read from the process' address space. We submitted a patch for the verifier to AOSP that ensured this check was performed.

3.1.2 Mixed float/int constant usage causes arguments to be passed incorrectly

While many arithmetic and logical operations in DEX bytecode are aware of the types of data they are using, other bytecodes such as data movement and constant loading instructions are not. Consider the following code sample.

```
const v0, 1
const v1, 1.0
invoke-static {v0}, void Main.doInteger(int)
invoke-static {v1}, void Main.doFloat(float)
```

This code loads two constants, 1 and 1.0, and passes them to methods that take integer and float arguments, respectively. The *const* bytecode is typeless, and just loads a bit pattern into a virtual register. As such, the load of the float value 1.0, and the integer 0x3f800000 (the IEEE 754 representation of 1.0) are indistinguishable in bytecode. This requires that type inference be performed - the compiler must look at the uses of constants to determine their types. Because *v1* is used as a float at line 4, it must be a float. If the VirtualRegisterChanger mutation changes the register on line 3 to *v1* instead of *v0*, then the constant 1.0 in *v1* is now being passed to both methods. Type inference will determine

Type	Description	Example
BranchShifter	Change the target of a branch by a small delta.	*if-eqz v0, +05 → if-eqz v0, +07*
ComparisonBiasChanger	Change the bias of a comparison operation.	*cmpg-double v0, v1 → cmpl-double v0, v1*
ConstantValueChanger	Change a constant used for a constant load, or an immediate in an arithmetic operation.	*add-int/lit8 v0, v1, 7 → add-int/lit8 v0, v1, **18***
InstructionDeleter	Delete a bytecode.	*const v0, 2; const v1, 4 → const v0, 2*
InstructionDuplicator	Duplicate a bytecode.	*or-int v0, v0, v2 → or-int v0, v0, v2; **or-int v0, v0, v2***
InstructionSwapper	Swap two bytecodes.	*monitor-enter v3; move v4, v2 → **move v4, v2; monitor-enter v3***
OperationChanger	Change the arithmetic or logical operation performed by a bytecode, preserving types.	*add-int/2addr v0, v1 → **div**-int/2addr v0, v1*
PoolIndexChanger	Change the index into a type/method/field pool used by a bytecode.	*new-instance v2, type@007 → new-instance v2, **type@023***
RandomInstructionGenerator	Generate a random bytecode, with random operands, and insert it into a random location within the method.	*nop; nop → nop; **throw v6**; nop*
TryBlockShifter	Move the boundaries of a try block.	*TRY { move v0, v1; } move v2, v6 → TRY { move v0, v1; move v2, v6 }*
VirtualRegisterChanger	Change one of the virtual registers specified by a bytecode.	*iget v1, v2, field@015 → iget v1, **v0**, field@015*

Table 1. A complete listing of all the DEX mutations currently performed by DEXFUZZ.

that *v1* contains both a float and an integer value, and this is legal according to DEX bytecode specifications.

This lead to a miscompilation in the *quick* backend of ART, however, because the code that passes arguments to the method using the appropriate calling convention would rely on this type-inference information, resulting in problems in an environment where integer and floating point (FP) values are passed in separate physical registers. Because the mutated register *v1* had been marked as a float type at line 3, the emitted native code would pass this argument in a FP physical register, when the callee method would expect to find its integer argument in a core (non-FP) register. The callee method would then use whatever data happened to be in that core register, and execute incorrectly. We have submitted a patch to AOSP that changes the calling convention compiler code to look at the specified types of the callee method instead of type-inference information.

3.1.3 Compiler crash from an unreachable check-cast

Verification of DEX bytecode is only performed on reachable code - code flow analysis takes place during verification, reporting errors like execution reaching the end without an explicit *return* bytecode. It is not intrinsically illegal to have unreachable bytecode, however. Consider the following DEX bytecode.

```
return-void
check-cast v0, V
return-void
```

The *check-cast* instruction is illegal when considered alone - it checks that it is acceptable to cast the value in *v0* to a *void* type, or throw a ClassCastException otherwise. *Void* is never a legal type to cast to, but because the *check-cast* is not reachable it is never rejected by the verifier. For most bytecode, this would not lead to any problems, however the *quick* backend performed a later optimization where it scanned across DEX bytecode it was to compile, to find *check-cast* instructions that it could elide because they would never throw the exception. This optimization would reach the unreachable check-cast and then cause the compiler to crash when an assertion was broken. While we have presented the simplest example of this bug here, this was found when the RandomInstructionGenerator mutation inserted such an invalid *check-cast* after a *return* statement. We submitted a patch for AOSP that makes this scan only consider instructions that were flagged as visited during verification.

3.1.4 Verifier allows jump to move-result

In DEX bytecode, every method invocation instruction that calls a result-returning method must be followed by a *move-result* bytecode to save the result. This means that verification must check that *move-result* always comes immediately after an invoke. Consider the following DEX bytecode.

```
002: if-nez v0, 008
004: invoke-static {}, int Main.getInteger()
007: move-result v1
008: add-int v0, v0, v1
```

Comparison of Mutations

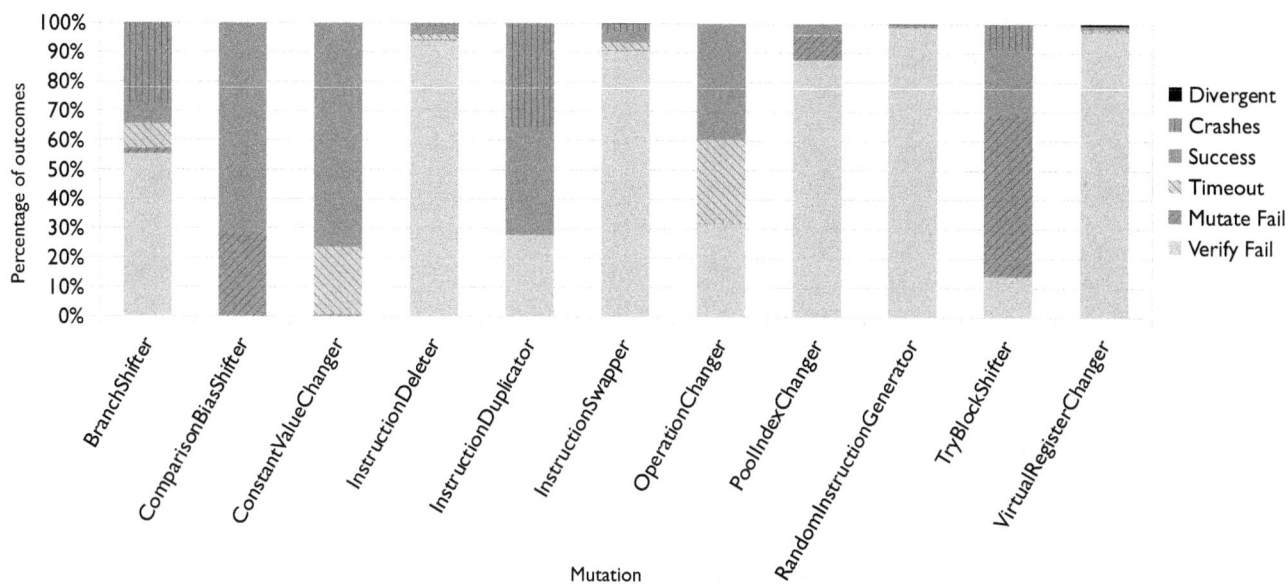

Figure 3. Breakdown of resulting programs created by individual bytecode mutations. In each case, we have run DexFuzz for 2,000 iterations, and report what percentage of these programs failed to be mutated, failed to verify, timed out, crashed, were successful, or produced program divergence, when run on the experimental version of Art available in Android KitKat (v4.4).

Mutation	Verify Fail	Mutate Fail	Timeout	Success	Crashes	Divergent
BranchShifter	1110	37	167	137	549	0
ComparisonBiasShifter	0	572	0	1428	0	0
ConstantValueChanger	0	13	459	1528	0	0
InstructionDeleter	1880	8	32	60	20	0
InstructionDuplicator	558	5	0	728	709	0
InstructionSwapper	1811	7	52	79	50	1
OperationChanger	636	2	571	791	0	0
PoolIndexChanger	1753	169	7	71	0	0
RandomInstructionGenerator	1979	10	2	5	2	2
TryBlockShifter	279	1098	0	444	179	0
VirtualRegisterChanger	1944	2	18	25	0	11

Table 2. Absolute counts of execution outcomes for each mutation shown in Figure 3.

We can see that the *move-result* instruction legally immediately succeeds the *invoke-static* instruction. For *move-result*, the *quick* compiler will typically emit native code that moves data from the return register of the platform's calling conventions into whatever storage location is associated with the specified virtual register, be it another physical register, or a stack location. For example on the Arm platform, the data will be read from the r0 register.

The verifier failed to check if there were any instructions that branched directly to a *move-result* instruction, however. If the BranchShifter mutation made the *if-nez* instruction jump to the *move-result* instruction instead of *add-int*, then we could have a case where we execute the *if-nez* instruction, and then the *move-result* instruction, although we have not returned from an invoke. Previously, the verifier would accept this, and invalid native code would be produced. In this case, if the branch was taken, then execution would jump directly to the copy of the r0 register, although it would no longer be known at this point what data r0 might contain. We submitted a patch to Aosp that ensures any form of branching directly to a *move-result* instruction is rejected.

3.2 Characterization of mutations

We have presented 11 mutations that can be applied to DEX bytecode that aim to highlight bugs within the ART VM. In this section, we characterise which mutations are more responsible for creating verified programs and finding program divergences. Because we have already used DEXFUZZ to find and patch a number of defects within ART, in this section all test programs were executed with the experimental version of ART released in Android KitKat (v4.4), where we are certain that there are bug-indicative divergences to be found. We use a single test program as a seed in these experiments—which was confirmed to work in this version of ART prior to mutation—in order to be sure we are evaluating the characteristics of mutation.

We ran DEXFUZZ 11 times, each time enabling only one of the available DEX mutations. For each mutation, we produced 2,000 candidate programs, and we report how many verified, how many failed to mutate at all, how many passed verification and ran successfully on the platform without divergence, how many crashed, and how many produced divergent behaviour that may indicate the presence of a defect. The differential testing we use in these experiments compares only the output of the interpreter and the compiler in this older version of ART.

In Figure 3 and Table 2, we present the breakdown of execution outcomes for the different mutations we perform. Some are clearly more successful at finding divergent behaviour than others, with the *VirtualRegisterChanger* most responsible for producing divergences. 97% of the programs generated by this mutation failed verification however, so this clearly demonstrates the necessity of allowing the generation of potentially illegal programs in order to find divergences. The other mutations that found divergences were *RandomInstructionGenerator*, and *InstructionSwapper*, which also generated a large percentage of programs that failed to verify, at 99% and 91%, respectively. A number of these divergent programs arose from the bug described in Section 3.1.1.

Many mutations were responsible for producing crashes in ART, with the *InstructionDuplicator* and *BranchShifter* mutations most likely to lead to a crash. From a cursory analysis of the backtraces of these crashes, it appeared that ART had problems with SSA transformation during the compilation stage, which may have been exacerbated by the variety of unique control flow graphs produced by the *BranchShifter* mutation in particular.

Looking at each mutation in turn, *BranchShifter* produced invalid programs for roughly half of its iterations, and was otherwise responsible for a large number of crashes. The *ComparisonBiasShifter* mutation either produced successful programs, or failed to mutate the program at all, due to maximum attempt thresholds mentioned in the description of DEXFUZZ's operation. *ConstantValueChanger* never produced any invalid programs, but created a number of long-running programs, presumably when changes to constants meant loops ran longer than the allowed timeout. *InstructionDeleter* was another mutation that led to a large percentage of invalid programs, but was also able to find a few crashes.

InstructionDuplicator had a roughly three-way split in terms of crashing, successful and invalid programs produced, with no divergences found, while *InstructionSwapper* found a few crashes, but mainly produced invalid programs. Despite *ConstantValueChanger* only changing an operation with a particular set of input types to an operation with the same set of input types, 30% of its programs failed to verify, contrary to expectation. This was traced to bytecodes that operated on 64-bit integers like *add-long* being changed to shift operations on longs, such as *ushr-long*, where the second input, the shift amount, is actually expected to be a 32-bit value, rather than 64-bit.

PoolIndexChanger resulted in a lot of invalid programs, as for example, method invocations were changed to call new methods with incompatible argument types. As might be expected, *RandomInstructionGenerator* lead to the largest percentage of invalid programs, but did also find crashes and divergences. The *TryBlockShifter* mutation found a large number of crashes too, which lends weight to the idea that control flow issues were a major source of crashes in the compiler at the time. Finally, as stated above, *VirtualRegisterChanger* was the most successful mutation, finding the largest number of divergences, but failed to find any crashes at all.

3.3 Effect of multiple mutations

We have seen that some mutations are capable of finding divergent behaviour on their own, and indeed some have been individually responsible for many of the bugs that we have discovered in ART so far. With the use of these small mutations there is a hope that a combination of these could perhaps find other bugs that individual mutations could not. We ranked the mutations of the previous experiment first by their ability to find divergent behaviour, and then by their ability to produce crashing programs. We took the top 5 of these mutations—*VirtualRegisterChanger*, *RandomInstructionGenerator*, *InstructionSwapper*, *InstructionDuplicator*, and *BranchShifter*—and ran DEXFUZZ with all 5 enabled, each with equal chance of being selected. This time, we ran DEXFUZZ for 10,000 iterations, and for each divergence we found, we checked to see if a combination of mutations was responsible for the divergence.

Table 3 presents the breakdown of execution outcomes when running the top 5 most successful mutations. As would be expected, the largest percentage of programs produced were invalid, since three of the top five mutations had extremely high invalid production rates. Like those mutations, divergences were also found. For each divergence found, we assessed if the divergence was produced by a combination of mutations, but found that this was not the case - in each

Execution Outcome	Observed
Verification Failure	9249
Timeout	129
Mutation Failure	28
Crashing	314
Successful	257
Divergent	23
Iteration Total	10000

Table 3. Breakdown of execution outcomes when running DEXFUZZ with only the top 5 most successful mutations enabled: VirtualRegisterChanger, RandomInstructionGenerator, InstructionSwapper, InstructionDuplicator, and BranchShifter.

program, a single instance of mutation created the divergent behaviour. It is easy to imagine a set of mutations that may result in divergence together - for example, creating a random legal *array-length* instruction, and then swapping it to a location where it becomes illegal and finds the bug mentioned in Section 1.1, where the swap without the *array-length* instruction would have also been legal. However, we have failed to find such occurrences in practice thus far, and so further investigation is required. More sophisticated mutations, such as those mentioned in Section 6 or fuzzing the *optimizing* compiler may provide better results.

3.4 Comparison with other mutative fuzzing strategies

While we showed in Section 2 that a naive fuzzing scheme was not ideal for fuzzing a strictly verified bytecode format, and while we have found no available fuzzing systems that specifically fuzz DEX programs for ART or Dalvik, there do exist target-program-agnostic fuzzers that attempt to intelligently perform mutative fuzzing. One such fuzzer is American Fuzzy Lop (AFL)[1], a system that fuzzes inputs for an instrumented binary program, observes the execution paths of the instrumented binary, and attempts to intelligently fuzz new inputs using basic bit-level flipping, such that it will aim to fuzz interesting programs further to explore new execution paths. It aims to maximise the number of unique execution paths it finds, as well as the number of crashes.

We have built a host (x86-64) version of ART with the compiler wrapper that AFL provides, that inserts the instrumentation required to be used with the version of AFL. We have specifically disabled the header verification of ART for this experiment as well, in order to give AFL a chance to explore more than the checksum calculation code of ART, as this is a known limitation of AFL. We ran AFL in its instrumented fuzzing mode for 24 hours, with a subset of 16 ART test programs as seeds, to see how many crashes and hangs it found, as well as programs with unique paths. Of these programs with unique paths, we ran them through our differential tester to see if any of the programs produced divergence between the interpreter's and the *quick* compiler's

output. We then ran DEXFUZZ for 24 hours with the same seed programs, to see how many crashes, hangs, and divergent programs it produced. In this experiment, DEXFUZZ's mutations have all been set to have an equal chance of being triggered.

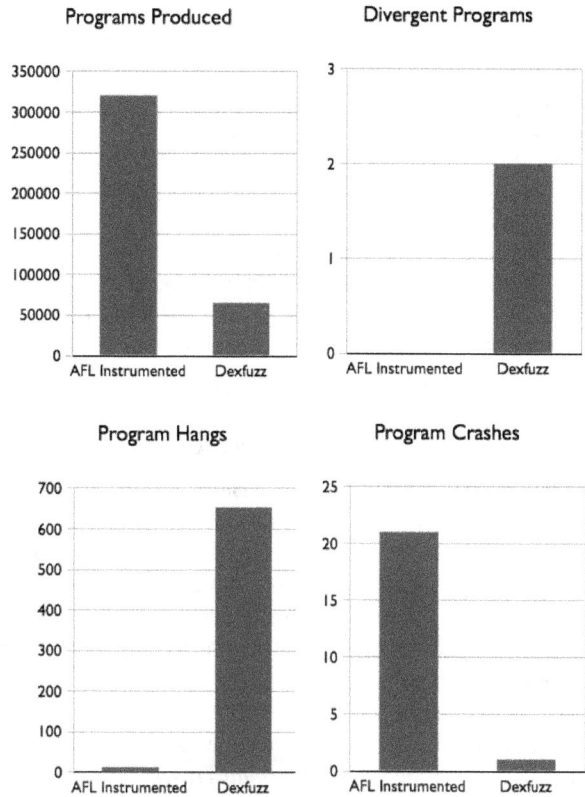

Figure 4. Comparison of success rates of AFL and DEXFUZZ after a 24-hour period of fuzzing.

Figure 4 shows how DEXFUZZ's ability to find divergent programs and crashes compares with AFL's. While it is clear that AFL is capable of producing a significantly larger number of programs within 24 hours, this could be explained by choice of implementation language (DEXFUZZ is written in Java, while AFL is written in C), and that very little time has currently been spent optimising DEXFUZZ, as most of the testing time in the tool is dominated by uploading programs to the test platform, and waiting for them to finish executing. Despite a comparatively small quantity of tests with respect to AFL, DEXFUZZ managed to find two programs that demonstrate divergent behaviour in ART while none of the programs that AFL marked as having unique execution paths demonstrated divergent behaviour. Indeed, of all the programs that AFL produced, none of them passed the verification stage of ART either. For all the hanging programs that AFL reported, none of these passed verification, and may have been an artefact of AFL's default timeout value. Despite having a more lenient timeout value, DEXFUZZ was able to find many more hanging programs in comparison to AFL, due to it actually producing programs that pass verification. Where AFL does excel in comparison to DEXFUZZ however, is its ability to find crashing behaviour. AFL has probably thoroughly tested the structural verification of ART, while DEXFUZZ's fuzzing is weaker in this regard. In general, however, we have shown that the use of domain-aware mutation is useful in discovering divergent behaviour.

4. Impact

In this paper, we have presented DEXFUZZ, a differential mutative fuzz testing tool for finding bugs in ART, and presented a number of bugs discovered in the AOSP version of ART. We have also presented some information about how many divergent programs we could have found in the experimental version of ART released in Android KitKat, if DEXFUZZ had been available at the time. Now we will discuss some of the impact on ART from our testing.

4.1 Improvements to ART Test Suite

Previously, the ART test suite consisted of a number of Java programs, that were compiled to DEX bytecode and executed. Our testing has uncovered bugs that are revealed using programs that cannot be produced directly from Java code, but require manipulation of already existing DEX bytecode. Since we started submitting patches to fix bugs uncovered by DEXFUZZ, the developers of ART in AOSP have added a new suite of tests to the existing ART suite, that allows for tests using mutated DEX bytecode to be checked. Now tests can be described using the *smali* DEX bytecode assembly format[6], which allows us to test for regressions in bugs found by DEXFUZZ. Our patches to AOSP were the catalyst for the creation of these tests, and we always aim to submit any patches with relevant tests for the test suite now.

4.2 Potential for future backends

Currently DEXFUZZ has only been put into practice with the *quick* compiler and interpreter of ART, as these are the only mature backends currently available. From looking at the AOSP code base, it is clear that significant work is going towards producing a new backend, the *optimizing* compiler. The *quick* backend treats DEX bytecode compilation in a simple manner, mapping directly from DEX bytecodes to sequences of native code and performing a few simple code optimizations on top. By comparison, the *optimizing* compiler focuses on much more significant optimization, of the DEX bytecode itself before lowering to native code, using much more sophisticated code optimization techniques, such as those found in modern JIT compilers. With such complexity comes the potential for bugs however, and as we have demonstrated DEXFUZZ's ability to find bugs in older versions of ART, we expect use of this tool to find bugs in the *optimizing* compiler early.

4.3 Contribution to AOSP

Since we have started developing DEXFUZZ, we have found a number of bugs in ART, and submitted patches for these bugs to the AOSP tree, most of which have been accepted, showing that DEXFUZZ finds bugs that the developers are interested in fixing. DEXFUZZ itself has been successfully submitted as a patch and merged into the AOSP code base, clearly indicating that DEXFUZZ is of considerable worth to the future development of ART.

5. Related Work

The use of fuzzing as a testing strategy started with Purdom[14], where a system that generates random sentences to test parsers was presented. Fuzzing was then used to test UNIX utilities for vulnerabilities by Miller et al.[13]. There have been a number of recent approaches to black-box fuzz testing for file formats, such as Peach[5] and AFL[1], as well as approaches to fuzzing of x86 instructions[11]. In this literature review we shall focus on the prior art of applying fuzzing to the testing of compilers and runtimes, considering other mutative approaches and the use of differential testing.

5.1 Differential testing of compilers

In [16], Yang et al. present Csmith, a tool that can generate millions of C99 compliant programs, and find over 300 bugs in open-source and commercial C compilers. They use differential testing to find these bugs, checking for a consensus in output between these different compilers, which inspired our use of multiple "backends" in the ART runtime. However, their main concern is with avoiding undefined behaviours of C programs, and as such their system does not actually use all features of any C standard. Because our tests are based on ART's available test suite, at a minimum we will test all the features of the VM that the test suite uses, which we then test in new combinations to explore for defects. We aim to quickly generate and throw away many programs that do not verify, in the hope of finding some that erroneously do verify, and lead to bugs. Finally, while their differential testing work focuses only on testing compilers, we test the verifier, compiler and complete runtime of a VM.

In [12], Vu et al. present Orion, a tool that uses Equivalence Modulo Inputs (EMI) to reveal more miscompilations than Csmith, which mainly highlights compiler crash defects. EMI is a form of mutative fuzzing, using code coverage information about programs to prune test programs into smaller programs with equivalent semantics. The set of equivalent programs are then executed with the same compiler to ensure they all produce the same result, with differences indicating compiler bugs. Using coverage information to direct mutations would be an interesting direction to take our work into in the future. Again, a concern of Orion is avoiding generating programs with undefined behaviours, a constraint we do not need to worry about.

5.2 Fuzz testing of runtimes

The published fuzzing of a Java virtual machine has been attempted before, in the tool jFuzz by Jayaraman et al. [10], built upon an explicit-state Java model checker and a system that fuzzes Java source code to find new program paths. However, we have not found any published literature concerning the application of fuzz testing at the bytecode-level for JVMs or the Dalvik/ART VMs. One advantage of fuzzing bytecode rather than source code is that features of the bytecode that the source language doesn't use can be tested. For example, while the *invoke_dynamic* JVM instruction isn't used by Java, it is used by other source languages that compile to JVM bytecode. Some preliminary research was performed into fuzzing ART by Sabanal at the Hack in the Box Amsterdam 2014 conference[4], but was not formally published.

Research has been made into other virtual machines that take source code rather than bytecode as their primary input. In particular, these tools have applied mutative and generative fuzzing to the source code using grammars. In [9], Holler et al. present LangFuzz, a language-agnostic system that has been tested against the JavaScript and PHP runtimes. The authors of [8] introduce the use of constraint logic programming into fuzzing, building upon the generation goals of stochastic context-free grammars that systems like LangFuzz use for program generation. They apply this technique to the JavaScript virtual machine. Our contribution in this paper, domain-aware binary fuzzing, is related to the use of stochastic context-free grammars, and it would be interesting to see if DEXFUZZ mutations could be described using context-free grammars in general.

The authors of [15] apply fuzz testing to the ActionScript virtual machine, and is probably most similar to our work, since ActionScript VMs accept compiled bytecode as input rather than source code. The authors' approach is to produce nearly valid ActionScript source code, parse this source and perform runtime class mutations to produce valid ActionScript programs, which then test the ActionScript VM. This approach is ultimately generative, and the authors compare its achieved code coverage against an existing test suite for ActionScript, whereas we use a test suite as a set of program seeds to perform our fuzzing.

6. Future Work

While DEXFUZZ has been submitted and merged into the ART code base in AOSP, we have a number of plans for extensions and improvements to DEXFUZZ.

As it is theoretically possible for bugs to arise from a set of multiple DEX mutations, we plan to add a feature to DEXFUZZ where once a divergent program is found, DEXFUZZ will automatically search for the minimal set of mutations that result in execution divergence. This can be done by, for example, finding if the mutations can be limited to a single method, and then performing a binary search from

there. This will aid users of the tool in finding the source of the bug, if they know exactly which methods and mutations are responsible for the issue.

In the case of multi-threaded programs, it is possible that while a test suite seed program produces deterministic output during normal execution, mutation could cause the program to produce non-deterministic output, either during normal execution, or during the process of error reporting. Currently DEXFUZZ will filter out any found divergences between backends due to this problem, by checking if one of the backends produces divergent output with itself when tested multiple times with the same program. However, a better solution might be to run a backend multiple times to find the range of divergent outputs it produces, and check that the other backends' outputs fall within this set of divergent outputs, such as performed in QuickCheck[7].

DEXFUZZ's testing strategy is currently predicated on the belief there are no bugs in the VM such that all backends of the VM will produce exactly the same incorrect output. In this case, there would be no divergence to indicate the presence of a bug. This is a general flaw with the differential testing methodology, and the only possible mitigation is to use more backends to perform testing. Alternatively, another VM that obeys the same specification could be used. While this is easily possible when testing JVMs, with the myriad of implementations available, the only feasible execution alternative to ART on Android is the previous VM, Dalvik, although there exist alternative Dalvik implementations such as Myriad's Alien Dalvik[2] and BlueStacks AppPlayer[3]. It would be useful to execute programs with both the ART and Dalvik VMs, provided that the compared output is filtered to remove known divergences between the two implementations - namely the way that they report errors.

Finally, we plan to add more mutations to DEXFUZZ, including "global" mutations such as changing the access flags of classes, methods, and fields. For example, the volatile flag of fields could be flipped randomly, to ensure that the loading and storing to and from the fields always holds the correct semantics in presence of other optimizations, although again this may require measures to check for self-divergence. Additional method-level mutations are planned, such as injecting the console printing of virtual register values at random locations, or calls to specific system methods such as the `System.gc()` method, to exercise random calls to the garbage collector.

7. Conclusion

In this paper we have presented a tool to augment the testing of the new ART VM in Android, called DEXFUZZ. We have shown how use of this tool in the past could have prevented the inclusion of security bugs in the original experimental release of ART. We have also described a number of bugs that we have found and fixed using this tool in the AOSP version of ART, to demonstrate the utility of this tool to prevent bugs being released in future versions of the software. DEX-FUZZ is built upon the combination of domain-aware binary fuzzing and differential testing, and we have evaluated what sorts of binary mutations that we have applied to DEX files lead to divergent behaviour in the experimental version of ART found in Android KitKat, to confirm which mutations were more useful for finding bugs. We find that mutating use of virtual registers, insertion of random instructions, and swapping instructions, while increasing the amount of invalid programs produced, are the mutations most likely to lead to divergent behaviour, and should be useful initial mutations to use if future VM designers wish to use this testing approach.

References

[1] american-fuzzy-lop on Google Code. https://code.google.com/p/american-fuzzy-lop/. Accessed: 2014-11-12.

[2] Alien Dalvik. http://www.myriadgroup.com/products/device-solutions/mobile-software/alien-dalvik/. Accessed: 2014-11-25.

[3] BlueStacks AppPlayer. http://www.bluestacks.com/app-player.html. Accessed: 2014-11-25.

[4] HITB2014AMS - Day 1 - State of the ART: Exploring the new Android KitKat Runtime. https://www.corelan.be/index.php/2014/05/29/hitb2014ams-day-1-state-of-the-art-exploring-the-new-android-kitkat-runtime/. Accessed: 2014-11-20.

[5] Peachfuzzer. http://peachfuzzer.com/. Accessed: 2014-11-20.

[6] smali - an assembler/disassembler for android's dex format on Google Code. https://code.google.com/p/smali/. Accessed: 2014-11-19.

[7] K. Claessen and J. Hughes. Quickcheck: A lightweight tool for random testing of haskell programs. In *Proceedings of the Fifth ACM SIGPLAN International Conference on Functional Programming*, ICFP '00, pages 268–279, New York, NY, USA, 2000. ACM. ISBN 1-58113-202-6. . URL http://doi.acm.org/10.1145/351240.351266.

[8] K. Dewey, J. Roesch, and B. Hardekopf. Language fuzzing using constraint logic programming. In *Proceedings of the 29th ACM/IEEE International Conference on Automated Software Engineering*, ASE '14, pages 725–730, New York, NY, USA, 2014. ACM. ISBN 978-1-4503-3013-8. . URL http://doi.acm.org/10.1145/2642937.2642963.

[9] C. Holler, K. Herzig, and A. Zeller. Fuzzing with code fragments. In *Proceedings of the 21st USENIX Conference on Security Symposium*, Security'12, pages 38–38, Berkeley, CA, USA, 2012. USENIX Association. URL http://dl.acm.org/citation.cfm?id=2362793.2362831.

[10] K. Jayaraman, D. Harvison, V. Ganesh, and A. Kiezun. jfuzz: A concolic whitebox fuzzer for java. In *NASA Formal Methods*, pages 121–125, 2009.

[11] A. Lanzi, L. Martignoni, M. Monga, and R. Paleari. A smart fuzzer for x86 executables. In *Proceedings of the Third International Workshop on Software Engineering for Secure Systems*, SESS '07, pages 7–, Washington, DC, USA, 2007. IEEE Computer Society. ISBN 0-7695-2952-6. . URL http://dx.doi.org/10.1109/SESS.2007.1.

[12] V. Le, M. Afshari, and Z. Su. Compiler validation via equivalence modulo inputs. In *Proceedings of the 35th ACM SIGPLAN Conference on Programming Language Design and Implementation*, PLDI '14, pages 216–226, New York, NY, USA, 2014. ACM. ISBN 978-1-4503-2784-8. . URL http://doi.acm.org/10.1145/2594291.2594334.

[13] B. P. Miller, L. Fredriksen, and B. So. An empirical study of the reliability of unix utilities. *Commun. ACM*, 33(12): 32–44, Dec. 1990. ISSN 0001-0782. . URL http://doi.acm.org/10.1145/96267.96279.

[14] P. Purdom. A sentence generator for testing parsers. *BIT Numerical Mathematics*, 12(3):366–375, 1972. ISSN 0006-3835. . URL http://dx.doi.org/10.1007/BF01932308.

[15] G. Wen, Y. Zhang, Q. Liu, and D. Yang. Fuzzing the actionscript virtual machine. In *Proceedings of the 8th ACM SIGSAC Symposium on Information, Computer and Communications Security*, ASIA CCS '13, pages 457–468, New York, NY, USA, 2013. ACM. ISBN 978-1-4503-1767-2. . URL http://doi.acm.org/10.1145/2484313.2484372.

[16] X. Yang, Y. Chen, E. Eide, and J. Regehr. Finding and understanding bugs in c compilers. In *Proceedings of the 32Nd ACM SIGPLAN Conference on Programming Language Design and Implementation*, PLDI '11, pages 283–294, New York, NY, USA, 2011. ACM. ISBN 978-1-4503-0663-8. . URL http://doi.acm.org/10.1145/1993498.1993532.

Exploring VM Introspection: Techniques and Trade-offs

Sahil Suneja

University of Toronto

sahil@cs.toronto.edu

Canturk Isci

IBM T.J. Watson Research

canturk@us.ibm.com

Eyal de Lara

University of Toronto

delara@cs.toronto.edu

Vasanth Bala

IBM T.J. Watson Research

vbala@us.ibm.com

Abstract

While there are a variety of existing virtual machine introspection (VMI) techniques, their latency, overhead, complexity and consistency trade-offs are not clear. In this work, we address this gap by first organizing the various existing VMI techniques into a taxonomy based upon their operational principles, so that they can be put into context. Next we perform a thorough exploration of their trade-offs both qualitatively and quantitatively. We present a comprehensive set of observations and best practices for efficient, accurate and consistent VMI operation based on our experiences with these techniques. Our results show the stunning range of variations in performance, complexity and overhead with different VMI techniques. We further present a deep dive on VMI consistency aspects to understand the sources of inconsistency in observed VM state and show that, contrary to common expectation, pause-and-introspect based VMI techniques achieve very little to improve consistency despite their substantial performance impact.

Categories and Subject Descriptors   C.4 [*Performance of Systems*]: Design studies; D.2.8 [*Metrics*]: Performance measures; D.4.2 [*Storage Management*]: Virtual memory; D.4.1 [*Process Management*]: Synchronization

Keywords   Virtualization; Virtual Machine; VMI; Taxonomy; Consistency

1. Introduction

Virtual machine introspection (VMI) [28] has been used to support a wide range of use cases including: digital foren-

sics [13, 14, 24, 31, 63]; touchless systems monitoring-tracking resource usage, ensuring system health and policy compliance [32, 67]; kernel integrity and security monitoring-intrusion detection, anti-malware, firewall and virus scanning [9, 23, 26–28, 34, 36, 38, 54, 64]; cloud management and infrastructure operations such as VM sizing and migration, memory checkpointing and deduplication, device utilization monitoring, cloud-wide information flow tracking and policy enforcement, cluster patch management, and VM similarity clustering [3, 8, 10, 15, 33, 58, 76].

There are different ways in which VMI gains visibility into the runtime state of a VM, ranging from exposing a raw byte-level VM memory view and traversing kernel data structures in it [5, 6, 14, 25, 40, 41, 46], to implanting processes or drivers into the guest [16, 29]. A security-specific survey of the VMI design space can be found in [37]. Although several techniques to expose VM state have been developed independently over the years, there is no comprehensive framework that puts all these techniques in context, and compares and contrasts them. Understanding the trade-offs between the competing alternatives is crucial to the design of effective new applications, and would aid potential VMI users in deciding as to which of the myriad techniques to adopt as per their requirements and constraints.

In this paper, we present a thorough exploration of VMI techniques, and introduce a taxonomy for grouping them into different classes based upon four operation principles: (i) whether guest cooperation is required; (ii) whether the technique creates an exact point-in-time replica of the guest's memory; (iii) whether the guest has to be halted; and, (iv) the type of interface provided to access guest state.

We present the results of a qualitative and quantitative evaluation of a wide range of VMI techniques. We compare software-only methods; VMI techniques that rely on hardware memory acquisition (e.g., System Management Mode (SMM) in x86 BIOS [7, 74], DMA [1, 9, 12, 47, 55], system bus snooping [43, 48]) are beyond the scope of this paper. The qualitative evaluation considers techniques available in

VEE '15,   March 14–15, 2015, Istanbul, Turkey..

Copyright © 2015 ACM 978-1-4503-3450-1/15/03... $15.00.

http://dx.doi.org/10.1145/2731186.2731196

VMware, Xen and KVM. The quantitative evaluation is restricted to a single hypervisor to minimize environmental variability. We use KVM as it has the highest coverage of VMI techniques and gives us more control, but its results can be extrapolated to similar VMware and Xen techniques that fall in the same taxonomy classes. We also present a detailed exploration of the memory consistency aspects of VMI techniques. We show the actual reasons behind potential inconsistency in the observed VM state, and the inability of pause-and-introspect based VMI techniques to mitigate all forms of inconsistency, contrary to common expectation.

Our evaluation reveals that VMI techniques cover a broad spectrum of operating points. Their performance varies widely along several dimensions, such as their speed (0.04Hz to 500Hz), resource consumption on host (34% to 140% for always-on introspection), and overhead on VM's workload (0 to 85%). VMI methods may be available out-of-box on different hypervisors or be enabled by third party libraries or hypervisor modifications, giving the user a choice between easy deployability vs. hypervisor specialization. Furthermore, higher performance may be extracted by modifying the hypervisor or host, yielding a performance vs. host/hypervisor specialization tradeoff. Therefore, application developers have different alternatives to choose from based on their desired levels of latency, frequency, overhead, liveness, consistency, and intrusiveness, constrained by their workloads, use-cases, resource budget and deployability flexibility.

The rest of this paper is organized as follows. Section 2 introduces our VMI taxonomy and groups existing VMI methods based on this taxonomy. Section 3 presents a qualitative evaluation of VMI techniques implemented on VMware, Xen and KVM. Sections 4 presents quantitative evaluation of VMI techniques based on KVM. Section 5 explores VMI state consistency. Section 6 present a summary of our key observations, best operational practices and our experiences with all the explored techniques. Finally, Section 7 offers our conclusions.

2. VMI Taxonomy

We characterize VMI techniques based on four orthogonal dimensions: (i) *Guest Cooperation*, whether the technique involves cooperation from code running inside the guest VM; (ii) *Snapshotting*, whether the technique creates an exact point-in-time replica of the guest's memory; (iii) *Guest Liveness*, whether the techniques halts the guest VM; and (iv) *Memory Access Type*, the type of interface provided to access guest state, which can be either via address space remapping, reads on a file descriptor, or through an interface provided by a VM manager or a debugger.

While there can be arbitrary combinations of these dimensions, in practice only a few are employed. Figure 1's taxonomy shows the specific attribute combinations that can categorize the current implementations for accessing in-VM memory state. Some of these methods are hypervisor ex-

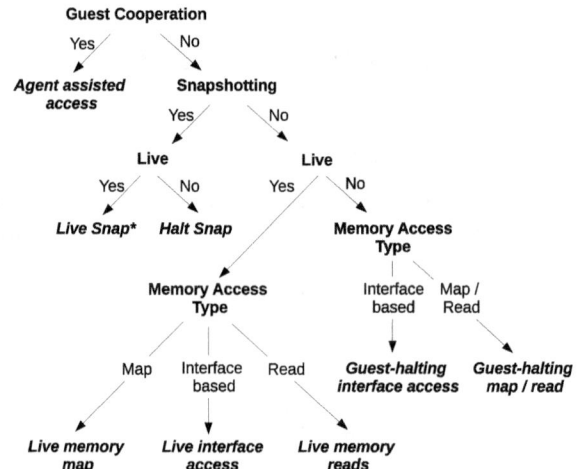

Figure 1: VMI Taxonomy: categorizing current implementations

posed, while others are either specialized use cases, or leverage low level memory management primitives, or enabled by third party libraries. The proposed taxonomy is general and hypervisor independent. The rest of this section describes the techniques' functionality.

I. Agent assisted access requiring guest cooperation

These techniques install agents or modules inside the guests to facilitate runtime state extraction from outside.

- **VMWare** VMSafe() **[72], XenServer's** XenGuestAgent **[17, 18], QEMU's** qemu-ga **[57]:** Access VM's memory directly via guest pseudo-devices (/dev/mem) or interface with the guest OS via pseudo filesystem (/proc) or kernel exported functions. The solutions then communicate either directly through their own custom in-VM agents [2, 22, 69–71], or mediated by the hypervisor [16, 36].

II. Halt Snap

These methods do not require guest cooperation and distinguish themselves for producing a full copy of the guest's memory image, while also pausing the guest to obtain a consistent snapshot.

- **QEMU** pmemsave**, Xen** dump-core**, Libvirt/Virsh library's** dump **and** save**, VMWare** vmss2core**:** These techniques dump the VM memory to a file. Example usages include Blacksheep [10], Crash [21].

- **QEMU** migrate **to file:** Migrates VM to a file instead of a physical host. Essentially similar to memory dumping, but smarter in terms of the content that actually gets written (deduplication, skipping zero pages etc.).

- **LibVMI library's** shm-snapshot **[11]:** Creates a VM memory snapshot inside a shared memory virtual filesystem at host. Implemented for both Xen and KVM (QEMU modified). Access to snapshot mediated by LibVMI after internally mapping the memory resident (/dev/shm/*) file.

III. Live Snap

These methods obtain a consistent snapshot without pausing the guest.

• HotSnap [20] for QEMU/KVM and similar alternatives for Xen [19, 35, 42, 66, 73] use copy-on-write implementations to create consistent memory snapshots that does not halt the guest. These approaches modify the hypervisor due to lack of default support.

IV. Live Memory Mapping

These methods do not require guest cooperation or a guest memory image capture, and support introspection while the guest continues to run. Methods in this class provide a memory mapped interface to access the guest state.

• Xen `xc_map_foreign_range()`, QEMU Pathogen [60]: Maps the target guest's memory into the address space of a privileged monitoring or introspection process. Used in libraries such as XenAccess [53] and LibVMI [11], and in cloud monitoring solutions such as IBMon [58] and RTKDSM [32].

• QEMU large-pages (`hugetlbfs`) based and VMWare `.vmem` paging file backed VM memory: Mapping the file that backs a VM's memory into the monitoring or introspection process' address space. Used in OSck [34] for monitoring guest kernel code and data integrity, and in [68] to expose a guest's video buffer as a virtual screen.

• QEMU and VMWare host physical memory access: Mapping the machine pages backing the VM's memory, into the introspection process' address space. Leveraging Linux memory primitives for translating the virtual memory region backing the VM's memory inside the QEMU or `vmware-vmx` process (via `/proc/pid/maps` psuedo-file) to their corresponding physical addresses (`/proc/pid/pagemap` file). Not straightforward in Xen, although the administrator domain can access the host physical memory, still need hypervisor cooperation to extract guest backing physical frames list (physical-to-machine (P2M) table).

V. Live Memory Reads

Methods in this class also enable live introspection without perturbing the guest, but access guest state through a file descriptor-based interface.

• QEMU and VMWare direct VM memory access: These methods directly read a guest's memory contents from within the container process that runs the VM. This can be achieved in different ways: (i) Injecting a DLL into the `vmware-vmx.exe` container process in VMWare to read its `.vmem` RAM file [45], (ii) Using QEMU's native memory access interface by running the introspection thread inside QEMU itself [8], (iii) Leveraging Linux memory primitives– reading QEMU process' memory pages at the hypervisor (via `/proc/pid/mem` pseudo-file) indexed appropriately by the virtual address space backing the VM memory (`/proc/pid/maps`) [67].

• LibVMI memory transfer channel: Requesting guest memory contents over a unix socket based communication channel created in a modified QEMU container process, served by QEMU's native guest memory access interface.

VI. Guest-Halting Memory Map and Reads

These methods achieve coherent/consistent access to the guest memory by halting the guest while introspection takes place (pause-and-introspect), but do not create a separate memory image and access guest memory contents directly. While all the live memory map and read methods can be included in this category by also additionally pausing the guest, we only select one direct read method, employed in literature, as a representative—QEMU semilive direct access, that encompasses the guest memory reads (QEMU `/proc/pid/mem`) between `ptrace()`- attach/detach calls. Used in NFM [67] for cloud monitoring under strict consistency constraints.

VII. Live Interface Access

Methods in this class also enable live introspection without perturbing the guest, but access guest state over an interface provided by a third party program.

• KVM with QEMU monitor's xp [75]: uses the hypervisor management interface to extract raw bytes at specified (pseudo) physical addresses.

VIII. Guest-Halting Interface Access

Methods in this class halt the guest and access guest state over an interface provided by a third party program.

• Xen's `gdbsx`, VMWare's `debugStub`, QEMU's `gdbserver` GDB stub for the VM: attach a debugger to the guest VM and access guess state over the debugger's interface. This method is used in IVP [62] for verifying system integrity. LibVMI when used without its QEMU patch defaults to using this technique to access guest state. We use the libVMI GDB-access version in our evaluation.

3. Qualitative Comparison

The various VMI techniques described in the previous section follow different operation principles and correspondingly exhibit different properties. Table 1 compares them in terms of the following properties:

• **Guest Liveness:** A live memory acquisition and subsequent VM state extraction is defined in terms of whether or not the target VM continues to make progress normally without any interruption.

• **Memory view consistency:** refers to coherency between the runtime state exposed by the method and the guest's actual state (Section 5).

• **Speed:** How quickly can guest state be extracted with a particular method?

• **Resource consumption on host:** How heavy is a particular approach in terms of the CPU resources consumed by

	Live	View consistency	Speed	Resource cost	VM perf impact	Host and Hypervisor Compatibility		
						Xen	KVM/QEMU	VMWare
Guest cooperation / agent assisted access	✓	✓ (not /dev/mem)	Medium	Medium	Low	VM /dev/mem support or module installation	VM /dev/mem support or module installation	Default; special drivers/tools in VM
Halt Snap		✓	Low	High	High	Default; - In-mem snap via library	Default; - In-mem snap via library + hypervisor modifications	Default
Live Snap	✓	✓	Medium	Low	Low	Hypervisor modifications	Hypervisor modifications	
Live Memory Mapping	✓		Very High	Very Low	Very Low	Default	Hypervisor modifications; - Default file backed mapping with special VM flags, large pages host reservation; - /dev/mem support for host phys mem access	via library; - Default file backed mapping; - /dev/mem support host phys mem access
Live Memory Reads	✓		High	Low	Very Low		Compatible (via /proc); - Mem transfer channel via library + hypervisor mod.	via library
Guest-Halting Memory Map and Reads		✓	Medium	Low	Medium	Compatible (+ guest pause)	Compatible (+ guest pause)	Compatible (+ guest pause)
Live Interface Access	✓		Very Low	Very High	Low		Default (via management interface)	
Guest-Halting Interface Access		✓	Very Low	Very High	Low	Default	Default + special VM initialization flags	Default + special VM config options

Table 1: Qualitative comparison of VMI techniques- empty cells in compatibility column do not necessarily indicate missing functionality in hypervisor.

it, normalized to monitoring 1 VM at 1Hz (memory and disk cost is negligible for all but snapshotting methods).

- **VM performance impact:** How bad does memory acquisition and state extraction hit the target VM's workload.
- **Compatibility:** How much effort does deploying a particular technique cost in terms of its host and hypervisor compatibility- whether available as stock functionality, or requiring hypervisor modifications, or third party library installation, or host specialization.

Table 1 only contrasts these properties qualitatively, while a detailed quantitative comparison follows in the next section. The compatibility columns in the table, do not indicate whether a functionality is available or missing from a hypervisor, rather whether the functionality has been 'shown' to work by virtue of it been exported as a default feature by the hypervisor or via libraries or hypervisor modifications.

As can be seen, no one technique can satisfy all properties at the same time, leading to different tradeoffs for different use cases. One tradeoff is between the conflicting goals of view consistency and guest liveness for almost all techniques. If the user, however, desires both, then he would either have to let go of guest independence by opting for the guest cooperation methods that run inside the guest OS scope, or choose a hardware assisted out-of-band approach using transactional memory [44]. COW based live snapshotting seems to be a good compromise, providing an almost-live and consistent snapshot.

Another tradeoff is between a VMI techniques' performance and generality in terms of requirements imposed on the host's runtime. For example, the live direct-reads method in KVM is sufficiently fast for practical monitoring applications and works out-of-box, still an order of magnitude higher speed can be achieved with live memory-mapping techniques by either enabling physical memory access on

host, or reserving large pages in host memory for file-backed method. Although the latter come with a tradeoff of increasing system vulnerability (/dev/mem security concerns) and memory pressure (swapping concerns [51, 65]).

4. Quantitative Comparison

To quantitatively compare VMI techniques, we use a simple generic use case of periodic monitoring. This entails extracting at regular intervals generic runtime system information from the VM's memory: CPU, OS, modules, N/W interfaces, process list, memory usage, open files, open network connections and per-process virtual memory to file mappings. This runtime information is distributed into several in-memory kernel data structures for processes (`task_struct`), memory mapping (`mm_struct`), open files (`files_struct`), and network information (`net_devices`) among others. These `struct` templates are overlaid over the exposed memory, and then traversed to read the various structure fields holding the relevant information [46], thereby converting the byte-level exposed memory view into structured runtime VM state. This translates to reading around 700KB of volatile runtime state from the VM's memory, spread across nearly 100K read/seek calls.

We compare the different VMI techniques along the following dimensions:

1. Maximum frequency of monitoring
2. Resource usage cost on host
3. Overhead caused to the VM's workload

We run different benchmarks inside the VM to measure monitoring's impact when different resource components are stressed - CPU, disk, memory, network and the entire system as a whole. The different targeted as well as full system benchmarks tested are as follows.

1. x264 CPU Benchmark: Measured is x264 video encoding benchmark's [50] (v1.7.0) frames encoded per second.

2. Bonnie++ Disk Benchmark: Measured is bonnie++'s [61] (v1.96) disk read and write throughputs as it processes 4GB of data sequentially. High performance `virtio` disk driver is loaded in the VM, and disk caching at hypervisor is disabled so that true disk throughputs can be measured, which are verified by running `iostat` and `iotop` on host. Host and VM caches are flushed across each of the 5 bonnie++ runs.

3. STREAM Memory Benchmark: Measured is STREAM benchmark's [39] (v5.10) `a[i] = b[i]` sort of in-memory data copy throughput. We modified the STREAM code to also emit the 'average' sustained throughput across all the STREAM iterations (N=2500), along with the default 'best' throughput. The array size is chosen to be the default 10M elements in accordance with STREAM's guidelines of array size vs. cache memory size on the system. The memory throughputs observed inside the VM are additionally confirmed to be similar to when STREAM is run on the host.

4. Netperf Network Benchmark: Measured is network bandwidth when a netperf [59] server (v2.5.0) runs inside the VM, while another physical machine is used to drive TCP data transfer sessions (N=6). High performance `virtio` network driver is loaded in the VM, and the network throughput recorded by the client is confirmed to be similar to when the netperf server runs on the host machine itself.

5. Full System OLTP Benchmark: Measured is Sysbench OLTP database benchmark's [4] (v0.4.12) throughput (transactions per sec) and response time. The benchmark is configured to fire in 50K database transactions, which includes a mix of read and write queries, on a 1M row InnoDB table. Optimal values are ensured for InnoDB's service thread count, cache size and concurrency handling, with the in-VM performance verified to be similar to on-host.

6. Full System Httperf Benchmark: Measured is the incoming request rate that a webserver VM can service without any connection drops, as well as its average and 95th percentile response latency. A 512MB working set workload is setup in a webserver VM, from which it serves different 2KB random content files to 3 different httperf clients (v0.9.0) running on 3 separate machines. The file size is chosen to be 2KB so that server is not network bound.

Experimental Setup: The host is an 8 core Intel Xeon E5472 @ 3GHz machine, with 16GB memory and Intel Vt-x hardware virtualization support. The software stack includes Linux-3.8 host OS with KVM support, Linux 3.2 guest OS, libvirt 1.0.4, QEMU 1.6.2, libvmi-master commit-b01b349 (for in-memory snapshot).

In all experiments except the memory benchmark, the target VM has 1GB of memory and 1 VCPU. Bigger memory impacts snapshotting techniques linearly, without any noticeable impact on other techniques as they are agnostic to VM size. Also, more VCPUs do not affect VMI perfor-

mance much, except for generating some extra CPU-specific state in the guest OS that also becomes a candidate for state extraction. We select 1 VPCU so as to minimize any CPU slack which could mask the impact of the VMI techniques on the VM's workload. However, in case of the memory benchmark, a multicore VM was necessary as the memory bandwidth was observed to increase with the number of cores, indicating a CPU bottleneck, with the peak bandwidth being recorded on employing 4 cores (almost twice as much as on a singe core; going beyond 4 had no further improvement).

Discussion: (i) We do not include live snapshotting in our quantitative evaluation because of the unavailability of a standalone implementation (patch or library) for our KVM testbed, while its qualitative performance measures are borrowed from [35]. Live snapshotting is expected to have a much better performance as indicated in Table 1. Quantitatively, while monitoring the target VM, live snapshotting is expected to achieve ~5Hz of monitoring frequency, with about 10% CPU consumption on host, and <13% hit on the VM's workload [35].

(ii) Also, we do not explicitly compare guest cooperation methods in the remainder of this section. This is because the default `qemu-ga` guest agent implementation on KVM/QEMU is pretty limited in its functionality. Absence of a dynamic `exec` capability with the agent means the generic monitoring process on host has to read all relevant guest `/proc/*` files to extract logical OS-level state [2], which takes about 300ms per transfer over the agent's serial channel interface. This translates to a maximum monitoring frequency of the order of 0.01Hz with <1% CPU consumption on host and guest. However, a better way would be for a custom agent to do the state extraction processing in-band and only transfer the relevant bits over to the host, along the lines of [52]. Emulating this with qemu agent, to extract the 700KB of generic VM runtime state, results in a maximum monitoring frequency of the order of 1Hz with about 50% CPU consumption on host, and a 4.5% hit on the VM workload.

4.1 Maximum Monitoring Frequency

Figure 2 compares the maximum attainable frequency at which an idle VM can be monitored while employing the different VMI techniques. The monitoring frequency is calculated from the average running time for 1000 monitoring iterations. We use an optimized version of LibVMI in this study that skips per iteration initialization/exit cycles. Disabling this would add over 150ms latency per iteration thereby lowering the maximum monitoring frequency, most noticeably of the live memory transfer channel implementation.

Interestingly, when sorting the methods in increasing order of their maximum monitoring frequency, each pair of methods shows similar performance, that jumps almost always by an order of magnitude across the pairs. This is be-

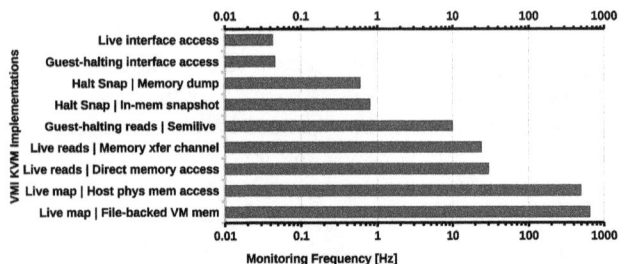

Figure 2: Comparing maximum monitoring frequency across all KVM instances of VMI techniques

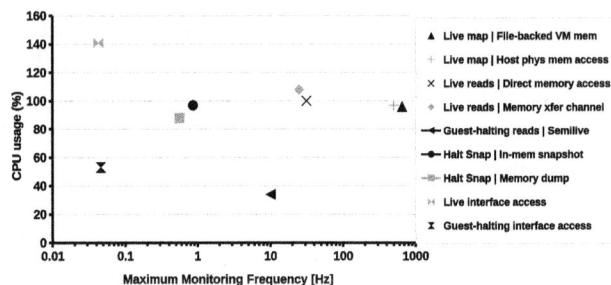

Figure 3: CPU used vs. maximum monitoring frequency

cause the candidates per pair belong to the same taxonomy category, hence they follow similar operation principles, except for interface based methods where the frequency is limited by the interface latency. Amongst the live memory access methods, mapping is much superior to direct reads primarily because of greater system call overheads in the latter (multiple `read()`/`seek()` vs. single `mmap()`). The next best is guest-halting direct reads that stuns the VM periodically for a few milliseconds, while still being much faster than guest-halting snapshotting methods that halt the VM for a few seconds. Finally, the methods interfacing with the management layer and GDB are the slowest because of yet another layer of indirection.

The maximum monitoring frequencies can vary with the workload inside the VM. Depending upon how active the VM is, it would change the amount of runtime state that exists in the VM, thereby leading to a change in the time required to extract this state. This can easily be observed in the maximum frequencies recorded with httperf in Section 4.4.1 which decrease by 4X due to a proportional increase in runtime state.

4.2 Resource Cost on Host

Monitoring with almost all methods has a negligible space footprint, except for snapshotting techniques that consume space, on disk or memory, equivalent to the VM's size. As for the CPU cost, Figure 3 plots the CPU resource usage on host while an idle VM is monitored at the maximum frequency afforded by each technique. The graph shows the same pairwise grouping of the methods as in the case of their maximum monitoring frequency. The exception here is that the management interface is much heavier than the debugger interface, although both deliver the same monitoring frequency.

The previous frequency comparison graph showed that the live memory mapping methods were an order of magnitude faster than live direct reads, which were themselves faster than guest-halting reads and snapshotting methods. This graph shows that the **better performance does not come at an added cost** as all of these except for halting-reads consume similar CPU resources. However, with the same CPU consumption, the methods situated more towards the increasing X axis are more efficient in terms of normalized CPU cost per Hz. Hence, amongst the live methods

having the same CPU consumption, the higher efficiency of guest memory mapping can be easily observed. Also, the lower CPU usage for the halting-reads method is misleading as the graph does not plot the impact on the VM with each technique. So even though the former can hit the 10Hz frequency while consuming <40% CPU as compared to live reads that consume 100% CPU for about 30Hz, yet it is costlier because it stuns the VM periodically thereby disturbing its workload heavily. The next section quantifies this impact.

4.3 Impact on VM's Performance

We run targeted workloads inside the VM stressing different resource components, and measure the percentage overhead on their corresponding performance metrics. VM impact is measured for the lowest monitoring frequency of 0.01 Hz, increasing in orders of 10 up to 10Hz or the maximum attainable frequency for each VMI technique. Each benchmark is run enough number of times to ensure sufficient monitoring iterations are performed for each method at each frequency. The graphs only plot the mean values while the error bars are omitted for readability (the experimental variation was within 5% of the means). We use the guest reported benchmark performance metrics, after having ensured that the guest timing matches with the host timings throughout the benchmarks' progress.

In the experiments, our VMI based monitoring application runs on a separate host core, while we experiment with two different configurations mapping the VM's VCPU to host's PCPU[1]. In the first 1VPCU-1PCPU configuration, we pin to a single core on host the QEMU process that runs the main VM thread and all other helper threads that get spawned to serve the monitoring process' memory access requests. In the second 1VCPU-2PCPU configuration, we taskset the QEMU process to two cores on host, the VM still having only one virtual core to itself . We do this to visualize the kind of overheads that would be seen if each technique was given unbounded CPU resources (a single extra core suffices, going beyond this has no additional effect).

---

[1] The hardware architecture influences the introspection application's as well as the VM's VPCPU-PCPU core mapping. The chosen configuration ensures the least impact on VM due to introspection.

(a) 1VCPU- 1PCPU

(b) 1VCPU - 2PCPU

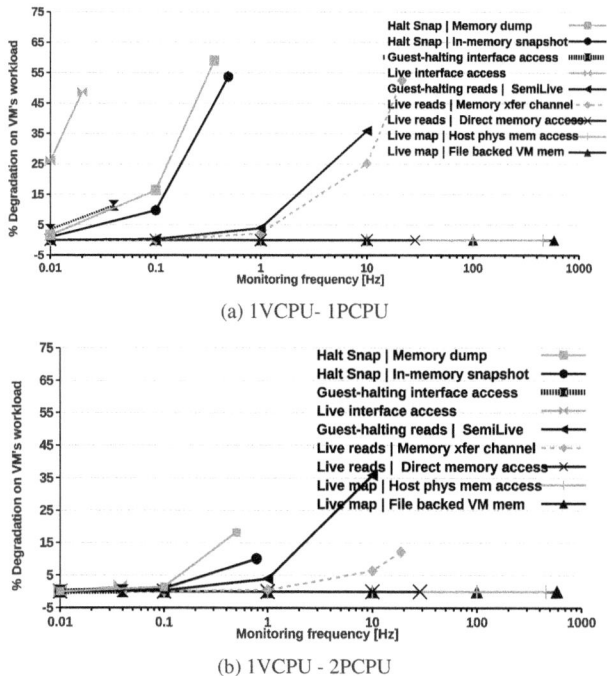

Figure 4: Comparing % degradation on x264 benchmark's frames-encoded/s as a function of monitoring frequency.

4.3.1 CPU Benchmark

Figure 4(a) plots the percentage degradation on x264's [50] frames encoded per second as a function of monitoring frequency for each technique. The rightmost points for each curve show the overheads for the maximum attainable monitoring frequency for each method. Each data point is obtained by averaging 10 x264 runs.

As can be seen, there is minimal overhead on x264's framerate with the live methods (except the libVMI memory transfer channel implementation), while for the rest, the overhead decreases with decreasing monitoring frequency. Biggest hit is observed for methods that quiesce the VM, as expected.

Figure 4(b) compares x264's performance degradation when each technique is given unbounded CPU resources in the 1VCPU - 2PCPU taskset configuration. As a result, the VM overhead is greatly reduced for methods that spawn QEMU threads to extract VM state, as the main QEMU thread servicing the VM now no longer has to contend for CPU with the other helper threads that get spawned to serve the monitoring process' memory access requests. The halting-read method, which wasn't using a full CPU to begin with, has no use for the extra CPU resources and thus the VM overhead remains the same owing to the periodic VM stuns.

This is the only case where we compare the performance of all candidate techniques. Our main focus is actually on how the categories themselves compare in terms of performance degradation of the target VM's workload. Hereafter, we only present results for one representative method from

each category- namely memory dumps (guest-halting snapshotting), management interface (interface access), semilive direct access (halting-reads), QEMU direct memory access (live memory reads), and file-backed VM memory (live memory map). Although not explicitly shown, the omitted methods follow performance trends similar to their sibling candidates from the same taxonomy category. The interface access methods are also observed to exhibit similar performance.

4.3.2 Memory, Disk and Network Benchmarks

Figure 5 plots the impact on the VM's memory, disk and network throughputs, owing to VMI based monitoring. Impact is mostly observed for only the methods that quiesce the VM, and does not improve markedly when extra CPU resources (1VPCU-2PCPU mapping) are provided to the techniques. This is because the CPU is not the bottleneck here, with the workloads either being limited by the memory subsystem, or bounded by network or disk IO.

The degradation on STREAM [39] benchmark's default 'best' (of all iterations) memory throughput was negligible even while monitoring with methods that quiesce the VM. However, the techniques' true impact can be seen in Figure 5(a) that compares the percentage degradation on STREAM's 'average' (across all iterations) memory throughput. In other words, the impact is only observed on the sustained bandwidth and not the instantaneous throughput.

For the impact on bonnie++ [61] disk throughputs, separate curves for disk writes are only shown for VM quiescing methods (Figure 5(b)), the rest being identical to those of reads, with the main noticeable difference being the minimal impact seen on the write throughput even with the halting-reads method. This can be attributed to the fact that the VM's CPU is not being utilized at its full capacity and spends a lot of time waiting for the disk to serve the write requests made from bonnie++. Hence, minor VM stunning doesn't hurt the benchmark so bad, as the work gets delegated to the disk. This, along with the writeback caching in the kernel, also means that the worst-case per-block write latency (not shown in the graphs) does not see a big hit even for methods that quiesce the VM, while their worst-case read latency is an order of magnitude higher.

Another interesting observation is the markedly high impact on the disk throughputs with memory dumping, as compared to the CPU intensive benchmark, which moreover shows no improvement even when the monitoring frequency is reduced from 0.1Hz to 0.01Hz. Netperf's [59] network bandwidth also sees a similar hit with guest-halting snapshotting (Figure 5(c)), with its impact curves being very similar to those of the disk (read) throughputs. The difference in this case is that that the overhead curve does not plateau out and eventually subsides to minimal impact at 0.01Hz. As demonstrated later in Section 4.4.1, these high overheads can

139

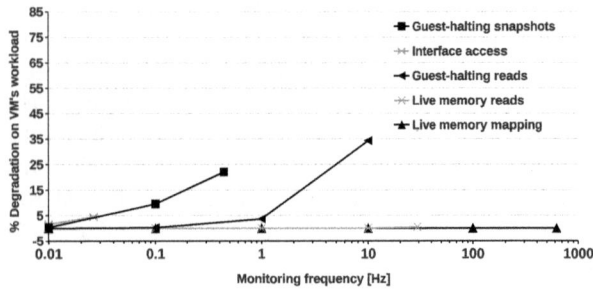

(a) Impact on STREAM benchmark's memory copy throughput

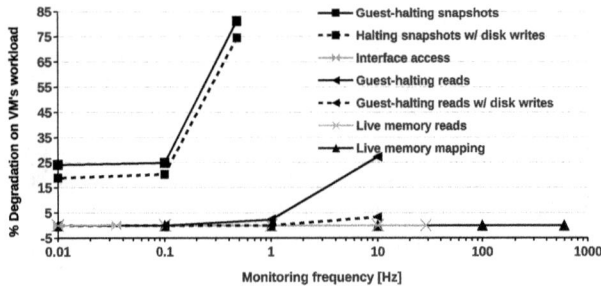

(b) Impact on bonnie++'s disk throughputs. Differing behaviour on writes shown separately.

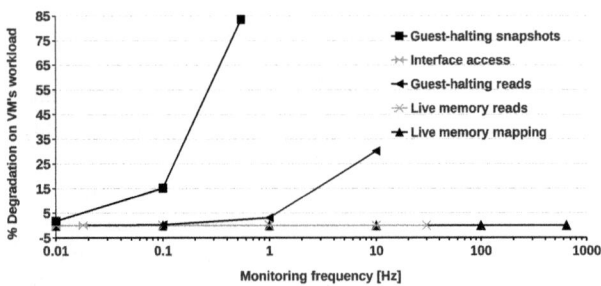

(c) Impact netperf's network transfer bandwidth

Figure 5: Comparing % degradation on memory, disk and network throughput as a function of monitoring frequency

attributed to the backlog of pending IO requests that dumping (and hence VM quiescing) creates in the network and disk IO queues.

4.4 Real Workload Results

After characterizing VMI based monitoring's impact on individual VM resources, we use two full system benchmarks to understand the impact on real world deployments-database and webserver. We omit the OLTP database benchmark [4] for brevity, as the graphs for impact on its transaction throughput and response times are pretty much identical to the disk read benchmark, being attributed to the backlogging in the database transaction queues. Instead we dig deep into the httperf benchmark to inspect these queue perturbations.

4.4.1 Full System Httperf Benchmark

Figure 6(a) plots the impact on the webserver VM's sustainable request rate as compared to the base case without any

monitoring, for the different VMI techniques under different monitoring frequencies. Each data point in the graph is obtained by averaging 3 httperf [49] runs, each run lasting for 320s.

Amongst all the benchmarks, httperf is hit the worst by methods that quiesce the VM, even at low monitoring frequency, with the halting-reads method recording ~25% impact even at 1Hz. With memory dumping, like in case of the disk and OLTP benchmarks, the impact on the sustainable request rate is not lowered even with extra CPU resources afforded to the QEMU process, as well as when the monitoring frequency is reduced from 0.1Hz to 0.01Hz. We explain this with an experiment later in this Section.

Also note the much lower maximum monitoring frequencies recorded for the different techniques as they monitor the httperf workload. The longer monitoring cycles are because the amount of state extracted is far more than other benchmarks (~4X), owing to several apache processes running inside the VM. This also prevents the interface based approaches from operating even at 0.01Hz, while the halting-reads method is unable to operate at its usual 10Hz (iteration runtime ~150ms).

The sustainable request rate is only one half of the story. Figure 6(b) also plots the impact on the webserver VM's average and 95th percentile response latencies. Shown are overheads for the practical monitoring frequencies of 0.1Hz for techniques that quiesce the VM, and for maximum attainable monitoring frequencies for the other live methods. As can be seen, even if a user was willing to operate the webserver at 75% of its peak capacity, while snapshotting once every 10s for view consistent introspection, they should be aware of the fact that the response times would shoot up 100% on an average, going beyond 200% in the worst case. The particular requests experiencing these massive degradations can be spotted in a server timeline graph, omitted for brevity, where the response times jump quite a bit for about 50s after a single dumping iteration (<2s).

Finally, we investigate why guest-halting snapshotting shows a horizontal impact curve from 0.1Hz to 0.01Hz in Figure 6(a), instead of the impact on server's capacity lowering on snapshotting it 10 times less frequently. As discussed above, when the webserver operates at 75% of its peak capacity (serving 1500 requests/s as opposed to 1950), the jump in response times eventually subsides after a single snapshotting iteration, and no requests are dropped. If the requests arrive at any rate greater than this, it is observed that a single <2s dumping cycle degrades the server capacity to ~700 serviced requests/s, with several connection drops, and the server doesn't recover even after 15 minutes. Figure 6(c) visualizes this observation for 5 httperf rounds of 320s each, plotting the (i) server capacity (reply_rate) (ii) avg. response time per request, and (iii) percentage connections dropped (Error %). In the end, the server has to be 'refreshed' with an apache process restart to clear up

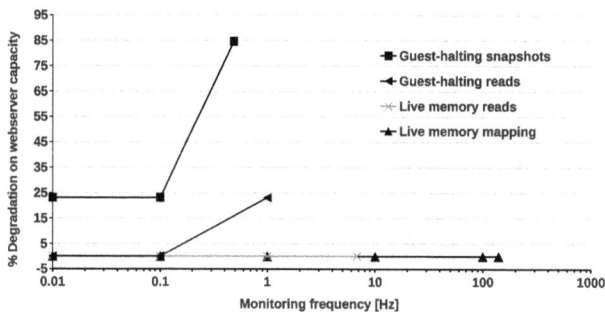

(a) Impact on httperf's sustainable request rate

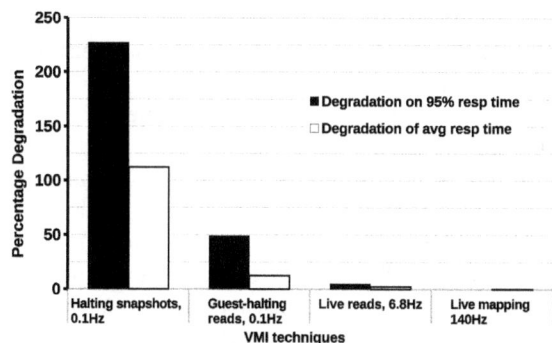

(b) Impact on httperf's response times

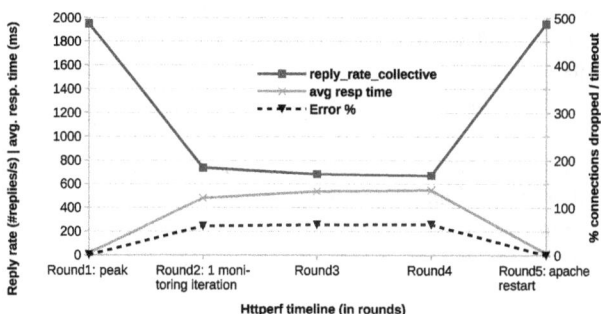

(c) httperf 1950 req/s + 1 round of memory dumping

Figure 6: Comparing % degradation on httperf's metrics as a function of monitoring frequency

all the wait queues to bring it back up to its base capacity. Hence, because the server is operating at its peak capacity in this case, the wait queues are operating at a delicate balance with the incoming request rate. Any perturbation or further queuing introduced by a single VM quiescing cycle destroys this balance, thereby creating a backlog of pending requests which the webserver never seems to recover from. The behaviour is same for any incoming rate >1500 requests/s. And this is why even for 0.01Hz monitoring frequency, the server can only handle 1500 requests per sec at best. Note that the measurements are made from the clients' side in httperf, so the requests from a new round also get queued up behind the pending requests from an earlier round. Hence, from the clients' perspective, a possible eventual server capacity recovery is not observed without a complete server queue flush.

5. Consistency of VM State

A key concern with VMI techniques is the consistency of the observed VM state. Particularly, introspecting a live system while its state is changing may lead to inconsistencies[2] in the observed data structures. An inconsistency during introspection may cause the monitoring process to fail, trying to access and interpret non-existent or malformed data. A common approach to mitigate inconsistencies is to pause/quiesce[3] the systems during introspection (halting-reads method). This is considered a safe approach as the system does not alter its state while the data structures are interpreted [11, 28, 30, 44, 56]. Therefore it is commonly employed for "safe" introspection despite its high overheads as we had shown in the prior sections. In this section we present a deeper exploration of what these inconsistencies are, their likelihood, and when pause-and-introspect (PAI) solutions help. Our investigation leads to some interesting key observations. First, we show that there are multiple forms of inconsistencies, both in intrinsic VM state and extrinsic due to live introspection. Second, contrary to common expectation, PAI does not mitigate all forms of inconsistency.

5.1 Inconsistency Types

We capture inconsistencies by recording the `read()` or `seek()` failures in the introspection process, while the VM being monitored runs workloads (Section 5.2) that continuously alter system state. Each of these failures denote an access to a malformed or non-existent data structure. Furthermore, by tracing back the root of these failures, we were also able to categorize every inconsistency observed as follows. We further verified the exact causes of each inconsistency occurrence by running Crash [21] on a captured memory snapshot of the paused VM under inconsistency.

I. Intrinsic Inconsistencies

This category of inconsistencies occur due to different but related OS data structures being at inconsistent states themselves—for a short period—in the OS, and not because of live introspection. These inconsistencies still persist even if PAI techniques are employed instead of live introspection. We subcategorize these into the following types:

I.A **Zombie Tasks:** For tasks marked as dead but not yet reaped by the parent, only certain basic `task_struct` fields are readable. Others such as memory mapping information, open files and network connections lead to inconsistency errors when accessed.

I.B **Dying Tasks:** For tasks that are in the process of dying but not dead yet (marked "exiting" in their `task_struct`), their memory state might be reclaimed by the OS. Therefore, although their state seems still available, accessing

---

[2] While the OS itself is not inconsistent, the observed inconsistencies arise because of a missing OS-context within VMI scope.

[3] We use pause/quiesce/halt to refer to the same guest state; not to be confused with the possibly different interpretations from the point of view of the OS.

these can lead to NULL or incorrect values being read by the monitoring process.

I.C **As-good-as-dead tasks:** We still optimistically go ahead and extract state for tasks of the previous type - tagged as exiting. We skip them only in cases where the memory info data structure `mm_struct` is already NULL which means not only are this task's memory mappings unavailable, but any attempt to extract its open files / network connections list is also highly likely to fail.

I.D **Fresh tasks:** For newly-created processes, all of their data structures do not instantaneously get initialized. Therefore, accessing the fields of a fresh process may lead to transient `read()` errors, where addresses read may be NULL or pointing to incorrect locations.

II. Extrinsic Inconsistencies

This second category of inconsistencies occur during live introspection and only these can be mitigated by PAI techniques. The reason for these inconsistencies is VM state changing during introspection. We subcategorize these into the following types:

II.A **Task Dies During Monitoring:** For tasks that die while their data structures were being interpreted, data fields and addresses read after the task state is recycled lead to `read()/seek()` errors.

II.B **Attributes Change During Monitoring:** In this case, while the tasks themselves keep alive, their attributes that point to other data structures might change, such as open files, sockets or network connections. In this case accessing these data structures based on stale/invalid memory references leads to inconsistency errors.

5.2 Quantitative Evaluation

We first create a benchmark, *cork*, that rapidly changes system state by forking and destroying processes at various rates, and use it with a process creation rate of 10Hz and a process lifetime of 1s. We quantify the occurrence probabilities of inconsistencies with two workloads: (i) our simple *cork* benchmark, which stresses the process create/delete dimension; and (ii) a webserver at its peak capacity serving incoming HTTP requests from three separate *httperf* clients for 2^{18} different 2KB files, which stresses both the process and file/socket open/close dimensions.

Figure 7 shows the observed probabilities for all the different inconsistency types for both benchmarks. These probabilities are computed from 3 separate runs, each of which repeat 10,000 introspection iterations (based on the live direct memory read approach) while the benchmarks are executed. The observed results are independent of the introspection frequency. As the figure shows, most inconsistencies are rather rare events (except for one corner case with *httperf*), and the majority of those observed fall into category I. While not shown here, when we perform the same experiments **with the halting-reads approach, all dynamic state**

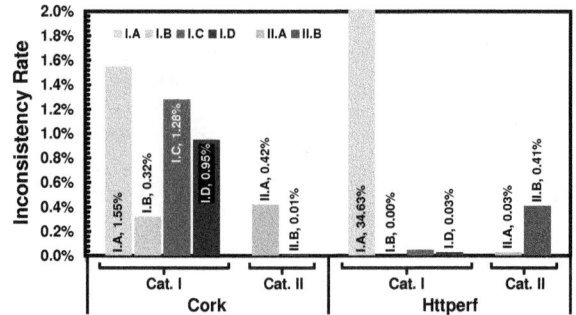

Figure 7: Observed inconsistency probabilities for all categories.

extrinsic inconsistencies of Category II disappear, while Category I results remain similar.

The quantitative evaluation shows some interesting trends. First, we see that Category II events are rather rare (less than 1%) even for these worst-case benchmarks. Therefore, for most cases PAI techniques produce limited return on investment for consistency. If strong consistency is what is desired regardless of cost, then PAI approaches do eliminate these dynamic state inconsistencies. The cost of this can be up to 35% with a guest-halting direct-reads approach for 10Hz monitoring, and 4% for 1Hz monitoring, in terms of degradation on VM's workload. *Cork* records more type $II.A$ inconsistencies, whereas the webserver workload exhibits more of type $II.B$. This is because of the continuous closing and opening of files and sockets, while serving requests in the webserver case. Both of these, however, occur infrequently—in only 0.4% of the iterations. *Cork* also exhibits type $I.C$ and $I.D$ inconsistencies for freshly created and removed tasks, as the OS context itself becomes temporarily inconsistent while updating task structures. One unexpected outcome of this evaluation is the very high rate of type $I.A$ inconsistencies with the webserver, which also has a significant occurrence in *cork*. The amount of time state is kept for zombie tasks varies by both system configuration and load, and can lead to substantial VMI errors (type $I.A$ inconsistency) as seen with the webserver. Zombies are alive until the parent process reads the child's exit status. If the parent process dies before doing so, then the system's `init` process periodically reaps the zombies. Under high loads, the webserver forks several `apache` worker threads and it takes a while before reaping them, thereby leading to their zombie state existence for longer durations.

6. Observations and Recommendations

In this section, we summarize our observations and present our suggestions to VMI users in selecting the technique best suited to their requirements and constraints.

• **Broad Spectrum of Choices:** There are several available VMI alternatives operating on different principles ranging from dumping to memory-mapping. Their performance varies widely along several dimensions such as their speed, resource consumption, overhead on VM's workload, view consistency, and more. These methods may be available out-of-box on different hypervisors or be enabled by third party libraries or hypervisor modifications, giving the user a choice between easy deployability vs. hypervisor specialization.

• **Guest Cooperation vs. Out-of-band:** If the user has sufficient resources allocated to his VMs, and installing in-VM components is acceptable, then guest-cooperation is a great way of bridging VMI's semantic gap. If this isn't acceptable, or security and inaccuracy of in-VM entities is an additional concern, then, the out-VM methods are a good alternative. The latter also helps against vendor lock-in, if the user prefers uninterrupted functionality with VM mobility across hypervisors without specializing his VMs for a particular hypervisor.

• **VMI use-case:** Some techniques are more suitable in certain scenarios. For example, high speed live methods are best for high frequency realtime monitoring such as process level resource monitoring, continuous validation, best effort security monitoring. On the other hand, snapshotting techniques are useful when all that is needed is an (infrequent) point in time snapshot, as in digital forensics investigation. For infrequent peeking into guest memory, a simple management interface access would suffice, while for guest debugging or crash troubleshooting, the guest-halting GDB-access interface would be the most suitable to freeze and inspect the guest in its inconsistent state without any regards to performance or overhead. Where strict view consistency is desired within acceptable overhead, guest-halting memory mapping/reads would work well such as for low frequency security scanning and compliance audits. Low frequency monitoring offers a lot more flexibility in terms of the choice of technique, except if the workloads are bound by specific resources as discussed next.

• **VM Workload:** Along with the intended VMI use-case, the target VM's workload can also influence the choice of introspection technique. If the user's workload is not bound by a particular VM resource, then there is more flexibility in selecting the introspection technique as well as its speed (frequency), even the ones that quiesce the VM. Even if it is CPU-intensive or memory bound, it can still tolerate guest-halting snapshotting better than if it were IO bound (disk / network / transactions), because the latter would be more sensitive to perturbation of the service queues, in which case snapshotting can be heavy even at very low monitoring frequencies. On the other hand, IO bound workloads can tolerate the lighter stuns of the guest-halting direct-reads method better than CPU intensive workloads, because the work gets handed off to other components while the CPU halts temporarily. But the halting-reads method's execution length, and hence the VM stun duration, depends on the amount of state to be extracted. So it might not be a good fit on an active VM with rapidly changing state (see rapidly spawning

apache processes in httperf evaluation in Section 4.4.1), or an application that accesses large memory such as virusscan.

• **Host/Hypervisor Specialization:** Different hypervisors support different techniques out-of-box, some faster than others (comparison across techniques, not across hypervisors). If the user has freedom of choice over hypervisor selection, e.g. if they are not vendor locked to a particular provider or constrained by enterprise policies, then they may choose the one offering the best technique- fastest or cheapest (resource consumption). Otherwise, if the hypervisor selection is fixed, but the user still has control over the host resources or is willing to modify the hypervisor or install third party libraries, they can further optimize the available option to extract the best performance. For example, a 'direct memory access' method in KVM is sufficiently fast for practical monitoring applications and works out-of-box, still an order of magnitude higher speed can be achieved by either modifying QEMU, or enabling physical memory access on host, or reserving large pages in host memory for file-backed method. Although the latter come with a tradeoff of increasing system vulnerability and memory pressure. This work also shows that libraries or hypervisor modification may not be needed to extract high performance, as depicted by the QEMU direct access live method (enabled by leveraging Linux memory primitives) being more efficient than the LibVMI library's live transfer channel implementation, while the latter also requiring QEMU modifications.

• **Mapping over direct reads:** Amongst the various methods compared in this study, the live methods are the best performing across several dimensions. Amongst these, guest memory mapping is much superior to direct memory reads (e.g. speed order of 100Hz vs 10Hz), primarily because of greater system call overheads in the latter (multiple read()/seek() vs. single mmap()). However, the previous observation's speed vs. hypervisor specialization tradeoff holds true here as well, atleast for KVM.

• **Guest-halting map/reads over snapshotting:** For strict view-consistent monitoring and other VM-snapshot based use-cases, it is better to use halting-reads than halting-snapshot based approaches, because although both techniques quiesce the target VM, the impact on the VM's workload is generally much lower with the former technique, and especially bearable for low monitoring frequency. Also, as shown in experiments, guest-halting snapshotting methods create backlogs in work queues thereby heavily impacting performance. Live snapshotting, on the other hand, is a much better alternative as indicated in Section 3's qualitative analysis and towards the end of Section 4 (as *Discussion*).

• **Consistency vs. Liveness, Realtimeness, and VM performance:** For almost all techniques, view consistency and guest liveness are conflicting goals. If the user, however, desires both, then they would either have to let go of guest independence by opting for the guest cooperation methods that run inside the guest OS scope, or choose a hardware assisted out-of-band approach using transactional memory [44]. One compromise option is COW snapshotting that provides an almost-live and consistent snapshot.

For the common non-live pause-and-introspect (PAI) based techniques (halting-reads), its maximum monitoring frequency can never equal live's because that would mean the VM is paused all the time and is thus making no meaningful progress. Thus, for PAI techniques, there exists a consistency vs. realtimeness tradeoff in addition to the consistency vs. VM performance tradeoff, the latter evident with high VM overheads with halting-reads.

Consistency Fallacy: Furthermore, as our experiments indicate, PAI techniques, employed for "safe" introspection despite their high VM performance impact, do not mitigate all forms of inconsistency, which are very rare to begin with. There is thus a need to synchronize with the guest OS to determine guest states safe for introspection.

• **Monitoring Overhead vs. Resource Usage:** In the KVM/ QEMU implementations of guest-halting snapshotting and interfaced based memory access methods, there exists a tradeoff between the resources available for monitoring versus the impact on the VM being monitored, except for when the target VM has CPU slack. This tradeoff does not hold true for the Live memory map/reads which already have negligible VM overhead in the base case, as well as the halting-reads method that doesn't consume a full CPU to begin with, while the overhead stems from periodic VM stuns.

• **Scalability of approaches:** If the user targets several VMs to be monitored at once, another important metric to consider is scalability. Although an explicit comparison is omitted for brevity, it is relatively straightforward to correlate a technique's maximum frequency with CPU usage, and observe that the live memory map/read techniques all consuming more or less a single CPU core on host would monitor the maximum number of VMs at 1 Hz (ranging between 30 to 500 VMs per dedicated monitoring core).

7. Conclusion

We presented a comparative evaluation of exisiting VMI techniques to aid VMI users in selecting the approach best suited to their requirements and constraints. We organized existing VMI techniques into a taxonomy based upon their operational principles. Our quantitative and qualitative evaluation reveals that VMI techniques cover a broad spectrum of operating points. We show that there is substantial difference in their operating frequencies, resource consumption on host, and overheads on target systems. These methods may be available out-of-box on different hypervisors or can be enabled by third party libraries or hypervisor modifications, giving the user a choice between easy deployability vs. hypervisor specialization. We also demonstrate the various forms of intrinsic and extrinsic inconsistency in the observed VM state, and show that pause-and-introspect based techniques have marginal benefits for consistency, despite their prohibitive overheads. Therefore application developers have different alternatives to choose from based on their desired levels of latency, frequency, overhead, consistency, intrusiveness, generality and practical deployability. We hope that our observations can benefit the community in understanding the trade-offs of different techniques, and for making further strides leveraging VMI for their applications.

Acknowledgments

We would like to thank our anonymous reviewers and our shepherd Kenichi Kourai for their helpful suggestions on improving this paper. We also thank Hao Chen for his insight during the initial phase of this work. This work is supported by an IBM Open Collaboration Research award.

References

[1] Adam Boileau. Hit by a Bus: Physical Access Attacks with Firewire. *RuxCon* 2006. www.security-assessment.com/files/presentations/ab_firewire_rux2k6-final.pdf.

[2] Adam Litke. Use the Qemu guest agent with MOM. http://https://aglitke.wordpress.com/2011/08/26/use-the-qemu-guest-agent-with-memory-overcommitment-manager/.

[3] F. Aderholdt, F. Han, S. L. Scott, and T. Naughton. Efficient checkpointing of virtual machines using virtual machine introspection. In *Cluster, Cloud and Grid Computing (CCGrid), 2014 14th IEEE/ACM International Symposium on*, pages 414–423, May 2014.

[4] Alexey Kopytov. SysBench Manual. http://sysbench.sourceforge.net/docs/#database_mode.

[5] Anthony Desnos. Draugr - Live memory forensics on Linux. http://code.google.com/p/draugr/.

[6] M. Auty, A. Case, M. Cohen, B. Dolan-Gavitt, M. H. Ligh, J. Levy, and A. Walters. Volatility - An advanced memory forensics framework. http://code.google.com/p/volatility/.

[7] A. M. Azab, P. Ning, Z. Wang, X. Jiang, X. Zhang, and N. C. Skalsky. Hypersentry: Enabling stealthy in-context measurement of hypervisor integrity. In *Proceedings of the 17th ACM Conference on Computer and Communications Security*, CCS '10, pages 38–49, New York, NY, USA, 2010. ACM.

[8] M. B. Baig, C. Fitzsimons, S. Balasubramanian, R. Sion, and D. Porter. CloudFlow: Cloud-wide policy enforcement using fast VM introspection. In *IEEE Conference on Cloud Engineering IC2E 2014*, 2014.

[9] A. Baliga, V. Ganapathy, and L. Iftode. Detecting kernel-level rootkits using data structure invariants. *IEEE Trans. Dependable Secur. Comput.*, 8(5):670–684, Sept. 2011.

[10] A. Bianchi, Y. Shoshitaishvili, C. Kruegel, and G. Vigna. Blacksheep: Detecting compromised hosts in homogeneous crowds. In *Proceedings of the 2012 ACM Conference on Com-*

puter and Communications Security, CCS '12, pages 341–352, New York, NY, USA, 2012. ACM.

[11] Bryan Payne. LibVMI Introduction: Vmitools, An introduction to LibVMI. http://code.google.com/p/vmitools/wiki/LibVMI Introduction.

[12] B. D. Carrier and J. Grand. A hardware-based memory acquisition procedure for digital investigations. *Digital Investigation*, 1(1):50–60, 2004.

[13] A. Case, A. Cristina, L. Marziale, G. G. Richard, and V. Roussev. Face: Automated digital evidence discovery and correlation. *Digit. Investig.*, 5:S65–S75, Sept. 2008.

[14] A. Case, L. Marziale, and G. G. RichardIII. Dynamic recreation of kernel data structures for live forensics. *Digital Investigation*, 7, Supplement(0):S32 – S40, 2010.

[15] J.-H. Chiang, H.-L. Li, and T.-c. Chiueh. Introspection-based memory de-duplication and migration. In *Proceedings of the 9th ACM SIGPLAN/SIGOPS International Conference on Virtual Execution Environments*, VEE '13, pages 51–62, New York, NY, USA, 2013. ACM.

[16] T.-c. Chiueh, M. Conover, and B. Montague. Surreptitious deployment and execution of kernel agents in windows guests. In *Proceedings of the 2012 12th IEEE/ACM International Symposium on Cluster, Cloud and Grid Computing (Ccgrid 2012)*, CCGRID '12, pages 507–514, Washington, DC, USA, 2012. IEEE Computer Society.

[17] Citrix. Citrix XenServer 6.2.0 Virtual Machine User's Guide. http://support.citrix.com/servlet/KbServlet/download/34971-102-704221/guest.pdf.

[18] Citrix Systems Inc. XenServer Windows PV Tools Guest Agent Service. https://github.com/xenserver/win-xenguestagent.

[19] P. Colp, C. Matthews, B. Aiello, and A. Warfield. Vm snapshots. In *Xen Summit*, 2009.

[20] L. Cui, B. Li, Y. Zhang, and J. Li. Hotsnap: A hot distributed snapshot system for virtual machine cluster. In *LISA*, 2013.

[21] David Anderson. White Paper: Red Hat Crash Utility. people.redhat.com/anderson/crash_whitepaper/.

[22] Dell Quest/VKernel. Foglight for Virtualization. quest.com/foglight-for-virtualization-enterprise-edition/.

[23] B. Dolan-Gavitt, B. Payne, and W. Lee. Leveraging forensic tools for virtual machine introspection. Technical Report GT-CS-11-05, Georgia Institute of Technology, 2011.

[24] J. Dykstra and A. T. Sherman. Acquiring forensic evidence from infrastructure-as-a-service cloud computing: Exploring and evaluating tools, trust, and techniques. *Digital Investigation*, 9:S90–S98, 2012.

[25] Emilien Girault. Volatilitux- Memory forensics framework to help analyzing Linux physical memory dumps. http://code.google.com/p/volatilitux/.

[26] Y. Fu and Z. Lin. Space Traveling across VM: Automatically Bridging the Semantic Gap in Virtual Machine Introspection via Online Kernel Data Redirection. In *IEEE Security&Privacy'12*.

[27] L. Garber. The challenges of securing the virtualized environment. *Computer*, 45(1):17–20, 2012.

[28] T. Garfinkel and M. Rosenblum. A Virtual Machine Introspection Based Architecture for Intrusion Detection. In *NDSS*, pages 191–206, 2003.

[29] Z. Gu, Z. Deng, D. Xu, and X. Jiang. Process implanting: A new active introspection framework for virtualization. In *Reliable Distributed Systems (SRDS), 2011 30th IEEE Symposium on*, pages 147–156. IEEE, 2011.

[30] B. Hay, M. Bishop, and K. Nance. Live analysis: Progress and challenges. *Security & Privacy, IEEE*, 7(2):30–37, 2009.

[31] B. Hay and K. Nance. Forensics examination of volatile system data using virtual introspection. *SIGOPS Oper. Syst. Rev.*, 42(3):74–82, 2008.

[32] J. Hizver and T.-c. Chiueh. Real-time deep virtual machine introspection and its applications. In *Proceedings of the 10th ACM SIGPLAN/SIGOPS International Conference on Virtual Execution Environments*, VEE '14, pages 3–14, New York, NY, USA, 2014. ACM.

[33] J. Hizver and T. cker Chiueh. Automated discovery of credit card data flow for pci dss compliance. In *Reliable Distributed Systems (SRDS), 2011 30th IEEE Symposium on*, pages 51–58, Oct 2011.

[34] O. S. Hofmann, A. M. Dunn, S. Kim, I. Roy, and E. Witchel. Ensuring operating system kernel integrity with OSck. In *ASPLOS*, pages 279–290, 2011.

[35] K.-Y. Hou, M. Uysal, A. Merchant, K. G. Shin, and S. Singhal. Hydravm: Low-cost, transparent high availability for virtual machines. Technical report, HP Laboratories, Tech. Rep, 2011.

[36] A. S. Ibrahim, J. H. Hamlyn-Harris, J. Grundy, and M. Almorsy. CloudSec: A security monitoring appliance for Virtual Machines in IaaS cloud model. In *NSS '11*, pages 113–120.

[37] B. Jain, M. B. Baig, D. Zhang, D. E. Porter, and R. Sion. SoK: Introspections on Trust and the Semantic Gap . In *35th IEEE Symposium on Security and Privacy S&P*, 2014.

[38] X. Jiang, X. Wang, and D. Xu. Stealthy malware detection through VMM-based out-of-the-box semantic view reconstruction. In *CCS '07*, pages 128–138.

[39] John D. McCalpin. Memory Bandwidth: Stream Benchmark. http://www.cs.virginia.edu/stream/.

[40] N. L. P. Jr., A. Walters, T. Fraser, and W. A. Arbaugh. Fatkit: A framework for the extraction and analysis of digital forensic data from volatile system memory. *Digital Investigation*, 3(4):197 – 210, 2006.

[41] I. Kollar. Forensic RAM dump image analyser. Master's Thesis, Charles University in Prague, 2010. hysteria.sk/~niekt0/fmem/doc/foriana.pdf.

[42] H. A. Lagar-Cavilla, J. A. Whitney, A. M. Scannell, P. Patchin, S. M. Rumble, E. de Lara, M. Brudno, and M. Satyanarayanan. Snowflock: Rapid virtual machine cloning for cloud computing. In *EuroSys*, 2009.

[43] H. Lee, H. Moon, D. Jang, K. Kim, J. Lee, Y. Paek, and B. B. Kang. Ki-mon: A hardware-assisted event-triggered monitoring platform for mutable kernel object. In *Proceedings of the*

22Nd USENIX Conference on Security, SEC'13, pages 511–526, Berkeley, CA, USA, 2013. USENIX Association.

[44] Y. Liu, Y. Xia, H. Guan, B. Zang, and H. Chen. Concurrent and consistent virtual machine introspection with hardware transactional memory. In *HPCA 2014*, 2014.

[45] Marco Batista. VMInjector: DLL Injection tool to unlock guest VMs. https://github.com/batistam/VMInjector.

[46] Mariusz Burdach. Digital forensics of the physical memory. 2005. http://forensic.seccure.net/pdf/mburdach_digital_forensics_of_physical_memory.pdf.

[47] Maximillian Dornseif. 0wned by an iPod. *PacSec Applied Security Conference* 2004. md.hudora.de/presentations/firewire/PacSec2004.pdf.

[48] H. Moon, H. Lee, J. Lee, K. Kim, Y. Paek, and B. B. Kang. Vigilare: Toward snoop-based kernel integrity monitor. In *Proceedings of the 2012 ACM Conference on Computer and Communications Security*, CCS '12, pages 28–37, New York, NY, USA, 2012. ACM.

[49] D. Mosberger and T. Jin. httperf - a tool for measuring web server performance. *SIGMETRICS Perform. Eval. Rev.*, 26(3):31–37, 1998.

[50] OpenBenchmarking/Phoronix. x264 Test Profile. http://openbenchmarking.org/test/pts/x264-1.7.0.

[51] Oracle's Linux Blog. Performance Issues with Transparent Huge Pages. https://blogs.oracle.com/linux/entry/performance_issues_with_transparent_huge.

[52] oVirt. oVirt guest agent. http://www.ovirt.org/Category:Ovirt_guest_agent.

[53] B. Payne, M. de Carbone, and W. Lee. Secure and Flexible Monitoring of Virtual Machines. In *Twenty-Third Annual Computer Security Applications Conference*, pages 385 –397, 2007.

[54] B. D. Payne, M. Carbone, M. Sharif, and W. Lee. Lares: An architecture for secure active monitoring using virtualization. In *Proceedings of the 2008 IEEE Symposium on Security and Privacy*, SP '08, pages 233–247, 2008.

[55] N. L. Petroni, Jr., T. Fraser, J. Molina, and W. A. Arbaugh. Copilot - a coprocessor-based kernel runtime integrity monitor. In *Proceedings of the 13th Conference on USENIX Security Symposium - Volume 13*, SSYM'04, pages 13–13, Berkeley, CA, USA, 2004. USENIX Association.

[56] J. Pfoh, C. Schneider, and C. Eckert. A formal model for virtual machine introspection. In *Proceedings of the 1st ACM workshop on Virtual machine security*, 2009.

[57] QEMU. Features/QAPI/GuestAgent. http://wiki.qemu.org/Features/QAPI/GuestAgent.

[58] A. Ranadive, A. Gavrilovska, and K. Schwan. Ibmon: monitoring vmm-bypass capable infiniband devices using memory introspection. In *HPCVirt*, pages 25–32, 2009.

[59] Rick Jones . Netperf Homepage. http://www.netperf.org/netperf/.

[60] A. Roberts, R. McClatchey, S. Liaquat, N. Edwards, and M. Wray. Poster: Introducing pathogen: a real-time virtual-machine introspection framework. In *Proceedings of the 2013 ACM SIGSAC conference on Computer & communications security*, CCS '13, pages 1429–1432, New York, NY, USA, 2013. ACM.

[61] Russell Coker. Bonnie++. http://www.coker.com.au/bonnie++/.

[62] J. Schiffman, H. Vijayakumar, and T. Jaeger. Verifying system integrity by proxy. In *Proceedings of the 5th International Conference on Trust and Trustworthy Computing*, TRUST'12, pages 179–200, Berlin, Heidelberg, 2012. Springer-Verlag.

[63] A. Schuster. Searching for processes and threads in microsoft windows memory dumps. *Digit. Investig.*, 3:10–16, Sept. 2006.

[64] A. Srivastava and J. Giffin. Tamper-Resistant, Application-Aware Blocking of Malicious Network Connections. In *RAID*, pages 39–58, 2008.

[65] Structured Data. Transparent Huge Pages and Hadoop Workloads. http://structureddata.org/2012/06/18/linux-6-transparent-huge-pages-and-hadoop-workloads/.

[66] M. H. Sun and D. M. Blough. Fast, lightweight virtual machine checkpointing. Technical report, Georgia Institute of Technology, 2010.

[67] S. Suneja, C. Isci, V. Bala, E. de Lara, and T. Mummert. Nonintrusive, out-of-band and out-of-the-box systems monitoring in the cloud. In *The 2014 ACM International Conference on Measurement and Modeling of Computer Systems*, SIGMETRICS '14, pages 249–261, New York, NY, USA, 2014. ACM.

[68] Toby Opferman. Sharing Memory with the Virtual Machine. http://www.drdobbs.com/sharing-memory-with-the-virtual-machine/184402033.

[69] VMware. VIX API Documentation. www.vmware.com/support/developer/vix-api/.

[70] VMware. VMCI Sockets Documentation. www.vmware.com/support/developer/vmci-sdk/.

[71] VMware. vShield Endpoint. vmware.com/products/vsphere/features-endpoint.

[72] VMWare Inc. VMWare VMSafe security technology. http://www.vmware.com/company/news/releases/vmsafe_vmworld.html.

[73] M. Vrable, J. Ma, J. Chen, D. Moore, E. Vandekieft, A. C. Snoeren, G. M. Voelker, and S. Savage. Scalability, fidelity, and containment in the potemkin virtual honeyfarm. In *SOSP*, 2005.

[74] J. Wang, A. Stavrou, and A. Ghosh. Hypercheck: A hardware-assisted integrity monitor. In *Proceedings of the 13th International Conference on Recent Advances in Intrusion Detection*, RAID'10, pages 158–177, Berlin, Heidelberg, 2010. Springer-Verlag.

[75] Wikibooks. QEMU/Monitor. http://en.wikibooks.org/wiki/QEMU/Monitor.

[76] T. Wood, P. Shenoy, A. Venkataramani, and M. Yousif. Black-box and gray-box strategies for virtual machine migration. In *NSDI*, 2007.

PEMU: A PIN Highly Compatible Out-of-VM Dynamic Binary Instrumentation Framework

Junyuan Zeng

Department of Computer Science
The University of Texas at Dallas
jzeng@utdallas.edu

Yangchun Fu

Department of Computer Science
The University of Texas at Dallas
yangchun.fu@utdallas.edu

Zhiqiang Lin

Department of Computer Science
The University of Texas at Dallas
zhiqiang.lin@utdallas.edu

Abstract

Over the past 20 years, we have witnessed a widespread adoption of dynamic binary instrumentation (DBI) for numerous program analyses and security applications including program debugging, profiling, reverse engineering, and malware analysis. To date, there are many DBI platforms, and the most popular one is PIN, which provides various instrumentation APIs for process instrumentation. However, PIN does not support the instrumentation of OS kernels. In addition, the execution of the instrumentation and analysis routine is always inside the virtual machine (VM). Consequently, it cannot support any out-of-VM introspection that requires strong isolation. Therefore, this paper presents PEMU, a new open source DBI framework that is compatible with PIN-APIs, but supports out-of-VM introspection for both user level processes and OS kernels. Unlike in-VM instrumentation in which there is no semantic gap, for out-of-VM introspection we have to bridge the semantic gap and provide abstractions (i.e., APIs) for programmers. One important feature of PEMU is its API compatibility with PIN. As such, many PIN plugins are able to execute atop PEMU without any source code modification. We have implemented PEMU, and our experimental results with the SPEC 2006 benchmarks show that PEMU introduces reasonable overhead.

Categories and Subject Descriptors D.3.4 [*Software*]: Processors—Code generation; Translator writing systems and compiler generators; D.4.6 [*Operating Systems*]: Security and Protection

General Terms Design, Security

Keywords Dynamic binary instrumentation; Introspection

Permission to make digital or hard copies of all or part of this work for personal or classroom use is granted without fee provided that copies are not made or distributed for profit or commercial advantage and that copies bear this notice and the full citation on the first page. Copyrights for components of this work owned by others than ACM must be honored. Abstracting with credit is permitted. To copy otherwise, or republish, to post on servers or to redistribute to lists, requires prior specific permission and/or a fee. Request permissions from permissions@acm.org.

VEE '15, March 14–15, 2015, Istanbul, Turkey..
Copyright © 2015 ACM 978-1-4503-3450-1/15/03... $15.00.
http://dx.doi.org/10.1145/2731186.2731201

1. Introduction

Dynamic binary instrumentation (DBI) is an extremely powerful technique for program analysis. At a high level, it dynamically inserts extra analysis code into the running binary program to observe how it behaves. It works similarly to a debugger but the analysis routine is programmed. Therefore, it can be used to automatically inspect the program state at instruction level and build many program analyses, such as performance profiling (e.g., [42, 46]), architecture simulation (e.g., [29]), program debugging (e.g., [25]), program shepherding (e.g., [23]), program optimization (e.g., [2]), dynamic data flow analysis (e.g., taint analysis [32, 36]), reverse engineering (e.g., [24]), and malware analysis (e.g., [12, 49]).

Today, there are many DBI platforms such as PIN [26], VALGRIND [31], DYNAMORIO [2], QEMU [4], and BOCHS [1]. Each platform is built atop its own virtual machine (VM), and has its own pros and cons. For example, process-level DBI such as PIN and VALGRIND provides rich APIs to analyze user level binary code execution, but the analysis code is executed inside the VM (i.e., in-VM) with the same privilege as the instrumented process. Moreover, it does not support any kernel-level code instrumentation. Some platforms only support a limited type of operating system (OS), e.g., VALGRIND only supports Linux binaries but provides no support for Microsoft Windows binaries. Some platforms are designed as a full system emulator (e.g., QEMU), but do not provide any general DBI APIs. As such, *can we build a cross-OS, API-rich, out-of-VM dynamic binary instrumentation framework that supports both user level and kernel level code?*

While there have been attempts to address this problem, they only partially achieved these goals. Specifically, PINOS [8] attempted to create a kernel instrumentation tool atop the XEN [3] hypervisor. However, it only supports inspecting the very low level instruction semantics (such as the executing instruction address), and does not support any high level instrumentation and introspection (e.g., get the running process ID inside the VM). Meanwhile, because of its implementation of stealing memory from the guest OS, it does not offer strong isolation and the analysis routine can be accessed by the instrumented process or kernel. Another attempt is

TEMU [48], which extends QEMU with its own APIs to allow end-users to develop TEMU-plugins for whole system instrumentation. Though it has greatly reduced developers' efforts in understanding the internals of QEMU in order to develop any useful plugins, it has only limited APIs compared to those provided by PIN. A recent effort, DRK [34], is able to perform kernel instrumentation. However, it is still an in-VM solution and does not isolate the analysis code (the analysis routine is executed as Linux Kernel modules), resulting in security issues when the kernel has malware.

To address these weaknesses, this paper presents PEMU (inherited from both PIN and QEMU), a new PIN-API compatible DBI framework that provides a whole system instrumentation but from out-of-VM introspection perspective. There are a number of goals PEMU aims to achieve. Specifically, it aims for PIN API-compatibility because of the large amount of users and rich-APIs PIN has. For instance, it has over 450 comprehensive, well-documented, easy to use instrumentation APIs. With the PIN compatible APIs, PIN plugins can be easily ported to PEMU with no or minimal modifications. Meanwhile, it aims for out-of-VM instrumentation because of the isolation requirement from security applications such as introspection. In addition, it aims for supporting a large number of different guest OSes without modification, considering that there are so many OSes with many different versions today.

The key idea to realize PEMU is to add *an additional software layer* atop an existing VM, and make our APIs self-contained. Such a design makes our system easily portable if the underlying VM has been upgraded. In addition to the engineering challenges (in support of the large number of PIN APIs), we also face a number of research challenges. One is how to bridge the semantic gap [9] while providing the out-of-VM instrumentation abstractions (e.g., APIs) for both process and kernel introspection, and also what those abstractions should be. The second is how to design our instrumentation engine such that it works seamlessly with the translation engine provided by the underlying VM but does not introduce large overhead. The third one is how to support the existing PIN APIs by using our framework.

We have addressed these challenges and implemented PEMU atop QEMU, and our experimental results with SPEC 2006 benchmarks show that PEMU has reasonable performance overhead compared to original QEMU and it will be useful for quickly developing PIN-style plugins atop PEMU or directly recompiling the existing PIN-plugins, for both instruction inspection and higher level semantic introspection.

Contributions. In summary, this paper makes the following contributions. We devise an additional software layer atop an existing binary code translation based VM with a set of standard APIs for both user level and kernel level DBI. This additional layer hides the low level VM details and contains a number of instrumentation related abstractions.

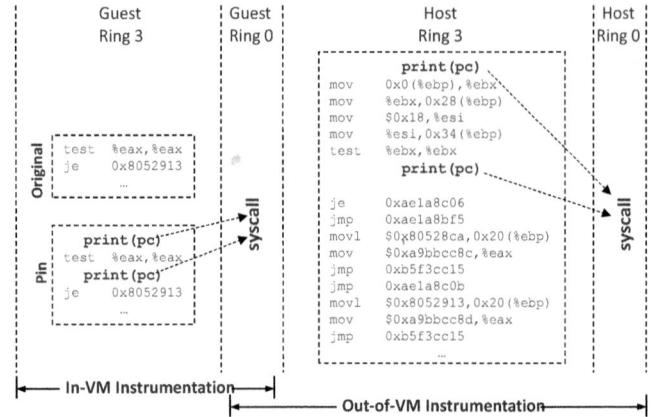

Figure 1. Differences Between in-VM and Out-of-VM Instrumentation.

With the additional layer and the abstractions, we present PEMU, a new DBI framework that enables end-users to develop instrumentation tools using many of the existing PIN APIs. We have implemented PEMU and tested with SPEC 2006 benchmark. Our experimental results show that PEMU introduces reasonable performance overhead.

2. Background and Overview

In this section, we first discuss the background related to our system in §2.1, and then motivate our research in §2.2. Next, we discuss how to develop a plugin using PEMU in §2.3, and finally we give an overview of PEMU in §2.4.

2.1 In-VM vs. Out-of-VM Instrumentation

The key technique behind any DBI is the just-in-time compilation (JIT) [4, 37]. Basically, all the executing instructions are translated by a JIT compiler, which provides an opportunity to interpose and instrument the binary code for analysis purposes. The entire DBI infrastructure can be considered as a VM, which could be a process level VM (e.g., PIN, VALGRIND), or a system level VM (e.g., QEMU). At a high level, a VM mediates program execution by dynamically translating blocks of native code and executing them from a code cache.

Given an analysis routine (e.g., printing the executed instruction addresses), there are two different ways of instrumenting the analysis routine with the original program code, as illustrated in Fig. 1.

- **In-VM instrumentation**. This is the easiest way. The analysis routine is directly translated together with the original code into the same code cache. The analysis routine and the original program code share the same address space, and they are executed inside the VM either at guest "ring 3" (application layer) or "ring 0" (OS kernel layer). Therefore, the analysis routine can feel free to call any guest OS abstractions, and access any code or data of the instrumented process or kernel. Most DBI systems (e.g., PIN and VALGRIND) are designed in this way.

```
1  static UINT64 icount;
2  FILE *pFile;
3  VOID docount(UINT32 c) { icount += c; }
4  VOID Trace(TRACE trace, VOID *v) {
5      for (BBL bbl = TRACE_BblHead(trace);
6          BBL_Valid(bbl); bbl = BBL_Next(bbl)) {
7          BBL_InsertCall(bbl, IPOINT_BEFORE,
8          (AFUNPTR)docount, IARG_UINT32, BBL_NumIns(bbl),
9          IARG_END);
10     }
11 }
12 VOID Fini(INT32 code, VOID *v) {
13     fprintf(pFile, "Count %lld\n", icount);
14     fclose(pFile);
15 }
16 INT32 Usage(VOID) {
17     return 0;
18 }
19 int main(int argc, char * argv[]) {
20     if(PIN_Init(argc, argv)) return Usage();
21     pFile = fopen("pemu_count", "w");
22     TRACE_AddInstrumentFunction(Trace, 0);
23     PIN_AddFiniFunction(Fini, 0);
24     PIN_StartProgram();
25     return 0;
26 }
```

Figure 2. A PEMU plugin to count the number of executed instructions.

- **Out-of-VM instrumentation**. Unlike in-VM instrumentation, the analysis routine is executed outside of the original program code (mostly at the virtual machine monitor layer, e.g., at "ring 3" of a host OS), though the original code and the analysis routine can be translated into the same cache. Therefore, the analysis routine and the original code does not share the same address space any more. There is a world switch for analysis routine from host "ring 3" to access the state of the monitored process or kernel at "ring 3" or "ring 0" of guest OS. Only a handful of systems (e.g., PINOS and TEMU) support out-of-VM instrumentation. However, their introspection supports are guest OS specific. Also, the isolation provided by PINOS is not as strong as TEMU. More specifically, while the instrumented code and instrumentation engine do not share any code in PINOS, the analysis routine and the original program code actually share the same address apace, because the analysis routine steals [8] the address space from the guest OS, which makes it possible to tamper with the analysis routine when used to analyze malware.

We can notice that in-VM instrumentation and out-of-VM instrumentation share the opposite pros and cons. In-VM instrumentation occurs inside the VM, and has rich abstractions. But it executes at the same privilege level as the monitored process. Out-of-VM instrumentation occurs outside of the VM, and has less abstractions. But the analysis routine is isolated with the original program code. To develop the analysis routine, we can still use host OS abstractions, but to inspect any guest OS state, there is a need for techniques to bridge the semantic gap.

2.2 Objectives

While there have been significant efforts in the past 20 years to build various DBI platforms, few works focus on out-of-VM instrumentation where the analysis routine and original program code are strongly isolated. In this paper, we would like to develop a new out-of-VM DBI with an emphasis on supporting security applications that satisfy the following constraints:

(1) **Rich APIs**. Similar to PIN tool, we would like to offer rich and well-defined APIs. Since PIN is one of the most popular DBI tools, we would like to make our API compatible with PIN. This will make an open source alternative to PIN, which will be useful when there is a need to customize the PIN engine.

(2) **Cross-OS**. Unlike VALGRIND, which only analyzes Linux binaries, we would also like to offer support to instrument both Windows and Linux binaries using the same platform. More importantly, since there are a large number of different OSes, we would like to make our system OS agnostic for the introspection.

(3) **Strong Isolation**. Unlike existing in-VM approaches, we would like to make our analysis code execute at the hypervisor layer (can be considered "ring -1") instead of at the guest OS "ring 3" for process introspection or "ring 0" for kernel introspection.

(4) **VM Introspection.** Unlike PINOS, which does not support higher level guest object introspection [16], we would like to provide APIs to retrieve the high level semantic state from the guest OS for the monitored process or guest kernel. Considering that there are too many guest OSes, we would like to design a general way to query the guest OS state.

2.3 An Example

Before describing the details of how we achieve these goals, we would like to first illustrate how to develop a PEMU plugin by using the provided APIs. As presented in Fig. 2, this is a very simple plugin with the functionality of counting the number of executed instructions. Similar to many other DBIs, to develop a PEMU plugin, users need to provide two sets of procedures: *Instrumentation Routine*, which specifies where the instrumentation should occur; and *Analysis Routine*, which defines analysis activities.

One important feature of PEMU is the API compatibility with the PIN tool. As illustrated in this example, the API we used is exactly identical to those used by a PIN tool. Therefore, many legacy PIN plugins can be recompiled and executed inside PEMU, but the distinctive feature is that both the analysis routine and instrumentation routine will be executed in the host OS, instead of inside the guest OS as would be done using PIN. For instance, the `fprintf` (line 13) and `fopen` (line 21) statements will be executed at

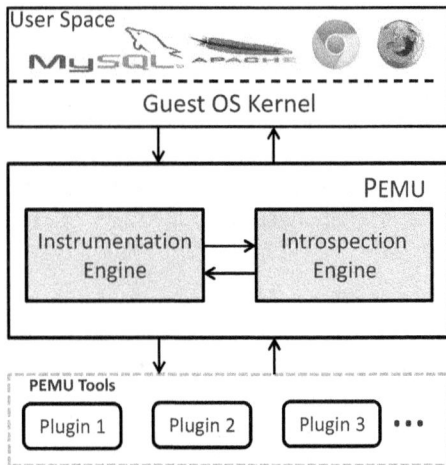

Figure 3. Architecture Overview of PEMU.

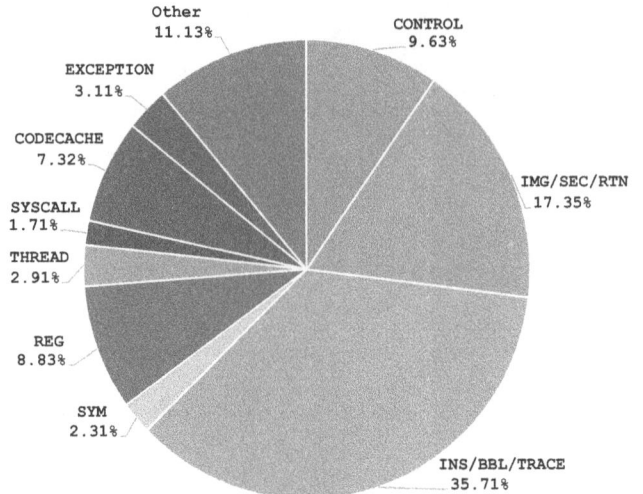

Figure 4. Distributions of PIN APIs.

the VMM layer and call host OS `fprintf` and `fopen`, but when we use PIN they will be executed inside the guest OS.

2.4 Architecture Overview

An overview of PEMU is presented in Fig. 3. There are two key components inside PEMU: *instrumentation engine* (§3) and *introspection engine* (§4). They both are located inside a virtual machine monitor.

To use PEMU, end users use the PIN compatible APIs provided by our *instrumentation engine* to develop the plugins, which will be compiled and linked at the VMM layer (namely, the host OS layer). If the analysis routine requires retrieving the state of the guest OS (e.g., `pid` of the instrumented process), it uses APIs provided by our *introspection engine*. In the following two sections, we describe how we design these two engines in greater detail.

3. Instrumentation Engine

Since PEMU aims for API compatibility with PIN, we have to first examine what those PIN APIs are. We take a recently released version of PIN (version 2.13), and we find there are in total 477 APIs. The distribution of these APIs are presented in Fig. 4.

PIN defines two sets of instrumentation: (1) *trace instrumentation* that occurs immediately before a code sequence is executed, and (2) *ahead-of-time instrumentation* that caches the instrumentation before the execution. There are three different types of *trace instrumentation* depending on the granularity:

- **Instruction Level**. The finest granularity is the instruction (INS) level instrumentation that allows for instrumenting a single instruction at a time by using the `INS_AddInstrument Function` call back. There are also many instruction insertion and inspection APIs starting with the `INS` prefix (e.g., `INS_InsertIfCall`,

`INS_IsBranch`, etc.). In total there are 142 `INS` related APIs.

- **Basic Block Level (BBL)**. A basic block (BB) is a single entrance, single exit sequence of instructions. Instead of one analysis call for every instruction, it is often more efficient to insert a single analysis call for a BB, thereby reducing the number of analysis calls. PIN does not offer a `BBL_AddInstrumentationFunction`, and instead developers have to instrument the TRACES (described next) and iterate through them to get the BB. There are in total 14 APIs related to BBL.

- **Trace Level**. A TRACE in PIN is defined as a sequence of instructions that begin at the target of a taken branch and end with an unconditional branch (i.e., `jmp/call/ret`). This is the set of instructions that are disassembled by a linear sweep algorithm, when giving a starting address. Therefore, a TRACE usually consists of a number of BBs. PIN provides `TRACE_AddInstrumentFunction` call back to instrument a TRACE. There are in total also 14 APIs related to TRACE. Note that PIN introduced the concept of TRACE for a trace-linking optimization [26], which attempts to branch directly from a trace exit to the target trace without trapping to the VM. TRACE is at a higher granularity than BB and INS, and sometimes instrumenting analysis routine at TRACE granularity can improve performance. For instance, TRACE-based BBL instruction counting (as shown in Fig. 2) is much faster than that of an INS based one.

Regarding the *ahead-of-time instrumentation*, PIN provides an image (IMG) instrumentation and routine (RTN) instrumentation. More specifically:

- **IMG instrumentation** allows a PIN-tool to inspect and instrument an entire image when it is loaded. A PIN-tool can walk the sections (SEC) of an image, the RTN of a section, and the INS of a routine. Image instrumentation relies on symbol information to determine an RTN boundary. An analysis routine can be inserted so that it is executed before or after a routine is executed, or before or after an instruction is executed. IMG instrumentation utilizes the `IMG_AddInstrumentFunction` API. In total, there are 27 APIs related to IMG, and 16 APIs related to SEC.

- **RTN instrumentation** allows a PIN-tool to inspect and instrument an entire routine when the image, it is contained in, is first loaded. A PIN-tool can walk the instructions of an RTN. An analysis routine can be inserted so that it is executed before or after a routine is executed, or before or after an instruction is executed. RTN instrumentation utilizes the `RTN_AddInstrumentFunction` API. In total, there are 39 APIs related to RTN.

Next, we discuss how to design PEMU in support of these APIs. As we base PEMU atop QEMU, we have to examine the difference between QEMU and PIN. In fact, there are substantial differences, leading to a number of new challenges while designing PEMU.

First, QEMU does not introduce any abstractions for TRACE, SEC, RTN, and IMG, and it only allows instrumentation at the INS or BB level. Therefore, we have to rebuild these missing abstractions. Second, QEMU's disassembling is based on BB, and the size of a BB has a limited value. For example, we notice that in QEMU-1.53 a BB needs to be split if the number of generated intermediate instructions is greater than 640. But there is no such constraint in PIN.

To address these challenges, we add our own disassembler rather than using the one in QEMU. Our own disassembler aims to reconstruct the abstractions for TRACE and we thus call this component *TRACE Constructor* (§3.1). To insert the analysis routine into the original program code, we leverage QEMU's dynamic binary translation (DBT) engine, on top of which to design our *Code Injector* (§3.2). In the rest of this section, we present the detailed design of these two components.

3.1 TRACE Constructor

The fundamental reason to introduce our own disassembler is to build the TRACE abstraction for PIN-APIs, from which to further build many other APIs such as those related to RTN, BB, and INS. Meanwhile, to uniformly support both trace and ahead of time instrumentation, we use a cache (we call hooking point hash table) to store all the call-back points where an analysis routine is instrumented. Then whenever these instruction points are executed, they will automatically invoke the analysis routine defined by users.

Since we aim to build TRACE abstractions, which contain BB and INS, we have to disassemble per TRACE. However, QEMU disassembles an instruction at a time (per BB). Therefore, when a starting address of a TRACE is to be disassembled by QEMU, we will disassemble all of the following

---

```
1: Global: TPC: a set storing the starting address of a TRACE;
         HPHT: the global hooking point hash table indexed by PC and
         storing function pointers of the user defined analysis routine.
2: Input: PC, the current trace starting instruction address;
3: Output: a TRACE, and updated TPC and HPHT.
4: Disassemble (PC) {
5:       TRACE ← GetTRACE();
6:       BB ← GetBB();
7:       do {
8:           INST ← DisasINST(PC);
9:           InsertINST(BB, INST);
10:          if (INST_Instrument ≠ NULL) {
11:              INST_Instrument(INST, HPHT);
12:          }
13:          if (INST.type ∈ {jcc, jmp, call, ret}) {
14:              InsertBB(TRACE, BB);
15:              if (BB_Instrument ≠ NULL) {
16:                  BB_Instrument(BB, HPHT);
17:              }
18:              BB ← GetBB();
19:              TPC ← TPC∪ GetTargetPC(INST) ;
20:          }
21:          PC ← PC + INST.InstLen();
22:      } while(INST.type ∉ {jmp, call, ret});
23:      if (TRACE_Instrument ≠ NULL) {
24:          TRACE_Instrument(TRACE, HPHT);
25:      }
26: }
```

Algorithm 1: *TRACE Construction*

---

instructions until we encounter an unconditional branch (e.g., `jmp`, `ret`, `call`), which is the end of a TRACE. As such, we will hold an entire TRACE before QEMU disassembles each instruction inside it.

However, there are also some practical challenges. One is that the instructions that belong to a TRACE may not exist in the guest OS memory (swapped or not loaded yet). The other is the instructions being disassembled are not currently being translated by QEMU-DBT, which is the underlying component for our Code Injector. Consequently, we cannot insert our analysis routines into the guest code while perform our disassembling.

To solve the first challenge, we use a proactive page fault injection approach that is triggered from the hypervisor layer and let the guest OS map the missing pages. For the second challenge, we use a global hooking point hash-table (HPHT) to cache the instruction point that will have analysis routine inserted. Later, when QEMU generates the translated code, our *Code Injector* will query this hash table to insert the analysis routine if there is any.

The Algorithm. To precisely describe how we build the TRACE abstraction and facilitate the instrumentation process, we use Algorithm 1 to show its details. For each PC that is a trace starting address, we will start disassembling the whole TRACE (line 4-26). This is the only point to invoke our own disassembler. To decide whether a given PC is a trace starting address, we query the TPC set that stores all the starting addresses of the TRACES. Note that some of the starting

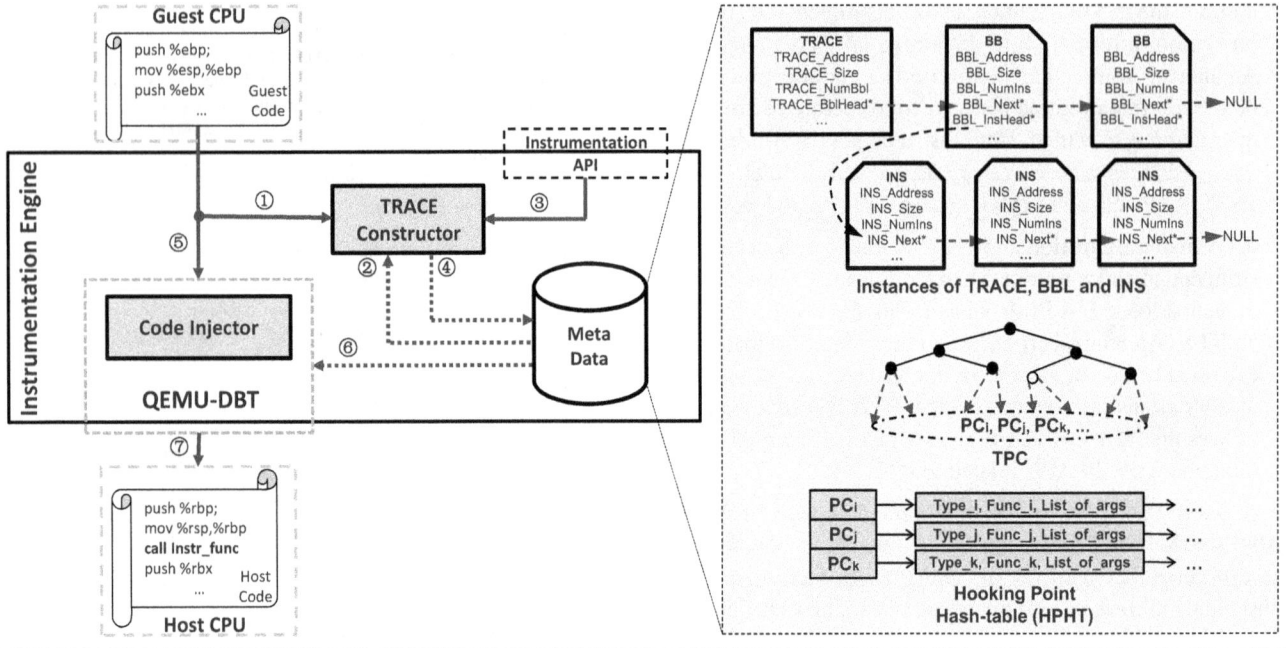

Figure 5. Detailed Design of Our Instrumentation Engine.

address is dynamically computed, especially for indirection control flow transfers.

To disassemble a TRACE, we first create a TRACE (line 5) and a BB instance (line 6), respectively. Then we disassemble and iterate each instruction inside the basic block, and add them into the corresponding BB (line 8-9). If there is any instruction level instrumentation (e.g., when `INS_InsertCall` is called in the PEMU plugin), we add the hooking point of the disassembling instruction into the HPHT (line 10-12). Next, if there is a control flow transfer instruction (line 13-20), then the current BB ends and we insert it into the current TRACE (line 14). Also, we insert a BB hooking point if there is any (line 15-17). Meanwhile, we allocate a new BB (line 18). To get a new TRACE starting address, we invoke a helper function, GetTargetPC (line 19), and we store the new starting address in our TPC. Next, we continue to get the next instruction (line 21), which can be the next instruction inside a BB or a starting address of a new BB. Until we encounter an unconditional control flow transfer instruction, we finish disassembling the current TRACE. If there is any TRACE instrumentation, we add the TRACE hooking points into HPHT (line 23-25).

Regarding the connection between TRACE, BB, and INS, we illustrate their data structures in the right hand side of Fig. 5. Each instance of these data structures is semantically compatible with the corresponding PIN counter-part. With these data structures, PIN's instrumentation and inspection APIs can be easily implemented. For example, when `BBL_Next` is called in a plugin, we will correspondingly traverse the BB instance list to return the next BB.

3.2 Code Injector

To inject the analysis routine that is specified in our HPHT, we leverage the QEMU's DBT for this goal. In particular, to translate the guest binary code into host code, QEMU uses a tiny code generator (TCG), which provides APIs to insert additional code. Having collected which instruction needs the instrumentation, our *Code Injector* will directly use the TCG API (e.g., `tcg_gen_helper`) to insert the analysis routine.

We can also notice that reconstructing TRACE abstractions as well as using the HPHT significantly alleviates the complexity of the instrumentation. With these data structures, we can uniformly achieve code injection anywhere regardless of the granularity. For instance, we can inject an analysis routine at an entry address of a BB, starting address of a TRACE, entry or exit address of an RTN, or just a particular instruction address. That is why we do not attempt to construct abstractions for RTN, SEC, and IMG. For them, we just perform ahead-of-time disassembling and extract the instruction address of interest. For instance, to hook the `malloc` routine, we just need to know the entry address of this function (which can be acquired by signature scanning in the guest memory), and then at runtime, we inject the analysis routine if there is a need for the function argument interpretation of `malloc`.

3.3 Putting it all together

To put it all together, we illustrate the overall execution steps of our *instrumentation engine* in Fig. 5. For each guest instruction, our *TRACE Constructor* will take control (**Step** ①). It first checks whether the current instruction is a starting address of a TRACE by querying the metadata (**Step** ②) that stores all the observed tracing starting addresses. Note that to disassemble a new TRACE, its starting address must have been observed by QEMU, and therefore it has already been included in our TPC set (we use a red-black tree to store this set). If this is not a trace starting address, then we directly continue the execution of *Code Injector* (**Step ⑤**) to generate the final host code (**Step ⑦**). During the code generation, our *Injector* may query the metadata, especially the HPHT data structure, to decide whether the current instruction needs an instrumentation (**Step ⑥**).

If the instruction is a TRACE starting address, then our disassembler will be invoked to disassemble the entire TRACE. During the disassembling, it will insert the corresponding instrumentation routine into the entry of the HPHT (**Step ④**), if such a routine is specified by instrumentation API in the user defined plugins (**Step ③**). When the disassembling finishes, the execution continues to Code Injector (**Step ⑤**) to generate the final host code.

4. Introspection Engine

Since the plugin of PEMU is executed below the guest OS, we have to design an introspection engine that supports the identification of the monitoring process/threads, as well as bridges the semantic gap when the plugins need to inspect the state of the monitored process or OS kernels.

4.1 Identification of Monitored Process/Threads

The instrumentation APIs and the execution of the analysis routine need to be executed when the monitored process is executing. In PIN, all of them are executed in the same address space as the monitored process. However, in PEMU, all of them are executed below the guest OS. Therefore, we have to precisely identify the target process or threads.

Given a running OS, there are a number of ways to differentiate and retrieve the process or thread execution context from a hypervisor layer. One intuitive approach is to traverse kernel data structure to locate the process name, but such an approach is OS-gnostic. Other approaches include using the value of page global directory (PGD) to differentiate each process (as shown in [21, 22]), or using PGD and the masked value of the kernel stack pointer (as shown in [15]).

In PEMU, we adopted the PGD and kernel stack pointer approach. However, we still need to extend it to capture the beginning of the process/thread execution because our instrumentation happens right before process execution. To this end, we propose to capture the data life time of PGD to identify the new process. This is based on the observation that the guest OS must allocate a new (unused) PGD when creating a new process. In x86, PGD is stored in control register CR3. Therefore, if we keep tracking the use of CR3, we can detect a new process.

More specifically, starting from the execution of the guest OS, we maintain a list of the used CR3 values. When a new value is used to update the CR3 (by monitoring `mov` instructions with the destination register `cr3`), we detect that a new process is created. However, we also need to capture when the process exits, because a dead process's CR3 value can be reused for new process. Therefore, we also monitor the execution of `exit` syscall, and the CR3 value used in this syscall will be removed from the CR3 list such that we can detect a new process when this value is used again.

Note that all threads share the same address space. Therefore they will have the same CR3. To differentiate threads, we use the masked value of kernel stack pointer, because each thread will have a corresponding kernel stack that keeps the return addresses and local variables of the functions executed in a syscall trapped from the thread.

4.2 Addressing the Semantic Gap Challenge

Once we have detected the newly created process/thread, our instrumentation will be performed on the monitored process/thread if the instrumentation is for it. Nearly all of our instrumentation APIs are self-contained, and many of them use the abstractions provided by the host OS. Therefore, for most of the instrumentation and analysis routines, there is no semantic gap. For instance, the analysis routine can call `fprintf` in the host OS to print the analysis result.

Unfortunately, for analysis routines that inspect the running process or kernel states, we have to reconstruct their abstractions (namely bridging the semantic gap). For instance, we cannot call the `getpid` syscall at the VMM layer, because the return value of this syscall will be the `pid` of the VMM. Instead, we need to retrieve the `pid` of the monitored process executed inside the VMM.

In the past decade, many approaches have been proposed to address the semantic gap challenge. These approaches include leveraging the kernel debugging information, as shown in the pioneer work Livewire [16]; analyzing and customizing kernel source code (e.g., [18, 35]); manually creating the routines to traverse kernel objects based on kernel data structure knowledge (e.g., [20, 33]); or using a dual-VM based binary code reuse approaches [11, 14, 15, 47]. Some of these approaches (e.g., [14, 18, 20]) have a strong semantic gap [19], which does not trust any guest OS code; Some of them (e.g., [47]) have a weak semantic gap, which trusts guest kernel code, but not application code.

To make PEMU more practical, we adopt the approach proposed in HyperShell [47]. Though it is a weak semantic gap approach, it is guest OS agnostic. More specifically, by taking this approach, we will forward the syscall execution into the guest OS if the syscall needs to inspect or retrieve the guest OS state. Regarding which syscall needs such forwarding, we let the PEMU plugin developers decide but we provide the corresponding APIs for them. For instance, if a plugin needs to retrieve the instrumented process ID, the plugin developers will invoke `PEMU_getpid`. If a plugin needs to open a file in the guest OS, it will use `PEMU_open`, and this file will be closed by `PEMU_close`. In other words, we provide a set of wrapper functions with PEMU prefix for state inspection

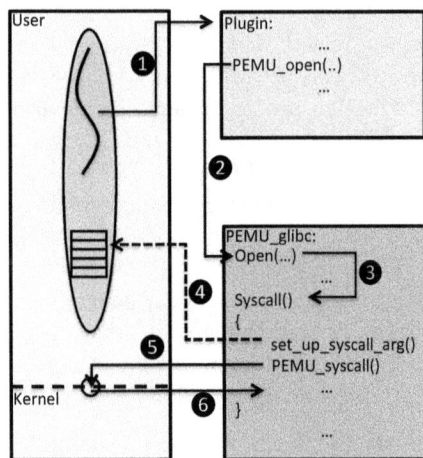

Figure 6. Detailed Steps For An Execution Forwarded Guest Syscall.

and file system related `glibc`-APIs. These APIs work as usual except that we have to detour the control flow of the entry point and exit point of these syscalls, such that the corresponding syscall execution can be forwarded to the guest OS. In total, there are 28 state inspection syscalls (including `getpid`, `gettimeofday` etc.), and 15 file system related syscalls (including `open`, `fstat`, `lseek`,etc.), which are forwarded to the guest OS if the plugin uses the PEMU prefix syscalls.

Though PEMU offers a weak semantic gap, we would like to note that for all other syscalls involved in the analysis routine, we offer a strong semantic gap. This is because we will not execute any guest code, will not traverse any guest kernel data structures, and the execution of the syscall will be directly executed on the host OS. If there is a strong security need, only the results for syscalls prefixed with PEMU cannot be trusted. In other words, a plugin developer is aware of this and can hence quantify the trustworthiness of her analysis routine.

Execution of a Forwarded Guest Syscall. To illustrate how a forwarded syscall really works, we present its detailed execution steps in Fig. 6. In general, there are three parts of code involved in an introspection process: (1) original program code, (2) the analysis routine, and (3) the modified `PEMU_glibc`.

Suppose the control flow is transferred to an analysis routine (**Step ❶**), which needs to open a file inside the guest VM by calling `PEMU_open`. Then, `PEMU_open` goes to the real `open` in PEMU_glibc (**Step ❷**). Next, it invokes the `syscall` function (**Step ❸**) where real `sys_open` is triggered. PEMU intercepts `syscall` so that it will not trap to host OS kernel. To forward the syscall execution to guest OS, it first needs to save the register context and set up the arguments (**Step ❹**). If the argument is a pointer, we

cannot directly pass that pointer to the guest VM because the guest OS can only access memory in its address space. To allow legal memory access inside the guest OS, we inject a `sys_mmap` to allocate a piece of memory and copy the argument content to the allocated memory (here it is the file name in this case). Next, it waits until the instrumented process executes in user space, and then it forces the execution of the syscall entry (**Step ❺**). The control flow goes back to the original program and a forwarded syscall gets executed. Finally, right after the execution of the syscall exit, PEMU copies the result and restores the register context (**Step ❻**).

5. Evaluation

We have implemented a proof-of-concept prototype of PEMU atop `qemu-1.5.3`. We use XED library to build our own disassembler. Meanwhile, we have implemented over one hundred PIN compatible instrumentation APIs for INS, RTN, BB, and TRACE, as well as 43 guest OS state inspection and file system related APIs. To implement the rest of the APIs is an engineering challenge, and we leave it for future work.

In this section, we present our evaluation result. We first test the compatibility of PEMU with PIN in §5.1. Then in §5.2 we evaluate the performance of PEMU using an instruction count plugin (shown in Fig. 2) with the SPEC CPU2006 benchmark. Next, we evaluate the memory cost of PEMU in §5.3. Finally, we perform case studies to demonstrate the unique benefits of PEMU in §5.4. Our host environment runs `Ubuntu 12.04` with 32-bit Linux kernel `3.0.0-31-generic-pae`, on Intel Core i7 CPU with 8G memory. Our guest OS is a 32-bit `Ubuntu 11.04` (Linux kernel `2.6.38-8-generic`) with 512M memory.

5.1 Compatibility Testing With PIN Plugins

To test how compatible PEMU is with PIN, we download the most recent released PIN tool, and use the plugins in `SimpleExamples` directory for this test. In total, there are 23 plugins. We recompile these plugins with PEMU's header files and library files. As shown in Table 1, a pleasant surprise is that 21 of them can be executed without any problem, considering that so far we only implemented over one hundred PIN APIs.

More specifically, we notice that most of these test plugins are mainly used to test the tracing of instructions (including opcode and operand), control flow transfers (branching, call, ret, etc.), memory access, and library calls. Since these are the basic functionalities for a DBI tool, the current implementation of PEMU fortunately supports all of them.

As shown in Table 1, we have two failures `dcache.so` and `opcodemix.so`. The main reason is that our current implementation does not support APIs for CODECACHE and CONTROLLER. Note that CODECACHE allows developers to inspect the PIN code cache and/or alter the code cache replacement policy, and CONTROLLER is used to detect the

Plugin	Description	Supported
calltrace.so	Call trace tracing	✓
extmix.so	Instruction extension mix profile	✓
inscount2_vregs.so	Counting executing instructions	✓
pinatrace.so	Memory address tracing	✓
xed-cache.so	Decode cache profile	✓
catmix.so	Instruction category mix profile	✓
fence.so	Runtime text modification guard	✓
jumpmix.so	Jmp/branch/call profiling	✓
regmix.so	Register usage mix profile	✓
xed-print.so	XED usage testing	✓
coco.so	Code coverage analyzer	✓
icount.so	Counting executing instructions	✓
ldstmix.so	Register/memory operand profiler	✓
topopcode.so	Opcode mix profiler	✓
xed-use.so	XED interface usage testing	✓
dcache.so	Data cache simulation	✗
ilenmix.so	Instruction length mix profiler	✓
malloctrace.so	Tracing calls to malloc	✓
toprtn.so	Hostest routines profiling	✓
edgcnt.so	Control flow edge profiler	✓
inscount2_mt.so	Counting executing instructions	✓
opcodemix.so	Opcode mix profiler	✗
trace.so	Compressed instruction tracer	✓

Table 1. Compatibility Testing with Existing PIN Plugins.

beginning or end of an interval of the execution of a program. We leave the support of these APIs for future work.

5.2 Performance Evaluation

Next, we test the performance of PEMU. We perform two sets of experiments: one is to measure how slow PEMU is when compared to a vanilla-QEMU, and the other is how slow when compared to PIN. We directly use the instruction counting plugin described in Fig 2. This plugin increases the number of instructions in a BB for an accumulated counter before the execution of each BB. We test this plugin with the SPEC 2006 benchmark programs. Each of the benchmark programs is executed 100 times, and we use the corresponding average number in our report.

Performance Comparison with vanilla-QEMU. In this experiment, we measure the overhead introduced by PEMU instrumentation. We compare the execution when running the benchmarks with PEMU, directly with QEMU without any instrumentation.

We report the detailed experimental result in Table 2. Specifically, we show the total number of instructions executed in the 2nd column and also the execution time of QEMU and PEMU is reported in the 3rd and 4th column (namely, T_{Qemu} and T_Pemu). We notice that on average there are 17649.1 million instructions traced for these benchmarks, and the average slowdown over QEMU is about 4.33X, which we believe it is reasonable for practical use. This overhead includes our TRACE Constructor, Code Injector, as well as runtime overhead of the analysis routine.

Performance Comparison with PIN. In the second experiment, we compare PEMU against PIN using the same plugin with the same benchmark. The execution time of running in PIN is presented in the 6th column, and the comparison between PEMU and PIN is presented in the last column.

We notice that the average slowdown between PEMU and PIN is over 83.61X. The main reason is that PIN is running natively while PEMU (based on QEMU) needs extra translation. The largest slowdown comes from 444.namd which is above 310X. However, we note that when running this program in vanilla-QEMU, it will have close to 100X slowdown. We carefully examine the reason and find the root cause due to the use of large amount of floating point instructions which needs time-consuming emulation inside QEMU.

It is also interesting to note that for 450.soplex, running in QEMU is faster than that of PIN. The main reason is this program contains more control flow instructions that will go to the middle of a TRACE, thereby breaking the TRACE. In this case, QEMU (based on BBL disassembling) will just redisassemble the basic block that has not been disassembled, but PIN (based on TRACE disassembling) will redisassemble the whole trace after a new trace is found. Meanwhile, the running time of this program is relatively short. Thus, the time is dominated by the disassembling time.

5.3 Memory Cost Evaluation

Since PEMU uses an ahead-of-time instrumentation that will store the hooking point to facilitate the instrumentation, we would like to measure how much memory space this hooking point table consumes. Again, we evaluate this memory cost with our instruction counting plugin against the SPEC2006 benchmark. The result is presented in Fig. 7. We notice that the average memory cost is about 9M.

More specifically, as shown in Fig. 7, the maximum memory cost comes from 465.tonto (about 22M) because this program contains the largest number of BB, resulting in the largest hash table to store the hooking points. More interestingly, 464.h264ref is one of the most time consuming programs but requires a relative small size of hash table. The reason is that this program contains lots of loops and thus certain instructions get executed repeatedly.

5.4 Case Studies

We have demonstrated using PEMU to analyze Linux binaries. In fact, our system is cross-OS, which is one of our design goals. To test this, we apply PEMU to analyze Windows binaries as we have evaluated with Linux binaries. In particular, we use a number of anti-PIN binaries during this test.

First, we test how PEMU would analyze the software protected by tElock and safengine shielden, which are two widely used tools to build anti-analysis software. We apply these protectors to the hostname binaries in a Win-XP SP3 machine, with anti-debugging and anti-instrumentation enabled, and produce two anti-analysis

Program	#Inst (M)	T_{Qemu} (s)	T_{Pemu} (s)	T_{Pemu}/T_{Qemu}	T_{Pin} (s)	T_{Qemu}/T_{Pin}	T_{Pemu}/T_{Pin}
401.bzip2	11500.27	24.55	81.15	3.31	11.17	2.20	7.26
403.gcc	4940.36	18.35	169.21	9.22	13.56	1.35	12.48
410.bwaves	29360.09	419.99	1336.57	3.18	7.44	56.45	179.65
416.gamess	2121.15	23.19	84.99	3.66	3.35	6.92	25.37
429.mcf	3562.67	23.91	70.58	2.95	3.55	6.74	19.88
433.milc	39509.49	779.07	2570.44	3.30	9.28	83.95	276.99
435.gromacs	4907.53	106.28	334.74	3.15	3.43	30.99	97.59
436.cactusADM	9730.11	304.89	1019.89	3.35	4.42	68.98	230.74
437.leslie3d	55857.54	900.01	3009.06	3.34	15.38	58.52	195.65
444.namd	74037.63	1523.78	5037.00	3.31	16.22	93.94	310.54
445.gobmk	314.88	2.43	4.17	1.72	1.71	1.42	2.44
450.soplex	63.67	1.49	2.22	1.49	1.80	0.83	1.23
453.povray	2987.41	36.16	193.17	5.34	3.52	10.27	54.88
454.calculix	187.33	2.53	6.61	2.61	2.46	1.03	2.69
456.hmmer	17862.2	46.43	260.56	5.61	6.95	6.68	37.49
458.sjeng	15514.49	48.40	432.79	8.94	14.38	3.37	30.10
462.libquantum	408.63	0.77	2.01	2.61	0.62	1.24	3.24
464.h264ref	98144.32	392.21	2751.31	7.01	34.01	11.53	80.90
465.tonto	3571.85	48.23	195.16	4.05	5.44	8.87	35.88
470.lbm	7744.81	161.22	692.51	4.30	2.92	55.21	237.16
471.omnetpp	2209.23	16.24	136.63	8.41	3.19	5.09	42.83
473.astar	26645.10	102.95	734.52	7.13	13.67	7.53	53.73
482.sphinx3	6198.21	77.95	322.26	4.13	4.94	15.78	65.23
999.specrand	6198.21	1.42	2.46	1.73	0.92	1.54	2.67
Avg.	17649.05	210.94	810.42	4.33	7.68	22.52	83.61

Table 2. Performance compared with vanilla-QEMU and PIN.

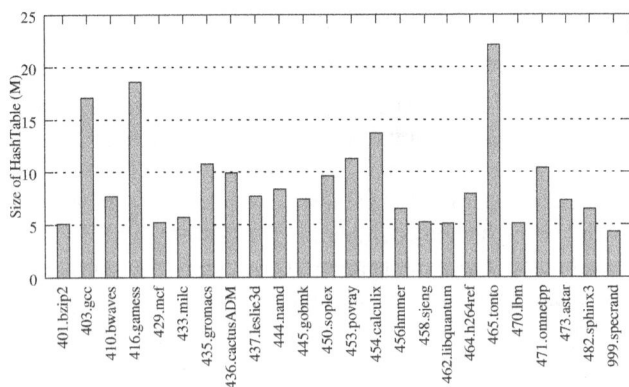

Figure 7. Memory Cost Comparison with SPEC2006 Benchmarks

```
1   FILE *trace;
2   VOID SysBefore(ADDRINT ip, ADDRINT num) {
3       fprintf(trace,"0x%lx: %ld\n",
4               (unsigned long)ip, (long)num);
5   }
6   VOID SyscallEntry(THREADID threadIndex,
7       CONTEXT *ctxt, SYSCALL_STANDARD std, VOID *v) {
8       SysBefore(PIN_GetContextReg(ctxt, REG_INST_PTR),
9               PIN_GetSyscallNumber(ctxt, std));
10  }
11  VOID Fini(INT32 code, VOID *v) {
12      printf("program exit()\n");
13  }
14  INT32 Usage(VOID){
15      return 0;
16  }
17  int main(int argc, char * argv[]){
18      if(PIN_Init(argc, argv)) return Usage();
19      trace = fopen("strace.out", "w");
20      PIN_AddSyscallEntryFunction(SyscallEntry, 0);
21      PIN_AddFiniFunction(Fini, 0);
22      PIN_StartProgram();
23      return 0;
24  }
```

Figure 8. A cross-OS PEMU plugin to trace the syscall.

hostname binaries. We then use PIN and PEMU to analyze the packed hostname.

More specifically, we developed a simple strace (as shown in Fig. 8) plugin to trace the syscall executed by the hostname binary. This plugin will print the syscall number at syscall entry point, and the return value at syscall exit point. We compiled it into a PIN plugin and PEMU plugin with the same source code. PIN failed on these two tests. Both packed programs detected the presence of PIN and exited at early stages. In contrast, hostname ran successfully on PEMU and displayed the host name.

In our other case study, we used eXait [13], a benchmark-like tool to test anti-instrumentation techniques. eXait has a plugin architecture, and each technique is implemented as a separated DLL. There are 21 plugins in total. Again we run PIN with strace plugin to instrument eXait and the loaded DLLs. We found that 17 anti-instrumentation techniques detect the presence of PIN. But none of them detect the presence of PEMU.

Through these case studies, we show there is a need for out-of-VM PIN alternatives. Also, even though future malware will be able to detect the presence of PEMU, we should be able to add countermeasures against them, given that the source code of PEMU is open.

In addition, PEMU can be used to build many out-of-VM introspection tools. In the past several years, we have been using its base internally to build introspection tools such as VMST [14], and EXTERIOR [15]. We believe there will be more use cases of PEMU in this regard.

6. Limitations and Future Work

The current design and implementation of PEMU has a number of limitations. The first one is the incomplete support of the PIN-APIs. Due to the grand engineering challenge, currently we are not able to support all of the PIN-APIs. Besides continuing to finish those unsupported APIs, we would also like to leverage the power from the open source community and make PEMU open source. Being an open source PIN alternative, we believe that there will be more users of PEMU, especially when there is a need to modify the instrumentation engine.

The second limitation is that we used a weak semantic gap [19] when designing the introspection API. That is, while we did not trust any instrumented application code, we did trust the guest OS kernel because we will forward the execution of state inspection related syscalls (e.g., PEMU_getpid) to the guest OS. A stronger semantic gap [19] will not trust the guest OS kernel at all. How to retrieve meaningful and trustworthy information from the hypervisor layer when guest OS is untrusted is still an open challenge. One of our future works will investigate how to address this problem.

The third limitation is that we have not attempted to optimize the generated instrumentation and analysis routine yet, though we have designed a number of optimized data structures (e.g., hooking point hash table) to speed up the instrumentation process. Currently, we directly leveraged the optimization from the tiny code generator (TCG) to optimize our instrumentation and analysis routine. We leave the investigation of other optimization techniques such as leveraging parallelism (e.g., [43]) for us to pursue in another future work.

7. Related Work

Over the past 20 years, many dynamic binary instrumentation (DBI) platforms have been developed. In this section, we compare PEMU with these platforms. Note that static binary code instrumentation or rewriting systems, including the first influential link-time instrumentation system ATOM [40], are not within our scope.

At a high level, these dynamic binary instrumentation platforms can be classified into (1) machine simulator, emulator, and virtualizer, (2) process level instrumentation framework, and (3) system wide instrumentation framework. In the following, we discuss these related works and compare PEMU with each of them. A summary of the comparison is presented in Table 3.

Platforms	Year	Emulator, Simulator, Virtualizer	Kernel Level Instrumentation	User Level Instrumentation	w/ API for instrumentation	Out-of-VM	Guest OS Agnostic	PIN API Compatible	Open Source
EMBRA [45]	1996	✓	✓	✓	✗	✓	✗	✗	✗
VMWARE [10]	1998	✓	✓	✓	✗	✓	✗	✗	✗
KERNINST [41]	1999	✗	✓	✓	✓	✗	✓	✗	✓
DYNINSTAPI [7]	2000	✗	✓	✓	✓	✗	✓	✗	✓
DYNAMO [2]	2000	✗	✓	✓	✗	✗	✓	✗	✗
BOCHS [1]	2001	✓	✓	✓	✗	✓	✗	✗	✓
SIMICS [27]	2002	✓	✓	✓	✗	✓	✗	✗	✗
VALGRIND [30, 31]	2003	✗	✗	✓	✓	✗	✓	✗	✓
STRATA [37]	2003	✗	✗	✓	✓	✗	✓	✗	✓
DYNAMORIO [2, 6]	2004	✗	✗	✓	✓	✗	✓	✗	✓
QEMU [4]	2005	✓	✓	✓	✗	✓	✗	✗	✓
PIN [26]	2005	✗	✗	✓	✓	✗	✓	✓	✗
NIRVANA [5]	2006	✗	✗	✓	✓	✗	✓	✗	✗
HDTRANS [39]	2006	✗	✗	✓	✓	✗	✓	✗	✓
VIRTUALBOX [44]	2007	✓	✓	✓	✗	✓	✗	✗	✓
PINOS [8]	2007	✓	✓	✓	✓	✗	✗	✓	✗
TEMU [48]	2010	✓	✓	✓	✓	✓	✓	✗	✓
DYNINST [28]	2010	✗	✓	✓	✓	✗	✓	✗	✓
DRK [34]	2013	✗	✓	✓	✓	✗	✓	✗	✓
DECAF [17]	2014	✓	✓	✓	✓	✓	✗	✗	✓
PEMU	2015	✓	✓	✓	✓	✓	✓	✓	✓

Table 3. Comparison with other dynamic binary instrumentation platforms.

Machine Simulator, Emulator, and Virtualizer. The very early development of dynamic binary code instrumentation originated from machine simulation or emulation. EMBRA [45] is such a simulation system. It performs whole system dynamic translation for MIPS architectures. BOCHS [1] and SIMICS [27] are also simulators that allow the instrumentation and inspection of all the executed x86 instructions. Targeting x86 architecture, the very early versions of VMWARE [10] also use dynamic binary translation to build virtual machine monitors (VMM). Another widely used VMM or emulator is QEMU [4], which supports a large number of architectures. When used as an emulator, QEMU uses a tiny code generator to emulate a CPU through a binary translation. QEMU can also be used as a virtualizer recently, and it can cooperate with the Xen hypervisor or KVM kernel module to achieve a near native performance through running the guest code directly on host CPU. VIRTUALBOX [44] is a faster VMM compared to QEMU, and it employs an in-situ patching to achieve better performance.

For all these out-of-VM works, they certainly can instrument both user level and kernel level code, but they do not offer any APIs for users to build dynamic binary instrumentation applications. Also, when used to analyze guest kernels, they all tend to be kernel specific.

Process Level Instrumentation Framework. Recognizing the importance and wide applications of DBI, many process level instrumentation frameworks (e.g., DYNINSTAPI [7], STRATA [37], DYNAMORIO [2], VALGRIND [30], PIN [26], NIRVANA [5], HDTRANS [39], DYNINST [28]) have been proposed. These frameworks offer APIs for developers to build plugins for various applications such as high performance simulation [37], program shepherding [23], and memory error detection [38].

Among them, VALGRIND [30, 31] is a comprehensive DBI framework that offers rich APIs for dynamic binary instrumentation. It supports various architectures (e.g., x86, ARM, MIPS) due to the use of an intermediate representation (IR) that is processor-neutral and SSA-based. Similar to VALGRIND, PIN [26] also works at user space, but it only supports IA-32 and x86-64 architectures. Developers can create PIN-tools using the APIs provided by PIN, and execute them atop either Windows or Linux. It is featured with 'ease of use' with rich APIs to abstract away the underlying instruction-set idiosyncrasies. Making PIN-API compatible is one of our design goals such that PIN users can easily switch to our platform, especially when there is a need to customize the underlying DBI engine. Unlike other DBI platforms, DYNINST [28] can instrument at any time in the execution of a program, from static instrumentation (i.e., binary rewriting) to dynamic instrumentation (i.e., instrumenting actively while executing the code). Also, it allows users to modify or remove instrumentation at any time, with such modifications taking immediate effect.

For process level instrumentation, they are efficient. They are built atop OS, and thus are OS-agnostic. It is also easier to develop the plugins. However, the analysis routine and the original program code share the same address space. Therefore, they are all in-VM approaches, and users have to be cautious when applying them for security sensitive applications.

System Wide Instrumentation Framework. In addition to process level instrumentation, there is also a need for OS kernel instrumentation. KERNINST [41], PINOS [8], TEMU [48], DRK [34], and DECAF [17] are such systems.

Among them, KERNINST and DRK are built atop in kernel dynamic binary code translation. They basically control all kernel instruction execution, and enable comprehensive instrumentation of the OS kernel code. PINOS [8] is a whole-system instrumentation extension of PIN. It takes advantage of Intel VT Technology to interpose between the subject system and hardware. PINOS has been implemented based on the Xen virtual machine monitor. Compared to PEMU, the instrumentation and analysis code of KERNINST, PINOS and DRK actually share the same address space. Even though PINOS steals the memory from the guest OS, the monitored process is still able to guess and access the memory used by

analysis routines. Therefore, they do not offer strong out-of-VM isolation.

TEMU [48] is a whole-system instrumentation tool built atop QEMU. A unique feature in TEMU is that it offers APIs for dynamic taint analysis and in-depth program behavioral analysis. It is an out-of-VM based instrumentation, but it installed a helper kernel module inside the guest OS to report the states to the outside analysis routine. The most recent effort, DECAF, extends TEMU. It does not use any in-VM kernel module anymore, but the way to bridge the semantic gap still requires the knowledge of kernel data structures. Therefore, DECAF is a more OS-specific solution. For TEMU, it is less since it is an in-VM based approach.

8. Conclusion

We have presented the design, implementation, and evaluation of PEMU, a new dynamic binary code instrumentation framework that allows end-users to develop out-of-VM plugins for various program analyses. One distinctive feature of PEMU is its PIN-API compatibility. Therefore, many of the PIN-tools can be recompiled and executed within our framework. Unlike other similar systems, it is guest-OS agnostic, and can execute many different guest OSes with different versions. Our experimental results with SPEC 2006 benchmarks show that PEMU introduces reasonable overhead.

Acknowledgement and Availability

We thank the anonymous reviewers for their insightful comments. We are also grateful to Erick Bauman for his invaluable feedback on an early draft of this paper. This research was supported in part by a AFOSR grant FA9550-14-1-0119 and a DARPA grant 12011593. Any opinions, findings, conclusions, or recommendations expressed are those of the authors and not necessarily of the AFOSR and DARPA. Finally, the source code of PEMU is available at https://github.com/utds3lab/pemu.

References

[1] bochs: The open source ia-32 emulation project, 2001. http://bochs.sourceforge.net/.

[2] BALA, V., DUESTERWALD, E., AND BANERJIA, S. Dynamo: A transparent dynamic optimization system. In *Proceedings of the ACM SIGPLAN 2000 Conference on Programming Language Design and Implementation* (New York, NY, USA, 2000), PLDI '00, ACM, pp. 1–12.

[3] BARHAM, P., DRAGOVIC, B., FRASER, K., HAND, S., HARRIS, T., HO, A., NEUGEBAUERY, R., PRATT, I., AND WARFIELD, A. Xen and the art of virtualization. In *Proceedings of the nineteenth ACM symposium on Operating systems principles* (2003).

[4] BELLARD, F. Qemu, a fast and portable dynamic translator. In *Proceedings of the annual conference on USENIX Annual Technical Conference* (Berkeley, CA, USA, 2005), ATEC '05, USENIX Association.

[5] BHANSALI, S., CHEN, W.-K., DE JONG, S., EDWARDS, A., MURRAY, R., DRINIĆ, M., MIHOČKA, D., AND CHAU, J. Framework for instruction-level tracing and analysis of program executions. In *Proceedings of the 2Nd International Conference on Virtual Execution Environments* (New York, NY, USA, 2006), VEE '06, ACM, pp. 154–163.

[6] BRUENING, D., ZHAO, Q., AND AMARASINGHE, S. Transparent dynamic instrumentation. In *Proceedings of the 8th ACM SIGPLAN/SIGOPS Conference on Virtual Execution Environments* (New York, NY, USA, 2012), VEE '12, ACM, pp. 133–144.

[7] BUCK, B., AND HOLLINGSWORTH, J. K. An api for runtime code patching. *Int. J. High Perform. Comput. Appl. 14*, 4 (Nov. 2000), 317–329.

[8] BUNGALE, P. P., AND LUK, C.-K. Pinos: A programmable framework for whole-system dynamic instrumentation. In *Proceedings of the 3rd international conference on Virtual execution environments* (2007), pp. 137–147.

[9] CHEN, P. M., AND NOBLE, B. D. When virtual is better than real. In *Proceedings of the Eighth Workshop on Hot Topics in Operating Systems* (2001), pp. 133–138.

[10] DEVINE, S. W., BUGNION, E., AND ROSENBLUM, M. Virtualization System Including a Virtual Machine Monitor for a Computer with a Segmented Architecture. *United States Patent 6,397,242* (1998).

[11] DOLAN-GAVITT, B., LEEK, T., ZHIVICH, M., GIFFIN, J., AND LEE, W. Virtuoso: Narrowing the semantic gap in virtual machine introspection. In *Proceedings of the 32nd IEEE Symposium on Security and Privacy* (Oakland, CA, USA, 2011), pp. 297–312.

[12] EGELE, M., KRUEGEL, C., KIRDA, E., YIN, H., AND SONG, D. Dynamic spyware analysis. In *2007 USENIX Annual Technical Conference on Proceedings of the USENIX Annual Technical Conference* (Berkeley, CA, USA, 2007), ATC'07, USENIX Association, pp. 18:1–18:14.

[13] FRANCISCO FALCÃSN, N. R. Dynamic binary instrumentation frameworks: I know you're there spying on me. In *recon* (2012).

[14] FU, Y., AND LIN, Z. Space traveling across vm: Automatically bridging the semantic-gap in virtual machine introspection via online kernel data redirection. In *Proceedings of the 2012 IEEE Symposium on Security and Privacy* (San Francisco, CA, May 2012).

[15] FU, Y., AND LIN, Z. Exterior: Using a dual-vm based external shell for guest-os introspection, configuration, and recovery. In *Proceedings of the Ninth Annual International Conference on Virtual Execution Environments* (Houston, TX, March 2013).

[16] GARFINKEL, T., AND ROSENBLUM, M. A virtual machine introspection based architecture for intrusion detection. In *Proc. Network and Distributed Systems Security Sym. (NDSS'03)* (February 2003).

[17] HENDERSON, A., PRAKASH, A., YAN, L. K., HU, X., WANG, X., ZHOU, R., AND YIN, H. Make it work, make it right, make it fast: Building a platform-neutral whole-system dynamic binary analysis platform. In *Proceedings of the 2014 International Symposium on Software Testing and Analysis* (New York, NY, USA, 2014), ISSTA 2014, ACM, pp. 248–258.

[18] HOFMANN, O. S., DUNN, A. M., KIM, S., ROY, I., AND WITCHEL, E. Ensuring operating system kernel integrity with osck. In *Proceedings of the sixteenth international conference on Architectural support for programming languages and operating systems* (Newport Beach, California, USA, 2011), ASPLOS '11, pp. 279–290.

[19] JAIN, B., BAIG, M. B., ZHANG, D., PORTER, D. E., AND SION, R. Sok: Introspections on trust and the semantic gap. In *Proceedings of the 2014 IEEE Symposium on Security and Privacy* (Washington, DC, USA, 2014), SP '14, IEEE Computer Society, pp. 605–620.

[20] JIANG, X., WANG, X., AND XU, D. Stealthy malware detection through vmm-based out-of-the-box semantic view reconstruction. In *Proceedings of the 14th ACM Conference on Computer and Communications Security (CCS'07)* (Alexandria, Virginia, USA, 2007), ACM, pp. 128–138.

[21] JONES, S. T., ARPACI-DUSSEAU, A. C., AND ARPACI-DUSSEAU, R. H. Antfarm: tracking processes in a virtual machine environment. In *Proc. annual Conf. USENIX '06 Annual Technical Conf.* (Boston, MA, 2006), USENIX Association.

[22] JONES, S. T., ARPACI-DUSSEAU, A. C., AND ARPACI-DUSSEAU, R. H. Vmm-based hidden process detection and identification using lycosid. In *Proc. fourth ACM SIGPLAN/SIGOPS international Conf. Virtual execution environments* (Seattle, WA, USA, 2008), VEE '08, ACM, pp. 91–100.

[23] KIRIANSKY, V., BRUENING, D., AND AMARASINGHE, S. P. Secure execution via program shepherding. In *Proceedings of the 11th USENIX Security Symposium* (Berkeley, CA, USA, 2002), USENIX Association, pp. 191–206.

[24] LIN, Z., ZHANG, X., AND XU, D. Automatic reverse engineering of data structures from binary execution. In *Proceedings of the 17th Annual Network and Distributed System Security Symposium (NDSS'10)* (San Diego, CA, February 2010).

[25] LU, S., TUCEK, J., QIN, F., AND ZHOU, Y. Avio: detecting atomicity violations via access interleaving invariants. In *Proceedings of the 12th international conference on Architectural support for programming languages and operating systems* (New York, NY, USA, 2006), ASPLOS XII, ACM, pp. 37–48.

[26] LUK, C.-K., COHN, R., MUTH, R., PATIL, H., KLAUSER, A., LOWNEY, G., WALLACE, S., REDDI, V. J., AND HAZELWOOD, K. Pin: building customized program analysis tools with dynamic instrumentation. In *Proceedings of the 2005 ACM SIGPLAN conference on Programming language design and implementation* (New York, NY, USA, 2005), PLDI '05, ACM, pp. 190–200.

[27] MAGNUSSON, P. S., CHRISTENSSON, M., ESKILSON, J., FORSGREN, D., HÅLLBERG, G., HÖGBERG, J., LARSSON, F., MOESTEDT, A., AND WERNER, B. Simics: A full system simulation platform. *Computer 35*, 2 (Feb. 2002), 50–58.

[28] MILLER, B. P., AND BERNAT, A. R. Anywhere, any time binary instrumentation.

[29] NARAYANASAMY, S., PEREIRA, C., PATIL, H., COHN, R., AND CALDER, B. Automatic logging of operating system

effects to guide application-level architecture simulation. In *Proceedings of the joint international conference on Measurement and modeling of computer systems* (New York, NY, USA, 2006), SIGMETRICS '06/Performance '06, ACM, pp. 216–227.

[30] NETHERCOTE, N., AND SEWARD, J. Valgrind: A program supervision framework. In *In Third Workshop on Runtime Verification (RV'03)* (2003).

[31] NETHERCOTE, N., AND SEWARD, J. Valgrind: A framework for heavyweight dynamic binary instrumentation. In *Proceedings of the 2007 ACM SIGPLAN Conference on Programming Language Design and Implementation* (New York, NY, USA, 2007), PLDI '07, ACM, pp. 89–100.

[32] NEWSOME, J., AND SONG, D. Dynamic taint analysis for automatic detection, analysis, and signature generation of exploits on commodity software. In *Proceedings of Network and Distributed Systems Security Symposium* (2005).

[33] PAYNE, B. D., CARBONE, M., AND LEE, W. Secure and flexible monitoring of virtual machines. In *Proceedings of the 23rd Annual Computer Security Applications Conference (ACSAC 2007)* (December 2007).

[34] PETER FEINER, A. D. B., AND GOEL, A. Comprehensive kernel instrumentation via dynamic binary translation. In *Proceedings of the seventeenth international conference on Architectural Support for Programming Languages and Operating Systems* (2012).

[35] PETRONI, JR., N. L., AND HICKS, M. Automated detection of persistent kernel control-flow attacks. In *Proceedings of the 14th ACM conference on Computer and communications security* (2007), CCS '07, pp. 103–115.

[36] SCHWARTZ, E. J., AVGERINOS, T., AND BRUMLEY, D. All you ever wanted to know about dynamic taint analysis and forward symbolic execution (but might have been afraid to ask). In *Proceedings of the 2010 IEEE Symposium on Security and Privacy* (Washington, DC, USA, 2010), SP '10, IEEE Computer Society, pp. 317–331.

[37] SCOTT, K., KUMAR, N., VELUSAMY, S., CHILDERS, B., DAVIDSON, J. W., AND SOFFA, M. L. Retargetable and reconfigurable software dynamic translation. In *Proceedings of the International Symposium on Code Generation and Optimization: Feedback-directed and Runtime Optimization* (Washington, DC, USA, 2003), CGO '03, IEEE Computer Society, pp. 36–47.

[38] SEWARD, J., AND NETHERCOTE, N. Using valgrind to detect undefined value errors with bit-precision. In *Proceedings of the Annual Conference on USENIX Annual Technical Conference* (Berkeley, CA, USA, 2005), ATEC '05, USENIX Association.

[39] SRIDHAR, S., SHAPIRO, J. S., NORTHUP, E., AND BUNGALE, P. P. Hdtrans: An open source, low-level dynamic instrumentation system. In *Proceedings of the 2Nd International Confer-*

ence on Virtual Execution Environments (New York, NY, USA, 2006), VEE '06, ACM, pp. 175–185.

[40] SRIVASTAVA, A., AND EUSTACE, A. Atom: A system for building customized program analysis tools. In *Proceedings of the ACM SIGPLAN 1994 Conference on Programming Language Design and Implementation* (New York, NY, USA, 1994), PLDI '94, ACM, pp. 196–205.

[41] TAMCHES, A., AND MILLER, B. P. Fine-grained dynamic instrumentation of commodity operating system kernels. In *Proceedings of the Third Symposium on Operating Systems Design and Implementation* (Berkeley, CA, USA, 1999), OSDI '99, USENIX Association, pp. 117–130.

[42] WALLACE, S., AND HAZELWOOD, K. Superpin: Parallelizing dynamic instrumentation for real-time performance. In *5th Annual International Symposium on Code Generation and Optimization* (San Jose, CA, March 2007), pp. 209–217.

[43] WANG, Z., LIU, R., CHEN, Y., WU, X., CHEN, H., ZHANG, W., AND ZANG, B. Coremu: A scalable and portable parallel full-system emulator. In *Proceedings of the 16th ACM Symposium on Principles and Practice of Parallel Programming* (New York, NY, USA, 2011), PPoPP '11, ACM, pp. 213–222.

[44] WATSON, J. Virtualbox: Bits and bytes masquerading as machines. *Linux J. 2008*, 166 (Feb. 2008).

[45] WITCHEL, E., AND ROSENBLUM, M. Embra: Fast and flexible machine simulation. In *Proceedings of the 1996 ACM SIGMETRICS International Conference on Measurement and Modeling of Computer Systems* (New York, NY, USA, 1996), SIGMETRICS '96, ACM, pp. 68–79.

[46] WU, Q., REDDI, V., WU, Y., LEE, J., CONNORS, D., BROOKS, D., MARTONOSI, M., AND CLARK, D. A dynamic compilation framework for controlling microprocessor energy and performance. In *Microarchitecture, 2005. MICRO-38. Proceedings. 38th Annual IEEE/ACM International Symposium on* (2005).

[47] YANGCHUN FU, J. Z., AND LIN, Z. Hypershell: A practical hypervisor layer guest os shell for automated in-vm management. In *USENIX ATC'14 Proceedings of the 2014 USENIX conference on USENIX Annual Technical Conference* (USENIX Association Berkeley, CA, USA, 2014), USENIX Association, pp. 85–96.

[48] YIN, H., AND SONG, D. Temu: Binary code analysis via whole-system layered annotative execution. Technical Report UCB/EECS-2010-3, EECS Department, University of California, Berkeley, Jan 2010.

[49] YIN, H., SONG, D., EGELE, M., KRUEGEL, C., AND KIRDA, E. Panorama: capturing system-wide information flow for malware detection and analysis. In *Proceedings of the 14th ACM conference on Computer and communications security* (New York, NY, USA, 2007), CCS '07, ACM, pp. 116–127.

Improving Remote Desktopping through Adaptive Record/Replay

Shehbaz Jaffer *

NetApp Inc., Bangalore

shehbaz.jaffer@netapp.com

Piyus Kedia †

Microsoft Research, Bangalore

piyuskedia@gmail.com

Sorav Bansal

IIT Delhi

sbansal@cse.iitd.ernet.in

Abstract

Accessing the *display* of a computer remotely, is popularly called "remote desktopping[1]". Remote desktopping software installs at both the user-facing client computer and the remote server computer; it simulates user's input events at server, and streams the corresponding display changes to client, thus providing an illusion to the user of controlling the remote machine using local input devices (e.g., keyboard/mouse). Many such remote desktopping tools are widely used.

We show that if the remote server is a virtual machine (VM) and the client is reasonably powerful (e.g., current laptop and desktop grade hardware), VM deterministic replay capabilities can be used adaptively to significantly reduce the network bandwidth consumption and server-side CPU utilization of a remote desktopping tool. We implement these optimizations in a tool based on Qemu/KVM virtualization platform and VNC remote desktopping platform. Our tool reduces VNC's network bandwidth consumption by up to 9x and server-side CPU utilization by up to 56% for popular graphics-intensive applications. On the flip side, our techniques consume higher CPU/memory/disk resources at the client. The effect of our optimizations on user-perceived latency is negligible.

Categories and Subject Descriptors D.4.9 [*Operating Systems*]: Systems Programs and Utilities; C.2.4 [*Dis-*

tributed Systems]: Client/Server; I.3.4 [*Computer Graphics*]: Graphics Utilities

Keywords Virtualization, Record/Replay, Deterministic Replay, Remote Desktop, Cloud Computing, Virtual Desktop Infrastructure

1. Introduction

"Remote Desktopping", the capability to *control* a computer remotely, is used for several applications including remote access (e.g., accessing office computer at home), collaboration (e.g., multiple users working on the same screen), technical support (e.g., support staff accessing user's machine), security surveillance (e.g., security personnel inspecting user machines), etc. Such tools and applications are popular and widespread. Some well-known remote desktopping tools are VNC, Windows Remote Desktop, TeamViewer, LogMeIn, Chrome Remote Desktop Extension, etc.

Virtualization and cloud computing has further increased the relevance of remote desktopping. Often, a server is implemented as a virtual machine (VM) and a remote desktopping client is used to access it. Another promising cloud computing paradigm, called "Virtual Desktop Infrastructure" (VDI), advocates running user desktops as VMs on a consolidated server and allows user access through remote desktopping tools. VDI has manageability, security, and cost advantages over traditional desktop computing, and improvements in remote desktopping directly impact the practicability of VDI.

All current remote desktopping tools work by streaming the display from the remote server to the user's client computer. The network bandwidth requirement of this display stream is usually the Achilles' heel of these tools. Although these tools use image/video compression, viewing high resolution videos or playing graphics-intensive games over a remote desktopping session is often impractical, due to network bandwidth constraints. Further, these tools require significant CPU usage at the server to compress and stream the display buffer. Our work alleviates these limitations.

We optimize remote desktopping tools to consume less bandwidth and server-side CPU while accessing a *virtual* remote server (i.e., the remote server is running as a VM) at the expense of higher client-side CPU consumption. (In Section 5, we discuss some remote desktopping applications

---

* This work was done while the author was pursuing his Masters degree at IIT Delhi.

† This work was done while the author was pursuing his Ph.D. degree at IIT Delhi.

[1] We use the term "remote desktopping" instead of "remote desktop" to avoid confusion with a commercial product with the same name

where this tradeoff is favourable). We propose the use of VM Record/Replay technology to achieve this objective. In our scheme, instead of streaming the *screen* of the server, we stream the *state* of the server to client. The state of the server is captured using VM Record/Replay technology and consists of an *initial snapshot* and a *record log*.

To implement remote desktopping using VM record/replay, the server's hypervisor begins *recording* the state of the server VM by snapshotting it, and then continuously generates a record log. The client's hypervisor *replays* the server VM using its initial snapshot and the generated record log. The initial snapshot is made available to the client through demand paging over the network. The generated record log is streamed continuously from server to client. This allows the client to reconstruct server's state (and hence its screen) continuously over time. All keyboard/mouse input at the client is simulated at the server to provide the illusion of a remote desktopping session.

The aforementioned mechanism is useful because for many important applications, the size of the streamed record log (including the partial transfer of the initial snapshot using demand paging) is often less than the size of the streamed screen contents. In this paper, we demonstrate this (somewhat counter-intuitive) result through many experiments.

Our work provides evidence of the practicability of using VM record/replay technology to reduce network bandwidth consumption and server-side CPU usage of remote desktopping tools. We have implemented our techniques in a tool based on Qemu/KVM [12] and VNC [18]. We achieve up to 9x bandwidth improvements and 56% improvement in server's CPU utilization over current tools for display-intensive applications, while consuming 30% more CPU at the client. We think this is a welcome tradeoff in most cases. Further, as we discuss in Section 5, the replay-based remote desktopping approach is stateful, i.e., repeat remote desktopping sessions consume less network bandwidth than the first session, as we avoid repeat transfers of the same state.

There are two limitations to our work. Firstly, our current implementation works only for compatible client and server machines, i.e., the client machine should support all CPU features of the server machine for it to be able to replay the server's execution. In general, this limitation can be addressed in either of the two ways: (1) by using a more advanced virtual machine monitor that can tide over slight differences in CPUs (using binary translation for example) and thus can replay across slightly divergent CPUs, or (2) by configuring the virtual machine to assume a less-featured virtual-CPU so it is compatible with both client and server[2].

Our second limitation is that our current implementation works only for uniprocessor VMs. Multiprocessor VM record/replay is less efficient, and while recent work promises significant advances, this still remains an open problem. For this paper, we posit that many (perhaps most) workloads are run on uniprocessor VMs (e.g., in cloud), and hence they can immediately benefit from our ideas.

The paper is organized as follows: Section 2 provides background on streaming VM deterministic replay and discusses our remote desktopping scheme, Section 3 discusses the challenges in our design and their solutions, Section 4 discusses our implementation, Section 5 discusses our experiments and results, Section 6 discusses related work, and Section 7 concludes.

2. Streaming VM Record/Replay

The ability to record the minimal set of non-deterministic events occurring in a VM, and then using this recorded log to replay the VM, is popularly known as VM Record/Replay [19]. For a uniprocessor VM execution, the sources of non-determinism are input I/O (e.g., network), interrupt timing, and certain non-deterministic instructions (e.g., reading the timestamp counter). A record log consists of a stream of non-deterministic events tagged with their *timestamp*. The timestamp of an event uniquely identifies the (deterministic) logical time epoch at which the event occurred. Modern x86 processors provide the capability to precisely monitor the number of branches executed (`branchcount`), and this together with the value of the current program counter (encoded by `rip` and `rcx` registers) provides a unique logical timestamp.

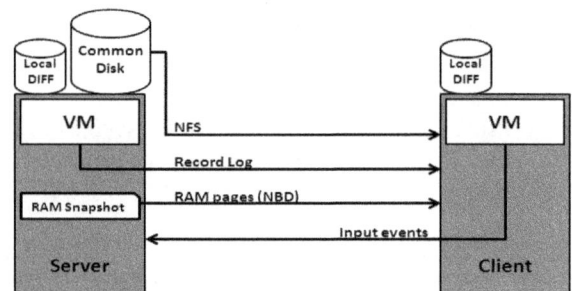

Figure 1. Architecture of record/replay-based remote desktopping

Replay involves first loading the snapshot created at the start of the recording session, and then injecting the recorded non-deterministic events into the VM at their respective time epochs. The x86 architecture provides the performance monitoring interrupt (PMI) mechanism to allow setting up of hypervisor traps at desired values of `branchcount` (somewhat imprecisely though [8]), and we use this for injecting non-deterministic events during replay.

Our proposed remote desktopping mechanism involves streaming the input keyboard/mouse events from client to server and streaming the record log from server to client. The record log contains the non-deterministic event stream at the

---

[2] Because successive processor generations are usually backward compatible, the vCPU need only be equivalent to either the server or the client CPU, whichever is older

server, and the client replays it to reconstruct the server state continuously. Figure 1 shows our solution's architecture. A sample sequence of events in this architecture involves (1) an input keyboard/mouse event being sent over network from client to server; (2) the server injecting this event into the VM; (3) the ensuing non-deterministic events getting recorded in the log which is streamed to the client; and (4) the log getting replayed at the client to provide a remote desktopping experience to the user. The first two steps (1) and (2), are common with existing remote desktopping tools. The difference is in the traffic generated from server to client — existing tools transfer server's screen contents, while we transfer server's state. We call our scheme *record/replay-based remote desktopping* to distinguish it from traditional *display-based remote desktopping*.

Notice that the log of non-deterministic events at server is generated continuously and includes events unrelated to client's input activity. For example, any network packets received at server also get recorded as non-deterministic events in the record log and are streamed to the client (so that it can reconstruct server's state). Thus, the user is provided the illusion of controlling the server and viewing its console remotely (even though the console is actually that of the client's replayed VM).

Our on-the-fly reconstruction of server state at the client using record/replay differs from previous work (e.g., Moka5 [10]) on streaming VM images over network (which we call *VM streaming*). In VM streaming, a VM's image is streamed on-demand from server to client, and this VM is executed stand-alone on the client computer with the client's environment. Hence, in VM streaming, the VM appears to the user as executing locally at client with a client-local network address. On the other hand, our remote desktopping architecture provides an illusion to the user of controlling a VM which is running on the remote server with the server's environment (e.g., the user observes a server-side network address). Also, unlike VM streaming, remote desktopping allows opening of multiple simultaneous sessions by multiple users for the same logical VM state (thus enabling collaborative applications of remote desktopping). We discuss this comparison between VM streaming and record/replay-based remote desktopping in more detail in Section 6.

Our record/replay-based solution is useful for remote desktopping *only if* record log sizes are lower than the corresponding (compressed and streamed) video framebuffer sizes generated by existing display-based remote desktopping tools. As we show in our experiments (Section 5), this is true for many display intensive workloads, and our solution is quite effective in these situations. Intuitively, the record log size is primarily a function of input I/O volume — hence, deterministic replay is likely to generate less traffic than display-transfers if the input I/O volume for a workload is less than the display activity it generates.

3. Architecture

In this section, we discuss the two primary challenges we faced (and their solutions) in making record/replay-based remote desktopping practical.

First, any streaming record/replay session involves creation and transfer of the initial VM snapshot. Because VM sizes can be huge (disks up to a few TBs, and memory up to a few 100GBs), the time and bandwidth required to create and transfer these snapshots could overshadow any improvements by our solution. In Section 3.1, we discuss fast and asynchronous creation of VM snapshot, and in Section 3.2, we discuss on-demand transfer of snapshot state to minimize network traffic.

Second, different workloads exhibit different video framebuffer (screen) activity and different non-deterministic record log activity. Depending on the workload, either display-based remote desktopping or record/replay-based remote desktopping may be the more performant option. We adaptively switch between the two options to optimize overall performance (Section 3.3).

3.1 Snapshot creation

Every streaming record/replay session (and hence, every record/replay-based remote desktopping session) requires VM snapshot creation, which involves snapshotting its CPU, memory, devices, and disk. The snapshot size of CPU and device state is small (less than 9 MBs uncompressed), and thus the dominant cost of snapshot creation and transfer is due to disk and memory.

We compare two methods of snapshotting and recording the disk. In the first method, we use standard copy-on-write snapshotting techniques (we call this method, the *snapshotted disk* method). In the second method, we do not create a disk snapshot, but instead record all disk reads in the record log, thus causing all disk reads to be replayed identically at the client (we call this method, the *output-replayed* disk method). In the snapshotted disk method, creation of copy-on-write disk snapshot is fast (sub-second), although future disk writes experience slightly higher latencies (due to extra copying). Output-replayed disks have zero snapshotting cost, but incur more network traffic if multiple reads, or reads-after-writes are made to the same disk blocks.

Snapshotting memory is more involved. Simply marking all memory copy-on-write (like disks) results in relatively higher costs of copy-on-write faults in memory. Our goal is to minimize any performance effects on server's execution due to snapshotting. To avoid user-visible slowdowns during application execution, memory snapshots are created asynchronously[3]. i.e., the VM continues to execute while a

---
[3] Asynchronous snapshotting could still result in user-visible slowdowns if the asynchronous thread contends for a common resource with the VM (e.g., CPU or bus bandwidth). We discuss the practical implications of this in our experiments (Section 5).

163

snapshotted memory copy is created in parallel. Here is a sequence of steps taken to create a snapshot asynchronously:

1. All memory pages of the VM are marked *clean*. The VM is stopped for a short duration (few milliseconds) during this step.

2. A separate snapshotting thread begins saving memory contents to a snapshot file. This file could be stored on-disk or in-memory.

3. Any concurrent modifications to memory pages by the VM, mark the corresponding pages *dirty*.

4. When the snapshotting thread finishes, the size of the set of dirty pages is compared with a threshold:

   a. If the dirty set size is below the threshold, the server is stopped and a snapshot of the pages in dirty set is taken synchronously. At this point, we have a separate copy of a complete memory snapshot at server.

   b. If the dirty set size is greater than the threshold, steps 1-4 are repeated.

   This threshold is chosen such that the server stops (in Step 4a) for less than a few milliseconds. In our experiments, this threshold was set to 2048 pages.

If this procedure does not converge in thirty iterations, we simply give up and disable record/replay-based remote desktopping.

Notice that this snapshotting procedure could take long (10-100 seconds), but because it is executed asynchronously, this time is largely hidden from the user. The user only observes a potential stall of a few milliseconds when the server is stopped in Step 1 at initialization time and in Step 4 at convergence-check time. Because the client can begin replay only after the server has finished snapshotting, we resort to display-based remote desktopping till then (for a continuous user experience). On completion of snapshot creation and its transfer from server to client, our tool switches from display-based remote desktopping to record/replay-based remote desktopping seamlessly (the full discussion of this switching is in Section 3.3). If the snapshotting procedure did not converge, we continue with display-based remote desktopping as before.

3.2 Snapshot transfer

Transfer of snapshotted state is done *on-demand* to minimize user-perceived latency and network traffic. All register and device snapshot state is transferred from server to client at the start of the streaming record/replay session.

For snapshotted disks, the disk snapshot is transferred on-demand from server to client over NFS [13]. Only those snapshotted disk blocks are transferred which are ever accessed at the client. Also, because the snapshot file is read-only, repeat accesses by client to the same disk block do not result in repeat network traffic.

Transfer of snapshot's memory state is performed on-demand at page granularity (4KB). Demand paging is implemented at client by modifying the VM's extended page tables, and only the pages touched by client are transferred over network. Because typical working set sizes of VMs are much smaller than their total memory allocations, demand paging saves significant network bandwidth and reduces user-perceived latency.

3.3 Adaptive switching

The application workload characteristics determine the amount of video framebuffer activity and the amount of non-determinism generated in the system. For example, execution of a graphics-intensive game involves large screen activity, but involves relatively smaller non-determinism (most non-determinism is only due to interrupt timing and keyboard/mouse inputs). On the other hand, an application involving large network downloads (e.g., P2P file sharing) results in large input non-determinism (due to a stream of incoming network packets) and relatively smaller screen activity. Thus, display-based remote desktopping is likely to be the more performant alternative for applications of the latter type, while record/replay-based remote desktopping perform better for the former type of applications. We use a dynamic adaptive mechanism to switch between the two modes depending on current workload behavior.

The adaption logic runs at both client and server. A remote desktopping session always starts in *display mode* (i.e., traditional display-based remote desktopping) and switches to *record/replay mode* (i.e., record/replay based remote desktopping), if required. The client decides the appropriate mode, and informs the server. On receiving a request to switch from display to record/replay mode, the server begins snapshotting asynchronously. Till snapshotting is complete, the client and server run in display mode, and together switch to record/replay mode after the snapshot is taken. If the client again decides to switch back to display mode (from record/replay mode), it simply stops replay and spawns a display mode client (e.g., VNC client) to connect to the display mode server (e.g., VNC server).

This scheme works well for low-latency ($<$ 1ms) networks; the transition from display mode to record/replay mode is seamless and translates to a blip of only 100-300 milliseconds (not noticeable by human user) at the client. With higher network latencies ($5 - 100$ms), the switchover from display to record/replay mode causes a longer human-visible stall at the user, as we discuss below [4].

A client that has freshly switched from display to record/replay mode generates many demand paging faults for memory (cold misses), and each fault results in a network round trip. The net effect is a client that is slower than the server in the first few seconds of the switchover. This client-side

---

[4] Transitions in the other direction (record/replay to display mode) are always quick ($< 50ms$).

slowdown is more for higher latency networks. A slow client causes record log traffic to get queued at the server, effectively making the client appear chronologically behind the server (resulting in overall poor user experience).

To deal with this problem, we introduce a transient *dual mode*, where the tool runs in both display and record/replay modes simultaneously. While switching from display to record/replay mode, the client runs in dual mode for up to 200 seconds after snapshotting is complete. In dual mode, the client computer streams-in both display and record/replay traffic, while the user facing screen displays the output of only the display mode client. This allows the record/replay client to "catch up" with the server, while keeping the user oblivious of this background switch. We consider a client to have *caught up* with the server if it reaches the end of the streamed record log network buffer (i.e., the client and the server are at the same execution epoch). This strategy of using a transient dual mode works well for both low-latency and high-latency networks. If the client does not catch up with the server in the 200 seconds of dual mode, the tool reverts back to display mode. 200 seconds are usually enough for a record/replay client to catch up (if it can), while still keeping dual mode overheads low. Typical catch-up times are lower and depend on the network latencies and workloads (see experiments in Section 5). The dual mode results in more network and CPU overhead during switch; this cost is recovered if the switch is successful and saves network and CPU over a longer duration.

The dual mode provides a convenient and simple switching strategy: if the client catches up during dual mode, the switch (from display to record/replay mode) is upheld, else it is cancelled. This end-to-end decision strategy holistically captures many system characteristics like network parameters, client-side resource capabilities, and workload behavior automatically. An attempted switch that gets cancelled in dual mode (due to the client not catching up in 200 seconds) results in wasted overhead, and so it is important to avoid failed switching attempts. As we discuss later, the switching decision from display to dual mode is based on traffic measurements and estimates. We also disallow a consecutive switching attempt within 20 minutes of a failed switch.

We use a similar end-to-end strategy for switching back from record/replay to display mode. If during record/replay mode, we find that the record log buffer has grown more than a threshold, we initiate a switch back to the display mode. In our current implementation, we switch back if the client falls behind the server by more than 500ms (we measure time difference by counting the number of in-flight timer interrupt entries). As we discuss next, we also switch from record/replay to display mode if traffic measurements and estimates suggest a possible benefit by doing so.

We measure and estimate network traffic in display and record/replay modes to aid the switching decision. In display mode, the record/replay mode traffic is estimated by mea-

suring the amount of non-deterministic input at the server VM. In record/replay mode, the display mode traffic is estimated by capturing the VGA virtual device activity. Both these measurements are lightweight ($< 1\%$ overhead) and are implemented in the hypervisor at the server, and are communicated to the client. We have tested our estimation routines on a variety of workloads, and they provide accurate estimates of traffic in each mode.

A switch from display to dual mode is initiated if record/replay-mode traffic is estimated to be at least 75% of the current display-mode traffic over the past 20 seconds. Similarly, a switch from record/replay mode to display mode is initiated if the display-mode traffic is estimated to be at least 1.1x less than the record/replay-mode traffic over the past 20 seconds. Notice that our strategy for switching from record/replay to display mode is more aggressive than our strategy for switching in the other direction. This is justified given the higher overhead of a bad switching decision in the latter case. The thresholds (1.5x, 1.1x, 20 seconds) have been chosen based on expected workload characteristics; they capture the important optimizations for display-intensive workloads, but ensure that overheads/bad-decisions do not occur for other workloads. The system is largely indifferent to small changes (10-60%) to these thresholds.

We call the duration between a *decision* to switch (by the client) and the *actual* switch, the "switching latency". We call the time for which the server actually stops (e.g., steps 1 and 4 in Section 3.1), the "switching stall time". The switching stall time is always smaller (often much smaller) than the switching latency.

The switching latency from display mode to record/replay mode is dominated by the time taken to snapshot the server's VM, and could be up to tens of seconds. The corresponding switching stall time is typically smaller (less than 0.35 seconds in all our experiments). The switching latency from record/replay mode to display mode is much lower and is always less than 10-50 milliseconds, as it only involves spawning a display mode client.

4. Implementation

We have implemented our remote desktopping tool [1] using Linux/Qemu/KVM [5], similar to previous work [19]. Record/replay of the disk controller, network card, and other devices was implemented by modifying the emulation logic of the respective devices appropriately. The record log entries have been structured to take minimal space, and no further compression is performed on them.

To implement record/replay-based remote desktopping, we extended our implementation to be able to read/write the record log from/to a network socket. The server runs the KVM process in record mode (outputting the record log to a network socket) and the client runs the KVM process in replay mode (inputting the log from the socket). If the client (consumer) is faster than the server (producer), the

165

socket's buffers eventually empty, causing the client to wait for the server to produce more log entries. Because the server generates at least one record log entry on every timer interrupt, the client never appears "inactive" to the user. Similarly, if the server is faster than the client, the socket's buffers eventually get full. We size the send socket buffer of Server and receive socket buffer of Client to 16MB to avoid the buffer from getting full due to network/traffic variations. We switch back to display mode if the socket buffer gets full. We also switch back to display mode if the client lags behind the server by more than 500ms in record/replay mode (such lags are allowed in dual mode).

Our remote desktopping client, when running in record/replay mode, runs a full VM on the client machine and displays its console to the user. All user input keyboard/mouse activity on that console is transmitted to the server. Demand paging (for transfer of snapshotted memory) is implemented by memory-mapping a "network block device" (NBD) [9] in the guest's address space. Thus, guest's memory accesses at the client cause appropriate network transfers from the server. If using snapshotted disks, the snapshotted disk is exported over NFS from server to client (NFS server process is run on the server machine, and NFS client process is run on the client machine). NBD's read-ahead parameter was set to 256 (default value).

TightVNC [18], an efficient open-source VNC implementation, is used to implement the display mode of our remote desktopping tool. A TightVNC server process runs on the server machine; the client connects to this server to run in display mode.

5. Experiments

We performed our experiments on a server machine with Intel Xeon X5650 2.67 GHz processor, 24GB memory, and 300GB disk, and a client laptop machine with Intel Core i5 2.40GHz processor, 4GB memory and 500GB disk. In our first set of experiments, we connected the machines through a 100Mbps network (effective download bandwidth of around 10-12MBps) with 0.2ms latency. We discuss the effect of network latency and bandwidth later in this section We report comparisons with VNC — our comparisons with other display-based remote desktopping tools had similar results (see Section 6 for details).

We first discuss the performance of our record/replay implementation. Table 1 lists some workloads and the corresponding record log growth rates for different workloads. We have chosen a mix of graphics-intensive, compute-intensive, disk and network intensive applications. The runtime overhead of record/replay for all these workloads is less than 10% (mostly 1-5%). For sleep, replay finishes 2x faster than a normal run, because CPU's idle periods (marked by the execution of the hlt instruction on x86) get skipped-over during replay. In general, any workload involv-

ing CPU idle time finishes faster during replay (i.e., client executes faster than server in our remote desktopping setup).

We next compare network bandwidth usage of our remote desktopping tool with existing display-based remote desktopping tools. Figure 2 presents our network bandwidth consumption results for display-intensive applications (video-local, video-stream, supertux, and tuxfootball). For each application, we show the cumulative network bandwidth consumed over time by display-based remote desktopping (VNC) and record/replay-based remote desktopping (RecRep). We show results for two videos of 240p and 480p resolutions. With VNC, we use two compression modes: lossy (VNC-6 for quality-level 6, and VNC-9 for quality-level 9) and lossless (VNC-lossless). VNC-lossy uses JPEG compression, while VNC-lossless uses the most efficient lossless compression method[5].

Applications involving large display activity perform significantly better with record/replay-based remote desktopping. Table 3 lists the average network traffic rates for each workload produced by VNC-6, VNC-lossless, and RecRep. Notice that for video and game workloads, RecRep provides a lossless viewing experience and yet consumes significantly less bandwidth than VNC-6. The measurements in Figure 2 include the startup cost (i.e., the cost of snapshot transfer at the start of the remote desktopping session). The extra traffic due to snapshot transfer at startup is seen as a steep vertical jump in bandwidth consumption in the first few seconds of each curve in Figure 2. However, the slope of the RecRep curve is significantly lower than VNC. Table 3 lists the steady-state traffic rates (steady-state slope of the curve in Figure 2) for each application.

RecRep's traffic consists of record log, memory demand paging traffic, and NFS traffic. For video-local applications, a majority of RecRep traffic is due to demand paging and NFS — client accesses the video stored on disk resulting in fresh memory and NFS file accesses, causing on-demand network traffic. For video-stream, the majority of RecRep traffic is due to the record log — all incoming network packets containing the video manifest as input non-determinism and get transferred from server to client as record log entries. In both cases, the traffic between server and client is proportional to the size of the original video (stored on disk or streamed over network). This is an improvement over VNC, where in comparison, video is first decompressed (to generate a screen) and then re-compressed (to transfer to client). The quality of this on-the-fly recompression (done by VNC) is evidently less than the quality of compression on the original video (which is a property of the video's file format, e.g., FLV, MP4, etc.).

RecRep performs even better for graphical games (supertux, tuxfootball) where there is low input non-determini-

---

[5] We set TightVNC parameters to minimize network traffic. TightVNC was the best performing VNC implementation we came across in terms of network bandwidth consumption.

Benchmark	Description	Log growth rate (KBps)	
		snapshotted disk	output-replayed disk
`video-local-` `(240, 360, 480)`	Viewing a video stored locally on the VM at 240p, 360p, and 480p resp.	59, 63, 64 resp.	79, 85, 86
`video-stream-` `(240, 360, 480)`	Viewing a video streamed from a LAN server at 240p, 360p, and 480p resp.	131, 208, 272 resp.	140, 221, 267
`emptyloop`	A process running a compute-intensive loop	32.3	36.3
`forkbomb`	Forks 1 million processes, each exiting gracefully	65.8	89.2
`cp`	Copies 100MB file within the same directory on ext3	10.6	58.3
`inet`	Receives data over TCP socket in 4-byte chunks	793	791
`onet`	Sends data over TCP socket in 4-byte chunks	714	732
`sleep`	Calls `sleep(10)` (idles for 10 seconds)	1.7	2.9
`iscp`	Copies 100MB from host to guest using `scp`	269.5	282.8
`lincompile`	Builds the Linux kernel from source	42.7	45.6
`supertux`	Playing a graphical game called `supertux`	48.6	82.75
`tuxfootball`	Playing a graphical game called `tuxfootball`	148.5	171.2

Table 1. Benchmark description and record log growth rates

Benchmarks	Server CPU Usage			Client CPU Usage		
	RecRep	VNC-lossless	VNC-6	RecRep	VNC-lossless	VNC-6
`video-local 240p`	16.21	39.14	36.12	54.36	17.97	18.30
`video-local 360p`	28.10	63.82	62.62	63.00	22.89	26.10
`video-local 480p`	34.90	85.40	79.87	71.33	24.33	27.50
`video-stream 240p`	17.17	36.82	35.96	65.13	18.41	19.13
`video-stream 360p`	33.93	70.95	64.88	72.03	23.62	27.97
`video-stream 480p`	37.05	81.57	80.17	73.89	23.33	28.32

Table 2. Average CPU usage at server and client for VNC and RecRep with snapshotted disk. Similar results are obtained with output-replayed disk .

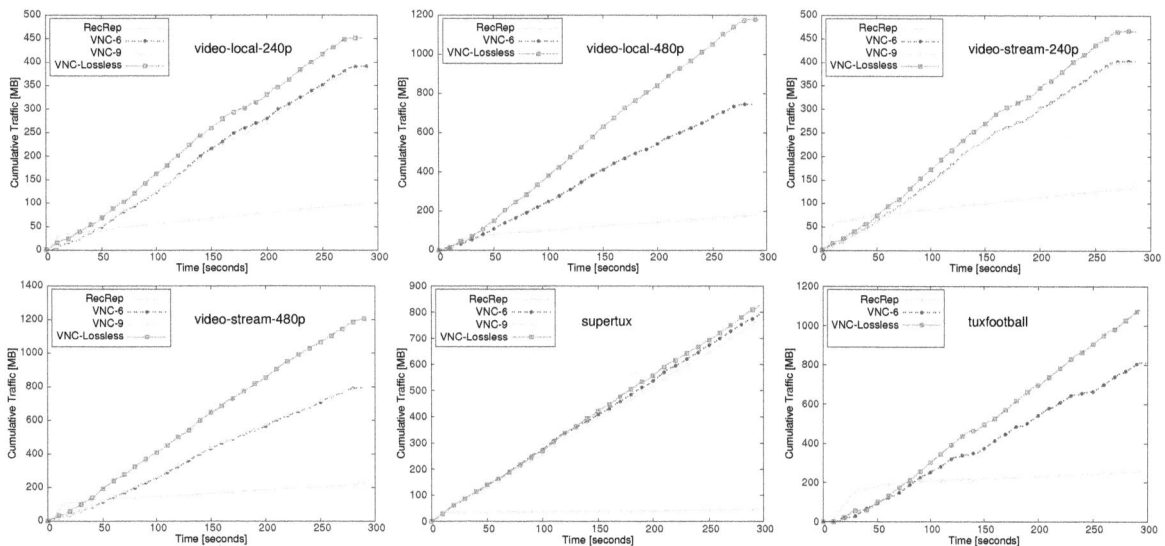

Figure 2. Comparisons on network bandwidth consumption for display-intensive applications. These results were obtained on a 100Mbps, 0.2ms latency network between client and server.

Application	VNC-lossless	VNC-6	RecRep			
			record log	demand paging	Snapshotted	total
video-local 240p	1867	1414	151	80	38	268
video-local 360p	3444	2390	157	113	107	377
video-local 480p	4605	2937	168	201	155	524
video-stream 240p	1763	1157	245	16	0	262
video-stream 360p	4030	2598	319	12	0	332
video-stream 480p	4688	2905	391	11	0	403
supertux	2421	1918	217	55	0	271
tuxfootball	4112	2941	301	464	0	767
lincompile	23	22	133	177	14	325
video-B-after-A 480p	4688	2905	158.51	159.27	155.12	470.41
video-A-repeat 480p	4688	2905	165.23	0	0.14	165.37

Table 3. Average network bandwidth rates with snapshotted disk (KBps). The measurements with output-replayed disks are similar .

sm and high screen activity. Most graphics are generated using local computation, and thus RecRep generates minimal traffic for supertux (92.8% reduction over VNC). With RecRep, the game's computation happens locally at client — this improves network and server CPU utilization at the expense of client CPU usage.

The initial traffic due to snapshot transfer is approximately 41MB, 47MB and 37MB for video-local-480p, video-stream-480p, and supertux respectively. This initial snapshot transfer size depends on the memory and disk footprints of the application. This traffic is compensated by reduction in steady-state traffic growth rates, and we break even at 28s, 21s, and 52s respectively for the three applications. Further, unlike display-based remote desktopping, record/replay-based remote desktopping has the advantage of being *stateful*. i.e., state once transferred from server to client can be reused without repeat transfers over the network. We next performed an experiment where the same video was played twice in the same session. To further distinguish application traffic (due to video-player) from data traffic (due to the played video), we also played another video in that session. Initially, all videos and applications were stored on disk (at server) when the client initiated a fresh remote desktopping session. Figure 3 plots the network usage results. The corresponding traffic rates are also presented in Table 3 (labels video-B-after-A, and video-A-repeat). Interestingly, compared to video-local-480, the total traffic rates for video-B-after-A and video-Arepeat are 10.30% and 68.51% lower. video-B-after-A requires only the video (and not the video-player) to be transferred from server to client; while video-A-repeat requires no new state transfer (only execution information is transferred). These improvements were seen both for snapshotted and output-replayed disks (the video gets cached in memory after first run). Because of our fetch-only-on-demand optimizations, the amount of RecRep traf-

fic is largely independent of VM's memory/disk size, and only depends on the workload's memory/disk footprints.

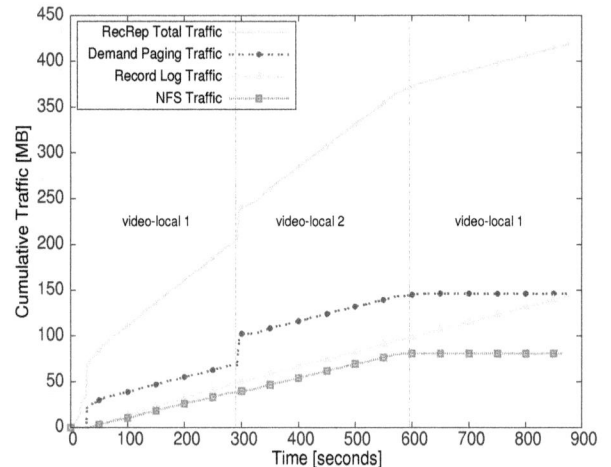

Figure 3. Network bandwidth consumption during a session involving three local video playbacks. During the first 60 seconds, video A is played; the next 60 seconds, video B is played using the same video player; and in the last 60 seconds, video A is played again. These results were obtained on a 100Mbps, 0.2ms latency network between client and server.

For other applications which do not exhibit rapid screen activity however, display-based tools (VNC) perform better. Our tool adaptively switches between the two approaches based on current workload behavior. We next discuss experiments involving multiple switches between display and record/replay modes. We ran a sequence of applications in the following order (we call this experiment the "sequence experiment"):

1. 5 minutes of video-local 360p
2. 100 seconds of idle

3. 5 minutes of `video-stream` 360p

4. 12MB file `download` over LAN

5. 300 seconds of playing `supertux`

Figure 4 plots the network bandwidth consumption of our remote desktopping tool over time, and compares it with VNC. Our tool starts in display mode (our display mode has identical performance as VNC-6) and switches to record/replay mode for `video-local`, `video-stream`, and `supertux`. It switches back to display mode for `idle` and `download`. The back-and-forth switching between modes is fast. The time between the decision to switch and the actual switch (switching latency) from record/replay mode to display mode is less than 10 milliseconds. The switching latency from display mode to record/replay mode was less than 10 seconds for all such switches in this experiment. The corresponding switching stall times ranged between 0.31 seconds and 0.35 seconds. Around half of this switching stall time (around 0.16 seconds) is due to the synchronous transfer of the last few memory pages (Step 4a in Section 3.1). The rest of the stall time is due to transfer of disk state metadata (to implement copy-on-write) and other processing at server to create a full snapshot. Switching latency is independent of VM's memory/disk size, and only depends on the workload's memory access pattern. Switching stall time is independent of VM size and workload's characteristics and only depends on the underlying hardware speed.

We next discuss comparisons on resource utilization at server and client. Table 2 lists average client/server CPU utilization for each workload. Figure 4 also plots the server-side CPU utilization for the sequence experiment over time. For applications involving small display activity (`idle` and `download`), both VNC and our tool (which switches to display mode) cause small CPU overheads. For video applications (`video-local` and `video-stream`), VNC consumes more CPU than RecRep. VNC requires more CPU to encode and compress the video framebuffer before streaming it to the client. On the other hand, RecRep's network stream is lighter and thus requires fewer CPU cycles. Overall, our tool consumes up to 56% less CPU on the server for video playback, streaming, and gaming applications. Our tool consumes less CPU on the server than on the client (even though they are executing the same instructions) for two reasons: first, unlike the client, the server does not execute the code to render the screen on its own display; second, replay is slightly more expensive (around 10% for CPU-intensive workloads) than record as it also involves instruction-level singlestepping for interrupt replay, as discussed in Section 4.

Figure 4 also plots the client's CPU utilization for the sequence experiment over time. At client, our tool in record/replay mode consumes significantly more CPU than VNC. VNC is only required to decode the network packets and produce a screen. On the other hand, our tool runs a full VM in re-play mode at client, resulting in higher CPU usage. This is the downside of our approach, and we discuss this tradeoff in Section 6.

We next measured keystroke latency while running in record/replay mode. We recorded the time elapsed between a client's keypress and the appearance of the corresponding character at client screen. This latency was between 10-70ms in all our experiments, ensuring a fast and comfortable user experience. (Any extra latency added by network will be common to both display-based and record/replay-based tools). Like other display-based remote desktopping tools, our tool supports concurrent access by multiple clients to one server. Even in collaborative settings, the network and CPU performance comparisons with display-based tools remain similar.

We next discuss the effect of network latency and bandwidth on our record/replay based scheme. Figure 5 plots the network traffic generated by our scheme on 0.2ms and 100ms networks for different bandwidths (10Mbps-1000Mbps) for `video-360p` application. For comparison, we also plot the traffic generated by VNC on a 100Mbps network in these graphs. To better understand the behavior of our tool, we disabled the limit on dual mode duration in this experiment, i.e., dual mode would go on till the client reaches the end of record log network buffer, and is not limited to 200 seconds.

Our scheme is more sensitive than VNC to network latency and bandwidth changes, as network parameters directly impact the switching time and the time the system remains in dual mode. The steady state bandwidth consumption of our tool remains largely independent of the network parameters. Slower networks (with higher latencies and lower bandwidths) cause our system to take longer to switch to steady-state record/replay operation, and thus cause higher traffic generation (longer time in dual mode). The overall comparison still remains favorable however, with break-even points reached at around 78s, 89s, and 195s for 0.2ms, 10ms, and 100ms latency networks respectively.

For bandwidths less than 30Mbps, the dual mode never finishes as the client is never able to catch up. For this experiment, dual mode bandwidth requirements of our tool are around 25Mbps, which are not met by a 20Mbps network. In contrast, VNC's bandwidth requirement for this experiment is only 18Mbps. Hence, our scheme has a drawback of requiring slightly higher network capacity during dual mode. After dual mode finishes, the bandwidth requirement of our scheme is much lower (3Mbps). If dual mode can be avoided (for example, by manual switch to record/replay mode), our scheme can run on lower capacity networks also.

Example Applications

Our experiments demonstrate that for applications where inputs are smaller than outputs, it is better to ship the inputs and reconstruct the outputs, thus saving shipping costs. VM record/replay is an enabling technology of this principle for

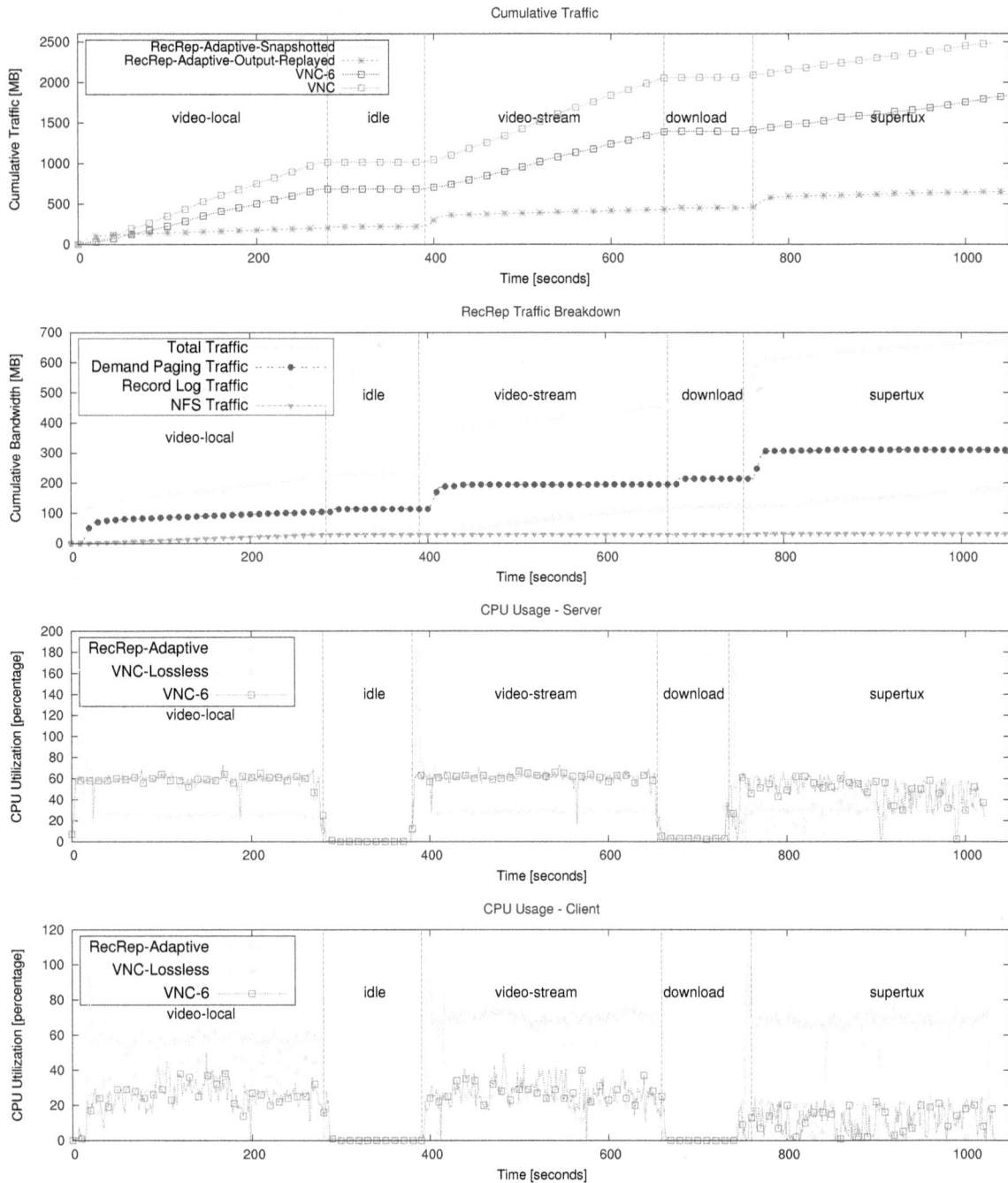

Figure 4. Running a sequence of applications (sequence experiment) over a 0.2ms latency, 100Mbps network.

remote desktopping tools. We discuss some intended applications of our tool:

Desktop-in-cloud: Being able to maintain your desktop state in the cloud has well-known advantages of cost, platform independence, mobility, flexibility, maintenance, security, backups, among others. Remote desktopping is a natural choice for accessing a desktop in cloud. The closest alternative to this desktop-in-cloud paradigm is the use of

cloud for storage (let's call this a *storage cloud*). In a storage cloud, applications are run locally on client, and the cloud maintains the data store. For display-intensive (and non-input-intensive) applications (e.g., game, video), a storage cloud offers a natural advantage over desktop-in-cloud. On the other hand, a storage cloud performs poorly if an application requires processing of lots of disk data (e.g., `grep`), as all data needs to be transported to client for computa-

170

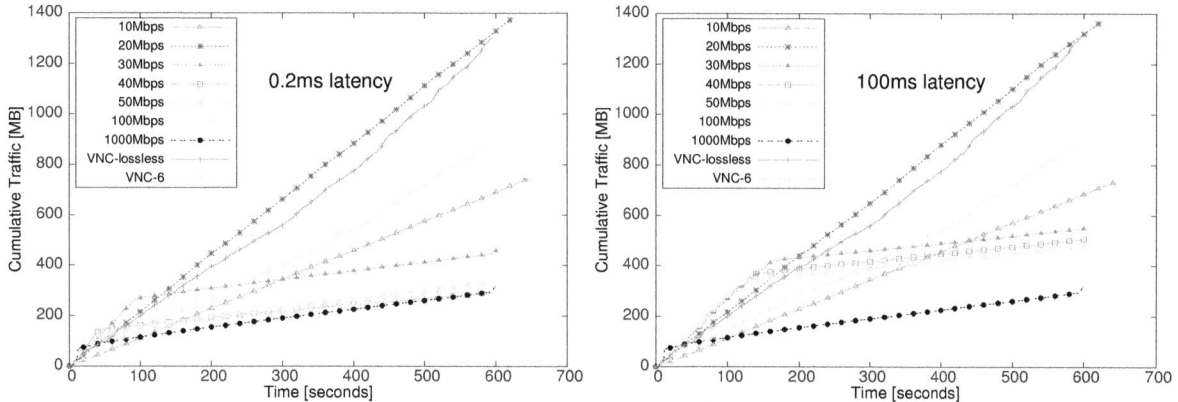

Figure 5. Cumulative Traffic consumed for varying bandwidth and varying latencies for `video-360p`.

tion. In a desktop cloud, such applications run locally on cloud and only their output needs to be shipped to the user-facing client. Our work allows the best of both worlds; input-intensive workloads like `grep` can run in display mode, while display-intensive workloads can run in record/replay mode, providing best performance in each case.

Network-level access control, **License Restrictions**: Often, organizations enforce network-level access control policies, whereby the server computers are allowed greater network visibility than client computers. In these situations, remote desktopping may be the only way to access applications depending on such network access. If such applications are also display-intensive (e.g., network games), our record/replay approach can help significantly. Similar situations can also arise due to license restrictions on an application (e.g., it can only run on one computer).

There remains a more fundamental question challenging our approach: if somebody has a client capable of running a workload, why will he/she use remote desktopping to run it? The alternative, of course, is to run the workload locally. We think that local installation and execution of an application entails its own challenges and usability headaches, and does not provide the mobility, inter-operability, maintenance, security and consolidation advantages of cloud computing. Our remote desktopping scheme allows the performance of local execution while retaining the benefits of "execution in the cloud".

6. Related Work

Previous efforts on improving remote desktopping technology have centered around designing the right abstractions and protocols for exchanging display information between the client and the server. While windowing systems like X [15] and NX [11] abstract display activities at the application layer, other tools like SLIM [16] and THINC [4] abstract at the device driver layer. Similarly, VNC [18] abstracts at the framebuffer layer. In our experiments with various tools including RDP [2], PCoIP [3], and X [7, 15], we found that

VNC's bandwidth consumption for video/graphical workloads is less than or comparable to these tools. VNC relaxes the video quality (frame rate, lossy JPEGs) aggressively for better compression. Similar comparisons reported in [4, 16] confirm this observation. Our experiments show that record/replay-based remote desktopping is capable of even outperforming VNC-lossy on network bandwidth, while still retaining full video quality. Because input non-determinism is recorded at the VM-level, our approach works generally across all OS/Application stacks.

While the use of record/replay for remote desktopping is novel, the central observation that using deterministic replay to generate machine state can be cheaper than transmitting it explicitly has previously been made in [6, 14] in the context of fault tolerance. The work closest to ours in our objectives is perhaps VM streaming (e.g., Moka5 [10], VMware VM Streaming [17]), where VMs stored at server are fetched *on-demand* to client. In VM streaming models, multiple clients may "checkout" the same VM simultaneously and consistency across parallel updates is maintained using a revision control system. Like us, these systems also use demand paging and copy-on-write optimizations to reduce network traffic. But, there are two important differences between our models:

First, in the VM streaming model, the server only acts as a VM repository, and the client accesses a VM and image and runs it locally and independently. This implies that the user observes client-local device environment inside the VM (e.g., the VM can only access client-visible network hosts). Our remote desktopping model, on the other hand, provides the illusion of operating a VM running on the server, with the server's environment (e.g., the VM will have a server-side IP address).

Second, in the VM streaming model, multiple clients may run the same VM image concurrently. At the time of "committing" the clients' updates back to the server, the user may be required to perform appropriate conflict resolution. In our remote desktopping model, only one master copy of the VM runs at server (with clients simply mimicking the master copy), thus alleviating such consistency problems. Notice that our model still provides concurrent access from multiple clients by serializing concurrent keyboard/mouse inputs (from concurrent clients) at server.

Because we run a full VM at client, the use of the term "remote desktopping" is deceptive. We use this term for lack of a better alternative, and for its resemblance in user experience to existing remote desktopping tools. Another term to describe our model could be "online VM streaming". Our approach trades off client resources for better utilization of network and server resources. Most studies show that user-facing client computers are under-utilized, and our work uses this under-utilized resource to improve network and server-side CPU utilization. Decentralizing resource consumption is usually a good thing in cloud computing environments.

If the client is untrusted, our approach to stream the memory pages from server to client, can potentially increase security risks, as data that was not supposed to be visible at the client (e.g., pages belonging to another user's process memory), may now become visible. A potential solution is to use trusted software at the client (e.g., through digital signatures). Characterizing the security risks of our scheme requires more work, and we do not address these issues in this paper.

Finally, we have evaluated our ideas only for uniprocessor VMs due to the unavailability of a complete and general method to deterministically replay a multiprocessor VM. There has been significant recent work on deterministic VM multiprocessor replay and we hope that a solution in this space can lend more generality to our optimizations. Our uniprocessor-based adaptive remote desktopping tool is publicly available for download.

7. Conclusion

We present a new method of remotely accessing a server VM using record/replay, and discuss its performance. Record/replay based approach outperforms traditional display based approaches by up to 9x in network bandwidth utilization for display-heavy workloads. We adaptively switch between record/replay and display modes to provide high resource utilization for all types of workloads. Overall, we show that our scheme holds promise, especially for cloud computing environments.

Acknowledgments

We thank Ankur Vijay, Anuj Kalia, Rohan Sharma and Shivam Handa for working on this tool at different stages of its development. The third author thanks NetApp for their support through the Faculty Fellowship program.

References

[1] Our prototype implementation source code. http://www.cse.iitd.ernet.in/~sbansal/rdrr.

[2] Remote desktop protocol. Microsoft KB Article Q186607.

[3] Teradici's PC-over-IP. http://www.teradici.com/pcoip-technology.

[4] Ricardo A. Baratto, Leonard N. Kim, and Jason Nieh. Thinc: A virtual display architecture for thin-client computing. In SOSP '05.

[5] Fabrice Bellard. Qemu, a fast and portable dynamic translator. In USENIX ATC, FREENIX Track, 2005.

[6] T. C. Bressoud and F. B. Schneider. Hypervisor-based fault tolerance. In SOSP '95.

[7] Citrix independent computing architecture. http://receiver.citrix.com.

[8] George W. Dunlap, Dominic G. Lucchetti, Michael A. Fetterman, and Peter M. Chen. Execution replay of multiprocessor virtual machines. In VEE '08: Proceedings of the fourth ACM SIGPLAN/SIGOPS international conference on Virtual execution environments, pages 121–130, New York, NY, USA, 2008. ACM.

[9] P.T.A. Marin Lopez and Arturo Gracia Ares. The network block device. In Linux Journal, volume 2000.

[10] MokaFive Inc. http://www.mokafive.com.

[11] Nomachine NX. http://www.nomachine.com.

[12] Qemu: open source processor emulator. http://fabrice.bellard.free.fr/qemu/.

[13] Russel Sandberg, David Goldberg, Steve Kleiman, Dan Walsh, and Bob Lyon. Design and implementation of sun network filesystem. In USENIX ATC, 1985.

[14] Daniel J. Scales, Mike Nelson, and Ganesh Venkitachalam. The design of a practical system for fault-tolerant virtual machines. Operating Systems Review, 44(4):30–39, 2010.

[15] Robert W. Scheifler and Jim Gettys. The x window system. ACM Trans. Graph., 5(2), 1986.

[16] Brian K. Schmidt, Monica S. Lam, and J. Duane Northcutt. The interactive performance of slim: A stateless, thin-client architecture. In SOSP '99.

[17] VMware Workstation 9.0. www.vmware.com/products/workstation/.

[18] XtightVNC-Viewer: Virtual network computing client software for X. http://packages.ubuntu.com/hardy/xtightvncviewer.

[19] Min Xu, Vyacheslav Malyugin, Jeffrey Sheldon, Ganesh Venkitachalam, and Boris Weissman. Retrace: Collecting execution trace with virtual machine deterministic replay. In Proceedings of the 3rd Annual Workshop on Modeling, Benchmarking and Simulation, MoBS, volume 3, 2007.

Migration of Web Applications with Seamless Execution

JinSeok Oh   Jin-woo Kwon   Hyukwoo Park   Soo-Mook Moon

School of Electrical Engineering and Computer Science
Seoul National University, Seoul 151-744, Korea
jjingoh@altair.snu.ac.kr, jwkwon@altair.snu.ac.kr, clover2123@altair.snu.ac.kr, smoon@snu.ac.kr

Abstract

Web applications (apps) are programmed using HTML5, CSS, and JavaScript, and are distributed in the source code format. Web apps can be executed on any devices where a web browser is installed, allowing one-source, multi-platform environment. We can exploit this advantage of platform independence for a new user experience called *app migration*, which allows migrating an app in the middle of execution seamlessly between smart devices. This paper proposes such a migration framework for web apps where we can save the current state of a running app and resume its execution on a different device by restoring the saved state. We save the web app's state in the form of a *snapshot*, which is actually another web app whose execution can restore the saved state. In the snapshot, the state of the JavaScript variables and DOM trees are saved using the JSON format. We solved some of the saving/restoring problems related to event handlers and closures by accessing the browser and the JavaScript engine internals. Our framework does not require instrumenting an app or changing its source code, but works for the original app. We implemented the framework on the Chrome browser with the V8 JavaScript engine and successfully migrated non-trivial sample apps with reasonable saving and restoring overhead. We also discuss other usage of the snapshot for optimizations and user experiences for the web platform.

Categories and Subject Descriptors   D.3.4 [**Programming Languages**]: Processors – code generation, run-time environments

General Terms   Algorithms, Design, Languages

Keywords   App migration; Web application; JavaScript; DOM; JSON; Snapshot

1. Introduction

For the last few years, many smart devices such as phones, tablets, TVs, and car infotainments have been actively used, especially by running diverse applications (apps) on top of those devices. Currently, Android apps or IOS apps constitute the main stream of the app platform, but a new platform of apps called *web apps* would soon join the mainstream with Tizen [31], webOS [33], and Firefox OS [12]. These *web platforms* have the advantage of portability and productivity compared to existing platforms. That is, web apps can be executed on any devices where a web browser is installed, supporting one-source, multi-platform environment. Moreover, programming based on the existing web technology allows a faster app development.

Web apps are programmed using HTML, CSS, and JavaScript. HTML expresses web components, CSS controls visual effects, and JavaScript performs computation and manipulation for the apps. The browser parses the HTML document and builds a document object model (DOM) tree, which is then displayed on the screen based on CSS by the rendering engine. The JavaScript engine executes the JavaScript code in the web app, mostly for handling the events and manipulating the DOM tree based on the events, which is then rendered for an updated display. Recently, HTML5 has been introduced for implementing multimedia components without plugins such as Adobe Flash [2]. Also, HTML5 provides APIs to control the hardware components of smart devices such as battery or camera [14], allowing the programmer to develop a "complete" application within the boundary of web technology.

Text-based source code distribution of the web apps may lead to a new user experience (UX) beyond the advantage of portability. That is, it would be interesting to move an executing app on a device to a different device and continue its execution seamlessly, which we call *app migration*. For example, we can migrate a game app being played on a smart phone to a smart TV and continue to play with it. Also, we can move a secretary app worked on a smart TV to a tablet, then to the in-vehicle infotainment (IVI) of a smart car for continuous secretary services on the move.

This app migration would also be possible if the app developer programs an app manually considering the migration between devices, or if a proxy server is used to add some instrumentation code to the app source code [11, 15]. However, it would be more useful if app migration works transparently for *any* app, supported entirely by the web browser, as in ours. Our proposed app migration is a more elaborate and convenient extension of the existing services such as the *chrome tab sync* to allow all the tabs of a browser on a desk-top to be browsed on a mobile browser [29], or the *dropbox* cloud service to access pictures and videos between devices [9]. App migration might also be possible for Android or IOS, but web apps allow easier extraction of properties from objects, and the text-based portability makes migration simpler, as explained shortly.

This paper proposes an app migration framework for web apps where we can capture a running app by saving its current state, and resume the app by restoring the saved state on a different device. We save the web app's state in the form of a *snapshot*, which is actually another web app composed of HTML/CSS/JavaScript, and if we execute the snapshot, it will restore the saved state automatically. That is, the snapshot has a text form where many of the web app states are saved in a platform-independent JSON format [18]. This is in sharp contrast to existing job migration used in the system VM where an app state on a desktop is migrated to a mobile device using VMware image [34]. Also, it is different from hibernation, where the whole process states are stored [23]. These techniques save the whole system image or whole process images, requiring a much higher memory overhead and restoration complexity. Our app migration saves the state of a single app, only the essential parts of the execution state after finding an appropriate time to save. Platform-independent text-form of the snapshot allows easier and more efficient migration between diverse devices with different CPUs, OS, browsers, and JavaScript engines, with a simple click of a button on the browser.

The contribution of this paper is as follows:

• We propose an app migration framework for saving and restoring the app state via a text-form of snapshot for its seamless, continuous execution on a different device.

• We propose a novel way to migrate app without any kind of instrumentation or modification on original app source code, which distinguishes our work from previous work [11, 15]. This approach allows more secure apps where the data-encapsulated objects the programmer do not want to expose can be protected. It also allows more generalized snapshot useful for other purposes.

We could successfully migrate three apps. We uploaded a video clip that demonstrates an example of app migration from a PC to a smart TV (http://youtu.be/pon7EDoYRVE). Our snapshot can also be useful for other optimization and UX purposes, which will be discussed.

The rest of the paper is composed of as follows. Section 2 overviews the proposed app migration framework and the scenario. Section 3 shows our approach to save and restore the web app state. Section 4 shows some of the technical problems and solutions of app migration. Section 5 discusses the implementation of the framework. Evaluation results are in Section 6 and other usage of the snapshot is discussed in Section 7. Related work is in Section 8 and a summary follows in Section 9.

2. App Migration Framework and Scenario

The current implementation of our app migration framework exploits the *extension* feature of a browser [6], a small program for enhancing the functionality of a browser. It can be programmed using HTML, CSS, and JavaScript, and be added as a button in the browser. For Google's Chrome browser, for example, a small button can be added at the end of the address bar as shown in Figure 1, which can be clicked

for the execution of the extension. Other browsers require a different implementation of the extension, yet it is similarly programmed. We do not need a separate proxy server for app instrumentation [11, 15], but just click the button to save the app state. We might need a more intuitive user interface as the swiping-based one used in Apple's Airplay [3] for saving, transferring, and restoring in real time, yet it is beyond the scope of this paper.

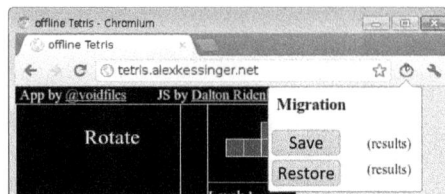

Figure 1. Browser extension of the Chrome browser.

App migration framework works as follows. A user runs a web app by pressing its icon installed in the device (platform-based app) or by entering an URL in the web browser (URL-based app). During execution, if the user wants to save the current execution state for app migration, he simply clicks the save button to execute the extension for the saving. The current state will be saved in the snapshot file, which will then be transferred to a different device.

The app restoration works similarly. The user runs an app by pressing its icon or entering its URL, but this time the user clicks the restore button of the extension to resume the execution of the migrated app. The snapshot file in the local storage is read and executed, which will resume the app execution seamlessly.

There can be variations on the scenario. As mentioned previously, the snapshot itself is a web app composed of HTML/CSS/JavaScript, so the user can directly run it on the browser without the extension. It might also be possible to save the files on a remote cloud server when we save the app state using the extension, which are then downloaded and executed when we want to resume its execution on a different device.

3. Approach to Save and Restore the App State

This section describes our approach to save and restore the app state, compared to the previous approaches. It also shows the basic structure of the proposed snapshot file. To make the paper self-contained, we start with how web app works and how JavaScript engine works, with a popular *tetris* app in Figure 2 as a running example.

3.1 How Web App Works

We first overview how web apps work. As a web page, a web app is run by executing an HTML file, embedded with JavaScript code fragments and the CSS. The web browser allocates a global object called *window*, which manages all the elements displayed for the HTML page. The *window* object has a property (which is similar to a field of an object) called a *document*, which is the root of the DOM tree, a format standardized for the document object. Each DOM

```
HTML(index.html)
 1 <html manifest="tetris.manifest">
 2 <head> …  <link href="tetris.css" … > </head>
 3 <body>
 4 <div id="tetris">
 5 ...
 6 <div class="game_area"> <div id="canvas">
 7 <div class = "square typ3" style="left:  100px; …"></div>
 8 <div class = "square typ3" style="left:   60px; …"></div>
 9 <div class = "square typ3" style="left:   80px; …"></div>
10 <div class = "square typ3" style="left:  100px; …"></div>
11 </div></div>
12 <div id="info">…<p id="lines">Score: … </div>
13 </div>
14 <div id="controls" class="show_controls">
15 <div class=…> <div class=…><span>L</span></div></div>
16 ..
17 </div>
18 <script type="text/javascript" src="tetris.js"></script>
19 </body>
20 </html>
```

```
JavaScript(tetris.js)
 1 var tetris = new Object();
 2 tetris.canvas = null, tetris.controls = null, …
 3 tetris.init = function() {
 4   this.canvas=document.getElementById("canvas");
 5   ...
 6   this.bindControlEvents(); this.play();
 7 },
 8 tetris.bindControlEvents = function() {
 9   var cb = function(e) { tetris.handleControl(e); }
10   this.controls = document.getElementById("controls");
11   this.controls.onclick = cb;
12 },
13 tetris.gameOver = function() {
14   ...
15   this.canvas.innerHTML = "<h1>GAME OVER</h1>";
16 },
17 tetris.play = function() { //gameLoop
18   var me = this;
19   ...
20   var gameLoop = function() {
21     me.move('D');
22     me.pTimer=setTimeout(gameLoop,me.speed);
23     ...
24   };
25   this.pTimer=setTimeout(gameLoop,me.speed);
26 },
27 tetris.incScore = function(amount) {
28   score = score + amount;
29   this.setInfo('score');
30 },
31 var score = 0, level = 1, lines = 0;
32 ...
33 tetris.init();
```

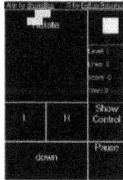

Figure 2. Example source code of the *tetris* web app.
(simplified and modified version of http://tetris.alexkessinger.net)

tree node corresponds to an element included in the HTML page such as text, image, and video component. The browser reads the HTML file and parses all of its components to build a DOM tree. Each component of the HTML page is separated by the tag such as <head> or <title>, so the HTML parser can identify each component and its hierarchy, which is added to the tree. The DOM tree is displayed with a visual effect of the CSS. When a script tag is encountered during the HTML parsing, the corresponding JavaScript *global code* is executed. When the last HTML tag is parsed and the *onload* event is fired by the browser, the loading process of the web app completes. Now the web app proceeds in an event-driven manner, such that a JavaScript function registered as an event handler is invoked when an event occurs such as the mouse click, the keyboard input, or the timer event. The event handler often changes the DOM tree for an updated display such that a DOM node belonging to a DOM tree can be changed or a new one is added to the tree via JavaScript execution using the DOM APIs.

For example, consider a simplified *Tetris* app shown in Figure 2 [25]. Its HTML file (*index.html*) is composed of HTML tags to describe the title, the game score, and the space information for the rectangle blocks, etc. (line 4-13). The CSS file is also included (line 2) to show the style information for the block color/shape and the layout of the game screen. A JavaScript file (*tetris.js*) is invoked (line 18) for controlling the game actions. It declares a *global variable tetris* and creates an object (line 1). Many objects including function objects such as *init()* or *play()* are created and saved as the properties of the *tetris* object (line 2-30). Other global variables are also declared and initialized (line 31). In this paper, we use *global variables* and *global objects* interchangeably, and they mean those JavaScript objects accessible from the global variables of the *window* object, which differ from local variables (objects) in a function. Finally, the function *tetris.init()* is invoked (line 33).

During the execution of *tetris.init()*, a DOM element created in the HTML file (line 14 of *tetris.html*) with an ID of "*controls*" is accessed using a DOM API, *getElementById()*, so that a reference to the element is saved in *tetris.controls* (line 10 of *tetris.js*). We call this variable a *DOM reference variable*. Then, an *onclick* event is registered for this DOM reference variable (line 11) so that when there is a mouse click on the control panel, the registered event handler *cb()* is invoked to move left/right (see Section 4.3). When *tetris.play()* is executed, a timer event is also registered (line 22, 25) using a *closure* variable (see Section 4.2), so that the current block moves down repetitively with some time interval. These event handlers will change the location of the current block using the *move()* function, so the DOM tree will show an updated shape when it is rendered. The function *tetris.gameOver()* will change the DOM tree by adding an innerHTML component when invoked to show the "Game Over" string. Some functions such as *tetris.incScore()* will update a global variable when invoked.

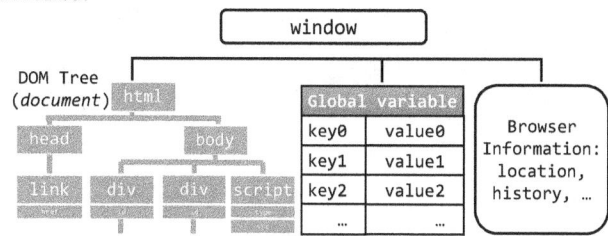

Figure 3. Window object structure.

Above description indicates that the execution state of a web app includes the DOM tree state and the JavaScript execution state. Both are the properties of the *window* object. Another property is the browser information. So, the *window* object has a property structure in Figure 3 (key0, key1, … are global variable names).

3.2 JavaScript Execution State

As to the JavaScript state, we first understand how the JavaScript works with its runtime data structures. The JavaScript engine is invoked when the first script tag is met during the HTML parsing. A heap area is assigned for it, and initialization is performed to make all built-in objects (which are also global variables) such as math objects in the heap. A runtime data structure called an *execution context* (EC), which roughly corresponds to the activation record in C, is generated in the heap when the JavaScript code is executed. A global execution context (GEC) is generated first, which contains all properties of the *window* object including the DOM tree, JavaScript global variables including those made by the programmer and those built-in variables, and the browser information. When a JavaScript function is invoked, its EC is also generated which contains its local variables and parameters. These ECs form an EC stack with GEC at the bottom, which correspond to the call stack of C. Independently, each function has a *scope chain* employed to find a variable name during execution, which is a linked list of ECs with GEC at the end. JavaScript requires the scope chain since it allows inner functions, so an inner function can use variables defined in outer functions; the scope chain is searched linearly to find a name. In real implementation, however, the scope chain is used only for the closure function to retrieve the closure variables (see Section 4.2) because other outer variables can be resolved when the JavaScript code is parsed. The JavaScript global code or function is parsed to the intermediate representation (IR), which is interpreted or JIT-compiled to machine code for execution. Figure 4 illustrates the EC stack and the scope chain, when *tetris.play()* and *gameLoop()* are in execution in Figure 2.

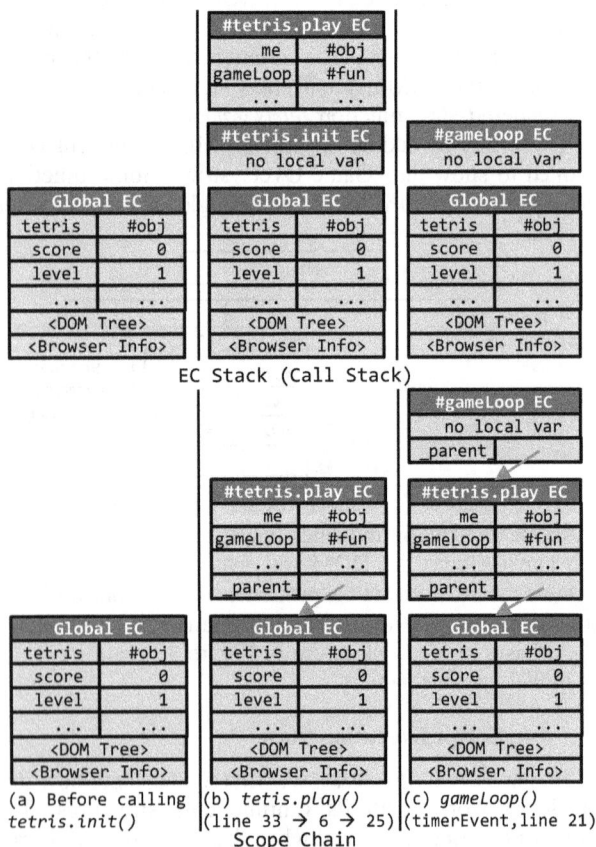

Figure 4. EC stack and scope chain for Figure 2.

A naïve way of saving the JavaScript execution state would be simply saving all the JavaScript global objects in the GEC, all other objects, all ECs in the call chain, the scope chains of closure functions, IRs, and even the JIT-compiled machine code. However, the amount of data to save and the time overhead would be substantial. More seriously, the restoration process will be complicated since all of these data structures should be relocated in the target machine, and restarting the JavaScript code in the EC stack would be tricky, especially if it is JIT-compiled. The process might require same JavaScript engine, same browser, or even same target machine. Maybe the app should also be installed in the target device in advance. Therefore, this approach is not convenient for app migration.

3.3 Saving and Restoring the App State

We take a different, simpler approach. Instead of saving the data structures as they are in the heap, we save them in a form of JavaScript code such that when it is executed, equivalent data structures will be restored automatically. This means that our snapshot is actually a JavaScript file. For example, if a global variable *x* has a value *0* when we save, we generate a JavaScript statement *var x=0;* in the snapshot file, so if it is executed at the target device, it will restore the GEC with *x* set to *0*. All the global variables can be restored in this way. However, the function execution state cannot be easily saved to JavaScript code. Fortunately, a JavaScript function as an event handler tends to be executed briefly to provide a fast user response time. So it is better to wait for an event handler to finish before we save, rather than saving in the middle of an event handler execution. That is, we take a snapshot only when no JavaScript code is in execution, in-between the execution of JavaScript event handlers. This would obviate the saving of the function execution state, so we need to save only the JavaScript global variables (and the DOM tree), shared among the event handlers.

For the *Tetris* app example, the game execution after loading is composed of the execution of a timer event handler that moves the current block downward, and the execution of a DOM event handler that manipulate the current block based on the mouse click. Between the execution of these event handlers, the DOM state and the JavaScript state do not change, thus being appropriate and safe for saving the app state.

The saving job itself will be done by a JavaScript function, *state_save()*, which we added for the browser extension. It will be executed when we click the save button. This function can access the *window* object of the app, so it can access all the global variables and the DOM tree. So, *state_save()* will collect all JavaScript global variables. This is possible since the extension mechanism allows the added JavaScript function to share the same browser session with the app when it is declared in *manifest.json*.

Before we describe how state_save() works, we first discuss the format used to save the JavaScript objects pointed by the JavaScript global variables. We use the JavaScript Object Notation (JSON), which is a string format used to send data between web applications using AJAX

(Asynchronous JavaScript and XML) or web services, and is useful to represent the objects in many programming languages [7, 13, 24]. Figure 5 (a) shows an example of JavaScript code and Figure 5 (b) shows the corresponding JSON-based JavaScript code. So, if we take a snapshot at the end of execution for the JavaScript code in Figure 5 (a) and generate the snapshot file as in Figure 5 (b), the execution of the snapshot file will generate the exact same JavaScript state. We can actually apply *JSON.parse()* to the JSON string (e.g., *var arr = JSON.parse([1,"a",true])*) as will be explained shortly, yet the result is the same. JSON is simple and supported by all browsers, thus useful for app migration.

```
var obj = new Object(); //Object
obj.x = 1; obj.y = "a"; obj.z = true;
var arr = new Array(); //Array
arr[0] = 1; arr[1] = "a"; arr[2] = true;
var fun = function() { return 1; }
var str = "abcd";
var num = 512;                              (a)
```
⇩ to JSON
```
var obj = {"x":1,"y":"a","z":true}
var arr = [1,"a",true]
var fun = function() { return 1; }
var str = "abcd";
var num = 512;                              (b)
```

Figure 5. JSON format examples.

The process of converting a JavaScript object to a JSON format string is called *serialization* (the opposite is *deserialization*) [28]. JavaScript provides an API for serialization (*JSON.stringify()*) and for deserialization (*JSON.parse()*). So the state saving and restoring can be implemented by invoking these APIs, as explained below.

Figure 6 (a) shows a sketch of the JavaScript function, *state_save()*, invoked when clicking the save button in the browser. The function accesses each global variable property of the *window* object, serializes it using *JSON.stringify()*, and saves its name and JSON string to an array. Finally, it

state_save()
```
function state_save(window) {
  //argument is window object
  var result = new Array();
  //for store JSON result
  for (var key in window) {
    //For each JavaScript global variable
    //name key of the window object
    var json = JSON.stringify(window[key]);
    //window property (global variable) to JSON
    result.push([key,json]);
  }
  makeOutput(result);
  //make output file(snapshot.js & snapshot.html)
  //based on result
}                                              (a)
```
snapshot.js
```
var {key1} = JSON.parse(<JSON string>);
//load value stored based on <JSON string>
var {key2} = JSON.parse(<JSON string>);
...                                            (b)
```
snapshot.html
```
<html>
<head> …
<script type="text/javascript"
        src="snapshot.js"> </script> </head>
<body> </body>
</html>                                        (c)
```

Figure 6. Simplified pseudo code for *state_save()* and the snapshot JavaScript and HTML files.

creates an output file using the array. The file includes not only the JSON strings, but the JavaScript code where *JSON.parse()* is invoked for the JSON strings, as shown in Figure 6 (b). So, it is actually a JavaScript file (*snapshot.js*), and if it is invoked, the saved JavaScript state can be restored as each JSON string is deserialized to a JavaScript object.

Another part of a web app state is the DOM state. Unlike the JavaScript global objects, *JSON.stringify()* does not work for the DOM objects since the DOM tree is a native property located in the web browser. Instead, we use the *JsonML* library to convert between the DOM tree and the JSON string [21]. So, we add the JSON string for the DOM tree obtained using the *JsonML* library, and a *JsonML* library call with the string as an argument, to *snapshot.js* (see Section 4.3). When this JavaScript file is executed, the DOM tree as well as the JavaScript global objects will be restored.

An HTML file is also generated (*snapshot.html*) as in Figure 6 (c), which will do the invocation of the JavaScript file. These two snapshot files are, in actuality, a legitimate full-fledged web app runnable on any browser. That is, our approach saves the execution state of a web app A by creating a new web app A' which evolved from the original app A, but captures the execution result so far. All of the JavaScript global objects (including the function objects) and the DOM tree will be included in the snapshot JavaScript file so that they are restored when the file is executed.

Previous work also used the JSON format using the *JSON.stringify()* and generate JavaScript code for restoration [11,15]. However, they modify the original JavaScript source code by adding instrumentation statements, and run the instrumented app to save the execution state, instead of the original app. The additional code retrieves the internal information needed to serialize the app state correctly. In our scheme, we run the original app and retrieve the internal information by accessing the browser and the JavaScript engine data structures. We think this is more practical for a web platform, which often requires a browser enhanced with additional features, so adding these new access APIs to the browser will be more straightforward than instrumenting every app. Moreover, we can pursue the next step of app migration based on a binary format for faster restoration, as will be discussed later. Our approach is also more advantageous in security (see Section 4.2), and allows generalizing the snapshot for other optimization and user experience purposes (see Section 7).

There are a few issues in saving and restoring the app state, which will be discussed below.

4. Issues for Saving and Restoring the App State

The previous section overviews our approach to saving and restoring the app state. There are a few technical issues to be solved, which will be presented in this section.

4.1 Object Reference Alias Problem

The existing *JSON.stringify()* cannot keep the original object reference information when it serializes an object to a JSON string, which can cause an alias problem when we deserialize, as often complained by the web programmers [19,20,22].

For example, the two variables, *obj1* and *obj2* in Figure 7 (a) point to the same object, but when they are serialized by *JSON.stringify()* as in Figure 7 (b), they are represented by two separate JSON strings. The problem is that when they are deserialized, they will be restored to two separate objects, which can make the program behave differently as shown in Figure 7. A similar problem can occur for a circular object structure as *obj3* in Figure 7 (a) where a property of an object points to itself; serialization for the object will fail with an exception as shown in Figure 7 (b) since it cannot handle recursive serialization.

```
var obj1 = new Object(); obj1.x = 1; obj1.y = 2;
var obj2 = obj1;
var obj3 = new Object(); obj3.x = 1; obj3.y = 2;
obj3.z = obj3;

alert(obj1 == obj2) // print "true"
alert(obj3 == obj3.z) // print "true"              (a)
```
snapshot.js   ⬇ State Save
```
var obj1 = JSON.parse('{"x":1, "y":2}');
var obj2 = JSON.parse('{"x":1, "y":2}');
alert(obj1 == obj2) // print "false"

var obj3  = JSON.parse('{"x":1, "y":2,
                     "z":{"x":1, "y":2, "z": … …
                                          Error    (b)
```

Figure 7. Reference alias and circular reference problems.

These problems occur since the original reference information is lost during serialization. So, we must keep track of the reference information when we save, to avoid duplicate serialization. We use an array of references, *sobj_ref[]*, to save *unique* objects during serialization. We define the same-sized array, *dobj_ref[]*, in the output JavaScript file to restore only those objects in *sobj_ref[]*, which are then assigned to global variables for correct deserialization.

```
JSON.stringify = function(arg) {
  if(arg.isObject()) {
    var index = sobj_ref.indexOf(arg);
    //check if arg is already in sobj_ref
    if(index == -1) { //arg is not in sobj_ref
      index = sobj_ref.push(arg); //register arg to sobj_ref
      var json = toJSON(arg); //serialize arg to JSON string
                        //(recursively for its properties)
      sobj_ref_value[index] = json;
    }
    return "dobj_ref[" +index + "]";
    //return string with dobj_ref index
  }
  … code for handling types other than an object …
}
```

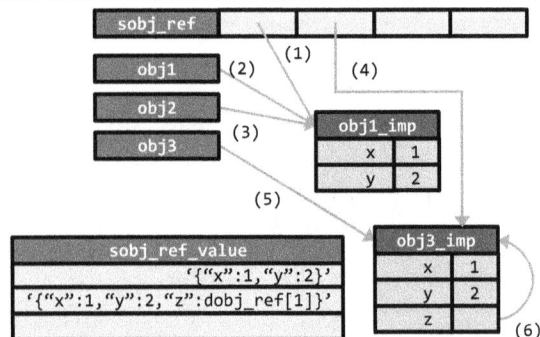

Figure 8. Pseudo code of JSON.stringfy() and an example using a reference array (*sobj_ref[]*) for Figure 7.

Figure 8 shows the modified *JSON.stringify()* using an array of references, *sobj_ref[]*. For each object we save its reference in this array, before we serialize/save its JSON string in *sobj_ref_value[]*. If an object reference is already available in the array, the object is not serialized. For the examples in Figure 7, we add the reference *obj1* to *sobj_ref[0]* and serialize/save its JSON string in *sobj_ref_value[0]*. Since the reference *obj2* is already in the array, we do not serialize it. We remember both variables correspond to index 0. For the circular object *obj3*, we add the reference to *sobj_ref[1]*, serialize/save the object in *sobj_ref_value[1]*, and remember the variable is in index 1. During the serialization of *obj3*, we can find that the property *z* is a reference to index 1, so we do not serialize recursively but saves *dobj_ref[1]* instead. This is illustrated in Figure 8. Now, *JSON.stringify()* for each object with an index *i* will return the "*dobj_ref[i]*" string to *state_save()*, which is then saved with its name (*key*) so that "*var key=dobj_ref[i];*" is printed in the output JavaScript file, as explained below.

The *dobj_ref[]* array is first declared in the snapshot JavaScript file as in Figure 9. Each array element is initialized by the object deserialized from the JSON string saved in the same-index element of *sobj_ref_value[]*. We then generate "*var key=dobj_ref[i];*" for each variable, which will restore the same state of objects.

```
var dobj_ref = new Array();
dobj_ref[0] = JSON.parse('{"x":1, "y":2}');
dobj_ref[1] = JSON.parse('{"x":1, "y":2,
                           "z":dobj_ref[1]}');

var obj1 = dobj_ref[0];
var obj2 = dobj_ref[0];
var obj3 = dobj_ref[1];
```

Figure 9. Snapshot JavaScript code using *dobj_ref[]*.

4.2 Saving Closure Function and Closure Variables

JavaScript treats functions as an object (first-class functions), so it allows functions to be passed as an argument or a return value and to be assigned to a variable. It also allows inner functions so that a function can be defined inside another function. A special inner function which accesses the local variables declared in its enclosing outer functions is called a *closure function*, and the outer function's variable is called a *closure variable*.

```
function createPerson() {
  var name = "alice";
  // local variable of outer function
  return {
    getName : function() { return name; },
    setName : function(n) { name = n; }
  };
};

var person = createPerson();
alert(person.getName()); //current name is "alice"
person.setName("bob");
alert(person.getName()); //current name is "bob"
```

Figure 10. An example of closure.

Figure 10 shows an example. The function *createPerson()* returns an object with *getName()* and *setName()* functions as its properties. These inner functions can access the variable, *name*, declared in the outer function, so they are closure functions and *name* is a closure variable. One issue is that when we invoke *person.getName()* or *person.setName()* after *person=createPerson();* is executed in Figure 10, the variable *name* will be inaccessible since it is a local variable of *createPerson()*, finished by then. So, the JavaScript engine keeps the closure variables even after the outer function finished, by making a scope chain for the closure functions (*getName()* and *setName()*) which includes the outer function's execution context.

Figure 11 depicts the structure of objects and the scope chain in the V8 JavaScript engine after the JavaScript code in Figure 10 completes. The object *person* has two property objects, *getName()* and *setName()*. Both functions point to the same scope chain via the *context* pointer, where the closure variable, *name*, is accessible.

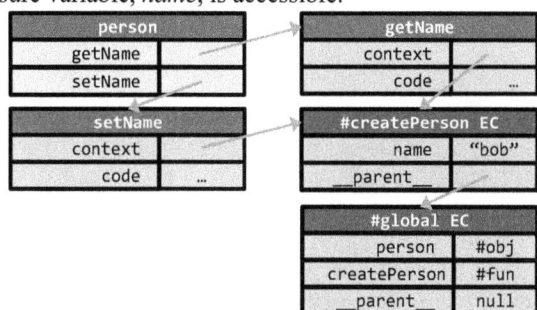

Figure 11. V8 implementation of the closure example.

Now, the problem is how to serialize the *person* object, hence the *getName()* and *setName()* objects. If we invoke *JSON.stringify()* for the global variable *person*, it can serialize *getName()* and *setName()* only, but not the closure variable, *name*. This is so because *JSON.stringify()* can serialize only the properties of an object, while the variable *name* is not a property of the *getName()* or the *setName()* object, but some property of the JavaScript engine. So, the restoration of the app state using deserialization can only recovers the closure functions, not closure variables, so we need a more elaborate, special way of serialization.

When we serialize a function object, we need to check if it is a closure function. If so, we need to obtain the current values of its closure variables. We also need to check if it shares the same scope chain with other closure functions to see if they have the same outer function instance. Based on these checks, we can identify all closure functions, the value of all closure variables, and their relationship. We added APIs to the browser to access these data.

Now we generate the snapshot JavaScript code for the closures. The only way to restore the closure variables and functions as in the original object state, especially with the scope chain, is simply regenerating them using the outer function call. So, for those closure functions sharing the same scope chain (thus the same closure variables), we construct an outer function object with the closure variables initialized to the current values and make an *anonymous* call to return an object with the closure functions as properties.

Figure 12 shows the JavaScript snapshot code to handle the closure functions and variables in Figure 10. It has an outer, anonymous function with the closure variable *name* initialized to the saved value "*bob*". An anonymous call is

made for this outer function, creating an object *closure1* with *func1* and *func2* as its properties. These two closure function objects are saved to *dobj_ref[]* array as previously, and the global variable *person* is restored using these objects. The closure variable is now accessible when the restored closure functions are invoked.

```
var dobj_ref = new Array();
dobj_ref[0] = JSON.parse('function() {var name = … }');
var createPerson = dobj_ref[0];

dobj_ref[1] = null;dobj_ref[2] = null;dobj_ref[3] = null;
//references used for closure recovery are initialized to null

var closure1 = function () {
   var name = "bob";
   return {
      func1 : function() { return name; },
      func2 : function(n) { name = n; }
   };
}();
dobj_ref[2] = closure1.func1; dobj_ref[3] = closure1.func2;
dobj_ref[1] = JSON.parse('{"getName" : dobj_ref[2],
                           "setName" : dobj_ref[3]}');
var person = dobj_ref[1];
```

Figure 12. Snapshot JavaScript code for the closure example.

Closures are tricky to save, yet they are used frequently in web apps. In our *tetris* example in Figure 2, an inner function, *gameLoop()*, is defined inside the outer *tetris.play()* function (line 17-26). The outer function defines a variable *me* which is used inside the inner function, so *gameLoop()* is a closure function and *me* is a closure variable. Actually, when *play()* is executed, it registers a timer event with *gameLoop()* as a handler, which will make *gameLoop()* be executed after a given time (*this.speed*). When *gameLoop()* executes, it moves down the current block using the closure variable *me* and then register a timer event again with itself. This makes *gameLoop()* executes repeatedly without a loop, which is a typical way for web apps to invoke a timer event handler repeatedly. We will see shortly how to save *gameLoop()* and register a timer event with it in the snapshot of the Tetris app (see Figure 14).

Actually, closures are used more heavily due to its advantage of *data encapsulation*. That is, many objects that would otherwise be declared as global variables are declared as local variables of an anonymous outer function. When the outer function executes, the local objects become closure variables, residing only in the internal data structure of the JavaScript engine, thus not accessible from the global variables of the app. Our Tetris app can be programmed in a form of *(function() {var tetris = {…, init=function{..}, play=function{..}}; tetris.init();})();* where *tetris* is now a closure variable (because *gameLoop()* accesses *me* which points to *tetris*), and then there is no global variable at all. If instrumentation were used as in the previous work [15], the *tetris* object would be accessible from some global variables added by instrumentation, compromising the data encapsulation (for example, a third-party widget which shares the same browser session with the instrumented Tetris app can access the *tetris* object via the app's global variables). In fact, most JavaScript framework implement its internal objects by closures. For the jQuery framework, *jQuery* (or $) is the only global object and its internal objects are data-encapsulated using closures [17]. For the Enyo framework, *enyo* is the only global object and all other objects including even the programmer-created objects can be implemented by closures [10]. Instrumentation would expose these framework objects to the outside as well.

4.3 DOM Tree and DOM Reference Variable

Everything depicted on the screen during the app execution is a DOM object. In our *tetris* app example, a block made of four rectangle DOM objects is shown with HTML in Figure 2 (line 7-10). We need to save the DOM objects when we save an app state.

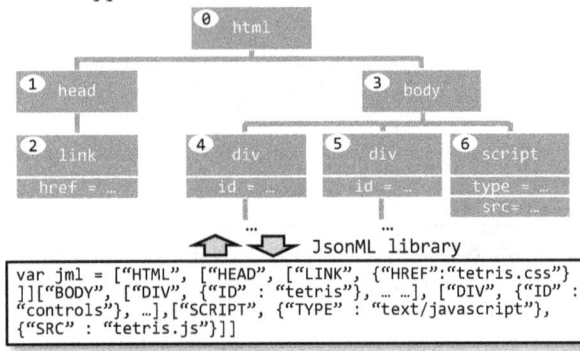

```
var jml = ["HTML", ["HEAD", ["LINK", {"HREF":"tetris.css"}
]]["BODY", ["DIV", {"ID" : "tetris"}, ... ...], ["DIV", {"ID" :
"controls"}, ...],["SCRIPT", {"TYPE" : "text/javascript"},
{"SRC" : "tetris.js"}]]
```

Figure 13. A JsonML example.

Since *JSON.stringify()* can serialize only JavaScript global variables, we save the DOM tree using the JsonML library. JsonML can serialize the DOM objects into the JSON format and deserialize the JSON string to the DOM objects. So, *state_save()* will invoke *JSON.stringify()* for JavaScript global variables and invoke JsonML for the DOM tree. Figure 13 shows the JSON format of a DOM tree. The tags, attributes, and contents are saved in the JSON format, which is assigned to a JavaScript variable in the *snapshot.js*.

One issue is that some JavaScript global variable (or its properties) may reference a DOM object using a DOM API (e.g., *tetris.controls = document.getElementById("controls")* to point to the control panel in the Tetris app), for interaction between DOM and JavaScript. Since the whole DOM tree is already serialized by JsonML, we do not have to serialize the DOM object referenced by the variable separately. The only requirement is that when the DOM tree is restored, the DOM-reference JavaScript variable should reference a correct, restored DOM object.

To handle this requirement, we perform a preorder traversal of the DOM tree during *state_save()* and save the reference of each DOM object in an array. Then, for each DOM reference variable, we save the index number of the array that matches its reference. Figure 13 shows the preorder index for each node.

When we restore the DOM tree, we also perform a preorder traversal for the restored DOM tree and save the reference of each DOM object in an array (i.e., *jsonML.DOM[]* in Figure 14). Now, each DOM reference variable is initialized by the array element value whose index matches the saved index number of the variable. This traversal and initialization is done by the JavaScript code in the *snapshot.js* (i.e., *jsonML.traverse(document)* in Figure 14).

Some DOM object referenced by a JavaScript variable might not exist in the DOM tree, though. For example, if the

createElement() DOM API is used in the JavaScript code, the DOM object is created yet is not in the DOM tree unless it is explicitly added by *appendChild()*. There are cases where the DOM object not in the DOM tree can be useful. For example, if an image DOM object is downloaded at runtime and is added to the DOM tree, there might be a delay in displaying the image because of the network traffic. Instead, the image can be accessed and created as a DOM object in the JavaScript code as early as possible to reduce the delay. We need to serialize these DOM objects separately using JsonML in *state_save()*.

4.4 Event Handler

After the loading of web apps, event-driven computation proceeds such that event handlers (JavaScript functions) are executed when events occur. For app migration, we need to save the current state of the events and the event handlers, which will then be restored after migration. One problem is that events are not accessible from the *window* object unlike global variables because events are not the properties of the *window* object. Events are actually maintained by the browser in its event queue, so we need to access the browser to find which events are registered and on wait. We re-register those events with the event handlers when we restore the app state.

Some event handlers are implemented by anonymous functions (e.g., *setTimeout(function(){...}, 1000);*, which makes an event fire after 1000ms and be handled by a function with no name), instead of a JavaScript global function. JavaScript global functions will be serialized when we make a snapshot. However, an anonymous function cannot be accessed by any JavaScript global variable, so we need to access the browser to find those anonymous event handlers and include them in the JavaScript snapshot file (e.g., *dobj_ref[i]=function(){...};).* We also need to register the event again (e.g., *setTimeout(dobj_ref[i], remaining time);).* There are two types of events: DOM event and Timer event.

4.4.1 DOM Event

A DOM event is a mouse-click or a keyboard-press event associated with a DOM tree node. For example, when you click a mouse for the *Tetris* app for the control panel, a DOM event associated with the "*controls*" DOM object (referenced by *tetris.controls*) occurs; it will invoke the registered event handler, *cb()*, for rotation or fast downward movement of the current block (it should be noted that *cb()* itself is a local variable which will disappear, so it should be handled as an anonymous event handler as described above).

We can attach a DOM event handler to a DOM tree node in the HTML tag (e.g., *<element onclick = "SomeJavaSciprtCode">*) or in the JavaScript code (e.g., *object.onclick=function(){...};* after obtaining the *object* using a DOM API function as in *object = document.getElementbyId("..");).* This will attach an event to the DOM tree node as an attribute. So, when we serialize the DOM tree, we check if there is an event associated with each node and generate a JavaScript statement to register an event handler (e.g., *JsonML.DOM[4].onkeydown = dobj_ref[5];* in Figure 14). There is one more way of attaching an event handler in the JavaScript code via *addEventListner()* (e.g., *object.addEventListner("click", function);*), yet this event handler is not attached to a DOM tree node as an attribute. For finding this type of event handlers and saving them, we made a special API.

4.4.2 Timer Event

A timer event is registered using a JavaScript API function. It is either an event that calls the event handler once after a given amount of time (*setTimeout(handler, time)*), or an event that calls the event handler repeatedly on a given interval (*setInterval(handler, interval)*). Registered timer events and their corresponding handlers are maintained by the browser, so they cannot be accessed from the *window* object and no APIs are provided to access them in the JavaScript specification. So, we made a new JavaScript API to be called from *state_save()* when we make a snapshot. The API accesses the current timer event list in the browser to return the current timer events registered, their corresponding event handlers, the event registration time, and the event firing time. In the JavaScript snapshot file, we generate the JavaScript code that registers these timer events, after computing the correct remaining time.

4.4.3 AJAX Event

AJAX is for asynchronous communication with the server. We create an XMLHttpRequest (XHR) object, make a server request after registering a call-back function as an event handler, and continue execution. When an answer comes from the server, an event occurs, executing the call-back function. If we need to migrate the app before the answer comes from the server, there will be a problem. To handle this, we made a new API to collect the current state of all XHR objects, so that we can make all pending requests again after migration and restoration.

5. Implementation

When we press the save button of the extension, the *state_save()* JavaScript function will be executed. Pressing the save button, in actuality, works as a timer event, so it is registered in the event queue of the browser (it is equivalent to executing *setTimeout(state_save(), 0)* with the timeout of zero second). When the browser dequeues the event immediately, it will invoke *state_save()* as an event handler. It should be noted that a JavaScript event handler is executed in a single-threaded manner such that only one JavaScript function is executed at a time during the app execution. So, when *state_save()* is executed, no other JavaScript function is in execution, meaning that neither the JavaScript global variables nor the DOM tree can be changed during the saving, and no event is fired. This will save the app state correctly.

Two files are created as a result of executing *state_save()*: one JavaScript file and one HTML file. The JavaScript file includes the JSON-based state restoration code and the event handlers. The HTML file simply calls the JavaScript file and loads the CSS of the original app. The two files can be stored

on the local storage or delivered to the server or the remote device, depending on the purpose of the snapshot.

The DOM tree is saved first after the indexing of DOM-tree nodes based on the preorder traversal is made. Then, the global variables of the *window* object is stored in the JSON format, with the DOM reference variables and other variables being saved separately in the file. Other states are saved including the JavaScript code to restore the DOM/time events and their corresponding event handlers.

For state restoration, we simply execute the snapshot HTML file, which, in turn, executes the JavaScript file thru the script tag in the HTML file. The *window* object's global variables other than the DOM reference variables will be restored first from the JSON format string included in the JavaScript file. Then, the DOM tree will be restored so that the DOM objects are allocated. Preorder traversal of the DOM tree is made to get the reference of the DOM objects, which are then assigned to the DOM reference variables. Finally, the timer events and the DOM events are restored to complete the restoration of the app state.

Figure 14 shows a sketch of the snapshot HTML and JavaScript files for Tetris, saved in the middle of execution.

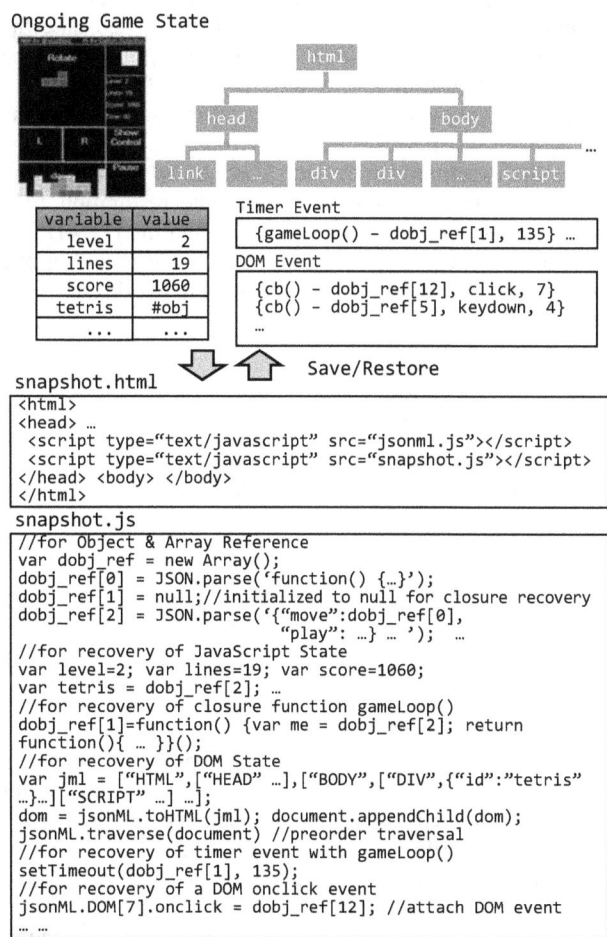

Figure 14. Snapshot JavaScript and HTML for Tetris app.

6. Evaluation

This section evaluates the proposed app migration framework, which works correctly for three apps currently.

6.1 Experimental Environment

The web apps we used for evaluation are listed in Table 1, with the video clips to illustrate app migration between browsers. They are game apps which manipulate the DOM tree using the event handlers, showing a dynamic behaviour.

Table 1. Sample web application (video clip at goo.gl/dVF5kZ)

A	Tetris (tetris.alexkessinger.net)
B	Sokoban (www.lutanho.net/play/sokoban.html)
C	Bunny Hunt (www.themaninblue.com/experiment/BunnyHunt)

We experimented with the X86 desktop and the ARM embedded board. The desktop has the i7-2600 3.4GHz CPU with 4GB memory, and the embedded board has the ARM Cortex-A8 1GHz CPU with 1GB memory. We use the Chrome browser r128665 with V8 JavaScript engine v3.9.24.

6.2 State Saving and Restoration Time Overhead

The app migration would be useful when the state restoring/saving time overhead is reasonable. For each app, we save and restore the app after running it for around 20 seconds. We repeat the experiment 10 times and take the average time overhead (since the exact save point would be slightly different from run to run).

Figure 15 shows the time overhead of each app for the x86 desktop and the ARM board environment. The save time means the execution time of the *state_save()* after pressing the saving button of the extension. The restoration time means the loading time spent for executing the HTML file. The time overhead even for embedded board is within one second, which do not make users feel a big overhead.

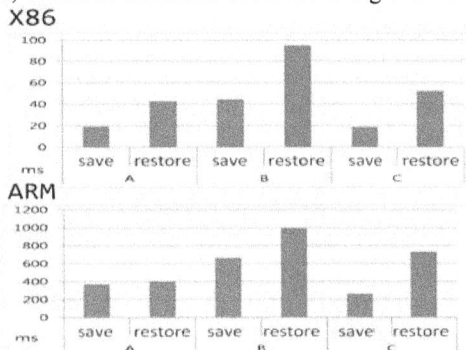

Figure 15. Save/restore time (ms) of our framework.

6.3 Snapshot File Size

Figure 16 shows the file size of the snapshot for each app and the distribution of the HTML, CSS, and JavaScript portions, compared to the original app. The HTML tags in the app source file are reduced to a single HTML tag to invoke the JS file in the snapshot, as shown in Figure 14, so the HTML portion is minimal.

The JavaScript portion increases significantly since it now includes the DOM tree in the JSON format. For the same DOM tree, the size of the HTML tags and the size of the JSON string would be similar (less than 5% difference in size). As the app execution proceeds, however, the DOM tree can be expanded as more nodes are added by the JavaScript code execution, so the corresponding JSON string is larger than the original HTML tags. Figure 16 shows that the JavaScript portion generally increases more than the reduced portion of the original HTML tags due to the expanded DOM tree. The increase is pronounced for the B app since its DOM objects were added significantly by the time when we take a snapshot.

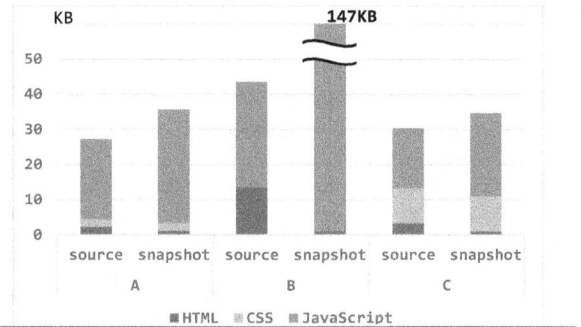

Figure 16. Size (KB) of app source and snapshot files.

6.4 Portion of State Save/Restoration

Figure 17 shows the distribution of the saving time (execution time of the *state_save()*) among the saving of the DOM tree, the saving of the JavaScript variables, and the saving of others (etc.) which includes the saving of the events, the event handlers, and the file I/O time. A larger DOM tree in the B app also makes the DOM saving time larger than the saving time of the JavaScript variables.

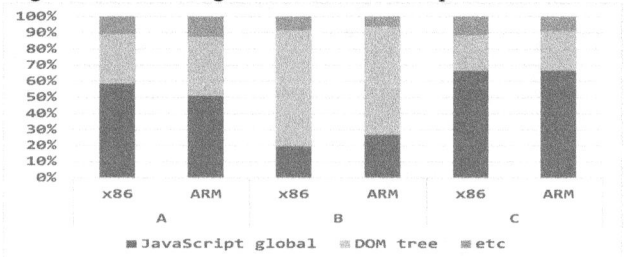

Figure 17. Saving time distribution.

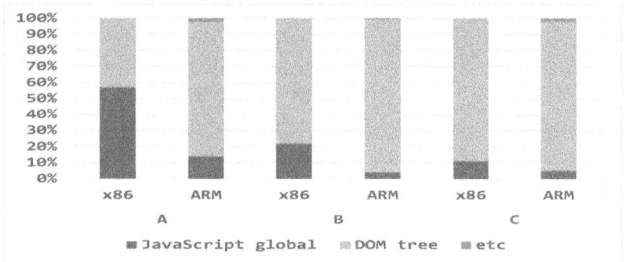

Figure 18. Restoration time distribution.

Figure 18 shows the same distribution of the restoration time of the app state from the snapshot. The etc. portion in Figure 18 also includes the file I/O time which is much smaller than that in Figure 17 because the file write takes much longer than the file read. One thing to note is that for the DOM objects the ARM restoration time is larger than the x86 restoration time. DOM restoration requires the invocation of the DOM and JsonML APIs, and it appears that the ARM Chrome browser is less optimized than the x86 Chrome browser. The restoration of the DOM tree of the C app takes a larger portion than the saving, and the C app displays image files unlike others, which might affect the DOM restoration overhead.

6.5 Number of Objects Saved and Restored

Table 2 shows the number of objects saved and restored for each app, for each type of objects discussed in this paper. It shows the number of JavaScript global objects created by the programmer (a). The number of closure functions is also shown (b). The number of DOM objects in the DOM tree (c) and the number of DOM reference variables (d) are also included, with the number of DOM objects not included in the DOM tree (e). Finally, the table shows the number of the timer events (f) and the DOM events (g) when we make a snapshot, which is the same as the number of event handlers saved. We did not see an example of circular references, but we saw a reference alias problem in the C app.

Table 2. Number of Objects Saved.

	(a)	(b)	(c)	(d)	(e)	(f)	(g)
A	109	4	59	23	0	2	2
B	61	16	786	0	14	0	17
C	35	4	56	4	16	7	5

Our sample apps do not use a web framework such as jQuery [17], Enyo [10], or ExtJS [27]. If an app is programmed using a framework, many API function objects will be created at the framework initialization time. We can save these objects in the snapshot with other app objects and migrate (this would work since we can save the framework objects in the binary form and restore [36]). Or, since most framework objects are functions unlikely to be changed by the programmer, we can save the minimum objects but invoke the framework initialization in the snapshot to re-create most framework objects at the target (as we do for JavaScript built-in objects which are not saved in the snapshot file but re-created on the target JavaScript engine when it is initialized). We might need to handle cases when the programmer adds his own APIs to the framework or when the APIs are invoked for a DOM object accessed via the framework. These are left as a future work.

7. Other Usage of the Snapshot

As mentioned before, our snapshot is a complete web app in itself. Compared to the original app, it is another app whose execution can restore the saved state and continue its execution. We can exploit the snapshot for other purposes.

The snapshot can be used for accelerating the app *launch time*. If the same job is repeated during the app launch time (e.g., initialization of the web framework such as jQuery), we can save the launched state as a snapshot and start from the snapshot when launching an app to reduce the launch time. For faster restoration, however, the JavaScript objects would better be saved in a binary form as they are in the heap,

rather than the JSON-based text form; the binary form of objects just need to be copied and relocated to the heap, while they need to be created by the execution of the JSON-based JavaScript code. We actually implemented this idea and found that app launch time can be reduced by 20% [36].

A snapshot can be used as a swap space in the web platform. That is, if there are too many apps running on a browser, the oldest app is forced to be deleted from the job queue, losing its current state. Instead, we can make a snapshot and save for the deleted job. When the job is restarted, its last state can be restored from the snapshot.

When we distribute a complex app (e.g., rich internet application), we can deliver it in a snapshot form after fully setting-up based on the customer's request. This can free the customer from time-consuming, complicated set-up process.

Web browsers save the URL for the bookmark or the history, so any dynamic change made for a web page is lost when we revisit it via the bookmark. If we save the snapshot instead, we can restore the exact same page when we revisit.

Another use of the snapshot is a new-type of app that can be *shared* and executed by multiple users. For example, when a group of people want to schedule a meeting, instead of using a scheduling site such as doodle.com, one person runs a scheduling app to mark his schedule and passes its snapshot to the next person, who then runs the snapshot to mark his and passes. In this way, an app in execution is circulated among multiple users, leading to a new collaborative user experience.

Finally, the snapshot can be used for *off-loading*. If an app includes some time-consuming computations for an event handler, we take a snapshot just before handling the event and send the snapshot to the server for faster execution. We take a snapshot again after the execution and send it back to the client for continuous execution. Our snapshot would make the communication and coordination overhead smaller than the one used in the Android platform [5].

The last two usages will generate the snapshot repeatedly, so the instrumentation approach would be too costly.

8. Related Work

Snapshot has originally been introduced for the database [1], but it has also been used to save the state of applications or the virtual machines for diverse purposes.

VMware employs job migration to send an app from the smartphone to the desktop so that the computation is made at the desktop and the result is sent back to the smartphone using the VMware image [34]. However, the VMware is a system VM, which includes the whole Linux image, so the memory overhead would be large for efficient job migration.

Process hibernation saves an intermediate state of the OS booting procedure repeated in every OS booting to reduce the booting time [23]. However, hibernation saves all the processes at once, not suitable to save a single app state.

There is a research work for saving the Java VM state and migrating it [30]. It saves the state of the Java heap and the stack during the interpretation of a Java application. A similar technique would not be applicable to saving an app state though, because it does not deal with app-specific activities such as event handling.

There are three researches for saving the web app's state, similarly to ours. *V8 serialization* saves the heap where the JavaScript objects created during the initialization of the V8 engine exist. Now the engine can start faster by restoring the serialized state [32]. This is for saving and restoring the initialized state of the JavaScript engine only, not a whole app including the DOM tree and the events.

Bellucci et al. [11] proposed to save the JavaScript and the DOM state using the JSON format for app migration. They solved the object reference alias problem similarly to ours. However, they provided no solution to save the closure variables, which occur frequently in real web apps and play an important role for data encapsulation, thus incomplete.

Lo et al. [15] completed the Bellucci's work by providing a solution to save the closure variables and event handlers. Their solution for closures is adding additional JavaScript code to create a scope object and save the closure variable as a property of the object. Then, whenever a closure variable is updated in a closure function, the object property is also made to be updated with additional code. Finally, the scope object is saved as a property of the closure function, which allows retrieving the current value of the closure variable when the closure function is saved in the snapshot. Event handling is also solved using additional code which manages the events using some wrapper functions (otherwise there is no way to access the browser event queue). This instrumentation-based approach is different from ours which accesses the browser and the JavaScript engine internals. One problem of instrumented app, apart from the instrumentation and space overhead, is that the closure objects that the programmer wants to hide at runtime (they are supposed to exist only at the scope chain of the JavaScript engine) are exposed through the scope objects via global variables, causing a security issue, as discussed in Section 4.2. Also, their snapshot is not appropriate for other optimizations and usages in Section 7.

There is also a research effort to restore a web app's state based on capture-and-replay [16]. They log all the events occurred during the app execution, so as to restore the app state by replaying the saved events one by one. This is useful for debugging and performance evaluation. However, restoration can complete only after all saved events are handled, so it would not be appropriate for app migration because the restoration overhead including the file size would be high, proportional to the running time before we capture. Logging and replaying is done by the client-side JavaScript, but is also done by a modified browser [35].

9. Summary and Future Work

Web platform is expected to become a viable app platform in a near future due to its advantage of portability and app productivity. As other app platforms, web platform is also expected to be available in diverse smart devices. One issue is how to benefit from these connected devices, installed with the same platform. The current wisdom appears to exploit the cloud service for sharing "static" digital contents such as pictures, audios, videos, and app binaries among those devices. One question is if the sharing can be extended to more of "dynamic" contents, more dynamic than PS4 Remote Play [26], AirPlay [3], or DLNA [8] which share at best the dynamic screen display of the static contents.

One good candidate that we propose to share is the app execution state. That is, if we share the app execution state among diverse devices so that the same app can be executed continuously and seamlessly, it would lead to a new user experience. This app migration will be simpler in the web platform due to its source code-based distribution and JSON-based data sharing between applications. We proposed a framework to save and restore the execution state of a web app with a snapshot based on the JavaScript code and the JSON strings. Unlike previous work with instrumentation, we save the state of an original app and access the browser internals to retrieve closures and events for correct saving. We showed app migration works for three apps.

The reason why we think app migration is valid is as follows. Since   an app by definition is small unlike a full application, the program state to save would be small. Also, the data used by an app is often available in the server if they are huge (e.g., for a map app, the map database itself is in the server, and the video/audio/picture files will be in the cloud server), and the app is just for the client-side display, so the client-side data state to save would also be small. So, app migration would requires a small overhead, yet it can give a new, interesting user experience. Apple Inc. has recently announced a similar idea called *handoff* for sharing apps between iPhone and iMac with new APIs [4].

There are still challenges left. One is accelerating the app migration, especially the app restoration. If the same web platform (CPU, OS, browser, JavaScript engine) is installed both at the source device and at the target device, faster restoration would be possible if we migrate the JavaScript objects in a binary form as they are in the heap, rather than the JSON-based JavaScript code, as we did for the launch-time optimization in Section 7. Space overhead would be higher, but not much, because some duplication in the JSON-based objects can be removed in the binary form (*e.g., var c ; function a(){ function b(){..} c=b ;} a();* where JSON-based snapshot include duplicated function strings for *b* and *c*, while binary-based snapshot include a single function object pointed by both *b* and *c*).

There will be more issues to be solved to save the state correctly, especially for HTML5 objects such as Application Cache, Local Storage, Canvas, or Video. We think that the state of most apps even with these objects is still local to the client browser, hence being savable by our technique, using the existing APIs or additional new APIs to access the browser. These are left as a future work.

Acknowledgements

This work was supported by the IT R&D program of MOTIE/KEIT [10045344, Development of Optimized Virtual Machine Acceleration Engine for Web Application Platform].

References

[1] M. Adiba and B. Lindsay. "Database snapshots." Proceedings of the sixth international conference on Very Large Data Bases, 1980.

[2] Adobe Flash runtime. http://www.adobe.com/products/flashruntimes.html

[3] Airplay. https://www.apple.com/airplay/

[4] Apple Handoff, Apple Worldwide Developers Conference (WWDC) 2014, https://developer.apple.com/videos/wwdc/2014/, Jun 2014.

[5] B. Chun et. al, CloneCloud: elastic execution between mobile device and cloud. In Proceedings of the sixth conference on Computer systems (EuroSys '11). 2011.

[6] Browser extension. http://en.wikipedia.org/wiki/Browser_extension

[7] D. Lee. JXON: an Architecture for Schema and Annotation Driven JSON/XML Bidirectional Transformations. In Proceedings of Balisage: The Markup Conference 2011.

[8] DLNA. http://www.dlna.org/

[9] Dropbox. https://www.dropbox.com

[10] Enyojs. http://enyojs.com

[11] F. Bellucci et. al, Engineering JavaScript state persistence of web applications migrating across multiple devices. In Proceedings of the 3rd ACM SIGCHI symposium on Engineering interactive computing systems (EICS '11). 2011.

[12] Firefox OS. http://www.mozilla.org/en-US/firefox/os

[13] G. Wang. Improving Data Transmission in Web Applications via the Translation between XML and JSON. In Proceedings of the 2011 Third International Conference on Communications and Mobile Computing (CMC '11). 2011.

[14] HTML5. http://www.w3.org/TR/html5/

[15] J. Lo et. al, Imagen: runtime migration of browser sessions for javascript web applications. In Proceedings of the 22nd international conference on World Wide Web (WWW '13). 2013.

[16] J. Mickens, J. Elson, and J. Howell. Mugshot: deterministic capture and replay for Javascript applications. In Proceedings of Networked Systems Design and Implementation, pages 159-174, 2010.

[17] jQuery. http://www.jquery.com

[18] JSON. http://www.json.org

[19] Json.NET - Preserving Object References. http://james.newtonking.com/json/help/index.html

[20] JSON-Circular. https://github.com/StewartAtkins/JSON-Circular

[21] JsonML. http://www.jsonml.org/

[22] JSON-R: A JSON Extension That Deals With Object References (Circular And Others). http://java.dzone.com/articles/json-r-json-extension-deals

[23] K. Baik et. al. Boosting up Embedded Linux device: experience on Linux-based Smartphone. In proceedings of the Linux Symposium. 2010.

[24] N. Nurseitov et al,. Comparison of JSON and XML Data Interchange Formats: A Case Study. In Proceedings of CAINE, 9, 157-162. 2009.

[25] Offline Tetris. http://tetris.alexkessinger.net/

[26] PS4 Remote Play. https://support.us.playstation.com/app/answers/detail/a_id/5065/~/ps4-remote-play-and-second-screen

[27] Ext JS. http://www.sencha.com/products/extjs

[28] Serialization. http://en.wikipedia.org/wiki/Serialization

[29] Sync tabs across devices. https://support.google.com/chrome/answer/2591582?hl=en

[30] Takashi Suezawa. Persistent execution state of a Java virtual machine. In Proceedings of the ACM 2000 conference on Java Grande (JAVA '00). 2000.

[31] Tizen. https://www.tizen.org

[32] V8 snapshot. https://developers.google.com/v8/embed

[33] webOS. http://www.openwebosproject.org

[34] Y.-Y. Su and J. Flinn. Slingshot: deploying stateful services in wireless hotspots. In Proceedings of the 3rd international conference on Mobile systems, applications, and services (MobiSys '05). 2005.

[35] B. Burg et al, Interactive record/replay for web application debugging. Proceedings of the 26th annual ACM symposium on User interface software and technology. 2013.

[36] J. Oh and S. Moon, Snapshot-based Loading-Time Acceleration for Web Applications. In Proceedings of the ACM/IEEE International Symposium on Code Generation and Optimization (CGO 2015). 2015

AppSec: A Safe Execution Environment for Security Sensitive Applicationst

Jianbao Ren

Xi'an Jiaotong University
renjianbao@stu.xjtu.edu.cn

Yong Qi

Xi'an Jiaotong University
qiy@mail.xjtu.edu.cn

Yuehua Dai

Xi'an Jiaotong University
xjtudso@stu.xjtu.edu.cn

Xiaoguang Wang

Xi'an Jiaotong University
mailwxg@foxmail.com

Yi Shi

Xi'an Jiaotong University
shiyi@mail.xjtu.edu.cn

Abstract

Malicious OS kernel can easily access user's private data in main memory and pries human-machine interaction data, even one that employs privacy enforcement based on application level or OS level. This paper introduces AppSec, a hypervisor-based safe execution environment, to protect both the memory data and human-machine interaction data of security sensitive applications from the untrusted OS transparently.

AppSec provides several security mechanisms on an untrusted OS. AppSec introduces a safe loader to check the code integrity of application and dynamic shared objects. During runtime, AppSec protects application and dynamic shared objects from being modified and verifies kernel memory accesses according to application's intention. AppSec provides a devices isolation mechanism to prevent the human-machine interaction devices being accessed by compromised kernel. On top of that, AppSec further provides a privileged-based window system to protect application's X resources. The major advantages of AppSec are threefold. First, AppSec verifies and protects all dynamic shared objects during runtime. Second, AppSec mediates kernel memory access according to application's intention but does not encrypts all application's data roughly. Third, AppSec provides a trusted I/O path from end-user to application. A prototype of AppSec is implemented and shows that AppSec is efficient and practical.

VEE '15, March 14–15, 2015, Istanbul, Turkey..
Copyright © 2015 ACM 978-1-4503-3450-1/15/03... $15.00.
http://dx.doi.org/10.1145/2731186.2731199

Categories and Subject Descriptors D.4.6 [*Operating Systems*]: Security and Protection

General Terms Design, Security, Performance

Keywords Privacy, VMM, Kernel, Human-machine interaction

1. Introduction

Operating system controls all system resources and is the root of trust, so compromising the OS compromises everything on the system. Compromised OS can freely get our sensitive information through accessing main memory or intercepting human-machine interaction. If an application could remain safe even if OS were compromised, then OS exploits would no longer have the security threats as today.

Previous works on untrusted OS mainly focus on memory data and simply isolate trusted code and data from OS kernel [11, 27, 36, 37] or encrypts all data flowing to kernel roughly [15, 16, 31, 48]. Applications and OS either need to be re-designed or compiled statically. Besides, this arbitrary encryption may make applications unusable. For example, a web browser whose data is encrypted by the privacy protection mechanism can not communicate with web servers which does not run the corresponding decryptor. Although some applications can operate on encrypted data [10, 40, 46], cryptographic schemes for general-purpose computing [28, 29] have severe performance overhead and some data cannot be encrypted, like keyboard input and screen output.

Because human-machine interaction data is processed in plaintext, protections are still incapable without considering the security of human-machine interaction. Some dedicated work has been done to enforce the human-machine interaction [17, 23, 50]. However, they either need to modify the device drivers to eliminate any dependencies on the OS kernel or hinder applications communicating with others. That is tedious and difficult to port on different systems.

This paper introduces AppSec, a hypervisor-based system in which **an untrusted operating system's behavior is verified according to application's intention and all human-machine interactions are enforced, without modifying OS kernel and applications**. To achieve these goals, we meet to solve the following problems on an untrusted OS:

1. How to infer application's intention and verify kernel's memory access transparently?

2. How to protect the security of all application linked dynamic shared objects (DSOes)?

3. How to protect human-machine interaction devices against a compromised OS?

4. How to enforce the security of application's X resource (e.g., clipboard, screen contents)?

AppSec provides several mechanisms to tackle these problems. AppSec intercepts every system call to infer application's intention. This includes the system call an application has invoked and the memory range that an application allows OS to access. During runtime, AppSec verifies whether a system call is invoked and whether the corresponding memory access is in accordance with application's intention. We know that all security sensitive applications pay much attention to their data security. So all application intended data transmission to a compromised kernel would not leak any privacy. To extract application's intention, AppSec intercepts security sensitive application's system calls. By analyzing the corresponding parameters, AppSec can validate OS kernel memory access at byte granularity. Verifying kernel memory access according to application's intention can protect user's privacy effectively and avoid encrypting all application data roughly.

Before verifying kernel memory access, we should identify which memory pages belong to a security sensitive application, but the dynamic memory allocation makes things a little more complicated. Previous work either instruments OS kernel or modifies applications to collect the page usage information explicitly [16, 31, 36]. While it may be bypassed when OS is compromised and it is not transparent to OS and applications. AppSec uses a skillful and non-bypassed page tracking based on hardware nested page table to deal with the dynamic memory allocation transparently. Its innovative features are that it does not instrument or modify OS kernel or applications and every physical pages once used by a protected application can be detected immediately.

DSOes are shared by all applications and their security is critical to user's privacy. Previous work compiles applications statically to avoid the security problem caused by DSOes [15, 16, 31, 48]. However, this loses the advantages of DSOes (e.g., updating during runtime). Besides, some close-source applications cannot be compiled stati-

cally. AppSec introduces a safe loader to check the code integrity of DSOes. During run-time, AppSec write-protects DSOes code and uses a skillful page tracking to verify the DSOes memory access.

For the security of human-machine interaction, AppSec uses an isolated dedicated customized OS to host the related input/output devices drivers and the X window server. All data transmissions between sensitive applications running on an untrusted OS and X server are encrypted. IOMMU and IOAPIC are used to protect the human-machine interaction devices from being attacked by the untrusted OS. On top of human-machine interaction devices protection, AppSec introduces a privilege-based window access control policy to prevent various attacks towards X window system, such as accessing chipboard and taking screenshot. All these protections are compatible with traditional applications and OS kernel.

In summary, we make the following contributions:

1. AppSec proposes a kernel memory access verifying mechanism based on applications' intention without redesigning or modifying applications and OS kernel.

2. AppSec introduces a safe loader to verify the code integrity of protected applications and DSOes which avoids compiling applications statically and keeps the advantages of DSOes.

3. AppSec proposes a security human-machine interaction channel and a privileged-based window system to protect all human-machine interaction data. Both mechanisms do not need to modify OS kernel or the corresponding drivers.

4. We have implemented a prototype of AppSec. All protections provided by AppSec are transparent to applications and OS kernel. An extra benefit of AppSec is that it can prevent ret2user [32] and ret2dir [33] attacks effectively. The experiments show that, with all protections, AppSec only incurs 6%~10% performance overhead.

In the next section, we give the threat model and some assumptions of AppSec. In Section 3, we give an overview of AppSec. In Section 4 and Section 5, we show how AppSec ensures the memory data security and human-machine interaction security respectively. The evaluation of AppSec is presented in Section 6.We discuss the limitation and our future work in Section 7. In Section 8, we compare AppSec with other work. In Section 9, we conclude our work.

2. Threat Model and Assumptions

In this section, we describe the threat model and our assumptions.

2.1 Threat Model

We consider an attacker who exploits the OS kernel vulnerabilities and has the full control of computer system but the CPU, the memory controller, system memory chips and the corresponding system bus. Example attacks are: accessing any memory pages, injecting code into OS kernel and the sensitive application, malicious DMA accessing, surreptitiously obtaining sensitive user-input data by recording key strokes, screenshot of sensitive application display etc.

2.2 Assumptions

We assume that all hardware is trusted, no bus traffic interception, no Trojan-Horse circuits or malicious microcode. We also assume the system firmware (e.g., BIOS) is trusted.

The protection object of AppSec is security sensitive applications. We assume they are conscious of flowing out data and encrypt it timely, for example, encrypting the file contents before writing them to disk and encrypting the network connection when communicating with others. AppSec does not prevent a private data leakage because of the vulnerabilities of an application itself. Denial-of-service attacks caused by a compromised kernel are also out of our scope. We also do not consider any side-channel attacks like timing, cache-collision.

AppSec is based on our previous work, a lightweight hypervisor whose interface has been verified [20, 21], we assume the hypervisor is trusted. And we assume that the CPU supports hardware virtualization, such as AMD Secure Virtual Machine (SVM) or Intel Trusted eXecution Technology (TXT) [18, 47].

3. System Overview

In this section, we start off by stating the desired properties to enforce the security of private data. Then we describe the challenges involved and present an overview of AppSec at last.

3.1 Desired Properties

In order to provide a safe and practical execution environment, AppSec seeks to meet the following properties.
Memory Access Verification. This is the cornerstone of a safe execution environment. AppSec must ensure that every memory access from kernel to a protected application should be verified according to application's intention.
Code and Control Flow Integrity. AppSec needs to guarantee the code integrity of sensitives application and all DSOes they linked during the whole life-cycle. During runtime, application may be interrupted at any time by OS kernel. AppSec must ensure the execution of an interrupted application begins at the interrupted site to prevent compromised kernel injecting malicious code into the protected application.
Trusted Human-Machine Interaction Path. Because all human-machine interaction data is plaintext, AppSec must protect it from being stolen or peeked by compromised OS and other applications.
Device Operation Verification. This consists of two different aspects. First, AppSec must prevent compromised OS ac-

cessing the human-machine interaction devices or intercepting their events. Second, AppSec must prevent the malicious device DMA accessing to sensitive application memory.
Compatibility and Transparency. Although these are not security properties, but are very important in practice. AppSec should not modify OS kernel and sensitive applications.
Low Performance Overhead. The safe execution environment provided by AppSec should incur acceptable overhead. And the performance overhead incurred to the other normal applications should be as little as possible.

3.2 Challenges

We now discuss the challenges we are facing in designing such a safe execution environment. The very first problem is the *semantic gap between guest OS and AppSec*. Because AppSec does not instrument the OS kernel or applications, it cannot get the exact information about the interactions between OS kernel and applications. This makes AppSec difficult to judge whether a memory access from kernel to application is application intended. The dynamic memory allocation makes things more complicated. It is difficult for AppSec to know which pages belong to a protected application and whether one page of a protected application is freed.

The next issue is raised by the *dynamic shared objects*. A tampered DSO may steal user's private data by changing application's original semantics. For example, the *strcpy* function can be modified to pass private data to a compromised kernel. So AppSec must ensure the code integrity of DSOes. Unfortunately, the random loaded location of DSOes makes this verification difficult. Besides, DSOes are shared by all applications. AppSec must distinguish whether the DSO code execution is in the context of a protected application or not. This is a premise for AppSec to judge if a memory access is from sensitive application itself.

Another problem we are facing is the *human-machine interaction devices security*. All devices drivers are hosted by OS kernel. Thus, once OS kernel is compromised, the adversary can capture all data passing through the human-machine interaction devices. What's more, the interrupt vector's mis-configuration can also cause a benign drivers' misbehavior and leak user's privacy.

The last issue is the *innate problem of X system*. The design philosophy of X system makes the trusted-path failure even if OS kernel and device drivers are trusted. For example, a malicious application can access the private data stored by a sensitive application in clipboard without any restriction. Applications can also use the corresponding functions (e.g., XGetImage) to get the screen contents. This exposes a sensitive application to risk.

3.3 AppSec Architecture Overview

Figure 1 illustrates the architecture of AppSec. The light weight VMM [20, 21] runs on bare-machine and provides a strong isolation to run two different OSes simultaneously.

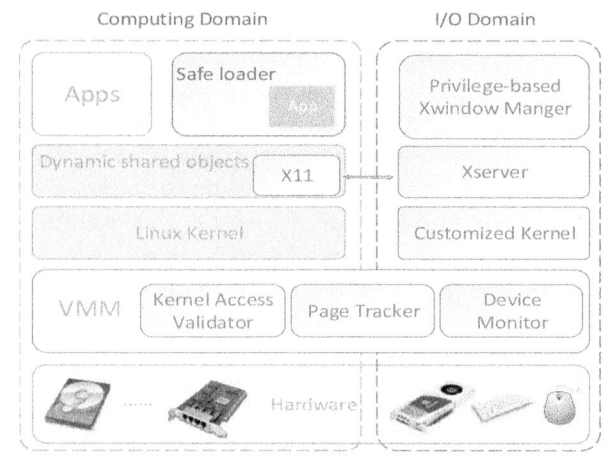

Figure 1. The architecture of AppSec.

One OS provides a normal computing environment and is called *computing domain*. The other one, running a customized kernel and only providing the X system service, is called *I/O domain*. I/O domain controls all human-machine interaction devices. Because I/O domain just serves the human-machine interaction requests and can only communicate with outside through X server's interface, we assume it is hard to be compromised.

A security sensitive application is loaded by the safe loader as depicted in Figure 2. The safe loader checks the integrity of DSOes and applications according to the hash values which are calculated in advance. Safe loader can distinguish which applications and DSOes are needed to check and invokes hypervisor to get the correct hash values transparently. We expect some third-parties could manage these hash values and provide them through Internet in the future. And now, we just store these hash values in hypervisor.

The hardware nested paging technique is leveraged by AppSec to construct a strong isolation between sensitive applications and OS kernel transparently. Sensitive applications can store their encryption keys in user space as normal. The un-bypassed and transparent page tracker collects application memory pages information in real-time. Everytime when kernel access sensitive applications' memory, a nested page table (NPT) fault is raised. In the NPT page fault handler, AppSec verifies kernel memory access according to application's intention. Access which is not in accordance with application's intention is denied.

AppSec encrypts all X connections to prevent computing domain kernel picking up the communication between sensitive applications and X server. Moreover, we retrofit the X system to support a privilege-based window management. The protected application is in the highest privilege level. AppSec ensures that the low privilege group windows cannot access the resource of high privilege group windows. This can effectively solve the aforementioned innate problem of X system.

4. Memory Data Security Enforcement

In this section, we discuss how AppSec tackles the aforementioned challenges to guarantee the memory data security of a security sensitive application. We start off by stating how AppSec constructs a trusted initial environment. And then, we show how AppSec protect application's private data during runtime. This includes tracking application's page in real-time, protecting application context switch and verifying kernel memory access.

4.1 Environment Initialization

4.1.1 Safe Loader

The very first problem to protect a security sensitive application is how to integrate it with AppSec transparently and ensure the code integrity of itself and all DSOes it linked. The easiest way is modifying the application to invoke hypervisor explicitly. However it conflicts with our transparency requirement. As we know, OS alway invokes the ELF (Extensible Linking Format) loader as a interpreter before transferring control flow to ELF applications. AppSec introduces a safe loader to replace the Linux traditional standard ELF loader.

The safe loader is aware of which application will run and invokes AppSec to verify its code integrity. It uses the hypercall to communicate with the core components of AppSec which run in the VMM. All these communication is imperceptible to OS kernel. The verification result is presented to user via a trusted dialog box. Such a dialog box, which executes under the control and with the privileges of hypervisor (not the OS), is often called a "powerbox" [41]. Except the verification results, the trusted dialog box also contains a user personal reserved information like a bank counterfoil. This can avoid OS faking the dialog box and bypassing the safe loader to run security applications.

The random loaded address of DSOes confuses AppSec with their code integrity checking. Previous works require the application to be compiled statically to eliminate this confusion. These conflicts with our transparency requirement and loses the advantage of DSOes. Because ELF loader is responsible for loading all DSOes into application's address space, the safe loader knows the memory mapping information of each linked DSO exactly. When the safe loader loads DSOes into application's address space, it records their virtual address and the corresponding inner offset.

As the demand paging mechanism used by OS kernel, before invoking AppSec to verify the code integrity, the safe loader touches all virtual pages to force OS loading the corresponding physical pages into memory. Combining with the address space isolation mechanism, AppSec can ensure the application and all DSOes it linked cannot be modified after they are verified.

190

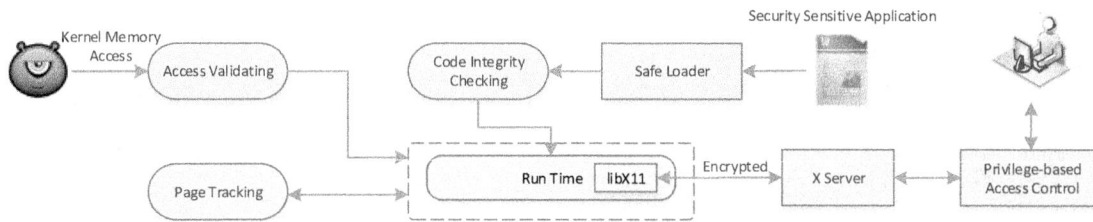

Figure 2. Overview of AppSec to protect a sensitive application for while life-cycle.

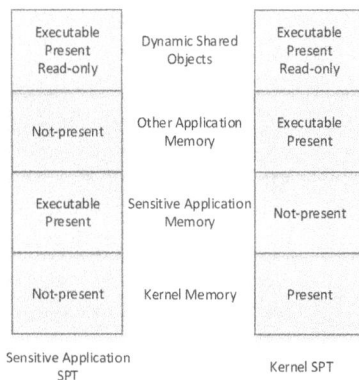

Figure 3. The SPT difference between the sensitive application and OS kernel.

4.1.2 Address Space Isolation

After the code integrity verification, AppSec isolates sensitive applications from OS kernel and other applications. The *nested paging* hardware virtualization is used to construct such isolation environment. Nested paging technology provides two levels of address translation (i.e., translation from guest liner address to guest physical address and translation from guest physical address to machine address). The page table which translates guest address to machine address is called *SPT (Shadow Page Table)*. The corresponding implementation of AMD and Intel processors are called *NPT* and *EPT* respectively.

AppSec provides different SPTs for sensitive applications and OS kernel. As Figure 3 shows, the SPT of sensitive applications contains all page mappings of their user space. Oppositely, all pages of sensitive applications are masked not-present in the SPT of OS kernel. Other applications share the same SPT with OS. As DSOes are shared by all applications, we mask all their pages present and read-only in every SPT. Because SPTs are maintained by hypervisor, OS kernel is unaware of the SPT page mapping and it can still manage the guest physical address mapping with its own page table. Everytime when OS access the protected application, a SPT fault will be triggered. In the SPT fault handler, AppSec can verify the kernel memory access transparently according to application's intention and the details are stated in Section 4.2.3. Because the SPT is transparent to OS, the memory access verification cannot be bypassed no matter what the attacker does to the OS kernel.

Currently, AppSec uses group-based policy to manage applications. All applications in the same group share one SPT and can communicate with each other as normal. Child processes belong to the same group with their parent in default. So child processes and parent process can communicate with each other based on shared memory freely. For un-shared memory communications like pipe, socket, AppSec assumes that applications encrypt private data by themselves or use an encrypted connection and does not intervene these communications.

Only isolating applications from OS kernel is inadequate to protect their private data. Compromised OS may map a page containing malicious codes into protected application's user space or replace a legal virtual page mapping with a malicious physical page and then transfers control flow to this page when a system call returns. As the malicious code resides in the same address space with the sensitive application, they can access the sensitive application memory data straightly. What's more, compromised OS kernel can also fork a fake child process to get it sharing the same SPT with a protected application. OS kernel can map the protected application's physical pages into the fake child process address space and access the protected application's memory indirectly through the fake child process. We will show how to prevent these attacks in Section 4.2.2.

4.2 Runtime Protection

During runtime, a sensitive application interacts with OS kernel frequently. This includes memory allocation, data transmission, context switch and so on. AppSec has to intercept these interactions and verifies the validity of these interactions according to application's intention.

4.2.1 Page Tracking

Before verifying OS memory access, we must know which memory pages belong to a protected application first. The very first problem to get the memory page usage information during runtime is caused by the dynamic memory allocation. Because of the semantic gap, it is difficult for AppSec to know if one page is allocated to an application or if one page is freed by an application. Instrumenting all memory allocation interfaces is the most obvious way to notify AppSec about the dynamic memory usage information. However, this is not transparent to OS kernel and may be bypassed if OS kernel is compromised. An optimum solution is implementing the page tracking into hypervisor.

AppSec uses a lazy memory page usage tracking mechanism to deal with the dynamic memory allocation. When a page is allocated to sensitive application by OS, AppSec does not know this allocation and the physical page is still not-present in the application's SPT. So, when the application touches this page for the first time, an SPT fault would be raised. In the SPT fault handler, AppSec knows a memory page allocation has occurred passively and updates the corresponding SPT (i.e., mask the page present in protected application's SPT and not-present in OS kernel's SPT). In order to make sure that all CPU cores have a coincident page mapping, AppSec must flush other CPU's TLB cache.

DSOes make things a little more complicated. As aforementioned, all applications share the same physical pages of DSOes. So when an SPT fault occurs in DSOes, we must identify if it is caused by a sensitive application. It is straightforward to use the different SPTs to identify the context. When an SPT fault occurs during the usage of sensitive application's SPT, we consider this SPT fault is caused by a sensitive application, otherwise it is caused by OS or other applications.

Unfortunately, it is likely that a sensitive application may execute with the OS kernel SPT sometimes. For example, when a sensitive application executes in DSOes code, OS may schedule other applications to run. AppSec switches the SPT and uses OS kernel SPT to run other applications. As all DSOes are masked present in OS kernel SPT, when the sensitive application is scheduled back, it will run with kernel SPT. To solve this problem, we compel the control flow to be transferred into a fixed address every time when the context switches from OS to protected applications. This fixed address could cause an SPT fault and in the SPT fault handler AppSec switches the SPT to run the protected application. The detail is presented in Section 4.2.2.

The global variables of DSOes would cause the whole system unusable if we use the aforementioned page tracking directly. For example, when sensitive application read its DSOes global variable for the first time and thus causes an SPT fault in the context of sensitive applications, AppSec masks the corresponding page not-present in the kernel SPT. This prevents other applications access the same DSOes variable.

We refine the aforementioned page tracking to tackle this problem. Figure 4 shows the page states transition graph. When the first access to a virtual page ("S") is a read operation, AppSec masks the corresponding page read-only and present on the SPTs of both kernel and sensitive application ("SR"). This is safe for the security sensitive application, because a memory page does not leak any privacy until it is written. While the first access to either "S" or "SR" state is a write operation, AppSec masks the corresponding page writable in the sensitive application SPT and not-present

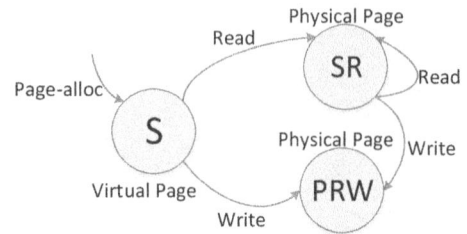

Figure 4. The state transition diagram of SPT page. "SR" means shared and readable, "P" means private and "W" means writable.

in the kernel SPT. Because of the COW (Copy On Write), OS will allocate a exclusive page to an application when a shared page is written. So masking this exclusive page not presented in kernel SPT would not cause whole system unusable.

Unlike the memory allocation, page free operation does not cause SPT fault. AppSec learns the memory page free operations by intercepting the corresponding system calls (i.e., *munmap* and brk). AppSec uses these system calls' parameters to infer which pages are freed and cleans their contents before masking them present in the OS kernel SPT.

4.2.2 Context Switch

AppSec need to intercept the context switch precisely to chose different SPTs and to protect the control flow integrity. Because security sensitive applications and OS kernel use different SPTs, when the context switch from user space to kernel space, a SPT fault will be raised. In the SPT fault handler, AppSec records the context switch site (i.e., system call return address and interrupt location) and changes the context switch back site to a fixed address directly. Besides, AppSec also records all system and their parameters to serve the later memory access verification. The fixed address can trigger a SPT fault proactively. So every context switch from kernel space to user space can be also intercepted.

When context switch from kernel space to user space, AppSec switches the SPT and drops the CPU privilege to level3. And then, AppSec pushes the original return address into application's stack and uses a ret instruction to take the control flow to application at the context switch site. AppSec ensures that every context switch from kernel space to user space can only transfer control flow to the aforementioned fixed address. OS can modify its stack to return at any address definitely. However, returning to other address makes CPU running with kernel NPT. When applications memory is touched (access, execute), AppSec can detect this malicious action in NPT fault handler. In order to tame the signal mechanism, AppSec records every signal handler address in a table by analyzing the corresponding system calls. Every time when OS does not transfer control flow to aforementioned fixed address, AppSec check if it transfers to a signal handler. If not, AppSec provides a warning information through a trusted dialog box to user.

As we mentioned in Section 4.2.1, malicious OS kernel may inject malicious codes into protected applications and transfer control flow to the malicious codes when a system call returns. AppSec ensures control flow can only be transferred from OS kernel to user space at some known sites (i.e., ether the fixed address or a signal handler). So malicious OS kernel has no chance to execute the injected malicious codes. For the virtual page remapping attacks, an NPT fault will be raised when CPU execute in the faked physical page. However, an NPT fault should not occur at text segment because the safe loader has already loaded all text segments into memory. So AppSec can detect this attack in NPT handler. To prevent the fake child process attack, AppSec verifies whether a corresponding "fork" system call has been invoked by sensitive applications. Because all child process share the same code segment with their parent, even if the compromised OS kernel create a faked child process during the sensitive application invokes a "fork" system call, AppSec still ensures that OS cannot inject malicious code in this fake child process.

In implementation, changing a context switch site to a fixed address may crash sensitive applications. That is because OS checks the switch site address in some cases. Fortunately, these cases are rare and we can deal with them respectively. For example, the "*time*" function uses "*vsyscall*" to get the time. OS checks if the context switch site locates between *0xffffffffff600000* and *0xffffffffff601000* which is the *vsyscall* mapping address range. If not, OS terminates the application. In this example, OS kernel returns back to the application according to a value stored in the user space stack instead of the context switch site. So AppSec modifies this value instead of the context switch site to pass the OS checking.

4.2.3 Memory Access Verification

During run-time, in order to get system service, a sensitive application must allow OS to access its memory. It is necessary for AppSec to distinguish the legitimate operations from the illegal operations according to application's intention. We use a straightforward mechanism to solve this problem. AppSec records every system call parameters when the system call is invoked. During runtime, when OS kernel accesses protected application memory, a SPT fault is raised. In the SPT fault handler, AppSec verifies if the kernel memory access is as security sensitive application wanted according to the system call parameters. If the memory access range is not the application wanted, the memory access will be denied or only ciphertext will be copied into kernel buffer depending on user's configuration. If the memory access range is as the application specified, AppSec copies the protected application memory content to OS kernel's buffer. So OS cannot get applications private data even if the private data locates in the same page with system call buffer.

AppSec uses IOMMU to prevent malicious OS kernel issuing illegal DMA operations to get a protected applica-

tion memory data. IOMMU uses another page table to translate all DMA operation addresses. We use the same mechanism as memory isolation to isolate security sensitive application's memory data from malicious DMA operations. All devices use the kernel SPT as their I/O page table in default. When a protected application needs to do DMA operation, AppSec constructs a temporary I/O page table to translate DMA address dynamically.

4.2.4 ret2user and ret2dir Attacks Defense

As the aforementioned mechanism used by AppSec, we have an extra benefit. That is AppSec can prevent the return-to-user (ret2user) [32] and ret2dir (return-to-direct-mapped memory) [33] attacks effectively.

ret2user attacks exploit the OS vulnerabilities to redirect corrupted kernel pointers to malicious code residing in user space and then run the malicious codes with kernel privilege. AppSec intercepts every context switch from kernel space to user space and drop the CPU privilege to level 3 compulsorily. So even if attackers transfer control flow to malicious codes, it still cannot be executed with kernel privilege.

ret2dir attacks are a little bit more complicated than ret2user attacks. They map the malicious codes which reside in user space memory page into OS kernel virtual address space by leveraging a kernel region that directly maps part or all of a system's physical memory. It can bypass all existing ret2user defenses, like SMEP, SMAP and kGuard [8, 30, 32]. However, with AppSec which uses different SPTs for applications and OS kernel, application's physical pages are masked not present in kernel's SPT. Codes with kernel privilege still cannot access data residing in user space even if the corresponding physical pages are mapped into kernel's virtual address space.

5. Trusted Human-Machine Interaction Path

Previous systems mainly focus on the security of memory data, and the security of I/O path is usually neglected. However, a practical computing environment facing end users involves a lot of human-machine interactions which are easily intercepted by a compromised kernel. It is necessary for AppSec to build such a trusted I/O path from end-user to the sensitive application against a compromised OS kernel.

It it challenging to protect the human-machine interaction path. The popular operating system integrates all device drivers into kernel space, like Linux and Windows. If OS kernel is compromised, all these device drivers are infected. To isolate the trusted path device drivers from OS, one method is to modify the commodity device driver to eliminate any dependencies on the OS like [50]. However, the close-couple design architecture makes it difficult to decouple device drivers from OS.

AppSec is inspired by exokernel [24], VirtuOS [38], Xen frontend backend driver model [26] and X system [7]. As depicted in Figure 1, AppSec uses a dedicated OS, *I/O do-*

main, to host all human-machine interaction device drivers. The computing domain can communicate with the I/O domain only through the X system interfaces. So, even if the OS kernel of computing domain is compromised, the I/O domain and user's I/O operation are still safe.

In this section, we first state how to isolate all human-machine interaction devices from the computing domain. On the top of human-machine interaction devices isolation, we show how to retrofit the traditional X system to enforce the communication between X client and X server and protect application's X resource.

5.1 Human-Machine Interaction Devices Isolation

The devices isolation comprise two aspects: device access isolation and device interrupt isolation.

5.1.1 Device Access Isolation

AppSec isolates human-machine interaction devices from the computing domain by intercepting the PCI/PCIe configuration space access. During booting, OS kernel traverses the PCI/PCIe configuration space to enumerate all presented devices. For the X86 architecture, the PCI/PCIe configuration space is accessed via two special I/O ports (i.e., *0xCF8* and *0xCFC* in default) or MMIO regions [5, 14]. AppSec intercepts the configuration space access and masks all human-machine interaction devices not-present when the computing domain booting. Similarly, AppSec masks other devices excluding the trusted path devices not-present when the I/O domain booting. For some devices whose absence may lead the OS to stall, AppSec creates these necessary virtual devices and provides the corresponding fake PCI/PCIe configuration information. All operations to these virtual devices will be discarded and AppSec just returns operation success to upper OS.

During runtime, compromised OS can capture all data passing through the human-machine interaction devices by configuring other devices to overlap these devices' I/O port space or physical memory space. In order to defend against these overlap attacks, AppSec verifies every device configuration operation. If computing domain tries to overlap I/O domain devices configuration range, AppSec denies the device configuration operation and generates an interrupt to the I/O domain. The I/O domain will show a corresponding attack information on the screen immediately.

5.1.2 Interrupt Isolation

All device accesses are interrupt-driven. Without interrupt isolation, computing domain can send out any spoofed interrupt to I/O domain which may cause I/O domain wrong reaction. To make matters worse, the computing domain can sniff the human-machine interaction interrupt events to infer user's privacy. For example, by analyzing the time series of keyboard interrupt with pattern recognition, attacker can get what an user inputs easily.

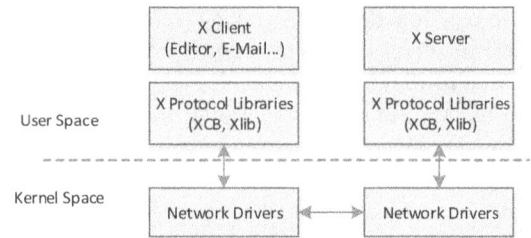

Figure 5. Data transmission path between X client and X server.

AppSec uses three different methods to isolate interrupts between computing domain and I/O domain. To prevent the computing domain sending spoofed interrupt to the I/O domain, AppSec intercepts all inter processor interrupts (IPI) and makes sure that all the IPI destination are confined in their own domain. To prevent the computing domain sniffing devices interrupt events and guarantee all human-machine interaction devices interrupts are delivered to the I/O domain directly, AppSec uses the other two methods for different interrupt source. For traditional interrupts which are signaled by asserting an interrupt line (pin), AppSec uses IOAPIC to route them to the I/O domain. For message signaled interrupts (MSI) which are signaled by writing a particular address, AppSec leverages the interrupt remapping features of IOMMU to route them to I/O domain.

5.2 X System Retrofit

X system is the native display technology on UNIX and Linux systems. It uses a client-server model to provide the basic framework for a GUI environment. X server renders screen contents on the display devices. It forwards the user inputs from input devices like keyboard, mouse and touchscreen to applications which are called X clients. The innate design of X system makes it inadequate for a safe computing environment. AppSec retrofits X system in two aspects to protect user's privacy.

5.2.1 Encrypted Channels

X client communicates with X server through a network connection. As shown in Figure 5, data is encapsulated by X protocol libraries and transmitted by OS. Most of the data transmission is not encrypted [3]. When the OS kernel is compromised, attacker can get all these transmitted data by sniffing the network connection.

AppSec modifies the X protocol libraries and adds encryption functions to build an secure channel between X client and X server. When an X client tries to get connection to X server, AppSec retrofits the original connection functions to make sure every connection is encrypted. Because AppSec guarantees the code integrity of DSOes, this encryption is un-bypassed and all data transmitted is safe even though the OS kernel is compromised.

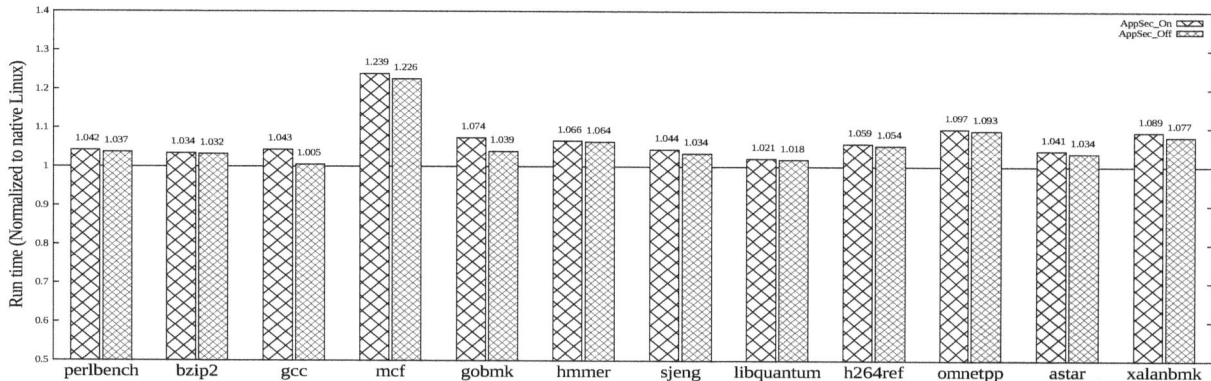

Figure 6. SPEC CPU2006 performance comparison between AppSec ON and OFF, which is relative to native Linux.

5.2.2 Privilege-based Window Access Control

One design philosophy of X system is that all applications are good and non-malicious. This leads to the lack of window-level isolation and allows any client to have full access other X client resource like clipboard and screen display. This is disastrous for a security sensitive computing environment.

AppSec introduces privilege-base window resource access control policy in X system. All windows are divided into different privilege groups, and low group cannot access high group's X resource. This is similar to the CPU ring. An application can be added into the high privilege group only if it is designated by user explicitly. We use two practical cases to show how this privilege-based access control work and what modification should be done to the X system.

Case 1. Clipboard: User uses a document editor to edit a top-secret document. At the same time, he/she may want to search on the Internet with a browser to enrich this document. Traditionally, the browser can access the document editor's clipboard by sending *XConvertSelection* request to the X server. X server forwards this request to the editor as a *SelectionRequest* request without any verification. After receiving *SelectionRequest*, the editor uses *XChangeProperty* to pass its clipboard contents, which may contain private data, to the web browser. With AppSec, user can add the text editor into the high privilege group manually and leaves the web browser in the low privilege group. In the *ProcChangeProperty* function of X server which serves client's *XChangeProperty* request, we check if the browser privilege is lower than the editor. If that, AppSec encrypts all clipboard contents and transmits the ciphertext to the browser.

Case 2. Screenshot: Similar to case 1, a text editor is used to edit a top-secret document. Attacker may get the screenshot by invoking the *XGetImage* function stealthily. In current implementation, AppSec modifies the *ProcGetImage* function, which serves the client getImage request, to check whether there are higher privileged windows than the invoker. If there are, AppSec draws a full-screen rectangle to overlap these high privileged windows before X server

Table 1. NPT performance for MCF (in seconds).

NPT Enabled	NPT Disabled
681.693	570.615

getting the display contents. At last, AppSec sends a *GraphicsExposure* event to all windows to recover their display contents.

6. Evaluation

In this section, we evaluate the performance overhead imposed by AppSec. We ran our evaluations on a Sugon A620r-G server with two AMD Opteron(tm) 6320 processors at 2.8 GHz, 16GB of DRAM, two integrated PCIe Gigabit Ethernet cards. The Debian wheezy were installed with the Linux version 3.10 in our experiments. We used the performance of native Linux as a base line in all experiments. *AppSec On* denotes we ran the test in a safe environment provided by AppSec and *AppSec Off* denotes we ran the test on the AppSec platform but not in the safe environment.

We evaluated AppSec performance overhead on application benchmarks as well as a few microbenchmarks. We used SPEC CPU2006, Apache Benchmark and Google V8 benchmark to obtain the effect of AppSec to application in practice. When AppSec provided a safe environment for a sensitive application, all processors NPT feature were enabled. In order to get the performance influence to other concurrent applications, we enabled all processors' NPT in all application benchmarks, no matter if AppSec was on or off. Microbenchmarks were used to see how AppSec affects primitive OS operations and we just disabled all processors' NTP when AppSec was off.

6.1 Application Benchmarks

Figure 6 shows the performance overhead incurred to SPEC CPU2006 benchmark suit. All results are normalized to native Linux. AppSec incurs at most 10% performance overhead to all tests excluding the mcf test. This is because these tests are CPU-bound and there are little OS interactions. The worst result is the mcf test. That is because there are a lot of

Table 2. Apache web server performance (requests per second).

Concurrent Transactions	Native Linux	AppSec On	AppSec Off
5	13655.58	12808.75	13600.53
7	14170.44	13592.32	14000.78

TLB misses during its execution. In the native Linux kernel, it only needs 4 times of memory access to handle one TLB miss at most. While when NPT is enabled, every TLB miss in the guest OS would incur 4*4 times of memory access to finish the TLB mapping at most. We executed mcf test with NPT enabled and disabled respectively. The result shown in table 1 confirms our analysis. The overhead is mainly caused by the hardware virtualization technology and could be reduced effectively if the hardware virtualization technology is improved.

Table 2 shows the performance overhead incurred to Apache web server. We used Apache Benchmark (ab) to issue 50,000 transactions with the specified number of concurrent transactions to the server. In each transaction, a 45-byte index page was transferred from the server to the Apache Benchmark client. Compared to native Linux, AppSec only incurs about 6% performance overhead. This is because we use extra pages to cache the frequent access memory content to reduce the number of interaction between AppSec and OS kernel. AppSec copies application buffer contents of the most frequently accessed page to a new page. The new page is mapped read-only in both NPTs of kernel and applications. Once the new is modified, the cache is invalid.

Table 3. Firefox web browser performance.

Native Linux	AppSec OFF	AppSec ON
3384	3306	3183
-	97.7%	94.1%

In order to obtain the effect of AppSec to user during the actual use, we chosen the Google V8 benchmark [2] running on mozilla firefox to evaluate the AppSec overhead. Table 3 shows the results. Higher score means higher performance. There is no more than 3% overhead AppSec incurred to the firefox when turning AppSec off. When turning AppSec on, the performance overhead is no more than 6%.

6.2 Microbenchmarks

We conducted some more micro experiments to obtain how much the overhead of AppSec interacting with OS kernel and user space contributes to the overall overhead. Table 4 shows the results of our experiments. We used *null system call* to evaluate the overhead of space switching between an application and OS. *mmap* and *page fault* were used to measure the performance of the proposed page tracking technology. *fork* expressed the overhead of creating a sensitive application process. File operations shown the overhead of AppSec incurring to some normal OS interaction operations.

Table 4. Latency microbenchmark results (in microsecond).

	Native	AppSec On	AppSec Off
null syscall	0.023	0.14	0.031
open/close	0.294	1.75	0.307
mmap	3841.8	42629.3	3862.4
page fault	2.21	8.85	2.33
file create	11.5	29.7	11.6
file delete	12.6	31.2	12.7
fork	65.22	3685.12	68.3

When we disable AppSec, there is no interaction between VMM and guest OS. So, compared to native Linux, AppSec incurs almost no performance overhead. However, when it is enabled, every space switch and OS interaction is intercepted and it incurs a little high performance overhead.

Compared with other tests, *mmap* and *fork* incur a little high performance overhead. That is because, when application mapping a file, AppSec marks the corresponding virtual address range and updates the NPT table when the application access this address. Similarly, when an application process being created, AppSec traverses its whole virtual address space, finds all physical pages it used to ensure no malicious pages are injected. However, the *fork* operation is unfrequent in the desktop environment and the user is oblivious to this performance overhead.

7. Discussion

7.1 Attestation Chain

In order to build an attestation chain to run a security sensitive application, AppSec leverages the trusted platform modules (TPM) [6]. The TMP chip ensures that the power-on boot process starts from a trusted condition and *OSV* VMM is not modified. *OSV* uses hardware virtualization technology to isolate its memory pages from guest OS which guarantees its integrity during runtime. Every time when a protected application is launched, AppSec checks the integrity of safe loader to provide a trust environment automatically. AppSec outputs all the integrity measurement results on screen directly or sends them to other computer for remote attestation. Any integrity check fault would be recorded and then AppSec terminates the guest OS.

7.2 Limitation and Future Work

AppSec ensures that OS kernel can only access protected application data according to application's intention. However, the correctness of OS cannot be verified which maybe used by attacker to exploit the Iago attacks. Although we can check some system call results during context switch, it is unlikely to be tractable for arbitrary applications given the complexity of OS interfaces (e.g., Linux includes more than 300 system calls and Windows well over 1000). We will leverage Drawbridge [12] to mitigate this problem. What's more, the security of human-machine interaction relies heavily on the security of X server. AppSec can leverage some control flow integrity tools [9, 49] to enforce the security of X server.

Now, every system call causes a lot of context or world switches (e.g, from guest user to guest kernel, from guest to host). This incurs a high performance overhead. In the future, we would use the FlexSC architecture [43] to reduce the performance overhead. Besides, we also plan to port our prototype to Intel platform with the help of Intel's Trust Execution Technology (TXT).

8. Related Work

In this section, we compare AppSec with the existing techniques of protecting user privacy in two different aspects.

8.1 Memory Data Protection

XOM [35], AEGIS [45] and Cryptopage [22] are proposed to protect sensitive data from being leaked or tampered. They do not trust the physical resources, like main memory and encrypt chips. In contract, we mainly focus on the software level attacks. Besides, these protections need to modify the CPU architecture, which makes them difficult to deploy.

PrivExe [39] provides an operating system service for private execution. Virtual Ghost [19] leverages LLVM compiler [34] to instrument OS and checks OS code in run-time. They all need to modify or re-compile OS kernel. In contract, AppSec protects full application from hostile OS transparently and excludes OS kernel from our TCB.

TrustVisor [36], Intel SGX instruction set [37], SICE [11] and Fides [44] partition an application into "secret" part and "public" part. They ensure that the secret part can only be accessed by the code in public part and the public part can only be invoked through the specified APIs. One significant drawback of these work is that the protected applications need to be modified or their architectures need to be re-designed. That need enormous efforts and is not available for some legacy commodity software. In contract, AppSec provides a whole application protection. AppSec does not need to re-design legacy software or re-compile them which is very important in practice.

Similar to AppSec, Overshadow [16], SP^3 [48], Ink-Tag [31] and Chaos [15] use a virtual machine monitor to isolate the security sensitive application from OS. The main idea of these work to protect the memory data is using the hardware virtualization to intercept kernel memory access and encrypt all data flowing to OS kernel. As we stated in Section 1, this arbitrary encryption would make applications unusable. Besides, some of them needs to instrument OS kernel or leverage the existing hypervisor paravirtualization interfaces [15, 31]. What's more, all of them compile applications statically to avoid the complexity of DSOes. In contract, AppSec introduces a safe loader to protect DSOes which avoids compiling applications statically. Kernel memory access is verified according to application's intention

which avoids the un-usability caused by encrypting all data arbitrarily. AppSec provides a secure human-machine interaction channel to enforce the security of input/output data. Besides, all of these work is based on sophisticated VMMs like VMware, Xen which have a very large performance overhead and are prone to be attacked [1, 4]. AppSec uses a lightweight hypervisor whose interfaces have been verified.

Haven takes a further step by using Intel SGX instruction to protect a whole application without any modification to protected application binary [13]. AppSec can leverage its LibOS mechanism to prevent against malicious behaviours like Iago attacks. However all human-machine interaction data is still unsafe and we have not found how Haven deal with the problems caused by DSOes. Another major advantage of AppSec is that AppSec introduces a trusted human-machine interaction channel to enforce the security of human-machine interactions. This is absence in previous related work.

8.2 Trusted Human-Machine Interaction

Zhou [50] and Dunn [23] use hypervisor to enforce human-machine interaction. However, they either need to modify device drivers to eliminate any dependencies on the commodity OS or hinder applications communicating with others.

DriverGuard [17] provides a trusted I/O flow between commodity peripheral devices and some privileged code blocks in device driver. UTP [25] uses the TPM chip to build a uni-directional trusted path. It ensures that user's transactions is indeed submitted by a human operating the computer. However, they all rely on the security of OS and the innate problem of X window system still expose X resource to risk.

EROS [42] Window System is a trusted window system for the EROS capability-based operating system. It is built on the primitive mechanisms of EROS operating system and is capable of enforcing mandatory access control. However, a compromised OS can still access all human-machine interaction devices to steal user privacy and the special operating system requirement makes it difficult to use for most traditional security sensitive application.

Compared to these work, AppSec first isolates all human-machine interaction devices from compromised OS kernel. On top of that, AppSec further proposes a privilege-based window system. It ensures that normal application cannot access the security sensitive application's X resource.

9. Conclusion

AppSec represents a significant step forward in protecting security sensitive applications' private data on an untrusted operating system. By protecting the code integrity of DSOes and tracking pages skillfully, we enable sensitive applications to use AppSec transparently. AppSec protects the security of memory private data by verifying kernel memory access according to application's intention. With human-machine interaction devices isolation and a privilege-based windows system, AppSec addresses the human-machine interaction issues such as keyboard interception and screen capture. The major advantages of AppSec are that AppSec secures both the memory data and human-machine interaction data and all protections provided by AppSec do not need to re-design, modify or recompile applications and OS. The prototype shows that AppSec only incurs 6%~10% performance overhead.

Acknowledgments

This research was supported in part by NSFC under Grant No.(60933003, 61272460), Ph.D. Programs Foundation of Ministry of Education of China under Grant No. (201202011 10010) and 863 Program (2012AA010904).

References

[1] Xen Arbitrary Code Execution. URL http://cve.mitre.org/cgi-bin/cvename.cgi?name=CVE-2014-3124.

[2] Google V8 Benchmark Suite. URL http://v8.googlecode.com/svn/data/benchmarks/v7/run.html.

[3] The connection methods to the X server. URL https://www.debian.org/doc/manuals/debian-reference/ch07.en.html#_the_connection_methods_to_the_x_server.

[4] VMWare Arbitrary Code Execution. URL http://cve.mitre.org/cgi-bin/cvename.cgi?name=CVE-2014-1209.

[5] PCI Local Bus Specification. URL http://www.math.uni.wroc.pl/~p-wyk4/so/pci23.pdf.

[6] Trusted Platform Module (TPM) Summary. URL http://www.trustedcomputinggroup.org/resources/trusted_platform_module_tpm_summary.

[7] X Window System. URL http://en.wikipedia.org/wiki/X_Window_System.

[8] INTEL® 64 AND IA-32 ARCHITECTURES SOFTWARE DEVELOPER'S MANUAL. Instruction Set Extensions Programming Reference. *Intel Corporation*, January 2013.

[9] M. Abadi, M. Budiu, Ú. Erlingsson, and J. Ligatti. Control-flow integrity principles, implementations, and applications. *ACM Transactions on Information and System Security (TISSEC)*, 13(1):4, 2009.

[10] A. Arasu, S. Blanas, K. Eguro, R. Kaushik, D. Kossmann, R. Ramamurthy, and R. Venkatesan. Orthogonal security with cipherbase. In *6th Conference on Innovative Data Systems Research*, Jan. 2013.

[11] A. Azab, P. Ning, and X. Zhang. SICE: a hardware-level strongly isolated computing environment for x86 multi-core platforms. In *Proceedings of the 18th ACM conference on Computer and communications security*, pages 375–388. ACM, 2011.

[12] A. Baumann, D. Lee, P. Fonseca, L. Glendenning, J. R. Lorch, B. Bond, R. Olinsky, and G. C. Hunt. Composing os extensions safely and efficiently with bascule. In *Proceedings of the 8th ACM European Conference on Computer Systems*, pages 239–252. ACM, 2013.

[13] A. Baumann, M. Peinado, and G. Hunt. Shielding applications from an untrusted cloud with haven. In *Proceedings of the 11th USENIX conference on Operating Systems Design and Implementation*, pages 267–283. USENIX Association, 2014.

[14] A. D. Central. BIOS and Kernel Developer's Guide for AMD Family 15h Models 00h-0Fh Processors.

[15] H. Chen, F. Zhang, C. Chen, Z. Yang, R. Chen, B. Zang, and W. Mao. Tamper-resistant execution in an untrusted operating system using a virtual machine monitor. 2007.

[16] X. Chen, T. Garfinkel, E. Lewis, P. Subrahmanyam, C. Waldspurger, D. Boneh, J. Dwoskin, and D. Ports. Overshadow: a virtualization-based approach to retrofitting protection in commodity operating systems. In *ACM SIGPLAN Notices*, volume 43, pages 2–13. ACM, 2008.

[17] Y. Cheng, X. Ding, and R. H. Deng. Driverguard: A fine-grained protection on i/o flows. In *Proceedings of European Symposium on Research in Computer Security*, pages 227–244. Springer, 2011.

[18] I. Corporation. Lagrande technology preliminary architecture specification. *Intel Publication*, (D52212), 2006.

[19] J. Criswell, N. Dautenhahn, and V. Adve. Virtual Ghost: Protecting Applications from Hostile Operating Systems. In *Proceedings of the nineteenth international conference on Architectural Support for Programming Languages and Operating Systems*. ACM, 2014.

[20] Y. Dai, Y. Shi, Y. Qi, J. Ren, and P. Wang. Design and verification of a lightweight reliable virtual machine monitor for a many-core architecture. *Frontiers of Computer Science*, pages 1–10.

[21] Y. Dai, Y. Qi, J. Ren, Y. Shi, X. Wang, and X. Yu. A lightweight VMM on many core for high performance computing. In *Proceedings of the 9th ACM SIGPLAN/SIGOPS international conference on Virtual Execution Environments*, pages 111–120. ACM, 2013.

[22] G. Duc and R. Keryell. Cryptopage: an efficient secure architecture with memory encryption, integrity and information leakage protection. In *Computer Security Applications Conference, 2006. ACSAC'06. 22nd Annual*, pages 483–492. IEEE, 2006.

[23] A. M. Dunn, M. Z. Lee, S. Jana, S. Kim, M. Silberstein, Y. Xu, V. Shmatikov, and E. Witchel. Eternal sunshine of the spotless machine: Protecting privacy with ephemeral channels. In *Proc. of the USENIX Symposium on Operating Systems Design and Implementation (OSDI)*, 2012.

[24] D. R. Engler, M. F. Kaashoek, et al. *Exokernel: An operating system architecture for application-level resource management*, volume 29. ACM, 1995.

[25] A. Filyanov, J. M. McCuney, A.-R. Sadeghiz, and M. Winandy. Uni-directional trusted path: Transaction confirmation on just one device. In *Dependable Systems & Networks (DSN), 2011 IEEE/IFIP 41st International Conference on*, pages 1–12. IEEE, 2011.

[26] K. Fraser, S. Hand, R. Neugebauer, I. Pratt, A. Warfield, and M. Williamson. Safe hardware access with the xen virtual

machine monitor. In *1st Workshop on Operating System and Architectural Support for the on demand IT InfraStructure (OASIS)*, pages 1–1, 2004.

[27] T. Garfinkel, B. Pfaff, J. Chow, M. Rosenblum, and D. Boneh. Terra: A virtual machine-based platform for trusted computing. In *ACM SIGOPS Operating Systems Review*, volume 37, pages 193–206. ACM, 2003.

[28] C. Gebtry, S. Halevi, and N. P. Smart. Homomorphic evaluation of the aes circuit. In *32nd International Cryptology Conference*, 2012.

[29] C. Gentry. *A fully homomorphic encryption scheme*. PhD thesis, Stanford University, 2009.

[30] V. George, T. Piazza, and H. Jiang. Technology Insight: Intel© Next Generation Microarchitecture Codename Ivy Bridge, 2011. URL www.intel.com/idf/library/pdf/sf_2011/SF11_SPCS005_101F.pdf.

[31] O. S. Hofmann, S. Kim, A. M. Dunn, M. Z. Lee, and E. Witchel. InkTag: Secure Applications On An Untrusted Operating System. In *Proceedings of the eighteenth international conference on Architectural support for programming languages and operating systems, (ASPLOS)*, pages 265–278. ACM, 2013.

[32] V. P. Kemerlis, G. Portokalidis, and A. D. Keromytis. kguard: Lightweight kernel protection against return-to-user attacks. In *Proceedings of the 21st USENIX Conference on Security Symposium*, Security'12, Berkeley, CA, USA, 2012. USENIX Association.

[33] V. P. Kemerlis, M. Polychronakis, and A. D. Keromytis. Ret2dir: Rethinking kernel isolation. In *Proceedings of the 23rd USENIX Conference on Security Symposium*, SEC'14, 2014.

[34] C. Lattner and V. Adve. LLVM: A compilation framework for lifelong program analysis & transformation. In *Code Generation and Optimization, 2004. CGO 2004. International Symposium on*, pages 75–86. IEEE, 2004.

[35] D. Lie, C. Thekkath, M. Mitchell, P. Lincoln, D. Boneh, J. Mitchell, and M. Horowitz. Architectural support for copy and tamper resistant software. *ACM SIGPLAN Notices*, 35 (11):168–177, 2000.

[36] J. M. McCune, Y. Li, N. Qu, Z. Zhou, A. Datta, V. Gligor, and A. Perrig. TrustVisor: Efficient TCB Reduction and Attestation. In *IEEE Symposium on Security and Privacy (SP)*, pages 143–158. IEEE, 2010.

[37] F. McKeen, I. Alexandrovich, A. Berenzon, C. V. Rozas, H. Shafi, V. Shanbhogue, and U. R. Savagaonkar. Innovative instructions and software model for isolated execution. In *Proceedings of the 2nd International Workshop on Hardware and Architectural Support for Security and Privacy*, page 10. ACM, 2013.

[38] R. Nikolaev and G. Back. Virtuos: an operating system with kernel virtualization. In *Proceedings of the Twenty-Fourth ACM Symposium on Operating Systems Principles (SOSP 2013)*, pages 116–132. ACM, 2013.

[39] K. Onarlioglu, C. Mulliner, W. Robertson, and E. Kirda. PRIVEXEC: Private Execution as an Operating System Ser-

vice. In *IEEE Symposium on Security and Privacy*. IEEE, 2013.

[40] R. A. Popa, C. M. Redfield, N. Xeldovich, and H. Balakrishnan. Cryptdb: Protecting confidentiality with encrypted query processing. In *23rd ACM Symposium on Operating Systems Principles*, pages 85–100, 2011.

[41] M. Seaborn. Plash: tools for practical least privilege, 2008. URL http://plash.beasts.org/index.html.

[42] J. S. Shapiro, J. Vanderburgh, E. Northup, and D. Chizmadia. Design of the eros trusted window system. In *Proceedings of the 13th conference on USENIX Security Symposium-Volume 13*, pages 12–12. USENIX Association, 2004.

[43] L. Soares and M. Stumm. Flexsc: flexible system call scheduling with exception-less system calls. In *Proceedings of the 9th USENIX conference on Operating systems design and implementation, OSDI*. ACM, 2010.

[44] R. Strackx and F. Piessens. Fides: Selectively hardening software application components against kernel-level or process-level malware. In *Proceedings of the 19th ACM conference on Computer and Communications Security (CCS 2012)*, 2012.

[45] G. E. Suh, D. Clarke, B. Gassend, M. Van Dijk, and S. Devadas. AEGIS: architecture for tamper-evident and tamper-resistant processing. In *Proceedings of the 17th annual international conference on Supercomputing*, pages 160–171, 2003.

[46] S. D. Tetali, M. Lesani, R. Majumdar, and T. Millstein. Mrcrypt: static analysis for secure cloud computations. In *Proceedings of the 2013 ACM SIGPLAN international conference on Object oriented programming systems languages & applications*, pages 271–286. ACM, 2013.

[47] A. Virtualization. Secure Virtual Machine Architecture Reference Manual. *AMD Publication*, (33047), 2005.

[48] J. Yang and K. Shin. Using hypervisor to provide data secrecy for user applications on a per-page basis. In *Proceedings of the fourth ACM SIGPLAN/SIGOPS international conference on Virtual execution environments*, pages 71–80. ACM, 2008.

[49] M. Zhang and R. Sekar. Control flow integrity for cots binaries. In *Usenix Security*, pages 337–352, 2013.

[50] Z. Zhou, V. Gligor, J. Newsome, and J. McCune. Building verifiable trusted path on commodity x86 computers. In *Security and Privacy (SP), 2012 IEEE Symposium on*, pages 616–630. IEEE, 2012.

Hardware-Assisted Secure Resource Accounting under a Vulnerable Hypervisor

Seongwook Jin, Jinho Seol, Jaehyuk Huh, and Seungryoul Maeng

Computer Science Department, KAIST

{swjin, jhseol, jhuh and maeng}@calab.kaist.ac.kr

Abstract

With the proliferation of cloud computing to outsource computation in remote servers, the accountability of computational resources has emerged as an important new challenge for both cloud users and providers. Among the cloud resources, CPU and memory are difficult to verify their actual allocation, since the current virtualization techniques attempt to hide the discrepancy between physical and virtual allocations for the two resources. This paper proposes an online verifiable resource accounting technique for CPU and memory allocation for cloud computing. Unlike prior approaches for cloud resource accounting, the proposed accounting mechanism, called Hardware-assisted Resource Accounting (HRA), uses the hardware support for system management mode (SMM) and virtualization to provide secure resource accounting, even if the hypervisor is compromised. Using a secure isolated execution support of SMM, this study investigates two aspects of verifiable resource accounting for cloud systems. First, this paper presents how the hardware-assisted SMM and virtualization techniques can be used to implement the secure resource accounting mechanism even under a compromised hypervisor. Second, the paper investigates a sample-based resource accounting technique to minimize performance overheads. Using a statistical random sampling method, the technique estimates the overall CPU and memory allocation status with 99% $\sim$ 100% accuracies and performance degradations of 0.1% $\sim$ 0.5%.

Categories and Subject Descriptors   D.4.8 [*Operating Systems*]: Performance

Keywords   resource accounting; cloud; virtualization

VEE '15,   March 14–15, 2015, Istanbul, Turkey.
Copyright © 2015 ACM 978-1-4503-3450-1/15/03...$15.00.
http://dx.doi.org/10.1145/2731186.2731203

1. Introduction

Although cloud computing provides elastic computing resources based upon service contracts between cloud users and providers, one of the critical concerns for such a utility-based computing model is whether the quantity of computing resources can be guaranteed by the cloud providers. Some cloud providers may choose to provide a fixed amount of resources, regardless of whether cloud users actually consume them or not. A different cost model may charge the cost based on the actual usage of resources. In both cost models, the accurate accounting of resources is critical for cloud computing, to provide fair and verifiable costs for outsourced computation.

Considering the importance of accountable resource allocation, cloud providers make their best effort to support the availability of the computing resources mandated by the service level agreement (SLA). However, compromised system administrators or remote attackers can potentially reduce the computing resources assigned for valid users, and redirect the stolen resources for their own benefit. Most of the current cloud computing systems employ virtualization, and a hypervisor in each physical system is responsible for allocating computing resources to each user VM. However, a compromised hypervisor or compromised administrator can assign an arbitrary amount of computing resources to user VMs, violating SLA. Furthermore, a malicious user may exploit the system vulnerability to steal computing resources from co-tenants.

Among cloud resources, explicit and coarse-grained resources such as a virtual machine (VM) itself or I/O operations can be relatively easily traced by users or guest OSes without significant performance overheads. However, CPU time shares or memory pages allocated for user virtual machines are very difficult to track its availability as cloud users can only observe virtual CPUs and memory, hiding actual allocation of physical resources. An alternative way to account such resources is to occasionally run benchmark applications to verify the resources based on performance outcome of benchmark runs. However, such a benchmark-based approach cannot account fine-grained resource allocation changes accurately. Furthermore, the performance of a benchmark application can be affected by various valid dynamic events including interference with co-tenants.

This paper proposes a resource accounting technique, called HRA (Hardware-assisted Resource Accounting) for CPU time shares and memory pages, even if a hypervisor or individual system administrator is compromised. To detect any violation of resource allocation for CPU time shares and memory pages, instead of running a benchmark application, this study uses a sample-based approach to check the status of CPU and memory allocation by random probing. The probing program, which is protected from the hypervisor, checks the CPU allocation status and the number of memory pages with random time intervals. The execution of such random probing mechanism must be isolated from a potentially compromised hypervisor, and its sampled execution must not be preempted by the hypervisor. We use the system management mode (SMM) for probing execution, which provides a higher privileged execution environment than the hypervisor execution as shown in Figure 1. The probing code checks CPU and memory status randomly in SMM, without any interference from the hypervisor.

This paper investigates two aspects of resource accounting under a vulnerable hypervisor. First, this paper discusses our probing mechanism based on SMM, which is implemented on a commodity system. We show that the probing mechanism incurs little performance interference, while providing accurate resource allocation status. Even system administrators cannot affect the execution of probing program in SMM unless they have accesses to BIOS, which requires rebooting of the system. The integrity of BIOS can be assured by remote attestation based on TPM (Trusted Platform Module). Even if a remote attacker acquires root permission to the hypervisor or management VM, the attacker cannot intervene on the SMM-based probing execution.

Second, we investigate the trade-off between sampling rates and accuracies with statistical modeling to prove that the proposed technique can verify CPU and memory resources with negligible performance impact. CPU and memory status is checked randomly, and by statistical inference, the total CPU time and memory amount are estimated. As probing occurs more frequently, the accuracy of estimation further increases. However, performance overheads can increase to run the probe program frequently. Using a statistical analysis and experimental evaluation on a real system, we show that the proposed sample-based approach does not cause significant performance overheads, while maintaining a high accuracy.

To the best of our knowledge, this is one of the first studies to verify cloud CPU and memory resources in an unobtrusive way, even under a vulnerable hypervisor. Although prior studies discussed the importance and potential challenges for resource accounting in cloud computing [7, 10, 15, 17, 23], solutions require a secure hypervisor and system administrator. However, there have been successful attacks on the security of hypervisors, and furthermore resource appropriation attacks even without compromising the hypervisor [28, 34]. In addition, prior studies incur some overheads due to an additional software layer [7]. Our system can report the accurate CPU and memory accounting for such cases with little performance overheads. Our experimental analysis shows that the proposed system can detect the CPU time share and memory allocation with accuracies of 99% $\sim$ 100% with performance losses of 0.1% $\sim$ 0.5%.

The rest of the paper is organized as follows. Section 2 presents the motivation for resource verification in cloud computing. Section 3 presents the background for system management mode (SMM). Section 4 discusses our sample-based probing technique and statistical analysis. Section 5 describes the architecture and implementation of the verification mechanism with SMM. Section 6 shows experimental results. Section 7 discusses prior work, and Section 8 concludes the paper.

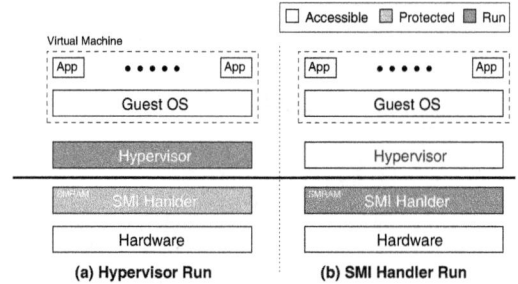

Figure 1: TCB of the proposed HRA system

2. Motivation

2.1 Cloud Security and Hypervisor Vulnerability

Along with the recent rapid growth in cloud computing, there have been increasing concerns over the security of cloud computing. Although cloud providers may make their best effort to keep the private data protected from remote attackers, cloud computing with multi-tenancy of sharing physical systems among cloud users can have an inherent potential vulnerability, which did not exist in in-house servers. In most of the commercial cloud services, cloud users can access only virtual machines (VMs), and the hypervisor provides an isolated execution environment for each VM. Furthermore, the hypervisor is responsible for allocating resources to VMs as mandated by SLA. Even though the hypervisor is critical for the security of virtualized clouds, hypervisor vulnerabilities have been growing gradually with its increasing code size for better performance and more complex functionality [16, 21, 22]. With such growing vulnerabilities of hypervisors, there have been several reports of attack cases [30, 31]. Furthermore, since the root-permission to the hypervisor or management domain (dom0 in Xen) can potentially provide unlimited accesses to user data in memory or resource allocation, a compromised system administrator can also have a full control over guest VMs.

202

To mitigate the security problem of hypervisors, there have several recent studies for protecting VMs. In SW-based approaches, support for nested virtualization adds an extra layer of virtualization to perform security-critical functions in the secure bottom-layer of virtualization [11]. An alternative design is to add a hardware-based security layer to provide such security functions [13]. However, in commercial systems, such proposals to improve the security of clouds with hypervisor vulnerabilities have yet to be adopted.

Most of the recent studies for hypervisor security have been focused on providing confidentiality and integrity of user data. However, a neglected aspect of security is the availability of resources. Even in the prior studies for securing hypervisors, the availability issue has not been addressed, since resource management still remains as an important role of hypervisors, and thus cannot be separated effectively from the hypervisors. In addition, the malicious administrator can assign an arbitrary amount of computing resources to a VM, by simply changing the resource allocation policy without breaking the hypervisor integrity.

2.2 Verifiable Resource Accounting

In virtualized clouds, users can only manage virtual CPUs and memory without direct accesses to the allocation of physical resources for their VMs. A VM has an illusion of having a contiguous virtual DRAM and CPU, but the hypervisor may dynamically change VM memory pages or schedule virtual CPUs, hiding the actual allocation of memory pages and CPU shares from guest VMs. Due to the virtualization of CPUs and memory, cloud users cannot directly account the CPU and memory allocation performed by the hypervisor. Since such CPU and memory usage information can only be reported by the potentially vulnerable hypervisor or administrator, the current cloud provider cannot provide secure user verification of resource accounting.

An alternative way to verify the CPU and memory allocation is to occasionally run a test benchmark application to measure the performance. The benchmark may infer any discrepancy between the reported resources and allocated resources based on the difference between the expected and measured performances. To verify the resource allocation, guest users must run the benchmark application occasionally. A major drawback of this benchmark approach is the difficulty of accounting fine-grained resource allocation changes. Furthermore, the performance of a benchmark application can be affected by various dynamic events including interference with co-tenants. Accurately inferring CPU usage or allocated physical memory indirectly from performance is not trivial. The second drawback of the benchmark approach is that a compromised hypervisor may detect the launch of the known test benchmark or even disable the test runs entirely, since it can access the memory of target VMs and modify the scheduled benchmark execution. This drawback can potentially abrupt the entire accounting mechanism by cloud users.

Another way to verify the allocated resources directly is to track application performance continuously. This type of application performance tracking can be used to a certain SLA type, which guarantees a maximum response time for some server workloads. For example, web servers running in clouds may have a target worst-case response time, and the cloud provider must meet the requirement with a very low rate of outliers. However, this type of SLA can be applied, only when the workloads are known a priori and their response time can be defined clearly. Commonly, it can be more easily applicable to platform-as-a-service (PaaS) clouds, than to infrastructure-as-a-service (IaaS). Due to the limited scope of the application-driven performance SLA, our system focuses on the resource-driven SLA, which verifies the amount of resources allocated to user VMs.

2.3 Threat Model

With various vulnerabilities [20, 21, 30, 31], a hypervisor can become malicious by external attacks or malicious insider. A malicious hypervisor or administrator can easily modify or access the private data of VMs and enforce an arbitrary resource management policy to allocate fewer resources to the guest VMs. In protecting guest VMs from these kinds of resource attacks, one of the most important components is to build a safe and privileged layer from the malicious hypervisor. The proposed HRA mechanism uses SMM as a higher privilege layer than the hypervisor execution. With SMM, HRA can exclude the hypervisor from the trusted computing base (TCB) and TCB includes only the hardware and BIOS loading the probing program. Since the system cannot guarantee the integrity of the proposed mechanism with a compromised BIOS, HRA uses Trusted Platform Module (TPM) [27] to verify the BIOS by writing the integrity information of the BIOS into Platform Configuration Register (PCR) when the system boots. With the TPM-based attestation, the client can rely on remote attestation to verify the proposed mechanism before a probing process.

To accelerate virtualization, current hardware manufactures developed hardware-assisted virtualization such as VT-x [12] and AMD-V [1], and most cloud providers use it for better performance. The proposed mechanism assumes that the hardware-assisted virtualization is available. The cloud providers manage all of the physical machine components including even the proposed mechanism. We assume that cloud providers, as an enterprise, are trustworthy, and they make their best effort to protect user VMs. Once provider attacks are detected, it has a fatal influence on their reputation and business. In opposition to the providers, some of individual administrators can be malicious. Each administrator has enough power to compromise the hypervisor of a subset of systems. Such malicious administrators can deallocate the resources by controlling the vulnerable hypervisor, allowing resource attacks even without altering hypervisor binaries. The administrators can steal the resources of VMs

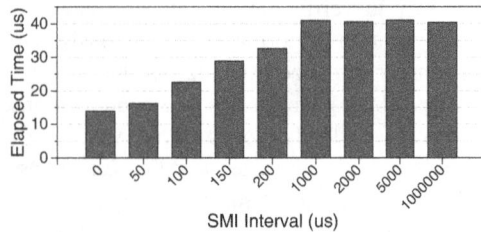

Figure 2: The Cost of Invoking SMM with intervals

by just altering VM configurations such as CPU allocation time or total memory.

However, the proposed mechanism does not provide memory protection to VMs. The previous studies [3, 4, 11, 13] can protect VMs against the malicious hypervisor for guest memory protection, and the proposed mechanism can be combined with them. The prior work for VM security protects the guest VM memory by adding an extra layer of hypervisor to perform security-critical functions, or requires a new architectural support for HW-based security operations. However, this work is based on the currently available hardware support for SMM and virtualization, and thus does not rely on an extra SW hypervisor, which can also be vulnerable and controlled by the administrator. However, we do not consider hardware attacks such as accessing DRAM after power-off or probing external buses, assuming the hardware system is protected by the cloud providers.

3. System Management Mode

To implement the proposed verifiable accounting mechanism under a vulnerable hypervisor, we use SMM to execute a resource probing program in an isolated execution environment protected even from the hypervisor. SMM [1, 12] is a special execution mode designed for processing maintenance functions in urgent circumstances. When the system software cannot handle abnormal system events such as high temperatures or hardware errors, SMM is invoked and execute the handlers for the abnormal events.

The x86 architectures use a special interrupt-driven mechanism to enter SMM. When a special interrupt called System Management Interrupt (SMI) is issued by predefined events or external requests, the current processor state is automatically saved in System Management RAM (SMRAM), part of memory configured for storing SMM states. SMRAM is inaccessible in any other modes except SMM. To process an SMI, a processor switches the current running task to the SMI handler located in SMRAM. After completing the SMI handling, the processor restores the saved processor state in processor registers by using a special instruction called *RSM* to resume the prior task.

SMRAM is normally configured by BIOS before the system software boots. After configured, SMRAM cannot be changed or disabled, protecting SMRAM from any software including the hypervisor which runs in a non-SMM mode. The system software cannot preempt the execution of SMM,

until SMM releases the current SMI handling, because all incoming interrupts or exceptions are pending in SMM. SMM is similar to a real mode which has full accesses to hardware resources. SMM can access the main memory and hardware devices with I/O port, being able to access even the memory area where the hypervisor and kernel are located. The proposed probing program resides in SMRAM protected from the hypervisor, and the hypervisor cannot know when the probing program is invoked.

The current SMM is designed for supporting management tasks such as power management and system hardware control tasks. These types of tasks require making all the current running tasks frozen. In addition to the lack of ability to control each core individually, there are several limitations in the current SMM design to consider for the implementation of the proposed secure accounting mechanism.

4GB Address Space Limit: SMM has privileged access permission to the main memory but it is restricted to $0 \sim 4GB$ memory space. Accessing the area beyond the 4GB limit leads to an undefined system behavior. To address this limitation in our implementation, the SMI handler modifies the SMM state-save area, replacing the saved context with stub codes. The stub codes are in charge of accessing the high memory region above the 4GB address limit, and run in the normal mode. Even if the stub code is running in the normal mode, all interrupts are disabled at the first SMI handling, so the stub code execution cannot be interrupted. After the execution of stub code for accessing the high memory region, the execution comes back to the SMI handler to re-enable interrupts.

All Cores SMM invocation: When an SMI occurs, all of the cores in a system must enter SMM synchronously. The HRA system checks the status of all cores simultaneously for resource verification operations to enter SMM together in all cores. However, some management operations such as creating and deleting VMs in our design need only one core to run the SMI handler, but the rest of cores also have to enter SMM due to the hardware restriction. This limited design causes performance degradations, but such management operations are very infrequent compared to resource probing operations.

Flushing write-back caches: An indirect performance overhead of entering SMM is the cost for flushing modified cache blocks. Before entering SMM, the modified write-back data in all the caches must be flushed to the main memory for coherence. To assess the performance overhead, Figure 2 shows the cost of invoking SMM with various intervals. To isolate the effect of cache flushing, the SMI handler immediately calls *RSM* instruction to exit as soon as entering SMM in this experiment. When SMIs are consecutively issued without intervals, it takes about $14\mu s$ per SMI. However, as the interval increases, the SMI handling time increases significantly to $40\mu s$, even for the same operation. The reason for the increasing latency is that with a longer

Resource	Time	Space
CPU	Allocation Time ✓	Number of CPU ✓
Memory	Bandwidth	Total Size ✓
Network	Latency, Throughput	Total Traffic
Storage	Latency, Throughput	Total Size

HRA verifies checked resources

Table 1: Resource Classification

interval until 1000 us, more cache blocks become modified, and the flushing operation takes a longer latency of $40\mu s$. However, as the cache capacity is limited, the cost for flushing dirty blocks does not increase further beyond $40\mu s$.

4. Sample-based Resource Accounting

This section describes our sample-based resource accounting mechanism for CPU and memory resources. To reduce the overhead of invoking SMM for probing resource allocation status, sampling rates should be reduced while a high accuracy is maintained. In this section, we describe a random sampling method, and analyze the accuracy and sampling rate trade-offs in the method.

4.1 Verifiable Resources

In cloud systems, all the resources are virtualized with time and space sharing by the hypervisor, although each guest VM has an illusion of dedicated resources. Time sharing is a virtualization of a resource by multiplexing virtual resource requests into a shared physical resource with fine-grained scheduling. Space sharing partitions resources in space and assigns each partition to a VM. Table 1 presents a classification of cloud resources and how they can be shared either by time and space partitioning. Among the resources with different sharing types, this paper focuses on two resources, which are difficult to account with the current virtualization techniques, CPU and memory resources.

CPU Resources: A hypervisor creates and schedules virtual CPUs (vCPU) for VMs, multiplexing vCPUs to limited physical cores by scheduling. The vCPUs share physical cores by time and space sharing, but the guest OS in each VM observes only the vCPUs without any direct knowledge of scheduling. Due to such CPU virtualization, a cloud user or guest OS is hard to identify the actual amount of CPU allocation by the hypervisor. Without any reliable hardware support in the current processors which cannot be altered by the hypervisor, the hypervisor can provide incorrect accounting information to the guest OS about CPU scheduling.

Memory Resources: The entire available memory is partitioned and allocated to VMs with space-sharing. To virtualize the memory, the current virtualization technique uses an additional address translation from guest physical address to machine address, for a contiguous guest-physical memory to each VM. The hypervisor can dynamically adjust the allocated memory pages of a VM by memory swapping without any permission from guest OSes. However, the hypervisor

cannot directly adjust memory bandwidth due to the lack of HW interface for bandwidth scheduling, even if its privilege level is high enough. Furthermore, common SLAs for clouds mandate only the capacity of memory allocation, without any guarantee on memory bandwidth due to the same lack of architectural support for adjusting memory bandwidth for a particular VM. In this paper, the proposed HRA mechanism reports the capacity of memory assigned for each VM.

I/O Resources: Unlike CPU or memory, I/O operations can be counted by the guest OS, since the guest VM generates I/O operation requested explicitly by the guest OS system call. Therefore, accounting I/O operations is relatively straightforward, unlike CPU and memory hidden by virtualization. However, one key problem can be the protection of accounting data from the potentially malicious hypervisor. The verifiable accounting system may provide an interface to guest VMs to record I/O operations securely. However, this paper focuses only on CPU and memory accounting, leaving the secure recording interface as future work.

4.2 Random Sampling based Resource Accounting

Our accounting system resides in SMM protected from the hypervisor. However, it cannot trace every context switch for CPUs or every allocation and deallocation of memory pages for two reasons. First, the accounting system in SMM is self-initiated not to be interfered by the hypervisor. In the current system architecture, system management interrupts (SMI) cannot be generated automatically by the hardware system for each context switch or memory page change. Therefore, the SMM-based accounting system should be launched by time-based scheduling to check the allocation status. Second, although the accounting program can quickly check the allocation status, there are non-negligible overheads for invoking SMM. Due to the overheads, there is a trade-off between sampling rates and accuracies for accounting. In this study, instead of tracking every context switch or page change, we use a sample-based accounting mechanism. The probing program is initiated by an SMI with random intervals, and checks the allocation status. In this section, we will discuss and analyze the random sampling method with an analytical model and simulation.

In this section, to simulate the effect of sampling with accuracy-overhead trade-offs, we use a scheduler simulator for examining estimation of the CPU resources under a potentially malicious hypervisor. The simulator emulates the Xen Credit Scheduler [32]. The simulator uses micro second as the minimum time unit and simulates vCPU scheduling based on VM traces collected from busy-waiting applications. To mimic the behavior of a malicious hypervisor, the simulator models that the hypervisor can force a context switch from a running VM any time. In real execution scenarios, the hypervisor can steal CPU resources after voluntary or forced VM exits any time. For example, even though CPU intensive applications are processed, the VM frequently exits and needs hypervisor interceptions for sys-

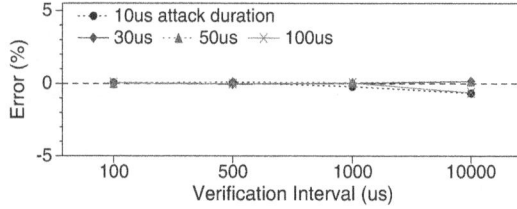

Figure 3: The Random Sampling Results on Simulation

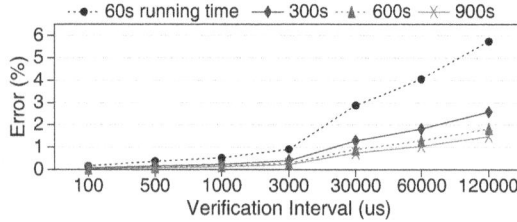

Figure 4: The Error on Various Running Time

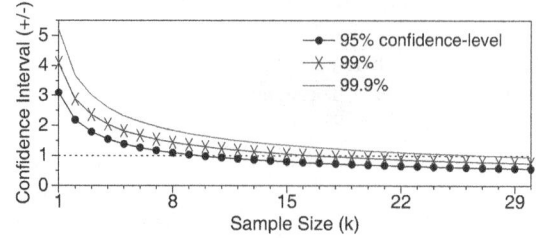

Figure 5: CPU Confidence Interval

tem calls and privileged executions. The malicious hypervisor can schedule the attacker VM as soon as the victim VM exits. Even exploiting Inter-Processor Interrupt (IPI) or timer interrupts, the hypervisor forces the victim VM to exit to schedule the attacker VM on any time. We have emulated such capability of the hypervisor stealing the CPU resources into the simulator.

Figure 3 shows the errors of random sampling on stealing 10% the CPU resources from the victim. The errors represent differences between the actual CPU allocation and one estimated by the sampling. In theory without considering the overheads of frequent context switches, the hypervisor may attempt to steal CPU resources with a very short duration not to be detected. To consider such extreme cases, fine-grained attack durations from 10μs to 100μs are selected in the experiment. In the figure, each curves shows different attack durations of the range. The x-axis represents different average verification intervals used by our random sampling method.

In the result, the random sampling correctly detects the hypervisor attack with the average 100μs verification interval. Even if the interval becomes longer, the random sampling generates relatively accurate results within 1% error. The error becomes as large as 1% in 10ms interval and 10μ attack duration, because the number of samples is not enough to generate correct results.

4.3 Statistical Analysis

With random sampling, it is critical to know the number of samples to have a certain level of confidence for the accuracy of estimated results. Figure 4 shows the number of samples must be large enough to produce correct CPU usage. In this figure, the x-axis represents different average verification intervals used by the probing program. Each curves shows different total execution times from 60 to 900 seconds. The error of 120000μs sample interval is as large as 6% with 60s, since with the 120000μs interval, it generates

only 500 samples during the 60s running time. With such a small number of samples, the random sampling cannot estimate CPU usages accurately. In this section, we use the Monte Carlo method for modeling the confidence of the random sampling and for inferring the sufficient quantity of samples [18].

First, we define an averaged CPU usage as the expected value of a random variable X, such as $\mu = \mathbb{E}(X)$. Each X is an independent sample from the same distribution. We calculate our estimation of μ by aggregating all of the generated random value X_i and dividing by the number of samples n: $\bar{X}_n = \frac{1}{n}\sum_{i=1}^{n} X_i$. In the Monte Carlo method, true variance δ^2 is usually unknown. However, it can be estimated from the sample values. The estimates of δ^2 are $s^2 = \frac{1}{n-1}\sum_{i=1}^{n}\left(X_i - \bar{X}_n\right)$. The s^2 will be very close to true variance δ^2 if the number of samples is large enough. According to Central Limit Theorem (CLT), $\bar{X}_n$ - μ has nearly a normal distribution with mean 0 and variance δ^2 [8]. Therefore, the random sampling has a confidence interval which can be estimated as:

$$\bar{x}_n \pm z_{\alpha/2}\frac{s}{\sqrt{n}} \tag{1}$$

For a 95% confidence interval, we use $\alpha = 0.05$, and therefore set $z_{\alpha/2} = z_{0.025} = 1.96$. According to the confidence interval equation, the length of confidence interval tends to be 0 as the number of sample n gets extremely huge. By rearranging the confidence interval equation, we can generates the minimum sample size n under the length of 100 $(1 - \alpha)$% confidence interval $2d$ for true mean μ as follows:

$$n \geq \left(z_{\alpha/2}\frac{s}{d}\right)^2 \tag{2}$$

To show the correlation between sample size and the length of confidence interval, we run the simulator emulating that hypervisor steals 10% of victim CPU resources with average intervals of 60ms. The Figure 5 presents the length of confidence interval associated with the sample size. The confidence interval is likely to drop sharply until 8000 samples. To narrow 1% length confidence interval, we needs about 16,000 samples. It indicates that the random sampling can have at least 1% error in 16,000 samples. If we sample more, we can more assure our results and the error can be more reduced.

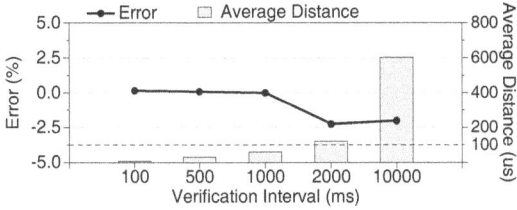

Figure 6: The Error on Long Intervals

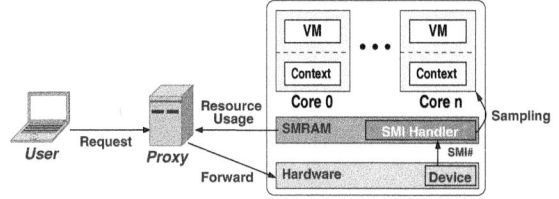

Figure 7: HRA Overview

However, the Monte Carlo method can generate misleading results if samples do not reflect a whole distribution. In random sampling, samples need to be uniformly distributed and cover whole VM scheduling stochastically. Suppose the sampling rate is $\frac{the\ number\ of\ samples}{time}$, and the interval can be defined as $\frac{time}{the\ number\ of\ samples}$. Longer intervals may miss more chances to detect hypervisor attacks, increasing the coverage error of sampling. With long sampling intervals, the random sampling does not cover the resource status occasionally in spite of a large number of samples.

With higher sampling rates, samples are more densely located within the same time interval. The average distance of samples is represented as follows:

$$Average\ Distance = \frac{Interval}{The\ Number\ of\ Samples} \quad (3)$$

Figure 6 shows that the random sampling does not produce correct CPU usage even with a large number of samples for long sampling intervals. In the experiment, the attack duration and the attack interval are $10\mu s$ and $100\mu s$ respectively. A malicious hypervisor steals 10% of CPU resources from the victim. The sampling interval is extremely increased from 100ms to 10000ms. The random sampling can produce correct results until 1000ms interval, but the error of 2000ms and 10000ms interval is beyond 2%. Nearly 50% of resource attacks cannot be detected with the long intervals, because the error is close to 2.5% and the average distance of samples is longer than the $100\mu s$ attack interval. In addition to the quantity of sample, the following equation for the restriction on sample distances must be satisfied to avoid large coverage errors.

$$Attack\ Interval \geq Average\ Distance \quad (4)$$

5. Architecture

5.1 Overview

This section describes the overall architecture of our resource accounting system, which is based on the random sampling described in the previous section. The probing program resides in SMRAM, and runs in SMM protected from the hypervisor. The system reports the amount of allocated CPU and memory resources even under a malicious hypervisor or administrator attempting to report false accounting. Figure 7 shows the overall architecture of the proposed accounting system. The system consists of a proxy system and computing machines. The proxy forwards accounting requests from users to a target system, issuing an SMI to generate the accounting summary. To be able to initiate SMIs by requests from a remote proxy, the computing machine must have an SMI-capable network device. The prototype system uses a serial device to invoke SMIs for the probing program from the proxy server. The serial device is excluded from the available devices for the hypervisor, which prevents any possible hypervisor intervention for the serial communication. For better bandwidth and scalability, the proposed accounting platform can use an out-of-band network channel. Most commercial servers are equipped with Ethernet as an out-of-band channel for IPMI (Intelligent Platform Management Interface). This out-of-band channel securely communicates with the proxy under a malicious hypervisor or administrators.

Once a user requests resource verification to a proxy while the user's application is running, the proxy enables the sample probing program in the computing machine, which schedules sample probing runs with random intervals set by the proxy. After aggregating samples, the probing program infers the actual usage of CPU and memory, and reports the result to the proxy. With a relatively minor overhead as will be discussed in the result section, the resource accounting system can be continuously running without noticeable performance degradation. The client can use the reported accounting information in different ways depending on the SLA. It can be used to verify whether the contracted amount of resources are actually allocated, or to verify the cost of CPU and memory, if the provider charges the cost based on the actual resource usage.

The accounting system depends on not only SMM but also hardware-assisted virtualization. For the hardware-assisted virtualization, the Virtual Machine Control Block (VMCB) [1] has an area to save the VM context information as well as the vCPU configurations. In our implementation, the VMCB is used to identify a VM and find the vCPU configurations. When a CPU enters SMM, the context of a running VM is saved in the SMM save-state area. The saved context contains the physical location of VMCB and indicates whether the running task belongs to the hypervisor or VM. In addition, the accounting system can identify which VM runs on a particular core by inspecting its VMCB.

Algorithm 1 Random sampling's algorithm

Proxy: Invoking VERIFY CPU at random
1: **for** $count \geq n$ **do**
2:    $interval \leftarrow rand(configured\,value * 2)$
3:    Invoking Verify CPU via SMI
4:    $sleep(interval)$
5:    $n \leftarrow n + 1$
6: **end for**

Algorithm 2 Verify CPU's algorithm

Probing: Verifying CPU
1: $save\_state \leftarrow SMRAM + STATE\_OFFSET[core\_id]$
2: **if** $save\_state.svm\_state$ is not host **then**
3:    $vmcb \leftarrow save\_state.vmcb$
4:    $vcpu \leftarrow rb\_tree\_search(vmcb.nCR3)$
5:    $vcpu.run\_count \leftarrow vcpu.run\_count + 1$
6: **end if**
7: $total\_count \leftarrow total\_count + 1$
8: RSM

5.2 Basic Operations

HRA supports several basic operations for managing VMs and estimating the resource allocation. Currently, HRA supports six operations. *Create VM* and *DeleteVM* are used for tracking VM life cycles. *Create vCPU* and *Delete vCPU* are provided for managing vCPUs. These management operations maintain mapping information between the physical entity such as the nCR3 register value and the virtual entity such as the VM name. Mapping information are necessary for *Verify CPU* and *Verify MEM*, which are used for verifying resource allocation status. The detailed explanation of operations will be described in the following section.

5.3 VM Identification

To distinguish each VM, our accounting system selects the value of nCR3 register as a unique key reflecting VM identification. The nCR3 register value represents the VM address space, pointing the top translation page for nested address mapping. To register a VM to the probing program, the proxy must request to add a VM to the probing program by a *create VM* operation. A user requests a new VM to the proxy, and then the proxy forwards this request to the hypervisor for creating a new VM. After creating a new VM, the hypervisor informs the proxy the about completion of the request. The steps are similar to the conventional cloud systems. In addition, the proxy invokes *Create VM* and *Create vCPU* on the probing program to discover the nCR3 register value of the new VM. With *Create VM* and *Create vCPU*, the proxy maintains the mapping information between the VM name and nCR3 values. Once the mapping information between a user VM and its nCR3 value is established, the HRA system uses the nCR3 value as a key for the VM.

Algorithm 3 Verify MEM's algorithm

Probing: Verifying MEM
1: $save\_state \leftarrow SMRAM + STATE\_OFFSET[core\_id]$
2: **if** $save\_state.svm\_state$ is not host **then**
3:    $vmcb \leftarrow save\_state.vmcb$
4:    $mem \leftarrow rb\_tree\_search(vmcb.nCR3)$
5:    $mfn\_list \leftarrow npt\_walk(vmcb.nCR3)$
6:    $mem.count \leftarrow npt\_verify(mfn\_list)$
7: **end if**
8: RSM

5.4 Estimation of Resources

Algorithm 1 describes the invocation of *Verify CPU* with a random interval. The proxy generates a random interval with a configured value. The random intervals are uniformly distributed between 0 and $2 \times configured\ value$. After issuing an SMI to call *Verify CPU*, the proxy waits for the next sampling run. Generating random intervals in the proxy is to mitigate the performance overhead for high quality random number generation in computing nodes and to create random numbers isolated completely from the hypervisor.

Algorithm 2 shows how to verify the CPU allocation from the probing program. The saved state area includes the last context information before the SMI invocation, automatically created on SMI. The *svm_state* fields of the saved state represents whether the core runs on the host mode or guest mode. If the core runs on the guest mode, the probing program retrieves the VMCB address from the saved state and the nCR3 value of VMCB is used for identifying which VM was running on the core. To quickly look up the vCPU list created by *Create vCPU*, the probing program maintains a red-black tree as an index structure. The red-black tree provides the worst-case guarantees, which is critical in a low latency system such as the proposed accounting system. After looking up the vCPU list, the probing program increases the run count of the vCPU data, and then *RSM* instruction is called to resume the execution of the VM. The accounting systems count the number of samples each vCPU is running, and infer the CPU allocation with the ratio of the count of each vCPU over the total number of samples.

For memory resources, the probing program also uses the nCR3 register to estimate the total allocated memory of a VM. The nCR3 value points the nested page table referenced on every page translation. As the nested page table contains mapping information from the guest physical address to machine address space, the total allocated memory can be estimated by traversing the nested page table. Algorithm 3 shows the estimation of memory resources. After the probing program accesses the physical location of VMCB by inspecting the saved state, it traverses the nested page table pointed by nCR3 and measures the total allocated memory of the VM.

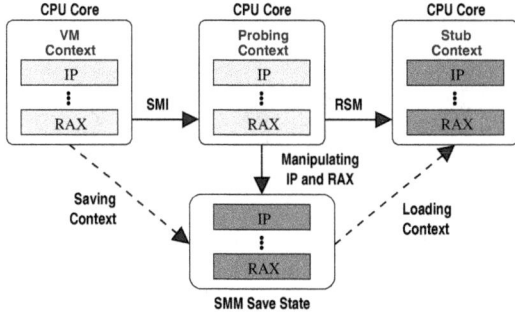

Figure 8: Snatching VM Context

To reduce latency of *Verify MEM*, the probing program only traverses addressable entries of nested page table. For example, if a VM has up to 1GB memory, the probing program just traverses the first 13 entries. Because the 13 entries cover the 1GB address space. The malicious hypervisor can share the same machine memory with multiple VMs. To detect these types of sharing attacks, the probing program inspects nested page tables of all VMs and identifies whether duplicated machine memory exists. The probing program also checks present bits in entries of nested page table due to memory swapping. The memory verification latency can be much longer than the CPU verification, and it may increase with larger memory capacities and small page sizes. We can reduce latency of *Verify MEM* by applying a spatial random sampling. The probing program randomly traverses a fixed number of entries, instead of traversing all of entries. Adopting random sampling, *Verify MEM* always generates the same latency regardless of memory configuration. In the result section, we discuss the effect of spatial sampling of memory allocation.

5.5 Avoiding Impersonating Attacks

A malicious hypervisor can allocate a duplicated nCR3 register value or dynamically change the nCR3 register at runtime. To detect such attacks, our accounting system maintains all the nCR3 register values of VMs in the system. However, the malicious hypervisor can use a more sophisticated attack impersonating a victim VM, switching the nCR3 values between the victim and attacker. For the attacker VM to run with the nCR3 value of the victim VM, the attacker VM must run on the address space of the victim. If the hypervisor simply extends the address space by altering the nested page table, the accounting system can detect this attack, inspecting entries of the nested page table. However, replacing memory contents with the attacker code is hard to detect without verifying the integrity of memory contents.

To detect this attack, our system uses a preliminary sample-based approach, which runs a stub code occasionally instead of running user VMs. This approach is similar to GINGER [24]. The system snatches a VM context switch and runs a stub code instead of the expected user VM. The stub code leaves integrity watermarks on its memory space and registers. The hypervisor, without knowing whether the

current context is for a guest VM or the stub code, may attempt to compromise the memory content or registers to run an attacker VM. If a malicious hypervisor attacks the running stub context, our system can detect the integrity violation. The stub context works as a trap for attacks and runs a simple job consuming allocated CPU resources. Since it wastes CPU cycles, it can be used only for a limited number of sampled periods. Figure 8 shows snatching a VM context switch on an SMI, the VM context is saved and the probing program copies the stub code and changes the instruction pointer and RAX register to run the stub code. Then the probing program calls the RSM instruction to return to the prior context. The current implementation of stub code just leaves known simple values on memory and registers in random locations to detect any changes by the malicious hypervisor. A more sophisticated implementation is our future work.

5.6 Limitation

CPU-intensive workloads mostly consume all the CPU resources allocated to users. However, CPU and I/O mixed workloads voluntarily release assigned CPU shares before consuming all CPU shares waiting for I/O completion. Our accounting system just samples the current CPU usage and cannot identify whether the sampled result are caused by voluntary release or preemption by hypervisor. The accounting system reports only how much CPU share each VM actually received from the hypervisor, but does not identify the reason for not using CPUs, if the measured CPU share is lower than the expected value.

How to use the CPU and memory accounting information depends on the cloud service model and SLA. If the cloud service must always guarantee a certain amount of CPU and memory without work-conserving scheduling, the estimated accounting results must match the resource amount mandated by SLA. In commercial public clouds, such non-work-conserving model is commonly used [28, 34]. An alternative cloud model is to charge the cost based on the actual usage of resources. In such models, the accurate accounting is also critical to verify the cost from resource consumption.

6. Evaluation

6.1 Experimental Setup

Our prototype HRA platform consists of a proxy machine and a computing machine. The computing machine has a single AMD hexa-core 2.8GHz CPU supporting the hardware-assisted virtualization and 8GB DDR3 Memory. The proxy machine has a single Intel quad-core 3.4GHz CPU and 8GB DDR3 Memory. The proxy does not affect the performance of the computing system due to the limited role in forwarding user requests. We use Xen 4.0.1 [32] as the hypervisor to run VMs and use Ubuntu 10.04 for the management VM and user VMs. The proposed mechanism can be applicable to not only a variant of Xen but also other hypervisors with

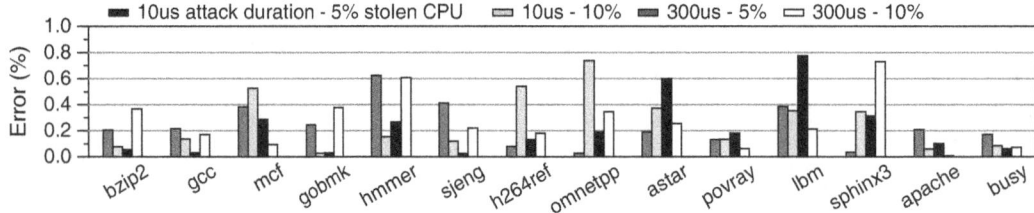

Figure 9: The CPU Verification Results on Real Environment

small modifications, since the HRA system does not modify the hypervisor or guest OS directly. A customized BIOS is installed on the computing machine to apply our probing program into SMM. The probing program has 16MB size in SMRAM where its codes and data reside. For communication between the proxy and computing systems, we use a serial device, which is excluded from the available devices to the hypervisor.

We run diverse experiments for evaluating the proposed mechanism. First, we run micro-benchmark tests to evaluate the performance of six basic operations of the proposed mechanism. HRA manages the data structures related to VMs through basic operations whenever a VM or vCPU is created. The experiment runs each operation 100 times, and the latencies are averaged. To estimate the CPU resources, HRA uses the aforementioned random sampling technique. We compare the actual CPU resources usage with the one estimated by the random sampling to show the accuracy and performance of the random sampling method.

As mentioned in Section 3, the overall system performance can be degraded because the running tasks have to stop when SMM is invoked. As a simple benchmark in each VM exercising CPUs, we first use a busy-waiting application, which constantly consumes CPU cycles. Furthermore, to investigate the trade-offs between the accuracy and performance, we use diverse workloads to reflect complex characteristics caused by multi-tenancy of clouds. The workloads consist of apache compile [2], SPECjbb 2005 [26], SPECCPU 2006 [25] and RUBis [19]. The apache compile is a CPU intensive workload compiling apache web server 2.2219. SPECjbb 2005 consumes a large amount of memory and is a typical memory intensive workload evaluating the server side java. SPECCPU 2006 is widely used in business and academia, measuring compute-intensive performance with a range of workloads. RUBis simulates an auction site for performance scalability. RUBis generates many TCP/IP packets, emulating various web interactions.

6.2 Micro-benchmark

HRA uses four operations as management operations, which are used for tracking and managing VM life cycle and vC-PUs. As invoked at VM management, these operations are not frequently used during a VM life cycle and do not affect the performance of VM workloads significantly. Table 2 shows that these operations take between $53\mu s$ and $63\mu s$. During these operations, a half of the elapsed time is spent

Operation	Time (μs)
Create / Delete VM	63.3 / 57.6
Create / Delete vCPU	61.7 / 58.1
Verify CPU	52.0
Verify MEM (1GB)	897
Verify MEM (20 entries)	111

Table 2: The Elapsed Time for Basic Operations

for entering and exiting SMM as discussed in Section 3. The rest of the time is spent on performing the actual operations. Considering these operations are rarely executed, the overhead of these operations is negligible.

Verify CPU identifies which VM runs on the current core by inspecting the saved context. It takes $52\mu s$ for *Verify CPU*, therefore it must be negligible overhead as a single operation. However, to estimate the CPU usage, a large number of the operations should be called, which can cause performance degradation in the system. As mentioned in Section 4.3, we have to call at least 16000 *Verify CPU* operations to keep error below 1%. It takes 8.3s for calling consecutively 16000 *Verify CPU*. We will discuss an effect of CPU verification on system performance in Section 6.5. *Verify MEM* measures the total allocated memory to VM. It takes about $897\mu s$ for *Verify MEM 1GB*, accessing all of entries in the nested page table. The performance of *Verify MEM* with various memory sizes will be discussed in Section 6.4.

6.3 Measuring CPU Resources

Figure 9 shows the accuracy of CPU verification as compared with the actual CPU usage. There are four attack types in the experiment according to the attack duration and amount of stealing CPU resources. The prefix of each legend is the attack duration and the postfix of each legend presents how much hypervisor steals the CPU resources from the victim. For example, 10us - 5% indicates that hypervisor steals the CPU resource as much as 5% from the victim with $10\mu s$ attack duration. Random intervals with an average 60ms are used for verifying CPU resources in this experiment. SPEC-CPU 2006, apache and busy-waiting workload are used in this experiment. The experiment results are averaged from five runs.

This experiment shows that the random sampling method produces a good accuracy with below 1% error on every workload. These results are similar to the estimated result from the simulation experiments as shown in Figure 3, with

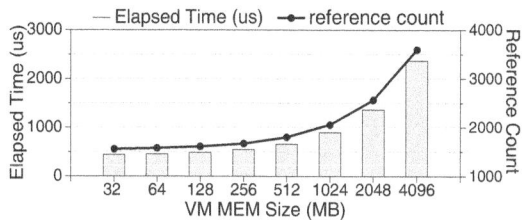

Figure 10: The Elapsed Time for Memory Verification

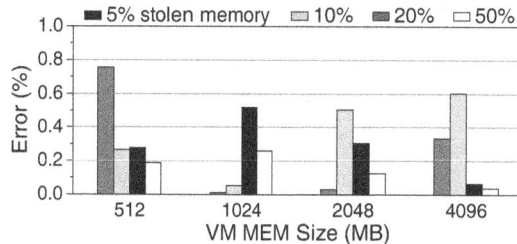

Figure 11: The Random Sampling for Memory Verification

minor variations. There is no clear correlation among errors, workloads, and attack types. Even with a short $10\mu s$ attack duration, random sampling can still produce a good accuracy with the average 60ms interval. A very short attack duration requires that attack must be frequently occurred as much as the reduced attack duration. In addition, such a short attack durations slow down system performance due to frequent VM switching which pollutes system locality. $10\mu s$ attack duration slow down 20% of system performance on the gcc workload of SPECCPU 2006. The slowdown for the short attack duration is caused by the attacking hypervisor, not by the probing program which is invoked only with 60ms average intervals.

6.4 Measuring Memory Resources

Figure 10 shows the total elapsed time and memory references for memory verification with various memory sizes. Unlike the prior experiments, we use DSL Linux 4.4 [9] to run a VM with a small OS memory footprint, to measure the latency for the *verify MEM* from 32MB to 4GB memory sizes. The baseline Linux has too large a memory footprint to fit in the small 32MB memory. It takes $442\mu s$ for memory verification on 32MB memory size and there is a very little time increase of latency until 256MB memory size. The reason for minor increases is that the cost for traversing nested page tables does not increase significantly. Since the hypervisor assigns memory with a large page unit (2MB) mostly, a small number of page table entries can cover a large memory, reducing the number of memory references during memory verification. An exception is that the current Xen hypervisor allocates the first 6MB memory with 4KB page unit, which requires about 1500 memory references. Due to the small pages for the first 6MB, it takes a non-negligible latency for 32MB memory.

The number of memory references increase significantly when the memory size increases beyond 1024MB, with the considerable increase of the elapsed time with 4096MB. Memory is mainly shared by space but a malicious hypervisor can steal memory from victim time sharing. Frequent memory verification can detect this attack but may slow down system performance. To deal with this constraint, we use a random spatial sampling for memory. In memory verification, our system just traverses 20 entries by random, which consumes only $111\mu s$. Figure 11 shows the accuracy of memory verification as compared with the actual allocation of memory. Four bars present the errors when 5%, 10%,

20% and 50% of the victim memory stolen by hypervisor. In this experiment, we enable the balloon driver of guest VM to mimic hypervisor attacks. Balloon driver repeats the allocation and deallocation memory every 5 seconds. The random sampling of memory verification produces a good accuracy even with a small amount of stolen memory. The error does not exceed 1% on any attack case. Unlike CPU verification, only 150 samples are needed to be produce reliable accuracy in Monte Carlo calculation. The performance of memory verification with random sampling will be discussed in the follow section.

6.5 Performance of Workloads

To evaluate HRA on a real environment, we run various workloads with different sampling intervals. Each guest VM has 3072MB memory and a virtual CPU. Workloads consist of SPECCPU 2006, apache compilation, SPECjbb and RUBis workload. The inverse elapsed time is used as the performance metric in the SPECCPU 2006 and apache compilation. For the SPECjbb, the performance score is used as the metric and we use the averaged throughput as the metric for the RUBis.

Figure 12 shows the normalized performance with random CPU verification runs against non-CPU verification runs. The performance degradation appears on every workload when CPU verification is launched on an average interval of a very short 3ms interval. The performance of the apache compilation, SPECjbb and RUBis decrease by 7%, 8% and 3% respectively. The performance of SPECCPU 2006 decreases broadly. All cores are forced to stop on every sampling interval, which takes about $60\mu s$ as shown in Table 2. Especially the entire dirty cache lines must be flushed on entering SMM, which affects the locality of running workloads and causes performance degradations. These effects stand out on the CPU intensive workloads. SPECjbb consumes not only a huge memory but also CPU resources, so the performance degradation is severe in SPECjbb as well as SPECCPU 2006.

For the average 30ms interval, the performance of most workloads decreases only by 1% $\sim$ 2% due to less verification overheads than 3ms. For the 60ms, the performance degradation is negligible and there is no performance difference between 60ms interval and non-CPU verification. In addition, some workloads of SPECCPU 2006 show better performance against non-CPU verification. The CPU verifi-

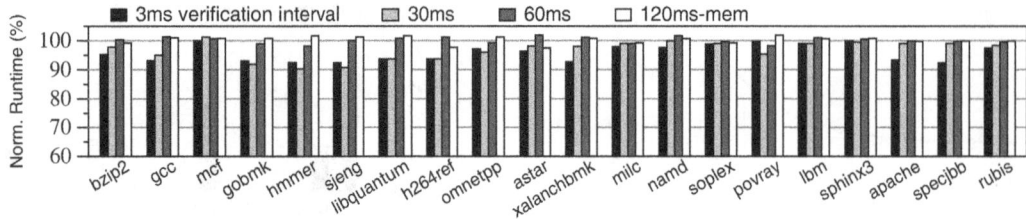

Figure 12: The Normalized Performance on Diverse Workloads

7. Related Work

There have been recent studies on attacks on resource allocation for clouds. Varadarajan et al. showed a new class of attack called RFA (Resource-Freeing Attack) in commercial cloud services. RFA compels a victim VM to free up resources by causing interference [28]. Zhou et al. demonstrated scheduler vulnerabilities in commercial cloud services [34]. Exploiting timing-based manipulation, a malicious customer breaks fair allocation of CPU resources and consume resources allocated to valid users. To defend these types of attacks fundamentally, Chen et al. introduced ALIBI, which monitors resource allocation underneath the cloud provider platform with nested virtualization [7]. ALIBI supports verifiable resource accounting to users, tracking guest memory and CPU-cycle consumption. However, it relies on nested virtualization with non-negligible overheads.

There have been several studies about SLA in cloud services. Baset analyzed and compared diverse SLAs of current public IaaS, and then indicated that the provider does not support performance SLA and users have to produce the evidence of SLA violations [5]. Lango introduced new SD-SLA (Software-Defined SLAs) which guarantees various SLOs (Service-Level Objectives) and satisfies minimum service requirements of users by runtime VM reconfiguration [14]. Bouchenak et al. investigated various tools and methods which can verify cloud services. They discussed the properties which must be satisfied on verifying cloud services [6]. They also introduced a new cloud model to guarantee performance SLA under a reliable hypervisor and management VM.

There has been studies about not only new designs of SLA but also possible detection of SLA violation [10, 15, 17]. CASVid [10] detects SLA violation at application layer by allocating and monitoring resources. Macias et al. introduced a policy of SLAs for better QoS, classifying clients according to the relationship with the provider and pay-

ment [15]. They preferentially guarantee the SLA of client regarded as a high priority in the cloud. Maurer et al. introduced the resource management framework which supports automatic resource allocation and guarantee SLAs by VM reconfiguration with minimizing violations of SLA and maximizing resource utilization [17]. These prior studies [10, 15, 17] depend on the integrity of administrator and privileged software such as a hypervisor. If administrators or privileged software is malicious, these studies cannot guarantee SLAs. However, our mechanism does not rely on the integrity of administrators or hypervisor.

There are several prior studies [3, 4, 29, 33] using SMM. Most of the studies focus on protecting execution environments. HyperCheck [29] and HyperSentry [3] verify the integrity of hypervisor with SMM. When SMI is invoked, the SMI handler checks the integrity of hypervisor to identify cleanness of system. SPECTRE [33] is an introspection framework detecting memory-based stealthy malware via SMM. To detect heap spray, heap overflow, and rootkit, SPECTRE introspects the operating system kernel, including its code and data. SICE [4] provides an isolated execution environment with hardware supports such as SMM without relying on any software of legacy host. SICE can extend a piece of software into VM level as isolated execution environment, protecting the VM from a malicious hypervisor.

8. Conclusions

This paper proposed a hardware-based secure resource verification framework for cloud computing. The framework can verify CPU and memory resources even under a vulnerable hypervisor, and it reduces the tracking overhead by sample-based measurements. In consolidated virtualized cloud systems with data-center scale deployment, it will become more difficult or inefficient to verify the resource allocation for each individual user without a low-overhead framework. The proposed framework showed the feasibility of hardware-oriented secure resource verification.

Acknowledgments

This work was supported by the National Research Foundation of Korea(NRF) grant funded by the Korea government(MSIP) (No. NRF-2013R1A2A2A01015514) and by the IT R&D program of MSIP/IITP [10041313, UX-oriented Mobile SW Platform].

References

[1] Advanced Micro Dvices. AMD64 Architecture Programmer's Mannual: Volume 2: System Programming, 2007.

[2] Apache HTTP Server. http://httpd.apache.org, 2011.

[3] A. M. Azab, P. Ning, Z. Wang, X. Jiang, X. Zhang, and N. C. Skalsky. HyperSentry: enabling stealthy in-context measurement of hypervisor integrity. In *Proceedings of 17th ACM Conference on Computer and Communications Security, CCS 2010.*

[4] A. M. Azab, P. Ning, and X. Zhang. Sice: a hardware-level strongly isolated computing environment for x86 multi-core platforms. In *Proceedings of the 18th ACM conference on Computer and communications security, CCS 2011.*

[5] S. A. Baset. Cloud SLAs: Present and Future. *ACM SIGOPS Operating Systems Review*, 46(2):57–66, 2012.

[6] S. Bouchenak, G. Chockler, H. Chockler, G. Gheorghe, N. Santos, and A. Shraer. Verifying Cloud Services: Present and Future. *ACM SIGOPS Operating Systems Review*, 47(2):6–19, 2013.

[7] C. Chen, P. Maniatis, A. Perrig, A. Vasudevan, and V. Sekar. Towards Verifiable Resource Accounting for Outsourced Computation. In *Proceedings of the 9th ACM SIGPLAN/SIGOPS International Conference on Virtual Execution Environments, VEE 2013.*

[8] K. L. Chung. *A Course In Probability Theory*. Academic press, 2001.

[9] Damn Small Linux. http://www.damnsmalllinux.org/, 2014.

[10] V. C. Emeakaroha, T. C. Ferreto, M. A. S. Netto, I. Brandic, and C. A. De Rose. CASViD: Application Level Monitoring for SLA Violation Detection in Clouds. In *Proceedings of the 36th IEEE Computer Software and Applications Conference, COMPSAC 2012.*

[11] H. C. Fengzhe Zhang, Jin Chen and B. Zang. CloudVisor: Retrofitting Protection of Virtual Machines in Multi-tenant Cloud with Nested Virtualization. In *Proceedings of the 23rd ACM Symposium on Operating Systems Principles, SOSP 2011.*

[12] Intel Corporation. Software Developer's Mannual vol. 3: System Programming Guide, 2009.

[13] S. Jin, J. Ahn, S. Cha, and J. Huh. Architectural support for secure virtualization under a vulnerable hypervisor. In *Proceedings of the 44th Annual IEEE/ACM International Symposium on Microarchitecture, MICRO 2011.*

[14] J. Lango. Toward Software-defined SLAs. *Communications of the ACM*, 57(1):54–60, 2014.

[15] M. Macias and J. Guitart. Client Classification Policies for SLA Enforcement in Shared Cloud Datacenters. In *Proceedings of the 12th IEEE/ACM International Symposium on Cluster, Cloud and Grid Computing, CCGrid 2012.*

[16] D. Magenheimer. Xen developer's mailing list: http://secunia.com/advisories/26986/, 2010.

[17] M. Maurer, I. Brandic, and R. Sakellariou. Self-adaptive and Resource-efficient SLA Enactment for Cloud Computing Infrastructures. In *Proceedings of the 5th IEEE International Conference on Cloud Computing, CLOUD 2012.*

[18] R. Y. Rubinstein and D. P. Kroese. *Simulation and the Monte Carlo method*, volume 707. John Wiley & Sons, 2011.

[19] RUBiS Benchmark. http://rubis.ow2.org, 2008.

[20] Secunia Vulnerability Report. http://secunia.com/advisories/15863/, 2010.

[21] Secunia Vulnerability Report. http://secunia.com/advisories/25985/, 2010.

[22] Secunia Vulnerability Report: Xen 3.x. http://secunia.com/advisories/product/15863/, 2010.

[23] V. Sekar and P. Maniatis. Verifiable Resource Accounting for Cloud Computing Services. In *Proceedings of the 3rd ACM Workshop on Cloud Computing Security Workshop, CCSW 2011.*

[24] S. Setty, V. Vu, N. Panpalia, B. Braun, A. J. Blumberg, and M. Walfish. Taking Proof-based Verified Computation a Few Steps Closer to Practicality. In *Proceedings of the 21st USENIX Conference on Security Symposium, Security 2012.*

[25] SPECCPU2006 Benchmark. http://www.spec.org/cpu2006, 2005.

[26] SPECjbb2005 Benchmark. http://www.spec.org/jbb2005, 2005.

[27] Trusted Platform Module. http://www.trustedcomputinggroup.org/developers/trusted_platform_module.

[28] V. Varadarajan, T. Kooburat, B. Farley, T. Ristenpart, and M. M. Swift. Resource-freeing Attacks: Improve Your Cloud Performance. In *Proceedings of the 19th ACM Conference on Computer and Communications Security, CCS 2012.*

[29] J. Wang, A. Stavrou, and A. K. Ghosh. HyperCheck: A Hardware-Assisted Integrity Monitor. In *Proceedings of 13th International Symposium on Recent Advances in Intrusion Detection, RAID 2010.*

[30] R. Wojtczuk. Subverting the Xen Hypervisor, 2008.

[31] R. Wojtczuk and J. Rutkowska. Xen 0wning trilogy, 2008.

[32] Xen Hypervisor. http://www.xen.org/, 2010.

[33] F. Zhang, K. Leach, K. Sun, and A. Stavrou. SPECTRE: A Dependable Introspection Framework via System Management Mode. In *Proceedings of the 43rd IEEE/IFIP International Conference on Dependable Systems and Networks, DSN 2013.*

[34] F. Zhou, M. Goel, P. Desnoyers, and R. Sundaram. Scheduler Vulnerabilities and Coordinated Attacks in Cloud Computing. In *Proceedings of the 10th IEEE International Symposium on Networking Computing and Applications, NCA 2011.*

PARS: A Page-Aware Replication System for Efficiently Storing Virtual Machine Snapshots

Lei Cui, Tianyu Wo, Bo Li, Jianxin Li, Bin Shi, Jinpeng Huai

SKLSDE lab, Beihang University, China.

{cuilei, woty, libo, lijx, shibin, huaijp}@act.buaa.edu.cn

Abstract

Virtual machine (VM) snapshot enhances the system availability by saving the running state into stable storage during failure-free execution and rolling back to the snapshot point upon failures. Unfortunately, the snapshot state may be lost due to disk failures, so that the VM fails to be recovered. The popular distributed file systems employ replication technique to tolerate disk failures by placing redundant copies across disperse disks. However, unless user-specific personalization is provided, these systems consider the data in the file as of same importance and create identical copies of the entire file, leading to non-trivial additional storage overhead.

This paper proposes a page-aware replication system (PARS) to store VM snapshots efficiently. PARS employs VM introspection technique to explore how a page is used by guest, and classifies the pages by their importance to system execution. If a page is critical, PARS replicates it multiple copies to ensure high availability and long-term durability. Otherwise, the loss of this page causes no harm for system to work properly, PARS therefore saves only one copy of the page. Consequently, PARS improves storage efficiency without compromising availability. We have implemented PARS to justify its practicality. The experimental results demonstrate that PARS achieves 53.9% space saving compared to the native replication approach in HDFS which replicates the whole snapshot file fully and identically.

Categories and Subject Descriptors   C.4 [*Performance of Systems*]: Reliability, availability, and serviceability;   D.4.5 [*Organization and Design*]: Checkpoint/restart

Keywords   Replication; Virtual machine snapshot; Availability; Storage space saving; Introspection

VEE '15,   March 14–15, 2015, Istanbul, Turkey..
Copyright © 2015 ACM 978-1-4503-3450-1/15/03... $15.00.
http://dx.doi.org/10.1145/2731186.2731190

1. Introduction

Virtualization has become the cornerstone of cloud infrastructures. The applications now run inside the virtual machine (VM) which provides an isolated and scaled computing paradigm, rather than physical machine [9, 12, 28, 29]. The VM snapshot is an essential part to support high availability in cloud infrastructures, it saves the running state of VM into persistent storage and recovers the VM from the saved state upon failures. The main advantage is that the VM can be rolled back to an intermediate state rather than the initial state, thereby reducing the computation loss [20, 32, 43].

However, storing snapshots in persistent storage faces several challenges. First, unlike process snapshot which only saves the memory footprint of the process, VM snapshot involves the entire memory state and thus is heavy. Consider that the virtual machines nowadays are always configured with several GB RAM, the snapshot size is up to GB accordingly. Second, the cloud infrastructure provides thousands of VMs to end-users, and each user may create dozens of snapshots, which will cost hundreds of TB storage totally. Third, disk failures are common nowadays [24, 46, 47], they lead to the loss of snapshot files resident in the disk so that the VM cannot be successfully recovered. This promotes the administrators to employ redundancy mechanism [26, 39, 45, 51] to provide high availability as well as long-term durability, however, at the cost of extra storage space. Overall, storing large amount of virtual machine snapshots in a space-efficient way without compromising availability is critical in large scale cloud infrastructures.

Several works have recognized this problem and proposed approaches which fall into two main categories. One category focuses on reducing the snapshot size when the VM snapshot is being taken. For example, they compress the memory state [30], save each memory page only once in post-copy manner rather than save iteratively [20, 49], or remove the data that exist in both memory pages and disk blocks[14, 43]. De-duplication technique is employed to save only one copy of the identical pages across multiple VM snapshots [21, 22, 42]. However, these works pay no attention to the availability of snapshot files, or in other words, they expect the underlying file system or storage device to provide the availability. Another category of approach, in contrast, attempts to improve availability to prevent data loss from disk failures. They either replicate multiple copies of the full file [26, 55], or utilize erasure code [19, 36, 38] to enhance availability with less storage space. Unfortunately, these methods lack the exploitation of file semantics, and consider that the data in the file have the same importance, so that they replicate the files identically and blindly.

In this paper, we investigate the problem of storing virtual machine snapshots in a distributed file system with the aim to achieve high availability with low storage usage, and propose a Page Aware Replication System, named as "PARS". The key insight behind PARS is the different page importance to system execution. Modern operating systems allocate most of the memory to a cache which stores data that has been recently read (or is to be written back), so that future requests for that data can be served faster than accessing external devices directly. It suggests that these (or at least a part of) cache pages are unnecessary for the guest OS and applications to work properly. In other words, the loss of them after recovery will not cause system crash, but only imposes performance loss. This inspires us to explore the page semantics related to system execution, classify pages by their importance, and then save multiple copies for critical pages while saving less copies for non-critical one, rather than replicate them fully and identically. To summarize, we make the following contributions:

- An analysis of practical memory usage in Windows desktop and Linux server cluster (§3).

- Categorization of memory pages by exploring the importance to system execution, and a page-aware policy to determine the replica count for different categories (§4).

- A mechanism to handle the loss of unnecessary cache pages after rollback recovery (§5).

- Implementation of PARS on QEMU/KVM platform and HDFS (§6), and evaluation under several workloads to prove its effectiveness (§7). The evaluation results show that PARS can reduce storage usage by 53.9% compared to native replication technique in HDFS [3] which replicates three full copies. In addition, PARS reduces 36.4% of snapshot duration without significant performance loss, and could reduce rollback latency by 65.8% for scenarios where performance requirement is not critical.

2. Background and Related Work

2.1 Virtual Machine Snapshot

VM snapshot is a file-based record of the memory state, disk data, and configuration of a virtual machine at a specific time point. It always records the full image of the in-memory state and saves the disk content in an incremental manner since the disk data updates much slowly. VM snapshot is essential for cloud management [10, 20, 32]. For virtual desktop usage, the users can backup the running system and resume the work whenever necessary, or perform intrusion analysis by continuously taking snapshots of the VM under attack. For scientific applications, the computation upon failure can continue from the previously recorded state instead of restarting from the initial state, so that the task can be completed within a limited period in the face of failures.

Although the snapshot mechanism can help the system to survive a majority of failures, the disk failures however may lead to data loss so that the virtual machine fails to be recovered. Distributed file system is an appealing way to provide high availability, it stripes redundant data across multiple disks through techniques such as replication [26, 51, 55] or erasure code [19, 36, 38], so that the data can be properly recovered from failure-free disks. Another benefit is that it employs a large amount of commodity disks to provide higher capacity cheaply. As a result, distributed file systems, such as Google FS [26], HDFS [3], are widely used in cloud infrastructures to store VM images and snapshots.

2.2 Related Work

2.2.1 Snapshot Size Optimization

There exist several optimization approaches which focus on reducing the VM snapshot size when snapshot is being taken. QEMU/KVM uses one byte to represent the entire zero page whose bytes are identical [33]. Jin el al. [30] find that a majority of memory pages have more than 75% similarity, they therefore compress the memory based on strong data regularities. Removing page cache from memory state is one compelling approach to reduce snapshot size effectively, and has been well studied [14, 17, 37, 43, 44]. However, these works still suffer from several drawbacks. Hines et al. [44] leverage balloon mechanism to reclaim temporarily unused memory pages, their method requires the modification and cooperation of guest OS and is not always accepted by users [15]. In addition, it is difficult to determine how many pages should be reclaimed [15]. Chiang et al. [17] remove free pages from snapshot state, but they ignore the removal of cache pages which take a large part of memory state. Park et al. [43] discard the duplicate pages that are resident in both memory and disk blocks, the main disadvantage is that they need to track IO operation to find the unchanged cache pages since guest OS boot up. Consider that snapshot creation is less frequent, their method incur non-trivial IO performance penalty. Koto [37] and Akiyama [14] insert a module into guest kernel to identify the cache pages and then eliminate them during memory state transfer. The modification of guest OS, as mentioned, may be refused by some users.

PARS is inspired by these works but is different. On snapshot, PARS identifies the cache pages and free pages via introspection which requires neither modification of guest OS nor IO tracking [31, 44]. Upon rollback, unlike the above works that reproduce all the cache pages from disk to build a full memory state [14, 37, 43], PARS is able to inform the loss to guest kernel. Thus, the kernel reads the data from disk until they are requested. This ability enables users to load no cache page upon rollback, so that fewer data transfer and faster rollback recovery can be achieved. Similarly, PARS achieves this feature of rollback in a transparent way.

2.2.2 Data Availability

Replication is one well known technique to enhance availability through placing multiple replicas of data in disperse disks. This mechanism has been adopted in many distributed file systems such as Google FS [26], Deep Store [51] and HDFS [3]. However, because the entire file needs to be replicated identically, large amount of storage space will be occupied to store extra replicas. For example, the distributed file systems always set the default replica count to 3, which will cost 2X extra storage. Erasure code splits the file into m stripes, and then codes the stripes to n fragments. The file can be reconstructed from any m of the n fragments. Compared to the replication approach which requires k replicas to survives $k-1$ failures, erasure code can tolerate $n-m$ failures with n/m storage usage. Obviously, appropriate selection of n and m would save storage space for achieving the same availability. Spanner [19], OceanStore [38], Azure Storage [16] and SafeStore [36] are popular distributed file systems which employ erasure code to improve data availability.

Although erasure code is an appealing way to achieve high availability with less storage, it incurs longer latency when recovering the data due to the decoding cost [45]. This implies that it is inappropriate for coding snapshots, because fast VM recovery from snapshot is essential upon failures. Moreover, it tends to reconstruct the entire fragment even if only one block is acquired. This feature is impractical when demand-paging based rollback technique is adopted [52, 53].

PARS employs replication technique to enhance data availability without sacrificing recovery latency. Instead of replicating the entire file, PARS explores the page semantics and saves multiple replicas for a fraction of snapshot state that is critical to system execution, it therefore provides the same availability without unnecessary storage cost.

2.2.3 Storage Space Saving

The existing approaches for space saving in storage system fall into two categories: intra-file compression [40, 41, 51] and inter-file compression [23, 54, 55]. Intra-file compression adopts the compression algorithms such as Lempel-Ziv to express the original data with less data based on statistical characteristics [51]. It can achieve 40% to 70% size reduction, but the drawback is the long access latency as a result of de-compression cost, which is similar to erasure code.

The inter-file compression, also known as de-duplication, merges several identical pages into one copy and several references, thereby reducing the storage usage [21, 27, 42]. The results from Zhang [54] and Nath [42] show that about 40% pages can be merged when large amount of virtual machine snapshots exist. However, inter-file compression

does not come for free, the loss of the merged page will lead to the loss of all pages referring to it and consequentially deteriorate data availability [39].

PARS achieves space saving by reducing the replicas for certain pages that are unnecessary for the system to work properly. Without doubt, we believe that PARS is orthogonal to the above methods for saving storage space further.

3. Motivation

3.1 OS Memory Usage

The OS allocates memory for kernel usage and user space usage. The kernel uses memory to store kernel images and kernel objects such as *inode* in file system, *sk_buffer* in TCP/IP stack, *page* in memory management, etc. In user space, the memory are allocated as BSS, Text or Data segments to store the static variables and application codes, or as heap and stack for dynamic objects.

Typically, the OS kernel and user applications always occupy a small part of the entire memory space and leave the remaining memory pages unused which are named as "free pages". Free pages mainly consists of two parts: i) the pages that are never allocated since system boot-up and ii) the pages that are ever used but now are freed. Linux kernel always fills the former one with zero, but leaves the freed pages unchanged with its old content and delays clearing the page until subsequent allocation. Windows adopts a different manner, it attempts to clear the freed pages with "zero page thread". Unfortunately, the priority of this thread is the lowest, the thread therefore has less opportunity to execute, so that most of the freed pages are unable to be cleared timely. The amount of zero pages gradually decreases due to memory allocation and finally becomes only a few after long-term program execution. This makes the snapshot optimizations such as zero page compression meaningless. We will show the results in §3.2.

Modern operating systems always utilize Buffered I/O to speed up data access to external devices. They allocate the free pages to cache the data that is read recently from (or is dirtied but not written back to) storage device to reduce the access latency, and name these pages as "cache pages". For example, Windows introduce SuperFetch [13] to improve interactive responsiveness by preloading applications or data into memory; Linux also employs a similar approach named Readahead [11] to reduce IO latency. Although OS provides reclamation mechanism to release the cache pages, the cache pages are still resident in memory for long. This is because reclamation is only invoked when the amount of free memory is below a specific threshold, or the allocation fails due to the memory shortage. Consequently, the amount of cache pages is large especially after long time execution.

3.2 Measurements

In this subsection, we collect the memory usage of two Windows VMs and twelve Linux VMs in our private cloud platform, and report the amounts of zero pages (whose bytes are all 0s or 1s), used pages (used by kernel or applications) and cache pages resident in the memory.

The Windows VMs are used as virtual desktop for daily office by research students. The Linux VMs are connected and served as a Elasticsearch cluster [2](a distributed, decentralized server used to search documents), which stores over 50 million microblogs from Weibo [7]. To acquire the number of used pages and cache pages, we call the *GlobalMemoryStatusEx* function in Windows and record the result in 15 minutes interval during four days of execution, and we leverage Ganglia monitor to acquire the results in Linux VMs over one month. Meanwhile, we create VM snapshots periodically to count zero pages.

Figure 1 reports the size of cache pages and used pages. As we can see, the cache pages take a large fraction of memory, for example, they take 48.3% and 32.2% for two Windows VMs after four days of execution, and take 53% on average for the Linux VM cluster. The used pages are much less, they take 17.2%, 16.9%, 23.8% and 40.5% of the memory respectively. The free pages (neither used nor cached) also takes a large part in Windows, they take about 50% of the memory. However, the free pages don't amount to zero pages. Table 1 compares the average amount of zero pages and free pages from ten random epochs, it can be found that the amount of zero pages is much less. This is because the page that has ever been allocated but now is freed will be left with the content uncleared, it therefore is a free page but not a zero page. The similar results can be found in other works, for example, Park et al. [43] demonstrate that the free pages and cache pages on average take 17% and 66% of the memory respectively.

	VM1	VM2	VM3	VM cluster
Free pages	1.8	2.2	1.1	22.8
Zero pages	0.31	0.61	0.23	1.37

Table 1. Amount of free pages and zero pages (GB).

3.3 Summary

The virtual machine snapshot size is always large, especially after long time execution since most of the memory pages are allocated and then polluted. The zero pages take much less than free pages, implying that the potential to reduce snapshot size through zero page compression is less than expected. Moreover, a large amount of cache pages are resident in memory. Note that the cache pages are always used to improve performance, this suggests that the loss of cache pages would not crash the guest OS or applications (§5.4). Therefore, storing the cache pages and free pages in snapshot, especially replicating multiple copies of them, plays no role in improving availability but imposes extra storage overhead, and thus is unnecessary. Consequentially, we need a page aware replication mechanism to reduce the storage cost without compromising availability.

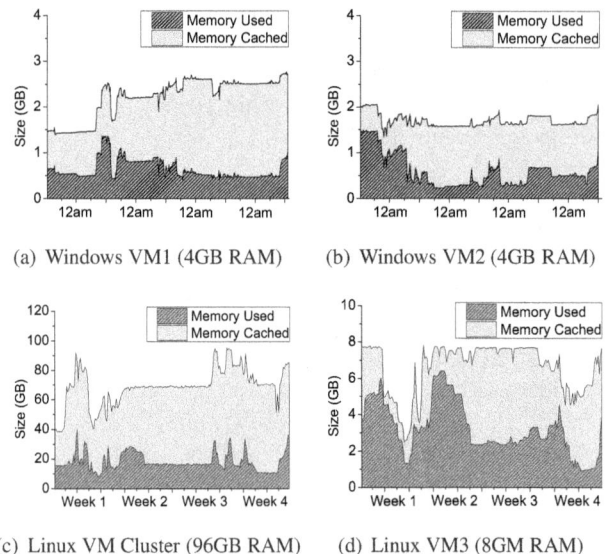

(a) Windows VM1 (4GB RAM)   (b) Windows VM2 (4GB RAM)

(c) Linux VM Cluster (96GB RAM)   (d) Linux VM3 (8GM RAM)

Figure 1. Amount of cache pages and used pages. For Linux VMs, we report the results of the entire cluster (c) and one randomly selected VM (d).

4. Page-Aware Replication Policy

PARS explores the page semantics and categorizes the page according to its importance to system execution, it then saves different number of replicas for different page types. Specifically, PARS replicates multiple copies of critical pages to survive disk failures for proper VM recovery, and saves at most one copy of non-critical pages to save storage usage. In the following subsections, we firstly describe how to categorize the memory pages, then introduce the determination of the replica count taking availability and space saving into account, and finally discuss the potential space saving.

4.1 Analysing Page Type

The memory pages can be divided into several mutually exclusive categories corresponding to how operating system uses the pages [34]. In Linux, we can acquire five categories by the page semantics. (1) Free pages, which are not used by any process or kernel. They are either never allocated since boot-up, or are ever used but now freed and left as is with old contents. (2) Cache pages, which are not currently used by any process. They are allocated to cache data to be read or written back to eliminate the access latency between application and external devices. (3) Inode pages, which are used by user process. These pages contain data from disk and are mapped into the virtual address space of process. (4) Anonymous pages, which are accessed frequently by user process. These pages are allocated to heap or stack through functions such as *malloc*. (5) Kernel pages, which are only used by kernel. These pages are used to store the kernel binaries or internal data structures.

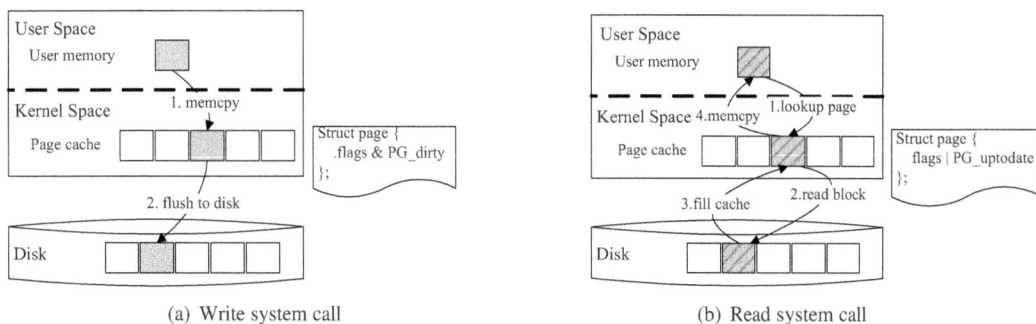

Figure 2. The procedure of filling page cache by read and write system calls.

The loss of the memory page produces different effects on system behavior, it may make no harm, or incur performance degradation, or even crash the system. Based on the effects, a memory page can be classified into one of the three categories: i) *unmeaningful pages*, ii) *performance related pages* and iii) *runtime critical pages*. The following paragraphs will explain the classification in detail.

The Free pages are currently not used by kernel or process, they are not linked in any way in the Linux kernel, and their loss makes no effects on the system execution. Thus, they are regarded as *unmeaningful pages*.

The Kernel pages, Inode pages and Anonymous pages are necessary for the application or kernel to work properly, missing such page will lead to misbehavior or even system crash, therefore they belong to *runtime critical pages*.

The Cache pages may lie in Page Cache which is used to cache the pages related to file, or in Buffer Cache which is related to block device. The Cache pages are difficult to be categorized directly, because they may be used to store the data either copied from user memory by *write* system call, or read from the underlying disk device by *read* system call.

The *write* system call is issued by user process, it uses the file descriptor, user buffer and associated size as the parameters. The write operation firstly calculates the page index through the file descriptor, and then attempts to lookup the *page*[1] in *radix tree* which is used in Page Cache to arrange *pages* efficiently. If the *page* is not present in *radix tree*, OS kernel will allocate a new one and append it into *radix tree*, mark the *page* as dirty (PG_dirty), and finally copy the content from user memory to the page, as illustrated in Figure 2(a). The kernel forks *pdflush* thread to flush the dirtied pages into disk asynchronously. The write operation related to Buffer Cache is similar except that it uses BH_dirty flag to indicate whether the *page* is dirtied. These dirtied cache pages containing the data to be written back are critical to the system execution, since their loss would lead to inconsistency between the application and disk blocks. Therefore, they are regarded as *runtime critical pages*.

The procedure of *read* system call, as illustrated in Figure 2(b), is a bit similar to *write*. It firstly lookups the *page* in *radix tree*, if the *page* is present and its flag is marked as up-to-date (PG_uptodate is set), the page content can be copied to user memory directly. Otherwise, the kernel allocates a new *page* into *radix tree*, reads the requested data from disk blocks, fills data into the page, and finally copies the page content to user memory. The read operation related to Buffer Cache is similar except it uses BH_uptodate flag to indicate that the *page* is up-to-date. This kind of cache page is just an identical copy of data resident in the block, so that the page loss only incurs longer latency when subsequent read operations access the same block. As a result, we treat these clean cache pages as *performance related pages*.

4.2 Replica Count Policy

Replica count plays an important role in availability and space saving. A large count can improve availability by tolerating more disk failures, but at the cost of more storage usage. On the other hand, a small count can save storage space, but sacrifices the availability. In many systems [3, 26, 51], the default replica count is 3, which achieves a well tradeoff between storage space and availability. We determine the replica count of pages according to their importance to system execution. Table 2 illustrates the page categories as well as the associated replica count in PARS.

Unmeaningful pages are irrelevant to system execution. Moreover, their page content are all 0s or 1s, or left with the old content when it is freed, and thus are meaningless. This suggests that saving these pages is unnecessary, therefore the replica count of this page type is set to 0.

Performance related pages can be discarded from snapshot state to save storage space [43, 44]. However, after rollback recovery, their loss will force the system to access the data from external device rather than the cache, resulting in longer latency and consequentially performance degradation. The degradation may be unacceptable for some workloads desiring low latency [48, 50], as a result, we by default save one copy of these pages for the sake of application performance. Meanwhile, the users can set the replica count to 0 if they prefer storage space saving to performance guarantee.

---

[1] The italic *page* here is a kernel object of "struct page" to describe one physical page.

Page category	Page semantics	Replica count
unmeaningful pages	Free pages	0
performance related pages	Clean cache pages	1
runtime critical pages	Dirtied cache pages; Inode pages; Kernel pages; Anonymous pages	k(default is 3)
metadata	Record the page address and page category	k

Table 2. Page categories and associated replica count.

Runtime critical pages are necessary for the system to perform properly, missing one such page may lead to runtime misbehavior or even system crash. As a result, we save k (default is 3) identical replicas of these pages to survive up to $k-1$ simultaneous disk failures. The users can specify a larger value if the underlying hardware suffers high failure rate or higher availability is required.

Metadata. Apart from the memory pages, the metadata, which records the page address and page type, should also be saved as part of the snapshot file. The metadata is undoubtedly critical, thus it is highly desired to save k copies to ensure the availability. Fortunately, the size of metadata is small. We use 8 bytes to represent the address and 1 byte to denote the page type. For a VM configured with 4GB RAM (1M pages), the metadata size is $k*1\text{M}*(8+1)\text{B} = 9k\text{MB}$.

4.3 Expected Storage Saving

In this part, we analyze the expected storage space saving yielded by PARS compared to the conventional replication technique when achieving the same availability. We suppose that the percentages of *runtime critical pages*, *performance related pages* and *unmeaningful pages* in the snapshot file are α, β, γ respectively, where $\alpha + \beta + \gamma = 1$. The size of snapshot file is denoted by S. The conventional storage system creates k identical replicas of the full file, therefore, the storage usage W is $k*S$. PARS saves no *unmeaningful pages*, and saves one copy of *performance related pages*, therefore the storage usage of PARS denoted by W' is determined by:

$$W' = k*\alpha*S + \beta*S \qquad (1)$$

And then the storage reduction r can be calculated by:

$$r = 1 - \frac{W'}{W} = 1 - \frac{k*\alpha*S + \beta*S}{k*S} = 1 - \frac{k*\alpha + \beta}{k}$$
$$= 1 - \alpha - \frac{\beta}{k} = \beta + \gamma - \frac{\beta}{k} = \frac{k-1}{k}*\beta + \gamma \qquad (2)$$

It can be concluded from (2) that the increase of *performance related pages* and *unmeaningful pages* has potential to reduce the storage usage. In practical cases as illustrated in Figure 1(c), where β is 0.53 and γ is 0.238, PARS can achieve 59.1% space saving when k is 3. In addition, if higher availability is required, PARS would save more storage space, for example, the reduction is 63.5% when k is 4 and 66.2% when k is 5. This also suggests that PARS can achieve much higher availability using the same storage by saving more replicas of *runtime critical pages*.

5. Data Loss Handling upon Recovery

One challenging task in PARS is to handle the page loss due to disk failures, especially for the *performance related pages* that are vulnerable to failures as a result of only one data copy. We assume that disks follow a simple fail-stop model rather than suffer silent errors [35], so that data loss can be detected easily. The following sections will describe how to handle the loss of snapshot state.

5.1 Loss of Metadata

We save k copies of metadata file. If there still exists one full copy of metadata, we can fetch the page address and the associated type, load the page content from snapshot into the guest memory space (supposing that the page content are available), and finally resume the virtual machine. Once all the copies of metadata are lost, the snapshot would be obsolete. One possible approach is to find an earlier available snapshot and then roll back the VM from it.

5.2 Loss of Unmeaningful Pages

The *unmeaningful pages* are useless and are not saved in the snapshot, their loss therefore is only considered as the result of metadata loss. Provided that the metadata exists, we identify the *unmeaningful pages* and simply fill zero into the associated memory pages upon rollback recovery.

5.3 Loss of Runtime Critical Pages

The *runtime critical pages* are replicated k times across disperse disks. Unless the k copies are lost simultaneously, the snapshot state could be reconstructed completely from any failure-free replica. Once the worst case happens, i.e., no replica is available, the rollback recovery from this snapshot would fail. Similarly, our advice is to roll back the VM from an earlier created snapshot or allow the user to specify a snapshot file for recovery.

5.4 Loss of Performance Related Pages

Handling the page loss of *performance related pages* is more challenging. First, they are saved only one copy and hence are more vulnerable to frequent disk failures. Second, the page loss without informing guest kernel would lead to data inconsistency which further results in application misbehavior. Specifically, if a page has been allocated to cache the data read from disk, the kernel would be aware of the existence of the page, that is, the kernel is able to index the *page* in *radix tree* and then accesses the proper page content. Supposing that the page now is lost due to disk failure, the memory content associated with this page are missing accordingly after recovery. However, the *radix tree* remains unchanged since it belongs to *runtime critical pages*. This implies that the kernel after recovery can still index the *page* in *radix tree* but cannot access the proper content because they are lost. Consequently, inconsistency arises and may result in application misbehavior or crash.

One possible solution for maintaining consistency is to remove the *page* from *radix tree* for the lost page through VM introspection. However, this method will cause chaos of kernel internal variables and is extremely complicated. For example, the *radix tree* reserves a variable *count* to record the number of *pages* in the tree, if a *page* is removed, the *count* should decrease accordingly. Moreover, the *page* is always linked to *active_list* or *inactive_list* for page reclamation, removing the *page* involves operations on these lists.

Our solution is simple and effective. Observed that when user application accesses data, the kernel firstly acquires the associated *page* from *radix tree*, and then tests if the page content is up-to-date (i.e., PG_uptodate flag is set). If it is not, the kernel will skip the cache and read the data from external device to update the page content. The related codes in kernel-2.6.32 are listed in Listing 1, some details are removed for clarity. Inspired by this, our approach is to clear the PG_uptodate flag of the lost pages upon recovery. Once the kernel after recovery requests the data which once existed in page cache but now is lost, it would realize that the page content is out of date. Therefore, it reads the data from the disk device, fills the proper data into the memory page, and finally copies the content to user. In this way, we hide the page loss to kernel. The procedure is similar for the Buffer Cache, the difference is that it removes the BH_uptodate flag.

Listing 1. Key codes of read operation.

```
1   do_generic_file_read(mapping, offset)
2   {
3     tree = mapping->page_tree;
4     page = radix_tree_lookup_slot(tree,offset)
5     if(page != NULL) {
6       if(!PageUptodate(page)) // PG_uptodate
7         // read data from external device
8         mapping->a_ops->readpage(page)
9     }
10    else {
11      page = page_cache_alloc_cold(mapping)
12      read_pages(page)
13    }
14    copy_to_user(page)
15  }
```

5.4.1 Safe Removal of PG_uptodate Flag

The OS kernel may not always perceive the removal of PG_uptodate flag after rollback. For example, in Listing 1, if the page content is up-to-date, then the kernel would execute the following steps: 1) get page from the radix tree (line 4), 2) find that the content is up-to-date (line 6), 3) copy the data

to user (line 14). Supposing that the VM state is checkpointed after step 2 but before step 3, the kernel after rollback recovery will continue to execute step 3 without checking PG_uptodate flag again. As a result, even if the PG_uptodate flag is removed upon rollback due to page loss, the kernel still copies the non-existent data to user space. This issue is attributed to that the *read* operation is not atomic, so that the snapshot procedure running concurrently may interfere with the kernel execution. Our solution is to delay the snapshot procedure so that the kernel is able to perceive all the removals of PG_update flag. Specifically, when snapshot operation is required, we start to intercept the *read* system call through VM introspection [25], and checkpoint the VM before the *read* execution. In this way, the *read* operation is considered to be atomic in the view of snapshot time point. One issue is that if *read* operation is rarely invoked, the snapshot procedure would be blocked for an unpredictable long time. To avoid this, we fork the snapshot procedure if no *read* is intercepted within 1 seconds. It is worth noting that the performance penalty due to interception is insignificant, because the interception lasts at most 1 seconds.

6. Implementation

6.1 Overall Architecture

PARS is implemented in the VMM layer using version qemu-kvm-0.12.5. PARS adopts introspection technology to acquire the page type, and thus requires no modification of guest OS. In addition, the QEMU snapshot mechanism is modified to save the page content following our page-aware policy. The architecture of PARS is illustrated in Figure 3, it consists of two key components: PageClassifier and Snap-Daemon. The two components are outlined below:

PageClassifier employs VM introspection to parse the internal data structure of guest kernel, explores the page semantics and then categorizes the pages. It is implemented in KVM module, and is transparent to the upper operating systems. Additionally, it supports multiple kernel versions, as will be described in §6.3.

SnapDaemon is responsible for taking snapshots of VM and rolling back the VM upon failures. SnapDaemon utilizes *libhdfs* [8], which provides C APIs to interact with HDFS, to write (read) data to (from) HDFS. In PARS, SnapDaemon only specifies the replica count when creating the file, and leaves the responsibility of replication to HDFS.

SnapDaemon provides two snapshot approaches: stop-and-copy snapshot [43] and copy-on-write (COW) based live snapshot [20]. In stop-and-copy snapshot, SnapDaemon involves three steps. First, it traverses the memory pages, for each page, it acquires the page category from PageClassifier and then saves the pair {page address, category} into the Metadata File which is replicated three copies. Second, it fetches the *runtime critical pages*, and saves them into Critical File which is replicated three copies. Finally, Snap-Daemon obtains the *performance related pages*, and writes

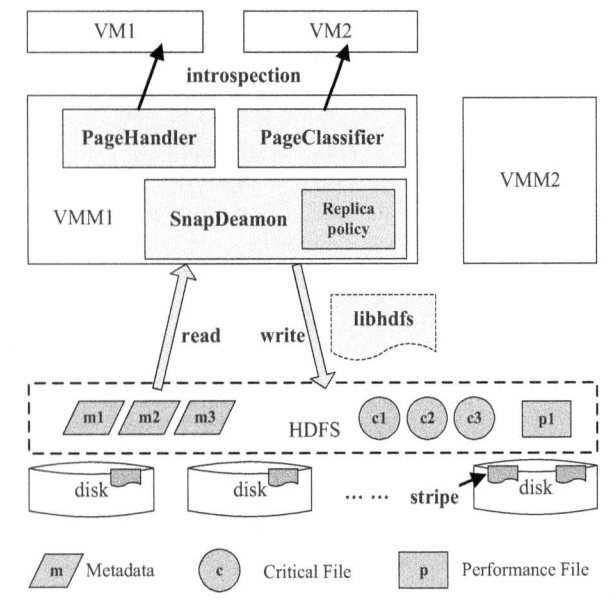

Figure 3. PARS architecture.

the content into Performance File. The procedures are similar for COW snapshot which saves the memory pages in demand-paging manner. If one page requires to be saved, SnapDaemon firstly explores the page type and then writes the content into corresponding file. Upon recovery, SnapDaemon firstly reads the metadata, and then fetches the page content from Critical File and Performance File. SnapDaemon considers the data to be lost if file *open* or *read* function returns invalid value. If the data are available, SnapDaemon fills them into the guest memory. Otherwise, SnapDaemon hides the page loss by employing PageHandler which clears the flag of lost pages as described in §5.

6.2 The Use of Introspection

VM introspection helps PARS to classify the memory pages (PageClassifier) and handle the page loss (PageHandler). It is specific to guest OS. We first describe the implementation details for Linux kernel 2.6.32.5, and then discuss the implementation on other Linux kernel versions in §6.3.

To explore the page semantics, the key is to acquire the object *page* which describes the information of a physical page. Fortunately, in Linux kernel, all the *page*s lie in *mem_map* which is a kernel array used to manage all the memory pages. *Mem_map* is located in the physical memory started from 0xffffea0000000000, it uses the page's physical frame number (pfn) as the index. Thus, we can locate the *page* by *mem_map* and pfn, and further read the value of *page* through *kvm_read_guest()* which is provided by KVM for reading data from a specified guest physical address.

Once the value of *page* is known, we can analyze its variables to determine the page category. Specifically, if the usage count (_count) of *page* is zero, the associated page therefore is not used by any process or the kernel, implying

that the page belongs to *unmeaningful pages*. If the page is in use but the map count (_mapcount) is zero, the page would be in cache. A page is in Page Cache if variable *private* is zero, otherwise it is in Buffer Cache. For a page in Page Cache, it belongs to *runtime critical pages* if one of the following flags in variable *flags* is set: i) PG_dirty which means that the page is dirtied, ii) PG_writeback which means that it will be written to disk and iii) PG_lock which means that the page is prepared for I/O. Otherwise, it is regarded as *performance related pages*. For a page in Buffer Cache, we acquire *buffer_head* of the *page* and categorize it into *runtime critical pages* if either of two flags in *b_state* is set: i) BH_dirty denoting a dirtied page and ii) BH_lock implying a locked page. Otherwise, the page belongs to *performance related pages*. The remaining pages are neither in cache nor are unmeaningful, and thus are *runtime critical pages*.

The procedure to handle page loss upon recovery using introspection is similar to how we categorize the page. We clear the PG_update flag of *page* or BH_uptodate flag of *buffer_head*, and then write the value of *page* back to *mem_map* through *kvm_write_guest()* which is used to write data to a specified guest physical address.

6.3 Multiple Platforms Support

We detect the guest kernel versions by distinguishing the interrupt descriptor table and system call table entry address which vary significantly across OS versions [18].

Our solution to categorize pages and handle page loss only involves one key kernel object, i.e., *page*, and thus is easy to support other Linux kernel versions. The difference across different versions lie in three aspects: i) the address of *mem_map*, ii) variables of *page* and iii) variables of *buffer_head*. The address of *mem_map* is denoted by VMEMMAP_START, it is 0xffffea0000000000 and is unchanged in Linux kernels from 2.6.32 to latest 3.14. The variables of *page* or *buffer_head* across different versions, however, are different. In a newer version, new variables may be added, variables may be renamed, and the offset of variable may be changed. Table 3 illustrates such cases in kernel 3.14 that are different from 2.6.32. Observed that only a few variables of *page* and *buffer_head* are used for introspection, we reserve an array to record these variables and their offsets along with the kernel version. Upon introspection, we firstly identify the kernel version, locate the *mem_map* by VMEMMAP_START, read the value of *page* and *buffer_head*, access the variables from the recorded offset, and finally categorize pages or handle page loss.

version	2.6.32	3.14
New variable		counters
Renamed variable	kmem_cache * slab	kmem_cache * slab_cache
Different offset	mapping=16	mapping=4

Table 3. Some changes of *page* between two kernels.

6.4 Storing Snapshots in HDFS

HDFS is designed to store large size files that are up to hundreds of MB or GB, and is suitable to store write-once, read-many-times data. The virtual machine snapshots have several features that are consistent with HDFS. First, the snapshot file are created and written only once, the subsequent operations are either reading the data for recovery or deleting the file for space reclamation. Second, the snapshot file is important and may be read multiple times, e.g., the snapshot contains important data, or new configured environment for software development. Third, the size of snapshot files is always large and up to several GB.

We leverage *libhdfs* to interact with HDFS. The *hdfsOpenFile* function treats replica count as one parameter. Thus, PARS focuses on the determination of file to be replicated and the replica count, yet leaves the responsibility of replication to HDFS. Implementation on HDFS involves only 70 lines of code. It is supposed to easily port to other distributed file systems due to the simplicity of the interfaces.

7. Evaluation

7.1 Experiment Setup

Our testbed consists of six physical severs, each is configured with 8-way quad-core Intel Xeon 2.4GHz processors, 48GB DDR memory, a 500GB WD disk, and Intel 82576 Gigabit NIC card. The servers are connected with switched Gigabit Ethernet. The virtual machines are configured with 4GB RAM unless specified otherwise. Both the physical servers and VMs are installed with Debian Linux 6.0. We setup HDFS on top of five physical servers, and use a separate server to run virtual machines. The snapshot files are stored into (or loaded from) HDFS via LAN rather than the local disk.

We evaluate PARS under several workloads. (1) Compilation, we compile Linux kernel 2.6.32.5 along with all the modules. (2) Mummer is a bioinformatics program for sequence alignment, it is CPU and memory intensive [4]. We align genome fragments obtained from NCBI [1]. (3) MPlayer is a video player, it prefetches a large fraction of movie file for performance requirements. (4) MySQL is a database management system [5], we employ SysBench tool [6] to read (write) data from (to) the database that stores 500,000 records. (5) Elasticsearch [2] is a file search server, it attempts to load as much data as possible into memory. The Elasticsearch server manages about 50 million microblogs, and the client continually requests the micorblogs with random generated user id.

7.2 Distribution of Different Page Types

We first report the percentages of three page categories in different epochs and under various workloads, and then compute the expected space saving.

Different times. We explore the memory usage in 60 seconds interval for over one hour running under Compilation

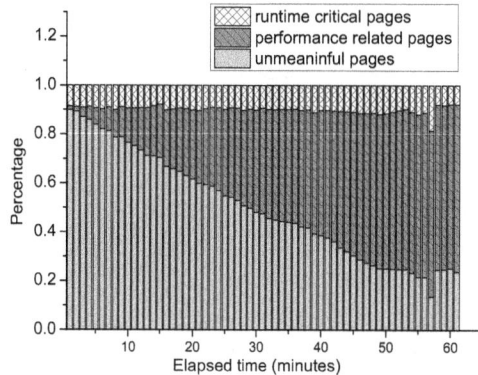

(a) Percentages under Compilation

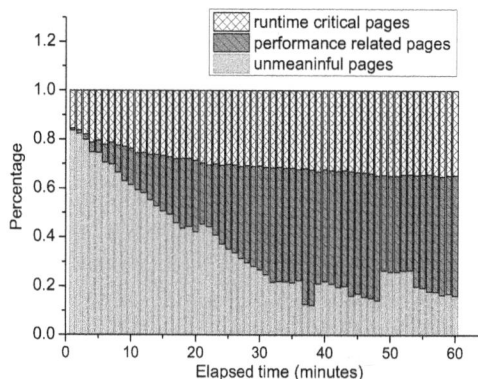

(b) Percentages under Elasticsearch

Figure 4. Percentages of different page categories.

and Elasticsearch. The percentages of three page categories are illustrated in Figure 4. As we can see from Figure 4(a), the percentage of *unmeaningful pages* decreases as the VM executes, for example, it is 90% at the start and gradually decreases to 21.6% in the 57th minute when the compilation completes. This is because more and more free pages are allocated to cache data. The percentage of *performance related pages*, as expected, increases with the time and takes a large fraction of memory pages. For example, it exceeds 50% since the 40th minute, and reaches 67.8% at the end of compilation. The percentage of *runtime critical pages* keeps almost steady, it is around 10% during the compilation. Figure 4(b) depicts the results under Elasticsearch. Different from Compilation, the *runtime critical pages* here occupies a large fraction of memory, e.g., its percentage exceeds 30% since the 30th minute. This is because Elasticsearch allocates its own buffer to fill data, and this buffer lies in the heap region which is regarded as *runtime critical pages* from the view of PARS. The percentage of *performance related pages*, as expected, gradually increases with the execution, and it finally takes about 50% of the memory pages at the end of the trace.

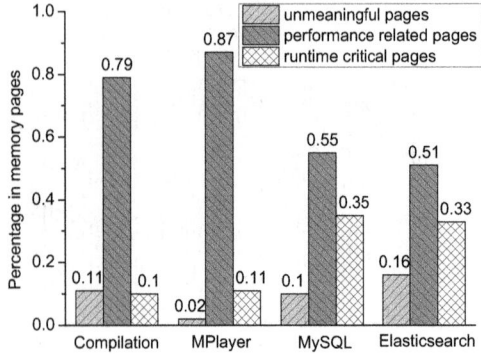

Figure 5. Percentages under various workloads.

Different workloads. The page count of different categories is specific to the workload and its temporal activity. We therefore count the pages on ten random epochs under various workloads after long time running, compute the percentage of page count to the whole memory size, and report the average percentage in Figure 5. As expected, *performance related pages* occupy the majority of memory state, they take 79%, 87%, 55% and 51% for Compilation, MPlayer, MySQL and Elastisearch respectively. The percentages for MySQL and Elasticsearch are a bit lower because the two applications allocate a number of memory pages as buffer to ensure low request latency. Consequently, we can compute the expected space saving by the equation (2). Compared to the conventional approach which replicates the file fully and identically, PARS is expected to reduce 63.7%, 60%, 46.7%, and 50% storage space when the replica count is 3.

7.3 Practical Storage Space Saving

In this subsection, we evaluate the practical storage saving yielded by PARS. We randomly collect 100 snapshots that are created by users of our private cloud platform during daily operations. The operations may be Linux kernel studying, software development and testing, or office usage. The associated guest kernel of these snapshots include CentOS 6.4 (2.6.32 kernel), Ubuntu 11.10 (3.0.3 kernel) and Debian 6.0 (2.6.32.5 kernel). We compare PARS with two approaches: 1) Native HDFS approach which stores 3 replicas of each file, 2) Compression approach, which is used widely in both storage system and snapshot system [30, 40, 41, 51], it compresses the snapshot first and then stores the files into HDFS. We employ *zlib* to compress data.

We first present detailed results to show the potential saving for a single snapshot. We load the snapshot state into guest memory and determine the page categories, and calculate the maximum, minimum, average and medium percentage of *runtime critical pages* in these snapshots. Meanwhile, we compress these snapshots and calculate the compression ratio. As we can see in Table 4, the percentage of *runtime critical pages* varies widely, e.g, the maximum percentage is

56.4% while the minimum value is only 13.7%. Smaller percentage implies less storage usage, because *runtime critical pages* are replicated three copies. The results of compression ratio are also varied, and they suggest that about half (52.7%) of the space can be saved with Compression approach.

We then re-create these snapshots with our PARS approach, compute the file size, and report the results in Table 5. The total size of 100 snapshots are 251GB. With Native HDFS approach, 753GB storage space will be occupied. The Compression approach reduces the usage to 356GB due to the benefit of compression. Our PARS approach uses 347G-B, which achieves a 53.9% reduction compared to the Native HDFS approach. These results strongly support our work on achieving storage efficiency. It's worth noting that the storage cost of PARS is almost identical to Compression approach, however, the time to create snapshot and roll back the VM is much less, which will be described in §7.4.

	max.	min.	avg.	med.
Compression ratio	72.7%	29.1%	47.3%	48.5%
Percentage of *runtime critical pages*	56.4%	13.7%	28.2%	26.1%

Table 4. Compression ratio and percentage of *runtime critical pages*. The smaller the better.

Modes	Native HDFS	Compression	PARS
Storage usage	753G	356G	347G
Space saving	N/A	52.7%	53.9%

Table 5. Storage usage of three approaches.

7.4 PARS Overhead

The overhead of PARS falls into two main aspects. One is the time overhead that involves introspecting the memory pages (introspection time), saving the memory pages to HDFS (snapshot duration), and loading the pages upon recovery (rollback latency). Another is the performance loss due to the introspection cost during live snapshot when saving the memory page on demand. In this section, we compare PARS with both Native snapshot approach in QEMU and Compression based snapshot approach which compresses the memory pages first and then writes them into HDFS.

7.4.1 Snapshot Duration

The snapshot duration of PARS using the stop-and-copy approach mainly consists of the time to introspect the guest memory, save Critical File and save Performance File. We also classify the pages in Native approach, to explore how much time can be saved by writing one replica of Performance File compared to three replicas. Figure 6 compares the detailed duration of PARS against Compression approach and Native approach. It can be seen that the introspection time is minor, it is less than 2 seconds for 4GB

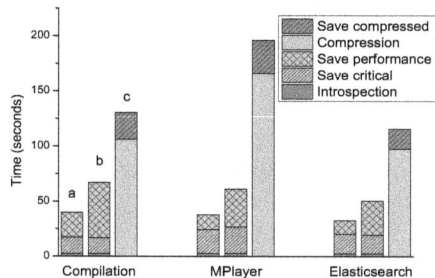

Figure 6. Time overhead on snapshot creation. a) PARS approach, b) Native snapshot, c) Compression based snapshot.

RAM (Table 6 summaries the introspection time for varying memory sizes on snapshot and rollback.). This is because our introspection method involves only a few bit operations. The time to save Critical File are almost identical between PARS and Native snapshot, because the two approaches both write three copies. However, PARS takes much less time to save Performance File than Native snapshot, for example, it spends 22.4 seconds while Native snapshot takes 50.4 seconds under Compilation. The reason is that PARS only saves one copy, while Native snapshot saves three copies which contend for network and disk I/O bandwidth. On average, PARS reduces the duration of Native snapshot by 36.4%. The Compression approach, as expected, spends much more time, mainly due to the long computation time which takes more than 80% of the full snapshot duration.

RAM size	1GB	2GB	4GB	8GB	16GB
snapshot	1.24	1.51	1.84	2.33	3.16
rollback	1.38	1.63	2.05	2.56	3.32

Table 6. Introspection time overhead (seconds).

7.4.2 Rollback Latency

The latency to roll back the virtual machine with PARS mainly involves the time to read Performance File and Critical File. Moreover, once the data of Performance File is lost, we need to handle the page loss. Therefore, apart from the rollback latency of the above three approaches, we also present the result of PARS without loading *performance related pages*. The results from Figure 7 show that the rollback latency are almost identical between PARS and Native snapshot, this is because the underlying HDFS supports parallel data loading from disperse disks when acquiring the file. On rollback recovery without loading *performance related pages*, PARS only reads the Metadata and Critical File, modifies the internal data of guest kernel to hide the page loss, and then resumes the VM. Consequentially, it results in less rollback latency. On average, PARS without loading *performance related pages* achieves a 65.8% latency reduction compared to PARS with loading all pages. The latency

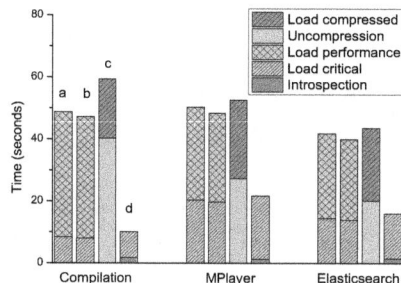

Figure 7. Details of rollback latency. a) PARS, b) Native snapshot, c) Compression based snapshot, d) PARS without loading *performance related pages*.

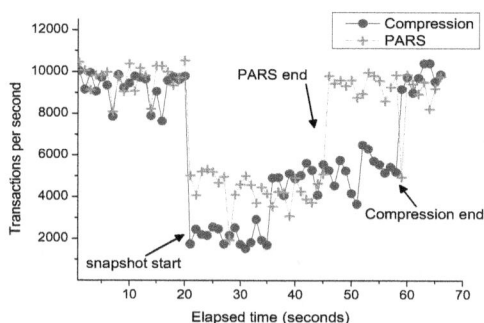

Figure 8. TPS of Elasticsearch during live snapshot.

of Compression approach is a bit larger than the other approaches, similarly, the cost is mainly attributed to the decompression time.

7.4.3 Performance Degradation during Live Snapshot

During live snapshot, PARS explores the page type for the page to be saved on demand. From Table 6, we can conclude that the introspection imposes negligible performance loss on native copy-on-write snapshot. Thus, the applications perform similar during PARS COW and native COW live snapshot. In this experiment, we compare PARS COW live snapshot (PARS) against Compression based live snapshot (Compression). We setup Elasticsearch server in a VM, and record the transactions per second (TPS) during normal execution and live snapshot.

Figure 8 compares the results of the two approaches. The TPS during PARS live snapshot drops from 10531 to 5015 since snapshot starts at the 20th second, and returns to normal at the 46th second when snapshot completes. The Compression approach performs much worse, the Elasticsearch server handles only half of the transactions compared to PARS. Specifically, the TPS on average is 2170 during Compression snapshot while it is 4463 during PARS snapshot from the 20th second to the 36th second. The TPS during Compression snapshot increases since the 36th second, we at-

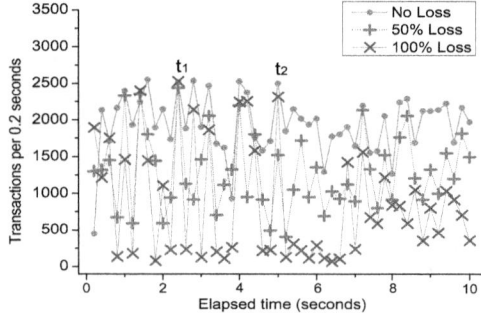

Figure 9. TPS with varying degrees of page loss.

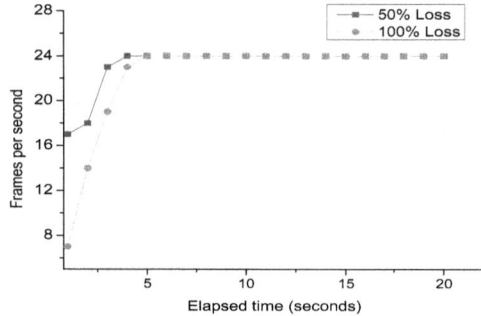

Figure 10. FPS with varying degrees of page loss.

tribute this to the benefit of access locality because the subsequent access to the page that has been saved will not trigger page fault again. It should be pointed out that the snapshot duration of PARS is shorter than that of Compression, implying that the Elasitcsearch server regains the full capacity early and thus is able to handle more transactions.

7.5 Performance Loss on Disk Failures

In this part, we evaluate PARS in the face of loss of *performance related pages* due to disk failures. HDFS stripes a file into disperse disks, so it is difficult to quantify the loss of file for real disk failures. Therefore, we randomly select pages and mark them as lost when reading them from HDFS. We consider three degrees of page loss: No Loss, 50% Loss and 100% Loss (equal to zero replica). We measure the application performance in terms of transactions per second (TPS, the TPS here actually refers to transactions per 0.2 second) of Elasticsearch and frames per second (FPS) of MPlayer.

Figure 9 compares the TPS of three degrees. It can be seen that TPS decreases seriously in 100% Loss case. Although some required data would hit in the private cache owned by Elasticsearch, making TPS in t_1 and t_2 be as high as that of No Loss, most of the desired data have to be fetched from disk rather than memory cache. On average, the server without loading *performance related pages* handles 884 transactions each epoch, a 54.9% loss compared to the No Loss case which is able to handle 1961 transaction-

s. The server in 50% Loss case handles 1321 transactions on average, which is better than 100% Loss. This is attributed to the low access latency since lots of data are loaded into the cache. Note that although loading no *performance related pages* could reduce the rollback latency by over 20 seconds as shown in Figure 7, the application here suffers serious performance degradation after recovery. The degradation may be intolerable for low-latency high-throughput scenarios [48, 50]. One solution is to trace working set cache pages during snapshot and only load these cache pages upon rollback [52], to offer a tradeoff between rollback latency and performance. We leave this as our future work.

The results of FPS are depicted in Figure 10. For the first three seconds, the FPS are 7, 14, 19 for the 100% Loss case, and are 17, 18, 23 if half of the data are lost. Note that 14 frames per second is sufficient to play the video fluently, this implies that the *performance related pages* might be eliminated from snapshot for some scenarios where applications are not time critical, such as virtual desktop, so that the storage usage can be further reduced.

Another point should be noted is that the FPS regains the full capacity from the 3rd second, while the TPS keeps low for a longer duration in the face of page loss. We owe the difference to the variety of mechanisms on how the application accesses the pages in cache. Specifically, MPlayer sequentially accesses the video file, so that the subsequent read operations will always hit the page prefetched in cache. In contrast, Elasticsearch client randomly requests the data which may be scattered in the cache. Thus, the hit rate is low.

8. Conclusions and Future Work

This paper proposes PARS, a page-aware replication system for storing VM snapshots efficiently. PARS explores the in-memory pages and categorizes them according to their importance to system execution. It enhances the data availability by replicating the critical pages, and reduces the storage space by saving one copy of performance related pages which take a large fraction of memory state. The advantage of PARS over naive replication is that it requires much lower storage for achieving the same availability, or is able to provide higher availability with the same storage cost.

For future work, we plan to identify the working set cache pages during snapshot and only save these active cache pages instead of the whole cache pages, to further reduce storage usage without compromising application performance after recovery. In addition, we plan to explore Windows kernels which are widely used for daily office work.

Acknowledgement

We would like to thank the anonymous reviewers for their valuable comments and help in improving this paper. This work is supported by China 863 Program (2013AA01A213), China 973 Program (2011CB302602), China HGJ Program (2013ZX01039-002-001) and NSFC Program (91118008).

References

[1] National center for biotechnology information. ftp://ftp.ncbi.nih.gov.

[2] Elasticsearch. http://www.elasticsearch.org/.

[3] Hdfs. http://hadoop.apache.org/.

[4] Mummer. http://mummer.sourceforge.net/.

[5] Mysql. http://www.mysql.com/.

[6] Sysbench. http://sysbench.sourceforge.net/.

[7] Weibo. http://weibo.com.

[8] libhdfs. http://hadoop.apache.org/docs/r1.2.1/libhdfs.html.

[9] Salesforce, 1999. http://www.salesforce.com.

[10] Using the snapshot, 2003. https://www.vmware.com/support/ws4/doc/preserve_snapshot_ws.html.

[11] readahead, 2005. https://lwn.net/Articles/155510/.

[12] Amazon ec2, 2006. http://aws.amazon.com/ec2/.

[13] Superfetch, 2007. http://en.wikipedia.org/wiki/\\Windows_Vista_I/O_technologies.

[14] S. Akiyama, T. Hirofuchi, R. Takano, and S. Honiden. Fast wide area live migration with a low overhead through page cache teleportation. In *Proceedings of CCGrid*, pages 78–82, 2013.

[15] N. Amit, D. Tsafrir, and A. Schuster. Vswapper: A memory swapper for virtualized environments. In *Proceedings of ASPLOS*, pages 349–366, 2014.

[16] B. Calder, J. Wang, A. Ogus, and N. N. et al. Windows azure storage: A highly available cloud storage service with strong consistency. In *Proceedings of SOSP*, pages 143–157, 2011.

[17] J.-H. Chiang, H.-L. Li, and T. cker Chiueh. Introspection-based memory de-duplication and migration. In *Proceedings of VEE*, pages 51–62, 2013.

[18] M. Christodorescu, R. Sailer, D. L. Schales, D. Sgandurra, and D. Zamboni. Cloud security is not (just) virtualization security: A short paper. In *Proceedings of the ACM Workshop on Cloud Computing Security*, pages 97–102, 2009.

[19] J. C. Corbett, J. Dean, and M. E. et al. Spanner: Google's globally-distributed database. In *Proceedings of OSDI*, pages 251–264, 2012.

[20] L. Cui, B. Li, Y. Zhang, and J. Li. Hotsnap: A hot distributed snapshot system for virtual machine cluster. In *Proceedings of USENIX LISA*, pages 59–73, 2013.

[21] L. Cui, J. Li, B. Li, and et al. Vmscatter: Migrate virtual machines to many hosts. In *Proceedings of VEE*, pages 63–72, 2013.

[22] U. Deshpande, X. Wang, and K. Gopalan. Live gang migration of virtual machines. In *Proceedings of HPDC*, pages 135–146, 2011.

[23] C. Dubnicki, L. Gryz, L. Heldt, and M. Kaczmarczyk. Hydrastor: A scalable secondary storage. In *Proceedings of FAST*, pages 197–210, 2009.

[24] D. Ford, F. Labelle, F. I. Popovici, M. Stokely, V.-A. Truong, L. Barroso, C. Grimes, and S. Quinlan. Availability in globally distributed storage systems. In *Proceedings of OSDI*, pages 1–14, 2010.

[25] T. Garfinkel and M. Rosenblum. A virtual machine introspection based architecture for intrusion detection. In *Proceedings of NDSS*, pages 191–206, 2003.

[26] S. Ghemawat, H. Gobioff, and S.-T. Leung. The google file system. In *Proceedings of SOSP*, pages 29–43, 2003.

[27] D. Harnik, O. Margalit, D. Naor, D. Sotnikov, and G. Vernik. Estimation of deduplication ratios in large data sets. In *Proceedings of MSST*, pages 1–11, 2012.

[28] M. Hibler, R. Ricci, L. Stoller, J. Duerig, S. Guruprasad, T. Stack, K. Webb, and J. Lepreau. Large-scale virtualization in the emulab network testbed. In *USENIX Annual Technical Conference*, pages 113–128, 2008.

[29] X. Jiang and D. Xu. Violin: Virtual internetworking on overlay infrastructure. In *Parallel and Distributed Processing and Applications*, pages 937–946, 2005.

[30] H. Jin, L. Deng, and S. Wu. Live virtual machine migration with adaptive memory compression. In *Proceedings of CLUSTER*, pages 1–10, 2009.

[31] S. T. Jones, A. C. Arpaci-Dusseau, and R. H. Arpaci-Dusseau. Geiger: Monitoring the buffer cache in a virtual machine environment. In *Proceedings of ASPLOS*, pages 14–24, 2006.

[32] A. Kangarlou, P. Eugster, and D. Xu. Vnsnap: Taking snapshots of virtual networked environments with minimmal downtime. In *Proceedings of DSN*, pages 87–98, 2011.

[33] A. Kivity, Y. Kamay, D. Laor, U. Lublin, and A. Liguori. Kvm: the linux virtual machine monitor. In *Proceedings of the Linux Symposium*, pages 225–230, 2007.

[34] J. F. Kloster, J. Kristensen, and A. Mejlholm. Determining the use of interdomain shareable pages using kernel introspection. Technical report, Aalborg University, 2007.

[35] G. Kola, T. Kosar, and M. Livny. Faults in large distributed systems and what we can do about them. In *Proceedings of Euro-Par*, pages 442–453, 2005.

[36] R. Kotla, L. Alvisi, , and M. Dahlin. Safestore: A durable and practical storage system. In *Proceedings of ATC*, pages 127–142, 2007.

[37] A. Koto, H. Yamada, K. Ohmura, and K. Kono. Towards unobtrusive vm live migration for cloud computing platforms. In *Proceedings of APSys*, pages 1–6, 2012.

[38] J. Kubiatowicz, D. Bindel, Y. Chen, and S. C. et al. Oceanstore: An architecture for global-scale persistent storage. In *Proceedings of ASPLOS*, pages 190–201, 2000.

[39] X. Li, M. Lillibridge, and M. Uysal. Reliability analysis of deduplicated and erasure-coded storage. *Proceedings of SIGMETRICS Performance Evaluation Review*, 38(3):4–9, 2010.

[40] C. Liu, D. Ju, Y. Gu, Y. Zhang, D. Wang, and D. H. Du. Semantic data de-duplication for archival storage systems. In *Proceedings of ACSAC*, pages 1–9, 2008.

[41] C. Marshall. Efficient and safe data backup with arrow. Technical report, 2008.

[42] P. Nath, M. A. Kozuch, D. R. OHallaron, and J. Harkes. Design tradeoffs in applying content addressable storage to enterprise-scale systems based on virtual machines. In *Proceedings of ATC*, pages 71–84, 2006.

[43] E. Park, B. Egger, and J. Lee. Fast and space-efficient virtual machine checkpointing. In *Proceedings of VEE*, pages 75–85, 2011.

[44] M. R, Hines, and K. Gopalan. Post-copy based live virtual machine migration using adaptive pre-paging and dynamic self-ballooning. In *Proceedings of VEE*, pages 51–60, 2009.

[45] R. Rodrigues and B. Liskov. High availability in dhts erasure-erasure code vs replication. In *Proceedings of IPTPS*, pages 226–239, 2005.

[46] B. Schroeder and G. A. Gibson. Understanding failures in petascale computers. *Journal of Physics*, 78:1–11, 2007.

[47] B. Schroeder and G. A. Gibson. Disk failures in the real world what does an mttf of 1,000,000 hours mean to you. In *Proceedings of FAST*, pages 1–16, 2007.

[48] P. Stuedi, B. Metzler, and A. Trivedi. jverbs: Ultra-low latency for data center applications. In *Proceedings of ACM SoCC*, 2013.

[49] M. H. Sun and D. M. Blough. Fast, lightweight virtual machine checkpointing. Technical report, 2010.

[50] Y. Xu, M. Bailey, B. Noble, and F. Jahanian. Small is better: Avoiding latency traps in virtualized data. In *Proceedings of ACM SoCC*, 2013.

[51] L. L. You, K. T. Pollack, and D. D. E. Long. Deep store: An archival storage system architecture. In *Proceedings of ICDE*, pages 804–815, 2005.

[52] I. Zhang, A. Garthwaite, Y. Baskakov, and K. C. Barr. Fast restore of checkpointed memory using working set estimation. In *Proceedings of VEE*, pages 534–533, 2009.

[53] I. Zhang, T. Denniston, Y. Baskakov, and A. Garthwaite. Optimizing vm checkpointing for restore performance in vmware esxi. In *Proceedings of USENIX ATC*, pages 1–12, 2013.

[54] W. Zhang, H. Tang, H. Jiang, T. Yang, X. Li, and Y. Zeng. Multi-level selective deduplication for vm snapshots in cloud storage. In *Proceedings of Cloud*, pages 550–557, 2012.

[55] B. Zhu, K. Li, and H. Patterson. Avoiding the disk bottleneck in the data domain deduplication file system. In *Proceedings of FAST*, pages 1–14, 2008.

Author Index